ADMINISTRATIVE LAW
AND
PROCESS

REVISED THIRD EDITION

edited by

DAVID W. ELLIOTT

Department of Law
Carleton University

CANADIAN LEGAL STUDIES SERIES

Captus Press

Canadian Legal Studies Series
Administrative Law and Process, Revised 3rd edition

This Selection Copyright © 1993–2003 by D.W. Elliott and Captus Press Inc.

First Captus Press edition, 1993
Second edition 1998
Third edition 1999
Revised Third edition 2003

Captus Press Inc.
Units 14 & 15, 1600 Steeles Avenue W.
Concord, Ontario L4K 4M2, Canada
Telephone: (416) 736–5537
Fax: (416) 736–5793
Email: info@captus.com
Internet: http://www.captus.com

Canada *We acknowledge the financial support of the Government of Canada through the Book Publishing Industry Development Program (BPIDP) for our publishing activities.*

National Library of Canada Cataloguing in Publication

Administrative law and process / edited by David W. Elliott — Rev. 3rd ed.

(Canadian legal studies series)
Includes bibliographical references.
ISBN 1–55322–054–4

1. Administrative law — Canada — Cases.   2. Administrative procedure — Canada — Cases.   I. Elliott, David W. (David William), Date.   II. Series.

KE5015.A7A36 2003   342.71'06   C2002–906123–7

0 9 8 7 6 5 4 3 2 1
Printed and bound in Canada

Table of Contents

4   Administrative Law: Scope of Natural Justice and Fairness 71

5   Administrative Procedure: Basic Aspects 89

6   Administrative Procedure: Disclosure 110

7   Administrative Procedure: Courts vs. Administrative Bodies 125

13 Research and Study. 265

14 Selected Readings 272

Note on Revised Third Edition of *Administrative Law and Process*

This Revised Third Edition reproduces the materials from the 1999 Third Edition of *Administrative Law and Process*, with minor editorial changes, and adds extracts from five recent Supreme Court decisions.

The Supreme Court's *Bell ExpressVu* decision demonstrates its current approach to general statutory interpretation. The decision is included in Chapter 3. The Court's most significant administrative law decision since the Third Edition is *Baker*. It is included in Chapter 4 (on the general scope and content of procedural fairness, oral hearings, and reasons); in Chapter 7 (on bias); and in Chapter 8 (on discretion). *Blencoe*, on administrative delay, is included in Chapter 5. The Court's immigration decision in *Suresh* is also included in Chapter 5. It illustrates the Court's factor-weighing approach to fundamental justice in s. 7 of *Charter*. The labour board decision in *Ellis-Don* epitomizes the ongoing tension between the court and administrative models of procedure, in regard to natural justice and internal consultation. It is included in Chapter 7. The full text of these decisions, and of other recent administrative law decisions, can be found in the court and tribunal data bases of online services such as Quicklaw.

In Chapters 9 to 12, agency websites are provided for ready access to recent information about the National Energy Board, the Canadian Radio-television Commission, the Canadian Transportation Agency, and the Canada Industrial Relations Board. For a general list of federal agencies, see *Government of Canada Departments and Agencies*: <http://canada.gc.ca/depts/major/depind_e.html>. For Ontario, see the Government of Ontario's home page, at: <http://www.gov.on.ca/MBS/english/government/index.html>.

As well, students are encouraged to supplement this edition with readings from recent texts and related works. See, for example: L. Braverman, *Administrative Tribunals: A Legal Handbook* (Aurora, Ont.; Canada Law Book, 2001): M. Mac Neil *et al.*, *Law, Regulation, and Governance* (Don Mills, Ont.: Oxford University Press, 2002); D.J. Mullan, *Administrative Law* (Toronto: Irwin Law, 2001); and J.M. Evans *et al.*, *Administrative Law: Cases, Text, and Materials*, 5th ed. (Toronto: Emond Montgomery, 2002).

Acknowledgment

My thanks to Joan Clarke and Barbara Higgins at the Department of Law, Carleton University, for their assistance in typing and formatting the first edition, and to Pauline Lai, Lily Chu, and other staff members of Captus Press for arranging copyright permissions and production of this publication. My thanks also to Pam Chapman, sessional lecturer at the Department of Law, for her kind support.

1 Introduction

(a) An Introductory Note

The materials in this sourcebook are intended to provide you with an introduction to Canadian administrative law and process. The focus is on the primary actors of the administrative process — public authorities, policy-makers, the courts, and those affected by administrative action — and on the legal world in which they operate.

The materials move from theory toward practice, from the more general to the more concrete. The first chapter recalls some constitutional principles that provide the framework for Canadian administrative law. *Dow Chemical* is referred to here because it is a microcosm of many of the key issues we will encounter throughout the book. The second chapter provides a (high-altitude!) bird's eye view of administrative law as a whole, with an emphasis on the federal level of government. Here, too, we will see issues that recur many times later on. In the third chapter we will we go to the earliest stages of the administrative process, and examine legal alternatives that confront policy-makers seeking to implement their ideas and mandates. Then we will carry the policy process a step further and explore the central tool for translating most policy options into action: the statute. We will look at the nature and making of statutes and subordinate legislation, at the controls on the making of legislation, and at the relationship between legislation and courts. This last topic will lead us to the special rules of statutory interpretation as applied in judicial control of administrative action.

In the chapters on judicial control, our focus will be on procedures, especially the common law presumptions of natural justice and fairness. We will see how these rules are intended to provide those affected by administrative action — sometimes called administrés — with procedural safeguards inside a court-like paradigm.

Not all administrative issues are procedural issues, so we will start Chapter 8 by looking at the use and control of discretion. The second part of that chapter deals with access to information, a topic with both procedural and discretionary aspects.

Having looked at the roles of policy-makers and courts, and at concerns of administrés, we then move to the filling in the sandwich, the public authorities themselves. Here we will focus on the mandates of a selected group of federal regulatory agencies, and consider how they have carried them out. These agencies seem to be involved in somewhat similar challenges — are they? How have they responded? How *well* have they responded? How *should* they — and the policy-makers — respond?

This is a selective volume. Important areas, from provincial and municipal authorities to judicial and non-judicial control outside the fields of procedure and discretion, are left for further studies. You are encouraged to supplement the materials in this volume with as many readings from the Selected Readings and other sources as possible. The materials should be also supplemented by a student research project. One possibility is a specific empirical assessment of the procedures of one or more of the four main agencies considered here (and, perhaps, some that are not considered here). Another possibility is an issue-based study that uses the materials as a starting point for exploring a current structural or procedural problem affecting the administrative process.

When you have mastered these materials — and have asked critical questions about them —

you should be ready for more advanced work in administrative law. You will also have a good understanding of two issues at the heart of administrative law:

1. what is the best balance between fairness and efficiency? and
2. who should set that balance?

(b) Some Definitions

What's in a word? In administrative law, as elsewhere, it is useful to begin with a common understanding of the meaning attributed to some basic terms. There is no magic in the definitions provided below; they are intended only to help ensure that we begin our explorations on a common wave length.

administrative law: the law relating to the administrative process

administrative process: all bodies that exercise public statutory power on behalf of the government (These bodies are also referred to as "public authorities" or "administrators.")

administrés: those who are directly affected by specific actions of the administrative process

constitutional law: the law relating to the ground rules of government and society

central administrative process: the part of the executive branch of government that is under the direct control of a Cabinet minister (e.g., the ministries and departments and central coordinating bodies)

Crown: the state acting in its formal executive capacity (When it is meant to refer to a specific executive, such as that of Manitoba, the term is more specific, "the Crown in right of Manitoba.")

executive: the branch of government whose characteristic functions are to initiate and administer policy and law and to administer the assets of the state

government: an institution that exercises general or shared sovereign power (or acts on behalf of one that does) and purports to act for all the people of a particular geographical area [where the institution exercises sovereign power, it is synonymous with the "state"]

judiciary: the branch of government with two characteristic functions: to resolve disputes according to law and to interpret and develop law

law: a body of rules enforceable in the courts (Arguably, law is much more than this, but all that is offered here is a starting point.)

legislature: the branch of government whose characteristic functions are to represent the interests of the electorate, to monitor the executive branch, and to formally enact law

outlying administrative process: the part of the executive branch of government that is outside the direct control of a Cabinet minister (e.g., the independent regulatory agencies and Crown corporations)

public law: the law relating to government (the state) and the relationship between government and society

quasi-administrative process: partly private institutions outside the executive branch of government that exercise public statutory power (e.g., statutory arbitrators; universities; disciplinary bodies of professional organizations)

(c) Basic Constitutional Elements

All students of Canadian administrative law should be familiar with its constitutional framework. You should be familiar with the key provisions of the *Constitution Act, 1982*,[1] proclaimed in effect on 17 April 1982. You should also be familiar with the *Constitution Act, 1867*[2] (formerly the *British North*

America Act, 1867), and the division of legislative (and executive) powers described there.

Note, too, that the Canadian constitution still comprises a number of basic principles and rules that are not guaranteed expressly in the *Constitution Act, 1982*, the *Constitution Act, 1867*, or in the other major written constitutional documents. These principles constitute the "unwritten" part of our constitution. Some of these principles have been given legal status by the Supreme Court of Canada; others have not. Still others are partly "written" and partly "unwritten."[3] What unites them all is their importance to the Constitution as a whole.

We will focus on those basic constitutional principles, rules, and other elements that are of special importance to administrative law.

1. DEMOCRACY

In the 1998 *Quebec Secession Reference*,[4] the Supreme Court described democracy as one of four "underlying" constitutional principles that have legal force. In a general sense, democracy might be described as a system of government that is accountable to the people at large. In regard to administrative law, the goal is to ensure that the government's vast and powerful administrative process does what the public, speaking through our elected representatives, have authorized. In the *Quebec Secession Reference*, the Supreme Court stated that democracy includes the notions of the expression of "the sovereign will of the people,"[5] "majority rule,"[6] voter participation in the electoral process,[7] "[t]he consent of the governed,"[8] and "the process of representative and responsible government."[9] The latter two concepts are especially significant to administrative law.

2. REPRESENTATIVE GOVERNMENT

Representative government is the principle by which elected legislators act on behalf of the people of the country as a whole.[10] Like responsible government, this principle supports the broader notion of democracy. It gives the public some control over the government as a whole and the administrative process in particular.

The responsible government principle accords a key role to the administrator's governing statute. The statute is the source of the administrator's mandate, and comes from a body that purports to speak on behalf of Canadians as a whole. Except

in unusual situations involving contracts or royal prerogative power, administrative action that is not authorized by statute is normally invalid.

3. RESPONSIBLE GOVERNMENT

(i) The General Principle[11]

Responsible government requires that the leadership of the executive branch of government must have the confidence of the majority, or the largest part, of the elected legislature, and conversely, that it must resign or call an election if it loses this confidence.

By convention, if the political party in power is defeated in the House of Commons on an important matter of policy, it may ask for a dissolution of Parliament, and appeal from Parliament to the electorate at large. If it loses this appeal, the government (i.e., the Cabinet and the Prime Minister) must resign in favour of the party winning a majority or plurality of seats. This party is called upon by the Governor General to form a new administration.

Responsible government has served two goals in Canada. First, it has facilitated an historic power shift from British to Canadian policy-makers, and thus had a key part in the evolution of national independence. Second, responsible government has helped secure public control of government and the administrative process. It gives the Canadian public some control — however tenuous and periodic — over the body that directs the administrative process: the leadership of the executive branch.

(ii) Ministerial Responsibility and Cabinet Control

A specific component of the concept of responsible government is the doctrine of ministerial responsibility. Under this doctrine, Cabinet ministers must be members of the Legislature, in most cases coming from the House of Commons, and are accountable to it for the operation of the government under their general control.[12]

Traditionally, a major error or wrong in a department could result in the resignation of the relevant minister. Today, however, such resignations are rare, and ministers tend not to resign unless they have been directly and personally involved. Ministerial responsibility has also been diluted by the growth of large sectors of the administrative process that are partly outside the formal control of individual ministers.

Nevertheless, ministerial control and responsibility for the administrative process is still important. Moreover, in many cases involving "independent agencies," the Canadian approach is to vest collective review, approval, or directive powers in the body controlled by ministers acting in their collective capacity — the Governor in Council. This contrasts with the American situation, where most independent administrative bodies are really independent of ongoing control by the central part of the executive branch of government.

4. SOVEREIGNTY OF PARLIAMENT

Although the Supreme Court did not expressly include sovereignty of Parliament among the "fundamental and organizing principles" discussed in detail in the *Quebec Secession Reference*,[13] there is no doubt about the importance of the limited form of Parliamentary sovereignty that exists in Canada today.

(i) The General Principle[14]

In its classic sense, as formulated by the 19th-century constitutional lawyer, A.V. Dicey, the doctrine of the Supremacy of Parliament means that Parliament — comprising the House of Commons (or legislative assembly), the House of Lords (or Senate, at the federal level in Canada) and the Queen (or Her representative) acting together — has the right to make or unmake any law whatsoever, and that no person or body can override or set aside the legislation of Parliament.[15]

This means that any Act passed by Parliament as constituted above will be obeyed by the courts. The supremacy of an Act of Parliament over the Crown prerogative power was established in the 1610 *Case of Proclamations*,[16] where it was held that the Crown cannot impose legal obligations by means of royal proclamation. The importance of the requirement that the legislature act by statute was confirmed in *Stockdale v. Hansard*[17] in 1839, where the courts decided that although each House of Parliament has complete control over its own proceedings, a mere resolution or declaration by either House is not by itself considered a law.

However, Parliamentary sovereignty in Canada is a limited form of sovereignty. How is it limited? We will look at a number of possible and actual limitations below.

(ii) Limitations on the Principle

Does international law limit Parliamentary sovereignty? Not in a legal sense. If the Canadian Parliament passed an Act violating the *North American Free Trade Agreement*, Canadian courts would not refuse to give that Act legal effect. Morality? Not directly. During World War II, courts upheld legislation drastically curtailing rights of Japanese Canadians.[18] Even today, a Canadian statute could violate moral principles and still have legal effect if it escaped the prohibitions in the *Charter*.

The executive prerogative power does not limit Parliamentary sovereignty. As seen above, it cannot be used to impose legal obligations by royal proclamation. Prerogative power can be curtailed and eliminated by Parliament. Where limited, it cannot be reconstituted as prerogative power. There has been a theory that the Canadian Parliament cannot "abdicate" its legislative power to another unrepresentative body, but the status and extent of the theory are uncertain.

In general, the Canadian courts will not strike down a Canadian statute for unconstitutionality unless the statute violates (a) the *Constitution Act, 1867* (formerly the *British North America Act, 1867*), the *Constitution Act, 1982* or one of the constitutional texts referred to in it; (b) one of the basic constitutional principles recognized as having legal force; or (c) "quasi-constitutional" statutes such as the Bills of Rights.

However, there is one very important non-legal limitation on Parliamentary sovereignty that must not be overlooked. This is the responsibility of Parliament to the electorate, and the possibility of popular resistance if the responsibility is not carried out. Yet the accountability to the people as a whole is essentially a political limit, enforced more by informed public opinion and democratic traditions than by judgments in courts of law.

5. CONSTITUTIONALISM

The Supreme Court has described constitutionalism as the requirement "that all government action comply with the Constitution."[19] Section 52(1) of the *Constitution Act, 1982* enforces this requirement by stipulating that "[t]he Constitution of Canada is the supreme law of Canada, and any law that is inconsistent with the provisions of the Constitution is, to the extent of the inconsistency, of no force and effect." As a result of this requirement, administrators in Canada are subject to two levels of legal restriction, the first in enabling statutes and other legislation, and the second in the Constitution. At the first level, an administrative decision may be invalid if it is not authorized by its enabling statute; at the second level, either the decision or its enabling statute is contrary to the Constitution.

6. FEDERALISM[20]

Federalism is a system that divides power between a government for an entire country and several relatively independent regional governments. The framework of the Canadian federal system is contained in the *Constitution Act, 1867*, which is one of the two main texts of the Constitution of Canada. A look at the *Constitution Act, 1867* makes it clear that neither the federal Parliament nor the provincial Legislatures have the more or less legally unrestricted legislative jurisdiction of the British Parliament. Sections 91, 92, 93, 94(A), 95, 101, and 132 of the Act divide legislative powers in Canada between the federal and provincial governments, mainly in terms of subject matter. Action by a given level of government outside its designated area of jurisdiction will be both unconstitutional and illegal. Changes to the division of federal and provincial powers are governed by the amendment procedures in the *Constitution Act, 1982*.[21]

The legal limitations imposed by the Canadian federal system have at least three major implications for Canadian administrative law: (i) they impose significant jurisdictional limits on the operation of the principle of the sovereignty of Parliament; (ii) they result in 11 (14, including the three territories) different administrative law systems in Canada; and (iii) they enhance the responsibilities and power of the official legal umpires of the system: the Canadian courts.

7. BASIC RIGHTS

The Supreme Court included the rights of minorities and individuals among the principles it described as "fundamental" in the *Quebec Secession Reference*.

Many of the most important minority and other basic rights are contained in the *Canadian Charter of Rights and Freedoms*.[22] Among the *Charter* provisions that have special relevance to administrative law are s. 32, describing the scope of the *Charter*; s. 2(a), guaranteeing freedom of expression; s. 8, protecting against unreasonable search or seizure; s. 7, guaranteeing the right to "life, liberty and security of the persons," and the right not to be deprived of these rights except in accordance with fundamental justice; s. 15, guaranteeing a variety of equality rights; and s. 1, permitting *Charter* violations to be justified in certain situations.

Like the other parts of the *Constitution Act, 1982*, the *Charter* prevails over ordinary laws where these conflict with the *Charter's* basic rights requirements. Thus, where *Charter* requirements are applied to administrative law, courts can go beyond the range of ordinary sub-constitutional control, which is limited to statutory interpretation. This new control capacity, applied to the wide and often subjective *Charter* guarantees, enhances the potential control power of Canadian courts and imposes additional legal limitations on the operation of the administrative process.

8. THE RULE OF LAW

Another fundamental principle of the Canadian constitution is the rule of law. Although the rule of law is proclaimed in the preamble to the *Canadian Charter of Rights and Freedoms*, its content is not expressly defined. Again, it is instructive to start by looking at Professor A.V. Dicey's definition. To Dicey, the rule of law meant first that no person could be punished or prejudiced by arbitrary, prerogative, or even wide discretionary power as opposed to a regular legal rule; second, that no persons, such as officials, were exempt from the ordinary law of the land, administered by the ordinary courts of law; and third, that constitutional guarantees result not from a general, abstract code, but from the ordinary law.[23]

Dicey's formulations were overstated. Wide discretionary powers have for long been recognized as a vital aspect of government administration, and a beneficial aspect if kept within proper bounds. And while government officials are as a rule liable for wrongs done in the course of action beyond the limits of power, Crown prerogatives and statutory immunities have resulted in exceptions of qualifications to this rule.

The Supreme Court has said that the rule of law requires (i) the supremacy of law over governments and private individuals, (ii) the existence of laws to maintain order, and (iii) all public power to be derived ultimately from a legal rule.[24] In most cases, this legal rule will be a statute enacted by elected representatives. In regard to the concepts of representative and responsible government, then, the purpose of the rule of law is to help ensure that the ultimate control of government and the administrative process is in the hands of the electorate.

9. INDEPENDENCE OF THE JUDICIARY

Dicey recognized that noble principles are worth very little if they cannot be readily enforced in concrete situations. He said that "the Habeas Corpus Acts declare no principle and define no rights, but they are for practical purposes worth a hundred constitutional articles guaranteeing individual liberty."[25] Similarly, the goals of the rule of law mean little if there is no effective system of courts to enforce them decisively and impartially.

The Canadian legal system contains numerous requirements to help secure judicial independence and impartiality. Superior court judges hold office during good behaviour, and there are statutory safeguards to ensure the independence of lower court judges. Judges of courts of record are exempt from legal liability for anything done or spoken in the exercise of their office and within the scope of their jurisdiction. Judges will be disqualified not merely for actual bias, but wherever there is a real likelihood of bias as well. Unlike some administrative tribunals, courts do not appear in the role of prosecutors and judges in the same cause. While appointments to the judiciary may sometimes appear to be rewards for political services, political partisanship is expected to cease after an appointment.

There is also a tradition of procedural safeguards, including full public hearings, decisions, and an elaborate system of appeals. All are designed to protect the rights of the citizen affected and to promote the general feeling that the courts *are*, by and large, fair and impartial. They are part of the complex phenomenon referred to as the "independence of the judiciary."

Some of the safeguards above have constitutional and legal status. For example, ss. 99 and 100 of the *Constitution Act, 1867* protect the tenure and salaries, respectively, of superior court judges in the provinces, while s. 11(d) of the *Charter* gives a person charged with an offence the right to "a fair and public hearing by an independent and impartial tribunal." Recently, the Supreme Court of Canada has included the independence of the judiciary as among those constitutional principles that the Court says have legal status. In *Re Remuneration of Provincial Court Judges*,[26] the Supreme Court stipulated a minimum floor for judicial salaries, compelled provincial legislatures to create independent salary advisory bodies, and required them to provide justifications based on "simple rationality" for departing from their advice.

Do the safeguards work? The answer depends on one's personal perspective. On one hand, the system is far from perfect, and allows for unconscious or indirect bias based on background, class, education, etc. On the other hand, specific allegations of deliberate judicial bias are relatively rare.

How do these safeguards relate to administrative law in particular? First, since procedural common law judicial review is modelled generally on court-like (although not court-identical) procedures, the law on the independence and bias of ordinary courts and judges can affect the law on the independence and bias of administrative tribunals and officials. Second, s. 11(d) of the *Charter* applies to all administrative tribunals with criminal or quasi-criminal functions. Third, the broader legally enforceable independence principle now recognized in the *Provincial Court Judges Reference* may extend additional legal-constitutional independence protections to the administrative process.

10. PREROGATIVE POWER

Letters Patent emanating from the Queen in Britain have created the office of Governor General in Canada, and delegate to the Governor General the Queen's personal powers. Most of the Governor General's powers[27] must be exercised on the advice of the Privy Council of Canada, which means that they are effectively exercised by the Prime Minister and his Cabinet. Only on rare occasions can the Governor General act without or against the advice of the Prime Minister or Cabinet. For example, a central responsibility of the Governor General is to ensure that there is a government in office at all times. So if a Prime Minister died in office, the Governor General would be responsible for selecting a new Prime Minister. In extreme conditions, a Governor General might be able to refuse a request for dissolution, but the general rule dictates that the Prime Minister's advice must be followed. This rule, which circumscribes prerogative power, is yet another corollary of the key constitutional concept of responsible government.

From the 10 basic elements described above, we can see how constitutional law gives our administrative law its basic shape. Thus, for example, the importance of statutory mandates, the subordination of regulations to statutes, the hierarchical structure of central government departments, the prevalence of judicial review interpretation presumptions, and the distinction between review and appeal, all reflect the constitutional principles of representative and responsible government and Parliamentary sovereignty. These principles ensure or assume that ultimate control is in the hands of the electorate. On the other hand, the growth of independent agencies with adjudicatory and court-like administrative procedures, and recurring battles over privative clauses, tend to reflect the countervailing principle of the rule of law, backed by the independence of the judiciary. In the past decade, the *Charter* has substantially limited Parliamentary sovereignty and responsible government, but has greatly expanded judicial power. Meanwhile, public authorities work within the constraints of a federal system, shaped by the *Constitution Act, 1867*. The subject matter and geographical scope of provincial or territorial authorities will likely be quite different from those created by the federal government. For administrators and all Canadians, the constitution is omnipresent and in law, at least, omnipotent.

Notes

1. Schedule B to the *Canada Act 1982 (U.K.)*, 1982, c. 11.
2. (U.K.), 30 & 31 Vict., c. 3, reprinted in R.S.C. 1985, App. II, No. 5.
3. For example, the "rule of law," which is affirmed but not defined in the Preamble to the *Canadian Charter of Rights and Freedoms*.
4. *Reference Re Secession of Quebec*, [1998] 2 S.C.R. 217.
5. *Ibid.* at para. 66.
6. *Ibid.* at para. 63. The Court cautioned, however, that in Canada, democracy means more than simple majority rule: paras. 76, 149.
7. *Ibid.* at para. 65.
8. *Ibid.* at para. 67.
9. *Ibid.* at para. 65.
10. Cf. the *Quebec Secession Reference*, *ibid.*, where the Court referred to the fact that "each of the provincial leg-

islatures and the federal Parliament is elected by popular franchise": para. 65.
11. See, generally, P.W. Hogg, *Constitutional Law in Canada*, 3d ed. (Scarborough, Ont.: Carswell, 1992) c. 9.
12. The obligation was described succinctly in the McRuer Report on administrative law, basic rights, and the state: "Ministers are held to be responsible and accountable for anything done within the segment of the public business under their control and direction, be it the ordinary business operations of government or the exercise of statutory powers conferred on them or on subordinates under their control and direction": Hon. J.C. McRuer, *Royal Commission of Inquiry into Civil Rights* (Toronto: Queen's Printer, 1968), Report No. 1, Vol. 1 at 44.
13. Indeed, the Court said [at para. 72] that "with the adoption of the *Charter*, the Canadian system of government was transformed to a significant extent from a system of Parliamentary supremacy to one of constitutional supremacy." As will be noted, though, Canadian legislatures exercise supreme powers that are legally supreme, subject to the *Charter* and the other parts of the Constitution.
14. See, generally, P.W. Hogg, *Constitutional Law in Canada*, *supra* note 11, c. 12.
15. A.V. Dicey, *An Introduction to the Study of the law of the Constitution*, 10th ed. (London: MacMillan, 1959, first published in 1895) at 39–40.
16. (1611) 12 Co. Rep. 74.
17. (1839) 9 Ad. & E 1.
18. *Co-operative Committee on Japanese Canadians v. Canada*, [1947] A.C. 87.
19. *Quebec Secession Reference*, *ibid.* at para. 72.
20. See, generally, P.W. Hogg, *Constitutional Law in Canada*, *supra* note 11, c. 5.
21. Sections 38–49.
22. The *Charter* comprises the first 34 sections of the *Constitution Act, 1982*. As well as containing the *Charter*, the *Constitution Act, 1982* stipulates the procedures for formally amending the Constitution of Canada, and makes a number of other changes affecting equalization and aboriginal and treaty rights.
23. Dicey, *supra* note 15 at 188.
24. *Reference Re Manitoba Language Rights*, [1985] 1 S.C.R. 721, 747–52 and *Quebec Secession Reference*, para. 71.
25. Dicey, *supra* note 13 at 199.
26. *Reference Re Remuneration of Judges of the Provincial Court of Prince Edward Island*, [1997] 3 S.C.R. 3.
27. Some of the more important of these are (i) the power to appoint judges and government officers; (ii) the right to remove Cabinet ministers and other government officers; (iii) the right to pardon and reprieve persons convicted of criminal offences; and (iv) the right to summon, prorogue, and dissolve Parliament.

(d)   Some *Charter* Provisions

CANADIAN CHARTER OF RIGHTS AND FREEDOMS[†]

Whereas Canada is founded upon principles that recognize the supremacy of God and the rule of law:

Rights and freedoms in Canada

1. The *Canadian Charter of Rights and Freedoms* guarantees the rights and freedoms set out in it subject only to such reasonable limits prescribed by law

---

[†] *Constitution Act, 1982*, Part 1, Schedule B.

as can be demonstrably justified in a free and democratic society.

Fundamental freedoms

2. Everyone has the following fundamental freedoms:
  (a) freedom of conscience and religion;
  (b) freedom of thought, belief, opinion and expression, including freedom of the press and other media of communication;
  (c) freedom of peaceful assembly; and
  (d) freedom of association.

. . . .

Legal Rights

Life, liberty and security of person

7. Everyone has the right to life, liberty and security of the person and the right not to be deprived thereof except in accordance with the principles of fundamental justice.

Search or seizure

8. Everyone has the right to be secure against unreasonable search or seizure.

. . . .

Proceedings in criminal and penal matters

11. Any person charged with an offence has the right
  (d) to be presumed innocent until proven guilty according to law in a fair and public hearing by an independent and impartial tribunal;

. . . .

Equality before and under law and equal protection and benefit of law

15.(1) Every individual is equal before and under the law and has the right to the equal protection and equal benefit of the law without discrimination and, in particular, without discrimination based on race, national or ethnic origin, colour, religion, sex, age or mental or physical disability.

Affirmative action programs

(2) Subsection (1) does not preclude any law, program or activity that has as its object the amelioration of conditions of disadvantaged individuals or groups including those that are disadvantaged because of race, national or ethnic origin, colour, religion, sex, age or mental or physical disability.

. . . .

Other rights and freedoms not affected by Charter

26. The guarantee in this Charter of certain rights and freedoms shall not be construed as denying the existence of any other rights or freedoms that exist in Canada.

. . . .

Application of Charter

Application of Charter

32.(1) This Charter applies
  (a) to the Parliament and government of Canada in respect of all matters within the authority of Parliament including all matters relating to the Yukon Territory and Northwest Territories; and
  (b) to the legislature and government of each province in respect of all matters within the authority of the legislature of each province.

Exception

(2) Notwithstanding subsection (1), section 15 shall not have effect until three years after this section comes into force.

Exception where express declaration

33.(1) Parliament or the legislature of a province may expressly declare in an Act of Parliament or of the legislature, as the case may be, that the Act or provision thereof shall operate notwithstanding a provision included in section 2 or sections 7 to 15 of this Charter.

Operation of exception

(2) An Act or a provision of an Act in respect of which a declaration made under this section is in effect shall have such operation as it would have but for the provision of this Charter referred to in the declaration.

Five year limitation

(3) A declaration made under subsection (1) shall cease to have effect five years after it comes

into force or on such earlier date as may be specified in the declaration.

Re-enactment

(4) Parliament or a legislature of a province may re-enact a declaration made under subsection (1).

Five year limitation

(5) Subsection (3) applies in respect of a re-enactment made under subsection (4).

. . . .

General

Primacy of Constitution in Canada

52.(1) The Constitution of Canada is the supreme law of Canada, and any law that is inconsistent with the provisions of the constitution is, to the extent of the inconsistency, of no force or effect.

(2) The Constitution of Canada includes
(a) the *Canada Act 1982*, including this Act;
(b) the Acts and orders referred to in the schedule; and
(c) any amendment to any Act or order referred to in paragraph (a) or (b).

(e) Dow Chemical†

Dow Chemical is one of the most dramatic cases in Canadian regulatory law. We will examine it in more detail in Chapter 9 in the context of the National Energy Board. However, the case illustrates so many tensions and challenges of administrative law that it is worth reading briefly now. Look through it with the following questions in mind:

1. What general kind of governmental technique was used to deal with Dow's application?
2. What governmental structure(s) was/were set up to deal with it?
3. Why would Dow, the Board, and the federal government want Dow's application processed as quickly and efficiently as possible?

4. In whose interest was it to ensure that the application was processed as fairly as possible?
5. Who were the actors involved in the Board's decision?
6. Describe the "unfairness" complained of.
7. What was the court's response?
8. Can you suggest possible alternatives to the approach taken by the Board?

Later, when you have progressed to the materials in Chapter 9 and read the case again, ask yourself the same questions.

---

† See Chapter 9 for extracts from the case.

Scope and History of the Administrative Process

(a) Growth and Structure of the Administrative Process

ADMINISTRATIVE LAW AND THE EXECUTIVE BRANCH

Administrative law[1] is part of the huge field of public law, which deals with the relationship between the government (the state) and society. In the first chapter,[2] we defined administrative law as the law relating to the administrative process,[3] comprising all bodies that exercise public statutory power on behalf of the government. These bodies are also referred to generally as "public authorities" or "administrators." We distinguished between a central administrative process and an outlying administrative process within the executive branch of government, and a quasi-administrative process that is outside the executive branch but exercises public statutory power.

By far the largest part of the administrative process is within the executive branch of government, the branch that accounts for the great size of modern government as a whole.

THE GROWTH OF THE EXECUTIVE

The size of the modern executive is a product of history. The last century has brought some dramatic changes in the nature and scale of government, particularly in the executive branch.

At the beginning of the 19th century, the British and colonial state was a very limited operation.[4] In Britain, for example, most civilian central government officers were associated with customs and revenue; departments such as the Home Office and the Board of Trade had only several dozen employees each.[5] Local government was carried out by an assortment of parish officials and specialized agencies such as the Commissioners of the Sewers. Most local government functions, from parish responsibilities to tavern licensing and road repair, were supervised by unpaid, part-time judicial officials called justices of the peace. In Britain and the colonies, the state's role was seen in essentially negative terms: defence, internal peace and order (this function was more in the hands of the judiciary than the executive), providing such basic services as road repair and drainage, and raising the revenue to support these functions. The picture in Canada was similar,[6] although Upper Canada had become actively involved in canal-building by the 1820s.[7]

In the second half of the 19th century and in the 20th century, Britain and Canada experienced a massive expansion in the role of the state in society. Government moved from the negative role described above to the positive role of the regulatory (especially in Canada), entrepreneurial (especially in Britain), and welfare (especially in Britain) state.[8]

In Canada today, statutes and subordinate legislation affect virtually every aspect of our lives. Government regulates almost all private industry, from mining to communications to professional services. Through legislation, government sets standards, issues licences, levies taxes, expropriates land and property, offers incentives and guarantees, protects health and safety, runs basic services, competes with private enterprise, manages education, and imposes penalties. Canada has federal, provincial, and territorial legislatures engaged in the business of formal law-making. This output is augmented by the by-laws of thousands of municipal councils and by myriads of other kinds of subordinate legislation.

In addition to enacting more laws, government has been spending more money as well. In 1950, government spending accounted for 21% of the

Canadian gross national product, and by 1991 it had risen to 48%.[9] In 1997, despite a decade of cost-cutting, it was still at 48%.[10] In most cases, this outpouring of legislation and money has been accompanied by a corresponding expansion of the executive branch of government. Members of the executive have been required to implement most statutes, by-laws, and other forms of subordinate legislation. Indeed, most subordinate legislation is not only administered but also *made* by the executive branch.

By 1992, the government employed one of every five members of the Canadian labour force.[11] In the federal government, for example, there were 555,759 employees.[12] Although spending cuts and layoffs made the 1990s a period of relative decline at all levels, the government — especially the executive branch — remained a major employer.[13]

Indeed, public employee numbers are only a partial indicator of the true reach of the Canadian government and its executive. How many additional jobs, for example, are dependent on government contracts? On government licences or incentives? On government trade tariffs or marketing programs? On government loans or assurances? How many people in the private sector are affected by government regulations?[14]

STRUCTURE OF THE ADMINISTRATIVE PROCESS TODAY

In Canada today, we have not one but 14 distinct administrative processes. This is a result of the federal system, which divides government between two main levels: federal and provincial. As well, the three territorial governments have powers — and administrative processes — that are modelled roughly on those of the provinces. The description below focuses on the federal level of government. Although the provincial and territorial models are generally similar, there can be significant variations between jurisdictions.

There are two main components to the federal executive branch — the traditional central administrative process of departments and the central coordinating organizations — and the newer and increasingly significant outlying administrative process of the independent agencies and Crown corporations.

At the federal level, there are approximately 20 government departments in the central administrative process. Some of the better known ones are

the departments of Finance, Health, Defence, and Natural Resources.

A government department is subject to the estimates system of budgeting, under which money is appropriated to it by Parliament and must be spent as Parliament directs.[15] The department's officers are selected through a merit system administered by the Public Service Commission. Finally, a deputy minister heads a government department. He holds office at pleasure, and is under the full control of a Cabinet minister. The minister is expected to answer to Parliament for the policies and actions of his or her department, and is expected to take responsibility for major departmental blunders.

The central administrative process also contains a number of general coordinating organizations. One is the Treasury Board Secretariat, proclaimed a department in 1966, but constituting the administrative arm of the Privy Council for Canada. Others are the Privy Council Office and the Prime Minister's Office. All are concerned with the formulation and coordination of general government policy. Another organization, the Public Service Commission, supervises the hiring of government employees. Like the ordinary government departments, the general coordinating organizations are subject to the direct control of a Cabinet minister.

Although the outlying administrative process is within the executive and thus considered a part of "government," it is *outside* the direct control of a Cabinet minister.

Independent government agencies[16] are an important part of the outlying administrative process. Typically, these agencies are distinct from the ordinary government departments; they report to Parliament through, but not to, individual Cabinet ministers. Although normally a minister is not answerable to Parliament for the day-to-day activities of independent agencies, there are usually a number of statutory devices (e.g., appeals, powers of approval, direction or review, or guidance power through orders in council) to ensure that the views of the Cabinet or the minister can prevail. Ministerial or Cabinet control is indirect, with the precise amount of control varying in individual cases. Ironically, while independence from partisan political influence is one of the commonest justifications given for independent government agencies, agency members are usually appointed by politically controlled orders in council rather than by competitive merit-based examinations administered by the Public Service Commission.

11

As well as freedom from partisan political control, greater flexibility, concentration of expertise, and avoidance of direct political responsibility for contentious decisions[17] appear to be some of the main reasons for creating independent government agencies.

These agencies go by a variety of names: commissions, boards, councils, agencies, and tribunals. The precise names are of only limited descriptive use. In general, the subject matter of a commission is wide and mainly regulatory or adjudicatory. A board has a similar but usually narrower scope. A tribunal is essentially adjudicatory. On the other hand, a council is more advisory and research-oriented. Except for the councils, most agencies usually have some adjudicatory functions. Well-known federal agencies include the Immigration and Refugee Board, the National Energy Board, the Canadian Radio-television and Telecommunications Commission, the Canada Industrial Relations Board, and the Canadian Transportation Agency.

The other main members of the outlying administrative process are the Crown corporations.[18] Like the independent government agencies, Crown corporations are within the executive, owned by the government, but outside direct ministerial control. In 1997, there were approximately 200 federal Crown corporations, including subsidiaries, associates, and related enterprises, down considerably from the total of over 300 in the early 1980s.[19] Two of the best-known remaining Crown corporations are the Canadian Broadcasting Corporation and Canada Post Corporation. As with independent government agencies, the rationale for the creation of Crown corporations has varied. Crown corporations can operate more flexibly than central government departments in quasi-commercial areas affecting the public interest. During the 1980s and 1990s, though, Canadian governments shrank both their budgets and their concept of the public interest, and privatized many Crown corporations.[20]

Exercising public statutory power outside the government are the members of the third main component of the administrative process, the quasi-administrative process. These are private institutions or individuals that exercise public statutory powers and perform public statutory duties. Statutory arbitrators, universities, and disciplinary boards of professional associations are the commonest examples.

Once again, let us not forget that the reach of the administrative process extends beyond the structures described here. Through regulations, contracts, franchises, licences, joint ventures, and dozens of other mechanisms, government policies and administrative initiatives extend well into the very core of so-called "private" activity. The administrative process and the rest of society are not isolated worlds separated by a fixed frontier, but rather the adjoining sides of a graduated spectrum.

Although the picture above is replicated at the provincial and territorial level, the structures are generally less elaborate, especially in the smaller provinces and in the territories. As well, the provinces and territories have jurisdiction over a form of government without an exact federal counterpart: the municipal government.

The key institution at the local level is the municipal corporation, a quasi-governmental organization that is normally created by statute. Although municipal corporations fall under provincial jurisdiction, they administer by-laws enacted by elected municipal councils. Although municipal corporations are a part of the executive branch, they are not regarded as Crown agents. A somewhat specialized body of administrative law principles has grown up around municipal by-laws.[21] One might imagine that since they were enacted by elected officials, reviewing courts would show them greater deference. However, the reverse often seems true!

CONCLUDING NOTE

All bodies — within and outside the executive branch of government — that exercise or discharge public statutory powers or duties comprise the administrative process. These bodies, their mandates, and the way these mandates are carried out are the concerns of administrative law.

Notes

1. See, for example, R. Dussault and L. Borgeat (trans.), *Administrative Law: A Treatise* (Scarborough, Ont.: Carswell, 1985–90) vols. 1 to 4; administrative law publications of the Law Reform Commission of Canada; S.A. de Smith et al., *de Smith's Judicial Review of Administrative Action*, 5th ed. (London: Sweet and Maxwell, 1985) [British]; C.T. Emery & B. Smythe, *Judicial Review: Legal Limits of Official Power* (London: Sweet and Maxwell, 1986) [British]; D.J. Baum, *Cases and Materials on Administrative Law* (Toronto: Butterworths, 1987); D.P. Jones & A.S. de Villars, *Principles of Administrative Law*, 2d ed. (Scarborough, Ont.: Carswell, 1994); H.W.R. Wade & C. Forsyth, *Administrative Law*, 7th ed. (Oxford: Oxford University Press, 1994) [British]; P.P. Craig, *Administrative Law*, 3d ed. (London: Sweet and Maxwell, 1994) [British]; J.M. Evans, H.N. Janisch & D.J. Mullan, *Administrative Law: Cases, Text, and Materials*, 4th ed. (Toronto: Emond Montgomery, 1995); D.J.M. Brown & J.M. Evans, *Judicial Review of Administrative Action in Canada*, looseleaf (Toronto: Canvasback Publishing, 1998); and other materials listed in *Introduction: General Works*, Chapter 14.
2. See Some Definitions in Chapter 1.

3. See also H. Hart Jr. & A. Sacks, *The Legal Process, Basic Problems in the Making and Application of Law* (Westbury, N.Y.: Liberty Foundation Press, 1984, based on unpub. ed., 1958); R. Dussault & L. Borgeat, *supra* note 1, vols. 1 to 3, 1985–89; Law Reform Commission of Canada, *Policy Implementation, Compliance and Administrative Law* (Working Paper 51) (Ottawa: Law Reform Commission of Canada, 1986), esp. 87–102; and K. Kernaghan & D. Siegel, *Public Administration in Canada: A Text*, 4th ed. (Scarborough, Ont.: Nelson Canada, 1999).

4. See generally, D. Roberts, *Victorian Origins of the Welfare State* (New Haven: Yale University Press, 1960); G. Fry, *The Growth of Government* (London: Cass, 1979); and P. Craig, *supra* note 1, c. 2.

5. See the table of government of civilian government employees compiled in *Victorian Origins of the British Welfare State, ibid.* at 14–16, and cited in *Administrative Law, ibid.* at 42.

6. In his Report of 1839 (references here are to G. Craig, ed., *Lord Durham's Report* (Toronto: McClelland & Stewart, 1963, first published, 1839)), Lord Durham said of Lower Canada that "A people can hardly be congratulated on having had at little cost a rude and imperfect administration of justice, hardly the semblance of police, no public provision for education, no lighting and bad pavements in its cities, and [extremely inadequate facilities for transporting articles to market]" (p. 77). Upper Canada had spent large sums on major public works such as canals, to the detriment of roads and local facilities such as post offices and schools (pp. 82–83, 99–104). Durham described the eastern colonies as peaceful but backward, with a "mortifying" lack of good roads and schools (pp. 108–09).

7. E. McInnis, *Canada: A Political and Social History*, 3d ed. (Toronto: Holt, Rinehart and Winston, 1969) at 237–40; and *ibid.* at 102–04.

8. Canada: R.I. Cheffins & R.N. Tucker, *The Constitutional Process in Canada*, 2d ed. (Toronto: McGraw-Hill Ryerson, 1976) at 51–56; Law Reform Commission of Canada, *Independent Administrative Agencies* (Working Paper 25) (Ottawa: Supply and Services Canada, 1980) c. 1; D. Olsen, *The State Elite* (Toronto: McClelland, 1980) c. 1; Economic Council of Canada, *Reforming Regulation* (Ottawa: Supply and Services Canada, 1981); T.L. Powrie, *The Growth of Government*, in T.C. Pocklington, ed., *Liberal Democracy in Canada and the United States* (Toronto: Holt, 1985) c. 2; and K. Kernaghan & D. Siegel, *supra* note 3 at 11–18. Britain: G. Fry, *The Growth of Government*, 1979.

9. K. Kernaghan & D. Siegel, *supra* note 3 at 14, and sources cited there.

10. See Statistics Canada, *Canadian Economic Overview: Gross Domestic Revenue by Income and Expenditures* (Ottawa: Statistics Canada, 1997), Catalogue #11-010, Tables 1 and 3.

11. In 1992, the number of employees in government entities, including universities, was 2,876,400: Statistics Canada, *Public Sector Employment and Remuneration 1992* (Ottawa: Statistics Canada, 1993) at 10 and 18.

12. Federal government structures and their employees as of December 1992: government departments, 235,343; Crown corporations, 152,383; other government agencies, 32,802; Canadian forces, 115,320; R.C.M.P., 19,911. See R. Dyck, *Canadian Politics: Critical Approaches* (Scarborough, Ont.: Nelson Canada, 1996) at 509.

13. In 1997, about 15% of all Canadians worked for government. There were about 2.1 million employees in the public sector, out of a total labour force of about 13.9 million: Statistics Canada, *Labour Force Historical Review: Labour Force Survey (CD ROM)* (Ottawa: Statistics Canada, 1997), Catalogue #71F004XCB, Table # TAB12AN.IVT.

14. On the importance of regulation in assessing the scope of the modern administrative state, see A.C. Cairns, "The Past and Future of the Administrative State" (1990) 60 U.T.L.J. 305 at 325.

15. For this, and a succinct discussion of the merit system and general structure of the federal bureaucracy, see R. Dyck, *Canadian Politics*, Concise Edition (Scarborough, Ont.: Nelson Canada, 1998) c. 14.

16. See Law Reform Commission of Canada, *Independent Administrative Agencies* (Working Paper 25); Law Reform Commission of Canada, *Independent Administrative Agencies* (Report 26), 1985.

17. For this motive, see M.J. Trebilcock et al., *The Choice of Governing Instrument* (Ottawa: Supply and Services Canada, 1982) at 90.

18. M.J. Trebilcock et al., *ibid.* at 74–76; J. Pritchard and S. Robert, *Crown Corporations in Canada: The Calculus of Instrument Choice*, 1983; P. Garant, "Crown Corporations as Instruments of Economic Intervention: Legal Aspects," in I. Bernier & A. Lajoie, eds., *Regulations, Crown Corporations and Administrative Tribunals*, 1985; R. Dyck, *supra* note 15 at 274–76; K. Kernaghan & D. Siegel, *supra* note 3, c. 9.

19. See Treasury Board figures reproduced in K. Kernaghan and D. Siegel, *supra* note 3 at 227.

20. Examples of former federal Crown corporations that were privatized during this period: Air Canada, Canadian National Railways, Petro-Canada, and Teleglobe Canada.

21. See, for example, F. Hoehn, *Municipalities and Canadian Law: Defining the Authority of Local Governments* (Saskatoon, Sask.: Purich Publishing, 1996).

(b)   Regulation and Regulatory Agencies[†]

John C. Strick

NOTE

Regulation is one of the oldest and most visible forms of government action. Regulation is usually more than bare legislative edicts, enforceable in courts in cases of non-compliance. In most cases, regulation is administered by special institutions of government, whether in the central, outlying, or

[†]   Excerpts from *The Economics of Government Regulation: Theory and Canadian Practice*, 2d ed. (Toronto: Thompson Educational Publishing, 1994) at 3, 5–18. Reproduced with permission.

quasi-administrative process. Here Strick discusses some of the kinds of regulation and varieties of public authorities that administer it.

EXTRACTS

Regulation is defined as government imposition of rules and controls which are designed to direct, restrict, or change the economic behaviour of individuals and business, and which are supported by penalties for non-compliance.

. . . .

Forms of Regulation

The design of regulation to influence economic behaviour in production, distribution and consumption can take a variety of forms. These include regulation in the form of price controls to modify market conditions; business licences and charters to influence supply; the promotion of fair competition to influence prices and output; and, regulation in the form of standards and codes governing measurement, quality, content, and production conditions. The following examines these forms of regulation.

Price Regulation

One of the most common forms of regulation is the regulation of prices of goods and services, and in some cases prices of factors. This type of government regulation is most frequently found in industries characterized by monopoly or a high degree of imperfect competition and market concentration. Such industries have the power to manipulate prices and set them substantially higher than prices that would prevail if left to the forces of supply and demand. Utilities, including hydroelectric power, water supply, telephone services and transportation services, have traditionally been viewed as natural monopolies and have come under this category of regulation. But, in addition to the highly monopolized industries, governments may occasionally intervene to control rising prices of services temporarily in short supply, such as rents when housing becomes scarce or the price of energy when that commodity comes under buying pressure. Furthermore, restrictions on price increases have been imposed through policies of wage and price controls applied as temporary measures to combat inflation.

In contrast to the imposition of price ceilings on goods and services to prevent them from rising, governments have also acted to establish price floors to prevent prices from falling below certain levels. Such price maintenance policies have most commonly been applied in the agriculture industry to avoid wide price fluctuations and subsequent fluctuations in farm income which frequently tend to occur in response to major fluctuations in the supply of agricultural products.

Licences and Charters

Businesses supplying goods and services require a licence, charter, or franchise from government in order to operate. Through licences, government can either permit or deny an individual the right to do business and can control the location of the business. In various activities restrictions are imposed on the number and types of entrants permitted into a particular industry such as banking, television, radio, and telephone. Along with the licences issued in some of these industries, conditions might be included specifying how the business is to be operated. Television stations, for example, are required in Canada to broadcast a specified amount of Canadian content. Regulations govern the ownership and the scope of operations of Canadian banks. Airlines and railways in Canada were at one time required to service specified areas. At the level of local government, in addition to a permit to operate, local zoning by-laws restrict the locations of various business establishments. Therefore, through licences, franchises and zoning, governments attempt to regulate the entry, exit, conditions of service, and even the location of a business.

Promotion of Competition

A major objective of government regulation is to promote fair competition in the market and prevent restrictive business practices such as collusion, price fixing, barriers to entry, and misleading advertising. The market system is basic to the economies of most Western democracies where free enterprise is emphasized. But an ideal functioning market economy requires competition as opposed to monopoly. Governments have assumed an obligation to monitor the operations of the market system and to introduce regulations to ensure fairness in competition. To this end, a variety of regulations can be found in anti-trust or anti-combines legislation prohibiting unfair business and marketing practices, and providing government with the authority to prevent and disband monopoly where it is deemed contrary to the public interest.

Standards

The establishment of standards is another very important form of government regulation which serves to protect the individual consumer, worker, and society. The standards may relate to the content and quality of products, the conditions of production, and various other aspects of economic activity. This is a form of regulation limiting choices particularly in the production and distribution processes. Consider some examples. There are engineering standards and building codes for the construction of buildings, bridges and various other engineered structures. Safety standards exist to protect workers on the job, particularly in reducing their exposure to hazardous products, noise, and dangerous equipment. There are safety standards for transportation and transportation vehicles. Quality and health standards are established for food products and drugs to prevent the production and marketing of unacceptably poor qualities of food products and health impairing drugs. Packaging and labelling standards and a standard set of weights and measures attempt to prevent the seller from exploiting the buyer. And, finally, governments attempt to establish standards for environmental protection, limiting pollutants being discharged into soil, air, and water.

These various forms of government regulation have recently been categorized into two groups, namely, economic regulation and social regulation.[1]

Economic and Social Regulation

Economic regulation is a term that has been used to describe the early type of government regulation, which of course continues to be applied, where regulations were concerned with industry practices involving pricing, marketing and competition. The regulations had a direct impact on industry structure and practices and were frequently aimed at specific industries or markets. From the characteristics of this type of regulation, it also became known as direct regulation and "old style" regulation.

Social regulation is the term which has been applied to describe that category or regulations which has become prominent in the last few decades and relates to the welfare of society. Regulations in this category tend to focus on the conditions under which goods and services are produced and distributed and on the attributes or physical properties of the products. They are primarily in the form of standards described above and relate to issues of safety, health, employment, the environment and a variety of social or welfare related issues. The regulations for the most part are not directed at any one specific industry or market but tend to cut across industries. Pressure for these regulations generally originated from social groups including consumer

interest groups, environmentalists, labour unions and others, and stem from social considerations related to improving the quality of life. This category of regulations has sometimes been referred to as the "new style" regulation or "new wave" regulation.

The concepts of both economic and social regulation are consistent with the definition of regulation presented in this work. Both are directed at modifying economic behaviour to achieve economic or social objectives and both relate to aspects of the economic activities of production, distribution, and consumption. For instance, when the government establishes safety standards for protecting workers, the need for these standards arises from dangers involved in the production process. The standards may force the producer to adopt changes in the production process and to introduce safer equipment or to reduce noise levels. This impacts on the production process and on the producer's choices, in other words, on the producer's economic behaviour.

Scope of Regulation

There are few economic activities which are not either directly or indirectly influenced by government regulations. These activities may range from regular, common-place activities where regulations might appear inconsequential to activities which are the mainstay of the economic structure. The regulations may range from those which are viewed as minor irritants by those affected, to those imposing major constraints and requiring considerable costs in terms of compliance.

It is impossible to measure accurately the scope of government regulations. Various proxies have been applied to attempt to do so but they are little more than general guides. One measure that has been applied is the proportion of gross national product that is affected by government regulation. It has been estimated that in excess of 25 percent of GNP in Canada and the United States is subject to some form of direct regulation of prices and production.[2] Direct regulation would include the regulation of public utilities, broadcasting, railroads, airlines, trucking, and agriculture.

But, in addition to direct regulation, government also regulates indirectly. Practically all economic activity is conducted within a framework of general rules and laws since one of the objectives of government is to provide a framework for the orderly conduct of production, distribution, and consumption. It is not possible, however, to place any type of meaningful, quantitative measures on such indirect regulations.

The specific economic activities where government regulations may be found are much too numerous to list.[3] Some of the general areas, however, may be identified.

One area of activity that has traditionally been subject to regulation is transportation. Because of their importance for national unity and east-west relations in Canada, trans-Canada transportation facilities, such as railroads, air transport, and trucking have been regulated from the beginning. Other modes of transportation subjected to some form of regulation include marine services, buslines, urban transit systems, and taxi services.

Communications is another field of activity that has been regulated from its inception. The communications spectrum is common property and a limited resource, and regulation has been justified to avoid congestion and abuse. In addition, regulation has been applied to communications to achieve economic, social, and cultural objectives. In the broadcasting area, radio and television, including cable and pay, are subjected to regulation. The telecommunication services of telephone and telegraph have also been quite closely regulated by the federal and provincial governments.

The regulation of the environment includes pollution control and the management of the nation's natural resources. Pollution control is a relatively new field of regulatory activity for governments but has reached wide-ranging proportions to cover practically all industry and consumer activities which may potentially damage the environment. Both the federal and provincial governments in Canada have become increasingly active in this area in the last two decades and a host of regulations concerning water, air, and land quality can be found in numerous government statutes. In addition to pollution, governments apply regulations as part of their policies to attempt to manage natural resources, such as energy, forests, minerals, wildlife and fisheries, and to manage land use, including parks, recreational uses and land use in urban centres.

The area of consumer protection relating to products and services is inundated with government regulations. These regulations govern the quality and content of products, and the conditions in which they are produced and sold, and include grading, labelling, weights and measures, advertising, and terms of sale. Regulations prohibit or restrict dangerous products including certain drugs, chemicals, and firearms. The quality of medical and health services and facilities [is] supervised, standards are established for buildings and related facilities, housing rentals are

monitored, and monopoly elements in production and distribution are closely observed.

Financial markets and institutions, including banks, trust and insurance companies, credit unions, and the stock and bond markets, operate within a set of government regulations. Regulations also apply to pension and financial retirement plans.

In Canada, cultural activities have been subjected to government regulation and supervision with a view to protecting and fostering the Canadian identity. Coverage involves regulations on the ownership of broadcasting facilities and in particular, Canadian-content regulations in radio and television programming and in theatrical film. Publishing and advertising relating to publishing are also subjected to regulations.

Governments have traditionally been concerned with business practices and the establishment of a framework that will assure fair business operations. Consequently, provisions exist governing property, contracts, patents, copyright, incorporation, competition, bankruptcy, importing and exporting, and foreign investment and ownership. Other regulations can be found pertaining to worker occupation and safety, licensing and certification of professions and professional groups, gambling, labour organization and collective bargaining, and the production and consumption of alcoholic and tobacco products.

The scope of government regulation is extremely wide, infringing in varying degrees on almost all types of economic activities relating to production, distribution and consumption.

Growth of Regulation

Government regulations have existed ever since the first forms of government were established. Early forms of economic organization of society, being uncomplicated and simple, required correspondingly simple regulations. But, as countries grew and developed, fostered by changing technology and industrial development, economies became increasingly more complex, requiring increasing government involvement in monitoring and regulating economic activities.

Numerous attempts have been made to apply some quantitative measure to determine the growth of government regulation. These include the growth in the number of government regulatory statutes over time, the increase in the number of pages of statutory regulation, and the increase in the number of regulatory agencies and commissions. The Economic Council of Canada attempted to employ such measures in tracing the growth of regulation in Canada.[4] The Council reported that between 1870 and

1978 the number of federal statutes increased from 25 to 140 while the number of provincial statutes increased from 125 to 1609. The increase in the number of statutes was not uniform but tended to fluctuate from decade to decade, and has accelerated in recent decades. During the period 1940 to 1949, new federal and provincial statutes numbered 3 and 148 respectively. During the period 1970–78, the federal government passed 25 new statutes while provincial governments passed 262 new statutes. The Council attributed the recent explosion in government regulations to "new style" or "social regulation" in areas primarily consisting of consumer protection and information, health and safety, and protection of the environment. The growth rate in the passage of new regulations does not appear to have slowed in the 1980s. In 1987 the federal government announced its intention of introducing over 800 new regulations during that year. These consisted primarily of new or changed provisions to existing statutes and included rules governing the transportation of dangerous goods, regulations pertaining to nuclear energy, a multitude of changes in fisheries regulations, new rules governing environmental contamination, food labelling, smoking on commercial airlines, noise levels for airports, a new grading schedule for french fried potatoes, new standards for thickness in spaghetti sauce, and numerous other major and minor regulations.

The Regulators

Regulation in Canada is conducted through a wide variety of institutions including government ministerial or executive department, boards, commissions, agencies, and tribunals. These institutions may be grouped into two categories: (1) government executive departments, and (2) statutory regulatory agencies (SRAs), which include the various commissions, boards, and agencies established by statutes. These two categories of regulatory bodies are found at both the federal and provincial government levels.

Government Departments

The government ministerial departments which are involved in regulatory activities are the ordinary executive departments of government. Each is controlled and directed by a Cabinet minister and is responsible for conducting the affairs of government within its particular jurisdiction. Executive departments are organized along functional lines. For example, government involvement in and administration of transportation activities is the responsibility of

the Department of Transportation; agricultural activities fall under the jurisdiction of the Department of Agriculture; and, health and social services are the domain of the Department of Health and Welfare. Each of these departments is involved in regulatory activity in varying degrees as part of their function of administering programs. Some departments, however, were created primarily to perform regulatory functions. Examples include the federal Department of Consumer Affairs and its similar counterpart at the provincial level, which administer a variety of legislation dealing with consumer protection. The duties of the federal department include: the enforcement of regulations regarding packaging and labelling of products; advertising; the enforcement of hazardous product standards programs; the establishment of specifications for weights and measures; and, services to assist consumers to organize for collective actions and resolve complaints. Similarly, the federal Department of Environment is heavily involved in administering environmental protection and environmental conservation services. The Department is responsible for administering the Environmental Protection Act and its specific duties include monitoring and regulating use, discharge and disposal of toxic and hazardous chemicals and wastes. Environmental protection is shared with other Departments, such as the Department of Indian Affairs and Northern Development, which administers legislation for environmental management in the northern territories, particularly the protection of the northern environment from the impact of oil and mineral exploration. As in the case of all government administrative departments, the Cabinet minister in charge of the department has the ultimate responsibility for its activities. In turn, the minister and the Cabinet collectively are accountable to the House of Commons for the department's activities, including its regulatory activities. The personnel within the government departments responsible for managing daily affairs are career public servants or bureaucrats generally appointed through the public service selection process. They enjoy continuity of service and over time acquire considerable expertise on the programs and activities of their departments. Consequently, they are in a position to exercise a great amount of influence on the Departmental minister in the initiation and design of regulatory policies through the information and advice they provide.

Statutory Regulatory Agencies (SRAs)[5]

Statutory regulatory agencies are government commissions, boards, tribunals, etc., established by legislation for the purposes of regulation. They form a component of a large number of federally and provincially incorporated entities known as Crown agencies or Crown corporations. SRAs obtain their mandate and terms of reference from the legislation under which they are created. At the federal level, their financial control and accountability is governed by the Financial Administration Act. SRAs are responsible to the cabinet through the appropriate departmental minister, who also exercises financial control and direction over the agency. The budget of the agency is part of the budget of the department to which it is related.

Prominent among this group of regulatory agencies are the National Transportation Agency (NTA) [now the Canadian Transportation Agency], formerly the Canadian Transport Commission (CTC), and the Canadian Radio-television and Telecommunications Corporation (CRTC). The NTA obtains its mandate from the National Transportation Act [now Canada Transportation Act] and the Aeronautics Act. It is responsible for coordinating and regulating various aspects of land, water, and air transportation. In the area of air transport, it formulates air carrier regulations, including the licensing of air carriers, but shares regulatory functions with the Air Navigation Services Branch and the Aviation Regulation Branch of the Department of Transport which establish standards and procedures for air traffic control and ensure adequate safety standards.

The CRTC operates under the terms of the Broadcasting Act. Its primary functions involve the regulation (including rates) of federally incorporated telecommunications carriers and the regulation and supervision of radio and television systems and cable and pay television systems. The Department of Communications is also involved through its regulation of radio frequency spectrum. In 1987–88, of the Department's total budget of approximately $150 million, $25 million was provided for the CRTC. The senior personnel within an SRA are generally appointed by the Cabinet. They may be former public servants, former elected politicians or political party supporters who are rewarded for their service to the party. Appointees may also be selected from the business community on the basis of the expertise and experience they may bring to the agency.

One of the primary reasons for the creation of SRAs to administer regulations is to provide some distance between political consideration and the administration of regulations. SRAs are provided with a greater degree of political autonomy, which varies among agencies. While some agencies require the approval of the appropriate minister for their decisions, others operate without this requirement

and even exercise power to establish new regulations without ministerial approval but within the limits of the legislation under which they operate. Cabinet power to over-ride SRA decisions is provided in the legislation governing the SRA, and this over-ride power generally applies to agencies with broad mandates to develop and apply policy. Appeals to the Cabinet on SRA decisions are generally on issues of major policy. The Cabinet in turn may uphold the agency's decision, over-ride it, or refer the issue back to the agency with a directive for further examination and consideration. Right of appeal of SRA decisions to the courts acts as a further restraint on SRA autonomy.

A number of factors may determine the degree of autonomy that an SRA may possess. Generally, the autonomy of an SRA may vary directly with the length of appointment of its members. Members of an agency who are appointed for a lengthy, fixed period of time and who can only be removed for very serious breach of office may tend to act more independently than agencies whose members are appointed for a short term. SRAs will also have greater autonomy if appeals in their areas of jurisdiction are not a tradition or commonplace. A distinguishing feature between Canadian SRAs and those in the United States is that SRA decisions in Canada may be appealed to the Cabinet whereas in the United States this right of appeal does not exist. It is consequently contended that SRAs in the United States enjoy greater autonomy than their counterparts in Canada. The generality of the SRA's terms of reference contained in the enabling legislation will also affect the degree of autonomy. If the terms of reference tend to be broad, the agency may possess considerable latitude in interpreting the legislation and freedom to establish subordinate or new regulations without requiring the approval of the executive or the legislature.

An example of an SRA with a large degree of autonomy in its operations is the CRTC. It is composed of nine [now thirteen] full-time members and ten [now six] part-time members appointed by the Governor-in-Council. The full-time members are appointed for a relatively lengthy term of seven years [now five]. The CRTC's freedom of operations stems from its very broad terms of reference. It was established to implement the Broadcasting Act which contains numerous general clauses regarding goals and objectives for broadcasting in Canada. This provided the CRTC, given its day-to-day responsibility for regulating Canadian broadcasting, with a great deal of latitude in interpreting its mandate and wide powers to develop broadcasting policies and corresponding rules and guidelines. Furthermore, the CRTC has successfully resisted the Cabinet's attempts to rein in its powers. In the words of the Caplan-Savenageau Task Force on Broadcasting Policy (1988):

> While the federal government has pursued a succession of projects to obtain power of direction over the CRTC, the Commission has continued, as it is entitled, to operate independently, holding hearings on issues, deciding on policy, making regulations, and putting these decisions into effect, with varying degrees of informal consultation with the government and the Department of Communications.[6]

Regulation in Question

Within the last decade there appears to have developed within various sectors of society and business, a disillusionment with regulation and a trend toward deregulation. Nowhere has this been more evident than in the U.S., particularly after 1980 when President Reagan took office. To a lesser degree, a trend toward deregulation also developed in Canada [Note: The trend continued in Canada in the 1990s]. An attitude appears to have developed that the economies were over-regulated and that inefficiencies were being created by regulation that were proving to be excessively costly. The inefficiencies could be eliminated or reduced by substituting market elements for regulation. The assumption underlying this position was that the market system is a more efficient allocator of resources and a more efficient regulator of prices and output than are regulatory agencies.

Consequently, there have been movements in Canada and the U.S. to deregulate various traditionally regulated industries such as the airlines, trucking, and the telephone industry. In conjunction with the deregulation movement, there has also been a trend towards privatization of formerly government-owned enterprises in both North America and in Europe. Numerous industries that had been nationalized or that were government-created, particularly following the Second World War, have recently been sold by governments to private interests. This privatization movement has stemmed primarily from the same attitudes that initiated the deregulation process — a belief that productivity and efficiency would be enhanced in the industries involved.

Over the years there have existed numerous conservative groups, individuals, and businesses who have opposed the ever increasing government encroachment in economic activities. But, interestingly enough, pressure for deregulation did not usu-

ally originate within the regulated industry. The telephone industry in Canada and the U.S. opposed the move by regulatory agencies to liberalize regulations and open the industry to competition. Frequently, the strongest supporters for continued regulation were the regulated firms and their employees who feared the adjustments and upheaval that could conceivably result. This lent credence to the charge that regulation benefitted the regulated and produced cartelization of the industry. The "old style" or "economic regulation" of prices and output consequently came under very careful scrutiny during the 1970s and 1980s with considerable pressure from consumer groups, as well as from potential competitors employing new technology, who wished to enter and compete with established firms in traditionally regulated industries.

Even in the area of social regulation, including the environment, health, and safety, continued and increasing regulation began to be seriously questioned. The prime concerns of the 1960s and early 1970s which led to numerous developments to reduce pollution, such as the pollutants from automobile emissions, appeared to subside in the early 1980s. In Canada, questions on the merits of the rapid escalation of regulation led the Economic Council of Canada to conduct a major investigation of regulation which produced a number of recommendations for the reform of the regulatory process. Proposals for reform on both sides of the Canada-U.S. border called for considerably closer scrutiny of the need for new regulations and the need for the continuation of existing regulations. A trend developed to apply benefit-cost analysis and cost-effectiveness analysis to evaluate existing and newly proposed regulations. While the need for continued regulation of various economic activities was recognized, the objective was to streamline the regulatory process, to cut some of the bureaucratic red tape which produced delays in decision making, and, where regulations are justified, to make them more effective.

Notes

1. These two categories of regulation are described in greater detail in Economic Council of Canada, [*Responsible Regulation: An Interim Report*, November, 1979], pp. 44–45.
2. *Ibid.*, p. 13.
3. A list of the more significant areas of regulation in Canada can be found in Economic Council of Canada, *Ibid.*, p. 11.
4. *Ibid.*, pp. 14–18.
5. A discussion of the various aspects of Statutory Regulatory Agencies in Canada is presented in Economic Council of Canada, *ibid.*, Ch. 5.
6. Canada, *Report of the Task Force on Broadcasting Policy* (Ottawa: Supply and Services, Canada, 1986), p. 18.

(c) Growth of Agencies†

Law Reform Commission of Canada

THE HISTORICAL PERSPECTIVE

The emergence of a complex federal administrative structure in Canada, including independent agencies which refine and apply the law under the aegis of special statutory powers, is not the product of a well-defined approach or design. The growth of this structure is best described as an aspect of the evolution of government rather than as a planned constitutional development. It takes its shape from pragmatic responses to emerging problems over the years. In some situations, especially in the early years, the choice of certain types of governmental bodies to perform particular functions may have been the product of a reasoned general approach. But the choice in many cases seems to have been *ad hoc*. The selection of a non-departmental rather than a departmental body to regulate, or an administrative tribunal rather than the courts to adjudicate, appears to have been influenced, more often than not, by the exigencies of the case and existing institutional precedents than by an overall plan or any particular attitudes respecting one type of governmental body rather than another.

. . . .

A. The Traditional Legal Context

. . . .

[The Law Reform Commission says that our traditional constitutional and administrative structure was based on a strict notion of responsible government. Cabinet ministers actively directed the business of public departments. Law-making powers were reserved mainly for elected officials, adjudicatory powers were reserved mainly for ordinary courts (which carried on much of the administrative work at the local level), discretion was limited, and statutory administrators (other than judges or jus- tices of the peace) were under the direct control of Ministers.]

While the constitutional arrangement outlined above was adequate for a small nation with limited governmental activity, new considerations have emerged in the context of the modern welfare state. Today, it is impossible for elected representatives effectively to supervise all aspects of the public business. Substantial areas of government are managed by officials who are only remotely responsible to Ministers or to Parliament and who have little direct contact with the public. Industries are controlled and regulated, taxes are levied. Welfare grants are dispensed, and land is expropriated by bureaucracies which are never required to stand for election. This expansion of government has conferred on government appointees and public servants great legislative, administrative and sometimes judicial power. The courts have attempted to adapt the principles of administrative law, first developed through judicial review of lower tribunals at a time when Justices of the Peace were still the main administrators in the English countryside, to contemporary conditions where comprehensive standards are needed to limit or structure the powers of public officials who enjoy wide authority under delegated legislation. Given the scope of current governmental operations and the degree of discretionary power exercised by administrative authorities, it is clear that sources of law additional to judicial ones will have to be depended upon if administrative law is to be bolstered to meet existing needs and to ensure that governmental action is carried out fairly, effectively and responsibly.

B. The Expansion of Government

At Confederation and for quite a few years thereafter the federal government and its administrators were preoccupied with the extension and protection of the frontier and the development of

---

† Excerpts from *Independent Administrative Agencies* (Working Paper 25) (Ottawa: Law Reform Commission of Canada, 1980) at 17–32. Source of Information: Department of Justice Canada. Reproduced with the permission of the Minister of Public Works and Government Services Canada, 2002. [For a useful index to federal agencies and departments today, see *Government of Canada Departments and Agencies*: <http://canada.gc.ca/depts/major/depind_e.html>.]

a national economy. Thus the opening of the West, relations with native peoples, building the great transcontinental railways, and the protection of the border were the great public questions. There was a handful of government offices in Ottawa as well as a number of officials scattered throughout the country to collect customs duties, administer land grants, carry out surveys, look after post and telegraphs and preserve order in the emerging nation.

The need for novel administrative structures reflecting the character of government functions in a young and developing country first became apparent in Canada in connection with the nascent railway industry. Even before Confederation the Province of Canada had resorted to a type of non-departmental regulatory body when it enacted a *Railway Act* in 1851 under which regulatory functions, principally the approval of rates, were assigned to a Board of Railway Commissioners, although in fact the functions were assumed by four Cabinet Ministers. This device, known after Confederation as the Railway Committee of the Privy Council, persisted until 1903.[37]

However, a debate over whether Cabinet Ministers should be replaced by full-time semi-independent officials began as early as the 1880's. The idea of establishing a railway regulatory commission to take over the function of rate-making from the Cabinet committee was considered but rejected in the Galt Royal Commission Report of 1888.[38] That Commission was reluctant to recommend the model of the recently established United States Interstate Commerce Commission[39], which it regarded as untried, and ventured the view that a commission format was inconsistent with the Canadian system of responsible government, ignoring the fact that the British Parliament was also then experimenting with a commission model.[40] But the problems associated with the employment of Cabinet Ministers as regulators did not go unnoticed by the Galt Commission. The fact that Railway Committee members served only part-time and were based in Ottawa, their lack of expertise and their vulnerability to political pressure were sensed as limitations on their effectiveness.

It is hardly surprising that the Galt Commission should have opted for keeping railway regulation within the confines of a government department. The system of public departments was well established when the Commission reported. Railways had been included in the responsibilities of the Department of Public Works after Confederation, and in 1879 had been placed under a newly constituted Department of Railways and Canals. Furthermore, the increased workload and complexity of the tasks entrusted to the Cabinet Committee seemed to call for the full-

time employment of knowledgeable people. The necessary expertise might conceivably have been built up within the department. However, there were certain drawbacks to this course.

Generally, there was less inclination at that time to involve the federal public service in complex programs. To a large extent the public service performed ministerial functions and gave support to more direct public service programs offered in the provinces. More specifically, the tradition of patronage in the public service of the day gave rise to fears that designated departmental personnel might have inappropriate backgrounds or lack the technical capacity to deal with the kinds of issues being raised in the context of railway regulation. Also, adjudicative functions were largely foreign to departments, and the considerations which supported the removal of these duties from the Cabinet Committee probably precluded as well their being vested in a department. In retrospect, it is interesting to speculate on the question whether the present *pot-pourri* of independent agencies would exist today if a professional and non-partisan Canadian federal public service had been available at the turn of the century to take up the slack from Cabinet ministers.

The move towards a non-elected full-time body outside any departmental structure to regulate railways matured with the reports of Professor S.J. McLean to the Minister of Railways and Canals on *Railway Commissions, Railway Rate Grievances and Regulative Legislation* between 1899 and 1902.[41] These reports suggested the appointment of an independent commission to take the place of the Railway Committee and drew the following conclusions:

1. There must be great care in the definition of the powers conferred upon the commission.
2. The matters to be dealt with are concerned with administration and policy, rather than formal judicial procedure.
3. Subject to an appeal to the Governor in Council the decision of the commission should be final.
4. There should be requirements in regard to technical qualifications for office; one commissioner should be skilled in law, and one in railway business.
5. The commissioners should hold office on the same tenure as judges.

The *Railway Act*[42] of 1903, which reflected in large part the recommendations of the McLean Reports, opted for a new administrative agency, the Board of Railway Commissioners, which appears to have served as a model for later legislative initiatives vesting all kinds of governmental functions in independent agencies. It is noteworthy, however, that the Act provided for an important measure of judicial and political control. There was an appeal to the courts on questions of law or jurisdiction, and the Governor in Council was authorized, either on petition or of its own motion, to vary or rescind any order, decision or rule of the Board. Thorny issues about the appropriate institutional relationships to establish between Cabinet, independent agencies, and individual ministers in charge of related departments still remain to be adequately dealt with today.

Within six years Canada again used a regulatory commission model to establish by treaty, jointly with the United States, the International Joint Commission[43] to replace the International Waterways Commission,[44] which had been a purely investigatory body. It marked a further important step in establishing a framework for government regulation in Canada similar in many respects to the type concurrently being set up in the United States. The practice of appointing experts to decide rather than merely to advise was becoming firmly established. There was much faith displayed at the time in the recruitment by government of specialists, especially those with backgrounds in business affairs, to bring their knowledge to bear on certain economic and political issues. The approach was again followed in 1912, when the *Canada Grain Act*[45] established a Board of Grain Commissioners charged with the administration of terminal warehouses and generally all matters related to the inspection, weighing, trading and storage of grain.

This was a period during our history when marked changes were taking place in the economy and in society at large. By 1900 the major economic and political problems which had precipitated Confederation had been resolved — the frontiers had been established and guaranteed, transportation and communication links had been forged and our national political and legal institutions had been established. During the first part of this century there was intense economic development, stimulated by waves of immigration, integration with the American economy, the assumption of responsibility in international affairs and the forced expansion of World War I. Immigration, which had been a mere 49,000 in 1901, rose to a phenomenal 402,000 in 1913. At the same time people were moving to the cities, especially Montreal, Toronto, Vancouver and Winnipeg.

C. World War I — Growth of Government Controls

With the advent of World War I and the commitment of Canada to the war effort, there was marked intervention in the economy by the federal government, including rent and price control, the prevention of hoarding, and the control of the marketing of Canada's principal products. This led to the creation of many administrative agencies such as the Board of Grain Supervisors (succeeded in 1919 by the Canadian Wheat Board), the Food Control Board (later the Canada Food Board), the Wage Trade Board, and municipal Fair Price Committees.

The government also took major initiatives in the health and welfare fields for the first time, although certain measures tangential to Agriculture, Immigration and Indian Affairs operations had been previously adopted. A Board of Pension Commissioners was established in 1916, to be replaced by the existing Canadian Pension Commission in 1933. The Department of Soldiers Civil Re-establishment was created in 1918, and the Department of Health in 1919. They were consolidated in 1928, only to be split again into Veterans Affairs and National Health and Welfare in 1944.

To finance the expansion of the public sector, direct taxation was introduced, first under the rubric of an excess business profits tax in 1916, and then in the much more significant form of an income tax on individuals and corporations in 1917. The income tax has greatly increased since then, and has provided guaranteed means for bureaucratic growth. It was also during the War, fifteen years after the installation of the first major regulatory agency, that the Union Government under Robert Borden placed the federal civil service on a truly professional footing by the *Civil Service Act*, 1918.[46] The Civil Service Commission, which had been given statutory powers over personnel in 1908, saw these powers expanded under the new legislation. At this point, the Commission assumed responsibility to pass upon the qualifications of candidates for admission to and classification, transfer and promotion in, the civil service. For the first time, it was explicitly provided that, save in exceptional cases provided for under the statute, neither the Governor in Council nor any minister, officer of the Crown, board or commission would have the power to appoint or promote anyone to a position in the civil service. It should be noted, however, that most independent agencies created in the years after the War were exempted from the provisions of the Act.

A final significant step taken by the Union Government was the passage of the *Public Service Rearrangement and Transfer of Duties Act* in 1918.[47] As expanded in 1925,[48] the Act provides that the Governor in Council may transfer any powers, duties or functions or the control or supervision of any part of the public service from one Minister to any other Minister, or from one department or portion of the public service to another. The Governor in Council may also amalgamate any two or more departments under one Minister of the Crown and under one deputy minister. Although a final section of the Act provided that all orders made under the authority of the Act must be tabled in the House of Commons, since the *Regulations Act*[49] was passed in 1950 no such orders are required to be tabled in the House. In recent years the executive has carried out numerous administrative reorganizations with minimal consultation. However, the practice has remained that any new departments or agencies have to be established by statute and, at least as a matter of courtesy, major reorganizations of existing departments and agencies have been ratified through legislation.

D. The Inter-War Period

At the end of the War the unusual economic controls were discontinued, with some temporary exceptions. Because of continuing high prices, many of the powers the government had exercised during war-time were conferred on a Board of Commerce, and the *Combines and Fair Prices Act*[50] gave the Board extensive powers to conduct investigations and to make determinations of fair prices and profits. But its activity was short-lived, and price-fixing had come to an end before the empowering statute was declared unconstitutional in 1922, although prohibitions against combines were revived in another form. As well, several schemes were developed to assist men who had served in the war in readjusting to life as civilians in a peacetime economy which gave birth to such structures as the Soldier Settlement Board and the Dominion Employment Services.

Nevertheless, the period following the War until the depression of the "30's" was one in which the federal government generally refrained from extensive new activities. A contributing factor to this quiescence was that the government was burdened with war debts and the obligations resulting from its absorption of the railways which became the Canadian National Railways (CNR). This latter step was to serve as a model for other public sector enterprises to become at least partially integrated with Canadian governmental structures. By 1939, fif-

teen Crown-owned companies had been created to operate in the fields of rail, ship and air transportation, banking and credit, harbour administration and commodity marketing.

The rapid dismantling of war-time controls should not obscure their long-term effects. Professional civil servants had acquired expertise in performing complex tasks which far out-stripped the involvement of their predecessors who, only a few years before, had been primarily involved in merely ministerial functions. The stage was set for departments to assume, in the long run, functions which up to that time might have been assigned only to specialists boards or commissions. As the Rowell-Sirois Report put it:

> People saw how governments could mould their lives and civil servants learned how to do it.... The belief grew that governments could and should use their powers to improve social conditions. The war-time experience with the regulation and direction of enterprise was an important factor in bringing on the wide extension of government control which economic and social chaos seemed to make desirable.[51]

Economic and social pressures, this time in the form of the Great Depression, comprised the motivating factor behind renewed federal legislative efforts in the "30's". The flurry of Canadian "New Deal" legislation in 1935 saw the creation of a number of regulatory and adjudicatory agencies, but several of these became entangled in constitutional difficulties. One such casualty was federal legislation to provide unemployment insurance, but the federal government later re-enacted legislation in this field, following a constitutional amendment in 1940, to create a commission with tripartite labour, business and government representation to oversee the functioning of a special Unemployment Insurance Account contributed to by employers and employees. Other casualties included several measures governing labour relations. Constitutional difficulties also frustrated several joint federal-provincial attempts to regulate marketing. Ultimately, various techniques, such as administrative delegation, were devised to overcome these difficulties, but these had certainly not been extensively developed when World War II again pushed constitutional distinctions into the background.

By no means were all the Crown entities created at this time unconstitutional, however. For example, the Canadian Broadcasting Corporation (CBC), created in 1932, regulated private radio and television broadcasting along with carrying on its own activities in the field until 1958. At that time an independent government agency, the Board of Broadcast Governors, later to give way in turn to the Canadian Radio-television Commission, was created to regulate the broadcasting industry. Administrative reforms also continued in areas of activity where the federal government had been active previously. In 1931, the Tariff Board was created as an independent agency to carry out advisory and quasi-judicial functions: first, it was to conduct inquiries into matters relating to tariffs and trade; second, it was to assume appellate functions previously handled by a departmental committee under the Minister of Finance which had been called the Board of Customs. In 1935, the Canadian Wheat Board was given the responsibility for marketing wheat in interprovincial and export trade. In 1936 the National Harbours Board was created, and the Departments of Railway and Canals and the Marine were merged with the Civil Aviation Branch of the Department of National Defence in a new Department of Transport. Trans-Canada Airlines, the precursor of Air Canada, was created in 1938. Also in 1938, the Board of Railway Commissioners, which had survived the vicissitudes of time and political criticism, was reconstituted as the Board of Transport Commissioners.

E. World War II and Its Aftermath

World War II again saw the federal government adopting close and detailed control over the economy. In many cases the chosen instrument of control was a Crown Corporation which itself "went into business" — for example, Eldorado Mining and Refining, the Polymer corporation, the Industrial Development Bank, and Defence Construction Ltd., to name a few. The technique of control through public ownership rather than regulation was, of course, not new, and has continued to be used. One has only to mention the CNR, the CBC and Air Canada to appreciate the importance of this type of entity. The distinction between government economic controls through the activities of Crown corporations, as opposed to controls through the use of regulatory mechanisms, is not always so clear-cut as these instances would seem to suggest, however. Thus such hybrid entities as the Bank of Canada and the Canadian Wheat Board combine both public ownership and regulatory functions.

What was said by the Rowel-Sirois Commission about the long term effects of governmental intervention during World War I applies with even greater force to the experience following World War II. Those who created Canada's war-time economic machine remained at the helm during the period of

reconstruction. And though most of the war-time state enterprises engaging in activities traditionally carried on by the private sector were discontinued after the War, many of the agencies created during World War II continued to operate afterwards.

Governmental organizations continued to proliferate in the post-war period. Further specialized bodies such as the Atomic Energy Control Board (1946) were set up. Canadian involvement in the setting up of NATO, the maintenance of a Department of Defence Production and the commitment of about one-third of the federal budget to defence matters, led to a substantial expansion of the federal public service during the early years of the Cold War.

During the economic booms of 1946–49 and the Korean War period, a network of marketing boards spread across the country. When, in 1952, the Supreme Court of Canada decided in the case of *P.E.I. Potato Marketing Board v. Willis* [1952] 2 S.C.R. 392, 4 D.L.R. (2d) 146, that regulatory power within the jurisdiction of the federal government could validly be delegated to boards created and operated by a provincial government, and vice versa, by implication this encouraged the creation of yet more independent administrative agencies, in the interests of cooperative federalism.

Welfare state activities blossomed. At the federal level, the Family Allowances Plan (1944), the Old Age Security Pension (1952) and the Canada Pension Plan (1965) joined the earlier established veterans' allowance and unemployment insurance benefits programs. Government intervention was also marked in respect of disposition and use of man-power, perhaps encouraged by large waves of immigrants. More recently, a rising tide of regulations, service and subsidization endeavours has added to the growth of government to the point where at least forty per cent of gross national income is expended on state-related activities. The number of civil servants has at least doubled since the end of World War II. In the words of John H. Deutsch writing in 1968:

> The life of the public service is closely bound up with the role of the state in society. One of the most striking features of the history of our time has been large and persistent increase in the activities of government. Over the hundred-year span of Canada's history, the changes have been truly remarkable. During this period, Canada's working population has increased about seven and a half times, but the number of employees in the public service of the federal government has risen by approximately one hundred times. In 1867, less than one out of every hundred of

24

the working population was employed by all governments — federal, provincial, and municipal. Today at least one in every eight is on a government payroll. At the time of Confederation, total government expenditures were in the order of 5 per cent of the total gross national production. Today, they are in the order of 32 per cent.[52]

All the agencies forming the subject of specific studies by the Commission — the Anti-dumping Tribunal (ADT), the Atomic Energy Control Board (AECB), the Canada Labour Relations Board (CLRB), the Canadian Radio-television and Telecommunications Commission (CRTC), the Canadian Transport Commission (CTC — created as an umbrella commission in 1967, under which the Board of Transport Commissioners, the Air Transport Board, and the Canadian Maritime Commission were merged), the Immigration Appeal Board (IAB), the National Energy Board (NEB), the National Parole Board (NPB), the Pensions Appeals Board (PAB), the Tariff Board and the Unemployment Insurance Commission (recently merged with the new Employment and Immigration Commission) — were either created or reconstituted in the post-war years.

However, these agencies are not the only kinds of non-departmental governmental organization that have developed in Canada over the years, and particularly since World War II. There are many others serving variegated functions, for example, purely advisory bodies such as the Law Reform Commission itself [now defunct]. There are as well quasi-departmental structures administering programs established to handle the overload of regular departments and which report through the same Minister. Crown Corporations also continue to grow in numbers and prosper as an institutional form.

•   •   •   •

Regardless of the proliferation of various governmental bodies, departments continue to play a central role in public administration. Deputy ministers and their senior policy advisers can have significant influence on the operations of related agencies sharing the same responsible minister with them, depending on arrangements between the Minister, the deputy minister and the chairman of the agency. It should not be forgotten either that the departments sometimes engage in functions similar to those performed by agencies. For example, several are engaged in licence granting and revocation. And income tax and immigration appeals were formerly dealt with by appeal procedures internal to departments, a way of proceeding still employed in connection with applications for patents, and food and drug regulations.

Notes

37. For a thumbnail sketch of railway regulatory developments in Canada up to 1903, see Hyson, *supra*, note 30, at 7–12.
38. *Report of the Royal Commission on Railways*. Sessional Paper No. 8A. 2nd Session of the 6th Parliament Canada (1888).
39. The Interstate Commerce Commission of the United States was created under the *Interstate Commerce Act*, Feb. 4, 1887, ch. 104, 24 U.S. Stat. 379.
40. The British Government set up a Board of Railway Commissioners in 1846 and abolished it in 1851. A new Railway and Canal Commission was established in 1873 and reconstituted with wider powers in 1888. See R.E. Wraith and P.G. Hutchesson, *Administrative Tribunals*. Allen & Unwin: London (1973), at 25–28.
41. *Reports upon Railway Commissions, Railway Rate Grievances and Regulative Legislation*. Sessional Paper No. 20a. 2nd Session of the 9th Parliament. Canada (1902).
42. *Railway Act*, S.C. 1903, 3 E. VII, c. 58.
43. See the *International Boundary Waters Treaty Act*, R.S.C. 1970, c. I-20 (an Act of 1911 ratifying the Boundary Waters Treaty of 1909 that provided for an International Joint Commission).
44. By the Rivers and Harbors Act of 1902, the United States Congress requested the President of the United States to invite Great Britain to jointly establish an international commission to be composed of three American and three Canadian representatives. This led to the establishment of the International Waterways Commission. See J.G. Castel, *International Laws Chiefly as Interpreted and Applied in Canada* (Toronto: Butterworths, 3rd ed., 1976), at 367–78.
45. *Canada Grain Act*, S.C. 1912, c. 27.
46. *Civil Service Act*, S.C. 1918, c. 12.
47. *Public Service Rearrangement and Transfer of Duties Act*, S.C. 1918, c. 6.
48. *Act to Amend the Public Service Rearrangement and Transfer of Duties Act*, S.C. 1925, c. 23.
49. *Regulations Act*, R.S.C. 1970, c. R-5, repealed by the *Statutory Instruments Act*, S.C. 1970-71-72, c. 38
50. *Combines and Fair Prices Act*, S.C. 1919, c. 45.
51. Report of the Royal (Rowell-Sirois) Commission on Dominion-Provincial Relations. (3 vol.) 1940. Book I, at 103.
52. J.J. Deutsch, "The Public Service in a Changing Society", (1968) 11 Can. Pub. Adm. 1.

(d)   Public Enterprise and Privatization†

Kenneth Kernaghan and David Siegel

DEFINITION OF PUBLIC ENTERPRISE

A number of different terms are used to denote the corporate form. The most common are "Crown corporation," "mixed enterprise," "joint enterprise," and "public enterprise." Sometimes these terms are used interchangeably, but this section will provide different definitions for each.

Separating the corporate form from other forms of government organization is relatively easy.[1] Crown corporations are established either through their own legislation, or through incorporation under the federal or provincial companies legislation in exactly the same way as any private sector corporation. Determining what constitutes a corporate form, as distinct from other organizational forms, is not difficult; the difficult part is determining what constitutes a *Crown corporation*.

Patrice Garant suggests that

> Crown corporations are companies in the ordinary sense of the term, whose mandate relates to industrial, commercial or financial activities but which also belong to the state, are owned by the government or the Crown or whose sole shareholder is the government or the Crown. This also includes wholly owned subsidiaries. Such companies must be considered part of the governmental public sector: they belong to the state and are exclusively controlled by it.
>
> On the other hand, institutions that are really administrative bodies rather than companies should be excluded from the family of Crown corporations: for example, organizations concerned with economic or social regulation, administrative management and consultation. On the other hand, semipublic companies, that is, majority or even minority subsidiaries in which there is coparticipation of public and private capital, are not Crown corporations, although they are often similar to them.[2]

This definition leaves out certain noncommercial entities that are defined as Crown corporations in the federal Financial Administration Act; these include the Canada Employment and Immigration Commission and the Agricultural Stabilization Board. While there are valid financial and political reasons for separating these organizations from their related departments, they are excluded from this definition because their *method of operation* is much more like an operating department than a corporation.

The federal government classifies its corporate holdings in a number of different categories.[3] *Parent corporations* are corporations that are one hundred percent owned by the federal government. There are three classes of subsidiaries of a parent corporation — *wholly-owned subsidiaries*, and *other subsidiaries* and *associates*, held at less than 50 percent.

There are four other types of corporations that are less directly controlled by the federal government.

Mixed enterprises are corporations whose shares are partially owned by the government of Canada with the balance owned by *private sector parties*. These can be corporations that have been partially privatized (Petro-Canada), or corporations that have been specifically created to work with a private sector corporation for a particular purpose (National Sea Products Limited).

Joint enterprises are similar to mixed enterprises except that the other shareholder is *another level of government*. Currently, all of these types are in the field of economic development — Lower Churchill Development Corporation Limited, North Portage Development Corporation, and Société du parc industriel et portuaire Québec-sud.

Other entities are

> corporate entities in which Canada holds no shares but, either directly or through a Crown corporation, has a right pursuant to statute, articles of incorporation, letters patent or by-law, to appoint or nominate one or more members to the board of directors or similar governing body.[4]

Some examples of these organizations are the Canadian Centre for Swine Improvement, the Canadian Sport and Fitness Administration Centre, and the Maritime Forestry Complex Corporation.

TABLE 9.1
FEDERAL CROWN CORPORATIONS BY METHOD OF OWNERSHIP

	1997	1982
Parent Crown Corporations	47	72
Wholly-Owned Subsidiaries	25	114
Other Subsidiaries and Associates	23	89
Mixed Enterprises	3	17*
Joint Enterprises	3	*
International Organizations	20	*
Other Entities	86	*

* Some changes have occurred as a result of differences in reporting methods.

Source: Treasury Board of Canada Secretariat, Crown Corporations and other Corporate Interests of Canada —
1997 and the comparable report for December 1982. Source of Information: Treasury Board of Canada Secretariat. Reproduced with the permission of the Minister of Public Works and Government Services Canada, 2002.

International enterprises are "corporate entities created pursuant to international agreements by which Canada has a right to appoint or elect members to a governing body."[5] Some examples are the International Monetary Fund, the Commonwealth War Graves Commission, and the International Porcupine Caribou Board.

Public enterprise is the most general term and is generally used to encompass all the above terms. This chapter will focus predominantly on parent corporations, although there will be some discussion of the various other types of organizations as well.

CHANGING TRENDS IN PUBLIC ENTERPRISE

Governments grew very rapidly in the 1960s and 1970s, and it is not surprising that public enterprise followed suit.[6] In more recent times, the growth of government has slowed considerably, and the size of the corporate sector has declined as a result of a growing trend toward privatization.

The Federal Scene

Table 9.1 shows the number of Crown corporations currently held by the federal government and illustrates the trend over the last fifteen years. The clear trend is toward a reduction in the number of corporate entities.[7] This has been effected both by high profile activities such as major privatizations, and by simply winding up some inactive corporations

and consolidating others. During the rapid growth of the 1960s and 1970s, the federal government almost lost control of all the various corporate entities in which it had some stake. New corporations were being created and subsidiaries added to existing corporations in a manner that made it difficult for the federal government to keep track of all these organizations.[8] In recent times, it has made a conscious effort to maintain better control.

Table 9.2 provides an idea of the size of the largest federal Crown corporations. Obviously, federal Crown corporations are major employers. The number of employees and levels of assets controlled have declined over the last few years, mostly as a result of privatizations, but a number of Crown corporations have followed their private sector counterparts by streamlining their workforces.

The activities in which federal Crown corporations have been involved have changed over the years. In the years immediately after Confederation, the federal government was most concerned with nation building, and so focused on transportation undertakings that would unify the diverse parts of the country. During World War II, the major theme of public policy changed from national unity to national defence, with the creation of many new corporations to supply the war effort.[9] Since the end of the war, federal Crown corporations have become more involved in the areas of finance, insurance, and real estate.

It is clear that Crown corporations no longer play as major a role in the economy as they once did. For example, with the sale of Air Canada and

TABLE 9.2
SIZE OF SELECTED LARGER CROWN CORPORATIONS
AND TOTAL CORPORATE SECTOR — 1997

	Employees	**Assets ($ millions)**
Canada Post Corporation	43831	2725.8
Canadian Broadcasting Corporation	7311	1664.7
Atomic Energy of Canada	3675	1040.5
VIA Rail	3000	712.5
Marine Atlantic	2011	326.1
Cape Breton Development Corporation	1894	252.6
Bank of Canada	1600	*
Business Development Bank of Canada	1066	4029.8
Export Development Corporation[a]	602	9706.0
Canadian Wheat Board[c]	454	8281.2
Farm Credit Corporation[b]	800	5022.5
Total Corporate Sector	75074	56661.2

* Financial information excluded because of the unique nature of its operations.

[a] Export Development Corporation has changed to Export Development Canada in December 2001.

[b] Farm Credit Corporation has changed to Farm Credit Canada in June 2001.

[c] The Canadian Wheat Board has changed from a Crown corporation to a shared-governance corporation effective December 31, 1998.

Source: Treasury Board of Canada Secretariat, Crown Corporations and other Corporate Interests of Canada — 1997, pp. 24–25. Source of Information: Treasury Board of Canada Secretariat. Reproduced with the permission of the Minister of Public Works and Government Services Canada, 2002.

Canadian National Railways, the federal involvement in transportation is more strategic and regional than predominant.

The question of which political party has employed the corporate form more frequently has always been contentious. Langford and Huffman point out that the federal Liberals have created an average of two corporations for each year they have been in power, which is more than twice the average of the Conservatives.[10] And the Liberal years of the 1960s and 1970s certainly saw the creation of a large *number* of Crown corporations. However, the Conservatives have created such major corporations as the Canadian Broadcasting Corporation, the Bank of Canada, Canadian National Railways, and the Canadian Wheat Board. This topic is likely to remain a subject of lively partisan debate.

The Provincial Scene

Defining the public enterprise sector in the provincial sphere is even more difficult than in the federal one. The ten jurisdictions each have slightly different definitions of Crown corporations, so that the data collection and comparability problems are significantly multiplied. However, it is usually suggested that provincial Crown corporations are both considerably larger and have grown more rapidly in recent years than federal Crown corporations.[11]

Provinces have adopted the Crown corporation form in a number of different functional areas. Industrial development, liquor sales, housing, power generation,[12] and research and development are the most popular, in terms of the number of provinces employing them. As measured by the total value of assets controlled, the two major fields are electrical power and banking, followed by housing, education, and telephone and communications. These five functions account for just over 80 percent of total assets.[13]

The major activities in which provincial Crown corporations have been involved have changed over the years. In the early years, one function was dominant — power generation.[14] This gave way to diversification into the trade, finance, insurance, and real estate sectors. More recently, provincial Crown corporations have become involved in industrial and resource development areas, with the newest area being insurance.[15] One of the recent trends is the privatization of portions of the electrical corporations in most provinces. It is likely that the next review of provincial Crown corporations will indicate considerably less involvement in this field.

Marsha Chandler suggests that this growth was the result of the presence of more left-wing (NDP and Parti Québécois) governments in provincial capitals. Her data indicate that left-wing governments not only use the corporate form more often, but they also use it for different purposes from those of their right-wing counterparts. "[N]on-socialist governments have used public ownership almost exclusively to facilitate economic development,"[16] e.g., hydroelectric and industrial development corporations. Left-wing governments have been more likely to use the corporate form for redistributive ends and to supplant private sector corporations, e.g. insurance and natural resources.

Notes

1. One of the most thoughtful considerations of the definition problem is found in: M.J. Trebilcock and J.R.S. Prichard, "Crown Corporations: The Calculus of Instrument Choice," in J. Robert S. Prichard, ed. *Crown Corporations in Canada: The Calculus of Instrument Choice* (Toronto: Butterworths, 1983), 8–15. John W. Langford also does an admirable job of grappling with this same difficult question in "The Identification and Classification of Federal Public Corporations: A Preface to Regime Building," *Canadian Public Administration* 23 (spring 1980): 76–104. For a different but equally plausible definition, see Royal Commission on Financial Management and Accountability, *Financial Report* (Hull: Minister of Supply and Services Canada, 1979), ch. 16.
2. Patrice Garant, "Crown Corporations: Instruments of Economic Intervention — Legal Aspects," in Ivan Bernier and Andrée Lajoie, eds., *Regulations, Crown Corporations and Administrative Tribunals*, Research study for the Royal Commission on the Economic Union and Development Prospects for Canada (Toronto: University of Toronto Press, 1985), 4.
... Reprinted by permission of the University of Toronto Press in cooperation with the Royal Commission on the Economic Union and Development Prospects for Canada and the Canadian Publishing Centre, Supply and Services Canada.
3. These categories are explained further and full information on the holdings are provided in: President of the Treasury Board, *Crown Corporations and Other Corporate Interests of Canada: 1992–93 Annual Report to Parliament* (1994), III-5 and passim.
4. Ibid., III-5.
5. Ibid.
6. A good history of the development of the public enterprise instrument in Canada is Economic Council of Canada, *Minding the Public's Business* (Ottawa: Minister of Supply and Services Canada, 1996), ch. 2.
7. The growth in number and complexity of Crown corporations is well documented in: John W. Langford and Kenneth J. Huffman, "The Uncharted Universe of Federal Crown Corporations," in J. Robert S. Prichard, ed., *Crown Corporations in Canada*, 219–301.
8. This embarrassing situation was described in more detail in previous editions of this book.
9. Sandford F. Borins, "World War Two Crown Corporations: Their Wartime Role and Peacetime Privatization," *Canadian Public Administration* 25 (fall 1982): 380–404.
10. John W. Langford and Kenneth J. Huffman, "The Uncharted Universe of Federal Public Corporations," in Prichard, ed., *Crown Corporations in Canada*, 276.
11. Marsha Gordon, *Government in Business* (Montreal: C.D. Howe Institute, 1981), 11–12.
12. In most provinces, power generation was one of the earliest Crown corporations, but this will remain in government hands in only one province — Quebec.
13. Aidan R. Vining and Robert Botterell, "An Overview of the Origins, Growth, Size and Functions of Provincial Crown Corporations," in Prichard, ed., *Crown Corporations in Canada*, 340.
14. For a discussion of the early history of the hydro-electric companies and their uneven development in different provinces, see: Aidan Vining, "Provincial Hydro Utilities," in Allan Tupper and G. Bruce Doern, eds., *Public Corporations and Public Policy in Canada* (Montreal: The Institute for Research on Public Policy, 1981), 152–75.
15. Gordon, *Government in Business*, 14–15.
16. Marsha A. Chandler, "State Enterprise and Partisanship in Provincial Politics," *Canadian Journal of Political Science* 15 (December 1982): 735.

(e) The Dramatis Personae of Administrative Law[†]

Albert Abel

NOTE

A. Abel says that the legal profession has found it hard to deal with administrative law because it doesn't know what it *is*. He says that the traditional means of defining "public administration," such as legal usage, the meaning given to it by public administrators, and continental European usage, are inadequate or no longer adequate. Instead, Abel starts with the term "administration," and suggests

[†] From (1972) 10 Osgoode Hall L.J. at 87–91. Reproduced by permission of M.L. Friedland.

that it "embraces all arrangements devised and put into effect within a social entity — a state, a business, a church, what you will — for correlating the authorities and responsibilities of members that bear on the achievement of the agency's goals." In regard to the term "public," Abel says that "Convention, not logic, fixes the line between the public and the private." If logic governed, he says, practically everything that exists at the sufferance of the state (almost everything there is!) would be public. Logically, he says, the family has many public characteristics, but traditionally it has been felt to involve values superior to those of the state. Private enterprise has a strong public component, but represents the traditional value of freedom of enterprise. The church is excluded because of the transcendent principle of freedom of religion. On the other hand, some institutions, such as the sports referee (and originally, but no longer, "domestic" tribunals), are also not included, because their concerns are regarded as relatively trivial. Some institutions, such as the military and the courts, *are* public, but have been treated separately from "public administration" as a whole; again, because of the transcendent needs or values they are supposed to serve (here, defence and the concept of the independence of the judiciary, respectively). Abel goes on to discuss the institutions that *are* normally included within the concept of public administration. He starts with the obvious example, that of central government departments, and goes on to discuss those that are not themselves part of government — such as occupational licensing and discipline boards — but are brought within the scope of public administration when they serve public functions. Abel continues:

EXTRACTS

Submissions Based on the Evidence as Presented

Neither a desire to swell my list of publications nor an academic delight at the wonders of administration inspired this discussion. Its object is utilitarian. Its recital of the range of matters falling legitimately within the purview of administrative law exposes how partial and inadequate has been the standard approach.

.   .   .   .

Talk and thought about administrative law have confined themselves to selected parts of it. These have been chosen for or warped into analogy with those tidier institutional models, the courts or the legislatures. The great organizing principles of natural justice (procedural due process) and ultra vires have been taken over from them. These have served well to cut the executive down to size. When the state's one important internal task was seen as the imposition of order, they were effective counterforces in the interest of freedom.

Examples scattered throughout the earlier discussion show that state action never did take only the forms of coercion and command. Subtler and more various public controls have long been exercised. But until recently they were uncommon. Regulation and adjudication swamped them. The fringes of public administration got scant attention. Administrative law took shape from templates appropriate to the commoner manifestations. In developing the ideas of ultra vires and natural justice to reconcile the claims of order and freedom, there was a true instinct for what was needed in the then situation. There has been weird extrapolation from those concepts, a cloud of misleading nonexplanation in the innocent double talk of characteristic discourse. Still there was a reasonable fit between the principles and standards applied and the great mass of administrative phenomena with which they had to deal.

They are no longer adequate. They become ever less so. They are not defective. They are deficient. The state becomes relatively less and less a master, more and more a manipulator. Regulation and adjudication continue but as adjuncts or alternatives to a heterogeneous array of official interventions into the life of the community. When the reconciliation of freedom and order was what administrative law was all about, promotion of inefficiency was up to a certain point a positive benefit. The stress on rules tending thereto was healthy. Now it is less so.

What do I propose? Nothing specific, really. Just a whole reorientation. Examination of the administrative universe has revealed how much of it has no resemblance to what the current fundamental concepts of administrative law assume. The devising of more suitable ones calls for a vast concourse of observation and deliberation. I do not claim to have given or to have the answers, only to suggest the pertinent kinds of questions.

Even that, it may be objected, is not achieved by a mere list of administrative actors with a description of their roles. Such an unsorted jumble of instances is a vexation of inquiry and no guide. The objection is a fair one. So I shall risk some reflections submitted only as one starting point for further analysis.

The law applicable to administrative agency operations ought to be responsible to the formal and functional particulars they are seen to exhibit. Form and function are often related. Some structures are used oftener and perhaps are better adapted to some functions. However there is no regular pattern of use. But, as an approach, a specification of functions and of formal features commends itself.

The state still has as one very important job the definition and enforcement of rights and duties between individuals. It has the further tasks of allocating the social increment and of operating the burgeoning public sector of the economy. For all three its major instrument is the administrative apparatus in the aggregate.

Certainly it is not the only one. The courts for the first, the legislature for the second keep their old hegemony. But they were conceived for the simpler needs of yesteryear. Their available resources of time and skill are fully employed in discharging their familiar assignments. They cannot be stretched to include primary handling of the phenomena emerging from increased urbanization and industrialization. The administrative branch has a wider potential range. The total administrative apparatus addresses itself to all three tasks but individual administrators or agencies may differ markedly. Some are primarily regulatory, others primarily allocative, others primarily businesslike and blends of all sorts and degrees occur.

The underlying values central to the functions differ. Their processes differ correspondingly.

Within the first safeguards for the individual are stressed. The demands of public order must be qualified by those of personal liberty. It approximates what courts do. The similarity has tended to blind them and the legal profession to the other functions of administration and to exalt this one. The result has been, if not to impose a strict court regime on all administration, at least to make all administrative processes fit the mould of natural justice. Sometimes complacency with the usual incidents of trial exaggerates this into a requirement of virtual parallelism. The expression "merely administrative" signals a sense that the court analogy is inappropriate. Ordinarily it manifests a fumbling recognition that protection of individual interests is subordinated to other values because the relevant administrative action relates primarily to other functions and is only incidentally regulatory. Conditioned by training and work environment, lawyers off and on the bench lean toward giving all administration a regulatory and

even a penal cast. Some is accepted as being only minimally of that character and best left to be ruled by other considerations. The result has been a treatment appreciably though perhaps not grossly skewed toward the compulsory or prohibitory features of administration and their consequences for individuals. What is most to be deplored is the absence of fundamental analysis and explanatory discourse.

The allocative function involves other values and other procedures. It seeks to effect a satisfying spread of social increments and decrements amongst the members of the political community. Its governmental archetype is the legislature. Its techniques are those of bargaining and compromise. The large accommodations of competing interests at the legislative level are made thus. Those turned over to administrators differ only in being of limited scope. The legislatures make policy wholesale, the administrators in the exercise of this function make it retail. The notion of *ultra vires* preserves the bargain which the legislature has struck by restricting ensuing subsidiary compromises within the range of concerns confided to the administrators. Inside that range the resolution of claims will reflect the considerations the legislature itself would respond to were it dealing directly. The calculus of constituency gratification governs. For political parties, properly absent, there are substituted public representatives, advisory committees or similar artificial equivalents. In the parcelling out of the social product, an acceptable reconciliation of discordant pressures is the objective. Ideally the content and the context of decision are unlike [*sic*], they may even contrast with those useful in connection with the function of supervising individual conduct — diffuse and relatively unstructured where that is focused, ambulatory where it is definitive, a dredge for materials of decision whereas that is a sieve. Effective demand for social — as for economic — goods, whether it be the best or not is the inescapable determinant of their distribution. Legal rules calculated to frustrate its operation are ultimately futile and hence unwise. The administrator should not be hampered in his use of the methods and materials useful for fashioning an acceptable settlement of competing claims in the social dividend.

Finally, government is big business. As such, it like other business has efficiency as a prime value. Both the courts, preoccupied with the regulatory function, and social scientists, sensitive to the allocative function of administration have at times denigrated efficiency. But it retains a very real importance. An inefficient, that is, wasteful deployment of resources human or material in the conduct of public as of private business has nothing to commend it. That is obvious when government comes to market as an entrepreneur. It is just as true when it is engaged in activities which have no private analogues. The collection and retention of redundant and overlapping reports, the excess stockpiling of personnel or inventory, the self-defeating diffusion of memoranda and other paperwork — who would question that these are bad in any connection? Not just in these specifics but in general, efficiency should be taken to be a legitimate objective of administrators in all matters relating to production processes rather than the end product. Other values may still be given more weight. But that should not be done automatically nor until after a preliminary functional analysis of the activity involved.

In practice the functions are all jumbled together. Many administrative actions and almost all agencies are not simply regulatory or simply allocative or simply conducting businesses. They are compounds. There is room for difference of judgment as to the relative significance of the different functions when they coexist. Such a difference of judgment is at the root of the recent pleas for more stress on regulations and less use of decisions. This is fine if the disagreement is deliberated disagreement. The essential thing is to dissect each act of administration to discover its functional characteristics and then shape the applicable law to maximize the realization of the values special to its particular set of functions. Most activities will be hybrids. One function with its values ought not [to] be allowed invariably to swamp the others.

From the catalogue of administrators, formal as well as functional distinctions appear. They too deserve consideration.

If one could assume diligent infallibility, the formal structure if quantitatively suitable with neither too few nor too many administrators for the handling of their business would be of little interest. Instead one not only must assume, one actually observes lethargy and fallibility. Hence the need of some kind of control to get enough and good enough performance. My postulate is that no administrator should be exempt from some control mechanism to that end.

Of the administrative arrangements examined, some lend themselves more readily than others to internal controls. For all, external controls are possible. But the need for them and their nature may differ for different administrative structures.

External controls are more dramatic and the legal profession or at least the law schools are obsessed with them. Internal controls are vastly more important, however.

Like freedom from prejudice, good administration cannot be brought into existence by courts or legislatures. They can at most condemn deviations considered unacceptable. Overindulgence in pejoratives, "arbitrary" and "abuse of discretion" has obscured the fact that the greatest shortcomings of administrators are inertia, procrastination, and slovenly adherence to routine. Hyperthyroid officiousness is rare. Elaborately safeguarding against active maladministration is often counter-productive. It aggravates the incentives to inaction, thereby costing more than it is worth on balance.

The diversities among the kinds of administrators suggest many particulars which seem to warrant investigation into their bearing on internal control in both its corrective and its dynamic aspects.

In classical hierarchical bureaucracies, there is a potential and an opportunity for revising lower echelon decisions. Its perfunctory exercise is valueless. A very active exercise is harmful alike in diverting agency resources from alternative uses for the reconsideration of a particular item and in reacting adversely on responsible initial performance. A discriminate exercise keeps all levels alert to the considerations and the procedures appropriate to the agency's function [in regard to] the matters at hand. Differences in internal structure — the number of levels, the pattern of division of labour both for sections and for individuals, the communications channels, the geographical dispersion or concentration of staff — may condition the efficiency of the inherent potential for internal control. Whether and how they facilitate or impede it [need] to be separately resolved for each of them in evolving a mature system of administrative law.

Whether the administrator whose activity is involved is an individual or a collegial body may be relevant. For efficiency the former, for representation and compromise of a range of sentiments the latter would seem to be preferable. Almost always when authority is vested in an individual, he has bureaucratic superiors and is subject to check by them. Plural member administration occurs at least as often outside as within departments. Control by superiors is lacking where there are no superiors.

There is nevertheless a possibility of internal control of a different kind where there is an appropriate diversity among members. There is with statutory arbitration boards. Often there is on advisory committees. On standing boards and commissions, representative diversity is less common. With them there is a tendency to appoint to membership from the department's staff or other civil service posts. There is also a tendency to develop over time a special rapport with their regular client groups. These weaken the operation of plural membership as a servomechanism reducing the need to rely on external controls.

Visibility of the administrator to the relevant community can be important.

In large bureaucratic establishments, anonymity of the participants in decision is not only characteristic, it is regarded as a desideratum. The decision is an institutional decision; interventions from outside are at a cost to the agency's performance as a system. If the agency task is seen as subordinate to other primary values, that cost may be justified, though such a partial stultification ought never [to] be inadvertently made. As a rule, the details of operation are best left to internal supervision. External controls ought to address themselves to the agency head who will be visible. He is properly accountable for how it operates but neither he nor anyone can fairly be held responsible if the particulars of its operation are tinkered with from outside.

Visibility is in itself a kind of external control or, more accurately, provides an external stimulus for internal control. Administrators who are exposed to continuous scrutiny by a concerned public — for instance, committees of adjustment in neighbourhood-sized communities, the Canadian [Radio-Television] Commission — in practice are not indifferent to how that public reacts to what they do. Persons with appropriate professional qualifications in administering technical or specialized programmes are not only conditioned by received professional ideals but monitored by their professional brethren outside government. This check fails, however, in the administration of occupational self-government; there a shared self-interest inverts the effect of professional scrutiny and supports increased use of external controls.

The latent potential of the structure for internal control should be exploited to the maximum. That is the way to raise the general quality of administration.

The administrative law we have has been too preoccupied with the prevention of bad administration. The administrative law we need is designed for the promotion of good administration.

External controls perforce deal mostly with the former. Even for that they are not very good instruments.

Legislators act when they vote the budget or at long intervals by recasting an agency's statutory delegations. They seldom retrench seriously either funds or powers. They act in relative ignorance of the full particulars of administrative performance. So indeed they must. Growth of the administrative apparatus has come about principally because government got too big for any legislator's personal attention. It is only the really dramatic discrepancy, real or alleged, between administrative performance and public expectations that is subject to legislative control.

The courts too are an imperfect instrument. Their habitual fixation on the regulatory function and relative insensitiveness to the allocative and business functions come naturally since property, civil rights, and criminal law are their daily grist. Nor is the judicial process in any event well adapted to the purpose at hand. Its great defect is that it is episodic. The self selection of litigation is not even a random sampling let alone a systematic quality control of the administrative work product. By rerouting administration to favour those who have the means to urge their claims thus, judicial controls can mess up rational administration. Moreover alacrity in their use chills administrative vigour and encourages the already endemic sluggishness.

It would nevertheless be foolish either to desire or to expect the discontinuance of legislative or of judicial supervision. Their presence cautions against laxness in making use of such internal controls as are available. Their value is in the contingency of discriminating use differentiating according to the various kinds of administrators and administrative action.

A sketch such as this cannot pretend to completeness. In proposing as a point of departure for a rational administrative law the work force of public administration of which a definition is attempted, in instancing important components central or peripheral [to] that work force, and in calling attention to functional and structural elements as possibly pertinent, it is but a preface to analysis. It serves as a broad panorama. A detailed mapping of the terrain is needed. The validity of the suggested bases for differentiation calls for examination, their consequences for elaboration, and no doubt others ought to be added.

The development of administrative law deductively from *a priori* propositions framed in other contexts has failed. An inductive approach is demanded.

(f)   The New Property†

Charles A. Reich

NOTE

This article is considered to be one of the classics of American administrative law. To what extent are its constitutional and philosophical underpinnings uniquely American, and to what extent do they reflect an experience common to Canadian administrative law?

Charles Reich's call for a broader concept of property did not go unheard. In *Goldberg v. Kelly*, 397 U.S. 254 (1970), the Supreme Court of the United States held that a claim to state welfare benefits was not necessarily just a privilege, but could qualify in some cases as a legal property interest. As such, it could meet the "life, liberty, or property" requirement for due process protection under the American constitution. This development occurred at about the same time as British and then Canadian courts began to widen the scope of the common law rules of natural justice: see Chapter 4, below.

Reich wrote before the wave of deregulation, privatization, and downsizing that hit the United States and much of the western world in the 1980s and 1990s. Nevertheless, the impact of this trend should not be overestimated. In the mid-1990s, for example, the proportion of Americans working for government was no less than what it was in the 1960s.

EXTRACTS

The institution called property guards the troubled boundary between individual man and the state. It is not the only guardian; many other institutions, laws, and practices serve as well. But in a society that chiefly values material well-being, the power to control a particular portion of that well-being is the very foundation of individuality.

One of the most important developments in the United States during the past decade has been the emergence of government as a major source of wealth. Government is a gigantic syphon. It draws in revenue and power, and pours forth wealth: money, benefits, services, contracts, franchises, and licenses.

Government has always had this function. But while in early times it was minor, today's distribution of largess is on a vast, imperial scale.

The valuables dispensed by government take many forms, but they all share one characteristic. They are steadily taking the place of traditional forms of wealth — forms which are held as private property. Social insurance substitutes for savings; and government contract replaces a businessman's customers and goodwill. The wealth of more and more Americans depends upon a relationship to government. Increasingly, Americans live on government largess — allocated by government on its own terms, and held by recipients subject to conditions which express "the public interest."

The growth of government largess, accompanied by a distinctive system of law, is having profound consequences. It affects the underpinnings of individualism and independence. It influences the workings of the Bill of Rights. It has an impact on the power of private interests, in their relations to each other and to government. It is helping to create a new society.

This article is an attempt to explore these changes. It begins with an examination of the nature of government largess. Second, it reviews the system of law, substantive and procedural, that has emerged. Third, it examines some of the consequences, to the individual, to private interests, and to society. Fourth, it considers the functions of property and their relationship to "the public interest." Finally, it turns to the future of individualism in the new society that is coming. The object is to present an overview — a way of looking at many seemingly unrelated problems. Inevitably, such an effort must be incomplete and tentative. But it is long past time that we [begin] looking at the transformation taking place around us.

I.   THE LARGESS OF GOVERNMENT

A.   The Forms of Government-Created Wealth

The valuables which derive from relationships to government are of many kinds. Some primarily concern individuals; others flow to business and organi-

---

† Reproduced by permission of The Yale Law Journal Company and Fred B. Rothman & Company from (1964) 73:5 Yale L.J. 733 at 733–34, 737–87 and by permission of the author.

zations. Some are obvious forms of wealth, such as direct payments of money, while others, like licenses and franchises, are indirectly valuable.

. . . .

[Reich goes on to illustrate the great variety of governmentally dispensed wealth: *income and benefits* (such as welfare benefits and unemployment compensation); *jobs* (Reich says that in the 1960s about 9 million people were employed by federal, state or local governments, approximately 13% of the total American labour force of 67 million. In comparison, in 1996 about 19 million people were employed in "traditional" governmental agencies in the United States, approximately 14% of the total labour force of 133 million: K.F. Warren, *Administrative Law in the Political System*, abr. 3d ed. (Upper Saddle River, New Jersey: Prentice Hall, 1997), 12); *occupational licences* (required for engaging in many kinds of work); *franchises* (Reich is referring here to partial monopolies created or assigned by government; his examples include New York City taxi medallions, television channels, pipeline certificates, and national park concessions); *contracts* (Reich cites defence spending, and notes that government contracts are sometimes the main source of income for businesses); *subsidies* (he compares assistance payments to industry to "welfare payments to individuals who cannot manage independently in the economy, *ibid.* at 26); *use of public resources* (Reich is referring to government ownership or control. He says public lands are used for mining, lumbering, and recreational and other purposes; airways, highways and rivers, for travel and commerce; and the radio-television spectrum for broadcasting); and *services* (examples include the postal service, used by advertisers and periodicals; insurance, used for activities such as house construction and banks; and technical information and education, used by businesses and individuals generally).

B. The Importance of Government Largess

How important is governmentally dispensed wealth in relation to the total economic life of the nation? In 1961, when personal income totalled $416,432,000,000,[19] governmental expenditures on all levels amounted to $164,875,000,000.[20] The governmental payroll alone approached forty-five billion dollars.[21] And these figures do not take account of the vast intangible wealth represented by licenses,

franchises, services, and resources. Moreover, the *proportion* of governmental wealth is increasing. Hardly any citizen leads his life without at least partial dependence on wealth flowing through the giant government syphon.

In many cases, this dependence is not voluntary. Valuables that flow from government are often substitutes for, rather than supplements to, other forms of wealth. Social Security and other forms of public insurance and compensation are supported by taxes. This tax money is no longer available for individual savings or insurance. The taxpayer is a participant in public insurance by compulsion, and his ability to care for his own needs independently is correspondingly reduced. Similarly, there is no choice about using public transportation, public lands for recreation, public airport terminals, or public insurance on savings deposits. In these and countless other areas, government is the sole supplier. Moreover, the increasing dominance of scientific technology, so largely a product of government research and development, generates an even greater dependence on government.[22]

Dependence creates a vicious circle of dependence. It is as hard for a business to give up government help as it is for an individual to live on a reduced income. And when one sector of the economy is subsidized, others are forced to seek comparable participation. This is true of geographical areas; government contracts can fundamentally influence the economy of a region.[23] It is also true of different components of the economy. If one form of transportation is subsidized, other types of transportation may be compelled to seek subsidies.[24] When some occupations are subsidized, others, which help to pay the bill, find themselves disadvantaged as a class. Thus, it is not strange to find musicians seeking a subsidy — perhaps to pay food bills that are made artificially high because of another subsidy.[25] Nor is it strange to find that an unemployed worker replaced by a machine seeks government funds to retrain, when in many cases the machine was created through government subsidized research and development. And it is not surprising that subsidies may be needed to enable workers to live in our large cities;[26] they must buy necessities at prices inflated to meet others' subsidized ability to pay.

The prospect is that government largess will necessarily assume ever greater importance as we move closer to a welfare state. Such a state, whatever its particular form, undertakes responsibility for the well-being of those citizens who, because of circumstances beyond their control, cannot provide minimum care, education, housing, or subsistence for themselves. This responsibility can only be carried out by means of what we have defined as government largess.

C. Largess and the Changing Forms of Wealth

The significance of government largess is increased by certain underlying changes in the forms of private wealth in the United States. Changes in the forms of wealth are not remarkable in themselves; the forms are constantly changing and differ in every culture. But today more and more of our wealth takes the form of rights or status rather than of tangible goods. An individual's profession or occupation is a prime example. To many others, a job with a particular employer is the principal form of wealth. A profession or job is frequently far more valuable than a house or bank account, for a new house can be bought, and a new bank account created, once a profession or job is secure. For the jobless, their status as governmentally assisted or insured persons may be the main source of subsistence.

. . . .

The kinds of wealth dispensed by government consist almost entirely of those forms which are in the ascendancy today. To the individual, these new forms, such as a profession, job, or right to receive income, are the basis of his various statuses in society, and may therefore be the most meaningful and distinctive wealth he possesses.[28]

II. THE EMERGING SYSTEM OF LAW

Wealth or value is created by culture and by society; it is culture that makes a diamond valuable and a pebble worthless. Property, on the other hand, is the creation of law. A man who has property has certain legal rights with respect to an item of wealth; property represents a relationship between wealth and its "owner." Government largess is plainly "wealth," but it is not necessarily "property."

Government largess has given rise to a distinctive system of law. This system can be viewed from at least three perspectives; the rights of holders of largess, the powers of government over largess, and the procedure by which holders' rights and governmental power are adjusted. At this point, analysis will not be aided by attempting to apply or to reject the label "property." What is important is to survey — without the use of labels — the unique legal system that is emerging.

A. Individual Rights in Largess

As government largess has grown in importance, quite naturally there has been pressure for the protection of individual interests in it. The holder of a broadcast license or a motor carrier permit or a grazing permit for the public lands tends to consider this wealth his "own," and to seek legal protection against interference with his enjoyment. The development of individual interests has been substantial, but it has not come easily.

From the beginning, individual rights in largess have been greatly affected by several traditional legal concepts, each of which has had lasting significance:

Right vs. privilege. The early law is marked by courts' attempts to distinguish which forms of largess were "rights" and which were "privileges." Legal protection of the former was by far the greater. If the holder of a license had a "right," he might be entitled to a hearing before the license could be revoked; a "mere privilege" might be revoked without notice or hearing.[29]

The gratuity principle. Government largess has often been considered a "gratuity" furnished by the state.[30] Hence it is said that the state can withhold, grant, or revoke the largess at its pleasure.[31]

Under this theory, government is considered to be in somewhat the same position as a private giver.

The whole and the parts. Related to the gratuity theory is the idea that, since government may completely withhold a benefit, it may grant it subject to any terms or conditions whatever. This theory is essentially an exercise in logic: the whole power must include all of its parts.[32]

Internal management. Particularly in relation to its own contracts, government has been permitted extensive power on the theory that it should have control over its own housekeeping or internal management functions. Under this theory, government is treated like a private business. In its dealings with outsiders it is permitted much of the freedom to grant contracts and licenses that a private business would have.[33]

. . . .

These sentiments are often voiced in the law of government largess, but individual interests have grown up nevertheless. The most common forms of protection are procedural, coupled with an insistence that government action be based on standards that are not "arbitrary" or unauthorized. Development has varied mainly according to the particular type of wealth involved. The courts have most readily granted protection to those types which are intimately bound up with the individual's freedom to earn a living. They have been reluctant to grant individual rights in those types of largess which seem to be exercises of the managerial functions of government, such as subsidies and government contracts.

Occupational licenses. After some initial hesitation, courts have generally held that an occupational or professional license may not be denied or revoked without affording the applicant notice and a hearing.[38] Doctors, lawyers, real estate brokers, and taxi drivers may not be denied their livelihood without some minimum procedure.[39] In addition to requiring notice and hearing, some courts may also review the evidence for sufficiency, to see if a basis for the official action exists in fact.[40] The need for procedural protection for occupational licenses is sufficiently well accepted that hearings have been required on denial of security clearances when these are tantamount to occupational licenses.[41]

Drivers' licenses. Licenses not specifically tied to a particular occupation, such as drivers' licenses, have to some extent been assimilated under the umbrella of occupational licenses. New York's highest court declared that a driver's license is "of tremendous value to the individual and may not be taken away except by due process."[42] Another court treated a driver's license not as an economic right but as an aspect of personal liberty....

. . . .

Franchises. A franchise is less of a "natural right" than an occupational license, because it confers an exclusive or monopoly position established by government. But the courts early took the position that certain types of franchises were "property" protected by the Constitution.[44] And even air route certificates, which are clearly not like the old-time franchise, are given judicial protection. The courts recognize the existence of "business and investment property" which must be protected.[45] Arguing that Congress intended an air carrier to enjoy "security of route," the Supreme Court has insisted on procedural safeguards before modification of a route.[46]

Benefits. With somewhat greater reluctance, the courts have moved toward a measure of legal protection for benefits. The District of Columbia Court of Appeals rejected an argument that a Veterans Administration decision (imposing a forfeiture of benefits because the veteran had rendered assistance to an enemy) is not reviewable by the courts.[47] The same court also questioned whether Congress could authorize an administrator to revoke a veteran's disability pension without some standards to guide him.[48] And the U.S. Supreme Court held that a state cannot deny unemployment benefits on grounds which interfere with freedom of religion.[49] In California, the courts held that unemployment compensation may not be denied one who refuses a job because he feels unable to take a required loyalty oath.[50]

Subsidies. A subsidy to a business is like a benefit to an individual, but the concept of "rights" in a subsidy is somewhat more attenuated. However, when the Postmaster General found the contents of Esquire Magazine to be objectionable, the Supreme Court made a strong stand for protection of the second class mail subsidy against arbitrary withdrawal.[51] And another court said that a condition attached by the Maritime Board to a subsidy could be attacked by the company which accepted the condition on the ground that it was illegally retroactive and discriminatory.[52]

Use of public resources. Although it is frequently stated that there are no property rights in public resources, the courts have afforded a measure of protection. They have given the holder of a grazing permit the right to prevent interference by others.[53] And the California Supreme Court has held that the use of a public school auditorium cannot be denied to a group because it refuses to sign a loyalty oath. The court said: "The state is under no duty to make school buildings available for public meetings.... If it elects to do so, however, it cannot arbitrarily prevent any members of the public from holding such meetings...."[54]

Contracts. Government contracts might seem the best possible example of a type of valuable which no one has any right to receive, and which represents only the government's managerial function. But even here, at least one court has said that a would-be contractor may not be wholly debarred from eligibility as a consequence of arbitrary government action:

> While they do not have a right to contract with the United States on their own terms, appellants do have a right not to be invalidly denied equal opportunity under applicable law to seek contracts on government projects.[55]

. . . .

In all of the cases concerning individual rights in largess the exact nature of the government action which precipitates the controversy makes a great difference. A controversy over government largess may arise from such diverse situations as denial of the right to apply, denial of an application, attaching conditions to a grant, modification of a grant already made, suspension or revocation of a grant, or some other sanction. In general, courts tend to afford the greatest measure of protection in revocation or suspension cases. The theory seems to be that here some sort of rights have "vested" which may not be taken away without proper procedure. On the other hand, an applicant for largess is thought to have less at stake, and is therefore entitled to less protection.[58] The mere fact that a particular form of largess is protected in one context does not mean that it will be protected in all others.

While individual interests in largess have developed along the lines of procedural protection and restraint upon arbitrary official action, substantive rights to possess and use largess have remained very limited. In the first place, largess does not "vest" in a recipient; it almost always remains revocable.

. . . .

When the public interest demands that the government take over "property," the Constitution requires that just compensation be paid to the owner. But when largess is revoked in public interest, the holder ordinarily receives no compensation. For example, if a television station's license were revoked, not for bad behavior on the part of the operator, but in order to provide a channel in another locality, or to provide an outlet for educational television, the holder would not be compensated for its loss. This principle applies to largess of all types.[62]

In addition to being revocable without compensation, most forms of largess are subject to considerable limitations on their use. Social Security cannot be sold or transferred. A television license can be transferred only with FCC permission. The possessor of a grazing permit has no right to change, improve, or destroy the landscape. And the use of most largess is limited to specified purposes. Some welfare grants, for example, must be applied to support dependent children. On the other hand, holders of government wealth usually do have a power to exclude others, and to realize income.

The most significant limitation on use is more subtle. To some extent, at least, the holder of government largess is expected to act as the agent of "the public interest" rather than solely in the service of his own self-interest. The theory of broadcast licensing is that the channels belong to the public and should be used for the public's benefit, but that a variety of private operators are likely to perform this function more successfully than government; the holder of a radio or television license is therefore expected to broadcast in "the public interest." The opportunity for private profit is intended to serve as a lure to make private operators serve the public.

The "mix" of public and private, and the degree to which the possessor acts as the government's agent, varies from situation to situation. The government contractor is explicitly the agent of the government in what he does; in theory he could equally well be the manager of a government-owned factory. Only his right to profits and his control over how the job is done distinguish his private status. The taxi driver performs the public service of transportation (which the government might otherwise perform) subject to regulation but with more freedom than the contractor. The doctor serves the public with still greater freedom. The mother of a child entitled to public aid acts as the state's agent in supporting the child with the funds thus provided, but her freedom is even greater and the responsibility of her agency still less defined.

The result of all of this is a breaking down of distinctions between public and private and resultant blurring or fusing of public and private. Many of the functions of government are performed by private persons; much private activity is carried on in a way that is no longer private.

B. Largess and the Power of Government

1. Affirmative Powers

When government — national, state, or local — hands out something of value, whether a relief check or a television license, government's power grows forthwith; it automatically gains such power as is necessary and proper to supervise its largess. It obtains new rights to investigate, to regulate, and to punish.[63] This increase in power is furthered by an easy and wide-ranging concept of relevance....

. . . .

The restrictions which derive from these expanded notions of relevance are enforceable not merely by withholding largess, but also by imposing sanctions. Along with largess goes the power to punish new crimes. Misuse of the gift becomes criminal, and hence new standards of lawful behavior are set: government can make it a crime to fail to spend welfare funds in such a manner as accords with the best interests of the children.

Government largess not only increases the legal basis for government power; it increases the political basis as well. When an individual or a business uses public money or enjoys a government privilege or occupies part of the public domain, it is easier to argue for a degree of regulation which might not be accepted if applied to business or individuals generally. Objections to regulation fade, whether in the minds of the general public or legal scholars, before the argument that government should make sure that its bounty is used in the public interest. Benefits, subsidies, and privileges are seen as "gifts" to be given on conditions, and thus the political and legal sources of government power merge into one.

2. The Magnification of Government Power by Administrative Discretion

Broad as is the power derived from largess, it is magnified by many administrative factors when it is brought to bear on a recipient. First, the agency granting government largess generally has a wide measure of discretion to interpret its own power. Second, the nature of administrative agencies, the functions they combine, and the sanctions they possess, give them additional power. Third, the circumstances in which the recipients find themselves sometimes makes them abettors, rather than resisters of the further growth of power.

The legislature generally delegates to an administrative agency its authority with respect to a given form of largess. In this very process of delegation there can be an enlargement of power. The courts allow the agencies a wide measure of discretion to make policy and to interpret legislative policy. Sometimes a legislature gives the agency several different, possibly conflicting policies, allowing it (perhaps unintentionally) to enforce now one and now another.[90]

There is little if any requirement of consistency or adherence to precedent and the agency may, instead of promulgating rules of general application, make and change its policies in the process of case-to-case adjudication.[91] For example, New Jersey's Waterfront Commission has power "in its discretion" to deny the right to work to any longshoreman if he is a person "whose presence at the piers or other

waterfront terminals in the Port of New York is found by the commission on the basis of the facts and evidence before it, to constitute a danger to the public peace or safety."[92] The discretion of an agency is even broader, and even less reviewable, when the subject matter is highly technical. In such fields, which are increasing in number, "experts" or professionals come to power, and their actions are even harder to confine within legislatively fixed limits. Discretion as to enforcement or punishment is one of the greatest of agency powers. A licensing agency often has power to choose between forgiveness, suspension, and permanent revocation of license after a violation.[93]

. . . .

Most dispensing agencies possess the power of delay. They also possess the power of investigation and harassment; they can initiate inquiries which will prove expensive and embarrassing to an applicant. Surveillance alone can make a recipient of largess uncomfortable. And agencies have so many criteria to use, so many available grounds of decision, and so much discretion, that they, like the FCC, can usually find other grounds to accomplish what they cannot do directly. This is a temptation to the honest but zealous administrator, and an invitation to the official who is less than scrupulous. In addition, the broader the regulation, the greater the chance that everyone violates the law in some way, and the greater the discretion to forgive or to punish. But even if a dispensing agency is self-restrained and scrupulous beyond the requirements of statutes, the function of dispensing will make its power grow. The dispensing of largess is a continuing process. The threat of an unfavorable attitude in the future should be sufficient persuasion for today.

The recipients of largess themselves add to the powers of government by their uncertainty over their rights, and their efforts to please. Unsure of their ground, they are often unwilling to contest a decision. The penalties for being wrong, in terms of possible loss of largess in the future, are very severe.[95] Instead of contesting, recipients are likely to be over-zealous in their acceptance of government authority so that a government contractor may be so anxious to root out "disloyal" employees that he dismisses men who could probably be retained consistently with government policy. Likewise a "think institute" existing primarily on government contracts, may be more eager to "think" along accepted lines because it has its next month's bills to "think" about.[96]

This penumbral government power is, indeed, likely to be greater than the sum of the granted powers. Seeking to stay on the safe side of an uncertain, often unknowable line, people dependent on largess are likely to eschew any activities that might incur official displeasure. Beneficiaries of government bounty fear to offend, lest ways and means be found, in the obscure corners of discretion to deny these favors in the future.

C. Largess and Procedural Safeguards

The procedural law of government largess is as distinctive as the substantive. In addition to the general law governing the grant and revocation of largess, there are special aspects of unusual interest: the power to conduct trials of persons for alleged violations of law, and the authority to apply sanctions and punishments.

1. Procedures: In general

The granting, regulation, and revocation of government largess is carried on by procedures which, in varying degrees, represent short-cuts that tend to augment the power of the grantor at the expense of the recipient. In the first place, the tribunal is likely to be an arm of the granting agency rather than independent and impartial....

. . . .

2. Trials

Among the matters which may be relevant to the granting or revocation of government largess are various types of law violations, civil and criminal in nature. Violations of law are normally determined by courts. But in dispensing largess government has not always been willing to rely on courts to determine whether laws have been violated. In an increasing number of cases it has undertaken to make such determinations independently. And thereby it has exercised an extraordinary procedural power — the power to try law violations in the executive branch, without benefit of judge or jury. It is true that these "trials" cannot result in imposition of criminal sanctions. But the ability to conduct trials and adjudications is of great significance in itself, and the denial of benefits which may follow approximates a sanction.

. . . .

Perhaps the greatest extreme reached by agency trial power is illustrated by motor vehicle bureaus, which sometimes find motorists "guilty" after courts have found them innocent. In New Jersey the Director of the Division of Motor Vehicles may suspend a driver's license (a) where the individual has been acquitted of the charge by a court or (b) where the individual has been convicted and punished, but the additional punishment of license suspension was expressly withheld by the sentencing court....

. . . .

3. New and unusual punishments

Administering largess carries with it not only the power to conduct trials, but also the power to inflict many sorts of sanctions not classified as criminal punishments. The most obvious penalty is simply denial or deprivation of some form of wealth or privilege that the agency dispenses. How badly this punishment hurts depends upon how essential the benefit is to the individual or business affected. The loss of some privileges or subsidies may be quite trivial. But for the government contractor placed on a blacklist the consequences may be financial ruin if the government is one of its major customers. The television station which loses its license is out of business. So is the doctor who loses his medical license.

Although the denial of benefits is consistently held not to be penal in nature, it is perfectly clear that on occasion the government uses this power as a sanction....

. . . .

Denial of benefits by no means exhausts the list of sanctions available to government. Severe harm can be inflicted by adverse publicity resulting from investigations, findings of violation, blacklisting, or forfeitures for cause. A striking instance is the SEC practice, upheld by the courts, of placing alleged violators of certain of its regulations on a public blacklist.[116] Forfeitures are imposed under agricultural stabilization programs.[117] The mere pendency of proceedings may be harmful, especially if accompanied by costly and harassing investigation and interminable delay.

III. THE PUBLIC INTEREST STATE

What are the consequences of the rise of government largess and its attendant legal system? What is the impact on the recipient, on constitutional guaranties of liberty, on the structure of power in the nation? It is important to try to picture the society that is emerging, and to seek its underlying philosophy. The dominant theme, as we have seen, is "the public interest," and out of it there grows the "public interest state."

A. The Erosion of Independence

The recipient of largess, whether an organization or an individual, feels the government's power. The company that is heavily subsidized or dependent on government contracts is subjected to an added amount of regulation and inspection, sometimes to the point of having resident government officials in its plant.[118] And it is subject to added government pressures. The well known episode when the large steel companies were forced to rescind a price rise, partly by the threat of loss of government contracts, illustrates this. Perhaps the most elaborate and onerous regulation of businesses with government contracts is the industrial security system, which places all employees in defence industries under government scrutiny, and subjects them, even high executives, to dismissal if they fail to win government approval.[119]

Universities also feel the power of government largess. Research and development grants to universities tend to influence the direction of university activities, and in addition inhibit the university from pursuing activities it might otherwise undertake.[120] In order to qualify for government contracts, Harvard University was required, despite extreme reluctance, to report the number of Negroes employed in each department. The University kept no such information, and contended that gathering it would emphasize the very racial distinctions that the government was trying to minimize. Nevertheless, the University was forced to yield to the Government's demand.[121]

Individuals are also subject to great pressures. Dr. Edward K. Barsky, a New York physician and surgeon since 1919, was for a time chairman of the Joint Anti-Fascist Refugee Committee.[122] In 1946 he was summoned before the House Committee on Un-American Activities. In the course of his examination he refused, on constitutional grounds, to produce records of the organization's contributions and expenditures. For this refusal he served six months in jail for contempt of Congress. Thereafter the New York State Education Department filed a complaint against him, under a provision of law making any doctor convicted of a crime subject to discipline. Although there was no evidence in any way touching Dr. Barsky's activities as a physician, the Depart-

ment's Medical Grievance Committee suspended his medical license for six months. The New York courts upheld the suspension....

. . . .

On appeal, the suspension was upheld by the United States Supreme Court.[124] The court declared that New York had "substantially plenary power" to fix conditions for the practice of medicine,[125] and concluded that the state's action was reasonable, especially "in a field so permeated with public responsibility as that of health."[126]

If the businessman, the teacher, and the professional man find themselves subject to the power of government largess, the man on public assistance is even more dependent. Welfare officials, often with the best of motivations, impose conditions intended to better a client, which sometimes are a deep invasion of his freedom of action.[127] In a memorable case in New York, an old man was denied welfare because he insisted on living under unsanitary conditions, sleeping in a barn in a pile of rags.

. . . .

Caught in the vast network of regulation, the individual has no hiding place.

B. Pressures Against the Bill of Rights

The chief legal bulwark of the individual against oppressive government power is the Bill of Rights. But government largess may impair the individual's enjoyment of those rights.

. . . .

It takes a brave man to stand firm against the power that can be exerted through government largess. This is nowhere better shown than by the case of George Anastaplo. [Mr. Anastaplo was denied admission to the bar of Illinois on the ground that he had exercised his constitutional right to refuse to answer a state subcommittee's question as to whether he had been a member of the Communist party. In *In re Anastaplo*, 366 U.S. 82, 83 n.1 (1961), the United States Supreme Court upheld the denial. They said the state's interest in having law-abiding lawyers outweighed the constitutional principle of freedom of speech and association on which Mr. Anastaplo had relied in refusing to answer the question.]

. . . .

The foregoing cases suggest that the growth of largess has made it possible for government to "purchase" the abandonment of constitutional rights. And government, for a variety of reasons, has used this power in many circumstances. In particular, government employees, defence employees, members of licensed occupations, and licensed businesses have felt pressure on their freedom of political expression and their right to plead the privilege against self-incrimination. Recipients of largess remain free to exercise their rights, of course. But the price of free exercise is the risk of economic loss, or even loss of livelihood.[156]

C. From Governmental Power to Private Power

The preceding description has pictured two fundamentally opposite forces: government versus the private sector of society. Emphasis on a sharp dichotomy highlights some of the relationships created by government largess. But to a considerable extent this picture distorts reality. First, the impact of governmental power falls unequally on different components of the private sector, so that some gain while others lose. Second, government largess often creates a partnership with some sectors of the private economy, which aids rather than limits the objectives of those private sectors. Third, the apparatus of governmental power may be utilized by private interests in their conflicts with other interests, and thus the tools of government become private rather than public instrumentalities.

Inequalities lie deep in the administrative structure of government largess. The whole process of acquiring it and keeping it favors some applicants and recipients over others. The administrative process is characterized by uncertainty, delay, and inordinate expense; to operate within it requires considerable know-how. All of these factors strongly favor larger, richer, more experienced companies or individuals over smaller ones. Only the most secure can weather delay or seemingly endless uncertainty. A company accused of misusing a license can engage counsel to fight the action without being ruined by the expenses of the defence; an individual may find revocation proceedings are enough to send him to the poorhouse regardless of the outcome. And the large and the small are not always treated alike. For example, small firms which deal with the government are sometimes placed on a blacklist because of delinquencies in performance, thus losing out on all government contracts.[157] But giant contractors who are guilty of similar delinquencies are apparently not subject to this drastic punishment. Similarly, regulation of taxicabs tends to be harder on the individual owner or driver, who may lose his driver's license, while little harm comes to the company controlling a fleet, which may lose drivers but not its precious franchises.[158]

Beside this unacknowledged double standard there is also the fact that sometimes the government quite openly favors one class of applicants — frequently the large and successful. Atomic energy benefits have generally gone to industry giants.[159] Television channels seem to be in the hands of large corporate applicants, often those which control newspapers or other stations. Another illustration of this tendency is in the award of franchises for turnpike restaurants; the business seems to go to large established chains, although they can hardly be said to provide service of outstanding culinary distinction.[160]

All these inequalities modify somewhat the simple picture of a government-private dichotomy. But a second modification is required: government and the private sector (or a favored part of that sector) are often partners rather than opposing interests. The concept of partnership covers many quite different situations. Sometimes government largess serves to aid the private objectives of an industry, as when government supplies grazing land to stockmen, timber to the lumber industry, and scientific know-how to the private investors in Telstar.[161] A second type of partnership exists where governmental action protects the recipient of largess from adverse forces with which he would otherwise have to contend; this is illustrated by the defense contract, with its virtual guarantee against losses due to most economic or management factors.[162] The Atomic Energy Commission provides insurance against public liability due to negligence.[163] Just as frequently, government largess offers protection against the disadvantages of competition....

. . . .

In any society with powerful or dominant private groups, it is not unexpected that governmental systems of power will be utilized by private groups. Hence the frequency with which regulatory agencies are taken over by those they are supposed to regulate.[174] Significantly, most of these agencies are also the chief federal dispensers of largess. They quarrel with the industries they regulate, but seen in a larger perspective these quarrels are all in the family. In sum, the great system of power created by government largess is a ready means to further some private groups, and not merely an advance in the position of government over that which is "private" in society as a whole.

D. The New Feudalism

The characteristics of the public interest state are varied, but there is an underlying philosophy that unites them. This is the doctrine that the wealth that flows from government is held by its recipients conditionally, subject to confiscation in the interest of the paramount state. This philosophy is epitomized in the most important of all judicial decisions concerning government largess, the case of *Flemming* v. *Nestor*.[175]

Ephram Nestor, an alien, came to this country in 1913, and after a long working life became eligible in 1955 for old-age benefits under the Social Security Act. From 1936 to 1955 Nestor and his employers had contributed payments to the government which went into a special old-age and survivors insurance trust fund. From 1933 to 1939 Nestor was a member of the Communist Party. Long after his membership ceased, Congress passed a law retroactively making such membership cause for deportation, and a second law, also retroactive, making such deportation for having been a member of the Party grounds for loss of retirement benefits. In 1956 Nestor was deported, leaving his wife here. Soon after his deportation, payment of benefits to Nestor's wife was terminated.

In a five to four decision, the Supreme Court held that cutting off Nestor's retirement insurance, although based on conduct completely lawful at the time, was not unconstitutional. Specifically, it was not a taking of property without due process of law; Nestor's benefits were not an "accrued property right."[176] The Court recognized that each worker's benefits flow "from the contributions he made to the national economy while actively employed," but it held that his interest is "noncontractual" and "cannot be soundly analogized to that of the holder of an annuity."[177] The Court continued:

> To engraft upon the Social Security system a concept of "accrued property rights" would deprive it of the flexibility and boldness in adjustment of ever-changing conditions which it demands.... It was doubtless out of an awareness of the need for such flexibility that Congress included ... a clause expressly reserving to it "[t]he right to alter, amend or repeal any provision" of the Act.... That provision makes express what is implicit in the institutional needs of the program.[178]

The Court stated further that, in any case where Congress "modified" social security rights, the Court should interfere only if the action is "utterly lacking in rational justification."[179] This, the Court said, "is not the case here." As the Court saw it, it might be deemed reasonable for Congress to limit payments to those living in this country; moreover, the Court thought it would not have been "irrational for Congress to have concluded that the public purse should not be utilized to contribute to the support of those deported on the grounds specified in the statute."[180]

The implications of *Flemming* v. *Nestor* are profound. No forms of government largess is more personal or individual than an old age pension. No form is more clearly earned by the recipient, who together with his employer, contributes to the Social Security fund during the years of his employment. No form is more obviously a compulsory substitute for private property; the tax on wage earner and employer might readily have gone to higher pay and higher private savings instead. No form is more relied on, and more often thought of as property. No form is more vital to the independence and dignity of the individual. Yet under the philosophy of Congress and the Court, a man or woman, after a lifetime of work, has no rights which may not be taken away to serve some public policy. The Court makes no effort to balance the interests at stake. The public policy that justifies cutting off benefits need not even be an important one or a wise one — so long as it is not utterly irrational, the Court will not interfere. In any clash between individual rights and public policy, the latter is automatically held to be superior.

The philosophy of *Flemming* v. *Nestor, of Barsky,* in *In Re Anastaplo,* and *Cohen* v. *Hurley,* resembles the philosophy of feudal tenure. Wealth is not "owned," or "vested" in the holders. Instead, it is held conditionally, the conditions being ones which seek to ensure the fulfilment of obligations imposed by the state. Just as the feudal system linked lord and vassal through a system of mutual dependence, obligation, and loyalty, so government largess binds man to the state.[181] And, it may be added, loyalty or fealty to the state is often one of the essential conditions of modern tenure. In the many decisions taking away government largess for refusal to sign loyalty oaths, belonging to "subversive" organizations, or other similar grounds, there is more than a suggestion of the condition of fealty demanded in older times.

The comparison to the general outlines of the feudal system may best be seen by recapitulating some of the chief features of government largess.

43

(1) Increasingly we turn over wealth and rights to government, which reallocates and redistributes them in the many forms of largess; (2) there is a merging of public and private, in which lines of private ownership are blurred; (3) the administration of the system has given rise to special laws and special tribunals, outside the ordinary structure of government; (4) the right to possess and use government largess is bound up with the recipient's legal status; status is both the basis for receiving largess and a consequence of receiving it; hence the new wealth is not readily transferable; (5) individuals hold the wealth conditionally rather than absolutely; the conditions are usually obligations owed to the government or to the public, and may include the obligation of loyalty to the government; the obligations may be changed or increased at the will of the state; (6) for breach of condition the wealth may be forfeited or escheated back to the government; (7) the sovereign power is shared with large private interests; (8) the object of the whole system is to enforce "the public interest" — the interest of the state or society or the lord paramount — by means of the distribution and use of wealth in such a way as to create and maintain dependence.

This feudal philosophy of largess and tenure may well be a characteristic of collective societies, regardless of their political systems. According to one scholar, national socialism regarded property as contingent upon duties owed the state; Nazism denied the absolute character of property and imposed obligations conditioning property tenure: "In practice the development seems to have been toward a concept of property based on the superior right of the overlord."[182] In Soviet Russia, the trend reportedly has been somewhat similar, although starting from a different theoretical point. After denying the existence of private property, the Soviets have developed a quasi-property, amounting to the right to use and to have exclusive possession for a period of years. Earnings in Russia are also in a sense property, but computed in accordance with the individual's contribution to the state.[183]

The public interest state is not with us yet. But we are left with large questions. If the day comes when most private ownership is supplanted by government largess, how then will governmental power over individuals be contained? What will dependence do to the American character? What will happen to the Constitution, and particularly the Bill of Rights, if their limits may be bypassed by purchase, and if people lack an independent base from which to assert their individuality and claim their rights? Without the security of the person which individual

wealth provides and which largess fails to provide, what, indeed, will we become?

IV. PROPERTY AND THE PUBLIC INTEREST: AN OLD DEBATE REVISITED

The public interest state, as visualized above, represents in one sense the triumph of society over private property. This triumph is the end point of a great and necessary movement for reform. But somehow the result is different from what the reformers wanted. Somehow the idealistic concept of the public interest has summoned up a doctrine monstrous and oppressive. It is time to take another look at private property, and at the "public interest" philosophy that dominates its modern substitute, the largess of government.

A. Property and Liberty

Property is a legal institution the essence of which is the creation and protection of certain private rights in wealth of any kind. The institution performs many different functions. One of these functions is to draw a boundary between public and private power. Property draws a circle around the activities of each private individual or organization. Within that circle, the owner has a greater degree of freedom than without. Outside, he must justify or explain his actions, and show his authority. Within, he is master, and the state must explain and justify any interference. It is as if property shifted the burden of proof; outside, the individual has the burden; inside, the burden is on government to demonstrate that something the owner wishes to do should not be done.

Thus, property performs the function of maintaining independence, dignity and pluralism in society by creating zones within which the majority has to yield to the owner. Whim, caprice, irrationality and "antisocial" activities are given the protection of law; the owner may do what all or most of his neighbors decry. The Bill of Rights also serves this function, but while the Bill of Rights comes into play only at extraordinary moments of conflict of crisis, property affords day-to-day protection in the ordinary affairs of life. Indeed, in the final analysis the Bill of Rights depends upon the existence of private property. Political rights presuppose that individuals and private groups have the will and the means to act independently. But so long as individuals are motivated largely by self-interest, their well-being must first be independent. Civil liberties must have a basis in property, or bills of rights will not preserve them.

Property is not a natural right but a deliberate construction by society. If such an institution did not exist, it would be necessary to create it, in order to have the kind of society we wish. The majority cannot be expected, on specific issues, to yield its power to a minority. Only if the minority's will is established as a general principle can it keep the majority at bay in a given instance. Like the Bill of Rights, property represents a general, long range protection of individual and private interests, created by the majority for the ultimate good of all.

Today, however, it is widely thought that property and liberty are separable things; that there may, in fact, be conflicts between "property rights" and "personal rights." Why has this view been accepted? The explanation is found at least partly in the transformations which have taken place in property.

During the industrial revolution, when property was liberated from feudal restraints, philosophers hailed property as the basis of liberty, and argued that it must be free from the demands of government or society.[184] But as private property grew, so did abuses resulting from its use. In a crowded world, a man's use of his property increasingly affected his neighbor, and one man's exercise of a right might seriously impair the rights of others. Property became power over others; the farm landowner, the city landlord, and the working man's boss were able to oppress their tenants or employees. Great aggregations of property resulted in private control of entire industries and basic services capable of affecting a whole area or even a nation. At the same time, much private property lost its individuality and in effect became socialized. Multiple ownership of corporations helped to separate personality from property, and property from power.[185] When the corporations began to stop competing, to merge, agree, and make mutual plans, they became private governments. Finally, they sought the aid and partnership of the state, and thus by their own volition became part of public government.

These changes led to a movement for reform, which sought to limit arbitrary private power and protect the common man. Property rights were considered more the enemy than the friend of liberty. The reformers argued that property must be separated from personality.[186] Walton Hamilton wrote:

As late as the turn of the last century justices were not yet distinguishing between liberty and property; in the universes beneath their hats liberty was still the opportunity to acquire property.

...

... the property of the Reports is not a proprietary thing; it is rather a shibboleth in whose name the domain of business enterprises has enjoyed a limited immunity from the supervision of the state.

...

In the annals of the law property is still a vestigial expression of personality and owes its current constitutional position to its former association with liberty.[187]

During the first half of the twentieth century, the reformers enacted into law their conviction that private power was a chief enemy of society and of individual liberty. Property was subjected to "reasonable" limitations in the interests of society. The regulatory agencies, federal and state, were born of the reform. In sustaining these major inroads on private property, the Supreme Court rejected the older idea that property and liberty were one, and wrote a series of classic opinions upholding the power of the people to regulate and limit private rights.

The struggle between abuse and reform made it easy to forget the basic importance of individual private property. The defence of private property was almost entirely a defence of its abuses — an attempt to defend not individual property but arbitrary private power over other human beings. Since this defence was cloaked in a defence of private property, it was natural for the reformers to attack too broadly. Walter Lippmann saw this in 1934:

But the issue between the giant corporation and the public should not be allowed to obscure the truth that the only dependable foundation of personal liberty is the economic security of private property.

...

For we must not expect to find in ordinary men the stuff of martyrs, and we must, therefore, secure their freedom by their normal motives. There is no surer way to give men the courage to be free than to insure them a competence upon which they can rely.[188]

The reform took away some of the power of the corporations and transferred it to government. In this transfer there was much good, for power was made responsive to the majority rather than to the arbitrary and selfish few. But the reform did not restore the individual to his domain. What the corporation had taken from him, the reform simply handed on to government. And government carried further the powers formerly exercised by the corporation. Government as an employer, or as a dispenser of wealth has used the theory that it was handing out gratuities to claim a managerial power as great as that which the capitalists claimed. Moreover, the corporations allied themselves with, or actually took over, part of government's system of power. Today it is the combined power of government and the corporations that presses against the individual.

From the individual's point of view, it is not any particular kind of power, but all kinds of power, that are to be feared. This is the lesson of the public interest state. The mere fact that power is derived from the majority does not necessarily make it less oppressive. Liberty is more than the right to do what the majority wants, or to do what is "reasonable." Liberty is the right to defy the majority, and to do what is unreasonable. The great error of the public interest state is that it assumes an identity between the public interest and the interest of the majority.

The reform, then, has not done away with the importance of private property. More than ever the individual needs to possess, in whatever form, a small but sovereign island of his own.

B. Largess and the Public Interest

The fact that the reform tended to make much private wealth subject to "the public interest" has great significance, but it does not adequately explain the dependent position of the individual and the weakening of civil liberties in the public interest state. The reformers intended to enhance the values of democracy and liberty; their basic concern was the preservation of a free society. But after they established the primacy of "the public interest," what meaning was given to that phrase? In particular, what values does it embody as it has been employed to regulate government largess?

Reduced to simplest terms, "the public interest" has usually meant this: government largess may be denied or taken away if this will serve some legitimate public policy. The policy may be one directly related to the largess itself, or it may be some collateral objective of government. A contract may be denied if this will promote fair labor standards. A television license may be refused if this will promote the policies of the antitrust laws. Veterans benefits may be taken away to promote loyalty to the United States. A liquor license may be revoked to promote civil rights. A franchise for a barber's college may not be given out if it will hurt the local economy, nor a taxi franchise if it will seriously injure the earning capacity of other taxis.

Most of these objectives are laudable, and all are within the power of government. The great difficulty is that they are simplistic. Concentration on a single policy or value obscures other values that may be at stake. Some of these competing values are other public policies; for example, the policy of the best possible television service to the public may compete with observance of the antitrust laws. The legislature is the natural arbiter of such conflicts. But the conflicts may also be more fundamental. In the regulation of government largess, achievement of specific policy goals may undermine the independence of the individual. Where such conflicts exist, a simplistic notion of the public interest may unwittingly destroy some values.

. . . .

Barsky v. *Board of Regents*[191] shows how one-sided the public interest concept may become. New York State suspended a doctor's license because he committed the crime of contempt of Congress. The Supreme court, upholding this, identified the public interest as the state's "broad power to establish and enforce standards of conduct relative to the health of everyone there,"[192] and the "state's legitimate concern for maintaining high standards of professional conduct."[193] But what about the importance of giving doctors security in their professions? What about the benefits to the state from having physicians who are independent of administrative control? Not only were these ignored by the state and the court; no effort was even made to show how the suspension promoted the one public policy that was named (high professional standards for those concerned with public health). As Justice Frankfurter said,

> It is one thing to recognize the freedom which the constitution wisely leaves to the States in regulating the professions. It is quite another thing, however, to sanction a State's deprivation or partial destruction of a man's professional life on grounds having no possible relation to fitness, intellectual or moral, to pursue his profession.[194]

In *Flemming* v. *Nestor*[195] the concept of the public interest is distorted even more. It was given a meaning injurious to the independence of millions of persons. At stake was the security of the old age Social Security pension system, together with all the social values which might flow from assuring old people a stable, dignified, and independent basis of retirement. Yet Congress and the Supreme Court jeopardized all these values to serve a public policy both trivial and vindictive — the punishment of a few persons for Communist Party membership now long past.

. . . .

It is not the reformers who must bear the blame for the harmful consequences of the public interest state, but those who are responsible for giving "the public interest" its present meaning. If "the public interest" distorts the reformers' high purposes, this is so because the concept has been so gravely misstated. Government largess, like all wealth, must necessarily be regulated in the public interest. But regulation must take account of the dangers of dependence, and the need for a property base for civil liberties. Rightly conceived, the public interest is no justification for the erosion of freedom that has resulted from the present system of government largess.[206]

. . . .

V.   TOWARD INDIVIDUAL STAKES IN THE COMMONWEALTH

Ahead there stretches — to the farthest horizon — the joyless landscape of the public interest state. The life it promises will be comfortable and comforting. It will be well planned — with suitable areas for work and play. But there will be no precincts sacred to the spirit of individual man.

There can be no retreat from the public interest state. It is the inevitable outgrowth of an interdependent world. An effort to return to an earlier economic order would merely transfer power to giant private governments which would rule not in the public interest, but in their own interest. If individualism and pluralism are to be preserved, this must be done not by marching backwards, but by building these values into today's society. If public and private are now blurred, it will be necessary to draw a new zone of privacy. If private property can no longer perform its protective functions, it will be necessary to establish institutions to carry on the work that private property once did but can no longer do.

In these efforts government largess must play a major role. As we move toward a welfare state, largess will be an ever more important form of wealth. And largess is a vital link in the relationship between the government and private sides of society. It is necessary, then, that largess begin to do the work of property.

The chief obstacle to the creation of private rights in largess has been the fact that it is originally public property, comes from the state, and may be withheld completely. But this need not be an obsta-cle. Traditional property also comes from the state, and in much the same way. Land, for example, traces back to grants from the sovereign. In the United States, some was the gift of the King of England, some that of the King of Spain. The sovereign extinguished Indian title by conquest, became the new owner, and then granted title to a private individual or group.[207] Some land was the gift of the sovereign under laws such as the Homestead and Preemption Acts.[208] Many other natural resources — water, minerals and timber, passed into private ownership under similar grants. In America, land and resources all were originally government largess. In a less obvious sense, personal property also stems from government. Personal property is created by law; it owes its origin and continuance to laws supported by the people as a whole. These laws "give" the property to one who performs certain actions. Even the man who catches a wild animal "owns" the animal only as a gift from the sovereign, having fulfilled the terms of an offer to transfer ownership.[209]

Like largess, real and personal property were also originally dispensed on conditions, and were subject to forfeiture if the conditions failed. The conditions in the sovereign grants, such as colonization, were generally made explicit, and so was the forfeiture resulting from failure to fulfil them. In the case of the Preemption and Homestead Acts, there were also specific conditions.[210] Even now land is subject to forfeiture for neglect; if it is unused it may be deemed abandoned to the state or forfeited to an adverse possessor. In a very similar way, personal property may be forfeited by abandonment of loss.[211] Hence, all property might be described as government largess, given on condition and subject to loss.

If all property is government largess, why is it not regulated to the same degree as a present-day largess? Regulation of property has been limited, not because society had no interest in property, but because it was in the interest of society that property be free. Once property is seen not as a natural right but as a construction designed to serve certain functions, then its origin ceases to be decisive in determining how much regulation should be imposed. The conditions that can be attached to receipt, ownership, and use depend not on where property came from, but on what job it should be expected to perform. Thus in the case of government largess, nothing turns on the fact that it originated in government. The real issue is how it functions and how it should function.

To create an institution, or to make an existing institution function in a new way, is an undertaking far too ambitious for the present article. But it is possible to begin a search for guiding principles. Such principles must grow out of what we know about how government largess has functioned up to the present time. And while principles must remain at the level of generality, it should be kept in mind that not every principle is equally applicable to all forms of largess. Our primary focus must be those forms of largess which chiefly control the rights and status of the individual.

A. Constitutional Limits

The most clearly defined problem posed by government largess is the way it can be used to apply pressure against the exercise of constitutional rights. A first principle should be that government must have no power to "buy up" rights guaranteed by the Constitution.[212] It should not be able to impose any condition on largess that would be invalid if imposed on something other than a "gratuity."[213] Thus, for example, the government should not be able to deny largess because of invocation of the privilege against self-incrimination.[214]

This principle is in a sense a revival of the old but neglected rule against unconstitutional conditions, as enunciated by the Supreme Court:

> Broadly stated, the rule is that the right to continue the exercise of a privilege granted by the state cannot be made to depend upon the grantee's submission to a condition prescribed by the state which is hostile to the provisions of the federal constitution.[215]

.   .   .   .

The courts in recent times have gone part of the distance toward this principle....

.   .   .   .

The problem becomes more complicated when a court attempts, as current doctrine seems to require, to "balance" the deterrence of a constitutional right against some opposing interest. In any balancing process, no weight should be given to the contention that what is at stake is a mere gratuity. It should be recognized that pressure against constitutional rights from denial of a "gratuity" may be as great or greater than pressure from criminal punishment. And the concept of the public interest should be given a meaning broad enough to include general injury to independence and constitutional rights.[222] It is not possible to consider detailed problems here. It is enough to say that government should gain no power, as against constitutional limitations, by reason of its role as a dispenser of wealth.

B. Substantive Limits

Beyond the limits deriving from the Constitution, what limits should be imposed on governmental power over largess? Such limits, whatever they may be, must be largely self-imposed and self-policed by legislatures; the Constitution sets only a bare minimum of limitations on legislative policy. The first type of limit should be on relevance. It has proven possible to argue that practically anything in the way of regulation is relevant to some legitimate legislative purpose. But this does not mean that it is desirable for legislatures to make such use of their powers. As Justice Douglas said in the *Barsky* case:

> So far as I know, nothing in a man's political beliefs disables him from setting broken bones or removing ruptured appendixes, safely and efficiently. A practicing surgeon is unlikely to uncover many state secrets in the course of his professional activities.[223]

.   .   .   .

It is impossible to confine the concept of relevance. But legislatures should strive for a meaningful, judicious concept of relevance if regulation of largess is not to become a handle for regulating everything else.

Besides relevance, a second important limit on substantive power might be concerned with discretion. To the extent possible, delegated power to make rules ought to be confined within ascertainable limits, and regulating agencies should not be assigned the task of enforcing conflicting policies. Also, agencies should be enjoined to use their powers only for the purposes for which they were designed.[226] In a perhaps naive attempt to accomplish this, Senator Lausche introduced a bill to prohibit United States government contracting officers from using their contracting authority for purposes of duress. This bill[,] in its own words, would prohibit officials from denying contracts, or the right to bid on contracts, with the intent of forcing the would-be contractor to perform or refrain from performing any act which such person had no legal obligation to perform or not perform.[227] Although this bill might not be a very effective piece of legislation, it does suggest a desirable objective.

A final limit on substantive power, one that should be of growing importance, might be a principle that policy making authority ought not to be delegated to essentially private organizations. The increasing practice of giving professional associations and occupational organizations authority in areas of government largess tends to make an individual subject to a guild of his fellows. A guild system, when attached to government largess, adds to the feudal characteristics of the system.

C.   Procedural Safeguards

Because it is so hard to confine relevance and discretion, procedure offers a valuable means for restraining arbitrary action. This was recognized in the strong procedural emphasis of the Bill of Rights, and it is being recognized in the increasingly procedural emphasis of administrative law. The law of government largess has developed with little regard for procedure. Reversal of this trend is long overdue.

The grant, denial, revocation, and administration of all types of government largess should be subject to scrupulous observance of fair procedures. Action should be open to hearing and contest, and based upon a record subject to judicial review. The denial of any form of privilege or benefit on the basis of undisclosed reasons should no longer be tolerated.[228] Nor should the same person sit as legislator, prosecutor, judge and jury, combining all the functions of government in such a way as to make fairness virtually impossible. There is no justification for the survival of arbitrary methods where valuable rights are at stake.

Even higher standards of procedural fairness should apply when government action has all the effects of penal sanction....

.   .   .   .

Today many administrative agencies take action which is penal in all but name. The penal nature of these actions should be recognized by appropriate procedures.[231]

Even if no sanction is involved, the proceedings associated with government largess must not be used to undertake adjudications of facts that normally should be made by a court after a trial. Assuming it is relevant to the grant of a license or benefit to know whether an individual has been guilty of a crime or other violation of law, should violations be determined by the agency? The consequence is an adjudication of guilt without benefit of constitutional criminal proceedings with judge, jury, and the safeguards of the Bill of Rights. In our society it is impossible to "try" a violation of law for any purpose without "trying" the whole person of the

alleged violator. The very adjudication is punishment, even if no consequences are attached. It may be added that an agency should not find "guilt" after a court has found innocence. The spirit, if not the letter, of the constitutional ban against double jeopardy should prevent an agency from subjecting anyone to a second trial for the same offense.

D.   From Largess to Right

The proposals discussed above, however salutary, are by themselves far from adequate to assure the status of individual man with respect to largess. The problems go deeper. First, the growth of government power based on the dispensing of wealth must be kept within bounds. Second, there must be a zone of privacy for each individual beyond which neither government nor private power can push — a hiding place from the all-pervasive system of regulation and control. Finally, it must be recognized that we are becoming a society based upon relationship and status — status deriving primarily from source of livelihood. Status is so closely linked to personality that destruction of one may well destroy the other. Status must therefore be surrounded with the kind of safeguards once reserved for personality.

Eventually those forms of largess which are closely linked to status must be deemed to be held as of right. Like property, such largess could be governed by a system of regulation plus civil or criminal sanctions, rather than a system based upon denial, suspension and revocation. As things now stand, violations lead to forfeitures — outright confiscation of wealth and status. But there is surely no need for these drastic results. Confiscation, if used at all, should be the ultimate, not the most common and convenient penalty. The presumption should be that the professional man will keep his license, and the welfare recipient his pension. These interests should be "vested." If revocation is necessary, not by reason of the fault of the individual holder, but by reason of overriding demands of public policy, perhaps payment of just compensation would be appropriate. The individual should not bear the entire loss for a remedy primarily intended to benefit the community.

The concept of rights is most urgently needed with respect to benefits like unemployment compensation, public assistance, and old age insurance. These benefits are based upon a recognition that misfortune and deprivation are often caused by forces far beyond the control of the individual, to rehabilitate him where necessary, and to allow him to be a valuable member of a family and a community; in theory they represent part of the individual's rightful share in the commonwealth.[232] Only by making such benefits into rights can the welfare state achieve its goal of providing a secure minimum basis for individual well-being and dignity in a society where each man cannot be wholly the master of his own destiny.[233]

CONCLUSION

The highly organized scientifically planned society of the future, governed for the good of its inhabitants, promises the best life that men have ever known. In place of the misery and injustice of the past there can be prosperity, leisure, knowledge, and rich opportunity open to all. In the rush of accomplishment, however, not all values receive equal attention; some are temporarily forgotten while others are pushed ahead. We have made provision for nearly everything, but we have made no adequate provision for individual man.

This article is an attempt to offer perspective on the transformation of society as it bears on the economic basis of individualism. The effort has been to show relationships; to bring together drivers' licenses, unemployment insurance, membership in the bar, permits for using school auditoriums, and second class mail privileges, in order to see what we are becoming.

Government largess is only one small corner of a far vaster problem. There are many other new forms of wealth: franchises in private businesses, equities in corporations, the right to receive privately furnished utilities and services, status in private organizations. These too may need added safeguards in the future. Similarly, there are many sources of expanded governmental power aside from largess. By themselves, proposals concerning government largess would be far from accomplishing any fundamental reforms. But, somehow, we must begin.

At the very least, it is time to reconsider the theories under which new forms of wealth are regulated, and by which governmental power over them is measured. It is time to recognize that "the public interest" is all too often a reassuring platitude that covers up sharp clashes of conflicting values, and hides fundamental choices. It is time to see that the "privilege" or "gratuity" concept, as applied to wealth dispensed by government, is not much different from the absolute right of ownership that private capital once invoked to justify arbitrary power over employees and the public.

Above all, the time has come for us to remember what the framers of the Constitution knew so well — that "a power over a man's subsistence amounts to a power over his will." We cannot safely entrust our livelihoods and our rights to the discretion of authorities, examiners, boards of control, character committees, regents, or license commissioners. We cannot permit any official or agency to pretend to sole knowledge of the public good. We cannot put the independence of any man — least of all our Barskys and our Anastaplos — wholly in the power of other men.

If the individual is to survive in a collective society, he must have protection against its ruthless pressures. There must be sanctuaries or enclaves where no majority can reach. To shelter the solitary human spirit does not merely make possible the fulfilment of individuals; it also gives society the power to change, to grow, and to regenerate, and hence to endure. These were the objects which property sought to achieve, and can no longer achieve. The challenge of the future will be to construct, for the society that is coming, institutions and laws to carry on this work. Just as the Homestead Act was a deliberate effort to foster individual values at an earlier time, so we must try to build an economic basis for liberty today — a Homestead Act for rootless twentieth century man. We must create a new property.

Notes

19. U.S. Dep't of Commerce, *op. cit. supra* note 1, at 328, table 439.
20. *Id.* at 417, table 546.
21. *Id.* at 434, table 564.
22. See generally Stover, The Government of Science (Center for the Study of Democratic Institutions, 1962). The vast scope of the government's research and development program is described by Lawrence Gallon in *Will Space Research Pay Off on Earth*, N.Y. Times, May 26, 1963, § 6 (Magazine), p. 29. He estimates government research expenditures of 15 billion dollars in Fiscal 1964.
23. The profound effect of research and developments contracts on the relative economic position of various regions of the country is described by James Reston in *The Scientific Revolution in America*, N.Y. Times, Aug. 1, 1962, p. 30, col. 3. See also *U.S. Aids Midwest in Arms Job Race*, N.Y. Times, Dec. 15, 1963, p. 38, cols. 308; *Space Funds Stir Political Storm*, N.Y. Times, March 1, 1964, p. 1, col. 3 ("The regional competition for the research and development dollars, which in many ways have become the modern-day 'pork barrel' for Congressmen, undoubtedly will intensify in the years ahead." P. 60, col. 3).
24. Greater transportation subsidies will soon be needed. See Text of President's Message to Congress on Nation's Transportation Problems, N.Y. Times, April 6, 1962, pp. 18–19. In 1962, by way of illustration, Eastern Airlines sought a 23.8 million dollar subsidy, N.Y. Times, July 10, 1962, p. 41, col. 5.
25. See N.Y. Times, Nov. 16, ;1961, § 2, p. 1, col. 1.
26. Subsidies have been proposed for law and middle income apartment tenants in New York City. N.Y. Times, April 8, 1962, § 8, p. 1, col. 8.

...

28. A story in the New York Times reports the plight of Stanley P. Truchlinsky, a one-armed newsdealer who lost his 26-year job at a kiosk opposite Carnegie Hall because he could not retain a license to operate the stand. Attempting to overcome his bitterness, Mr. Truchlinsky said he would take an aptitude test to see "what I can do." N.Y. Times, March 11, 1964, p. 34, col. 2.
29. See generally Gellhorn, *op. cit. supra* note 5, at 105–51.
30. For example, the District of Columbia Court of Appeals declared that veterans' disability benefits "fall within the legal principles respecting gratuities." *Thompson v. Gleason,* 317 F.2d 901, 906 (1962).
31. See, *e.g., Lynch v. United States,* 292 U.S. 571, 577 (1934).
32. See Note, *Unconstitutional Conditions,* 73 Harv. L. Rev. 1595, 1609 (1960), which rejects the theory and states that the imposition of such conditions is "a distinct exercise of power which must find its own justification."
33. *Perkins v. Lukens Steel Co.,* 310 U.S. 113, 127 (1940):
    Like private individuals and business, the Government enjoys the unrestricted power to produce its own supplies, to determine those with whom it will deal, and to fix the terms and conditions upon which it will make needed purchases.

...

38. For example, *Willner v. Committee on Character and Fitness,* 373 U.S. 96 (1963).
39. See, *e.g., Hecht v. Monaghan,* 307 N.Y. 461 (1954). See generally Kneier, *Licensing by Local Governments in Illinois,* 1957 U. Ill., L.F. 1 (1957); Note, *Entrance and Disciplinary Requirements for Occupational Licenses in California,* 14 Stan. L. Rev. 533 (1962).
40. *Schware v. Board of Bar Examiners,* 353 U.S. 232 (1957); *Konigsberg v. State Bar,* 353 U.S. 252 (1957); *Green v. Silver,* 207 F. Supp. 133 (D.D.C. 1962). In the *Schware* case the Court said:
    A State cannot exclude a person from the practice of law or from any other occupation in a manner or for reasons that contravene the Due Process or Equal Protection Clause of the Fourteenth Amendment.... A state can require high standards of qualification, such as good moral character or proficiency in its law, before it admits an applicant to its bar, but any qualification must have a rational connection with the applicant's fitness or capacity to practice law. 353 U.S. at 238–39.
41. *Parker v. Lester,* 227 F.2d 708 (9th Cir. 1955); *Graham v. Richmond,* 272 F.2d 517 (D.C. Cir. 1959); *Homer v. Richmond,* 292 F.2d 719 (D.C. Cir. 1961).
42. *Wignall v. Fletcher,* 303 N.Y. 435, 441, 103 N.E.2d 728, 731 (1952). See also *Hecht v. Monaghan,* 307 N.Y. 461 121 N.E.2d 421 (1954).

...

44. *City of Owensboro v. Cumberland Tel. & Tel. Co.,* 230 U.S. 58 (1913); *Frost v. Corporation Commission,* 278 U.S. 515 (1929); *Seatrain Lines v. United States,* 64 F. Supp. 156 (D. Del. 1946).
45. *Great Lakes Airlines, Inc. v. CAB,* 294 F.2d 217, 225 (D.C. Cir. 1961). On the procedures required for modifying an air carrier's certificate, see *CAB v. Delta Airlines, Inc.,* 367 U.S. 316, 331–32 (1961).
46. *CAB v. Delta Air Lines, Inc.,* 367 U.S. 316 (1961). The trend toward judicial protection of franchises is further illustrated by a Fifth Circuit decision that arbitrary denial of a liquor license gives rise to a cause of action under the Civil Rights Act. *Hornsby v. Allen,* 326 F.2d 605 (5th Cir. 1964).
47. *Wellman v. Whittier,* 259 F.2d 163 (D.C. Cir. 1958), *rev'd per curiam on other grounds,* 354 U.S. 931 (1959).
48. *Thompson v. Gleason,* 317 F.2d 901, 906 (D.C. Cir. 1962).
49. *Sherbert v. Verner,* 374 U.S. 398 (1963).
50. *Syrek v. California Unemployment Ins. App. Bd.,* 2 Cal. Rptr. 40, 47 (1960), *off'd,* 54 Cal. 2d 519, 7 Cal. Rptr. 97, 354P.2d 625 (1960). See also *Ault Unemployment Compensation Case,*

398 Pa. 250, 157 A.2d (1960); *Darin Unemployment Compensation Case,* 398 Pa. 259, 157 A.2d 407 (1960); *Fino v. Maryland Employment Security Bd.,* 218 Md. 504, 147 A.2d 738 (1958); *but see Ostrofsky v. Maryland Employment Security Bd.,* 218 Md. 509, 147 A.2d 741 (1958).
51. *Hannegan v. Esquire, Inc.,* 327 U.S. 146 (1946).
52. *American President Lines, Ltd. v. United States,* 291 F.2d 931, 936 (Ct Cl. 1961):
    The administration of a statute cannot be carried on like horse-trading or haggling in a market place for private trading. What one can be induced to agree to, after he has become deeply involved with the Government by several years of action based upon reasonable assumptions, cannot impair his right under the statute to non-discriminatory treatment, and freedom from unreasonably retroactive treatment.
53. *Oman v. United States,* 179 F.2d 738 (10th Cir. 1949). The court indicated that it would protect rights as between private parties even though the government could revoke the permit at any time. *Id.* at 742.
54. *Danskin v. San Diego Unified School Dist.,* 28 Cal. 2d 536, 545, 171 P.2d 885 (1946). See also *ACLU v. Board of Educ.,* 55 Cal.. 2d 167, 10 Cal. Rptr. 647, 359 P.2d 45 (1961).
55. *Copper Plumbing & Heating Co. v. Campbell,* 290 F.2d 368, 370–71 (D.C. Cir. 1961).

...

58. For example, the grant of a valuable federal savings and loan association charter is said to rest in the virtually unreviewable discretion of the Federal Home Loan Bank Board. *Federal Home Loan Bank Bd. v. Rowe,* 284 F.2d 274 (D.C. Cir. 1960).

...

62. See *Osborn v. United States,* 145 F.2d 892, 896 (9th Cir. 1944), holding that a grazing permit on public lands may be revoked without payment of just compensation, and see *ibid.,* n.5 for other illustrations. Compare *Kanarek v. United States,* 314 F.2d 802 (Ct. Cl. 1963), holding that withdrawal of the security clearance of a government contractor's employee, causing him to lose his employment, was not a taking of property for public use entitling the employee to compensation.
63. For a general description of the powers gained by the government through contracting, see Miller, *Government Contracts and Social Control: A Preliminary Inquiry,* 41 Va. L. Rev. 27 (1955); Miller, *Administration by Contract: A New Concern for the Administrative Lawyer,* 36 N.Y.U.L. Rev. 957 (1961). On the powers derived from unemployment compensation, see Note, *Charity versus Social Insurance in Unemployment Compensation Laws,* 73 Yale L.J. 357 (1963).

...

90. For example, in California the State Board of Barber Examiners may dispense certificates for operating barber colleges in any given area after considering:
    (a) The economic character of the community.
    (b) The adequacy of existing barber shops and barber colleges in that community.
    (c) The ability of the community to support the proposed barber college.
    (d) The character of adjacent communities and the extent to which the college would draw patrons from such adjacent communities.
    (e) The social and economic effect of the establishment of a barber college on the community where it is proposed to be located, and on the adjacent communities. Cal. Bus. and Prof. Code § 6534.7.
91. See generally Jaffe & Nathanson, Administrative Law ch. 3 (1961).
92. New Jersey Stat. Ann. § 32:23-29(c) (1963).
93. See *Associated Securities Corp. v. SEC,* 293 F.2d 738, 741 (10th Cir. 1961).

...

95. The dangers of contesting are shown by *Nadiak v. CAB,* 305 F.2d 588 (5th Cir. 1962). A pilot of 12 years' experience was

suspended for 60 days because of minor violation. He contested this order and appealed to the Civil Aeronautics Board. Thereupon the Board commenced a full scale investigation of his entire 12-year career, an investigation which ended with revocation of all of his certificates for a minimum period of one year. *Id.*, 590–91.

96. See Hart. The Research Enterprise and Defense Planning, May, 1963 (unpublished paper in Yale Law Library).

...

116. *Kukatush Mining Corp.* v. *SEC*, 309 F.2d 647 (D.C. Cir. 1962).
117. *Holden* v. *United States*, 187 F. Supp. 790 (E.D. Ark. 1960).
118. Peck & Scherer, The Weapons Acquisition Process: An Economic Analysis 85 (1962).
119. See, *e.g.*, *Kanarek* v. *United States*, 314 F.2d 802 (Ct. Cl. 1963).
120. Kirk, *Massive Subsidies and Academic Freedom*, 27 Law & Contemp. Prob. 607 (1963). *But see* Kidd, *The Implications of Research Funds for Academic Freedom*, 27 Law & Contemp. Prob. 613 (1963).
121. Harvard Summer News, July 12, 1962. p. 1, col. 1. The report states that Harvard officials felt that to keep such records would be an invasion of the privacy of the individual, and that a "visual survey" would be "surreptitious and unhealthy and repugnant to the dignity of the individual." However the report said that the government insisted that the check be made.
122. *Barsky* v. *Board of Regents*, 347 U.S. 442 (1954).

...

124. 347 U.S. 442 (1954).
125. *Id.* at 451.
126. *Id.* art 453.
127. A report on the Aid to Dependent Children Program (ADC) in Chicago comments:

> The climate in the department which places such emphasis on denying assistance, and the lack of consistent application of IPAC [Illinois Public Aid Commission] policies in the ADC program, is damaging to the applicant or recipient and serves to prolong and perpetuate dependency. Some of the staff treat the families with consideration and decency and try to be helpful and understanding while at the same time adhering strictly to policy. Others are rigid and punitive, with little regard for human dignity. Their attitudes are destructive of personality, ambition and self-respect — and intensify existing problems.

Greenleigh Associated, Inc., Facts, Fallacies and the Future, A Study of the Aid to Dependent Children Program of Cook County, Illinois 64 (1960).

...

156. Speaking of the attempt to deny public housing to members of certain organizations designated as "subversive," the Wisconsin Supreme Court said:

> If a precedent should be established, that a governmental agency whose regulation is attacked by court action can successfully defend such an action on the ground that plaintiff is being deprived thereby only of a privilege, and not of a vested right, there is extreme danger that the liberties of any minority group in our population, large or small, might be swept away without the power of the courts to afford any protection.
>
> The more that government engages in any activity formerly carried on by private enterprise, the more real is the peril. For example, the number of rental units for residence housing in the Authority's Hillside Terrace housing project constitutes a very small percentage of the total of all such units in Milwaukee, so that the number of people subjected to pressure by enforcement of Resolution 513 would constitute but a nominal percentage of the total population of

the city. On the other hand, if the government, or an agency thereof, owned 90 per cent of all rental units available for private housing in the nation as a whole, or even in a particular state or municipality, the number of people subjected to pressure by such a plan, of requiring a certificate of nonmembership as a condition of tenancy, would be very considerable....

Lawson v. *Housing Authority*, 270 Wis. 269, 275, 70 N.W.2d 605, 608–09 (1955).

157. See Garratt, Blacklisting of Contractors from "Government Contracting and Federally Financed Construction, November, 1962 (unpublished paper in Yale Law Library).
158. See Taylor, Licensing and Control of the Taxicab Industry in New York, November, 1962 (unpublished paper in Yale Law Library).
159. Fraidin, How AEC Contracts Are Awarded — And To Whom, April, 1963 (unpublished paper in Yale Law Library).
160. Smith, Restaurant and Service Station Concessions on the Connecticut Turnpike, November, 1962 (unpublished paper in Yale Law Library).
161. Cohen, The Communications Satellite Act of 1962: An Inquiry Into the Use of Research and Development, November, 1962 (unpublished paper in Yale Law Library).
162. Peck & Scherer, *op. cit. supra* note 118, at ch. 2–3.
163. Atomic Energy Act, 68 Stat. 919 (1954), as amended, 42 U.S.C. §§ 2011–2281 (1958).

...

174. See, *e.g.*, Huntington, *The Marasmus of the ICC: The Commission, The Railroads, and The Public Interest*, 61 Yale L.J. 467 (1952).
175. 363 U.S. 603 (1960).
176. *Id.* at 608.
177. *Id.* at 609–10.
178. *Id.* at 610–11.
179. *Id.* at 611.
180. *Id.* at 612.
181. See generally *Block, Feudal Society (1961)*. Personal dependence was a fundamental element of feudalism, expressed in the concept of being the "man" of another man. *Id.* at 145.
182. Wunderlich, *The National Socialist Conception of Landed Property*, 12 Social Research 60, 75 (1945).
183. See Gsovski, Soviet Civil Law 106–07, 573–74, 582 (1948); Hazard and Social Change in the U.S.S.R. 133 (1953).
184. See generally Philbrick, *Changing Conceptions of Property in Law*, 86 U. Pa. L. Rev. 691 (1983); Hamilton & Till, *Property*, 12 Encyc. Soc. Scl. 528 (1934; Freund, The Supreme Court of the United States 31–40 (1961).
185. See generally Berle & Means, The Modern Corporation and Private Property (1932); and Berle, Power Without Property (1957).
186. Philbrick, *Changing Conceptions of Property in Law*, 86 U. Pa. L. Rev. 691–732 (1938).
187. Hamilton, *Property — According to Locke*, 41 Yale L.J. 864, 877–78 (1932); see also Hamilton & Till, *supra* note 184, at 528.
188. Lippmann, the Method of Freedom 101 (1934). See also Philbrick, *Changing Conceptions of Property in Law*, 86 U. Pa. L. Rev. 691 (1938):

> It is not, however, the *use* of ordinary property, nor the property of ordinary or "natural" persons that presents today serious problems of adjusting law to new social conditions. Those problems arise in connection with property for *power*, and therefore primarily in connection with industrial property.

...

191. *Barsky* v. *Board of Regents*, 347 U.S. 442 (1954).
192. *Id.* at 449.
193. *Id.* at 451.
194. *Id.* at 470 (dissenting opinion).
195. 363 U.S. 603 (1960).

206. See generally Gellhorn, Individual Freedom and Governmental Restraints 105–57 (1956) (Chapter III, "The Right to make a Living"). Although it speaks in different terms, and is limited to occupational licensing Professor Gellhorn's discussion is a most perceptive analysis of the meaning of "the public interest." See also Schubert, The Public Interest (1960) for an elaborate analysis of differing public interest theories.

207. *Johnson* v. *McIntosh*, 21 U.S. (8 Wheat.) 543 (1823).

208. 5 Stat. 453, 455 (Sept. 4, 1941), 12 Stat. 392 (May 20, 1962).

209. *Pierson* v. *Post*, 3 Cal. R. 175 (1805).

210. The Homestead Act had conditions of age, citizenship, intention to settle was cultivated, and loyalty to the United States. 12 Stat. 392 (1862).

211. *Mullett* v. *Bradley*, 24 Misc. 695, 53 N.Y. Supp. 781 (1898): *Bridges* v. *Hawkesworth*, 21 L.J. Rep. 75 (Q.B. 1851).

212. Note, *Unconstitutional Conditions*, 73 Harv. L. Rev. 1595, 1599 (1960).

213. Compare Calabresi, *Retroactivity: Paramount Powers and Contractual Changes*, 71 Yale L.J. 1191 (1962). In the context of legislation dealing with government obligations, Professor Calabresi argues that certain regulation can only be justified by a "paramount power of government" (*e.g.*, the commerce power) rather than power incidental to the obligation itself.

214. Judge Curtis Bok wrote:
We are unwilling to engraft upon our law the notion, nowhere so decided, that unemployment benefits may be denied because of raising the bar of the [Fifth] Amendment against rumor or report of disloyalty or because of refusing to answer such rumor or report. The possible abuses of such a doctrine are shocking to imagine....
Ault Unemployment Compensation Case, 398 Pa. 250, 259, 157 A.2d 375, 380 (1960).

215. *United States* v. *Chicago*, M., St. P. & P.R.R., 282 U.S. 311, 328–29 (1931).

222. The approach of the Court of Appeals for the Ninth Circuit in *Parker* v. *Lester*, 227 F.2d 708 (9th Cir. 1955) might serve as a model:
What we must balance in the scales here does not involve a choice between any security screening program and the protection of individual seamen. Rather we must weigh against the rights of the individual to the traditional opportunity for notice and hearing, the public need for a *screening system which denies such right to notice and hearing*. Granted that the Government may adopt appropriate means for excluding security risks from employment on merchant vessels, what is the factor of public interest and necessity which requires that it be done in the manner here adopted?
Id. at 718.
Later the Court added:
It is not a simple case of sacrificing the interest of a few to the welfare of the many. In weighing the considerations of which we are mindful here, we must recognize that if these regulations may be sustained, similar regulations may be made effective in respect to other groups as to whom Congress may next choose to express its legislative fears....
Id. at 721.

223. *Barsky* v. *Board of Regents*, 347 U.S. 442, 472, 474 (1954) (Douglas, J., dissenting).

226. Compare *Housing Authority* v. *Cordova*, 130 Cal. App. 2d 883, 889 279 P. 2d 215, 218 (1955):
[W]e fail to find in the act, pursuant to which the plaintiff Housing Authority was created, anything to suggest that it is authorized to use the powers conferred upon it to punish subversives or discourage persons from entertaining subversive ideas by denying to such the right of occupying its facilities....

227. 109 Cong. Rec. 3258–59 (daily ed., March 4, 1963). The Senator, while denouncing coercion and government by men rather than laws, failed to discuss the question whether there is any "right" to a government contract.

228. The Administrative Conference of the United States has recommended "drastic changes" in the procedures by which persons or firms may be debarred from government contracting. The Conference said that such action should not be taken without prior notice, which includes a statement of reasons, and a trial-type hearing before an impartial trier of facts, all within a framework of procedures. Thus, protections would surround even that form of largess which is closest to being a matter within the managerial function of government. Final Report of the Administrative Conference of the United States, p. 15 and Recommendation 'No. 29' (1962).

231. Recently the Supreme Court, in a case involving revocation of citizenship for evading the draft, held that any action that is in fact punishment cannot be taken "without a prior criminal trial and all its incidents, including indictment, notice, confrontation, jury trial, assistance of counsel, and compulsory process for obtaining witnesses." *Kennedy* v. *Mendoza-Martinez*, 372 U.S. 144, 167 (1963).

232. The phrase is adapted from Hamilton and Till's definition of the word "property": "a general term for the miscellany of equities that persons hold in the commonwealth." Hamilton & Till, *Property*, 12 Encyc. Soc. Sci.

233. Experts in the field of social welfare have often argued that benefits should rest on a more secure basis, and that individuals in need should be deemed "entitled" to benefits. See Ten Brock & Wilson, *Public Assistance and Social Insurance —A Normative Evaluation*, 1 U.C.L.A.L. Rev. 237 (1954); Kieth-Lucas, Decisions About People in Need (1957). The latter author speaks of a "right to assistance" which is a corollary of the "right to self-determination" (*id.* at 251) and urges public assistance workers to pledge to respect the rights and dignity of welfare clients (*id.* at 263). See also Wynn, Fatherless Families 78–83, 162–63 (1964). The author proposes a "fatherless child allowance," to which every fatherless child would be entitled.
Starting from a quite different frame of reference — the problem of the rule of law in the welfare state — Professor Harry Jones has similarly argued that the welfare state must be regarded as a source of new rights, and that such rights as Social Security must be surrounded by substantial and procedural safeguards comparable to those enjoyed by traditional rights of property. Jones, *The Rule of Law and the Welfare State*, 58 Colum. L. Rev. 143, 154–55 (1958). See also Note, *Charity Versus Social Insurance in Unemployment Compensation Laws*, 73 Yale L.J. 357 (1963).
A group called the Ad Hoc Committee on the Triple Revolution recently urged that, in view of the conditions created by the "cybernation revolution" in the United States, every American should be guaranteed an adequate income as a matter of right whether or not he works. N.Y. Times., March 23, 1964, p. 1, cols. 2–3.

3 Policy Options, Statutes, and Statutory Interpretation

(a) Policy Options

Modern government is much more than drafting statutes and hiring public servants. Policy-makers must choose from an astounding variety of legislative and executive options in deciding how to respond to social problems. A look at some of these options illustrates the complexity of government, and provides a starting point for assessing the appropriateness of individual government structures. One interesting analysis[1] of alternative legislative techniques is discussed by two American writers, H. Hart and A. Sacks.[2] Much of their analysis has equal application in the Canadian context.[3]

At the most general level, Hart and Sacks *distinguish between* (i) legislative techniques for influencing primary private conduct,[4] (ii) legislative techniques for influencing secondary private conduct,[5] and (iii) legislative options for assigning public powers.[6]

(i) Legislative Techniques for Influencing Primary Private Conduct

Often policy-makers respond to a social problem by trying to encourage or discourage certain kinds of private conduct. Where they do this at first instance, rather than dealing with non-compliance with previous government action, they are attempting to influence primary private conduct.

Hart and Sacks point out that for a policy-maker confronted with a social problem, the most elementary choice is between doing something or nothing.[7] The costs of doing nothing must be weighed against the costs of various forms of action. Where there is already a government response in place, a shift to government inaction, such as a move to deregulation, can be costly and complex. For regulation of primary private con-duct, both authors distinguish between government action that is coercive[8] and one that is not,[9] and further divide coercive government action into regulation[10] and direct coercion.[11] They note that regulation can either be addressed directly to the general public, without the help of a member of government ("self-applying"[12]) or administered by government officials ("administered"[13]). Examples of the first category are most of tort, property, contract, and criminal law. They require little official action, except in cases of alleged or actual non-compliance. However, for many reasons, such as the complexity of the subject matter, government officials are often necessary to administer a law in the first place. Hart and Sacks give licences,[14] exactions[15] (such as income tax) and expropriation[16] as examples of this kind of administered coercive government action.

They add, though, that "in pursuit of the ultimate goal of maximizing the satisfactions of valid human wants, the law finds many a tool besides force that suits its purpose."[17] They identify a wide array of non-coercive (and, we might add, less typically "legal") government techniques.[18]

The usefulness of this general approach can be seen in its analysis of the characteristic strengths and weaknesses of individual legislative techniques. For example, one important form of coercive technique is the licence.[19]

A licence is a requirement of a government permission in order to carry out a desired activity (or, in exceptional cases, to validate an activity already carried out). Like other kinds of administered government action, the licence requires a special bureaucratic structure instead of self-applying action, and is typically more costly. Because a licence generally involves assessment on an individual case-by-case basis, it can require particularly large numbers of officials. The licence can also slow down useful private activity. Its case-by-case, often adjudicatory structure attracts arguments that court-like protections should be imposed. This, in turn, can lead to greater formality and further delays.

Moreover, the licence has a coercive element. Failure to obtain a necessary licence or breach of the terms of an existing licence can result in penalties. The prevalence and coerciveness of the licence may be seen as a potential threat to individual freedom. The extent to which the American public was dependent on government mechanisms such as the licence, and the potential abuses that could result, were documented in Charles Reich's 1964 article, "The New Property."[20] The licence is just as omnipresent in Canada today. It may be inappropriate where the desired government objective is considered less urgent, or where non-coercive alternatives are readily available.

On the other hand, the licence is vital to almost all schemes for rationing limited resources, such as the use of radio waves.[21] It is useful in controlling monopolistic enterprises, such as the transport of oil and natural gas. It can facilitate careful case-by-case control where public safety is a paramount need. By requiring permission before activity starts, it can prevent irreparable harm. As well, it gives government an effective means of collecting information and revenue.[22]

(ii) Legislative Techniques for Influencing Secondary Private Conduct (Enforcing Compliance)

Policy-makers have also many options available for enforcing compliance with existing laws. These include various structures of enforcement and forms of penalty. Among the many structural options available are: (a) leaving enforcement substantially to the courts (the early 19th-century approach); (b) creating police forces (the approach in Britain and the Canadian colonies after the mid-19th century); or (c) supplementing or partially replacing police forces with special administrative enforcement structures (e.g., human rights commissions).

Penalties for breach of laws include fines, publicity, licence revocation or suspension, or imprisonment. Selecting an appropriate penalty involves a compromise between one that is disproportionate to the harm penalized, or causes undue harm or prejudice, and one that is too light to discourage the undesirable conduct.

In all these situations, the administrator as well as the private individual or group may react differently to different techniques, depending on the circumstances. When a technique seems unduly severe and may produce undesirable side effects, or seems inappropriate for one reason or another, an administrator might elect simply not to apply it, and resort instead to an informal alternative that seems less inappropriate. If the alternative is acceptable to the regulated party and unknown to or unchallenged by third parties, it may prevail despite formal legal provisions to the contrary.

(iii) Legislative Options for Assigning Public Powers

A third general set of techniques referred to by Hart and Sacks is relevant where policy-makers have decided to create or change an institution in the executive branch or some other part of the administrative process. In the Canadian context, some of the most important options here are associated with the issues of independence, court-like powers, subordinate legislative powers, discretion, and finality.

A. Independence

Many government structures in Canada today have been deliberately given a degree of independence of the control and responsibility of an elected Cabinet minister.[23] For example, while Treasury Board and the departments and ministries are under direct Cabinet control, the various regulatory boards and commissions and the Crown corporation are, to some extent, free of this control. Relatively independent administrative bodies are not entirely new phenomena, but a significant proportion of the growth of the executive branch in 20th century Canada has taken this form.

There are various reasons for seeking this independence. The growth of independent agencies in Canada has usually been an *ad hoc* process.[24] Often the motive appears to be to prevent or remove suspicion of perceived abuses from partisan politics. This is especially true where adjudicatory bodies are involved. Sometimes the motive is to facilitate flexible hiring practices free of the constraints imposed on the central public service, or flexible administrative structures free of the hierarchical framework of the traditional departments and ministries. With Crown corporations, independence may be seen as a means of moving the structure closer to the private commercial model, with its greater flexibility and emphasis on profitability. At the same time, independence decreases cabinet control and dilutes direct government responsibility for its action. Accordingly, factors suggesting independence should be weighed carefully in the light of available alternative controls.[25]

B. Court-Like Functions

How closely should an administrative authority's functions approximate those of ordinary courts of law? Often, legislatures have delegated to the executive branch functions that were originally discharged mainly by the judiciary. The massive increase in legislation has placed a special strain on the courts, with their ultimate responsibility of interpreting all the new laws. Also, as government has taken an increasingly active role in society, there has been a need for institutions that can judge government-individual disputes and administer legislative schemes with greater speed, specialized expertise, and flexibility, and at less cost than ordinary courts.

As a result, most of the administrative functions exercised by the judiciary were transferred in the 19th and 20th centuries to specialized institutions in the executive branch,[26] and new administrative functions were given to that branch rather than the judiciary. A more recent example was the creation of labour relations boards after World War II, relegating ordinary courts to a more residual role in labour relations.

Where the new executive bodies are called upon to discharge adjudicatory functions similar to those of ordinary courts, it is reasonable to expect that the legislature will subject them to at least some of the procedural and other safeguards imposed on ordinary courts. How extensive should these safeguards be? Which of the positive features of the judicial process — independence, impartiality, extensive procedural safeguards, enforceable decisions, etc. — can be readily transplanted to the administrative process? Can we transplant the strengths without the weaknesses? Can we achieve them without excessive delay, cost, formality, rigidity, etc.? Moreover, should courts themselves impose judicial safeguards when the legislature has not done so expressly? These are important questions that we will encounter later in the chapters on judicial procedural control.

C. Rule-Making Power

Rule-making by the executive[27] is a vital feature of modern Canadian government. Rules are often an efficient way of communicating requirements to large numbers of people, or of dealing with recurring situations. They can help make policy implementation more predictable. However, the size and complexity of modern government makes it impossible for Parliament and the legislatures to formulate all the necessary or desired rules themselves. Hence, they often delegate this function to the executive.

The making of ordinary statutes is a complex process, involving opportunities for comment by elected representatives. Executive-made rules have almost the same legal effect as statutes, and can affect as many people. How are they made? Are they subject to comparable safeguards and controls? We will explore the whole question of rule-making later in this chapter.

D. Discretion

Administrators have always exercised discretion or choice. The very fact of administering implies at least some choice. A police officer may have to choose between enforcing and not enforcing a by-law about jaywalking; an inspector may have discretion to recommend immediate or gradual compliance with a pollution-control law; and a licensing board may have discretion to reject or accept an application. The distinguishing mark of modern government is not the presence but the extent of its discretion, and the tendency of modern policy-makers to confer large grants of discretion intentionally and explicitly. This phenomenon creates challenges for administrators, administrés, and reviewing courts alike.[28]

E. Finality

In government, few things are absolutely final. Nevertheless, policy-makers do have access to a number of different options in regard to the finality of statutory powers. At the low end of the finality spectrum, an administrator might be empowered merely to recommend, with provision for extensive further consideration by another body. On the other hand, recommendations subject merely to approval by a second body may still carry considerable weight in normal situations.

A decision carries greater finality than a recommendation. However, it may be made expressly subject to reconsideration by way of administrative or judicial appeal. If no appeal is provided, the decision will normally still be subject to judicial review. If the legislature desires to restrict or preclude judicial review, it may attempt to do so by means of privative clauses. Even here, the attempt may prove unsuccessful.

The degree of finality required will vary with individual circumstances, such as the need for speed, the relative importance of reconsidering the decision, constitutional restrictions (which may apply to some provincial but not federal privative clauses), and the relative expertise of the administrator and the courts.

In all these areas, where power is granted, there is a potential for both good and abuse. Just as it is important to choose the most appropriate and effective technique and function, it is also wise to prepare in advance for potential abuses of power. This question, the question of controls for the administrative process, will be an important concern in chapters to come.

Notes

1. For another helpful approach, see Robert S. Summers, *Law: Its nature, Functions and Limits*, 2d ed. (Englewood Cliffs, N.J.: Prentice-Hall, 1972); 198–208; 275–278.
2. H. Hart & A. Sacks, *The Legal Process, Basic Problems in the Making and Application of Law*, unpublished (Westbury, N.Y.: Liberty Foundation Press, 1984, based on unpub. ed., 1958) especially 120–22, 127–34, 283–86, and 844–63.
3. For somewhat similar approaches in the Canadian context, see M. Trebilcock et al., *The Choice of Governing Instrument*, 1982; G.B. Doern & R.W. Phidd, *Canadian Public Policy: Ideas, Structures, Process*, 1983; and Law Reform Commission of Canada, Working Paper 51, 1986.
4. Discussed in part (i), below.
5. Discussed in part (ii), below.
6. Discussed in part (iii), below.
7. *Supra* note 2 at 845.
8. (That is, containing either a legislative penalty for non-compliance or some other legislatively authorized use of force: *ibid.* at 121 and 845–53.) Hart and Sacks distinguish between two main kinds of coercive government action: legislative techniques for influencing primary private behaviour (behaviour other than non-compliance) and legislative techniques for controlling secondary private behaviour (i.e., for enforcing compliance). We will be focusing here on control of primary private behaviour;

techniques for enforcing compliance are discussed in part (ii), below

9. *Ibid.* at 853–57.
10. A regulation is a statement of a duty, plus a sanction for non-compliance: see *ibid.* at 121, 845–46.
11. Direct coercion is an application of force with no prior opportunity for non-compliance: *ibid.* at 853–55.
12. *Ibid.* at 120–21.
13. In Hart and Sacks's terminology, "individualized": *ibid.* at 846.
14. Hart and Sacks distinguish the usual kind of licence, the prerequisite (prior check), from the postrequisite (after check).
15. An exaction is a duty to render something to government.
16. They see expropriation as an example of what they call "direct coercion" (an application of force with no prior opportunity for non-compliance (*ibid.* at 854)). Another example might be a compulsory evacuation order for safety or medical reasons.
17. *Ibid.* at 855.
18. For example, rewards and contracts and the many forms of direct government action, such as education, publicity, research services, public works, assurances, loans, and government enterprises.
19. *Ibid.* at 847–50.
20. (1963–64) 73 Yale Law J. 733: see Chapter 2(f).
21. Hart & Sacks, *supra* note 2 at 849.
22. See further, Law Reform Commission of Canada, *supra* note 3 at 40–44.
23. See generally Law Reform Commission of Canada, *Independent Administrative Agencies* (Working Paper 25) (Ottawa: Law Reform Commission of Canada, 1980); *Independent Administrative Agencies* (Report 26) (Ottawa: Law Reform Commission of Canada, 1985); and H.N. Janisch, "Independence of Administrative Tribunals: In Praise of 'Structural Heretics'" (1987) 1 Cdn. J. Administrative Law and Practice 1.
24. See *Independent Administrative Agencies* (Report No. 26) *ibid.* at 5: Chapter 2(c).
25. We will look at the question of independence further in regard to specific public authorities in Chapters 9 to 12.
26. See P. Craig, *Administrative Law*, 3d ed. (London, U.K.: Sweet and Maxwell, 1994) c. 2; H.W. Arthurs, *"Without the Law": Administrative Justice and Legal Pluralism in Nineteenth-Century England* (Toronto: University of Toronto Press, 1985) c. 4.
27. See R.I. Cheffins and R.N. Johnson, The *Constitutional Process in Canada*, 2d ed. (Toronto: McGraw-Hill Ryerson, 1976) c. 3.
28. We will consider some of these challenges in Chapter 7.

(b) The Making and Control of Legislation

(i) Some Definitions

Our concern here is with legislation: legal rules made by government. We will look at statutes (primary legislation), which are legal rules enacted by legislatures; and subordinate legislation, which are legal rules made by the administrative process.

(ii) Role of Statutes

Statutes and subordinate legislation are the key tools for translating policy initiatives into action.

Statutes give policy decisions legal force. They either address the public directly or confer mandates on members of the administrative process. In the latter role, statutes provide the legal foundation for virtually all actions by the administrative process. You and I can do as we please, as long as we do not contravene the law; members of the administrative process, acting in their official capacity, can do only what statutes (or subordinate legislation made pursuant to statutes) permit them to do. The reason for this emphasis on statutory mandates is simple: Statutes are enacted by people who are elected by the public at large. If the public is to have any residual control over the administrative process, then that process must comply with its statutory mandates.

(iii) Making and Control of Statutes

There are numerous safeguards built into the statute-making process to ensure, among other things, input by elected people. On the other hand, there are limits to the time and expertise of ordinary MPs or MLAs, so safeguards must strike a compromise between expertise and elected authority. Who supplies most of the expertise? The higher ranks of the executive branch! Thus, to a considerable extent at least, the mandates for the administrative process are crafted within the administrative process itself.

Statutes that derive from government public bills undergo an extensive formative stage, moving from memorandum to Cabinet to draft bill to bill.[1] Memoranda to Cabinet (usually prepared within a minister's department and signed by a minister) are reviewed by a special Cabinet policy committee and then by the Cabinet as a whole. Then a draft bill is prepared on instructions from a minister, and reviewed by a Cabinet committee or by the Cabinet as a whole. In the House of Commons (where most bills are considered first) the bill undergoes three readings, but the most important consideration happens at the second reading (full debate; approval in principle), by a House of Commons committee, and at report stage (when the House committee's report is debated). There are three further readings in the Senate until the bill is approved by the Governor General. The process is broadly similar in the provincial and territorial legislatures.

(iv) Nature of Subordinate Legislation

Subordinate legislation is subordinate to statutes because normally it can only be made where a statute authorizes it. The only exception is legislation made pursuant to prerogative power. Prerogative legislation is very rare, and cannot be used to affect the existing rights of citizens.

Subordinate statutory legislation cannot go beyond the scope of its enabling statute, but it can be amended or abolished by that statute or any other explicit statute of the relevant government. Subject to these qualifications, subordinate

legislation has the same legal effect as statutes, and is considerably more numerous than statutes. It comprises a significant part of the legislative mandates of the administrative process. Although it must be made pursuant to statutes, it can be made without any direct participation by elected officials. It is important, then, to consider just how subordinate legislation *is* made, and what safeguards are provided.

(v) Making and Control of Subordinate Legislation

In fact, there is no single process, but rather a variety of processes. At the federal level, there are four main categories of subordinate legislation:

1. Orders in Council (Governor in Council regulations),[2] which must be preceded by advance notice, impact statements, and drafts, approved by at least four Cabinet members and signed by the Governor General;
2. ministerial regulations,[3] which must be preceded by advance notice, impact statements, and drafts;
3. regulations that are subject only to the requirements of the *Statutory Instruments Act*; and
4. simple statutory instruments,[4] which are subject only to the *Statutory Instruments Act*'s requirement of referral to the standing Parliamentary committee on statutory instruments.

Each category usually includes the requirements of the category below, as well as its own. Orders in Council, for example, are normally a form of pre-publication regulation. Pre-publication regulations include the normal requirements of regulations, and regulations themselves are a form of statutory instrument.

The federal government's pre-publication process dates back to 1986. It is non-statutory, based on government policy, and supplements statutory requirements. It requires that departments (and independent agencies, on a voluntary basis) publish general advance notice of their planned regulations, together with statements of anticipated impact,[5] in an annual publication called the *Federal Regulatory Plan*.[6] The 299-page 1997 *Plan* includes information about regulatory initiatives from 20 government departments (and including those of the National Parole Board, Correctional Services Canada, and the Royal Canadian Mounted Police) and 14 major federal regulatory agencies.

Then, at least 30 days before planned publication in Part II of the *Canada Gazette*, a draft regulation plus a summary of anticipated regulatory impact must (except where exempted) appear in Part I of the *Canada Gazette*.

For draft Orders in Council (which comprise about 90% of regulations by departments), decisions on (a) whether to approve Justice-checked drafts and (b) whether the normal pre-publication requirements should be followed, are made by the "Special Committee" of Council. This is a Cabinet committee with a quorum of four ministers and normally meets just prior to regular weekly Cabinet sessions. As well, regulations that directly affect government spending require approval by the Treasury Board.

Whether or not they have pre-publication requirements, most regulations are under the legislative régime of the *Statutory Instruments Act*. This requires review by the Department of Justice officials; registration with the Clerk of the Privy Council in order to become law; publication in Part II of the *Canada Gazette* within 23 days of being registered; referral to MPs; and referral to the Standing Joint Committee (of Parliament) on Scrutiny of Regulations. While regulations become law when they are registered, they are not enforceable until they have been published in the *Gazette*.

Although all regulations are part of a broader category called "statutory instruments," a large group of "simple" statutory instruments[7] are not classified as regulations.[8] They need only be referred to the standing committee and be available for inspection.

Beyond these formal categories of subordinate legislation, there are many informal rules and guidelines that do not constitute statutory instruments. These may play a big role in governing internal departmental and agency behaviour, but are not subject to any of the above requirements.[9]

(vi) Adequacy of safeguards

Are these processes adequate? Does the statute-making process permit sufficient input by elected officials *outside* Cabinet? How stringent should the rule-making process be for subordinate legislation? Which subjects should be dealt with in statutes, and which can be relegated to subordinate legislation? Presumably, more important subject matter should be reserved for statutes, but how should importance be assessed? Within the field of subordinate legislation, is the more important subject matter reserved for initiation or approval by ministers or the Cabinet as a whole? Is there any means of systematically reviewing the existing allocation of statutory and subordinate rule-making, as well as planning new allocations?

The phenomenon of administrator's informal guidelines based only on implied statutory authorization raises further problems and choices. These guidelines are widespread, often directed to administrators, but affecting the way administrators deal with the public. A good example is the Unemployment Insurance Commission Manual, an internal guidebook on procedure to be followed by Commission employees.[10] Where should such rules be allowed? When should they be confirmed by express statutory authorization? How do and how should they fit into the procedures for controlling formal subordinate legislation?

Both formal subordinate legislation and informal guidelines make up the "regulations" referred to in an article by Roderick Macdonald.[11] Macdonald says regulations are only one aspect of the general question of "regulation," which he describes as all forms of state activity — including those delegated to private persons — that affect citizens' economic behaviour. He says regulations should be applied more sparingly, where the object is to affirm impersonal norms. In most other cases, he says, regulations and statutes should be either avoided entirely or softened by consultation, accessibility, and flexibility.

[Note: Bill C-25, a new *Regulations Act*, would have reformed and replaced the *Statutory Instruments Act*, R.S.C. 1985, c. S-2. The proposed new federal law contained a simpler definition of "regulation"; a shorter production process for regulations not requiring legal review; a revised set of criteria for exempting regulations from the regulatory process; consultation, registration and publication by electronic means; and measures to enhance Parliamentary scrutiny. Unfortunately, like its predecessor, Bill C-84 died on the Order Paper in February 1996; Bill C-25, in April 1997.]

Notes

1. As well as the brief account here, see R.J. Van Loon & M.S. Whittington, *The Canadian Political System: Environment, Structure, and Process* 4th ed. (Toronto: McGraw-Hill Ryerson, 1987) at 30–32 and 628–32; Canada, Department of Justice, *The Federal Legislative Process in Canada*, 1987; R. Sullivan, *Driedger on the Construction of Statutes*, 3d ed. (Toronto: Butterworths, 1994); Treasury Board Secretariat, *Regulatory Policy 1995: Regulatory Affairs Guide* (Ottawa: Treasury Board of Canada, 1995); Treasury Board Secretariat, *Managing Regulation in Canada: Regulatory Affairs Guide* (Ottawa: Treasury Board of Canada, 1996); Treasury Board Secretariat, *Fed-*

eral Regulatory Process: Regulatory Affairs Guide (Ottawa: Treasury Board of Canada, 1996).

2. Subordinate legislation made by Cabinet.

3. Subordinate legislation made by departments and major agencies.

4. Roughly speaking, statutory instruments are formal rules, orders, or regulations, etc., including those made under prerogative power and those under non-legislative statutory power: see, further, s. 2(1)(d) of *Statutory Instruments Act*.

5. Called Regulatory Impact Analysis Statements (RIAS).

6. See, for example, Government of Canada, *Federal Regulatory Plan 1997: A Guide to Planned Regulatory Initiatives* (Ottawa: Treasury Board of Canada, 1996).

7. Those statutory instruments that are not also regulations. The term is not used in the *Statutory Instruments Act, infra* note 8.

8. Although the definition in the *Statutory Instruments Act* is complex, a regulation might be described generally as a statutory instrument which is made pursuant to statutory legislative power or is enforced by a statutory penalty.

9. As we will see later, they may be subject to judicial review.

10. Law Reform Commission of Canada, *Unemployment Insurance Benefits* by Pierre Issalys & Gaylord Watkins (Ottawa: Supply and Services Canada, 1977) at 45.

11. R.A. Macdonald, "Understanding Regulation by Regulations" in I. Bernier & A. Lajoie, eds., *Regulations, Crown Corporations and Administrative Tribunals* (Toronto: University of Toronto Press, 1985) (vol. 48 the of Macdonald Commission) at 82–154.

(c) Quebec Regulations Act[†]

NOTE

Quebec is the only Canadian jurisdiction to require by statute that proposed versions of regulations must be published before the regulations are formally made. For two non-statutory pre-publication and consultation régimes, see the *Federal Regulatory Plan*,[1] in place since 1985, and the Saskatchewan *Code of Regulatory Conduct*,[2] in place since 1993.

EXTRACTS

8. Every proposed regulation shall be published in the *Gazette officielle du Québec*.

9. Section 8 does not require the publication in the *Gazette officielle du Québec* of any text referred to in a proposed regulation.

10. Every proposed regulation published in the *Gazette officielle du Québec* shall be accompanied with a notice stating, in particular, the period within which no proposed regulation may be made or submitted for approval but within which interested persons may transmit their comments to a person designated in the notice.

11. No proposed regulation may be made or submitted for approval before the expiry of 45 days from its publication in the *Gazette officielle du Québec*, or before the expiry of the period indicated in the notice accompanying it or in the Act under which the proposed regulation may be made or approved, where the notice or Act provides for a longer period.

12. A proposed regulation may be made or approved at the expiry of a shorter period than the period applicable to it, or without having been published, if the authority making or approving it is of the opinion that a reason provided for in the Act under which the proposed regulation may be made or approved, or one of the following circumstances, warrants it:

    (1) the urgency of the situation requires it;

    (2) the proposed regulation is designed to establish, amend, or repeal norms of a fiscal nature.

13. The reason justifying a shorter publication period shall be published with the proposed regulation, and the reason justifying the absence of such publication shall be published with the regulation.

14. A proposed regulation may be amended after its publication without being published a second time.

[†] R.S.Q. c. R-18.1 (first enacted as S.Q. 1986, c. 22).

[1] E.g., Government of Canada, *Federal Regulatory Plan 1997* (Ottawa: Canada Communications Group, 1998).

[2] Government of Saskatchewan, *Code of Regulatory Conduct* (Regina: Government of Saskatchewan, 1993).

(d) Compliance†

Law Reform Commission of Canada

NOTE

All public authorities must ensure that the policies behind their governing legislation are effectively carried out. For public authorities required to influence behaviour in the private sector, this means attempting to ensure private sector compliance. The following extracts identify several main forms of instrument that may be available to administrators for implementing policy. They also highlight some key problems in securing compliance.‡ Not the least of these is a disconcerting gap between theory and practice.

EXTRACTS

Three basic groups of instruments[1] used for policy implementation are examined [here]: command-penalty, financial incentives and persuasion. Command-penalty instruments include criminal offences, regulatory offences and licences; compulsion is a central element of each in the sense that non-compliance could result in a financial penalty, imprisonment or the withholding of permission to engage in an activity.

Financial incentives[2] encompass such instruments as conditional grants, low-interest loans, loan guarantees and tax subsidies. There is no immediate element of government coercion associated with financial incentives: they are designed to encourage compliance. Persuasion instruments or "techniques" include education and public information campaigns, advertising and "advice-giving" activities of government, intended to alter or influence private sector behaviour.

Instruments may be used in combination or in sequence. However, each possesses distinctive legal, political and economic characteristics and capabilities, rendering it more or less appropriate in a given context. For example, financial incentives and persuasion are often used to adjust or influence private sector behaviour of a non-life-threatening variety; because they do not involve a coercive component, they are usually subject to less onerous procedural requirements than command-penalty techniques.

[Our focus is] on problems relating to the implementation of policies that require private sector *compliance*. In order to understand how government goes about doing this, it is not enough to examine the *legal instruments* available to government officials. These often provide only a backdrop for what really occurs. Administrators do not apply law mechanically: an analysis of day-to-day implementation activity reveals its more typical, informal nature. Implementation is a human process, involving ongoing interactions among government and private parties: policy implementation is mainly a *relational* process. In such a context, administrative law is called upon to address more than defects in decision making, to become that branch of law which, among other things, provides structure and guidance for policy implementation. Law relies heavily on coercive instruments. This reliance emphasizes unduly the contentious or adversarial components of the implementation process, and can give rise to many implementation problems. First, it can cause relationships to start off on the wrong foot, by framing interactions in an adversarial mode when compliance may more likely be achieved through co-operation. Secondly, it does not always provide administrators (namely, those who implement the policy), *administrés* (that is, those members of the private sector who are the subject of administrative action), or third parties (that is, all those other than administrators and *administrés*) with practical guidance as to how the policy is actually to be implemented.

The administration of *regulatory offences* characteristically involves many government officials and institutions, including "front-line" enforcers, inspectors, Department of Justice prosecutors, and the courts. Each official and institution may have its own priorities and concerns about prosecution. Administrators face difficulties related to their "wearing different hats": one day an administrator may be acting

---

† Excerpts from *Policy Implementation, Compliance and Administrative Law* (Working Paper 51) (Ottawa: Law Reform Commission, 1986) at 16–17, 75–77. Source of Information: Department of Justice Canada. Reproduced with the permission of the Minister of Public Works and Government Services Canada, 2002.

‡ The Law Reform Commission defines "compliance" as "action in response to government requests or commands": *ibid.* at 17.

as an adviser to *administrés*, on another as inspector, and on the next as enforcer. The government institution may sometimes provide its administrators with some strategic guidance; more often than not, however, such decisions are left to personal judgment. The administrator's operational and prosecutorial discretion poses difficult problems for policy implementation: how administrators apply the law may be different from what legislators intended.

Some of the parties to a prosecution come into action later in the process than others. Thus, for example, once proceedings have begun, the front-line administrator relinquishes control over the prosecution to the Department of Justice prosecutor. However, prosecutors may not be as familiar as administrators with the policy underlying regulatory offences. As a result, prosecutions may be poorly handled, or inappropriately plea bargained. On the court docket, a regulatory offence prosecution may not receive high priority, because of competing demands such as criminal prosecutions, heavy caseloads, and so on. Its outcome may be difficult to predict. Furthermore, depending upon factors such as court, media and community reactions to the prosecution, publicity arising from prosecutions can either further or detract from policy goals, and bolster or harm the reputation of *administrés* (regardless of conviction), all of which is beyond the control of the administrator. As a result, in many contexts reliance on offence provisions in legislation can prove to be an inappropriate emphasis for policy implementation.

Licensing is also a coercive instrument: it permits an activity which would otherwise be subject to prosecution and can restrict the nature of permitted activity. Licences can be administered with or without public hearings, depending on the regime. Administrators face considerable logistical and practical burdens in order to satisfy the formal evidentiary demands of the public hearing process. Moreover, licence standards are frequently complicated and subject to interpretation and change; thus it is difficult to make determinations about levels of compliance. Where licences are not revoked or suspended following detection of non-compliance, licensees may acquire *de facto* tenure in the licence. On the positive side, licences are flexible instruments: through licence conditions and other requirements, the Administration can develop standards specific to the individual licensee.

While the formal legal structure is heavily weighted to framing and constraining the use of coercion, in practice government resorts more and more to incentives and persuasion. Here the role of law is less defined. The administration of grants, for

example, is usually informal: details are negotiated without the participation of third parties. This may give rise to suspicion on their part, as they are not allowed to participate in the process. While in appropriate circumstances the use of incentives can be highly effective, the broader implementation picture may suffer. Issues such as the legal characterization of grants, the rights and obligations of parties, methods of participation and the enforcement obligations of administrators cry out for further study.

The Administration resorts extensively to *persuasion* in policy implementation, whether or not enabling legislation addresses or authorizes such practices. Persuasion can help change attitudes and improve efficiency: persuasion activities can lead to decreased reliance on more costly activities associated with other instruments. As well, persuasion can be used to "test the waters" and otherwise influence behaviour in areas where the Administration lacks substantive jurisdiction. However, the lack of safeguards is for many a cause for concern. If only for this reason the various forms of persuasion used by government merit separate study.

The preceding summary underlines only a few of the difficulties in the area of policy implementation. Many others need to be examined with a view to reform. The role of *inspectorates* calls for much more research; we hope to offer an overview of the issues in the near future. Our examination of licences and incentives confirms that much of policy implementation relates to *bargaining, agreements and arrangements*. Indeed, the Administration sometimes relies on *compliance contracts* to implement policies (Barton *et al.*, 1984; Daintith, 1979). This attempt to call on the language and practice of private law also merits exploration, since the threats it may pose could be as great as the potential it offers.

A final area in need of immediate attention concerns the use of publicity to stigmatize non-compliant behaviour. The effects of this are poorly understood. Should such measures be taken, say, where non-compliance adversely affects third parties? What identifiable effects does publicity have in the minds of the audience and on the *administré*'s bottom line? Does the *administré* suffer a boycott as soon as the constituency knows that a charge has been laid? What information about *administré* conduct should administrators publicize? Policy makers need to better understand and to recognize explicitly the effects of stigmatization from publicity about non-compliance in their implementation policies.

Notes

1. Power may be a better term, although it does not readily lend itself to legal analysis. Our discussion of instruments and activities was inspired by the literature about the uses of coercive, compensatory and conditioning power (Russell, 1938; Galbraith, 1983).

2. An incentive is essentially an inducement to behave in a certain way; the incentive is defined by the entity offering the incentive. To be an incentive the money transfer must be conditional on some action by a private actor; an incentive is not, therefore, merely an unrequited transfer.

(e) Statutory Interpretation

1. REFERENCES

J. Willis, "Statutory Interpretation in a Nutshell" (1938) 16 Can. Bar Rev. 1; P.-A. Côté, *The Interpretation of Legislation in Canada*, 2d ed. (Cowansville, Québec: Yvon Blais, 1991); R. Sullivan, *Driedger on the Construction of Statutes*, 3d ed. (Toronto, Butterworths, 1994); D.J. Gifford et al., *How to Understand Statutes and By-Laws* (Scarborough, Ont.: Carswell, 1996); R. Sullivan, *Statutory Interpretation* (Concord, Ont.: Irwin Law, 1997).

2. GENERAL CONSTRUCTION

Statutory construction has three main general rules: plain meaning, absurdity-injustice, and mischief. Although called rules, they are in fact presumptions.

The plain meaning rule is that if the ordinary grammatical and dictionary meaning of words is available, this is the meaning that should normally be given. Where relevant, this meaning may be modified by (a) the definition section of the relevant statute, (b) the relevant federal or provincial interpretation act, and (c) the special legal dictionary meanings.

The absurdity-injustice rule says that the ordinary grammatical sense of words should be altered if this is required to avoid an absurd or manifestly unjust result. In this case, an alternative construction is necessary.

The mischief rule applies where the meaning of words is ambiguous. This rule invites courts to look at the evil or mischief the statute was designed to prevent, and to give the statute an interpretation that will best accomplish this result. It involves a look at the social policy of the act and its relevant sections.

In reality, whether the meaning of a word is plain or ambiguous is often debatable, and there is always a need to avoid absurd, illogical, and unjust results. Hence courts generally try to combine the three interpretation approaches described above. The Supreme Court has described this integrated perspective as follows:

> ... [T]he proper construction of a statutory provision flows from reading the words of the provision in their grammatical and ordinary sense and in their entire context, harmoniously with the scheme of the statute as a whole, the purpose of the statute, and the intention of Parliament: *R. v. Gladue*, [1999] S.J.C. No. 19, para. 25.

Thus, while there are interpretation criteria to consider, these cannot be applied mathematically; the interpretation process requires flexibility and exercise of individual judgment.

3. GRAMMATICAL CONTEXT

As Professor Willis has observed, "Words, like people, take their colour from their surroundings." Although this is always so in statutory interpretation, in some cases the grammatical context of a word plays a special role in influencing its meaning. In such cases, courts may refer to the general principle *noscitur a sociis*, which simply means that a word is influenced by those surrounding it. A rule that applies this principle to a more specific situation is *ejusdem generis*, which means that general words or phrases are modified by those that accompany them. Another more specific rule is *expressio unius, exclusio alterius*, which means that the express mention of one thing raises a presumption against the inclusion of other things that otherwise may have been contemplated.

4. FORMAL CONTEXT

The written text of a statute, including the long title, section numbers, and punctuation, has the force of law. Schedules have the same force as the written text if they are incorporated into the latter. Preambles do not have the same legal weight as the written text, although they may be considered in determining the general purpose of the statute. Headings can be considered in interpreting federal, but not Ontario, statutes. Marginal notes have the force of law in some jurisdictions (i.e., at the federal level), but not in others (i.e., in Ontario).

Other statutes may affect the construction of a statute in some cases. Where provisions in different statutes appear to conflict, the principle of the sovereignty of Parliament requires that the more recent and specific provision prevails. Where the statutory language is insufficient to shed light on legislative intent, courts may look at extrinsic evidence such as legislative history as well, but should do so cautiously: *M. v. H.*, [1999] S.C.J. No. 23, para. 186.

The interpretation and validity of all legislation is subject to the paramount requirements of the legal components of the Constitution of Canada. This is required by s. 52(1) of the *Constitution Act, 1982*, and has been described as the principle of "constitutionalism": *Reference Re Secession of Quebec*, [1998] 2 S.C.R.217, para. 72.

5. ADMINISTRATIVE LAW PRESUMPTIONS

Although all presumptions described earlier can affect administrative law, a few apply mainly in this particular field. These include the general presumption that government power requires statutory authorization (for an early application involving government fees, see *Goudie v. Langlois* (1819), Stuarts K.B.R. 142 (L.K.B.)); the presumption that a delegated statutory discretionary power cannot be re-delegated to another person or agency (see, for example, *Re Chemicals Regulations*, [1943] S.C.R. 1 (S.C.C.) and *Forget v. Quebec (A.G.)*, [1988] 2 S.C.R. 96 (S.C.C.)); the presumption that power conferred on a Minister of the Crown can be exercised by an appropriate official in the Minister's department (see *Carltona Ltd. v. Commissioners of Works*, [1943] 2 All E.R. 560 (D.A.) and *Interpretation Act*, R.S.C. 1985, c. I-21, s. 24(2)); the presumption that a statute does not bind or limit the Crown, in the absence of express wording or necessary implication to the contrary (see, for example, *Oldman River Society v. Canada (Min. of Transport)*, [1992] 1 S.C.R. 3); and, last but not the least, the presumptions that comprise the specific grounds of judicial control (Chapters 4 to 8, below).

(f)   Ejusdem Generis: *Brampton*†

NOTE

The Ontario *Milk Industry Act* empowered the Milk Control Board of Ontario to refuse a milk distribution licence to an applicant "not qualified by experience, financial responsibility and equipment to properly conduct the proposed business or for any other reason that the Board may deem sufficient". The Board refused Brampton Jersey's application to distribute milk in Brampton on the ground that this area was already adequately served. Brampton Jersey's application for Mandamus to compel the issue of a licence was rejected by the Ontario High Court. They appealed to the Ontario Court of Appeal.

EXTRACTS

[HOGG J.A.:]

. . . .

In the present instance the appellant's application to the Board for a licence to distribute milk was refused solely upon the ground announced by the Board on March 2, 1955, as follows:

> Upon a careful review of the respective arguments by Counsel representing the various interests concerned in this application, and having regard to the fact that the area involved is being adequately served, it was resolved that the Board

---

† *Brampton Jersey Enterprises Ltd. v. The Milk Control Board of Ontario* (1955), 1 D.L.R. (2d) 130 (O.C.A.).

is of the opinion that the present relationship between the Producers and Distributors in the market should be continued and, therefore, is not prepared to approve the application at this time.

The authority for the refusal to issue a licence is to be found in s. 12(1)(*g*) to which reference has already been made. This provision of the Act reads:

> The Board may, "(*g*) refuse to grant a licence where the applicant is not qualified by experience, financial responsibility and equipment to properly conduct the proposed business or for any other reason that the Board may deem sufficient".

Regulation 6(1) (O. Reg. 79/55, 88 Ont. Gaz. 987) made by the Board pursuant to the authority given by the statute sets out that: "No person shall be a regular distributor, or producer-distributor, or peddler [of milk] without a licence from the Board, obtainable on application therefor." Regulation 6(2) states that an application for a licence shall be in Form 3. One of the requirements of Form 3 is information as to the number of producers of milk at the date of the application. No request is made for the number of distributors. It may be inferred from this fact that the number of distributors is not an element to be considered by the Board in granting a licence to distribute milk.

The problem presented to the Court may be approached from several viewpoints. It is trite to say that the Board, being a creature of statute, must act within the ambit of the powers given it by statute. A power conferred upon a wholly statutory body to interfere with or prohibit, by regulation or licence, the common law right of persons to carry on a lawful business in a lawful manner and to engage in competition with other persons also carrying on the same business, is strictly construed by the Courts. The refusal by the Board to grant a licence to distribute milk must be based upon and be related to the purpose and object of the statute, and it is not, in my opinion, an object or a purpose of the *Milk Industry Act* that a person should be prohibited from distributing milk for the reason that there are already persons engaged in the same business within the same district or area and the Board is of the opinion that, therefore, such district is adequately served and supplied with milk. The powers given to the Board are all of a regulatory character and in no instance except in those already mentioned under ss. (1)(*d*) and (*e*) of s. 12 is the Board given express power to prohibit any act. The powers given to the Board do not include or embrace within

their ambit authority to prevent absolutely the distribution of milk on the ground that milk is already being supplied to the citizens of the Town of Brampton and vicinity in sufficient quantity by other distributors who have already received a licence. The reason given by the Board for its refusal to grant a licence to the appellant is not, in my view, related to the object or purpose of the statute.

. . . .

Turning now to the consideration of another aspect of the subject, it was argued with force by Mr. Sedgwick for the appellant that the concluding words of s. 12(1)(*g*), which are "or for any other reason that the Board may deem sufficient", must be interpreted as being *ejusdem generis* with the preceding specific words of the subsection, namely, "qualified by experience, financial responsibility and equipment to properly conduct the proposed business".

. . . .

The *ejusdem generis rule* cannot be applied unless there is a genus.

In the present instance the concluding words of ss. (1)(*g*) of s. 12 cannot be related only to the one word "qualified" for in such case, as was said by Duff J. in *Ferguson* v. *MacLean*, the possible number of categories might be indefinitely great — but to the word "qualified" as limited and circumscribed by the following words, "by experience, financial responsibility and equipment to properly conduct the proposed business".

In the *Tillmanns & Co. case*, [1908] 2 K.B. 385, already referred to, Kennedy L.J. expressed the principle at p. 409 in this way: "The genus must first be found, and then you must find whether the words that follow are applicable to the species enumerated belonging to the one genus." This judgment was affirmed by the House of Lords, [1908] A.C. 406.

In s. 12(1)(*g*) the common category or genus is the qualification of the appellant to conduct the proposed business properly by reason of (*a*) his experience, (*b*) his financial responsibility, and (*c*) his possessing or having the ability to acquire suitable equipment.

The words of general signification "or for any other reason that the Board may deem sufficient" are not to be taken in their larger sense but must be limited to things *ejusdem generis* with the prior specifically-mentioned words and must relate in some manner to the applicant's qualification to conduct properly the business of distributing milk. Even if, as is argued by counsel for the respondent, the *ejusdem generis* rule should be used sparingly in construing a statute conferring discretionary powers on a public Board, as suggested in *Re Ollmann*, [1925] 3 D.L.R. 1196, 57 O.L.R. 340, nevertheless the sweeping and general words of this subsection have a limitation imposed upon them, having regard to the context in which they are found, and having regard to the scope and intent of the legislation and of the Regulations passed pursuant thereto. As has been said, a perusal of the statute, and an examination into its terms, makes it clear that the Legislature intended to confer only regulatory powers on the Board. Had it been intended to confer an unlimited and untrammelled discretion on this body, the Legislature would have said so in express terms and the words descriptive of the qualification to be looked for in an applicant for a licence to distribute milk would then be wholly superfluous.

It is my opinion that the Board has acted in excess of the power conferred upon it by the statute. The statute gives the Board numerous powers for the regulation and control of the production, transportation, distribution, marketing and sale of milk, but the power to dictate who and how many shall distribute milk in the area in question, and to refuse a licence to an applicant, on the ground that there are sufficient distributors now supplying the area in question, is not to be found within the confines of the statute. This is the exercise of a power of restraint on the business of distributing milk which is not warranted by the legislation. If it had been the intention of the Legislature to give the Board power to determine who and how many should be entitled to distribute milk, and to prohibit any others except those chosen by the Board, the statute would have contained such express power. An example of legislation of this character is to be found in ss. 264 and 413 of the *Municipal Act*.

For reasons given I am of the opinion that the appeal should be allowed with costs of the appeal and of the application. It is possible that the Board considers the appellant has satisfied the requirements set out in s. 12(1)(g) of the statute and no indication is given, in the reasons of the Board, of any ground for refusing the application other than that the area in question is adequately served and that existing conditions should not be changed. However, I think the application should be referred back to the Board for determination as to whether the appellant has satisfied or has failed to satisfy, the requirements of the said ss. (1)(g) of s. 12, with the direction of this Court to issue the licence if the Board is satisfied with the qualifications of the appellant.

Appeal allowed.

(g) "Integrated" Statutory Interpretation: *Bell ExpressVu*†

NOTE

Bell ExpressVu was a licensed distributor of satellite direct-to-home (DTH) television programming in Canada. Bell ExpressVu became concerned about what it regarded as illegal competition from "grey market" satellite dish dealers. It sought an injunction under s. 9(1)(c) of the *Radiocommunication Act* to prohibit these dealers from selling decoding systems (and U.S. mailing addresses) to Canadian customers to enable them to receive DTH programming from the United States. Section 9(1)(c) said that:

No person shall ... (c) decode an encrypted subscription programming signal or encrypted network feed otherwise than under and in accordance with an authorization from the lawful distributor of the signal or feed.

Bell ExpressVu claimed that this provision prohibited all decoding, except where authorized by a lawful distributor of a given signal. The grey market dealers claimed that the provision allowed all decoding except in cases where there *is* a lawful distributor, and this distributor has not authorized their decoding. The dealers said that because there was no lawful distributor for the American signals

---

† *Bell ExpressVu Limited Partnership v. Rex*, [2002] S.C.J. No. 43, rev'g. (2000), 191 D.L.R. (4th) 662 (B.C.C.A.), which aff'd. [1999] B.C.J. No. 3092 (QL) (B.C.S.C.), refusing to grant an injunction.

in Canada, the prohibition in s. 9(1)(c) did not apply.

Note that *Bell ExpressVu* did not directly involve a public administrative authority. Instead of conferring power on a regulator such as Canada Radio-television and Communications Commission, the relevant statute provided for private litigation. On the other hand, the Court faced the same question that haunts nearly all administrative law cases: what is the meaning of the relevant statutory provision? Note the Supreme Court's reaffirmation of the "integrated" approach to statutory interpretation described in Part (e) of Chapter 3. What would the Court have done if it had found the grammatical meaning and the broader context in conflict?

EXTRACTS

[IACOBUCCI J. for the Court:]

(1) Principles of Statutory Interpretation

[para26] In Elmer Driedger's definitive formulation, found at p. 87 of his *Construction of Statutes* (2nd ed. 1983):

> Today there is only one principle or approach, namely, the words of an Act are to be read in their entire context and in their grammatical and ordinary sense harmoniously with the scheme of the Act, the object of the Act, and the intention of Parliament.

Driedger's modern approach has been repeatedly cited by this Court as the preferred approach to statutory interpretation across a wide range of interpretive settings....

[para27] The preferred approach recognizes the important role that context must inevitably play when a court construes the written words of a statute: as Professor John Willis incisively noted in his seminal article "Statute Interpretation in a Nutshell" (1938), 16 Can. Bar Rev. 1, at p. 6, "words, like people, take their colour from their surroundings". This being the case, where the provision under consideration is found in an Act that is itself a component of a larger statutory scheme, the surroundings that colour the words and the scheme of the Act are more expansive....

[para28] Other principles of interpretation — such as the strict construction of penal statutes and the "Charter values" presumption — only receive application where there is ambiguity as to the meaning of a provision....

[para29] What, then, in law is an ambiguity? ... Major J.'s statement in *CanadianOxy Chemicals Ltd. v. Canada (Attorney General)*, [1999] 1 S.C.R. 743, at para. 14, is apposite: "It is only when genuine ambiguity arises between two or more plausible readings, each equally in accordance with the intentions of the statute, that the courts need to resort to external interpretive aids" (emphasis added), to which I would add, "including other principles of interpretation".

[para30] For this reason, ambiguity cannot reside in the mere fact that several courts — or, for that matter, several doctrinal writers — have come to differing conclusions on the interpretation of a given provision....

(2) Application to this Case

[para31] The interpretive factors laid out by *Driedger* need not be canvassed separately in every case, and in any event are closely related and interdependent (*Chieu, supra*, at para. 28). In the context of the present appeal, I will group my discussion under two broad headings....

(a) Grammatical and Ordinary Sense

[para32] In its basic form, s. 9(1)(c) is structured as a prohibition with a limited exception....

The provision opens with the announcement of a broad prohibition ("No person shall"), follows by announcing the nature ("decode") and object ("an encrypted programming signal") of the prohibition, and then announces an exception to it ("otherwise than under and in accordance with authorization from the lawful distributor")....

[para33] The forbidden activity is decoding. Therefore, as noted by the Court of Appeal, the prohibition in s. 9(1)(c) is directed towards the reception side of the broadcasting equation. Quite apart from the provenance of the signals at issue, where the impugned decoding occurs within Canada, there can be no issue of the statute's having an extra-territorial reach. In the present case, the reception that the appellant seeks to enjoin occurs entirely within Canada.

[para34] The object of the prohibition is of central importance to this appeal. What is interdicted by s. 9(1)(c) is the decoding of "an encrypted subscription programming signal" (in French, *un signal*

d'abonnement) (emphasis added). The usage of the indefinite article here is telling:

> it signifies "one, some [or] any" (*Canadian Oxford Dictionary* (1998)). Thus, what is prohibited is the decoding of any encrypted subscription programming signal, subject to the ensuing exception.

[para35] The definition of "subscription programming signal" suggests that the prohibition extends to signals emanating from other countries. Section 2 of the Act defines that term as, "radiocommunication that is intended for reception either directly or indirectly by the public in Canada <u>or elsewhere</u> on payment of a subscription fee or other charge" (emphasis added)....

. . . .

[para39] The Court of Appeal relied upon the definite article found in this portion of s. 9(1)(c) ("the signal"), in order to support its narrower reading of the provision. Before this Court, counsel for the respondents submitted as well that the definite article preceding the words "lawful distributor" confirms that the provision "is only intended to operate where there is a lawful distributor"....

. . . .

[para41] In my view, the definite articles are used in the exception portion of s. 9(1)(c) in order to identify from amongst the genus of signals captured by the prohibition (any encrypted subscription programming signal) that species of signals for which the rule is "otherwise". Grammatically, then, the choice of definite and indefinite articles essentially plays out into the following rendition: No person shall decode any (indefinite) encrypted subscription programming signal unless, for the (definite) particular signal that is decoded, the person has received authorization from the (definite) lawful distributor. Thus, as might happen, if no lawful distributor exists to grant such authorization, the general prohibition must remain in effect.

. . . .

[para43] In the end, I conclude that when the words of s. 9(1)(c) are read in their grammatical and ordinary sense, taking into account the definitions provided in s. 2, the provision prohibits the decoding in Canada of any encrypted subscription programming signal, regardless of the signal's origin, unless autho-

rization is received from the person holding the necessary lawful rights under Canadian law.

(b) Broader Context

[para44] Although the *Radiocommunication Act* is not, unfortunately, equipped with its own statement of purpose, it does not exist in a vacuum ... [and should be read in tandem with the *Broadcasting Act*].

. . . .

[para47] Canada's broadcasting policy [in the *Broadcasting Act*] has a number of distinguishing features, and evinces a decidedly cultural orientation. It declares that the radio frequencies in Canada are public property, that Canadian ownership and control of the broadcasting system should be a base premise, and that the programming offered through the broadcasting system is "a public service essential to the maintenance and enhancement of national identity and cultural sovereignty". Sections 3(1)(d) and 3(1)(t) enumerate a number of specific developmental goals for, respectively, the broadcasting system as a whole and for distribution undertakings (including DTH distribution undertakings) in particular. Finally, s. 3(2) declares that "the Canadian broadcasting system constitutes a single system" best regulated and supervised "by a single independent public authority".

[para48] In this context, one finds little support for the restrictive interpretation of s. 9(1)(c). Indeed, as counsel for the Attorney General of Canada argued before us, after consideration of the Canadian broadcasting policy Parliament has chosen to adopt, one may legitimately wonder why would Parliament enact a provision like the restrictive interpretation? Why would Parliament provide for Canadian ownership, Canadian production, Canadian content in its broadcasting and then simply leave the door open for unregulated, foreign broadcasting to come in and sweep all of that aside? What purpose would have been served?

[para49] On the other hand, the interpretation of s. 9(1)(c) that I have determined to result from the grammatical and ordinary sense of the provision accords well with the objectives set out in the Broadcasting Act. The fact that DTH broadcasters encrypt their signals, making it possible to concentrate regulatory efforts on the reception/decryption side of the equation, actually assists with attempts to pursue the statutory broadcasting policy objectives and to regulate and supervise the Canadian broadcasting system

as a single system. It makes sense in these circumstances that Parliament would seek to encourage broadcasters to go through the regulatory process by providing that they could only grant authorization to have their signal decoded, and thereby collect their subscription fees, after regulatory approval has been granted.

. . . .

[para55] After considering the entire context of s. 9(1)(c), and after reading its words in their grammatical and ordinary sense in harmony with the legislative framework in which the provision is found, I find no ambiguity. Rather, I can conclude only that Parliament intended to create an absolute bar on Canadian residents decoding encrypted programming signals. The only exception to this prohibition occurs where authorization is acquired from a distributor holding the necessary legal rights in Canada to transmit the signal and provide the required authorization. There is no need in this circumstance to resort to any of the subsidiary principles of statutory interpretation.

(h) Questions

1. Distinguish between
   (a) techniques for influencing primary private behaviour, enforcing compliance, and assigning public powers;
   (b) the main kinds of techniques for assigning public powers;
   (c) coercive and non-coercive techniques for influencing private behaviour;
   (d) self-applying and administered techniques for influencing private behaviour.

2. Why is licence such a popular technique? Does its popularity affect the techniques for assigning public powers?

3. Compare the Law Reform Commission's groups of instruments for policy implementation with Hart and Sack's categories of techniques.

4. What is compliance? What are the main problems in securing it?

5. You are a deputy minister in charge of Fitness and Amateur Sport. Enthusiastic junior members of your department have presented you with a variety of proposals designed to enhance the physical fitness of Canadians. Identify the legislative technique(s) represented by each proposal below, and comment about the strengths and weaknesses of the techniques involved:
   (a) a statute requiring every Canadian between ages 20 and 40 to do 10 push-ups per day unless excused by a written medical certificate;
   (b) a new Department of Public Works' policy of refusing to contract with firms that lack physical exercise programs for their employees;
   (c) a TV and radio advertising campaign exhorting Canadians to get more exercise;
   (d) a government pamphlet detailing the ill effects of low physical fitness;
   (e) refraining from the above or any other governmental measure, and leaving it to the good sense of Canadians themselves to exercise and stay fit.

6. Compare the safeguards used in making statutes with those used in making subordinate legislation. What are the main categories of subordinate legislation and their safeguards?

7. Concerned about the growing number of taxi-cabs involved in local motor vehicle accidents, the township of Prudence enacted a special Safe Taxi by-law, which created a Safe Tax Licensing Board. Applicants were required to receive from the Board a Safe Taxi licence before they could operate their vehicles on the streets of Prudence.

   Harry Hiccup, son of the president of Prudence Chamber of Commerce, but known to his friends as "Hot-Rod Harry," was refused a Safe Taxi licence by the Board, "because of your seventeen speeding convictions over the past year and a half." Harry's father storms into your office and asks if you can help Harry challenge the Board's decision in the courts.

The relevant provision of the Safe Taxi Licensing by-law provides that "The Board may refuse to issue a Safe Taxi license if the applicant's vehicle has poor brakes, poor lights, an inoperative horn, obstructed vision through the windows or loose steering, or for any other reason the Board deems sufficient." The by-law also states that "A decision of the Board is final and shall not be reviewed in any court." Advise Harry's father.

4

Administrative Law:
Scope of Natural Justice and Fairness

(a) Natural Justice and Fairness

The statutory mandates initiated by policy makers may be either substantive, telling administrators *what* to do, or procedural, telling them *how* to act. This question of *how*, which is the procedural aspect of administrative law, will be considered at some length in this sourcebook.

Both questions on "what" and "how" relate to fairness as well as to efficiency. Indeed, fair procedure is an important aspect of the general efficiency/fairness dichotomy that permeates administrative law.

Fair procedure is the responsibility of many of the central actors in administrative law. The starting point is the governing statute that, subject to the overriding provisions of the *Charter* and the rest of the Constitution, may have imposed procedural requirements on the decision in question. Even if it has not, the administrator has a responsibility to act fairly, which he or she may have regularized by means of administrative guidelines or even procedural regulations. Where neither statute, Constitution, nor administrative guidelines provides procedural direction, and the administré feels threatened by a procedural injustice, he or she may be able to obtain help from the courts. Even without express statutory direction, the courts may impose certain procedural requirements derived from the common law. These procedural requirements[1] are known as the rules of natural justice and the rules of procedural fairness. The rules of procedural fairness (often known as the "duty to act fairly") are best understood as an aspect of the rules of natural justice.

There are two main branches to the rules of natural justice: the *audi alteram partem* and partiality or bias rules. In each case, there are two main aspects to the rules: scope (to what parts of the administrative process do they apply?) and content (where they *do* apply, what procedural standards do they require?)

In this chapter, we will concentrate on the general question of the scope of the rules of natural justice, focusing on the more common branch, which is *audi alteram partem*. In subsequent chapters, we will look at some special questions of scope and content.

Note

1. Common law judicial review can also impose *non*-procedural limitations on decisions of public authorities. These include presumptions against defects such as fraud, lack of evidence, bad faith, improper purpose, irrelevant considerations, and fettering of discretion, at least where there is no privative clause or similar signal for restraint. Where there is a privative clause, review is generally limited to jurisdictional errors or patent unreasonableness.

(b) Classic Natural Justice: *Cooper*†

NOTE

The Wandsworth Board of Works demolished Mr. Cooper's partly built house because he had violated a statutory notification requirement. They didn't give Mr. Cooper any advance notice of their planned demolition, or any opportunity to defend his own failure to give them with prior notice.

Mr. Cooper sued the Board for damages (monetary compensation) for the common law tort of trespass. Justice Willis issued the Board a *rule nisi*. This was a conditional order that said the Board needn't pay damages for trespass if it could show sufficient reason not to do so.

This issue was referred to the Court of Common Pleas. Here the Board relied on its statutory power to demolish property in order to penalize statutory violations. It argued that its statutory power prevailed over the common law tort of trespass.

Cooper is one of the best-known cases in administrative law. It shows how an action for damages must be preceded by judicial review to establish that the decision causing the damages was not authorized by statute. Also, the case shows how judicial review for breach of the rules of natural justice may be available even though no statutory provision expressly imposes a procedural obligation.

Cooper further illustrates what might be called "classic natural justice." Under this approach, natural justice is patterned — but only loosely — on judicial functions. The notion is that if an administrator acts — even remotely — like a court, the administrator may be required to provide court-like procedural protections, however minimal these might be in specific situations. The content of classic natural justice is not fixed. It is a sliding scale, aimed at providing whatever procedural help is necessary in the circumstances to provide a fair opportunity to be heard (the *audi alteram partem* rule) or an opportunity to be heard before an impartial decision-maker (the rule against bias). The scope, too, is flexibly drawn. The presumptions of classic natural justice apply wherever a public statutory decision seriously affects the interests of individuals.

In *Cooper*, note the judicial analogy and how loosely it is drawn. Consider, too, that the court offers functional justifications for providing notice to Cooper.

EXTRACTS

[ERLE, C.J.:]

I am of the opinion that this rule ought to be discharged [i.e., dismissed ... thus ending the conditional order against damages]. This was an action of trespass by the plaintiff against the Wandsworth district board, for pulling down and demolishing his house; and the ground of defence that has been put forward by the defendants has been under the 76th section of the *Metropolis Management Act* [1855], 18 & 19 Vict. C., 120. By the part of that section which applies to this case, it is enacted that, before any person shall begin to build a new house, he shall give seven days' notice to the district board of his intention to build; and it provides at the end that, in default of such notice it shall be lawful for the district board to demolish the house. The district board here say that no notice was given by the plaintiff of his intention to build the house in question, wherefore they demolished it. The contention on the part of the plaintiff has been that, although the words of the statute, taken in their literal sense, without any qualification at all, would create a justification for the act which the district board has done, the powers granted by that statute are subject to a qualification which has been repeatedly recognized, that no man is to be deprived of his property without his having an opportunity of being heard. The evidence here shews that the plaintiff and the district board had not been quite on amicable terms. Be that as it may, the district board say that no notice was given, and that consequently they had a right to proceed to demolish the house without delay, and without notice to the party whose house was to be pulled down, and without giving him an opportunity of shewing any reason why the board should delay. I think that the power which is granted by the 76th section is subject to the qualification suggested. It is a power carrying with it enormous consequences. The house in question was built only to a certain extent. But

---

† *Cooper v. Wandsworth Board of Works* (1863), 14 C.B. (N.S.) 180; 143 E.R. 414 (U.K. Common Pleas).

the power claimed would apply to a complete house. It would apply to a house of any value, and completed to any extent; and it seems to me to be a power which may be exercised most perniciously, and that the limitation which we are going to put upon it is one which ought, according to the decided cases, to be put upon it, and one which is required by a due consideration for the public interest. I think the board ought to have given notice to the plaintiff, and to have allowed him to be heard. The default in sending notice to the board of the intention to build, is a default which may be explained. There may be a great many excuses for the apparent default. The party may have intended to conform to the law. He may have actually conformed to all the regulations which they would wish to impose, though by accident his notice may have miscarried; and, under those circumstances, if he explained how it stood, the proceeding to demolish, merely because they had ill-will against the party, is a power that the legislature never intended to confer. I cannot conceive any harm that could happen to the district board from hearing the party before they subjected him to a loss so serious as the demolition of his house; but I can conceive a great many advantages which might arise in the way of public order, in the way of doing substantial justice, and in the way of fulfilling the purpose of the statute, by the restriction which we put upon them, that they should hear the party before they inflict upon him such a heavy loss. I fully agree that the legislature intended to give the district board very large powers indeed: but the qualification I speak of is one which has been recognised to the full extent. It has been said that the principle that no man shall be deprived of his property without an opportunity of being heard, is limited to a judicial proceeding, and that a district board ordering a house to be pulled down cannot be said to be doing a judicial act. I do not quite agree with that; neither do I undertake to rest my judgment solely upon the ground that the district board is a court exercising judicial discretion upon the point: but the law, I think, has been applied to many exercises which in common understanding would not be at all more a judicial proceeding than would be the act of the district board in ordering a house to be pulled down. The case of the corporation of the University of Cambridge, who turned out Dr. Bentley, in the exercise of their assumed power of depriving a member of the University of his rights, and a number of other cases which are collected in *The Hammersmith Rent-Charge case* in the judgment of Parke, B., shew that the principle has been very widely applied. The district board must do the thing legally; there must

be a resolution; and, if there be a board, and a resolution of that board, I have not heard a word to shew that it would not be salutary that they should hear the man who is to suffer from their judgment before they proceed to make the order under which they attempt to justify their act. It is said that an appeal from the district board to the metropolitan board (under s. 211) would be the mode of redress. But, if the district board have the power to do what is here stated, I am not at all clear that there would be right of redress in that way. The metropolitan board may not have a right to give redress for that which was done under the provisions of the statute. I think the appeal clause would evidently indicate that many exercises of the power of district board would be in the nature of judicial proceedings; because, certainly when they are appealed from, the appellant and the respondent are to be heard as parties, and the matter is to be decided at least according to judicial forms. I take that to be a principle of very wide application, and applicable to the present case; and I think this board was not justified under the statute, because they have not qualified themselves for the exercise of their power by hearing the party to be affected by their decision.

[BYLES, J:]

... It seems to me that the board are wrong whether they acted judicially or ministerially. I conceive they acted judicially, because they had to determine the offence, and they had to apportion the punishment as well as the remedy. That being so, a long course of decisions, beginning with *Dr. Bentley's case*, and ending with some very recent cases, establish that, although there are no positive words in a statute requiring that the party shall be heard, yet the justice of the common law will supply the omission of the legislature. The judgment of Mr. Justice Fortescue, in *Dr. Bentley's case*, is somewhat quaint, but it is very applicable, and has been the law from that time to the present. He says,

> The objection for want of notice can never be got over. The laws of God and man both give the party an opportunity to make his defence, if he has any. I remember to have heard it observed by a very learned man, upon such an occasion, that even God himself did not pass sentence upon Adam before he was called upon to make his defence. "Adam" (says God), "where art thou? Hast thou not eaten of the tree whereof I commanded thee that thou shouldest not eat?" And the same question was put to Eve also.

If, therefore, the board acted judicially, although there are no words in the statute to that effect, it is plain they acted wrongly. But suppose they acted ministerially — then it may be they were not bound to give the first sort of notice, *viz.*, the notice of the hearing; but they were clearly bound, as it seems to me, by the words of the statute, to give notice of their order before they proceeded to execute it....

WILLES and KEATING, JJ., delivered concurring judgments.

Rule discharged.

(c) Return to the Classic Approach?: *Ridge†*

NOTE

In the early 20th century, both British and Canadian courts turned away from the classic flexible approach and moved on to natural justice. There was a tendency to require specific "judicial" features — such as a dispute between two parties before a third party "judge," or an absence of discretion — before the rules of natural justice would apply. Where natural justice did apply, courts tended to require the fixed, relatively high-level requirement of an oral hearing.

This was the prevailing law when the Brighton Watch Committee dismissed Charles Ridge from his job as Chief Constable. Ridge was given no prior notice or information about the case against him. Legislation required notice and a hearing, but counsel for the Committee claimed that it did not apply in the circumstances of this case. Neither did natural justice, they argued, because the Committee's functions were not judicial. There was no dispute between two parties, and the dismissal power was a broad statutory discretion.

Although a majority of the House of Lords held that the legislative procedural requirements did apply, a small majority went on to hold that the rules of natural justice applied, too. For those who understood its significance, this latter finding and the reasons given in support of it (by Lords Reid, Morris, and Hodson) marked a judicial revolution.

EXTRACTS

[LORD REID:]

My Lords, the appellant, Mr. Ridge, became Chief Constable of the County Borough of Brighton in 1956, after serving in the Brighton Police Force for some thirty-three years. At a meeting of the watch committee, the police authority, on Mar. 7, 1958, it was resolved that he should be dismissed and he now maintains that resolution was void and of no effect because he had no notice of the grounds on which the committee proposed to act and no opportunity to be heard in his own defence.

The appellant had been arrested on Oct. 25, 1957, and subsequently tried on a charge of conspiring with the senior members of his force and others to obstruct the course of justice, and had been suspended from duty on Oct. 26. He was acquitted on Feb. 28 but the other two members of the force were convicted and in sentencing them the trial judge, Donovan, J. made a statement which included grave reflections on the appellant's conduct. He was then indicted on a charge of corruption and was on Mar. 6 acquitted, no evidence having been offered against him. On this occasion Donovan, J., made a further statement. On the day following that statement the watch committee met and summarily dismissed the appellant. I shall not deal further with these matters because my noble and learned friend Lord Morris of Borth-y-Gest intends to do so.

The power of dismissal is contained in s. 191 (4) of the *Municipal Corporations Act*, 1882. So far as I am aware that subsection is the only statutory provision regarding dismissal, and the respondents purported to act under it. It is in these terms:

> The watch committee, or any two justices having jurisdiction in the borough, may at any time suspend, and the watch committee may at any time dismiss, any borough constable whom they think negligent in the discharge of his duty, or otherwise unfit for the same.

The appellant maintains that the watch committee ought to have proceeded in accordance with reg-

---

† *Ridge v. Baldwin et al.*, [1964] A.C. 170; [1963] 2 All E.R. 66 (H.L.).

ulations made under the *Police Act*, 1919, s. 4(1), which authorised the Secretary of State to make regulations as to, *inter alia*, the conditions of service of the members of all police forces in England and Wales. Regulations were duly made but the respondents maintain that they do not apply to this case.[43] For the moment I shall assume in their favour that that is so and consider whether the *Act* of 1882 taken by itself authorised them to do as they did.

The appellant's case is that in proceeding under the *Act* of 1882 the watch committee were bound to observe what are commonly called the principles of natural justice, that before attempting to reach any decision they were bound to inform him of the grounds on which they proposed to act and to give him a fair opportunity of being heard in his own defence. The authorities on the applicability of the principles of natural justice are in some confusion and so I find it necessary to examine this matter in some detail. The principle *audi alteram partem* goes back many centuries in our law and appears in a multitude of judgments of judges of the highest authority. In modern times opinions have sometimes been expressed to the effect that natural justice is so vague as to be practically meaningless. But I would regard these as tainted by the perennial fallacy that because something cannot be cut and dried or nicely weighed or measured therefore it does not exist....

. . . .

[In the course of an exhaustive survey of the earlier case law respecting the application of the rules of natural justice, Lord Reid distinguished three potential kinds of fact situation that might arise: dismissal of a servant by his master, dismissal from an office held at pleasure, and dismissal from an office where there must be some grounds to warrant dismissal. He noted *inter alia*, that the wartime cases in which the rules had been applied very restrictively must be considered in the light of their unusual fact situations, and continued:]

. . . .

The matter has been further complicated by what I believe to be a misunderstanding of a much quoted passage in the judgment of Atkin, L.J., in *R. v. Electricity Comrs.*[44]. He said:

> The operation of the writs [of prohibition and certiorari] has extended to control the proceedings of bodies which do not claim to be and would not be recognised as courts of justice. Whenever any body of persons having legal authority to determine questions affecting the

rights of subjects, and having the duty to act judicially, act in excess of their legal authority, they are subject to the controlling jurisdiction of the King's Bench Division exercised in these writs.[45]

A gloss was put on this by Lord Hewart, C.J., in *R. v. Legislative Committee of the Church Assembly*[46]. There it was sought to prohibit the Assembly from proceeding further with the *Prayer Book Measure*, 1927. That seems to me to have no resemblance to a question whether a person should be deprived of his rights or privileges, and the case was decided on the ground that this was a deliberative or legislative body and not a judicial body. SALTER, J., put it in a few lines:

> The person or body to whom these writs are to go must be a judicial body in this sense, that it has power to determine and decide, and the power carries with it, of necessity, the duty to act judicially. I think that the Church Assembly has no such power and, therefore, no such duty.[47]

But Lord Hewart, C.J. said, having quoted the passage from Lord Atkin's judgment:

> The question therefore which we have to ask ourselves in this case is whether it is true to say in this matter, either of the Church Assembly as a whole or of the Legislative Committee of the Church Assembly, that it is a body or persons having legal authority to determine questions affecting the rights of subjects and having the duty to act judicially. It is to be observed that in the last sentence which I have quoted from the judgment of Atkin, L.J.[48], the word is not 'or' but 'and'. In order that a body may satisfy the required test it is not enough that it should have legal authority to determine questions affecting the rights of subjects; there must be super-added to that characteristic the further characteristic that the body has the duty to act judicially. The duty to act judicially is an ingredient which if the test is to be satisfied must be present. As these writs in the earlier days were issued only to bodies which without any harshness of construction could be called and naturally would be called courts so also today these writs do not issue except to bodies which act or are under the duty to act in a judicial capacity.[49]

I have quoted the whole of this passage because it is typical of what has been said in several subsequent cases. If Lord Hewart, C.J. meant that it is never enough that a body simply has a duty to determine what the rights of an individual should be, but that there must always be something more to impose on it a duty to act judicially before it can be found to observe the principles of natural justice, then that appears to me impossible to reconcile with the earlier authorities. [Lord Reid referred to statements in ten 19th and early 20th century cases, including *Cooper* v. *Wandsworth Board of Works*[50], which he said were inconsistent with this proposition.] ... [T]hat is only a selection of the earlier authorities. And, as I shall try to show, it cannot be what Lord Atkin[51] meant.

In *R.* v. *Electricity Comrs.*[52] the commissioners had a statutory duty to make schemes with regard to electricity districts and to hold local inquiries before making them. They made a draft scheme which in effect allocated duties to one body which the Act required should be allocated to a different kind of body. This was held to be ultra vires and the question was whether prohibition would lie. It was argued that the proceedings of the commissioners were purely executive and controllable by Parliament alone. Bankes, L.J., said:

> On principle and on authority it is, in my opinion, open to this court to hold, and I consider that it should hold, that powers so far-reaching, affecting as they do individuals as well as property, are powers to be exercised judicially and not ministerially, or merely, to use the language[53] of Palles, C.B., as proceedings towards legislation.[54]

So he inferred the judicial element from the nature of the power. I think that Atkin, L.J.[55], did the same. Immediately after passage which I said has been misunderstood, he cited a variety of cases and in most of them I can see nothing "superadded" (to use Lord Hewart's word) to the duty itself. Certainly Lord Atkin did not say that anything was superadded. A later passage in his judgment convinces me that he, like Bankes, L.J.[56], inferred the judicial character of the duty from the nature of the duty itself. Although it is long, I am afraid I must quote it:

> In the present case the Electricity Commissioners have to decide whether they will constitute a joint authority in a district in accordance with law, and with what power they will invest that body. The question necessarily involves the withdrawal from existing bodies of undertakers of some of their existing rights, and imposing upon them of new duties including their subjection to the control of the new body, and new financial obligations. It also provides in the new body a person to whom may be transferred rights of purchase which at present are vested in another authority. The commissioners are proposing to create such a new body in violation of the Act of Parliament and are proposing to hold a possibly long and expensive inquiry into the expediency of such a scheme, in respect of which they have the power to compel representatives of the prosecutors to attend and produce papers. I think that in deciding upon the scheme and in holding the inquiry they are acting judicially in the sense of the authorities I have cited....[57]

There is not a word in Lord Atkin's judgment to suggest disapproval of the earlier line of authority which I have cited. On the contrary, he goes further than those authorities.

Notes

43. [Police Regulation #1709 required that when a "report" or "allegation" of an offence was received, a watch committee must inform the constable of it in writing and must give him or her an opportunity to make a written statement on his or her own behalf. Question: Had there been a "report" or "allegation" in this case?]
44. [1942] 1 K.B. 171.
45. [1923] All E.R. Rep. at p. 161; [1924] 1 K.B. at p. 205.
46. [1927] All E.R. Rep. 696 at p. 699; [1928] 1 K.B. 411 at pp. 415–16.
47. [1927] All E.R. Rep. at p. 701; [1928] 1 K.B. at p. 419.
48. [1923] All E.R. Rep. at p. 161; [1924] 1 K.B. at pp. 204–05.
49. [1928] 1 K.B. at p. 415; [1927] All E.R. Rep. at p. 699.
50. (1863), 14 C.B.N.S. 180.
51. [1923] All E.R. Rep. at pp. 160, 161; [1924] 1 K.B. at p. 204.
52. [1923] All E.R. Rep. 150; [1924] 1 K.B. 171.
53. In *R.* v. *Kingstown Comrs.* (1885), 16 L.R. Ir. 150.
54. [1923] All E.R. Rep. at p. 157; [1924] 1 K.B. at p. 198.
55. [1923] All E.R. Rep. at p. 157 et seq.; [1924] 1 K.B. at pp. 198 et seq.
56. See [1923] All E.R. Rep. At p. 157; [1924] 1 K.B. at p. 198.
57. [1923] All E.R. Rep. At pp. 161–62; [1924] 1 K.B. at pp. 206–07.

(d) Duty to Act Fairly: *Nicholson*†

NOTE

Nicholson, a probationary constable, phoned police headquarters about obtaining an overtime slip. His superior, Sergeant Burger, said this was disobedience to a direct order and told Nicholson he was being suspended indefinitely. When Nicholson asked if any charges would be laid, he was told

---

† *Re Nicholson and Haldimand-Norfolk Regional Board of Commission of Police* (1979), 88 D.L.R. (3d) 671 (S.C.C.).

there wouldn't be any charges. When Nicholson went to see an inspector, the inspector said he supported what Burger had done. Six days later, Nicholson was dismissed by the Haldimand-Norfolk Regional Board of Commissioners of Police.

Note how the majority and dissenting judgments both seem to assume that the dismissal of a probationary constable is outside the scope of the traditional rules of natural justice because it involves functions that are "administrative" rather than *quasi-judicial*. Does this assumption reveal a misunderstanding of *Ridge v. Baldwin*? The majority judgment in this case is the Canadian origin of the "duty to act fairly." Since *Nicholson*, though, courts have tended not to draw a firm distinction between the duty to act fairly and natural justice, except where compelled to do so by statute. Today, Laskin C.J.C.'s quotation from de Smith is probably more apt than his quotation from Megarry J.

EXTRACTS

Appeal from a judgment of the Ontario Court of Appeal, 69 D.L.R. (3d) 13, 12 O.R. (2d) 337, allowing an appeal from a judgment of the Divisional Court, 61 D.L.R. (3d) 36, 9 O.R. (2d) 481, granting an application to quash a decision of the respondent Regional Board of Commissioners of Police dismissing the appellant.

Ian Scott, Q.C., for appellant.

P.D. Amey, for respondent, Haldimand-Norfolk Regional Board of Police Commissioners.

Dennis Brown, for intervenant, Attorney-General of Ontario.

[LASKIN, C.J.C.:]

The issue in this appeal arises out of a letter of June 10, 1974, written to the appellant by the Deputy Chief of Police of the Regional Municipality of Haldimand-Norfolk advising him the "the Board of Commissioners of Police have approved the termination of your services effective June 4, 1974". The appellant, then a second class constable of the regional municipality, had been in its service since April 1, 1974, but he carried over his service as a police constable with the Town of Caledonia, which had been amalgamated with the Town of Haldimand on that date as an area municipality within the Regional Municipality of Haldimand-Norfolk.

The appellant was engaged as a constable, third class, by the Town of Caledonia on March 1, 1973,

under an oral hiring of which a term was that he would serve a probationary period of 12 months. On March 1, 1974, he was promoted to constable second class, and pursuant to the *Regional Municipality of Haldimand-Norfolk Amendment Act*, 1973 (Ont.), c. 155, s. 75, he became a member of the regional police force, carrying over his previous service to the same extent as if appointed by the Haldimand-Norfolk Police Board.

Subject to some observations to be made later in these reasons on the question whether the appellant knew why his services had been terminated, the formal record indicates that he was not told why he was dismissed nor was he given any notice, prior to dismissal, of the likelihood thereof or of the reason therefor, nor any opportunity to make representations before his services were terminated. Counsel for the appellant does not assert any right on his behalf to an adjudication of the existence of proper cause but rests primarily on the contention that, however fragile was the appellant's security of position, he was in law entitled to be treated fairly and there was a corresponding duty on the respondent to act fairly toward the appellant. This, it is said, the respondent did not do.

The fragility of the appellant's tenure, the allegation that in law he had no security of position and was [dismissible] at pleasure, is at the foundation of the respondent's case; and from this base it was contended that there was no obligation to give any notice or to assign any reason or to hear any representations from the appellant before dispensing with his services.

It is common ground that the relevant legislation within which the respective contentions of the parties are to be assessed is the *Police Act*, R.S.O. 1970, c. 351, and, particularly, s. 27(*b*) [am. O. Reg. 296/73, s. 1] of R.R.O. 1970, Reg. 680, made pursuant thereto. Section 27 of the Regulation is as follows:

> 27. No chief of police, constable or other police officer is subject to any penalty under this Part except after a hearing and final disposition of a charge on appeal as provided by this Part, or after the time for appeal has expired, but nothing herein affects the authority of a board or council,
> (a) subject to the consent of the Commission, to dispense with the services of any member of a police force for the purpose of reducing the size of or abolishing the police force, where the reduction or abolition is not in contravention of the Act;
> (b) to dispense with the services of any constable within eighteen months of his becoming a constable;

(c) to make rules or regulations for the retirement of members of the police force who are entitled to a pension under a pension plan established for the members of the force, under which the municipality contributes an amount not less than 5 per cent of the amount of the salaries of the members participating in the plan, and to retire the members in accordance with those rules or regulations;

(d) to act in accordance with a report or recommendation of the Commission made under section 28; or

(e) to discharge or place on retirement, if he is entitled thereto, any member of the force who, on the evidence of two legally qualified medical practitioners is, due to mental or physical disability, incapable of performing his duties in a manner fitted to satisfy the requirements of his position but any decision of the board or council made pursuant to this clause may be appealed to the Commission.

Following his dismissal, the appellant instituted proceedings to quash the decision of June 4, 1974, made by Haldimand-Norfolk Board of Police Commissioners. They came before the Ontario Divisional Court under the *Judicial Review Procedure Act*, 1971, (Ont.), c. 48. In giving the appellant the relief that he sought, Hughes, J., who spoke for the Court, took three points to which I wish to refer [61 D.L.R. (3d) 36, 9 O.R. (2d) 481]. He cleared out any issue arising from the transfer of service and status from Caledonia to Haldimand-Norfolk by declaring that whatever benefits of employment may have been conferred upon the appellant by Caledonia, his status as a police officer was neither impaired nor enhanced thereby. I agree with this assessment. Second, he concluded that a collective agreement entered into between the Haldimand-Norfolk Board of Police Commissioners and the regional police had no bearing on the case before the Divisional Court. That was common ground at the hearing in this Court and nothing more need be said about it.

This left for consideration a third point, central there as here, namely, whether, in the case of a constable who has served less than the 18 months specified in s. 27(*b*), the Board may dismiss peremptorily without obligation to give previous notice or assign a reason or give any opportunity to contest the proposed dismissal. Hughes, J., in the course of his reasons, put the point in terms of whether a hearing was required as well as notice of the complaint against a constable. Arnup, J.A., speaking for the Court of Appeal, which reversed the Divisional Court, took a like view of the issue, putting it as follows at the very front of his reasons [69 D.L.R. (3d) 13 at p. 14, 12 O.R. (2d) 337]:

Can the services of a police constable be dispensed with within 18 months of his becoming a constable, without observance by the authority discharging him of the requirements of natural justice, including a hearing?

Counsel for the appellant did not, in his main submission here, put his case that high, as I have already noted.

. . . .

... At bottom, however, Hughes, J., was of the view that *Ridge* v. *Baldwin*, [1964] A.C. 40, was in point in obliterating the distinction between those who perform ministerial acts and those who perform judicial acts, and in proclaiming a duty to act fairly applicable to the former as to the latter. He posed and answered the issue in the following passage of his reasons [61 D.L.R. (3d) at pp. 44–5]:

Can it be that the disclaimer in s. 27(*b*) of Reg. 680, which otherwise enshrines the principles of natural justice as they affect the dismissal or suspension of a police officer, confers an immunity from the application of those principles on members of a board when dealing with a police officer, who has taken the oath of office and upon whom has been conferred the province-wide powers prescribed in the *Police Act*, but who has not yet completed 18 months of service? I do not believe that it can. It may relieve them from complying with the Regulations and preclude the officer's appeal to the Ontario Police Commission, but it cannot relieve them of the duty to act judicially with all which that implies.

He concluded his reasons by stating that a duty to act fairly rested squarely upon the Board of Police Commissioners of Haldimand-Norfolk, adding this:

Their deliberations may be untrammeled by Regulations made under the *Police Act*, but this Court should not allow them to proceed as if the principles of natural justice did not exist.

Hughes, J., did not spell out the elements of the duty to act fairly but, in the course of his reasons, and adverting to s. 27(*b*), he stated that [at p. 40]: "What this Court has to decide is whether s. 27(b) by 'not specifically requiring a hearing', confers upon the Haldimand-Norfolk board power to dismiss a constable, not having served for 18 months, without one." In a later part of his reasons, he said the crucial question was whether the dismissal could be made without any notice of the complaint against the appellant and without a hearing. It can be taken from his reasons that he was asserting a duty of compliance with the rules of natural justice in their traditional sense of notice and hearing, with an opportunity to make representations, and with reviewability of the decision as much as a less onerous duty of acting fairly.

. . . .

For Arnup, J.A., the consequence of the appellant being short of 18 months' service when he was separated from his position was that (to use his words [69 D.L.R. (3d) at p. 22]) "the Board may act as it was entitled to act at common law, *i.e.*, without the necessity of prior notice of allegations or of a hearing, and *a fortiori*, with no right of appeal by the constable". He also relied on the *expressio unius* rule of construction by noting that "the Legislature has expressly required notice and hearing for certain purposes and has by necessary implication excluded them for other purposes". There is no recognition in his reasons, as there was in those of Hughes, J., that there may be a common law duty to act fairly falling short of a requirement of a hearing or, indeed, falling short of duty to act judicially. Counsel for the appellant asserted that there is an emerging line of authority on this distinction which this Court should approve, and that although it may be regarded as an aspect of natural justice it has a procedural content of its own. It does not, however, rise to the level of what is required to satisfy natural justice where judicial or *quasi*-judicial powers are being exercised. I shall come to this line of authority later in these reasons.

. . . .

The position at which I have arrived to this point is this: a constable is "the holder of a police office" (to use the description of the Privy Council in A.-G. *New South Wales* v. *Perpetual Trustee Co.* (Ld.), [1955] A.C. 457 at p. 489), exercising, so far as his police duties are concerned, an original authority confirmed by s. 55 of the *Police Act* and by the oath of office prescribed by s. 64 of the Act (wherein reference is made to "the duties of his office", among which are duties specified in the *Criminal Code*). He is a member of civilian force, and I take his assimilation to a soldier, as stated by the Privy Council in the *Perpetual Trustee Co.* case, *supra*, to be an assimilation related only to whether an action *per quod* lies against a tortfeasor at common law for the loss of

his services, and not to assimilation for other purposes, such as liability to peremptory discharge, if that be the case with a soldier.

The effect of the judgment below is that a constable who has served 18 months or more is afforded protection against arbitrary discipline or discharge through the requirement of notice and hearing and appellate review, but there is no protection at all, no half-way house, between the observance of natural justice aforesaid and arbitrary removal in the case of constable who has held office for less than 18 months. In so far as the Ontario Court of Appeal based its conclusion on the *expressio unius* rule of construction, it has carried the maxim much too far. This Court examined its application in *L'Alliance des Professeurs Catholiques de Montreal* v. *Labour Relations Board of Quebec*, [1953] 4 D.L.R. 161, [1953] 2 S.C.R. 140, 107 C.C.C. 183, and rejected an argument for its application to deny notice and hearing in that case. Rinfret, C.J.C., referred, *inter alia*, to the judgment of Farwell, L.J., in *Lowe* v. *Darling & Son*, [1906] 2 K.B. 772 at p. 785, where mention is made of *Colquhoun* v. *Brooks* (1888), 21 Q.B.D. 52, and of the statement of Lopes, L.J., at p. 65, that "the maxim ought not to be applied, when its application, having regard to the subject-matter to which it is applied, leads to inconsistency or injustice". This statement commends itself to me and I think it relevant to the present case where we are dealing with the holder of public office, engaged in duties connected with the maintenance of public order and preservation of the peace, important values in any society.

Again, in so far as the judgment of the Ontario Court of Appeal is based on reading the words "at pleasure" (as importing arbitrary power) into s. 27(*b*), or the term "probationary" (with similar import), it results in reducing the status of the office of police constable to that involved in a master-servant relationship merely because there has been less than 18 months' service in the office, and I do not regard this as either an obvious or a necessary gloss on s. 27(*b*). The view so taken by the Ontario Court of Appeal, and supported strongly in this Court by counsel for the respondent, relied heavily on the three-fold classification of dismissal situations formulated by Lord Reid in *Ridge* v. *Baldwin*, *supra*, at p. 65. Since the present case is not one where the constable holds office at pleasure, he fits more closely into Lord Reid's third class of dismissal from an office where there must be cause for dismissing him, rather than into his second class of dismissal from an office held at pleasure.

I would observe here that the old common law rule, deriving much of its force from Crown law, that a person engaged as an office holder at pleasure may be put out without reason or prior notice ought itself to be re-examined. It has an anachronistic flavour in the light of collective agreements, which are pervasive in both public and private employment, and which offer broad protection against arbitrary dismissal in the case of employees who cannot claim the status of office holders. As S.A. de Smith has pointed out in his book *Judicial Review of Administrative Action*, 3rd ed. (1973), at p. 200, "public policy does not dictate that tenure of an office held at pleasure should be terminable without allowing its occupant any right to make prior representations on his own behalf; indeed, the unreviewability of the substantive grounds for removal indicates that procedural protection may be all the more necessary"....

. . . .

This case does not, however, fall to be determined on the ground that the appellant was [dismissible] at pleasure. The dropping of the phrase "at pleasure" from the statutory provision for engagement of constables, and its replacement by a regime under which regulations fix the temporal point at which full procedural protection is given to a constable, indicates to me a turning away from the old common law rule even in cases where the full period of time has not fully run. The status enjoyed by the office holder must now be taken to have more substance than to be dependent upon the whim of the Board up to the point where it has been enjoyed for 18 months. Moreover, I find it incongruous in the present case to insist on treating the appellant as engaged at pleasure when he was first taken on as a third class constable (and not, as was possible, as a fourth class one) and when he was promoted to second class constable after serving 12 months.

In short, I am of the opinion that although the appellant clearly cannot claim the procedural protections afforded to a constable with more than 18 months' service, he cannot be denied any protection. He should be treated "fairly" not arbitrarily. I accept, therefore, for present purposes and as a common law principle what Megarry, J., accepted in *Bates* v. *Lord Hailsham of St. Marylebone*, [1972] 1 W.L.R. 1373 at p. 1378, "that in the sphere of the so-called *quasi*-judicial the rules of natural justice run, and that in the administrative or executive field there is a general duty of fairness".

The emergence of a notion of fairness involving something less than the procedural protection of traditional natural justice has been commented on in de Smith, *Judicial Review of Administrative Action*, supra, at pp. 208–9, as follows:

> That the donee of a power must "act fairly" is a long-settled principle governing the exercise of discretion, though its meaning is inevitably imprecise. Since 1967 the concept of a duty to act fairly has often been used by judges to denote an implied procedural obligation. In general it means a duty to observe the rudiments of natural justice for a limited purpose in the exercise of functions that are not analytically judicial but administrative. Given the flexibility of natural justice, it is not strictly necessary to use the term "duty to act fairly" at all. But the term has a marginal value because of (i) the frequent re-emergence of the idea that a duty to observe natural justice is not to be imported into the discharge of "administrative" functions and (ii) a tendency to assume that a duty to "act judicially" in accordance with natural justice means a duty to act like a judge in a court of law. It may therefore be less confusing to say that an immigration officer or a company inspector or a magistrate condemning food as unfit for human consumption is obliged to act fairly rather than obliged to act judicially (or to observe natural justice, which means the same thing). However, close analysis of the relevant judgments is apt to generate its own confusion; for sometimes one judge will differentiate a duty to act fairly from a duty to act judicially and another will assimilate them, both judges being in full agreement as to the scope of the procedural duty cast on the competent authority. [Footnotes omitted.]

What rightly lies behind this emergence is the realization that the classification of statutory functions as judicial, *quasi*-judicial or administrative is often very difficult, to say the least; and to endow some with procedural protection while denying others any at all would work injustice when the results of statutory decisions raise the same serious consequences for those adversely affected, regardless of the classification of the function in question: see, generally, Mullan, "Fairness: The New Natural Justice", 25 Univ. of Tor. L.J. 281 (1975).

. . . .

... [T]he Privy Council also took up the notion of fairness in a New Zealand appeal, *Furnell* v. *Whangarei High Schools Board*, [1973] A.C. 660. Lord Morris of [Borth-y-Gest], speaking for the majority of three said, at p. 679 that "natural justice is but fairness writ large and juridically. It has been described as 'fair play in action.' Nor is it a leaven to be associated only with judicial or *quasi*-judicial occasions. But as was pointed out by Tucker L.J. in *Russel* v. *Duke of Norfolk* [1949] 1 All E.R. 109, 118, the requirements of natural justice must depend on the circumstances of each particular case and the subject matter under consideration." The majority concluded in that case that "the scheme of the procedure gives no scope for action which can properly be described as unfair and there are no grounds for thinking that the sub-committee acted unfairly" (at p. 682). The two dissenting Judges were of a different view. The importance of the case lies in the respect paid by both the majority and the dissenting Judges to a duty to act fairly.

. . . .

The present case is one where the consequences to the appellant are serious indeed in respect of his wish to continue in a public office, and yet the respondent Board has thought it fit and has asserted a legal right to dispense with his services without any indication to him of why he was deemed unsuitable to continue to hold it.

In my opinion, the appellant should have been told why his services were no longer required and given an opportunity, whether orally or in writing as the Board might determine, to respond. The Board itself, I would think, would wish to be certain that it had not made a mistake in some fact or circumstance which it deemed relevant to its determination. Once it had the appellant's response, it would be for the Board to decide on what action to take, without its decision being reviewable elsewhere, always premising good faith. Such a course provides fairness to the appellant, and it is fair as well to the Board's right, as a public authority to decide, once it had the appellant's response, whether a person in his position should be allowed to continue in office to the point where his right to procedural protection was enlarged. Status in office deserves this minimal protection, however brief the period for which the office is held.

It remains to consider whether the appellant should not be heard to complain of want of fairness because he was aware of the reason for his dismissal. The only evidence in the record that goes to this point [is] his cross-examination on his affidavit in support of his application for judicial review. Questions were put to him respecting the performance of various of his duties, and among them was a reference to a telephone call made by Nicholson to police headquarters in Simcoe, asking for instructions for obtaining and completing an overtime slip. It

apparently angered his superior, one Sergeant Burger, that the appellant "was going over his head" in making the call (which Nicholson charged to himself and not to the police department). He was told by Burger that this was disobedience to a direct order (Nicholson said he was unaware of any relevant order) and that he was being suspended indefinitely. The cross-examination shows that Nicholson asked if any charges would be laid and the answer he got was "there won't be any charges." All of this happened on May 29, 1974, some six days before the dismissal by the Board. An inspector, whom Nicholson went to see the same day, had been told by Burger of his suspension of Nicholson, and the inspector said he supported what Burger had done and that Nicholson had no future in the department.

The cross-examination also revealed that the inspector invited or offered to let Nicholson resign. Nicholson denied that he was told by the inspector that "subject to the confirmation of the Board, [he was] no longer a policeman", these words being put to him by counsel for the Board on his cross-examination. When asked what he thought his position was when he left the inspector's office, Nicholson said this:

> I thought that if they felt I was dispensed with, I thought it was illegal. There were no charges, there was no lawful suspension, there was no lawful firing and I was in a quandary. I knew that I was off probation, so I decided to go and see a lawyer, and retain a lawyer.

If the making of the telephone call of which Burger disapproved (and which he said was disobedience of direct order, Nicholson saying he was unaware of any relevant order) was the basis of the proposed dismissal, it would have been simple enough to say so. I can hardly credit that in itself it could be reason for dismissing a constable who had served for 15 months. If it was an allegedly culminating event this too could be easily stated, or if there was another ground Nicholson could have been told of it prior to dismissal. I do not regard it as giving a reason for dismissal to tell Nicholson that he had no future in the department. Moreover, there is nothing in the record to show that an inspector, the particular inspector, had the power to dismiss a constable with less than 18 months' service.

I would allow the appeal, set aside the judgment of the Ontario Court of Appeal and restore the order of the Divisional Court, with costs to the appellant throughout.

. . . .

[Martland J., for four judges, dissenting, held that because Nicholson's status was only probationary, the Board's decision was administrative (not *quasi*-judicial), so it had no obligation to observe the rules of natural justice.]

(e) More Questions of Scope: *Knight*†

NOTE

A school board fired an education official without holding a formal hearing or providing official reasons beforehand. However, board members did advise the official of their concerns in advance, and gave him an opportunity to make representations. The statutory or the contractual provisions did not contain procedural protections relevant to the matter at hand.

The board claimed that it could dismiss the official without "cause" (reasons). As a result, they said that this was a case of tenure "at pleasure," exempt from the rules of natural justice or fairness. The official challenged the validity of the dismissal. He claimed that (i) he was entitled to cause, (ii) common law procedural fairness or natural justice did apply, and (iii) natural justice requirements had been violated because he had been denied a hearing and advance reasons for the dismissal.

In *Martineau v. Matsqui Institution*, [1980] 1 S.C.R. 602 (*Martineau #2*), the Supreme Court clarified that the duty to act fairly (sometimes referred to as procedural fairness) is really just an aspect of the general concept of natural justice. The Court said that the concepts need only be distinguished where a statute expressly precludes review of judicial or non-judicial functions. In this situation, the duty to act fairly might be able to supply a "low-level" form of natural justice protection. Elsewhere, though, since *Knight* the Supreme Court has used the two concepts more or less interchangeably.

But what are the threshold criteria that must be met before natural justice protections of *any* kind are available? And what about the special case of dismissals involving tenure at pleasure? Should they be immune to natural justice requirements? Finally, should courts impose natural justice requirements where the parties themselves had the opportunity to include them in a contract, but did not do so? These were some of the general issues that confronted the Court in *Knight*.

EXTRACTS

[L'HEUREUX-DUBÉ J. for herself, DICKSON C.J., La FOREST, and CORY JJ.:]

. . . .

[L'Heureux-Dubé J. found that neither the statute nor the contract required "cause" for dismissal.]

The conclusion that the respondent's employment could be legally terminated without a showing of just cause does not necessarily entail that the procedure involved can be arbitrary. There may be a general right to procedural fairness, autonomous of the operation of any statute, depending on consideration of three factors which have been held by this Court to be determinative of the existence of such a right (*Cardinal* v. *Director of Kent Institution*, [1985] 2 S.C.R. 643). If consideration of these factors in the context of the present appeal leads to the conclusion that the respondent was entitled to procedural fairness, the *Education Act* and, in this case, the terms of the contract of employment, must then be considered to determine whether this entitlement is either limited or excluded entirely. It should be noted at this point that the duty to act fairly does not depend on doctrines of employment law, but stems from the fact that the employer is a public body whose powers are derived from statute, powers that must be exercised according to the rules of administrative law. It is in that context that the employee-employer relationship between the respondent and the appellant Board must be examined, with the result that the analysis must go beyond the contract of employment to encompass arguments of public policy.

---

† *Knight v. Indian Head School Division No. 19*, [1990] 1 S.C.R. 653; rev.'g. (1988), 66 Sask. R. 308 (Sask. C.A.); which rev'd. (1986), 53 Sask. R. 278 (Sask. Q.B.).

Obviously, if either the statute or the contract confer upon the employee a right to procedural fairness, there is no need to consider the factors I have alluded to above in order to determine the existence of a similar general right, such a right becoming redundant. Since, however, I believe that in the case at bar neither the statute nor the contract do accord such a right, I will begin with an analysis of those factors.

A. General Duty of Fairness

The existence of a general duty to act fairly will depend on the consideration of three factors: (i) the nature of the decision to be made by the administrative body; (ii) the relationship existing between that body and the individual; and (iii) the effect of that decision on the individual's rights. This Court has stated in *Cardinal* v. *Director of Kent Institution*, *supra*, that whenever those three elements are to be found, there is a general duty to act fairly on a public decision-making body (Le Dain J. for the Court at p. 653).

(i) the nature of the decision

There is no longer a need, except perhaps where the statute mandates it, to distinguish between judicial, quasi-judicial and administrative decisions. Such a distinction may have been necessary before the decision of this Court in *Nicholson* v. *Haldimand-Norfolk Regional Board of Commissioners of Police*, [1979] 1 S.C.R. 311. Prior to this case, the "duty to act judicially" was thought to apply only to tribunals rendering decisions of a judicial or quasi-judicial nature, to the exclusion of those of an administrative nature. Following *Nicholson*, that distinction became less important and was found to be of little utility since both the duty to act fairly and the duty to act judicially have their roots in the same general principles of natural justice (see *Syndicat des employés de production du Québec et de l'Acadie* v. *Canada (Canadian Human Rights Commission)*, [1989] 2 S.C.R. 879, at pp. 895–96, per Sopinka J. for the majority).

On the other hand, not all administrative bodies are under a duty to act fairly. Over the years, legislatures have transferred to administrative bodies some of the duties they have traditionally performed. Decisions of a legislative and general nature can be distinguished in this respect from acts of a more administrative and specific nature, which do not entail such a duty (see Dussault and Borgeat, *Traité de droit administratif*, Tome III, 2e éd., at p. 370;

Attorney General of Canada v. *Inuit Tapirisat of Canada*, [1980] 2 S.C.R. 735, at p. 758, per Estey J. for the Court). The finality of the decision will also be a factor to consider. A decision of a preliminary nature will not in general trigger the duty to act fairly, whereas a decision of a more final nature may have such an effect (Dussault and Borgeat, *supra*, p. 372).

In the case at bar, the decision made by the appellant Board was of a final and specific nature, directed as it was at terminating the employment of the respondent. As such, the decision to dismiss could possibly entail the existence of a duty to act fairly on the part of the appellant Board.

(ii) the relationship between the employer and the employee

The second element to be considered is the nature of the relationship between the Board and the respondent. In an oft-cited decision of the House of Lords, *Ridge* v. *Baldwin*, [1963] 2 All E.R. 66, Lord Reid classified the possible employment relationship between an employer and an employee into three categories (at pp. 71–72): (i) the master and servant relationship, where there is no duty to act fairly when deciding to terminate the employment; (ii) the office held at pleasure, where no duty to act fairly exists, since the employer can decide to terminate the employment for no other reason than his displeasure; and (iii) the office from which one cannot be removed except for cause, where there exists a duty to act fairly on the part of the employer. These categories are creations of the common law. They can of course be altered by the terms of an employment contract or the governing legislation, with the result that the employment relationship may fall within more than one category (see *Nova Scotia Government Employees Association* v. *Civil Service Commission of Nova Scotia*, [1981] 1 S.C.R. 211, at p. 222 per Laskin C.J. for the majority). Lord Reid did not examine the possible implications of the non-renewal of a fixed-term employment contract, but since it was not alleged in the present appeal that the employment was terminated by non-renewal of the employee's contract, I will not address this question.

In the case at bar, the office held by the respondent was not of a pure master and servant type since it encompassed some elements of a public nature....

. . . .

Being an office, the respondent's situation would fall into one of the last two of Lord Reid's categories. As I have already analyzed the employment contract and *The Education Act* with regard to the question of whether the respondent could be dismissed only for cause, and concluded in the negative, the employment relation existing between the respondent and the appellant Board would fall into the second of Lord Reid's category, i.e., an office held at pleasure. I find, however, that this conclusion does not ineluctably lead to the conclusion that the appellant Board was not under a duty to act fairly, as may seem to flow from the judgment of the House of Lords in *Ridge* v. *Baldwin, supra.* Administrative law has evolved in recent years, particularly in the Canadian context, so as to make procedural fairness an essential requirement of an administrative decision to terminate either of the last two classes of employment described by Lord Reid. In *Nicholson,* supra, although the employee was found to be [dismissible] for cause, Laskin C.J., after referring to the three-class system developed by Lord Reid in *Ridge* v. *Baldwin,* expressed some doubts about limiting the duty to act fairly to cases of dismissal for cause, to the exclusion of cases where offices are held at pleasure....

. . . .

... I would adopt Wade's reasoning when he writes about offices held at pleasure (*Administrative Law* (5th ed, 1982), at p. 500-1):

> If the officer is subject to some accusation, justice requires that he should be allowed a fair opportunity to defend himself, whatever the terms of his tenure....

. . . .

There is also a wider public policy argument militating in favour of the imposition of a duty to act fairly on administrative bodies making decisions similar to the one impugned in the case at bar. The powers exercised by the appellant Board are delegated statutory powers which, as much as the statutory powers exercised directly by the government, should be put only to legitimate use. As opposed to the employment cases dealing with pure master and servant relationships, where no delegated statutory powers are involved, the public has an interest in the proper use of delegated power by administrative bodies....

. . . .

I conclude accordingly that the characterization of the respondent's employment as an office held at pleasure is not incompatible with the imposition of a duty to act fairly on the part of the appellant Board.

(iii) the impact of the decision on the employee

This point can be dealt with summarily. There is a right to procedural fairness only if the decision is a significant one and has an important impact on the individual. Various courts have recognized that the loss of employment against the office holder's will is a significant decision that could justify imposing a duty to act fairly on the administrative decision-making body....

On the whole, the nature of the decision, the relationship existing between the respondent and the appellant Board and the impact on the respondent of the impugned decision lead to the conclusion that there was a general duty to act fairly on the part of the appellant Board in the circumstances of this case.

. . . .

[L'Heureux-Dubé J. found that the right to procedural fairness had not been modified or excluded by statute or contract].

Like the principles of natural justice, the concept of procedural fairness is eminently variable and its content is to be decided in the specific context of each case. In *Nicholson,* supra, at p. 326–27, Laskin C.J. adopts the following passage from the decision of the Privy Council in *Furnell* v. *Whangarei High School Board*, [1973] A.C. 660, a New Zealand appeal where Lord Morris of Borth-y-Gest, writing for the majority, held (at p. 679):

> *Natural justice is but fairness writ large and juridically. It has been described as 'fair play in action'.* Nor is it a leaven to be associated only with judicial or quasi-judicial occasions. But as was pointed out by Tucker L.J. in *Russell* v. *Duke of Norfolk*, [1949] 1 All. E.R. 109, at p. 118, the requirements of natural justice must depend on the circumstances of each particular case and the subject matter under consideration. [Emphasis added.]

This was underlined again very recently by this Court in *Syndicat des employés de production du Québec et de l'Acadie* v. *Canada (Canadian Human Rights Commission), supra,* where Sopinka J. was writing for the majority at pp. 895–96:

Both the rules of natural justice and the duty of fairness are variable standards. Their content will depend on the circumstances of the case, the statutory provision and the nature of the matter to be decided. The distinction between them therefore becomes blurred as one approaches the lower end of the scale of judicial or quasi-judicial tribunals and the high end of the scale with respect to administrative or executive tribunals. Accordingly, the content of the rules to be followed by a tribunal is now not determined by attempting to classify them as judicial, quasi-judicial, administrative or executive. Instead, the court decides the content of these rules by reference to all the circumstances under which the tribunal operates. [Emphasis added.]

. . . .

In the case at bar the Saskatchewan Court of Appeal found that the basic requirements of the duty to act fairly are the giving of reasons for the dismissal and a hearing, adding that the content will vary according to the circumstances of each case. Since the respondent could be dismissed at pleasure, the content of the duty of fairness would be minimal and I would tend to agree that notice of the reasons for the appellant Board's dissatisfaction with the respondent's employment and affording him an opportunity to be heard would be sufficient to meet the requirement of fairness. This Court in *Nicholson, supra*, at p. 328, per Laskin C.J. for the majority, found similar requirements to be sufficient in a case where the employee was [dismissible] from office only for cause.

. . . .

In the present case, the trial judge found as a fact that the respondent knew or should have known why the appellant Board was unhappy with his employment contract and that if he did not accept a one year contract he would be dismissed. In my view, the record amply supports this finding, which was not disputed by the Court of Appeal. I recognize the Court of Appeal's concern that the respondent was never officially notified of the reasons for his dismissal, but it is clear that he was informed of those reasons through his meetings with the appellant Board, sometimes personally, sometimes through his solicitor. In conformity with s. 2 of the contract of employment, the respondent was present at the appellant Board's meeting on May 30, 1983, where his contract was not renewed, and had the opportunity to make representations if he so wished. Further, during the summer, the respondent's

attorney met twice with the appellant Board to negotiate a new contract, and all issues appeared to have been settled except as to the duration of the contract, the respondent pressing for a minimum two year term while the Board insisted on a one year contract. Both parties appear to have been adamant on this point and it can be presumed that it caused the negotiations to fall through. Since I accept the trial judge's finding of facts that "everything that had to be said had been said" (at p. 283), the requirement of the formal giving of reasons and the holding of a hearing would achieve no more, in my respectful view, than to impose upon the appellant Board a purely procedural requirement, against the above stated principles of flexibility of administrative procedure.

In my view, the appellant Board has made itself sufficiently available for discussion through meetings with the respondent and his lawyer so that each party's concerns were made fully known to the other. This can only lead to the conclusion that the respondent knew the reasons for his dismissal and was provided with every opportunity to be heard. The requirements of the duty to act fairly in the scope of the employer-employee relationship in the case at bar have been met. I therefore conclude that the respondent was properly dismissed and that his action must fail.

Disposition

Accordingly I would allow the appeal, set aside the judgment of the Court of Appeal and restore the judgment of Lawton J. in the Court of Queen's Bench, the whole with costs throughout.

. . . .

[SOPINKA J., for himself, WILSON, and McLACHLIN JJ., delivered a separate concurring judgment. Sopinka J. disagreed that the board owed a duty of fairness to the official.]

In her reasons, my colleague concludes that a common law duty of fairness arises from "the nature of the decision, the relationship existing between the respondent and the appellant Board and impact on the respondent of the impugned decision". This precedes her detailed examination of the statute, the regulations and the contract with a view to identifying therein the indicia of a duty of fairness. An examination in detail of the statute, regulations and contract is made after a common law duty is "presumed to exist" and then only to determine whether such a duty has been ruled out.

In my respectful opinion, that approach converts the exception into the rule. The correct approach requires an examination of the statute, regulations and contract to determine whether the respondent has brought himself within the exception to the general rule that an office terminable at pleasure does not attract the duty of fairness....

. . . .

I conclude that where the statute intended to create a right to be heard or to make representations, it was careful to say so. This is apparent in s. 113 and the provisions dealing with teachers' con-tracts. If the legislature intended to provide both a teacher and a director of education with a hearing before a Board of Reference or Review and a right to be heard by the Board, it is peculiar that it specified both these rights in the case of a teacher but only one, a more limited right of review, in the case of the director of education.

I further conclude that in the case of a director of education, the legislature left to agreement between the parties the matter of how the contract was to be terminated....

[R]eading in a duty of procedural fairness would be to rewrite the contract for the parties. This is something that the legislature left to them.

I would therefore dispose of the appeal as proposed by L'Heureux-Dubé J.

(f) Oral Hearings and Reasons: *Baker*†

NOTE

Ms. Baker applied for a humanitarian and compassionate considerations exemption that would have stopped her deportation from Canada and would have increased her chances of permanent residence here. Through her lawyer, she claimed that if she were deported she would be separated from her Canadian-born children, and her medical condition would deteriorate because of the inadequate medical facilities in her native country. She made these claims in writing, as no oral hearing was provided.

The Immigration Department rejected the application in a letter, without reasons. When Ms. Baker asked for reasons, the Department provided her with the notes made by the investigating officer, Officer Lorenz. These had been supplied to the senior officer, Officer Caden. He had made the decision to reject the application.

Ms. Baker challenged the decision on several grounds, some of which are of special interest here. She argued that (i) she was entitled to an oral hearing; (ii) she was entitled to full reasons from the senior officer who actually made the decision; and (iii) the investigating officer's notes gave rise to a reasonable apprehension of bias.

In making its decision, the Supreme Court commented on the general scope and content of procedural fairness. Some of these comments, and the Court's comments on the oral hearing and reasons issues, are reproduced here.

EXTRACTS

[L'HEUREUX-DUBÉ for herself, GONTHIER, McLACHLIN, BASTARACHE and BINNIE JJ.]

[para5] Upon request of the appellant's counsel, [Mrs. Baker] was provided with the notes made by Immigration Officer G. Lorenz, which were used by Officer Caden when making his decision. After a summary of the history of the case, Lorenz's notes read as follows:

> PC is unemployed — on Welfare. No income shown — no assets. Has four Cdn.-born children — four other children in Jamaica — HAS A TOTAL OF EIGHT CHILDREN
>
> Says only two children are in her "direct custody". (No info on who has ghe [sic] other two). There is nothing for her in Jamaica — hasn't been there in a long time — no longer close to her children there — no jobs there — she has no skills other than as a domestic — children would

---

† *Baker v. Canada (Minister of Citizenship and Immigration)*, [1999] 2 S.C.R. 817, rev'g, [1997] 2 F.C. 127 (F.C.A.), answering a question certified by Simpson J. in [1995] F.C.J. No. 1441 (F.C.T.D.).

suffer — can't take them with her and can't leave them with anyone here. Says has suffered from a mental disorder since '81 — is now an outpatient and is improving. If sent back will have a relapse. Letter from Children's Aid — they say PC has been diagnosed as a paranoid schizophrenic. — children would suffer if returned —

Letter of Aug. '93 from psychiatrist from Ont. Govm't. Says PC had post-partum psychosis and had a brief episode of psychosis in Jam. when was 25 yrs. old. Is now an out-patient and is doing relatively well — deportation would be an extremely stressful experience.

Lawyer says PS [sic] is sole caregiver and single parent of two Cdn born children. Pc's mental condition would suffer a setback if she is deported etc.

This case is a catastrophy [sic]. It is also an indictment of our "system" that the client came as a visitor in Aug. '81, was not ordered deported until Dec. '92 and in APRIL '94 IS STILL HERE!

The PC is a paranoid schizophrenic and on welfare. She has no qualifications other than as a domestic. She has FOUR CHILDREN IN JAMAICA AND ANOTHER FOUR BORN HERE. She will, of course, be a tremendous strain on our social welfare systems for (probably) the rest of her life. There are no H&C factors other than her FOUR CANADIAN-BORN CHILDREN. Do we let her stay because of that? I am of the opinion that Canada can no longer afford this kind of generosity. However, because of the circumstances involved, there is a potential for adverse publicity. I recommend refusal but you may wish to clear this with someone at Region.

There is also a potential for violence — see charge of "assault with a weapon" [Capitalization in original.]

. . . .

[para20] Both parties agree that a duty of procedural fairness applies to H & C decisions. The fact that a decision is administrative and affects "the rights, privileges or interests of an individual" is sufficient to trigger the application of the duty of fairness....

. . . .

[para22] ... [T]he purpose of the participatory rights contained within the duty of procedural fairness is to ensure that administrative decisions are made using a fair and open procedure, appropriate to the decision being made and its statutory, institutional, and social context, with an opportunity for those affected by the decision to put forward their views and evidence fully and have them considered by the decision-maker.

[para23] Several factors have been recognized in the jurisprudence as relevant to determining what is required by the common law duty of procedural fairness in a given set of circumstances. One important consideration is the nature of the decision being made and the process followed in making it. In *Knight...*, at p. 683, it was held that "the closeness of the administrative process to the judicial process should indicate how much of those governing principles should be imported into the realm of administrative decision making"....

[para24] A second factor is the nature of the statutory scheme and the "terms of the statute pursuant to which the body operates". ... Greater procedural protections, for example, will be required when no appeal procedure is provided within the statute, or when the decision is determinative of the issue and further requests cannot be submitted....

[para25] A third factor in determining the nature and extent of the duty of fairness owed is the importance of the decision to the individual or individuals affected....

[para26] Fourth, the legitimate expectations of the person challenging the decision may also determine what procedures the duty of fairness requires in given circumstances....

[para27] Fifth, the analysis of what procedures the duty of fairness requires should also take into account and respect the choices of procedure made by the agency itself, particularly when the statute leaves to the decision-maker the ability to choose its own procedures, or when the agency has an expertise in determining what procedures are appropriate in the circumstances....

[para28] I should note that this list of factors is not exhaustive....

[para29] ... In my view, however, the articles of the *Convention* and their wording did not give rise to a legitimate expectation on the part of Ms. Baker that when the decision on her H & C application was made, specific procedural rights above what would normally be required under the duty of fairness would be accorded, a positive finding would be made, or particular criteria would be applied. This *Convention* is not, in my view, the equivalent of a government representation about how H & C applications will be decided, nor does it suggest that any

rights beyond the participatory rights discussed below will be accorded....

[para30] The next issue is whether, taking into account the other factors related to the determination of the content of the duty of fairness, the failure to accord an oral hearing and give notice to Ms. Baker or her children was inconsistent with the participatory rights required by the duty of fairness in these circumstances....

[para31] ... First, an H & C decision is very different from a judicial decision, since it involves the exercise of considerable discretion and requires the consideration of multiple factors. Second, its role is also, within the statutory scheme, as an exception to the general principles of Canadian immigration law. These factors militate in favour of more relaxed requirements under the duty of fairness. On the other hand, there is no appeal procedure, although judicial review may be applied for with leave of the Federal Court — Trial Division. In addition, considering the third factor, this is a decision that in practice has exceptional importance to the lives of those with an interest in its result — the claimant and his or her close family members — and this leads to the content of the duty of fairness being more extensive. Finally, applying the fifth factor described above, the statute accords considerable flexibility to the Minister to decide on the proper procedure, and immigration officers, as a matter of practice, do not conduct interviews in all cases. The institutional practices and choices made by the Minister are significant, though of course not determinative factors to be considered in the analysis. Thus, it can be seen that although some of the factors suggest stricter requirements under the duty of fairness, others suggest more relaxed requirements further from the judicial model.

[para32] Balancing these factors, I ... [feel that] the circumstances require a full and fair consideration of the issues....

[para33] However, it also cannot be said that an oral hearing is always necessary to ensure a fair hearing and consideration of the issues involved....

[para34] I agree that an oral hearing is not a general requirement for H & C decisions.... In this case, the appellant had the opportunity to put forward, in written form through her lawyer, information about her situation, her children and their emotional dependence on her, and documentation in support of her application from a social worker at the Children's Aid Society and from her psychiatrist.

These documents were before the decision-makers, and they contained the information relevant to making this decision. Taking all the factors relevant to determining the content of the duty of fairness into account, the lack of an oral hearing or notice of such a hearing did not, in my opinion, constitute a violation of the requirements of procedural fairness to which Ms. Baker was entitled in the circumstances, particularly given the fact that several of the factors point toward a more relaxed standard....

．　．　．　．

[para37] More generally, the traditional position at common law has been that the duty of fairness does not require, as a general rule, that reasons be provided for administrative decisions....

．　．　．　．

[para43] In my opinion, it is now appropriate to recognize that, in certain circumstances, the duty of procedural fairness will require the provision of a written explanation for a decision. The strong arguments demonstrating the advantages of written reasons suggest that, in cases such as this where the decision has important significance for the individual, when there is a statutory right of appeal, or in other circumstances, some form of reasons should be required. This requirement has been developing in the common law elsewhere. The circumstances of the case at bar, in my opinion, constitute one of the situations where reasons are necessary....

[para44] In my view, however, the reasons requirement was fulfilled in this case, since the appellant was provided with the notes of Officer Lorenz. The notes were given to Ms. Baker when her counsel asked for reasons....

．　．　．　．

[para77] ... I would allow the appeal, and set aside the decision of Officer Caden of April 18, 1994, with party-and-party costs throughout. The matter will be returned to the Minister for redetermination by a different immigration officer.

[Two judges gave a separate majority opinion. Although they felt that the main majority gave too much effect to a signed but unratified international convention, they agreed with the main majority on the procedural issues above.]

5   Administrative Procedure: Basic Aspects

(a)   Scope, Procedure, Statutes, and *Charter*

We have seen that the common law norms of fair procedure — the rules of natural justice — have two main aspects. The question of scope asks where these rules apply, and the question of content asks what is required where they do apply. One limit to the scope of the rules of natural justice has been their general inapplicability to legislative functions. Law-making normally affects large sectors of the public, and it usually bears little resemblance to the adjudicatory context in which the rules of natural justice normally apply. Moreover, legislators are elected officials, accountable to the public through the ballot. However, as the *Wiswell* case demonstrates with regard to legislative functions, the outer boundaries of the rules of natural justice are capable of moving.

Another question of scope, not addressed in this chapter, is how far the rules of natural justice extend — and should extend — beyond the institutions that are normally regarded as part of government. Although the rules of natural justice are generally limited to "public, statutory" bodies, they have been applied outside the traditional sphere of government in a number of areas. For example, the rules may apply to membership or disciplinary decisions of self-governing bodies such as churches, private clubs, trade unions, professional self-regulating organizations, hospitals and universities ... to the extent they are not excluded by contract.

As for the content of the common law rules of natural justice, the key point is that it is not fixed, but varies with the circumstances of the individual case. There is a spectrum of possible procedural safeguards, ranging from the requirement of notice to more rigorous protections like cross-examination. Even notice can be more demanding in special situations, as seen in *Morrissey*. The challenge is to isolate the factors that tend to suggest higher or lower level safeguards in a given situation.

As noted earlier, the common law rules of natural justice are only a part of the procedural framework within which administrative bodies must operate. The terms of the individual enabling act can be crucial here, and other key procedural safeguards can be found in statutory procedural codes, such as the Ontario *Statutory Powers Procedure Act*; in quasi-constitutional enactments, such as the *Canadian Bill of Rights*; and in the constitutional *Canadian Charter of Rights and Freedoms*. Extracts from these important general enactments are included in this chapter.

(b) Wiswell†

NOTE

A municipal council was not required by its enabling statute to post notice of a hearing before amending a zoning law. However, its own internal rules did require notice, both by way of advertisements in at least two local papers and signs on the property affected. The council passed a by-law rezoning land from single to multiple family status. They gave notice of the by-law hearing in two newspapers, but failed to put the signs on the property. As a result, a homeowners association that had been strongly and publicly opposed to the rezoning of the property failed to see the notice of the hearing, and no one appeared to speak against it. When the association challenged the by-law in court, the municipality argued that the enactment of a by-law is a legislative process, immune from natural justice requirements.

EXTRACTS

[HALL, J.]

This is an appeal from the judgment of the Court of Appeal for Manitoba [45 D.L.R. (2d) 348, 48 W.W.R. 193] allowing the appeal of the respondent from the judgment of Smith, J., of the Court of Queen's Bench in which he held that By-law 177 of the Metropolitan Corporation of Greater Winnipeg was invalid.

On April 13, 1962, the Council of the Metropolitan Corporation of Greater Winnipeg passed By-law 177 rezoning from "R1" Single-Family District to "R4A" Multiple-Family District the following land:

> In the City of Winnipeg, in the Province of Manitoba, being in accordance with the Special Survey of the said City and being Lots Forty to Forty-Five, both inclusive, which lots are shown on a plan of survey of part of Lot Forty-Five of the Parish of Saint Boniface registered in the Winnipeg Land Titles Office as No. 308, excepting out of said Lots Forty-four and Forty-five all that portion coloured pink on Plan 5262 taken for a road diversion by the City of Winnipeg.

This land is situated at the north-west corner of the intersection of Academy Road and Wellington Crescent and comprises approximately 3.4 acres.

. . . .

The appellants who are members of an unincorporated association known as the Crescentwood Home Owners Association brought action on their own behalf and on behalf of all other members of the association to have said By-law 177 of the respondent declared invalid. The Crescentwood Home Owners Association is comprised of residents of the Crescentwood area in the City of Winnipeg which includes the tract covered by By-law 177. The over-all objective of the association has been to maintain the area in question as a single-family dwelling area. The association had consistently opposed any attempts to have the area or any part of it rezoned or used for any purpose other than for single-family units.

In 1956 Dr. Ginsburg obtained two orders from the Zoning Board of the City of Winnipeg permitting him to erect on his property an 8-storey 64-suite apartment block. The granting of these orders was opposed by the association which also unsuccessfully appealed both orders to the Municipal and Public Utility Board. The orders were for one year and were renewed from year to year *ex parte* and without notice to the association and were in force and effect on April 1, 1961, when the Metropolitan Corporation of Greater Winnipeg succeeded the City of Winnipeg in jurisdiction over zoning matters.

On November 22, 1961, Messrs. Johnston, Jessiman, Gardner & Johnston, as solicitors for the appellants, wrote the respondent as follows:

> The Metropolitan Corporation of
>   Greater Winnipeg,
>
> 100 Main Street,
> Winnipeg, Manitoba
> *Attention: Mr. John Pelletier*
>
> Dear Sirs:
> *Re: City of Winnipeg Zoning Board Orders*
> We act on behalf of the Crescentwood Home Owners Association.

---

† *Wiswell et al. v. Metropolitan Corporation of Greater Winnipeg* (1965), 51 D.L.R. (2d) 754 (S.C.C.). (Cartwright, Martland, Judson, Hall and Spence JJ.).

As you know, the City of Winnipeg Zoning Board granted one year extensions to many of the orders made by it just prior to all zoning functions being taken over by Metro in April, 1961. We are interested in what our client's position is in respect to two such orders....

. . . .

[The solicitors for the homeowners association then asked to be advised of the municipality's policy in regard to applications to renew zoning orders such as those affecting the Ginsberg property, and to be given notice of any new applications for renewal. Shortly after this, after a hearing at which the homeowners association's solicitor was present, the municipal council extended the zoning order again for Dr. Ginsberg. Meanwhile Dr. Ginsberg applied to the municipal council to have the property rezoned to permit the building of the apartment. The municipality posted advertisements of the rezoning hearing in the Winnipeg Free Press and the Winnipeg Tribune, but put no notice of the hearing on the property itself. The homeowners and their representatives failed to see the newspaper notices, so they did not appear at the hearing to oppose the proposed rezoning by-law. The by-law was passed on 13 April 1962. In the meantime, Dr. Ginsberg had died.]

The appellants rely on paragraph 10 of the Metropolitan Council's resolution which it adopted as the procedure to be followed in connection with applications to amend zoning by-laws and town planning schemes. Para. 10 of that resolution reads:

10. Public notice shall be given by advertising in at least two newspapers having a general circulation in the Metropolitan Area each week for at least two weeks before the hearing.... The Director of planning shall give to the applicant notices to be posted by the applicant on the premises which are the subject of the proposed amendment. Such notices must be erected by the applicant not less than 14 days before the date set for the hearing and shall be in such form as the Director of Planning may from time to time prescribe....

Notice of Dr. Ginsburg's application to re-zone was published in two newspapers having a general circulation in the metropolitan area, the Winnipeg Tribune and the Winnipeg Free Press in the issues of March 1st and March 8, 1962. The size of the advertisements was criticized, but it must be accepted that the advertisements were in the type and format usually used for legal notices of various kinds. The

notice in question dealt with four applications, two in the City of Winnipeg, one in the Rural Municipality of Assiniboia and one in the Rural Municipality of St. Vital. In so far as it dealt with the area in question in this appeal, the notice read:

THE METROPOLITAN
CORPORATION OF
GREATER WINNIPEG
ZONING NOTICE

Take notice that the Planning Committee of the Metropolitan Corporation of Greater Winnipeg will hold a public hearing at 2:00 p.m., Monday, March 12, 1962, in the Council Chambers, 100 Main Street, for the purpose of considering a re-zoning of the following areas and permitting certain specific uses on particular properties:

1. City of Winnipeg

. . . .

(b) Northwest corner Wellington Crescent and Academy Road. From "R1" (One-family) District to "R4A" (Multiple-family) District property situated on the Northwest corner of Wellington Crescent and Academy Road more particularly described as Lots 40 to 45 inclusive, Plan 308, D.G.S. 45 Parish of St. Boniface except that portion of Lot 45 shown on Plan 5262 reserved for a road diversion by the City of Winnipeg. It is proposed to erect a multi-storey luxury apartment block on this property.

However, the second requirement of para. 10 above as to notices to be posted by the applicant on the premises was not complied with. No notices were posted on the premises. No reason for this omission or explanation therefor was given and it appears that the Metropolitan Council proceeded to deal with the application on the basis that the requirements of said para. 10 had been complied with.

The respondent took the position that in enacting By-law 177 it was engaged in a legislative function and not in a *quasi*-judicial act and that it had the right to proceed without notice to interested parties despite its own procedure resolution before mentioned.

I agree with Freedman, J.A., when, on this aspect of the matter, he says [45 D.L.R. (2d) at pp. 350–1]:

But to say that the enactment by By-law 177 was simply a legislative act is to ignore the realities and the substance of the case. For this was not a by-law of wide or general application, passed by the Metropolitan Council because of a conviction that an entire area had undergone a change in character and hence was in need of reclassification for zoning purposes. Rather this was a specific decision made upon a specific application concerned with a specific parcel of land. Metro had before it the application of Dr. Ginsberg, since deceased, for permission to erect a high-rise apartment building on the site in question. Under then existing zoning regulations such a building would not be lawful. To grant the application would require a variation in the zoning restrictions. Many residents of the area, as Metro well knew, were opposed to such a variation, claiming that it would adversely affect their own rights as property holders in the district. In proceeding to enact By-law 177 Metro was essentially dealing with a dispute between Dr. Ginsberg, who wanted the zoning requirements to be altered for his benefit, and those other residents of the district who wanted the zoning restrictions to continue as they were. That Metro resolved the dispute by the device of an amending by-law did indeed give to its proceedings an appearance of a legislative character. But in truth the process in which it was engaged was *quasi*-judicial in nature; and I feel I must so treat it.

Then Counsel argues as well that the governing statute does not call for notice. Hence, he says, notice was not required. I am unable to accept this contention. A long line of authorities, both old and recent, establish that in judicial or *quasi*-judicial proceedings notice is required unless the statute expressly dispenses with it. The mere silence of the statute is not enough to do away with notice. In such cases, as has been said, the justice of the common law will supply the omission of the Legislature. Some of the authorities dealing with this subject are referred to by Kirby, J., in the recent case of *Re Camac Exploration Ltd. and Alberta Oil & Gas Conservation Bd.* (1964), 43 D.L.R. (2d) 755, 47 W.W.R. 81.

The fact is that the association did not see the notice which was published in the Winnipeg Tribune and the Winnipeg Free Press on March 1st and 8th, 1962. An explanation as to why the association did not see the advertisement published in the Winnipeg Tribune and the Winnipeg Free Press is that Mr. S. Greene who was secretary of the association at the relevant time and who died prior to the trial was out of Winnipeg on holidays at that period in March, 1962. Metro could not, of course, be expected to know this. However, it was stated in evidence by Mr. Johnston who was president of the association at the time in question that if the placards contemplated by para. 10 of the procedure resolution had been

erected on the premises for the 14-day period before the date set for the hearing he would certainly have seen them.

. . . .

The point to be decided is whether the failure to post the placards on the premises and proceeding to hold hearings on Dr. Ginsburg's application to re-zone in the absence of the association when Metro knew that the association would oppose any such application and was actually opposing the extension applications at that very time, vitiated By-law 177 and rendered it a nullity.

I am of opinion that the by-law was void in the particular circumstances of this case. It was not merely the failure to post the placards but the manifest ignoring of the fact known to it that the association would oppose the by-law and that the association had been advised by the letter of January 23, 1962, (ex.1) that the orders of 1956 had been extended to April 30, 1963, for the 8-storey 64-suite apartment block, leaving the association with no reason to believe or expect that the concurrent application to re-zone was at that very time being processed without its knowledge.

The obligation on a body with the power to decide not to act until it has afforded the other party affected a proper opportunity to be heard is aptly stated by Lord Reid in *Ridge v. Baldwin*, [1963] 2 All E.R. 66 at p. 81 as follows:

> Then there was considerable argument whether in the result the watch committee's decision is void or merely voidable. Time and again in the cases I have cited it has been stated that a decision given without regard to the principles of natural justice is void and that was expressly decided in *Wood v. Wood* (1874), L.R. 9 Exch. 190. I see no reason to doubt these authorities. The body with the power to decide cannot lawfully proceed to make a decision until it has afforded to the person affected a proper opportunity to state his case.

. . . .

In view of my finding that the by-law was void for lack of notice and for failure to give the appellants an opportunity to oppose the application to re-zone, I do not find it necessary to deal with the second ground that By-law 177 was not passed in good faith and in the public interest.

I would accordingly allow the appeal and restore the judgment of Smith, J., with costs throughout.

[Martland J. concurred with Hall J. Cartwright and Spence JJ. concurred with Hall J. in separate reasons. Judson J. dissented. He agreed that the municipality was obliged to give notice to those affected, but he felt the newspaper advertisements met this requirement, and that the municipality's failure to comply with its own internal requirement did not affect its jurisdiction.]

(c)   Notice: *Morrissey*†

NOTE

The Ontario Racing Commission suspended Orwell Morrissey from racing horses for 60 days. The suspension followed a Commission hearing. Morrissey had attended the hearing with his counsel after being advised of it by a telephone call two days before. In the circumstances of this case, was this adequate notice? Cf. s. 6 of the *Statutory Powers Procedure Act*.

EXTRACTS

Application for an order in lieu of *certiorari* to quash a ruling of the Ontario Racing Commission.

.   .   .   .

[HAINES, J.:]

This is an application for an order in lieu of *Certiorari*, to quash a ruling of the Ontario Racing Commission, dated September 5, 1968, whereby the Ontario Racing Commission suspended Orwell W. Morrissey from racing for a period of 60 days.

At the opening of this application, it was conceded by both the counsel for the applicant and counsel for the respondent, that the Ontario Racing Commission acted or purported to act on the occasion in question in a judicial capacity and that therefore this Court has jurisdiction in the matter. It was admitted by both counsel that there were no allegations of wilful wrongdoing by either the applicant or the respondent in the circumstances. The facts, briefly, are as follows:

Orwell W. Morrissey is the owner, trainer and driver of standard bred horses licensed by the Ontario Racing Commission. Some time in November, 1967, after consultation with three duly qualified veterinarians whose practices included the caring and feeding of race horses, and who gave their approval to the practice, Morrissey began to add a common food supplement to the feed administered to his horses. Morrissey contends that he had been advised by the veterinarian that it was permitted to use such food supplement known as "Ferogen" for horses in racing and he had no reason to doubt the veterinarian's advice. This practice continued from November, 1967, until August 19, 1968. During this period, Morrissey acknowledges that he had between 15 and 20 horses in training at any given date and all were fed with the food supplement in question. During this period, he estimates that his horses won approximately 60 races and since the Commission requires each winning horse be tested, Morrissey estimates that about 60 urine tests were conducted on his horses during the period, and none of these yielded a positive result. In addition thereto, several spot checks were made upon his other horses, again a common practice, and no positive tests were received. However, some time in May or June, 1968, one of his horses showed a "cloudy test" which was attributed at the time to some medicinal solution, but no mention was made at this time of the potential danger of the "Ferogen" food supplement.

On May 29, 1968, the Ontario Racing Commission issued and circulated the following notice:

NOTICE TO HORSEMEN

In recent weeks the Commission has been obliged to consider three cases involving horses which had positive tests in urine samples following races. It was discovered that the source of the drugs came from a common food supplement fed to the horses. The trainers had no knowl-

---

† *R. v. Ontario Racing Commission Ex parte Morrissey* (1969), 8 D.L.R. (3d) 624 (O.H.C.).

edge of any drug in such food nor were they aware that over-feeding of such supplement and failure to follow prescribed directions accompanying the packaged food could result in such positive drug tests.

The Commission has dealt leniently with these cases owing to the above facts. However, in the future, positive tests indicating drugs in any urine, saliva or other sample, even though originating from feeding practices as above, will not be dealt with leniently.

It is clear from reading this notice that as late as May 29, 1968, the Ontario Racing Commission itself was uncertain as to the nature of the supplement itself, in fact, the name of the product in question was not given. Morrissey does not deny reading the circular, but claims that it misled him in that none of his horses at that date showed a positive result, and therefore he assumed he was not overfeeding the supplement and could safely continue to use it, which he did, carefully complying with the instructions of the veterinarian and the manufacturer of the product.

On August 19, 1968, Morrissey raced a horse named "Favronian Major" at Mohawk Raceway. After the said race a spot check conducted on "Favronian Major" yielded a positive test, which was immediately forwarded to the judges of the race, as was the required procedure. Morrissey attended before the racing judges to discuss the positive tests, and provided the judges with some of the food supplement in question. The ensuing discussion was transcribed on a tape recorder. Morrissey was informed by the judges that the matter would automatically be referred to the Racing Commission as is the required procedure with all positive tests. He was instructed that until the Commission dealt with the matter, he was able to continue racing but that the horse in question was under suspension until a final disposition of the case.

On September 3, 1968, Mr. Morrissey was informed by telephone that the Commission would hear the matter on September 5, 1968. He attended before the Ontario Racing Commission on September 5th with his counsel. Some oral evidence was given at the hearing, but no transcript was made and no records of the proceedings were kept; therefore, it is difficult to ascertain just what did occur. There was no dispute that Morrissey was not fully co-operative with the judges and racing staff. Furthermore, there was no suggestion as to any wilful misconduct on his part. It was not argued or suggested that he administered the food supplement to affect the results of the races. During the hearing,

Dr. Sherman, a veterinarian called by counsel on behalf of the Commission, stated that strychnine, which is an ingredient of "Ferogen", can build up in the kidney of a horse over a period of time even though the horse is not overfed the food supplement and the manufacturer's directions are followed. He acknowledged that most veterinarians do not and would not possess this knowledge and that he was more familiar with the problem because of his recent practical work in this field for the Commission.

There is rule 21 of the Rules and Regulations of the Canadian Trotting Association which deals with "drugs". There are several offences under rule 21, including those set out in ss. 3, 4, 5, 6 and 7 thereof. At no time during the hearing did the Racing Commission indicate to Morrissey that he was alleged to have broken any rule or regulation of the Commission, and there was no suggestion that his conduct was contrary to the public interest. However, on cross-examination of Morrissey by counsel for the Commission, near the end of the hearing, Morrissey states he was asked if he was aware of s. 7 of the said Rule 21, which section is known as the "Trainer Responsibility Rule".

At the end of the hearing, the following ruling was given:

> Trainer-Driver Orwell W. Morrissey of Ayr, Ontario, License 961/68 dob 6 May 26, who on August 27, 1968 was referred to the Commission and whose horse Favronian Major was suspended from racing by the judges at Mohawk Raceway for a positive test of a urine sample from the said horse which raced at Mohawk Raceway on August 19, 1968 is suspended by the Commission for 60 days effective this date.

> By ORDER of the Commission. The Horse Favronian Major is now eligible to race.

The main grounds upon which this application is brought are:

1. That the hearing as conducted by the Ontario Racing Commission was a denial of natural justice; and
2. That the Commission acted in want of jurisdiction.

First, I would like to deal with the issue of natural justice. Under s. 11 of the *Racing Commission Act*, R.S.O. 1960, c. 342, the Ontario Racing Commission is a statutory body empowered to govern, direct, control, and regulate horse racing in Ontario and to license owners, trainers, etc., as it deems expedient, and to revoke or suspend any licence for conduct that the Commission considers contrary to the public interest. The Commission is further empowered by s. 11 to hold hearings relating to the carrying out of its objectives and powers. It is contended by the applicant that the Commission failed to observe the rules of natural justice in that, if the Ontario Racing Commission intended to place the applicant in jeopardy by suspension by reason of his conduct, the Commission was obliged to do two things in order to satisfy the requirements of natural justice, namely:

1. It should have given notice of the hearing in writing wherein it set out the conduct which was the subject matter of the complaint to which it was going to set its mind, so that the applicant would clearly know it was not merely an investigatory type of hearing but rather an accusatory type and that it should further have set out sufficient facts so that it would be obvious to a reasonable man that his conduct was in jeopardy;
2. It should have given clear and unequivocal notice in writing to the applicant that the conduct of which he was being accused may warrant suspension by the Commission if the complaints were substantiated.

I agree with this submission; the Commission was acting in a judicial or *quasi*-judicial capacity; it is required therefore to observe the rules of natural justice, those basic principles of fair procedure which are an indispensable concept and the basis of the safeguards of individual rights in our judicial system. There can be no doubt that the Commission is obliged to conduct the hearing in accordance with the rules of natural justice and that it failed in this respect having regard to the notice of the hearing. There was nothing in the telephone call which might have led Morrissey to believe that his occupation and means of livelihood would be placed in jeopardy by a suspension handed down at this hearing; there was no indication that this hearing was anything more than a continuation of the investigation into the probable cause of the positive urine sample; and investigatory hearing that is automatically held every time there is a positive testing. Morrissey had no forewarning that he was being accused of a breach of the Rules and Regulations of the Canadian Trotting Association. He arrived at the hearing having received only oral communication of the hearing and with no reason to believe it would be anything other than investigatory in nature. There was no notice to give him an indication of the extent of his jeopardy or of the nature of the complaints to which the Commission was to address itself. Indeed, there was nothing to forewarn Morrissey that the hearing concerned him in particular, because it was a routine investigation to complete the earlier investigation begun by the racing officials at the track. Furthermore, he had no advance knowledge of the accusations to be dealt with, therefore, he had no way of knowing that he could suffer a suspension as a result of the hearing. I find that the Commission if it were acting in accordance with the principles of natural justice should have sent out a written notice, setting out the date and subject matter of the hearing, the grounds of the complaint against Morrissey, the basic facts in issue and the potential seriousness of the possible result of such hearing. I find that this type of notice is the minimum which would satisfy the requirements of natural justice, especially in the case where a man's occupation and livelihood is placed in jeopardy and he has no forewarning of the case he must prepare to meet the accusations against him.

. . . .

For these reasons I allow the application and quash the suspension.

There is one final point I would like to set out. In my opinion, this case illustrates the power of the Ontario Racing Commission having regard to its objects and powers under the statute. The Commission has a great obligation to use these powers to promote racing in the interests of the public in general; therefore, it seems to me to be a great misfortune that it has not seen fit to have recorded all proceedings of every hearing where a man's occupation and source of livelihood is placed in jeopardy, and while I do not attempt to advise the Commission, it is hoped that they will see fit in the future, not only to give adequate notice which sets out the charges a person must meet, but further that all proceedings of the Commission will be recorded for the benefit of the public, the assistance of this Court, and the protection of the Commission itself.

Order accordingly.

(d) Bill of Rights and *Charter*: *Singh*†

NOTE

Extracts from the reasons of Wilson J. are given here. Beetz J. for three other judges held that because the situation involved "rights" of Mr. Singh and six other refugee claimants, s. 2(e) of the *Canadian Bill of Rights* guaranteed them "the right to a fair hearing in accordance with the principles of fundamental justice for the determination of [their] rights and obligations." He held that for serious interests, where issues of personal credibility are involved, this requires the opportunity for an oral hearing. As the relevant provision of the *Immigration Act* denied Singh and the others an oral hearing, it should be declared inoperative in regard to them. Beetz J. did not consider directly whether common law natural justice would apply, and refrained from considering whether the *Charter* applied.

EXTRACTS

[The reasons of DICKSON C.J. and of LAMER and WILSON J. were delivered by WILSON J.:]

The issue raised by these appeals is whether the procedures set out in the *Immigration Act*, 1976, 1976–77 (Can.), c. 52 as amended, for the adjudication of the claims of persons claiming refugee status in Canada deny such claimants rights they are entitled to assert under s. 7 of the *Canadian Charter of Rights and Freedoms*.

On February 16, 1984 the Court granted leave to appeal in these seven cases and they were consolidated for hearing on April 30, 1984.

. . . .

... Each appellant, in accordance with the procedures set out in the *Immigration Act*, 1976 asserted a claim to Convention refugee status as defined in s. 2(1) of the Act. The Minister of *Employment and Immigration*, acting on the advice of the Refugee Status Advisory Committee, made determinations pursuant to s. 45 of the Act that none of the appellants were Convention refugees. Each of the appellants then made an application for redetermination of his or her refugee claim by the Immigration Appeal Board pursuant to s. 70 of the Act. In accordance with s. 71(1) of the Act the Immigration Appeal Board in each case refused to allow the application to proceed on the basis that it did not believe that there were "reasonable grounds to believe that a claim could, upon the hearing of the application, be established...." Each applicant then sought judicial review of the Board's decision pursuant to ... section 28 of the *Federal Court Act*. These applications were denied by the Federal Court of Appeal.

. . . .

The term "Convention refugee" is defined in s. 2(1) of the Act as follows:

"Convention refugee" means any person who, by reason of a well-founded fear of persecution for reasons of race, religion, nationality, membership in a particular social group or political opinion,
(a) is outside the country of his nationality and is unable or, by reason of such fear, is unwilling to avail himself of the protection of that country, or
(b) not having a country of nationality, is outside the country of his former habitual residence and is unable or, by reason of such fear, is unwilling to return to that country;

As noted above, the procedures for determination of whether an individual is a Convention refugee and for redetermination of claims by the Immigration Appeal Board are set out in ss. 45 to 48 and 70 to 71 respectively. Focussing first on the initial determination, s. 45 provides as follows:

45.(1) Where, at any time during an inquiry, the person who is the subject of the inquiry claims that he is a Convention refugee, the inquiry shall be continued and, if it is determined that, but for the person's claim that he is a Convention refugee, a removal order or a departure notice would be made or issued with respect to that person, the inquiry shall be adjourned and that person shall be examined under oath by a senior immigration officer respecting his claim.

(2) Where a person who claims that he is a Convention refugee is examined under oath pursuant to subsection (1), his claim, together with a transcript of the examination with respect thereto, shall be referred to the Minister for determination.

---

† *Singh et al. v. Minister of Employment and Immigration*, [1985] 1 S.C.R. 177.

(3) A copy of the transcript of an examination under oath referred to in subsection (1) shall be forwarded to the person who claims that he is a Convention refugee.

(4) Where a person's claim is referred to the Minister pursuant to subsection (2), the Minister shall refer the claim and the transcript of the examination under oath with respect thereto to the Refugee Status Advisory Committee established pursuant to section 48 for consideration and, after having obtained the advice of that committee, shall determine whether or not the person is a Convention refugee.

(5) When the Minister makes a determination with respect to a person's claim that he is a Convention refugee, the Minister shall thereupon in writing inform the senior immigration officer who conducted the examination under oath respecting the claim and the person who claimed to be a Convention refugee of his determination.

(6) Every person with respect to whom an examination is to be had pursuant to subsection (1) shall be informed that he has the right to obtain the services of a barrister or solicitor or other counsel and to be represented by any such counsel at his examination and shall be given a reasonable opportunity, if he so desires and at his own expense, to obtain such counsel.

. . . .

Under s. 70(1) of the Act a person whose refugee claim has been refused by the Minister may, within a period prescribed in Regulation 40(1) as fifteen days from the time he is so informed, apply for a redetermination of his claim by the Immigration Appeal Board. Section 70(2) requires the refugee claimant to submit with such an application a copy of the transcript of the examination under oath which was conducted pursuant to s. 45(1) and a declaration under oath setting out the basis of the application, the facts upon which the appellant relies and the information and evidence the applicant intends to offer at a redetermination hearing. The applicant is also permitted pursuant to s. 70(2)(d) to set out in his declaration such other representations as he deems relevant to his application.

The Immigration Appeal Board's duties in considering an application for redetermination of a refugee status claim are set out in s. 71 which reads as follows:

71.(1) Where the Board receives an application referred to in subsection 70(2), it shall forthwith consider the application and if, on the basis of such consideration, it is of the opinion that there are reasonable grounds to believe that a claim could, upon the hearing of the application, be established, it shall allow the application to pro-

ceed, and in any other case it shall refuse to allow the application to proceed and shall thereupon determine that the person is not a Convention refugee.

(2) Where pursuant to subsection (1) the Board allows an application to proceed, it shall notify the Minister of the time and place where the application is to be heard and afford the Minister a reasonable opportunity to be heard.

(3) Where the Board has made its determination as to whether or not a person is a Convention refugee, it shall, in writing, inform the Minister and the applicant of its decision.

(4) The Board may, and at the request of the applicant or the Minister shall, give reasons for its determination.

If the Board were to determine pursuant to s. 71(1) that the application should be allowed to proceed, the parties are all agreed that the hearing which would take place pursuant to s. 71(2) would be a *quasi*-judicial one to which full natural justice would apply. The Board is not, however, empowered by the terms of the statute to allow a redetermination hearing to proceed in every case. It may only do so if "it is of the opinion that there are reasonable grounds to believe that a claim could, upon the hearing of the application, be established ...". In *Kwiatkowsky* v. *Minister of Employment and Immigration*, [1982] 2 S.C.R. 856, this Court interpreted those words as requiring the Board to allow the claim to proceed only if it is of the view that "it is more likely than not" that the applicant will be able to establish his claim at the hearing....

. . . .

... [T]he Act imposes limitations on the scope of the hearing afforded to refugee claimants which it is difficult to reconcile with the principles of natural justice....

. . . .

... In the present instance ... it seems to me that s. 71(1) is precisely the type of express provision which prevents the courts from reading the principles of natural justice into a statutory scheme for the adjudication of the rights of individuals.

. . . .

We must ... ask ourselves whether the deprivation of these rights constitutes a deprivation of the right to life, liberty and security of the person within the meaning of s. 7 of the *Charter*. Even if we accept the "single right" theory advanced by counsel for the Minister in interpreting s. 7, I think we must recognize that the "right" which is articulated in s. 7 has three elements: life, liberty and security of the person. As I understand the "single right" theory, it is not suggested that there must be a deprivation of all three of these elements before an individual is deprived of his "right" under s. 7. In other words, I believe that it is consistent with the "single right" theory advanced by counsel to suggest that a deprivation of the appellants' "security of the person", for example, would constitute a deprivation of their "right" under s. 7, whether or not it can also be said that they have been deprived of their lives or liberty. Rather, as I understand it, the "single right" theory is advanced in support of a narrow construction of the words "life", "liberty" and "security of the person" as different aspects of a single concept rather than as separate concepts each of which must be construed independently.

Certainly, it is true that the concepts of the right to life, the right to liberty, and the right to security of the person are capable of a broad range of meaning.... [In the U.S. Supreme Court it has been said that a similar guarantee in the American constitution includes the right "to contract, to engage in any of the common occupations of life, to acquire useful knowledge, to marry, establish a home and bring up children, to worship God according to the dictates of his own conscience, and generally to enjoy those privileges long recognized ... as essential to the orderly pursuit of happiness by free men."]

The "single right" theory advanced by counsel for the Minister would suggest that this conception of "liberty" is too broad to be employed in our interpretation of s. 7 of the *Charter*. Even if this submission is sound, however, it seems to me that it is incumbent upon the Court to give meaning to each of the elements, life, liberty and security of the person, which make up the "right" contained in s. 7.

To return to the facts before the Court, it will be recalled that a Convention refugee is by definition a person who has a well-founded fear of persecution in the country from which he is fleeing. In my view, to deprive him of the avenues open to him under the Act to escape from that fear of persecution must, at the least, impair his right to life, liberty and security of the person in the narrow sense advanced by counsel for the Minister. The question, however, is whether such an impairment constitutes a "deprivation" under s. 7.

It must be acknowledged, for example, that even if a Convention refugee's fear of persecution is a well-founded one, it does not automatically follow that he will be deprived of his life or his liberty if he is returned to his homeland. Can it be said that Canadian officials have deprived a Convention refugee of his right to life, liberty and security of the person if he is wrongfully returned to a country where death, imprisonment or another form of persecution may await him? There may be some merit in counsel's submission that closing off the avenues of escape provided by the Act does not per se deprive a Convention refugee of the right to life or to liberty. It may result in his being deprived of life or liberty by others, but it is not certain that this will happen.

. . . .

It seems to me that even if one adopts the narrow approach advocated by counsel for the Minister, "security of the person" must encompass freedom from the threat of physical punishment or suffering as well as freedom from such punishment itself. I note particularly that a Convention refugee has the right under s. 55 of the Act not to "... be removed from Canada to a country where his life or freedom would be threatened...." In my view, the denial of such a right must amount to a deprivation of security of the person within the meaning of s. 7.

. . . .

I should note, however, that even if hearings based on written submissions are consistent with the principles of fundamental justice for some purposes, they will not be satisfactory for all purposes. In particular, I am of the view that where a serious issue of credibility is involved, fundamental justice requires that credibility be determined on the basis of an oral hearing. Appellate courts are well aware of the inherent weakness of written transcripts where questions of credibility are at stake and thus are extremely loath to review the findings of tribunals which have had the benefit of hearing the testimony of witnesses in person.... I find it difficult to conceive of a situation in which compliance with fundamental justice could be achieved by a tribunal making significant findings of credibility solely on the basis of written submissions.

. . . .

I should note, however, that even if hearings based on written submissions are consistent with the principles of fundamental justice for some purposes, they will not be satisfactory for all purposes. In particular, I am of the view that where a serious issue of credibility is involved, fundamental justice requires that credibility be determined on the basis of an oral hearing. Appellate courts are well aware of the inherent weakness of written transcripts where questions of credibility are at stake and thus are extremely loath to review the findings of tribunals which have had the benefit of hearing the testimony of witnesses in person.... I find it difficult to conceive of a situation in which compliance with fundamental justice could be achieved by a tribunal making significant findings of credibility solely on the basis of written submissions.

. . . .

It seems to me that the basic flaw in Mr. Bowie's characterization of the procedure under ss. 70 and 71 is his description of the procedure as non-adversarial. It is in fact highly adversarial but the adversary, the Minister, is waiting in the wings. What the Board has before it is a determination by the Minister based in part on information and policies to which the applicant has no means of access that the applicant for redetermination is not a Convention refugee. The applicant is entitled to submit whatever relevant material he wishes to the Board but he still faces the hurdle of having to establish to the Board that on the balance of probabilities the Minister was wrong. Moreover, he must do this without any knowledge of the Minister's case beyond the rudimentary reasons which the Minister has decided to give him in rejecting his claim. It is this aspect of the procedures set out in the Act which I find impossible to reconcile with the requirements of "fundamental justice" as set out in s. 7 of the Charter.

It is perhaps worth noting that if the Immigration Appeal Board allows a redetermination hearing to proceed pursuant to s. 71(1), the Minister is entitled pursuant to s. 71(2) to notice of the time and place of the hearing and a reasonable opportunity to be heard. It seems to me that, as a matter of fundamental justice, a refugee claimant would be entitled to discovery of the Minister's case prior to such a hearing. It must be acknowledged, of course, that some of the information upon which the Minister's case would be based might be subject to Crown privilege. But the courts are well able to give the applicant relief if the Minister attempts to make an overly broad assertion of privilege: see *Canada Evidence Act*, 1980-81-82-83 (Can), c. 111, Schedule III, s. 36.1.

Under the Act as it presently stands, however, a refugee claimant may never have the opportunity to make an effective challenge to the information or policies which underlie the Minister's decision to reject his claim.

Because s. 71(1) requires the Immigration Appeal Board to reject an application for redetermination unless it is of the view that it is more likely than not that the applicant will be able to succeed, it is apparent that an application will usually be rejected before the refugee claimant has had an opportunity to discover the Minister's case against him in the context of a hearing.... Indeed ... I find it difficult to see how a successful challenge to the accuracy of the undisclosed information upon which the Minister's decision is based could ever be launched.

I am accordingly of the view that the procedures for determination of refugee status as set out in the *Immigration Act*, 1976 do not accord refugee claimants fundamental justice in the adjudication of these claims and are thus incompatible with s. 7 of the Charter.

(e) Statutory Powers Procedure Act[†]

NOTE

The *Statutory Powers Procedure Act*, first enacted in 1971, provides a code of minimum rules of fair procedure for most Ontario tribunals. For these tribunals, procedural requirements may derive from (i) the *Charter*, (ii) the *S.P.P.A.*, (iii) the tribunal's specific enabling act, (iv) the common law rules of

---

[†] *Statutory Powers Procedure Act*, R.S.O. 1990, c. S. 22 (first enacted as S.O. 1971, c. 47, assented to July 23, 1971), as am. by S.O. 1993, c. 27, Sched.; S.O. 1994, c. 27, s. 56; S.O. 1997, c. 23. s. 13 (section hearings and citations omitted). See also *Judicial Review Procedure Act*, R.S.O. 1990, c. J.1 (first enacted as S.O. 1971, c. 48 (streamlining judicial review remedies); and *Courts of Justice Act*, R.S.O. 1990, c. C. 43, ss. 18–21 (first enacted as *Judicature Act Amendment*, S.O. 1971, c. 97) and *Judicature Amendment Act (No. 4)*, S.O. 1970, c. 97) (creating a separate division of the Ontario High Court (the General Division of the Ontario Court of Justice) called the Divisional Court).

natural justice and fairness, and (v) the tribunal's own procedural rules.

Since constitutional requirements prevail over those in statutes, and since legislative requirements prevail over those in the common law, constitutional and legislative requirements should be looked at first. The *S.P.P.A.* can apply except where it is expressly excluded by statute: s. 32. But before *S.P.P.A.* requirements apply in the first place, the tribunal in question must be required by statute "or otherwise by law to hold or to afford to the parties to the proceeding an opportunity for a hearing before making a decision" (s. 3(1)). "Or otherwise by law" refers to the rules of natural justice, so in the absence of a specific statutory direction, the application of the *S.P.P.A.* depends on the common law.

In 1995, the *S.P.P.A.* was amended

(i) to require separate procedures for oral, electronic, and written hearings;
(ii) to give tribunals special powers to:
 (a) address procedural or interlocutory matters by panels;
 (b) hold pre-hearing conferences in certain situations to expedite matters;
 (c) consolidate or simplify procedures where two or more proceedings involve the same issue;
 (d) make interim orders;
 (e) correct typographical or similar errors in their decisions or orders at any time;
 (f) review, confirm, vary, suspend or cancel all or part of their own decisions or orders; and
 (g) make rules governing their practice and procedure;
 and
(iii) to abolish the Statutory Powers Procedure Rules Committee, a rule-making supervisory body that had been created under the original act.

There were a number of further clarifications and changes in 1997, including a provision permitting tribunals to combine written, electronic and oral hearings, and a provision permitting public electronic hearings in some cases.

EXTRACTS

1.(1) In this Act,

"electronic hearing" means a hearing held by conference telephone or some other form of electronic technology allowing persons to hear one another;

"hearing" means a hearing in any proceeding;

"licence" includes any permit, certificate, approval, registration or similar form of permission required by law;

"oral hearing" means a hearing at which the parties or their counsel or agents attend before the tribunal in person;

"proceeding" means a proceeding to which this Act applies.

"statutory power of decision" means a power or right, conferred by or under a statute, to make a decision deciding or prescribing,

(a) the legal rights, powers, privileges, immunities, duties or liabilities of any person or party, or

(b) the eligibility of any person or party to receive, or to the continuation of, a benefit or licence, whether the person is legally entitled thereto or not;

"tribunal" means one or more persons, whether or not incorporated and however described, upon which a statutory power of decision is conferred by or under a statute.

"written hearing" means a hearing held by means of the exchange of documents, whether in written form or by electronic means.

. . . .

2. *Repealed.*

3.(1) Subject to subsection (2), this *Act* applies to a proceeding by a tribunal in the exercise of a statutory power of decision conferred by or under an Act of the Legislature, where the tribunal is required by or under such Act or otherwise by law to hold or to afford to the parties to the proceeding an opportunity for a hearing before making a decision.

(2) This *Act* does not apply to a proceeding,

(a) before the Assembly or any committee of the Assembly;

(b) in or before ... [ordinary courts of law] ...

(c) to which the Rules of Civil Procedure apply;

(d) before an arbitrator to which the *Arbitrations Act* or the *Labour Relations Act* applies;

(e) at a coroner's inquest;

(f) of a commission appointed under the *Public Inquiries Act*;

(g) of one or more persons required to make an investigation and to make a report, with or without recommendations, where the report is for the information or advice of the person to whom it is made and does not in any way legally bind or limit that person in any decision he or she may have power to make; or

(h) of a tribunal empowered to make regulations, rules or by-laws in so far as its power to make regulations, rules or by-laws is concerned.

. . . .

4.(1) Any procedural requirement of this Act, or of another Act or a regulation that applies to a proceeding may be waived with the consent of the parties and the tribunal.

(2) Any provision of a tribunal's rules made under section 25.1 may be waived in accordance with the rules.

4.1 If the parties consent, a proceeding may be disposed of by a decision of the tribunal given without a hearing, unless another Act or regulation that applies to the proceeding arises provides otherwise.

4.2 [tribunals empowered to decide interlocutory matters in panels]

. . . .

5.1(1) A tribunal whose rules made under section 25.1 deal with written hearings may hold a written hearing in a proceeding.

(2) The tribunal shall not hold a written hearing if a party objects.

(3) In a written hearing, all the parties are entitled to receive every document that the tribunal receives in the proceeding.

5.2(1) A tribunal whose rules made under section 25.1 deal with electronic hearings may hold an electronic hearing in a proceeding.

(2) The tribunal shall not hold an electronic hearing if a party satisfies the tribunal that holding an electronic rather than an oral hearing is likely to cause the party significant prejudice.

(3) Subsection (2) does not apply if the only purpose of the hearing is to deal with procedural matters.

(4) In an electronic hearing, all the parties and the members of the tribunal participating in the hearing must be able to hear one another and any witnesses throughout the hearing.

5.2.1 A tribunal may, in a proceeding, hold any combination of written, electronic and oral hearings.

5.3(1) [prehearing conferences]

5.4(1) [tribunals empowered to make interim orders]

6.(1) The parties to a proceeding shall be given reasonable notice of the hearing by the tribunal.

(2) A notice of a hearing shall include a reference to the statutory authority under which the hearing will be held.

(3) A notice of an oral hearing shall include,

(a) a statement of the time, place and purpose of the hearing; and

(b) a statement that if the party notified does not attend at the hearing, the tribunal may proceed in the party's absence and the party will not be entitled to any further notice in the proceeding.

(4) A notice of a written hearing shall include,

(a) a statement of the date and purpose of the hearing, and details about the manner in which the hearing will be held;

(b) a statement that the party notified may object to the hearing being held as a written hearing (in which case the tribunal is required to hold it as an electronic or oral hearing) and an indication of the procedure to be followed for that purpose;

(c) a statement that if the party notified neither acts under clause (b) nor participates in the hearing in accordance with the notice, the tribunal may proceed without the party's participation and the party will not be entitled to any further notice in the proceeding.

(5) A notice of an electronic hearing shall include,

(a) a statement of the time and purpose of the hearing, and details about the manner in which the hearing will be held;

(b) a statement that the only purpose of the hearing is to deal with procedural matters, if that is the case;

(c) if clause (b) does not apply, a statement that the party notified may, by satisfying the tribunal that holding the hearing as an electronic hearing is likely to cause the party significant prejudice, require the tribunal to hold the hearing as an oral hearing, and an indication of the procedure to be followed for that purpose; and

    (d) [a statement regarding non-participation similar to 6(5)(c)]

7. Where notice of *an oral* hearing has been given to a party to a proceeding in accordance with this Act and the party does not attend at the hearing, the tribunal may proceed in the absence of the party and the party is not entitled to any further notice in the proceeding.

[Subsections 2 and 3 contain similar provisions for non-participation in written and electronic hearings.]

8. Where the good character, propriety of conduct or competence of a party is an issue in a proceeding, the party is entitled to be furnished prior to the hearing with reasonable information of any allegations with respect thereto.

9.(1) An oral hearing shall be open to the public except where the tribunal is of the opinion that,

    (a) matters involving public security may be disclosed; or

    (b) intimate financial or personal matters or other matters may be disclosed at the hearing of such a nature, having regard to the circumstances, that the desirability of avoiding disclosure thereof in the interests of any person affected or in the public interest outweighs the desirability of adhering to the principle that hearings be open to the public, in which case the tribunal may hold the hearing in the absence of the public.

(1.1) In a written hearing, members of the public are entitled to reasonable access to the documents submitted, unless the tribunal is of the opinion that clause (1)(a) or (b) applies.

(1.2) An electronic hearing shall be open to the public unless the tribunal is of the opinion that,

    (a) it is not practical to hold the hearing in a manner that is open to the public; or

    (b) clause (1)(a) or (b) applies.

(2) A tribunal may make such orders or give such directions at an oral or electronic hearing as it considers necessary for the maintenance of order at

the hearing, and, if any person disobeys or fails to comply with any such order or direction, the tribunal or a member thereof may call for the assistance of any peace officer to enforce the order or direction, and every peace officer so called upon shall take such action as is necessary to enforce the order or direction and may use such force as is reasonably required for that purpose.

9.1 [consolidation of proceedings involving similar subject matter]

10. A party to a proceeding may be represented by counsel or an agent.

10.1 A party to a proceeding may, at an oral or electronic hearing,

    (a) call and examine witnesses and present evidence and submissions; and

    (b) conduct cross-examinations of witnesses at the hearing reasonably required for a full and fair disclosure of all matters relevant to the issues in the proceeding.

11.(1) A witness at an oral hearing is entitled to be advised by counsel or an agent as to his or her rights but such counsel or agent may take no other part in the hearing without leave of the tribunal.

   (2) Where an oral hearing is closed to the public, the counsel or agent for a witness is not entitled to be present except when that witness is giving evidence.

12.(1) A tribunal may require any person, including a party, by summons,

    (a) to give evidence on oath or affirmation at an oral or electronic hearing; and

    (b) to produce in evidence at a hearing documents and things specified by the tribunal, relevant to the subject-matter of the proceeding and admissible at an oral or electronic hearing.

. . . .

14. [protection for witnesses from subsequent court proceedings]

15. [and new sections 15.1 and 15.2: evidence]

16. [judicial notice]

16.1(1) A tribunal may make interim decisions and orders.

(2) A tribunal may impose conditions on an interim decision or order.

(3) An interim decision or order need not be accompanied by reasons.

17. A tribunal shall give its final decision or order in any proceeding in writing and shall give reasons in writing therefor if requested by a party.

(2) A tribunal that makes an order for the payment of money shall set out in the order the principal sum, and if interest is payable, the rate of interest and the date from which it is to be calculated.

18.(1) The tribunal shall send each party who participated in the proceeding, or the party's counsel or agent, a copy of its final decision or order, including the reasons if any have been given....

. . . .

20. A tribunal shall compile a record of any proceeding in which a hearing has been held which shall include,

(a) any application, complaint, reference or other document, if any, by which the proceeding was commenced;

(b) the notice of any hearing;

(c) any interlocutory orders made by the tribunal;

(d) all documentary evidence filed with the tribunal, subject to any limitation expressly imposed by any other Act on the extent to or the purposes for which any such documents may be used in evidence in any proceeding;

(e) the transcript, if any, of the oral evidence given at the hearing; and

(f) the decision of the tribunal and the reasons therefor, where reasons have been given.

21. A hearing may be adjourned from time to time by a tribunal of its own motion or where it is shown to the satisfaction of the tribunal that the adjournment is required to permit an adequate hearing to be held.

21.1 A tribunal may at any time correct a typographical error, error of calculation or similar error made in its decision or order.

21.2(1) A tribunal may, if it considers it advisable, and if its rules made under section 25.1 deal with

the matter, review all or part of its own decision or order, and may confirm, vary, suspend or cancel the decision or order.

(2) The review shall take place within a reasonable time after the decision or order is made.

(3) In the event of a conflict between this section and any other Act, the other Act prevails.

22. A member of a tribunal has power to administer oaths and affirmations for the purpose of any of its proceedings and the tribunal may require evidence before it to be given under oath or affirmation.

23.(1) A tribunal may make such orders or give such directions in proceedings before it as it considers proper to prevent abuse of its processes.

(2) A tribunal may reasonably limit further examination or cross-examination of a witness where it is satisfied that the examination or cross-examination has been sufficient to disclose fully and fairly all matters relevant to the issues in the proceeding.

(3) A tribunal may exclude from a hearing anyone, other than a barrister and solicitor qualified to practise in Ontario, appearing as an agent on behalf of a party or as an adviser to a witness if it finds that such person is not competent properly to represent or to advise the party or witness or does not understand and comply at the hearing with the duties and responsibilities of an advocate or adviser.

24.(1) [Tribunal can provide reasonable notice of the hearing or of its decision by public advertisement or otherwise.]

(2) A notice of a decision given by a tribunal under clause (1)(b) shall inform the parties of the place where copies of the decision and the reasons therefor, if reasons were given, may be obtained.

25.(1) An appeal from a decision of a tribunal to a court or other appellate body operates as a stay in the matter unless,

(a) another Act or a regulation that applies to the proceeding expressly provides to the contrary; or

(b) the tribunal or the court or other appellate body orders otherwise.

25.1(1) A tribunal may make rules governing the practice and procedure before it.

(2) The rules may be of general or particular application.

(3) The rules shall be consistent with this Act and with the other Acts to which they relate.

(4) The tribunal shall make the rules available to the public in English and in French.

(5) Rules adopted under this section are not regulations as defined in the Regulations Act.

(6) The power conferred by this section is in addition to any power to adopt rules that the tribunal may have under another Act.

[Provisions creating the Statutory Powers Procedure Act Rules Committee repealed.]

26. The Lieutenant Governor in Council may make regulations prescribing forms for the purpose of section 12.

. . . .

32. Unless it is expressly provided in any other Act that its provisions and regulations, rules or by-laws made under it apply despite anything in this Act, the provisions of this Act prevail over the provisions of such other Act and over regulations, rules or by-laws made under such other Act which conflict therewith.

[Former sections 26 to 31, 33, and 34 and Forms 1 and 2 repealed.]

(f)   Delay: *Blencoe*†

NOTE

Delayed proceedings can cause unfairness just as much as denial of proper notice or of a chance to refute an allegation. On the other hand, procedural safeguards require time, and there may be a fine line between caution and procrastination. How much delay is too much? What should courts do about it?

Before *Blencoe*, courts had said relatively little about delay as a basis for constitutional or common law control. Delay could result in a breach of natural justice, but only if it deprived a person of a fair opportunity to be heard.

In *Blencoe*, a human rights commission took two years to process a complaint. Mr. Blencoe, the object of the human rights complaint, argued that this delay cost him his career, his health, and his friends. The Supreme Court considered the question of delay from the standpoint of fundamental justice in s. 7 of the *Charter*, and under common law natural justice and "abuse of process". The majority looked at both s. 7 and the common law; the minority thought it sufficient to consider the common law. After *Blencoe*, are courts likely to do much about delay either way?

EXTRACTS

[BASTARACHE   J.   for   himself,   McLACHLIN, L'HEUREUX-DUBÉ, GONTHIER, and MAJOR JJ.:]

[para54] ... In the circumstances of this case, the state has not prevented the respondent from making any "fundamental personal choices". The interests sought to be protected in this case do not in my opinion fall within the "liberty" interest protected by s. 7 [of the *Charter*].

. . . .

[para57] ... The words "serious state-imposed psychological stress" delineate two requirements that must be met in order for security of the person to be triggered. First, the psychological harm must be <u>state imposed</u>, meaning that the harm must result from the actions of the state. Second, the psychological prejudice must be serious....

. . . .

[para65] ... [On the basis of the facts in this case, t]he harm to the respondent resulted from the publicity surrounding the allegations themselves coupled with the political fall-out which ensued rather than

---

† *Blencoe v. British Columbia (Human Rights Commission)*, [2000] 2 S.C.R. 307; rev'g. (1998) 160 D.L.R. (4th) 303 (C.A.); which rev'd. [1999] 1 W.W.R. 139 (S.C.), dismissing Mr. Blencoe's petition for judicial review and ordering that proceedings be terminated due to delay.

any delay in the human rights proceedings which had yet to commence at the time that the respondent began to experience stigma.

. . . .

[para83] It is only in exceptional cases where the state interferes in profoundly intimate and personal choices of an individual that state-caused delay in human rights proceedings could trigger the s. 7 security of the person interest. While these fundamental personal choices would include the right to make decisions concerning one's body free from state interference or the prospect of losing guardianship of one's children, they would not easily include the type of stress, anxiety and stigma that result from administrative or civil proceedings.

. . . .

[para97] To summarize, the stress, stigma and anxiety suffered by the respondent did not deprive him of his right to liberty or security of the person. The framers of the *Charter* chose to employ the words, "life, liberty and security of the person", thus limiting s. 7 rights to these three interests. While notions of dignity and reputation underlie many *Charter* rights, they are not stand-alone rights that trigger s. 7 in and of themselves. Freedom from the type of anxiety, stress and stigma suffered by the respondent in this case should not be elevated to the stature of a constitutionally protected s. 7 right.

. . . .

[para99] Because of my conclusion that there was no deprivation of the respondent's right to liberty or security of the person, I need not proceed to the second stage of the analysis to determine whether the alleged deprivation was in accordance with the principles of fundamental justice. However, for the reasons that immediately follow in the administrative law section, I express the view that the delay, in the circumstances of this case, would not have violated the principles of fundamental justice.

. . . .

[para102] There is no doubt that the principles of natural justice and the duty of fairness are part of every administrative proceeding. Where delay impairs a party's ability to answer the complaint against him or her, because, for example, memories have faded, essential witnesses have died or are unavailable, or evidence has been lost, then administrative delay

may be invoked to impugn the validity of the administrative proceedings and provide a remedy.... It is thus accepted that the principles of natural justice and the duty of fairness include the right to a fair hearing and that undue delay in the processing of an administrative proceeding that impairs the fairness of the hearing can be remedied....

. . . .

[para104] ... The respondent also argued before Lowry J. that he was not provided with a copy of Ms. Schell's timeliness submissions for a two-month period and that he had not received proper disclosure. Lowry J. did not consider the respondent prejudiced in this regard. With respect to the alleged failure to disclose information to the respondent, this is not, in my opinion, a case in which the unfairness is so obvious that there would be a denial of natural justice, or in which there was an abuse of process such that it would be inappropriate to put the respondent through hearings before the Tribunal. I would therefore adopt the finding of Lowry J. that the delay in this case is not such that it would necessarily result in a hearing that lacks the essential elements of fairness. The respondent's right to a fair hearing has not been jeopardized. Proof of prejudice has not been demonstrated to be of sufficient magnitude to impact on the fairness of the hearing.... The question which must be addressed is therefore whether the delay in this case could amount to a denial of natural justice or an abuse of process even where the respondent has not been prejudiced in an evidentiary sense.

. . . .

[para115] ... I caution that in cases where there is no prejudice to hearing fairness, the delay must be clearly unacceptable and have directly caused a significant prejudice to amount to an abuse of process. It must be a delay that would, in the circumstances of the case, bring the human rights system into disrepute. The difficult question before us is in deciding what is an "unacceptable delay" that amounts to an abuse of process.

. . . .

[para121] To constitute a breach of the duty of fairness, the delay must have been unreasonable or inordinate.... There is no abuse of process by delay *per se*. The respondent must demonstrate that the delay was unacceptable to the point of being so oppressive as to taint the proceedings.

. . . .

[para 126] ... Clearly much of this delay resulted from the respondent's actions [in challenging the complaints], although there appear to be other delays cause by the Commission.

. . . .

[para131] A review of the facts in this case demonstrates that, unlike the aforementioned cases where there was complete inactivity for extremely lengthy periods, the communication between the parties in the case at bar was ongoing. While Lowry J. acknowledged the five-month delay of inactivity, on balance, he found no unacceptable delay and considered the time that elapsed to be nothing more "than the time required to process complaints of this kind given the limitations imposed by the resources available"....

. . . .

[para135] Nevertheless, I am very concerned with the lack of efficiency of the Commission and its lack of commitment to deal more expeditiously with complaints. Lack of resources cannot explain every delay in giving information, appointing inquiry officers, filing reports, etc.; nor can it justify inordinate delay where it is found to exist. The fact that most human rights commissions experience serious delays will not justify breaches of the principles of natural justice in appropriate cases....

[para136] I would allow the appeal. The Court of Appeal decision is set aside and the Tribunal should proceed with the hearing of the Complaints on their merits. Considering the lack of diligence displayed by the Commission, I would nevertheless exercise. the Court's discretion under s. 47 of the *Supreme Court Act*, R.S.C., 1985, c. S-26, to award costs against the appellant Commission in favour of Robin Blencoe, Andrea Willis and Irene Schell.

[LeBEL J. for himself, IACOBUCCI, BINNIE, and ARBOUR JJ.:]

. . . .

[para154] Abusive administrative delay is wrong and it doesn't matter if it wrecks only your life and not your hearing. The cases that have been part of this evolution have sometimes expressed the point differently, but the key consideration is this: administrative delay that is determined to be unreasonable based on its length, its causes, and its effects is abusive and contrary to the administrative law principles that

exist and should be applied in a fair and efficient legal system.

[para155] Unreasonable delay is not limited to situations that bring the human rights system into disrepute either by prejudicing the fairness of a hearing or by otherwise rising above a threshold of shocking abuse. Otherwise, there would not be any remedy for an individual suffering from unreasonable delay unless this same individual were unlucky enough to have suffered sufficiently to meet an additional, external test of disrepute resulting to the human rights system....

. . . .

[para160] As indicated above, the central factors toward which the modern administrative law cases as a whole propel us are length, cause, and effects. Approaching these now with a more refined understanding of different kinds and contexts of delay, we see three main factors to be balanced in assessing the reasonableness of an administrative delay:

(1) the time taken compared to the inherent time requirements of the matter before the particular administrative body, which would encompass legal complexities (including the presence of any especially complex systemic issues) and factual complexities (including the need to gather large amounts of information or technical data), as well as reasonable periods of time for procedural safeguards that protect parties or the public;

(2) the causes of delay beyond the inherent time requirements of the matter, which would include consideration of such elements as whether the affected individual contributed to or waived parts of the delay and whether the administrative body used as efficiently as possible those resources it had available; and

(3) the impact of the delay, considered as encompassing both prejudice in an evidentiary sense and other harms to the lives of real people impacted by the ongoing delay. This may also include a consideration of the efforts by various parties to minimize negative impacts by providing information or interim solutions....

. . . .

[Applying these factors, Lebel J. concluded that the delay was sufficient to warrant a court order for an expedited hearing, but not a stay of proceedings.]

(g)   Fundamental Justice: *Suresh*†

NOTE

On 17 September 1997, an immigration adjudicator ordered Mr. Manickavasagam Suresh to be deported from Canada. Section 53 of the former *Immigration Act* protected Convention refugees from being sent back to a country where their life or freedom would be threatened. However, paragraph 53(1)(b) of the Act deprived a refugee of this protection if he or she was a member of an inadmissible class and if the Minister of Citizenship and Immigration "is of the opinion that the person constitutes a danger to the security of Canada." In effect, the provision enabled the Minister to order deportation if she thinks the risk of torture is outweighed by the risk of keeping the individual in Canada.

The Minister sent Mr. Suresh notice that she was proposing to act under paragraph 53(1)(b) and invited written submissions from him. In response, Mr. Suresh claimed that there was a substantial risk that he would be tortured if he were returned to Sri Lanka. Mr. Suresh's written submissions and other publicly available material were considered by an Immigration officer. On 19 October 1997, the officer sent the Minister a formal memorandum recommending that she should declare Mr. Suresh to be a danger to the security of Canada. She did this, and once again, an adjudicator ordered Mr. Suresh to be deported.

One of many issues in this case was whether the process constituted an unjustified denial of fundamental justice. When looking at the Supreme Court's answer, note the relevance of common law natural justice to *Charter* fundamental justice, and the modern "factor-weighing" approach to both. How does s. 15 of the *Charter* fit in, if factor weighing is carried out within the confines of s. 7?

EXTRACTS

[THE COURT:]

[para113] This appeal requires us to determine the procedural protections to which an individual is entitled under s. 7 of the *Charter*. In doing so, we find it helpful to consider the common law approach to procedural fairness articulated by L'Heureux-Dubé J. in *Baker*, supra. In elaborating what is required by way of procedural protection under s. 7 of the *Charter* in cases of this kind, we wish to emphasize that our proposals should be applied in a manner sensitive to the context of specific factual situations. What is important are the basic principles underlying these procedural protections. The principles of fundamental justice of which s. 7 speaks, though not identical to the duty of fairness elucidated in *Baker*, are the same principles underlying that duty....

.   .   .   .

[para115] What is required by the duty of fairness — and therefore the principles of fundamental justice — is that the issue at hand be decided in the context of the statute involved and the rights affected.... More specifically, deciding what procedural protections must be provided involves a consideration of the following factors: (1) the nature of the decision made and the procedures followed in making it, that is, "'the closeness of the administrative process to the judicial process'"; (2) the role of the particular decision within the statutory scheme; (3) the importance of the decision to the individual affected; (4) the legitimate expectations of the person challenging the decision where undertakings were made concerning the procedure to be followed; and (5) the choice of procedure made by the agency itself: *Baker*, supra, at paras. 23–27. This is not to say that other factors or considerations may not be involved. This list of factors is non-exhaustive in determining the common law duty of fairness: *Baker*, supra, at para. 28. It must necessarily be so in determining the procedures demanded by the principles of fundamental justice.

[para116] The nature of the decision to deport bears some resemblance to judicial proceedings. While the decision is of a serious nature and made by an individual on the basis of evaluating and weighing risks, it is also a decision to which discretion must attach. The Minister must evaluate not only the past actions of and present dangers to an individual under her

---

† *Suresh v. Canada (Minister of Citizenship and Immigration)*, [2002] S.C.J. No. 3 (QL); rev'g. [2000] 2 F.C. 592, 183 D.L.R. (4th) 629 (F.C.A.); aff'g. (1999), 173 F.T.R. 1, 50 Imm. L.R. (2d) 183, [1999] F.C.J. No.865 (QL) (F.C.T.D.) (McKeown J.).

consideration pursuant to s. 53, but also the future behaviour of that individual. We conclude that the nature of the decision militates neither in favour of particularly strong, nor particularly weak, procedural safeguards.

[para117] The nature of the statutory scheme suggests the need for strong procedural safeguards. While the procedures set up under s. 40.1 of the Immigration Act are extensive and aim to ensure that certificates under that section are issued fairly and allow for meaningful participation by the person involved, there is a disturbing lack of parity between these protections and the lack of protections under s. 53(1)(b). In the latter case, there is no provision for a hearing, no requirement of written or oral reasons, no right of appeal — no procedures at all, in fact. As L'Heureux-Dubé J. stated in *Baker, supra*, "[g]reater procedural protections ... will be required when no appeal procedure is provided within the statute, or when the decision is determinative of the issue and further requests cannot be submitted" (para. 24). This is particularly so where, as here, Parliament elsewhere in the Act has constructed fair and systematic procedures for similar measures.

[para118] The third factor requires us to consider the importance of the right affected. As discussed above, the appellant's interest in remaining in Canada is highly significant, not only because of his status as a Convention refugee, but also because of the risk of torture he may face on return to Sri Lanka as a member of the LTTE. The greater the effect on the life of the individual by the decision, the greater the need for procedural protections to meet the common law duty of fairness and the requirements of fundamental justice under s. 7 of the *Charter*. Deportation from Canada engages serious personal, financial and emotional consequences. It follows that this factor militates in favour of heightened procedural protections under s. 53(1)(b). Where, as here, a person subject to a s. 53(1)(b) opinion may be subjected to torture, this factor requires even more substantial protections.

[para119] As discussed above, Article 3 of the CAT, which explicitly prohibits the deportation of persons to states where there are "substantial grounds" for believing that the person would be "in danger of being subjected to torture", informs s. 7 of the *Charter*. It is only reasonable that the same executive that bound itself to the CAT intends to act in accordance with the CAT's plain meaning. Given Canada's commitment to the CAT, we find that the appellant had the right to procedural safeguards, at

the s. 53(1)(b) stage of the proceedings. More particularly, the phrase "substantial grounds" raises a duty to afford an opportunity to demonstrate and defend those grounds.

[para120] The final factor we consider is the choice of procedures made by the agency. In this case, the Minister is free under the terms of the statute to choose whatever procedures she wishes in making a s. 53(1)(b) decision. As noted above, the Minister must be allowed considerable discretion in evaluating future risk and security concerns. This factor also suggests a degree of deference to the Minister's choice of procedures since Parliament has signaled the difficulty of the decision by leaving to the Minister the choice of how best to make it. At the same time, this need for deference must be reconciled with the elevated level of procedural protections mandated by the serious situation of refugees like Suresh, who if deported may face torture and violations of human rights in which Canada can neither constitutionally, nor under its international treaty obligations, be complicit.

[para121] Weighing these factors together with all the circumstances, we are of the opinion that the procedural protections required by s. 7 in this case do not extend to the level of requiring the Minister to conduct a full oral hearing or a complete judicial process. However, they require more than the procedure required by the Act under s. 53(1)(b) — that is, none — and they require more than Suresh received.

[para122] We find that a person facing deportation to torture under s. 53(1)(b) must be informed of the case to be met. Subject to privilege or similar valid reasons for reduced disclosure, such as safeguarding confidential public security documents, this means that the material on which the Minister is basing her decision must be provided to the individual, including memoranda such as Mr. Gautier's recommendation to the Minister. Furthermore, fundamental justice requires that an opportunity be provided to respond to the case presented to the Minister. While the Minister accepted written submissions from the appellant in this case, in the absence of access to the materials she was receiving from her staff and on which she based much of her decision, Suresh and his counsel had no knowledge of which factors they specifically needed to address, nor any chance to correct any factual inaccuracies or mischaracterizations. Fundamental justice requires that written submissions be accepted from the subject of the order <u>after</u> the subject has been provided with an opportunity to examine the material being used against him

or her. The Minister must then consider these submissions along with the submissions made by the Minister's staff.

[para123] Not only must the refugee be informed of the case to be met, the refugee must also be given an opportunity to challenge the information of the Minister where issues as to its validity arise. Thus the refugee should be permitted to present evidence pursuant to s. 19 of the Act showing that his or her continued presence in Canada will not be detrimental to Canada, notwithstanding evidence of association with a terrorist organization. The same applies to the risk of torture on return. Where the Minister is relying on written assurances from a foreign government that a person would not be tortured, the refugee must be given an opportunity to present evidence and make submissions as to the value of such assurances.

. . . .

[para126] The Minister must provide written reasons for her decision. These reasons must articulate and rationally sustain a finding that there are no substantial grounds to believe that the individual who is the subject of a s. 53(1)(b) declaration will be subjected to torture, execution or other cruel or unusual treatment, so long as the person under consideration has raised those arguments. The reasons must also articulate why, subject to privilege or valid legal reasons for not disclosing detailed information, the Minister believes the individual to be a danger to the security of Canada as required by the Act. In addition, the reasons must also emanate from the person making the decision, in this case the Minister, rather than take the form of advice or suggestion, such as the memorandum of Mr. Gautier. Mr. Gautier's report, explaining to the Minister the position of Citizenship and Immigration Canada, is more like a prosecutor's brief than a statement of reasons for a decision.

[para127] These procedural protections need not be invoked in every case, as not every case of deportation of a Convention refugee under s. 53(1)(b) will involve risk to an individual's fundamental right to be protected from torture or similar abuses. It is for the refugee to establish a threshold showing that a risk of torture or similar abuse exists before the Minister is obliged to consider fully the possibility. This showing need not be <u>proof</u> of the risk of torture to that person, but the individual must make

out a prima facie case that there <u>may</u> be a risk of torture upon deportation. If the refugee establishes that torture is a real possibility, the Minister must provide the refugee with all the relevant information and advice she intends to rely on, provide the refugee an opportunity to address that evidence in writing, and after considering all the relevant information, issue responsive written reasons. This is the minimum required to meet the duty of fairness and fulfill the requirements of fundamental justice under s. 7 of the *Charter*.

[para128] The Minister argues that even if the procedures used violated Suresh's s. 7 rights, that violation is justified as a reasonable limit under s. 1 of the *Charter*. Despite the legitimate purpose of s. 53(1)(b) of the Immigration Act in striking a balance between the need to fulfil Canada's commitments with respect to refugees and the maintenance of the safety and good order of Canadian society, the lack of basic procedural protections provided to Suresh cannot be justified by s. 1 in our view. Valid objectives do not, without more, suffice to justify limitations on rights. The limitations must be connected to the objective and be proportional. Here the connection is lacking. A valid purpose for excepting some Convention refugees from the protection of s. 53(1) of the Act does not justify the failure of the Minister to provide fair procedures where this exception involves a risk of torture upon deportation. Nor do the alleged fundraising activities of Suresh rise to the level of exceptional conditions contemplated by Lamer J. in *Re B.C. Motor Vehicle Act*, [[1985] 2 S.C.R. 486 at 50]. Consequently, the issuance of a s. 53(1)(b) opinion relating to him without the procedural protections mandated by s. 7 is not justified under s. 1.

. . . .

[para130] Applying these conclusions in the instant case, we find that Suresh made a *prima facie* showing that he might be tortured on return if expelled to Sri Lanka. Accordingly, he should have been provided with the procedural safeguards necessary to protect his s. 7 right not to be expelled to torture. He was not provided the required safeguards. We therefore remand the case to the Minister for reconsideration in accordance with the procedures set out in these reasons.

6   Administrative Procedure: Disclosure

(a)   Disclosure

Disclosure is the provision of information to one or more parties in an administrative proceeding. Disclosure is a corollary of the natural justice principle that a person affected by an administrative proceeding should have a fair opportunity to be heard on his or her own behalf. In order to be effectively heard, you must know the case against you.

Disclosure may arise as a general issue, or in the context of a specific form of a natural justice safeguard such as notice or cross-examination. Some statutory or administrative proceedings, such as pre-hearing conferences and interrogatories, are created specifically to help facilitate disclosure.

A request for disclosure may be directed either to another party to the proceedings, or to the administrative body itself. In the latter case a party may wish to see information the administrative body has generated itself, material commonly known as staff studies. Subject to competing factors, disclosure is normally permitted in the former case. Disclosure *may* be permitted in the latter case, especially if the information is factual material specific to the subject matter of the proceedings, as opposed to general knowledge or policy advice.

Like the other natural justice safeguards, disclosure can serve purposes beyond enhancing the knowledge and participation of the immediate parties to the proceedings: for the administrator as well as the parties, it can be a vital source of accurate information. On the other hand, there are a number of factors that may be considered sufficiently important in specific situations to outweigh the case for disclosure. Five examples come to mind.

First, the information sought may be simply irrelevant to the subject matter of the proceedings. Second, the information may be superfluous, as the case may be already apparent from other information. Third, the information sought may be subject to valid claims to confidentiality. For example, it may involve intimate or potentially ruinous personal details. Fourth, in the case of administrative staff studies, a disclosure requirement might be thought to inhibit the candour and freedom of administrative staff and to prevent the administration from taking full advantage of its internal expertise. Fifth, it may be that the disclosure forum sought, such as oral cross-examination, exacts too high a toll on the cost or formality of the proceedings in proportion to its likely benefit.

Disclosure, then, requires the courts to perform a balancing act in which the results in one situation may be very different from those in the next. The best a student can do is to become familiar with the factors likely to tip the balance in one direction or the other.

(b) *London Cable*†

NOTE

Section 19(2) of the *Broadcasting Act* required a public hearing once the Executive Committee of the CRTC decided that it would be in the public interest to hold such a hearing. A cable subscribers' group was opposed to London Cable's plans to raise its monthly cable fees. At the public hearing to consider London Cable's application for a fee increase, counsel for the subscribers' group sought to cross-examine certain witnesses for London Cable, and sought disclosure of CRTC staff documents relating to the application, the audited financial statement, and the projected future earnings of London Cable. The CRTC refused these requests and granted the fee increase. The subscribers' group challenged this decision in the Federal Court of Appeal.

EXTRACTS

APPEAL from an APPLICATION to review a decision of the Canadian Radio-Television Commission granting an amendment of a cable television licence.

> *Andrew J. Roman*, for applicant.
> *C.C. Johnston*, for respondent.
> *R.J. Wright*, Q.C., for intervenor.

[The judgment of the Court was delivered by JACKETT, C.J.:]

This is an appeal under s. 26 [am. R.S.C. 1970, c. 10 (2nd Supp.), s. 65] of the *Broadcasting Act*, R.S.C. 1970, c. B-11, and a s. 28 application, joined together in a single proceeding under Rule 1314, in respect of a decision of the Canadian Radio-Television Commission[1] (75-513) dated October 28, 1975, whereby an application by London Cable TV Limited[2] to amend its cable television licence, *inter alia*, so as to permit it to charge $6 per month for "basic service" was approved.[3]

The applicants were intervenants in a "public hearing", which was held as a condition precedent to granting such an amendment as required by s. 19(2) of the *Broadcasting Act*.[4] They attacked the decision

of the Commission because (a) they were not permitted to see certain documents either before or during the hearing, and (b) the Commission refused to permit cross-examination of witnesses at the hearing.

In so far as the cross-examination is concerned, it was not, in my opinion, demonstrated that such refusal resulted, in this case, in a failure to permit the applicants to exercise their rights as members of the "public" under the statute. I am of the same view with reference to the withholding of certain documents that have been referred to as "staff-documents".

That leaves for consideration the effect on the validity of the order attacked of the withholding from the applicants of an audited financial statement of the licensee and projections as to future earnings at the pre-existing rate ($5 per month) and at the proposed rate ($6 per month), which had, at the request of the Commission, been put before the Commission in support of the application by the licensee before the Commission proceeded with the "public hearing".

In so far as these documents are concerned, an attack was made on the granting of the amendment on the basis that their having been withheld was a breach of the fundamental rule of natural justice that *prima facie* no decision or order is to be made against a person by a statutory authority without affording him a reasonable opportunity of answering the case against him. The applicants, as subscribers, or as the representatives of subscribers, to the cable system here in question, attempted to bring themselves within that rule. I do not find it necessary to express any opinion as to whether the applicants can succeed in this proceeding on the basis of that rule because I have come to a conclusion in their favour for another reason that I am about to express. For the same reason, I do no find it necessary to come to any conclusion as to whether there was, by virtue of the withholding of such documents, such a failure to comply with the Commission's own rules of procedure as to entitle the applicants to an invalidation order.

I am of opinion that it was, by virtue of s. 19(2), a condition precedent to the valid making

---

† *Re Canadian Radio-Television Commission and London Cable TV Ltd.* (1976), 67 D.L.R. (3d) 267. (Federal Court of Appeal, Jackett, C.J. Pratte and Heald, JJ., April 9, 1976)

of the amending order attacked by this application that a "public" hearing have been held in connection with the proposed amending order. In my view, at the very minimum, what the statute required, by requiring a "public hearing", was a hearing at which, subject to the procedural rules of the Commission and the inherent jurisdiction of the Commission to control its own proceedings, every member of the public would have a status "to bring before" the Commission anything relevant to the subject-matter of the hearing so as to ensure that, to the extent possible, everything that might appropriately be taken into consideration would be before the Commission, or its Executive Committee, when the application for the amendment was dealt with.[5] To be such a public hearing, it would, in my view, have had to be arranged in such a way as to provide members of the public with a reasonable opportunity to know the subject-matter of the hearing, and what it involved from the point of view of the public, in sufficient time to decide whether or not to exercise their statutory right of presentation and to prepare themselves for the task of presentation if they decide to make a presentation. In other words, what the statute contemplates, in my view, is a *meaningful* hearing that would be calculated to aid the Commission, or its Executive Committee, to reach a conclusion that reflects a consideration of the public interest as well as a consideration of the private interest of the licensee; it does not contemplate a public meeting at which members of the public are merely given an opportunity to "blow off steam".

In this case it seems clear to me, from a study of the "Case" and from argument in this Court, that there was not made available to the applicants as members of the public a reasonable opportunity to know what was involved in the application.[6] The refusal to provide them with the financial statements and projections in question — and the failure to provide the fundamental basic facts relevant to the proposed increase in rates by some other method — left members of the public, including the applicants, in a position where they knew that the licensee was asking leave to increase its charges to the public but where they had no means of forming a considered opinion as to whether such increase was justified by the circumstances and had no means, if they concluded that it was not, of preparing themselves to put forward their position at the hearing.

When the Commission not only failed to make such basic information available with its notice to the public of the statutory "public hearing" but refused, when asked by interested members of the public, to supply such basic information, in my view, it failed

to take a step that, in the circumstances of this case, was a condition precedent to the holding of a s. 19 "public hearing"; and, as such a hearing was a condition precedent to the power of the Commission or Executive Committee to make the order under attack, I am of opinion that it must be set aside.[7]

I propose that the decision made by the Canadian Radio-Television Commission (or its Executive Committee) on October 28, 1975 (75-513), permitting London Cable TV Limited to amend its cable television licence be set aside and that the matter be referred back for reconsideration after the requirements of s. 19 of the *Broadcasting Act* have been complied with.

Appeal and application allowed.

Notes

1. Replaced by the Canadian Radio-Television and Telecommunications Commission. See Bill C-5 of 1975–76 Session, proclaimed April 1, 1976.
2. Now amalgamated with other companies to form Canadian Cablesystems (Ontario) Limited.
3. The power of the Commission to grant Cable television licences was established, as far as this Court is concerned, in an application, *Re Capital Cities Communications Inc. et al. and Canadian Radio Television Com'n* (1975), 52 D.L.R. (3d) 415, 19 C.P.R. (2d) 51, [1975] F.C. 18. No question has been raised in this matter as to the Commission's jurisdiction to insert a condition in such a licence concerning service charges and that question does not, therefore, have to be decided for the purpose of this proceeding.
4. Section 19(1) and (2) read as follows:
   "19(1) A public hearing shall be held by the Commission
   (a) in connection with the issue of a broadcasting licence, other than a licence to carry on a temporary network operation; or
   (b) where the Commission or the Executive Committee has under consideration the revocation or suspension of a broadcasting licence.
   (2) A public hearing shall be held by the Commission, if the Executive Committee is satisfied that it would be in the public interest to hold such a hearing, in connection with
   (a) the amendment of a broadcasting licence;
   (b) the issue of a licence to carry on a temporary network operation; or
   (c) a complaint by a person with respect to any matter within the powers of the Commission."
   While a public hearing is clearly mandatory in every application to which s. 19(1) applies, in my view, a public hearing is also mandatory in every case to which s. 19(2) applies if the Executive Committee decides that "it would be in the public interest to hold such a hearing".
5. Compare *Re A.-G. Man. et al. and National Energy Board et al.* (1974), 48 D.L.R. (3d) 73 at pp. 85–6, [1974] 2 F.C. 502 at pp. 518–9, *per* Cattanach, J.
   I express no view as to whether other grounds exist for invalidating the order attacked. For example, I express no opinion as to whether what was contemplated was a hearing during which a record would be made on the basis of which the matter would have to be determined (in which case, on the reasoning in

Minister of National Revenue v. Wright's Canadian Ropes Ltd., [1947] 1 D.L.R. 721, [1947] A.C. 109, [1974] 1 W.W.R. 214, this proceeding would probably succeed) and I express no opinion as to whether what was contemplated was a hearing at which every intervenant would be entitled to the rights implied by the rules of natural justice in favour of parties against whom it is proposed to make or refuse an order (in which case also the proceeding would probably succeed).

6. What pre-hearing information, if any, is necessary to make a "public hearing" a meaningful hearing will obviously vary according to the circumstances.
7. If, of course, such information had not been supplied in a preliminary way to the Commission by the licensee, the Commission could not have supplied it to the public. As it seems to me, however, some such information has to be put before the Commission before the Commission has a *prima facie* case to consider with reference to an increase in rates.

(c) *Ciba-Geigy*†

NOTE

The Patented Medicine Prices Review Board had scheduled a hearing that could result in a finding that Ciba-Geigy was selling a drug at an excessive price. Ciba-Geigy sought disclosure of all Board staff documents that related to its investigation of Ciba-Geigy. The key issue here was the relevance to a non-criminal administrative law proceeding of the Supreme Court's requirement in *R. v. Stinchcombe*, [1991] 3 S.C.R. 326 that in a criminal case the Crown must disclose all materials to the defence.

EXTRACTS

[MacGUIGAN J. for himself, MARCEAU and DÉCARY JJ.:]

[para1] ... This appeal has to do with the extent of the disclosure required to the appellant of documents in the hands of the Patented Medicine Prices Review Board ("the Board").

[para2] Utilizing its powers under the Patent Act ("the Act"), the Board scheduled a hearing to determine whether the drug Habitrol marketed in Canada by the appellant is being sold at an excessive price. The consequences of such a finding under s. 83 of the Act could be an order for a price reduction in the selling price, a payment to Her Majesty in the Right of Canada of an offset amount from estimated excess corporate revenue, and, on a finding of a policy of selling the medicine at an excessive price, an offset of up to twice the amount of the estimated

excess revenues. This last kind of remedial order is not in play in the instant case in its current state.

[para3] In deciding to hold a formal hearing, once a patentee has refused to make a voluntary compliance order the Chairman of the Board considers a report from the Board staff to the effect that the market price charged for the drug in Canada exceeds the Board's guidelines. The appellant seeks the disclosure to it of all documents in the Board's possession which relate to the matters in issue in the s. 83 hearing, particularly the report on which the Chairman acted in ordering the hearing. In its view such disclosure should extend to all the facets of the staff investigation and to all documents in the hands of the Board or its Chairman.

[para4] The Board refused the appellant's request for such exhaustive disclosure for the following reasons (Appeal Board, I, 3):

> In the Board's view, in a hearing before it, the party to whom the hearing relates must be provided with a level of disclosure and production which ensures that the party is fully informed of the case to be made against it. Further, the procedure followed must provide the party to whom the hearing relates a reasonable opportunity to meet that case by bringing forward its own position and by correcting or contradicting any statement or evidence related to the case which is prejudicial to its position.
>
> It is the Board's view that, in matters of the disclosure and production of information and documents in the context of a public hearing, the Board must balance its duty to give every opportunity to a Respondent to be heard against its

---

† *Ciba-Geigy Canada Ltd. v. Canada (Patent Medicine Prices Review Board)*, [1994] 3 F.C. 425 (F.C.A.); aff'g. an unreported decision of McKeown J. (F.C.T.D.).

responsibility to ensure that its orders do not have the effect of limiting its ability to discharge its responsibilities in the public interest on an ongoing basis. In order to discharge such responsibilities, the Board must be confident that it is getting candid, complete and objective advice from its staff. This is particularly the case in respect of the preliminary views it receives as to whether there is sufficient evidence to justify calling a hearing into a matter. This balancing need not in any way affect the Board's duty in law to make its decisions on the basis of the evidence placed and tested before it during a hearing.

[para5] On a judicial review proceeding McKeown J. upheld the Board's decision as follows (Appeal Book, I, 17):

The Board has made a decision refusing disclosure of the documents requested and I should give such a decision curial deference unless fairness or natural justice requires otherwise. Disclosure cannot be decided in the abstract. The Board is supposed to proceed efficiently and to protect the interest of the public. This requires, *inter alia*, that a hearing shall not be unduly prolonged. Certainly, the subject of an excess price hearing is entitled to know the case against it, but it should not be permitted to obtain all the evidence which has come into the possession of the Board in carrying out its regulatory functions in the public interest on the sole ground that it may be relevant to the matter at hand. The Board's function is not to obtain information solely for investigative purposes; its primary role is to monitor prices. In its decision, the Board recognized the need to balance its duty to the applicant against limiting its ability to discharge its responsibilities in the public interest on an ongoing basis. The Board has exercised its duty properly in the case at bar.... [W]hen the statutory scheme of this Board is looked at, the Board is a regulatory board or tribunal. There is no point in the legislature creating a regulatory tribunal if the tribunal is treated as a criminal court. The obligations concerning disclosure imposed by the doctrine of fairness and natural justice are met if the subject of the inquiry is advised of the case it has to meet and is provided with all the documents that will be relied on. CIBA has been provided with much more than the minimum disclosure required to enable it to meet the case. Law and policy require that some leeway be given an administrative tribunal with economic regulatory functions, if, in pursuing its mandate, the tribunal is required by necessity to receive confidential information. It is not intended that proceedings before these tribunals be as adversarial as proceedings before a

court. To require the Board to disclose all possibly relevant information gathered while fulfilling its regulatory obligations would unduly impede its work from an administrative viewpoint. Fairness is always a matter of balancing diverse interests. I find that fairness does not require the disclosure of the fruits of the investigation in this matter.

We are all agreed that the Motions Judge has correctly stated and applied the law.

[para6] Indeed, in emphasizing that its case is one of *audi alteram partem* and not of bias, counsel for the appellant expressly agreed with the law as stated by the respondent that "the concept of procedural fairness is eminently variable, and its content is to be decided in the specific context of each case" (*Knight* v. *Indian Head School Division No. 19 of Saskatchewan*, [1990] 1 S.C.R. 653, 682 (per L'Heureux-Dubé J.) and the context to be thus taken into account consists of the nature and seriousness of the matters in issue, the circumstances, and of course the governing statute. This was precisely the approach of the Motions Judge.

[para7] The only real issue between the parties is as to the effect to be given in this non-criminal case to the powerful reasons for decision of Sopinka J. in *R.* v. *Stinchcombe*, [1991] 3 S.C.R. 326 that in a criminal case the Crown has a legal duty to make total disclosure to the defence. Stinchcombe was applied by a Divisional Court in Ontario to the requirements of natural justice under an Ontario Human Rights Code Board of Inquiry in *Ontario Human Rights Commission* v. *House*, decided 8 November 1993 (No. 520/93). The Court in House analogized the proceedings in question to criminal proceedings and the role of Commission counsel to that of the Crown in criminal proceedings. It concluded that (p. 12):

There is no dispute in these proceedings that the allegations made by the complainants are indeed extremely serious. Any racial discrimination strikes at the very heart of a democratic pluralistic society. It is, of course, of the utmost seriousness if any such racial discrimination exists or has existed in an important public institution such as a major hospital. The consequences attendant on a negative finding by a Board of Inquiry would be most severe for the Respondents as any such finding could and should seriously damage the reputation of any such individual.

[para8] This is where any criminal analogy to the proceedings in the case at bar breaks down. There are admittedly extremely serious economic conse-

quences for an unsuccessful patentee at a s. 83 hearing, and a possible effect on a corporation's reputation in the market place. But as McKeown J. found, the administrative tribunal here has economic regulatory functions and has no power to affect human rights in a way akin to criminal proceedings.

[para9] A trustful relationship with its investigative staff and proceeding "as informally and expeditiously

as the circumstances of fairness permits" are valid Board objectives.

[para10] We are all agreed with McKeown J. that "law and policy require that some leeway be given an administrative tribunal with economic regulatory functions ... in pursuing its mandate."

[para11] The appeal must therefore be dismissed with costs.

(d) Privacy Commissioner†

NOTE

Sometimes a disclosure claim may be made on a statutory ground independent of natural justice principles. For example, s. 12 of the *Privacy Act*, R.S.C. 1985, P-21 gives an individual the right to access to personal information about himself or herself if it is "under the control" of the relevant government institution. Section 22(1)(b) permits an institution to refuse disclosure where disclosure would be "injurious to the enforcement of any law." After the Canada Labour Relations Board dismissed a bus driver's complaint against his union, the driver made a *Privacy Act* request for all personal information about him in the Board's possession. The Board sent him the information, except for the personal notes of its panel members who adjudicated at the hearing. However, the *Privacy Act*'s disclosure requirement did not contain an exemption for personal notes of adjudicatory officials. Acting on the driver's behalf, the Privacy Commissioner sought judicial review of the Board's refusal to disclose the notes. Would Noel J.'s reasoning about "adjudicative privilege" apply to a natural justice-based disclosure claim?

EXTRACTS

[NÖEL J:]

. . . .

[para79] It is the duty and role of courts to ensure that administrative tribunals make their decisions in

accordance with the rules of natural justice.... As such, courts are called upon to warrant the fairness of the process. To do so the court must ensure that the tribunal possesses the freedom to decide matters independently, as it sees fit, without interference from anyone at any time. In my view, regulated and systematic intrusions by outsiders into the thought process of a decision maker as it stands to be revealed by the hearing notes would impact negatively on the integrity of the decision-making process.

. . . .

[para82] I am ... satisfied that the respondent has met the burden placed upon it by s. 22(1)(b) and has established that disclosure of the Notes, by revealing the mental processes and ultimately, the decision-making processes of its members, would compromise its operations. Specifically, I am satisfied that the workings of the CLRB as an adjudicative tribunal called upon to dispose of substantive rights would be impeded to the point that a reasonable expectation of probable harm to the performance of its statutory functions under the Code would result from the requested disclosure. The regulated disclosure of hearing notes under the *Privacy Act* would take away from the Board a tool that is, in my view, essential to the performance of its duty. In so stating, I stress that if the notes are not exempt from disclosure, any "personal information" which they may contain, including all expressions of opinions pertaining to litigants, lawyers and witnesses would by law have to be systematically collated and retained by the CLRB in an information bank for a

---

† *Canada (Privacy Commissioner) v. Canada (Labour Relations Board)*, [1996] 3 F.C. 609 F.C.T.D. (August 12, 1996).

minimum period of two years in view of their disclosure upon request to the individual concerned.

... That prospect, in my view, raises a reasonable expectation of probable harm to the performance by the CLRB of its statutory functions under the Code and on that basis I conclude that the notes are exempt from disclosure under section 22(1)(b) of the Act.

. . . .

[para98] In my view ... the absence of an exemption in the *Privacy Act* for accounts of consultations and deliberations involving decision makers is not necessarily evocative of a desire to do away with the adjudicative privilege under that Act. It is more likely that the legislator simply did not envisage that accounts of consultations and deliberations were susceptible of containing "information", let alone "personal information" as that term is defined under the *Privacy Act*.

[para99] Before leaving this issue, it is significant that while accounts of consultations and deliberations of decision makers in the exercise of a discretionary power were exempted from disclosure under the *Access Act*, notes of decision makers taken in the course of a hearing, such as the ones in issue, were not.... Yet hearing notes are as intimately linked to the adjudicative privilege as are consultations and deliberations amongst decision makers. While this omission may be the result of an oversight, I rather think that hearing notes were not brought under the exemption because they are not, in the normal course, thought to be "under the control" of government.

. . . .

[Nöel J. held that the personal notes were not "under the control" of the Board.]

. . . .

[para119] The [Privacy] Commissioner, without relying on any authority, simply chose to disregard the long established judicial practice which guards decision makers from intrusion into the thought process leading to their decision. He did so on the basis that, in his view, this practice was unnecessary and indeed harmful to the proper functioning of our legal system and despite the clear pronouncements of the Courts which are primarily concerned with the due process of law. In professing to know how to better run the legal system, I believe that the Commissioner lost sight of the purpose and the limits which are inherent in his own legislation.

[para120] For these reasons, the application is dismissed with costs.

(e) *Dynar*†

NOTE

As a result of an F.B.I. investigation, Mr. Dynar was charged in the United States with money laundering. Since Mr. Dynar was a Canadian citizen in Canada, the American government requested his extradition to the United States. After a hearing under the *Extradition Act*, Mr. Dynar was committed for extradition. Mr. Dynar sought to re-open the hearing, arguing that the American government had failed to disclose the extent of the Canadian involvement in the investigation. The Minister refused to re-open the hearing, and ordered his surrender to the United States. Mr. Dynar appealed the committal decision to the Ontario Court of Appeal and then cross-appealed this decision on the ground that the non-disclosure breached the fundamental justice guarantee in the *Canadian Charter of Rights and Freedoms*.

EXTRACTS

[CORY and IACOBUCCI JJ. for themselves and for LAMER C.J. and La FOREST, L'HEUREUX-DUBÉ, and GONTHIER JJ.:]

---

† *United States of America v. Dynar*, [1997] 2 S.C.R. 462 (June 26, 1997). Appeal and cross-appeal from a judgment of the Ontario Court of Appeal (1995), 25 O.R. (3d) 559, 85 O.A.C. 9, 101 C.C.C. (3d) 271, (i) allowing the respondent's appeal from a decision of the Ontario Court (General Division), [1994] O.J. No. 3940 (QL) committing him for extradition and (ii) granting his application for judicial review of the Minister's surrendered decision. Appeal allowed and cross-appeal dismissed.

[para115] Mr. Dynar cross-appeals from the decision of the Ontario Court of Appeal on the basis that he was not given a fair hearing. He argues that he did not receive adequate disclosure of the involvement of the Canadian investigating authorities in the gathering of the evidence that was the basis for the committal order. This lack of disclosure, he submits, justifies a new hearing at which full disclosure should be given, which in turn may provide him with the basis for arguing that a stay of proceedings is warranted.

[para116] Alternatively, it is submitted that he will argue at a new hearing that there was a violation of his right to be free from unreasonable search and seizure under s. 8 of the *Charter* because the wiretap evidence was gathered without judicial authorization. He also contends that there was a violation of his s. 7 rights on the basis of entrapment because the "sting" operation was allegedly set up without reasonable grounds to believe that an offence was being committed. The respondent conceded in oral argument that the ultimate goal of these endeavours is either the exclusion of the evidence of the sting operation from the extradition proceedings, or a stay of proceedings. However, the nature of the extradition hearing, and the evidence relied upon by the Requesting State in the committal hearing, demonstrate that a new hearing is not warranted.

(1) The Nature of the Extradition Hearing

[para117] The extradition process in Canada is governed by the *Extradition Act*, which translates into domestic law Canada's international obligations to surrender fugitives who have committed crimes in other jurisdictions: *McVey, supra,* at p. 508. The Act establishes a two-step process for determining whether a particular fugitive should be surrendered to a foreign jurisdiction for trial.

[para118] The first step, the committal hearing, is the judicial phase of the process in which the fugitive is brought before a judge who determines whether the evidence justifies surrender of the fugitive. If the Requesting State has made out its case, the fugitive is committed. If not, the fugitive is discharged. If the fugitive is committed for surrender, the warrant of committal, as well as any report from the judge presiding over the committal hearing, is forwarded to the Minister of Justice, who then makes the final decision whether the fugitive should be surrendered. This second phase of the process is political in nature and is not in issue in the cross-appeal. Rather, the cross-appeal puts in issue the level of procedural protection that the fugitive is entitled to receive dur-

ing the judicial phase of the process — the committal hearing.

[para119] Under s. 13 of the *Extradition Act*, the committal proceeding is to be conducted "in the same manner, as nearly as may be, as if the fugitive was brought before a justice of the peace, charged with an indictable offence committed in Canada". The purpose of the extradition hearing for a fugitive accused of a crime in another jurisdiction is outlined in s. 18(1)(b), which provides:

> 18.(1) The judge shall issue a warrant for the committal of the fugitive to the nearest convenient prison, there to remain until surrendered to the foreign state, or discharged according to law,
>
> ...
>
> (b) In the case of a fugitive accused of an extradition crime, if such evidence is produced as would, according to the law of Canada, subject to this Part, justify the committal of the fugitive for trial, if the crime had been committed in Canada.

The extradition judge must determine whether the fugitive should be committed for surrender, which is to say whether a *prima facie* case has been demonstrated that would justify his committal for trial if his conduct had taken place in Canada.

[para120] ... the role of the extradition judge has been held to be a "modest one", limited to the determination of whether or not the evidence is sufficient to justify committing the fugitive for surrender....

. . . .

[para122] A judge hearing an application for extradition has an important role to fulfil. Yet it cannot be forgotten that the hearing is intended to be an expedited process, designed to keep expenses to a minimum and ensure prompt compliance with Canada's international obligations. As La Forest J. stated for the majority in *McVey, supra,* at p. 551, "extradition proceedings are not trials. They are intended to be expeditious procedures to determine whether a trial should be held". In fact, in some contexts, a requirement for more "trial-like" procedures at the extradition committal stage may "cripple the operation of the extradition proceedings": *McVey, supra,* at p. 528. See also *Schmidt, supra,* at p. 516.

(2) The Application of the Charter to Extradition Proceedings

[para123] There is no doubt that the *Charter* applies to extradition proceedings. Yet s. 32 of the *Charter*

provides that it is applicable only to Canadian state actors. Pursuant to principles of international comity as well, the *Charter* generally cannot apply extra-territorially....

[para124] The *Charter* does therefore guarantee the fairness of the committal hearing. The Minister's discretion in deciding to surrender the fugitive may also attract *Charter* scrutiny. In both instances, s. 7 of the *Charter*, which provides that an individual has a right not to be deprived of life, liberty or security of the person, except in accordance with the principles of fundamental justice, will be most frequently invoked. It is obvious that the liberty and security of the person of the fugitive are at stake in an extradition proceeding. The proceedings must therefore be conducted in accordance with the principles of fundamental justice: see A. W. La Forest, *La Forest's Extradition To and From Canada* (3rd ed. 1991), at p. 132; *Schmidt, supra*, at pp. 520–21.

[para125] Even where there is a sufficient involvement of Canadian authorities in the proceedings to justify applying the *Charter*, courts must proceed with caution. It has been observed that "judicial intervention must be limited to cases of real substance": *Schmidt, supra*, at p. 523. To do otherwise might all too easily place Canada in a position of violating its international obligations: see La Forest's *Extradition, supra*, at p. 25.

[para126] Mr. Dynar has not argued that the situation he will face in the United States is in any way oppressive or unacceptable. Indeed, before such an argument could succeed the fugitive would have to demonstrate that he will be subjected to egregious conduct that would "shock the conscience" or that would be "simply unacceptable": *Schmidt, supra*, at p. 522; *Allard, supra*, at p. 572. Rather the focus of Mr. Dynar's argument is on his entitlement under s. 7 of the *Charter* to procedural safeguards in the form of disclosure in connection with the extradition hearing.

(3) *Applicable Procedural Safeguards at the Extradition Hearing*
(A) THE RIGHT TO DISCLOSURE OF MATERIALS IN THE HANDS OF THE REQUESTING STATE

[para127] Mr. Dynar's submission is that he was entitled to a high level of disclosure in the extradition proceeding so that he could make full answer and defence in accordance with his s. 7 *Charter* rights. The essence of Mr. Dynar's argument is that an attenuated version of the rules set out in *R. v.*

Stinchcombe, [1991] 3 S.C.R. 326, *R. v. O'Connor*, [1995] 4 S.C.R. 411, and *R. v. Chaplin*, [1995] 1 S.C.R. 727, should apply. Although the level of disclosure required in an extradition proceeding does not have to be definitively resolved in this case, some comments pertaining to this issue should be made.

[para128] Even though the extradition hearing must be conducted in accordance with the principles of fundamental justice, this does not automatically entitle the fugitive to the highest possible level of disclosure. The principles of fundamental justice guaranteed under s. 7 of the *Charter* vary according to the context of the proceedings in which they are raised. It is clear that there is no entitlement to the most favourable procedures imaginable: *R. v. Lyons*, [1987] 2 S.C.R. 309, at pp. 361–62. For example, more attenuated levels of procedural safeguards have been held to be appropriate at immigration hearings than would apply in criminal trials. See *Chiarelli v. Canada (Minister of Employment and Immigration)*, [1992] 1 S.C.R. 711. The same approach is equally applicable to an extradition proceeding. While it was stated in *Idziak v. Canada (Minister of Justice)*, [1992] 3 S.C.R. 631, at p. 658, that the committal hearing in the extradition process is "clearly judicial in its nature and warrants the application of the full panoply of procedural safeguards", it was held that the extent and nature of procedural protection guaranteed by s. 7 of the *Charter* in an extradition proceeding will depend on the context in which it is claimed (at pp. 656–57).

[para129] The context and purpose of the extradition hearing will shape the level of procedural protection that is available to a fugitive. In *Kindler v. Canada (Minister of Justice)*, [1991] 2 S.C.R. 779, at p. 844, the position was put by the majority in this way:

> While the extradition process is an important part of our system of criminal justice, it would be wrong to equate it to the criminal trial process. It differs from the criminal process in purpose and procedure and, most importantly, in the factors which render it fair. Extradition procedure, unlike the criminal procedure, is founded on the concepts of reciprocity, comity and respect for differences in other jurisdictions.

See also *Mellino, supra* at p. 551.

[para130] It follows that it is neither necessary nor appropriate to simply transplant into the extradition process all the disclosure requirements referred to in *Stinchcombe, supra*, *Chaplin, supra*, and *O'Connor, supra*. Those concepts apply to domestic criminal

proceedings, where onerous duties are properly imposed on the Crown to disclose to the defence all relevant material in its possession or control. This is a function of an accused's right to full answer and defence in a Canadian trial. However, the extradition proceeding is governed by treaty and by statute. The role of the extradition judge is limited and the level of procedural safeguards required, including disclosure, must be considered within this framework.

[para131] Procedures at the extradition hearing are of necessity less complex and extensive than those in domestic preliminary inquiries or trials. Earlier decisions have wisely avoided imposing procedural requirements on the committal hearing that would render it very difficult for Canada to honour its international obligations. Thus, in *Mellino*, *supra*, at p. 548, reservations were expressed about procedures that would permit an extradition hearing to become the forum for lengthy examinations of the reasons for delay in either seeking or undertaking extradition proceedings. La Forest J., for the majority, held that this would be "wholly out of keeping with extradition proceedings".

[para132] ... [D]isclosure of the relationship between United States and Canadian authorities in an investigation is not a requirement imposed on the Requesting State under either the Act or the treaty.

. . . .

[para136] Quite simply, no justiciable *Charter* issue arises in light of the evidence adduced and the nature of an extradition hearing. Mr. Dynar took advantage of telephone facilities to carry out his activities in the United States. He also sent Mr. Cohen to Buffalo to pick up the money. It does not matter that he physically did not leave Canada at any point. The actions of Dynar and Cohen were sufficient to bring them within the jurisdiction of the United States. The affidavit evidence submitted by the Requesting State discloses that the evidence was gathered by American authorities, on American soil, for an American investigation. Any attempt to demonstrate involvement of Canadian authorities acting in conjunction with American authorities simply cannot alter this basic fact.

. . . .

[para141] Mr. Dynar contends that as a result of the Requesting State's non-disclosure, there is no evidentiary record on the basis of which he can even attempt to make a *Charter* argument. Yet the evidence presented by the Requesting State does disclose enough information to conclude that there is simply no "air of reality" to the contention that Mr. Dynar could establish a *Charter* violation by the Canadian officials in the gathering of the evidence. The evidence before Keenan J. included the affidavit of Agent Matthews. It clearly reveals that the FBI had been interested in the activities of Mr. Dynar for some time; that Matthews himself was aware of previous occasions on which Mr. Dynar had admitted to laundering large sums of money in the State of Nevada, and that he initiated the investigation on the basis of his suspicions regarding Mr. Dynar's telephone call to Lucky Simone. The affidavit provides a sufficient basis to conclude that the investigation, the evidence and the prosecution were essentially American. No amount of cooperation by the Canadian authorities could change this.

. . . .

[para145] Mr. Dynar argued that even if he was not entitled to additional disclosure from the American authorities, he was entitled to disclosure of the materials in the hands of the Canadian authorities. Since no justiciable *Charter* issue can arise from the potential involvement of the Canadian authorities in the gathering of evidence in this case, it is not necessary to consider the degree of disclosure that might be required in other circumstances.

. . . .

[para147] The facts presented in this case preclude any recourse to the *Charter* in the committal hearing and the cross-appeal must be dismissed.

VI. Conclusion

[para148] In the result, therefore, the appeal is allowed, the judgment of the Court of Appeal is set aside, and the cross-appeal is dismissed. The order of Keenan J. committing the fugitive for extradition and the Minister of Justice's decision to surrender the fugitive are reinstated.

. . . .

[Major, Sopinka, and McLachlin JJ. delivered separate concurring reasons.]

(f)   Cross-Examination: *Globe*†

NOTE

The *audi alteram partem* branch of the rules of natural justice includes a wide spectrum of possible procedural safeguards. These range from the nominal requirement of notice to the more court-like protections associated with an oral hearing, such as the right to cross-examination, legal counsel, and strict evidentiary standards. What is needed to provide a fair opportunity to be heard varies with the circumstances of each case. On the other hand, it may be possible to isolate some factors that influence a reviewing court's decision to require a particular level of protection.

The *Globe* case involved a certification application. If a majority of the employees in a bargaining unit belonged to a particular union, that union could apply for certification. The Toronto Newspaper Guild applied for certification in regard to employees at the Globe Printing Co. The employer opposed the application, claiming that resignations since the application had deprived the union of its majority membership. When the Board refused to investigate the alleged resignations, counsel for the employer sought to cross-examine the union about them. The cross-examination request was refused, the Toronto Newspaper Guild was certified, and the employer challenged the certification decision in the courts.

Gale J. upheld the challenge and ruled that there should have been an opportunity to cross-examine. (His decision was upheld on appeal, although on slightly different grounds.) What were the key factors prompting Gale J. to require this high-level and highly court-like form of safeguard? What factors did they outweigh? Do you agree with the result?

EXTRACTS

[GALE J.:]

.   .   .   .

That which next happened is set forth in paras. 10 and 11 of the affidavit of Mr. Hicks, counsel for the Company, and those paragraphs read as follows:

> 10. I thereupon submitted to the Chairman of the Board that the documents filed by Counsel for the Applicant Union did not show that the Applicant represented a majority of members of the Applicant Union in good standing as alleged and stated that I wished to cross-examine the representative of the Applicant Union who had given evidence. The Chairman asked me the purpose of this submission and of the proposed cross-examination. I advised the Chairman that I had information to the effect that a number of employees in the department in question had sent in their resignation as members of the Applicant Union. The Chairman stated he saw no relevancy to resignations. Argument then ensued addressed to the Board by Counsel for the Applicant Union and myself in which I pointed out that to refuse me the right to cross-examine was directly at variance with the Board's policy of checking the alleged membership of a union with employers' lists as of the date of the application and of the date of the hearing; and that since I was precluded by previous rulings of the Board from examining the membership cards or other evidence filed by the Applicant Union, the right to cross-examination was vital in order to bring out the relevant and material facts. Counsel for the Applicant Union submitted that the matter of resignations was irrelevant, that I was on a 'fishing expedition' and, after some further exchange, stated that while he objected to any cross-examination of the Union officials all of the cards did represent members in good standing according to 'the constitution of the Applicant Union'. He refused to deny receipt of resignations from membership in the Union received from employees in the said Circulation Department. The Chairman of the Board ruled against my right to cross-examine.

> 11. I thereupon submitted to the Board that since the Company was precluded by the Board's own regulation from soliciting evidence from employees to avoid being charged with interference with their rights under the regulations and since the Board had ruled against the right to cross-examine a heavy onus lay upon the Board

---

† *Re Ontario Labour Relations Board et al. and Globe Printing Co.*, [1951] 3 D.L.R. 162 (O.H.C.), aff'd. in [1952] 2 D.L.R. 302 (O.C.A.) and [1953] 3 D.L.R. 561 (S.C.C.).

to make a full and fair investigation in order to satisfy itself that a majority of the employees of the unit were members in good standing of the Applicant Union and I submitted that the Board should question the witness called on behalf of the Applicant Union and examine the documents filed for that purpose. Counsel for the Applicant Union objected thereto and the Board sustained the objection. I thereupon submitted to the Board that it ought to make a full and fair investigation, including the examination of some or all of the employees of the Company in the department concerned so that it might be satisfied that a majority of the employees were members of the Applicant Union and that they were members in good standing. Counsel for the Applicant Union objected to any such investigation on the ground of delay and I thereupon submitted to the Board that the issue could be resolved by a vote by secret ballot, as requested in the Reply. The hearing was concluded and the Board reserved its decision.

.   .   .   .

It is my view that the Company did not receive a proper hearing in this instance in that it was not allowed to see the documents filed by the Union or to cross-examine the person who made a statement as to their effect and thus it was denied a reasonable opportunity of meeting the case which was made against it. In one sense it might be said that the Company ought not to be concerned with the consequences of certification and accordingly that any irregularities at the hearing of the application are of no significance. But from the Company's standpoint extremely important results flow from the fact of certification. Indeed, so vital are the changes which may be wrought that usually the employer is as affected as any of the other parties involved. Its relations with its employees and its future wage-structure are two matters which may be materially altered. It is wrong, therefore, to contend that here the Company is any less touched by the certification than the Union or the employees. Its interest in the proceedings, though quite different, is certainly substantial.

.   .   .   .

It will be seen, therefore, that the case advanced by the Union, which the Company had to answer to resist certification successfully, was that the Union had as members in good standing 56 to 59 employees in a unit which the Board found to consist of 95 employees. How was the Company to answer the allegations thus made?

It might be thought that the Company could have called as witnesses the persons who were said to have resigned from the Union but it is to be pointed out that because of previous rulings of the Board the Company and its counsel had studiously refrained from indulging in any investigation concerning those resignations and they were not in possession of the names of those persons at the time of the hearing. That the Company's conduct in this regard was prudent is demonstrated by earlier decisions of the Board. I have in mind, for example, the views expressed by it in *Nat'l Paper Employees' Ass'n v. Nat'l Paper Goods Ltd.* 1 Dominion Labour Service, 7-1163 at p. 7-1164, where this was said:

> We cannot but feel, however, that Mr. Turnbull, who was fully cognizant of his legal position in the matter, as appears from his letter of September 24, 1943, addressed to a group of employees, was, to say the least, unwise in suggesting that they might obtain assistance from the man who had been acting as legal adviser to the respondent company. Without in any way casting any reflection on learned counsel concerned, it seems to us that such a suggestion may, in a proper case, provide evidence of a scheme on the part of the employer to interfere with the formation of a trade union or employees' organization. Coupled with even fragmentary additional evidence of unfair practices by an employer, we would probably be warranted in finding that the employer has violated section 19(1) of the Regulations.

.   .   .   .

... [T]he Company and its counsel were left with no alternative but to divert any effort of an employee to discuss his standing or position in the Union. Thus the respondents ignore reality when they argue that the Company might have met the factual allegations of the Union by calling the employees who were thought to have resigned. Even had their names been known, considerable suspicion might have been attendant upon the circumstance that the Company had persuaded them to come forward as its witnesses.

It might next be suggested that the Company could have called as a witness some official of the Union who could give information as to the number of employees in the Department who were then members of the Union, but that, of course, was quite unnecessary in view of the fact that Mr. Barnes, who had sworn the affidavit verifying the facts set forth on the application was present at the hearing and ought to have been made available for the purpose of cross-examination since he also made certain statements of fact on that occasion. The most effective way in which the Company could have tested the merits of the application was to cross-examine the person who was presenting it to the Board. Unfortunately, in this case the right to cross-examination was not granted and in that fact alone I think the Company was improperly excluded from a cardinal privilege which it enjoys under our jurisprudence; that exclusion, of itself, was tantamount to a denial of basic justice.

Lastly, the Company might have been able to defeat the application had it been allowed to see the bundle of membership cards or other documents handed to the Board by counsel for the Union. There is in evidence before me a statement to the effect that the Board has consistently ruled that employers are not entitled to examine membership cards filed by Unions upon applications for certification. Whatever might be said in favour of the

Board's policy in that respect if resort is to be had to the ruling, then full and fair opportunity ought always to be conferred upon the parties to the application other than the Union to challenge by cross-examination or otherwise the Union's assertion that it has as members in good standing a majority of the employees affected, for that is the most vital issue to be determined by the Board before it can certify the Union.

I reluctantly conclude, therefore, that in hearing the application in this matter the Board conducted itself in a manner which offends the principles of justice by declining to permit the Company to adduce evidence in the form of cross-examination or by denying to it the right to examine the documents which were filed by the Union. Accordingly, I have no hesitation in saying that the remedy of *certiorari* is available to the Company to quash the certificate unless s. 5 of the Act precludes that relief.

(g) Timing and Confidentiality: *Krever*†

NOTE

The Krever Commission was appointed to examine the Canadian blood system after thousands contracted HIV and Hepatitis C from blood and blood products. After devising detailed rules of procedure agreed to by all parties, the Commission held extensive hearings. On the last day of the hearings, the Commission sent out confidential notices warning certain parties that it might reach certain conclusions that could amount to misconduct within the meaning of s. 13 of the *Inquiries Act*.

Recipients of the misconduct notices argued, *inter alia*, that (i) if the Commissioner originally had jurisdiction, he lost it by sending out the notices too late in the proceedings; and that (ii) Commission counsel should be prohibited from taking part in the drafting of the final report because they had received confidential information that had not been disclosed to the Commissioner or the other parties.

Do you think the fact that the parties had all agreed to the general procedural rules influenced

the Court's decision about the timing of the notices? On issue (ii), above, compare the Court's approach to the role of agency counsel here and in *Régie des permis d'alcool*, [1996] 3 S.C.R. 919 (Chapter 7, below). Should agencies be required to disclose to parties information generated by agency staff members as well as information received from other parties? (cf. *London Cable* case, above.)

EXTRACTS

[CORY J., for the Court:]

. . . .

[para29] Commissions of inquiry have a long history in Canada, and have become a significant and useful part of our tradition. They have frequently played a key role in the investigation of tragedies and made a great many helpful recommendations aimed at rectifying dangerous situations.

---

† *Canada (Attorney General) v. Canada (Commission of Inquiry on the Blood System in Canada — Krever Commission)*, [1997] 3 S.C.R. 440; aff'g. [1997] F.C.J. No 17 (QL) (F.C.A.); aff'g. [1996] 3 F.C. 259, 115 F.T.R. 81, 136 D.L.R. (4th) 449, 37 Admin. L.R. (2d) 260, [1996] F.C.J. No. 864.

. . . .

[para30] ... Undoubtedly, the ability of an inquiry to investigate, educate and inform Canadians benefits our society. A public inquiry before an impartial and independent commissioner which investigates the cause of tragedy and makes recommendations for change can help to prevent a recurrence of such tragedies in the future, and to restore public confidence in the industry or process being reviewed.

[para31] The inquiry's roles of investigation and education of the public are of great importance. Yet those roles should not be fulfilled at the expense of the denial of the rights of those being investigated. The need for the careful balancing was recognized by Décary J.A. when he stated at para. 32 "[t]he search for truth does not excuse the violation of the rights of the individuals being investigated". This means that no matter how important the work of an inquiry may be, it cannot be achieved at the expense of the fundamental right of each citizen to be treated fairly.

[para55] ... [P]rocedural fairness is essential for the findings of commissions may damage the reputation of a witness. For most, a good reputation is their most highly prized attribute. It follows that it is essential that procedural fairness be demonstrated in the hearings of the commission.

Fairness in Notices

[para56] That same principle of fairness must be extended to the notices pertaining to misconduct required by s. 13 of the *Inquiries Act*. A commission is required to give parties a notice warning of potential findings of misconduct which may be made against them in the final report. As long as the notices are issued in confidence to the party receiving them, they should not be subject to as strict a degree of scrutiny as the formal findings. This is because the purpose of issuing notices is to allow parties to prepare for or respond to any possible findings of misconduct which may be made against them. The more detail included in the notice, the greater the assistance it will be to the party. In addition, the only harm which could be caused by the issuing of detailed notices would be to a party's reputation. But so long as notices are released only to the party against whom the finding may be made, this cannot be an issue. The only way the public could find out about the alleged misconduct is if the party receiving the notice chose to make it public, and thus any harm to reputation would be of its own

doing. Therefore, in fairness to witnesses or parties who may be the subject of findings of misconduct, the notices should be as detailed as possible. Even if the content of the notice appears to amount to a finding that would exceed the jurisdiction of the commissioner, that does not mean that the final, publicized findings will do so. It must be assumed, unless the final report demonstrates otherwise, that commissioners will not exceed their jurisdiction.

. . . .

b.   Timing of the Notices

[para68] The appellants submit that because the Commissioner waited until the last day of hearings to issue notices identifying potential findings of misconduct which might be made against them, their ability to cross-examine witnesses effectively and present evidence was compromised. They submit that there is no longer any opportunity to cure the prejudice caused by the late delivery of the notices, and that they must therefore be quashed. For the following reasons, I must disagree.

[para69] There is no statutory requirement that the commissioner give notice as soon as he or she foresees the possibility of an allegation of misconduct. While I appreciate that it might be helpful for parties to know in advance the findings of misconduct which may be made against them, the nature of an inquiry will often make this impossible. Broad inquiries are not focussed on individuals or whether they committed a crime; rather they are concerned with institutions and systems and how to improve them. It follows that in such inquiries there is no need to present individuals taking part in the inquiry with the particulars of a "case to meet" or notice of the charges against them, as there would be in criminal proceedings. Although the notices should be given as soon as it is feasible, it is unreasonable to insist that the notice of misconduct must always be given early. There will be some inquiries, such as this one, where the Commissioner cannot know what the findings may be until the end or very late in the process. So long as adequate time is given to the recipients of the notices to allow them to call the evidence and make the submissions they deem necessary, the late delivery of notices will not constitute unfair procedure.

[para70] The timing of notices will always depend upon the circumstances. Where the evidence is extensive and complex, it may be impossible to give the notices before the end of the hearings. In other

situations, where the issue is more straightforward, it may be possible to give notice of potential findings of misconduct early in the process. In this case, where there was an enormous amount of information gathered over the course of the hearings, it was within the discretion of the Commissioner to issue notices when he did. As Décary J.A. put it at para. 79:

> ... the Commissioner enjoys considerable latitude, and is thereby permitted to use the method best suited to the needs of his inquiry. I see no objection in principle to a commissioner waiting until the end of the hearings, when he or she has all the information that is required, to give notices, rather than taking a day to day approach to it, with the uncertainty and inconvenience that this might involve.

In light of the nature and purposes of this Inquiry, it was impossible to give adequate detail in the notices before all the evidence had been heard. In the context of this Inquiry the timing of the notices was not unfair.

[para71] Further, the appellants were given an adequate opportunity to respond to the notices, and to adduce additional evidence, if they deemed it necessary. The notices were delivered on December 21, 1995, and parties were initially given until January 10, 1996 to decide whether and how they would respond. This period was then extended following requests from the parties. The time permitted for the response was adequate. It cannot be said that

the timing of the delivery of the notices amounted to a violation of procedural fairness.

. . . .

[para72] The appellant Red Cross Society argues that because Commission counsel received confidential documents concerning allegations against the appellants, they should be forbidden from taking part in the drafting of the report. This argument too is premature, because there is no indication that the Commissioner intends to rely upon his counsel to draft the final report. In addition, it is not clear from the record what was contained in the confidential submissions reviewed by counsel. If the submissions were composed merely of suggested allegations, then I do not believe that there is any merit to this complaint. However, in the unlikely event that the submissions also included material that was not disclosed to the parties, there could well be valid cause for concern. As Décary J.A. put it at para. 103:

> The method adopted at the very end of the hearings for inviting submissions from the parties was particularly dangerous in that it opened the door to the possibility that a person in respect of whom unfavourable findings of fact would be made in the final report might not have had knowledge of all of the evidence relating to that person.

If the submissions did contain new, undisclosed and untested evidence, the Commissioner should not seek advice regarding the report from counsel who received the confidential submissions.

7

Administrative Procedure: Courts vs. Administrative Bodies

(a) Administrative Law and the Court Model

As suggested in Chapter 3, a key question for administrative law is the extent to which administrative bodies should resemble or differ from ordinary courts of law. On the one hand, Canadian and British administrative law have strong judicial roots. Some of the earliest administrators were justices of the peace, supervised by the higher ordinary courts of law. Today, many administrative bodies perform functions — such as dispensing licences to competing applicants — that seem to call for court-like safeguards. For these situations, many of us expect to see court-like institutional independence from political interference and judge-like impartiality in individual decisions. For these cases, we expect that those affected will have at least some opportunity to be heard and perhaps more specific protection from the centuries-old judicial norms of fair procedure. The court process hearing model serves an additional purpose by providing interested parties with the opportunity to participate directly in administrative decision-making.

One the other hand, administrative bodies are *not* courts. They are normally cheaper, more accessible, more informal, and more flexible than courts. Their decision-makers tend to have more specialized expertise than judges. Statutes generally give administrative bodies specific policy goals. They usually require administrators to do much more than to adjudicate competing claims. They give often give administrators important investigatory and regulatory functions, and may impose on them wide-ranging duties of a financial, managerial, or social nature. To help administrators pursue these goals, statutes may appear to contemplate decision-making processes that are far removed from formal trials in courts. Enabling acts may equip administrators with large staffs — rather than

a handful of court clerks — to help with their decisions. Moreover, to help ensure fair administrative decision-making, statutes may provide for internal review processes and a variety of other non-judicial safeguards. Some legislation may purport to restrict judicial safeguards.

Not surprisingly, then, the question of how far administrators *should* resemble courts, and *should* be subject to court-like procedural safeguards[1] is as difficult as it is important. Paradoxically, perhaps, it is often the courts themselves who must address this question. In applying the various forms of judicial control of administrative action, it is courts who must interpret the statutory and constitutional mandates of administrators and give them meaning in individual situations. At least in part, then, the scope of the court model in administrative law depends on judicial interpretation. The extracts in this chapter provide a few examples of this model and of the challenges involved in deciding whether and how to apply it.

Note

1. Other important practical matters may also hinge on the similarities or differences between administrators and courts. For example, on the extent to which administrative tribunals (unlike ordinary courts) may have standing to participate in appeals from their own decisions, see *Northwestern Utilities Ltd. v. City of Edmonton*, [1979] 1 S.C.R. 684, 708–10; and *CAIMAW v. Paccar of Canada Ltd.*, [1989] 2 S.C.R. 983. On the extent to which administrative tribunals (like ordinary courts) can decide about the constitutionality of laws, see *Douglas/Kwantlen Faculty Assn. v. Douglas College*, [1990] 3 S.C.R. 570; *Cuddy Chicks Ltd. v. Ontario (Labour Relations Board)*, [1991] 2 S.C.R. 5; *Tétreault-Gadoury v. Canada (Employment and Immigration Commission)*, [1991] 2 S.C.R. 22; *Bell v. Canada (Canadian Human Rights Commission); Cooper v. Canada (Canadian Human Rights Commission)*, [1996] 3 S.C.R. 854 (and note the critical reconsideration by Lamer C.J. at paras. 1–65).

(b) Role of Judge: *Jones*†

NOTE

Lord Denning's eloquent judgment in *Jones* illustrates the length to which our system goes to promote impartiality and objectivity in the ordinary courts of law. In this case, a widow had sued the National Coal Board in regard to her husband's death. Anxious to determine exactly what had happened, the trial judge had intervened actively in the examination-in-chief and cross-examination. With the best of intentions, said Lord Denning, the trial judge had overstepped the mark, and there must be a new trial.

Impartiality and objectivity are usually valuable goals in the administrative process too. Reviewing courts try to promote them through the *audi alteram partem* and bias branches of the rules of natural justice. But in the administrative process these goals must often be balanced against other needs — making use of administrative expertise, considering policy, preserving accountability, and promoting efficiency. How to set this balance, and where to abandon or relax the strict judicial model, is one of the most difficult challenges of administrative law.

EXTRACTS

[DENNING L.J.:]

. . . .

No one can doubt that the judge, in intervening as he did, was actuated by the best motives. He was anxious to understand the details of this complicated case, and asked questions to get them clear in his mind. He was anxious that the witnesses should not be harassed unduly in cross-examination, and intervened to protect them when he thought necessary. He was anxious to investigate all the various criticisms that had been made against the board, and to see whether they were well founded or not. Hence he took them up himself with the witnesses from time to time. He was anxious that the case should not be dragged on too long, and intimated clearly when he thought that a point had been sufficiently explored. All those are worthy motives on which

judges daily intervene in the conduct of cases and have done for centuries.

Nevertheless, we are quite clear that the interventions, taken together, were far more than they should have been. In the system of trial which we have evolved in this country, the judge sits to hear and determine the issues raised by the parties, not to conduct an investigation or examination on behalf of society at large, as happens, we believe, in some foreign countries. Even in England, however, a judge is not a mere umpire to answer the question "How's that?" His object above all is to find out the truth, and to do justice according to law; and in the daily pursuit of it the advocate plays an honourable and necessary role. Was it not Lord Eldon, L.C., who said in a notable passage the "truth is best discovered by powerful statements on both sides of the question" (see *Ex p. Lloyd* (1) (1822), Mont. 70, n.) and Lord Greene, M.R., who explained that justice is best done by a judge who holds the balance between the contending parties without himself taking part in their disputations? If a judge, said Lord Greene, should himself conduct the examination of witnesses,

"he, so to speak, descends into the arena and is liable to have his vision clouded by the dust of the conflict."

See *Yuill* v. *Yuill* (2) ([1945] 1 All E.R. 183 at p. 180).

Yes, he must keep his vision unclouded. It is all very well to paint justice blind, but she does better without a bandage round her eyes. She should be blind indeed to favour or prejudice, but clear to see which way lies the truth: and the less dust there is about the better. Let the advocates one after the other put the weights into the scales — the "nicely calculated less or more" — but the judge at the end decides which way the balance tilts, be it ever so slightly. So firmly is all this established in our law that the judge is not allowed in a civil dispute to call a witness whom he thinks might throw some light on the facts. He must rest content with the witnesses called by the parties; see *Re Enoch & Zardsky, Book & Co.* (3) ([1910] 1 K.B. 327). So also it is for the advocates, each in his turn, to examine the witnesses, and not for the judge to take it on himself lest by so

---

† *Jones v. National Coal Board*, [1957] 2 All E.R. 155 (C.A.).

doing he appear to favour one side or the other; see *R.* v. *Cain* (4) ((1936), 25 Cr. App. Rep. 204); *R.* v. *Bateman* (5) ((1946), 31 Cr. App. Rep. 106); and *Harris* v. *Harris* (6) (Apr. 8, 1952, The Times, Apr. 9, 1952) by Birkett L.J., especially. And it is for the advocate to state his case as fairly and strongly as he can, without undue interruption, lest the sequence of his argument be lost; See *R.* v. *Clewer* (7) ((1953), 37 Cr. App. Rep. 37). The judge's part in all this is to hearken to the evidence, only himself asking questions of witnesses when it is necessary to clear up any point that has been overlooked or left obscure; to see that the advocates behave themselves seemly and keep to the rules laid down by law; to exclude irrelevancies and discourage repetition; to make sure by wise intervention that he follows the points that the advocates are making and can assess their worth; and at the end to make up his mind where the truth lies. If he goes beyond this, he drops the mantle of a judge and assumes the robe of an advocate; and the change does not become him well. Lord Bacon spoke right when he said that:

> "Patience and gravity of hearing is an essential part of justice; and an ever-speaking judge is no well-tuned cymbal."

Such are our standards. They are set so high that we cannot hope to attain them all the time. In the very pursuit of justice, our keenness may out-run our sureness, and we may trip and fall. That is what has happened here. A judge of acute perception, acknowledged learning, and actuated by the best of motives, has nevertheless himself intervened so much in the conduct of the case that one of the parties — nay, each of them — has come away complaining that he was not able properly to put his case; and these complaints are, we think, justified.

(c) Trial and Administrative Hearing Patterns

TYPICAL STAGES OF A CIVIL TRIAL

1. **Opening statements**
   (a) by counsel for plaintiff (summary of relevant facts, introduction of documents, and statement of relief sought);
   (b) by counsel for defendant (optional)

2. **Examination-in-chief**
   (a) examination of plaintiff's witnesses by counsel for plaintiff;
   (b) examination of defendant's witnesses by counsel for defendant

3. **Cross-examination**
   (a) of defendant's witnesses by counsel for plaintiff;
   (b) of plaintiff's witnesses by counsel for defendant

4. **Closing statements**
   (a) [by] counsel for plaintiff;
   (b) [by] counsel for defendant

POSSIBLE STAGES OF AN ADMINISTRATIVE AGENCY ORAL HEARING[†]

Applicant Presents His [or Her] Case

Calls first witness examination-in-chief by applicant
cross-examination by respondents
re-examination by applicant
clarification questions by decision-maker

Calls second witness
examination-in-chief by respondent
cross-examination by applicant
cross-examination by respondents
re-examination by applicant
clarification questions by decision-maker

and so forth until the applicant has no further witnesses

Respondent Presents His [or Her] Case

Calls first witness
examination-in-chief by respondent
cross-examination by applicant
re-examination by respondent
clarification questions by decision-maker

[†] Excerpts from R.W. Macaulay and J.L. Sprague, *Hearings Before Administrative Tribunals* (Scarborough, Ont.: Carswell, 1995) at 12–14. Reproduced by permission of Carswell, a division of Thomson Canada Limited.

and so forth until the respondent has no further witnesses

> Summary of evidence and argument by applicant
> Summary of evidence and argument by respondent
> examination-in-chief by respondent
> cross-examination by applicant
> cross-examination by respondents
> re-examination by applicant
> clarification questions by decision-maker

Macaulay and Sprague go on to note that "[w]hile in some cases this process may be very effective, there no rule that an oral hearing may be structured this way": *Hearings Before Administrative Tribunals* at 14. Many administrative decisions are made much more informally and simply than this.

(d) Bias and Expertise: *Crowe*†

NOTE

Most members of regulatory agencies and other public authorities are expected to have special expertise in their field. Not surprisingly, many administrators have had prior experience in the areas they are supposed to regulate as administrators. However, where an administrator is expected to resolve disputes between individual parties, too close a connection with one or more of the parties can create the appearance of bias.

In this classic case on bias, Marshall Crowe, chairman of the National Energy Board, was the member of a Board panel formed to hear an application to ship Arctic gas to southern Canada. However, Mr. Crowe had been associated with this project prior to his membership on the Board. Was this association close enough to create a reasonable apprehension of bias? Note how, although the majority and dissenting judges agreed on the "reasonable apprehension" test for bias, they were at odds on how to measure it. What factors were used to assess the proximity between Mr. Crowe's position on the panel and his earlier involvement? Which opinion do you prefer? That of the majority or the dissent? Why?

EXTRACTS

[LASKIN, C.J.C.:]

On March 11, 1976, this Court gave judgment in an appeal from a decision of the Federal Court of Appeal which answered in the negative a question referred to it by the National Energy Board pursuant to s. 28 (4) of the *Federal Court Act*, R.S.C. 1970, c. 10 (2nd Supp.). The question so referred was as follows:

> Would the Board err in rejecting the objections and in holding that Mr. [Marshall] Crowe was not disqualified from being a member of the panel on grounds of reasonable apprehension or reasonable likelihood of bias?

This Court allowed the appeal, set aside the decision of the Federal Court of Appeal and declared that the question should be answered in the affirmative. It stated in its formal judgment on March 11, 1976, that reasons of the majority and dissenting Judges would be delivered later. The reasons of the majority now follow. The issue referred to the Federal Court of Appeal and which came by leave to this Court arose in connection with the organization of hearings by the National Energy Board to consider competing applications for a Mackenzie Valley pipeline, that is, applications for a certificate of public convenience and necessity under s. 44 of the *National Energy Board Act*, R.S.C. 1970, c. N-6. One of the applications, filed on March 21, 1974, by Canadian Arctic Gas Pipeline Limited was in respect of a proposed natural gas pipeline and associated works to move natural gas in an area of the Northwest Territories (the Mackenzie River Delta and Beaufort Basin) to markets in southern Canada and also to move natural gas in Alaska to markets in other States of the United States. This application was supplemented by other material filed on January 23, 1975, on March 10, 1975, and on May 8, 1975.

---

† *Committee for Justice and Liberty et al. v. National Energy Board (Crowe case)* (1976), 68 D.L.R. (3d) 716 (S.C.C.).

The competing application, filed in March, 1975, by Foothills Pipe Lines Ltd., was for a natural gas pipeline to move natural gas only from the area in the Northwest Territories, mentioned above, to southern Canada markets and not from Alaska as well.

On April 17, 1975, the National Energy Board assigned Mr. Crowe, Chairman of the Board and two other members (of eight members in all who then constituted the Board) to be the panel, with Mr. Crowe presiding, to hear the applications, beginning on October 27, 1975. Under s. 45 of its governing statute the Board was empowered to give standing at its s. 44 hearings to "interested persons", and it was then obliged to hear their objections to the granting of a certificate of public convenience and necessity. The three appellants in this case, the Committee for Justice and Liberty Foundation, the Consumers' Association of Canada and the Canadian Arctic Resources Committee were recognized by the Board as "interested persons" as were other organizations and individuals. In all, some 88 parties were represented at the commencement of the hearings, and of these 80 indicated that they had no objection to Mr. Crowe continuing as a member and presiding over the hearings. One of the non-objectors was Canadian Arctic Gas Pipeline Limited, one of the applicants for a certificate. It was its counsel who raised on July 9, 1975, the question of reasonable apprehension of bias on Mr. Crowe's part in favour of his client by reason of Mr. Crowe's association with a Study Group out of whose deliberations and decisions the applicant was born.

When the hearings opened on October 27, 1975, as scheduled, Mr. Crowe read a statement detailing his involvement with the Study Group. Objections were then invited. In the result, the question mentioned at the beginning of the reasons was referred to the Federal Court of Appeal on October 29, 1975. I turn now to deal with the facts upon which the issue of reasonable apprehension of bias is raised.

Mr. Marshall Crowe became chairman of the National Energy Board and its chief executive officer on October 15, 1973. Immediately prior to that date he was president of the Canada Development Corporation, assuming that position late in 1971, after first being a provisional director following the enactment of the *Canada Development Corporation Act* by 1970-71-72 (Can.), c. 49....

. . . .

As president of the Canada Development Corporation and as its representative, Mr. Crowe became associated with the Gas Arctic-Northwest Project Study Group which, pursuant to an agreement of June 1, 1972 (hereinafter referred to as the Study Group Agreement), embarked on a consideration of the physical and economic feasibility of a northern natural gas pipeline to bring natural gas to southern markets.

The Study Group Agreement brought together two groups of companies which had previously been exploring separately the feasibility of a natural gas pipeline. The participating companies merged their efforts and resources to that end, and pursuant to the Study Group Agreement they set up two companies, Canadian Arctic Gas Study Limited and Canadian Arctic Gas Pipeline Limited. The first-mentioned company was the vehicle for seeing to the various studies involved in carrying out the pre-construction purposes of the Study Group, and the second company, which was incorporated on November 3, 1972, was to be the operating vehicle which would apply for permission to build the pipeline in implementation of the project....

. . . .

The Canada Development Corporation became a member of the Study Group on November 30, 1972. Mr. Crowe was its designated representative and, as such, became, on December 7, 1972, a member of the Management Committee. He had attended a meeting of the executive committee as an observer on October 25, 1972, when the participation of the Canada Development Corporation was being worked out, but he did not later become a member of that committee, although he attended two other meetings thereof. In addition to being a member of the powerful Management Committee, Mr. Crowe became also a member of its finance, tax and accounting committee, and was elected vice-chairman thereof on January 25, 1973. During the period of his membership of the Management Committee, from December 7, 1972, until October 15, 1973, he participated in the seven meetings that it held in that span of time and joined in a unanimous decision of that committee on June 27, 1973, respecting the ownership and routing of a Mackenzie Valley pipeline.

. . . .

Although Mr. Crowe resigned from the presidency of the Canada Development Corporation as of October 15, 1973, when he became chairman and chief executive officer of the National Energy Board, the Canada Development Corporation continued as a full participant in the Study Group until October 31, 1975, becoming an associate member as of November 1, 1975, pursuant to a resolution of the Management Committee. As such, it had the following rights (as stated by counsel for the Canadian Arctic Gas Pipeline Limited to the Federal Court of Appeal on December 8, 1975):

1. For so long as an Equity Commitment Letter dated April 22, 1975, remains in effect CDC will be entitled to receive notice of, and attend, through a non-voting representative all meetings of all Committees of the Study Group except the Executive Committee of the Management Committee.
2. To receive all materials that a full participant would be from time to time entitled to receive.

In turn the CDC agrees to be bound by the confidentiality rules binding all participants.

This relationship may after 31 December, 1975, be terminated by either party.

The equity commitment letter of April 22, 1975 indicates a provisional interest in subscribing for $100 million of [equity] in the capital of CAGPL subject to the terms and conditions set out in that letter.

In brief, the Canada Development Corporation remained a full participant long after the applications were made for certificates of public convenience and necessity and after the hearings thereon commenced, and, in effect, until the National Energy Board referred to the Federal Court of Appeal the question concerning reasonable apprehension of bias in Mr. Crowe. During the period of Mr. Crowe's association with the Study Group as the representative of the Canada Development Corporation the latter contributed a total of 1.2 million dollars to the activities of the Study Group as its share of expenses.

Section 44 of the *National Energy Board Act*, the central provision respecting certificates of public convenience and necessity, reads as follows:

44. The Board may, subject to the approval of the Governor in Council, issue a certificate in respect of a pipeline or an international power line if the Board is satisfied that the line is and will be required by the present and future public convenience and necessity, and, in considering an application for a certificate, the Board shall take into account all such matters as to it appear to be relevant, and without limiting the generality of the foregoing, the Board may have regard to the following:
(a) the availability of oil or gas to the pipeline, or power to the international power line, as the case may be;

(b) the existence of markets, actual or potential;
(c) the economic feasibility of the pipeline or international power line;
(d) the financial responsibility and financial structure of the applicant, the methods of financing the line and the extent to which Canadians will have an opportunity of participating in the financing, engineering and construction of the line; and
(e) any public interest that in the Board's opinion may be affected by the granting or the refusing of the application.

. . . .

What must be kept in mind here is that we are concerned with a s. 44 application in respect of which, in my opinion, the Board's function is *quasi-judicial* or, at least, is a function which it must discharge in accordance with rules of natural justice, not necessarily the full range of such rules that would apply to a Court (although I note that the Board is a Court of record under s. 10 of its Act) but certainly to a degree that would reflect integrity of its proceedings and impartiality in the conduct of those proceedings. This is not, however, a prescription that would govern an inquiry under ss. 14(2) and 22.

I am of the opinion that the only issue here is whether the principle of reasonable apprehension or reasonable likelihood of bias applies to the Board in respect of hearings under s. 44. If it does apply — and this was accepted by all the respondents — then, on the facts herein, I can see no answer to the position of the appellants.

Before setting out the basis of this conclusion I wish to reiterate what was said in the Federal Court of Appeal and freely conceded by the appellants, namely, that no question of personal or financial or proprietary interest, such as to give rise to an allegation of actual bias, is raised against Mr. Crowe....

. . . .

... I do not think that Mr. Crowe's representative capacity is a material consideration on the issue in question here, any more than representative capacity would be a material consideration if the president or chairman of one of the other participants in the Study Group had been appointed chairman of the National Energy Board and had then proceeded to sit on an application which he had a hand in fashioning, albeit he was divorced from the Study Group at the time the application was filed. Mr. Crowe was not a mere cipher carrying messages from the board of directors of the Canada Development Corporation and having no initiative or flexibility in the manner and degree of his participation in the work of the Study Group. Nowhere in the Study Group Agreement nor in the minutes of proceedings of the Management Committee is there any indication that the representatives came to the meetings with fixed instructions from which they could not depart without a reference back. The nature of the exercise carried on under the Study Group Agreement required the representatives to apply their own judgment and their own talents to the joint project, with of course concern for the interests of the companies that they represented and subject, of course, to such directions as the companies might give.

. . . .

... The application of Canadian Arctic Gas Pipeline Limited was filed five months after the resignation and the consequent departure of Mr. Crowe from the Study Group. Be that as it may, we are not dealing with a case where Mr. Crowe's association with the Study Group is by virtue of that fact alone urged as a disqualification, for example, in relation to some application that the Study Group has initiated or promoted after Mr. Crowe's termination of his relationship with the Group. While I would not see any vice in Mr. Crowe sitting on an application coming from or through the Study Group in relation to a matter in which he was not involved, even though it was decided upon shortly after his dissociation from the Study Group, that is not this case.

. . . .

... To say ... therefore, that the issues before the Board are different than those to which the Study Group directed itself is not entirely correct, save as it reflects the different roles of the Board and of the Study Group. Moreover, it does not meet the central issue in this case, namely, whether the presiding member of a panel hearing an application under s. 44 can be said to be free from any reasonable apprehension of bias on his part when he had a hand in developing and approving important underpinnings of the very application which eventually was brought before the panel.

. . . .

... The vice of reasonable apprehension of bias lies not in finding correspondence between the decisions in which Mr. Crowe participated and all the statutory prescriptions under s. 44, especially when that provision gives the Board broad discretion "to

take into account all such matters as to it appear to be relevant", but rather in the fact that he participated in working out some at least of the terms on which the application was later made and supported the decision to make it. The Federal Court of Appeal had no doubt that Mr. Crowe (to use its words) "took part in [the] meetings and in the decisions taken which ... dealt with fairly advanced plans for the implementation of the pipeline project".

I come then to the question whether the Federal Court of Appeal's negative answer to the question propounded to it is supportable. I have already indicated that the Court introduced considerations into its test of reasonable apprehension of bias which should not be part of its measure. When the concern is, as here, that there be no prejudgment of issues (and certainly no predetermination) relating not only to whether a particular application for a pipeline will succeed but also to whether any pipeline will be approved, the participation of Mr. Crowe in the discussions and decisions leading to the application made by Canadian Arctic Gas Pipeline Limited for a certificate of public convenience and necessity, in my opinion, cannot but give rise to a reasonable apprehension, which reasonably well-informed persons could properly have, of a biased appraisal and judgment of the issues to be determined on a s. 44 application.

The Court in fixing on the test of reasonable apprehension of bias ... was merely restating what Rand, J. said in *Szilard* v. *Szasz*, [1955] 1 D.L.R. 370 at p. 373, [1955] S.C.R. 3 at pp. 6–7, in speaking of the "probability of reasoned suspicion of biased appraisal and judgment, unintended though it be". This test is grounded in a firm concern that there be no lack of public confidence in the impartiality of adjudicative agencies, and I think that emphasis is lent to this concern in the present case by the fact that the National Energy Board is enjoined to have regard for the public interest.

For these reasons, the appeal is allowed and the question submitted to the Federal Court of Appeal is answered in the affirmative. As stated in the formal judgment of this Court, delivered on March 11, 1976, there will be no order as to costs.

MARTLAND and JUDSON, JJ., concur with de GRANDPRE, J.

RITCHIE, SPENCE, PIGEON and DICKSON, JJ., concur with LASKIN, C.J.C.

[de GRANDPRE, J. (dissenting):]

. . . .

... [T]he National Energy Board is a tribunal that must be staffed with persons of experience and expertise. As was said by Hyde, J., of the Quebec court of Appeal in *R. v. Picard et al., ex p. Int'l Longshoremen's Ass'n, Local 375* (1967), 65 D.L.R. (2d) 658 at p. 66, [1968] Que. Q.B. 301:

> Professional persons are called upon to serve in judicial, *quasi* judicial and administrative posts in many fields and if Governments were to exclude candidates on such ground, they would find themselves deprived of the services of most professionals with any experience in the matters in respect of which their services are sought. Accordingly, I agree with the Court below that this ground was properly rejected.

. . . .

... The Board is not a Court nor is it a *quasi*-judicial body. In hearing the objections of interested parties and in performing its statutory functions, the Board has the duty to establish a balance between the administration of policies they are duty bound to apply and the protection of the various interests spelled out in s. 44 of the *Act*. The decision to be made by the Board transcends the interest of the parties and involves the public interest at large. In reaching its decision, the Board draws upon its experience, upon the experience of its own experts, upon the experience of all agencies of the Government of Canada and, obviously, is not and cannot be limited to deciding the matter on the sole basis of the representations made before it. It is not possible to apply to such a body the rules of bias governing the conduct of a Court of law.

II

Such being the legal principles involved, what would a reasonable and right-minded person have discovered if he had taken the time and trouble of informing himself of the true situation?

He would first have discovered[,] in the words of the representative of the Committee for Justice and Liberty Foundation before the Board on October 27, 1975, that the industry "had foreseen the need to transport northern natural gas south several years ago" and that "Mr. Crowe was actively involved in a sequence of decisions based on the presupposition that a pipeline was required". In other words, the basic decision to build a pipeline or at least to make an application to the National Energy Board was taken in principle long before Mr. Crowe became involved in the Study Group and for that matter the CDC....

. . . .

What else would the reasonable and right-minded person have discovered had he decided to inform himself of the true situation? He would have found that

. . . .

the Study Group which during the participation of Mr. Crowe had decided only two things, namely, routing and ownership, had split and that the applications now before the Board, competing as they are for the obtaining of the certificate under s. 44 of the Act, are in fact being made by parties who during Mr. Crowe's participation in the work of the Study Group, had expressed concurrence in the decision of June 27, 1973, which is the major gun in appellant's arsenal.

Thus it follows that to a considerable degree the sole decision taken by Mr. Crowe and his partners, namely, that relative to routing and ownership, was now being contested by some of the participants who at the time agreed therewith.

. . . .

The reasonable and right-minded person would also have learned that the applications had been from time to time modified so that the proposal put forth by Arctic Gas and which the Board was to examine in the course of the hearings which started on October 27 last would be different from that examined by the Study Group between December, 1972, and November, 1973.

. . . .

He would also have learned that the Government of Canada as well as the Governments of British Columbia, Saskatchewan, Manitoba, Ontario and Quebec have expressly recognized that they cannot entertain any reasonable apprehension of bias on the part of Mr. Crowe. Nothing has been heard from the Province of Alberta but considering its vital interest in the subject-matter, it is reasonable to infer that its silence is a complete acceptance of Mr. Crowe's ability to render justice. It is not unreasonable to assume that these seven Governments together would look after the public interest and would be the first to raise the question of bias if any reasonable apprehension existed that the basic principles would be offended by the presence of Mr. Crowe.

In my opinion, the Court of Appeal was right in concluding that no reasonable apprehension of bias by reasonable, right minded and informed persons could be entertained.

For all these reasons, as well as for those of the Court of Appeal, I would dismiss the appeal with costs.

Appeal allowed.

(e) Bias and the *Charter*: *Idziak*†

NOTE

The common law presumption against bias arises in several different situations. It can range from *simple prejudgment* as the result of an earlier statement or action of the decision-maker,[1] to *prior involvement*, as in the *Crowe* case; and *undue proximity* between the decision-maker and one or more of the parties (also a factor in *Crowe*). Moreover, the alleged bias may be institutional, derived from the structure of the administrative body, or individual, derived from the actions or position of the individual administrator. The content of the common law presumption against bias ranges from the reasonable apprehension of bias test, applied in more *quasi*-judicial situations, to the closed mind test, applied where policy and discretion are paramount.

Charter provisions such as s. 7 add another dimension to bias. Although the courts have established that s. 7 fundamental justice includes the common law rules of natural justice, it is not yet clear how far these are altered by s. 7. For example, although statutes can expressly override common law presumptions against bias, they cannot directly immunize administrators against *Charter*-based bias allegations. But can they protect administrators indirectly by designing structures that attract only minimal bias safeguards? *Idziak* touched on some of these questions.[2] How satisfactory were its answers?

The United States government sought to extradite Mr. Idziak, a 67-year-old prospector, to face fraud charges. Prosecution by Department of Justice lawyers at an extradition hearing led to a warrant of committal. The Minister of Justice then decided to sign a warrant of surrender releasing Mr. Idziak to U.S. authorities. Among other things, Mr. Idziak challenged the Minister of Justice's involvement in both the extradition hearing and the warrant of surrender decision. Mr. Idziak claimed this raised a reasonable apprehension of bias, contrary to fundamental justice in s. 7 of the *Charter*. The challenge failed in the Ontario courts and in the Supreme Court of Canada.

EXTRACTS

[CORY J. (for himself, L'HEUREUX-DUBÉ, and IACOBUCCI JJ.):]

. . . .

... [D]id the Minister of Justice breach the principles of fundamental justice guaranteed by s. 7 of the *Charter* in reaching the decision to surrender Mr. Idziak?

. . . .

... [*The Extradition Act*, R.S.C., 1985, c. E-23 provides that]:

25. Subject to this Part, the Minister of Justice, on the requisition of the foreign state, may, under his hand and seal, order a fugitive who has been committed for surrender to be surren-

---

† *Idziak v. Minister of Justice et al.*, [1992] 3 S.C.R. 631 (November 19, 1992. Present: Lamer C.J. and La Forest, L'Heureux-Dubé, Sopinka, Cory, McLachlin and Iacobucci JJ.)

[1] See, for example, *R. v. Pickersgill*, (1970), 14 D.L.R. (3d) 717 (Man. Q.B.) where it was alleged that a speech by the chairman of the former Canadian Transport Commission two months before a hearing showed that he had made up his mind in favour of discontinuing uneconomic railway lines. The court rejected the allegation, mainly on the ground that the speech addressed general government policy and not the merits of the hearing in question.

[2] The other main procedural issue in this case was whether the Minister should have disclosed to Mr. Idziak a memorandum prepared for the Minister by a Department of Justice lawyer.

dered to the person or persons who are, in the Minister's opinion, duly authorized to receive the fugitive in the name and on behalf of the foreign state, and the fugitive shall be so surrendered accordingly.

. . . .

Two positions were put forward on behalf of Mr. Idziak. First, it was said that the procedure followed by the Minister in deciding to surrender the applicant contravened the principles of fundamental justice guaranteed by s. 7 of the *Charter*. Second, it was argued that even if the procedure survives constitutional scrutiny the decision to surrender the appellant breached the substantive component of s. 7.

. . . .

It is clear ... that the application of the *Charter* to the extradition procedure empowers the courts to examine the fairness of the extradition procedure set out in the legislation. Further, the authorities make it clear that the decision of the Minister to issue a warrant of surrender pursuant to s. 25 of the *Extradition Act* must be exercised in accordance with the principles of fundamental justice.

. . . .

The elements of fairness form a minimum standard of s. 7 protection. The extent and nature of that protection, which is based upon the common law notion of procedural fairness, will depend upon the context in which it is claimed.... To determine the nature and extent of the procedural safeguards required by s. 7 a court must consider and balance the competing interest of the state and the individual. See *R.* v. *Lyons*, [1987] 2 S.C.R. 309, at p. 361, and *Chiarelli* v. *Canada (Minister of Employment and Immigration)*, [1992] 1 S.C.R. 711, at p. 744.

Did the Minister's Review Raise a Reasonable Apprehension of Bias?

(a) Is there Institutional bias created by the extradition process?

The extradition process in which Mr. Idziak was involved must then meet the minimal standards of procedural fairness. These standards will include the right to be heard by an unbiased decision-maker. It is the appellant's position that the *Extradition Act* creates an impermissible apprehension of bias. The issue of institutional bias was considered in *R.* v. *Lippé*, [1991] 2 S.C.R. 114. Chief Justice Lamer, with

whom the majority agreed on this point, defined the threshold test for a party claiming institutional bias in this way at p. 144:

> Step One: Having regard for a number of factors including, but not limited to, the nature of the occupation and the parties who appear before this type of judge, will there be a reasonable apprehension of bias in the mind of a fully informed person in a *substantial number* of cases?
>
> Step Two: If the answer to that question is no, allegations of an apprehension of bias cannot be brought on an institutional level, but must be dealt with on a case-by-case basis. [Emphasis in original.]

The requirement that the alleged bias occur in a substantial number of cases is met in this case as the challenged overlapping of the roles of the Minister of Justice in the extradition process would apply to every extradition proceeding. The difficulty arises in applying step two which requires a court to consider the "nature of the occupation" and the parties. In order to comply with this aspect of the test, it is necessary to examine the character of the impugned provisions.

It has been seen that the extradition process has two distinct phases. The first, the judicial phase, encompasses the court proceedings which determine whether a factual and legal basis for extradition exists. If that process results in the issuance of a warrant of committal, then the second phase is activated. There, the Minister of Justice exercises his or her discretion in determining whether to issue a warrant of surrender. The first decision-making phase is certainly judicial in its nature and warrants the application of the full panoply of procedural safeguards. By contrast, the second decision-making process is political in its nature. The Minister must weigh the representations of the fugitive against Canada's international treaty obligations. The differences in the procedures were considered in *Kindler* v. *Canada (Minister of Justice)*, [1991] 2 S.C.R. 779, at pp. 798–99:

> In this two-step process any issues of credibility or claims of innocence must be addressed by the extradition judge. Kindler had ample opportunity before Pinard J. to challenge the credibility of the evidence led against him at his trial. This he did not do. It was therefore not open to him to seek to adduce fresh evidence before the Minister of Justice as to the credibility of witnesses or his innocence of the offence. The Minister was obliged neither to consider such issues, nor to hear *viva voce* evidence.

. . . .

Parliament chose to give discretionary authority to the Minister of Justice. It is the Minister who must consider the good faith and honour of this country in its relations with other states. It is the Minister who has the expert knowledge of the political ramifications of an extradition decision. In administrative law terms, the Minister's review should be characterized as being at the extreme legislative end of the continuum of administrative decision-making.

The appellant contends that a dual role has been allotted to the Minister of Justice by the *Extradition Act*. The Act requires the Minister to conduct the prosecution of the extradition hearing at the judicial phase and then to act as adjudicator in the ministerial phase. These roles are said to be mutually incompatible and to raise an apprehension of bias on their face. This contention fails to recognize either the clear division that lies between the phases of the extradition process, each of which serves a distinct function, or to take into account the separation of personnel involved in the two phases.

It is correct that the Minister of Justice has the responsibility to ensure the prosecution of the extradition proceedings and that to do so the Minister must appoint agents to act in the interest of the requesting state. However the decision to issue a warrant of surrender involves completely different considerations from those reached by a court in an extradition hearing. The extradition hearing is clearly judicial in its nature while the actions of the Minister of Justice in considering whether to issue a warrant of surrender are primarily political in nature. This is certainly not a case of a single official acting as both judge and prosecutor in the same case. At the judicial phase the fugitive possesses the full panoply of procedural protection available in a court of law. At the ministerial phase, there is no longer a *lis* in existence. The fugitive has by then been judicially committed for extradition. The Act simply grants to the Minister a discretion as to whether to execute the judicially approved extradition by issuing a warrant of surrender.

It is significant that the appellant's argument has already been rejected by this Court in *United States of America* v. *Cotroni*, [1989] 1 S.C.R. 1469. At page 1500, La Forest J. noted:

> ... I find the argument that the fact that the executive discretion to refuse surrender and the duty to present requests for extradition in court, both fall within the responsibilities of the Minis-

ter of Justice, somehow create an unacceptable conflict to have no merit.

I agree with this comment. Certainly the arrangement could not raise apprehension of bias in a fully informed observer. The appellant's allegation of institutional bias must fail.

(b) Is there actual bias demonstrated by the Acts of the Minister?

The appellant next raised the argument that in the particular circumstances of this case, the reasonably informed person could have had a reasonable apprehension of bias by the Minister against the appellant. The determination of bias in a specific case will depend upon the characterization of the decision-maker's function. Administrative decision-making covers a broad spectrum. At the adjudicative end of the spectrum, the appropriate test is: could a reasonably informed bystander reasonably perceive bias on the part of the adjudicator? At the opposite end of the continuum, that is to say the legislative end of the spectrum, the test is: has the decision-maker pre-judged the matter to such an extent that any representations to the contrary would be futile? See *Newfoundland Telephone Co.* v. *Newfoundland (Board of Commissioners of Public Utilities)*, [1992] 1 S.C.C. 623, at p. 638.

The basis for the distinction is that, in an adjudicative proceeding, the parties' confidence in the result will depend upon the decision-maker's adhering to a standard of judicial impartiality. On the other hand, an administrative body created to determine policy issues may need the expert knowledge of members who are representative of interested parties. The legislative goal in creating such administrative bodies would be frustrated if courts held their members to the strict reasonable apprehension of bias standard. The exercise by the Minister of Justice of the authority to surrender an individual already judicially committed for extradition clearly falls in the legislative end of the continuum. The closed mind test applied in *Newfoundland Telephone, supra*, is applicable in this case.

There is no suggestion that the Minister was improperly influenced by anyone involved in prosecuting the extradition proceedings against Mr. Idziak nor is there any evidence that the Minister in any way pre-judged the matter. The appellant has certainly not established that the Minister as decision-maker held an impermissible bias against him. This submission of the appellant cannot be sustained.

. . . .

Summary

In summary, it can be said that:

(a) there is no institutional bias or unfairness in the statutory procedures enacted for the extradition of an individual;

(b) there was no apprehension of bias demonstrated at any point in the course of Mr. Idziak's hearings;

(c) viewed in light of the nature of the ministerial decision whether to issue a warrant of surrender, no unfairness was demonstrated by the refusal to produce the memorandum of a Department of Justice lawyer prepared for the Minister. Taken in the context of the ministerial decision, the document was properly entitled to solicitor-client privilege and need not have been produced.

Disposition

In the result the appeal must be dismissed.

[The following is the judgment of LAMER C.J. and McLACHLIN J. delivered by LAMER C.J.:]

I concur with the reasons of my colleague Justice Cory, except with respect to the issue of the solicitor-client privilege. While it may well be that the nature of the relationship involved here makes this document confidential, I would not want to decide in this case whether the confidentiality is grounded on the solicitor-client privilege. Given the conclusion that s. 7 of the *Canadian Charter of Rights and Freedoms* has not been violated, we do not need to deal with this issue in this case.

[The following is the judgment delivered by La FOREST J.:]

I fully agree with Mr. Justice Cory including (apart from some reservation as to nomenclature) his reasons regarding the Minister's privilege to refuse to reveal a confidential document. In my view, in considering the issue of surrender in the present case, the Minister was engaged in making a policy decision rather in the nature of an act of clemency. In making a decision of this kind, the Minister is entitled to consider the views of her officials who are versed in the matter. I see no reason why she should be compelled to reveal these views. She was dealing with a policy matter wholly within her discretion; see *Attorney General of Canada* v. *Inuit Tapirisat*, [1980] 2 S.C.R. 735, at pp. 753–54. It is thus unnecessary to hold that the Minister's privilege to keep the memorandum confidential falls within the solicitor-client privilege, and I prefer not to do so because I have not weighed the full implications of so holding.

[The following is the judgment delivered by SOPINKA J.:]

Subject to the reservation expressed by the Chief Justice which I share, I agree with Mr. Justice Cory.

(f) Board Counsel: *Régie des permis d'alcool*†

NOTE

The Régie des permis d'alcool du Québec cancelled a numbered company's liquor permit because of a "disturbance of public tranquility." The company challenged the decision in the courts, arguing that Régie breached the independence and impartiality guarantees in s. 23 of the Quebec *Charter of Human Rights and Freedoms*, R.S.Q., c. C-12. The company said this was because (i) Régie staff members, especially its lawyers, were involved in the investigation of cases, the filing of complaints, the presentation of cases to the directors, and the drafting of decisions; (ii) the directors of the Régie had tenure for only five years; and (iii) the Minister of Public Security, who was responsible for the police forces that conducted investigations for the Régie, also had a large role in the administration of the Régie's enabling Act.

---

† *2747-3174 Québec Inc. v. Quebec (Régie des permis d'alcool)*, [1996] 3 S.C.R. 919 (21 November 1996).

EXTRACTS

[GONTHIER, J. for himself, LAMER C.J. and La FOREST, SOPINKA, CORY, McLACHLIN, IACOBUCCI and MAJOR JJ.:]

. . . .

II — Relevant Statutory Provisions

[para5]

. . . .

Charter of Human Rights and Freedoms, R.S.Q., c. C-12

> 23. Every person has a right to a full and equal, public and fair hearing by an independent and impartial tribunal, for the determination of his rights and obligations or of the merits of any charge brought against him.

. . . .

[para39] The applicability of s. 23 having been established [because the Régie's functions are "quasi-judicial" as required by section 56 of the *Charter*], it is now necessary to consider the merits of the present case. Before doing so, however, I wish to note that, even in cases not involving s. 23, administrative agencies may be required to comply with the principles of natural justice under general law rules. It is clear that the purpose of those principles is to ensure in certain ways the impartiality and independence of the decision maker (see, for example, *Old St. Boniface Residents Assn. Inc.* v. *Winnipeg (City)*, [1990] 3 S.C.R. 1170; *Newfoundland Telephone Co.* v. *Newfoundland (Board of Commissioners of Public Utilities)*, [1992] 1 S.C.R. 623). The exact content of the rules to be followed will depend on all the circumstances, and in particular on the language of the statute under which the agency acts, the nature of the task it performs and the type of decision it is required to make. Conversely, the fact that an agency is subject to s. 23 does not mean that its structure must have the same characteristics as that of the courts. The flexibility this Court has shown in such matters is just as appropriate where s. 23 is concerned.

. . . .

[para44] As a result of *Lippé, supra*, and *Ruffo* v. *Conseil de la magistrature*, [1995] 4 S.C.R. 267, *inter alia*, the test for institutional impartiality is well established. It is clear that the governing factors are

those put forward by de Grandpré J. in *Committee for Justice and Liberty* v. *National Energy Board*, [1978] 1 S.C.R. 369, at p. 394. The determination of institutional bias presupposes that a well-informed person, viewing the matter realistically and practically — and having thought the matter through — would have a reasonable apprehension of bias in a substantial number of cases. In this regard, all factors must be considered, but the guarantees provided for in the legislation to counter the prejudicial effects of certain institutional characteristics must be given special attention.

. . . .

[para46] The arguments against the Régie des permis d'alcool relate primarily to its role at various stages in the liquor permit cancellation process. The Act authorizes employees of the Régie to participate in the investigation, the filing of complaints, the presentation of the case to the directors and the decision.

[para47] I note at the outset that a plurality of functions in a single administrative agency is not necessarily problematic. This Court has already suggested that such a multifunctional structure does not in itself always raise an apprehension of bias....

. . . .

[para48] Although an overlapping of functions is not always a ground for concern, it must nevertheless not result in excessively close relations among employees involved in different stages of the process. The lack of separation of roles within the Régie des permis d'alcool was the principal basis for the Court of Appeal's decision in the present case, which means that a thorough review of its institutional structure will be necessary.

. . . .

[para52] In practice, employees of the Régie are involved at every stage of the process leading up to the cancellation of a liquor permit, from investigation to adjudication. Thus, the Act authorizes the Régie to require permit holders to provide information (s. 110). Members of the Régie's staff designated by the chairman, or members of police forces, may also inspect establishments during business hours (s. 111). The Régie has signed memorandums of understanding with certain police forces to establish a framework for their role of inspection and seizure. The Régie can thus initiate the investi-

137

gation process. However, a formal investigation is not an absolute prerequisite for cancellation of a permit. The Régie may summon a permit holder of its own initiative or on the application of any interested person, including the Minister of Public Security (s. 85). As the annual report indicates, legal services lawyers participate in the preliminary review of files before the decision to summon a permit holder is made. Where the application for cancellation is made by a third party, s. 26 of the Regulation respecting the procedure applicable before the Régie des permis d'alcool du Québec, requires that the Régie summon the permit holder if the facts mentioned call prima facie for the enforcement of ss. 86 to 90 of the Act. The Act and regulations do not, however, specify the circumstances in which the Régie may proceed *proprio motu*.

[para53] If the Régie decides to hold a hearing, a notice of summons drafted by a legal services lawyer is sent to the permit holder. In the case at bar, the notice was signed by the chairman of the Régie. Where a ground related to public tranquility is involved, a hearing is then held before at least two directors designated by the chairman (ss. 15 and 16). One of the legal services lawyers acts as counsel for the Régie at that hearing. The directors must decide the matter and, in the case of a tied vote, the matter is referred to the Régie sitting in plenary session. The proceedings are completed with the publication of written reasons.

(ii) Role of the Régie's Lawyers

[para54] This detailed description of the Régie's structure and operations shows that the issue of the role of the lawyers employed by legal services is at the heart of this appeal. In my view, an informed person having thought the matter through would in this regard have a reasonable apprehension of bias in a substantial number of cases. The Act and regulations do not define the duties of these jurists.

The Régie's annual report, however, and the description of their jobs at the Régie, show that they are called upon to review files in order to advise the Régie on the action to be taken, prepare files, draft notices of summons, present arguments to the directors and draft opinions. The annual report and the silence of the Act and regulations leave open the possibility of the same jurist performing these various functions in the same matter. The annual report mentions no measures taken to separate the lawyers involved at different stages of the process. Yet it seems to me that such measures, the precise limits of which I will deliberately refrain from outlining,

are essential in the circumstances. Evidence as to the role of the lawyers and the allocation of tasks among them is incomplete, but the possibility that a jurist who has made submissions to the directors might then advise them in respect of the same matter is disturbing, especially since some of the directors have no legal training.

. . . .

[para56] Similarly, in the case at bar, the Régie's lawyers could not advise the directors and make submissions to them without there being a reasonable apprehension of bias.

This is not to say that jurists in the employ of an administrative tribunal can never play any role in the preparation of reasons. An examination of the consequences of such a practice would exceed the limits of this appeal, however, as I need only note, to dispose of it, that prosecuting counsel must in no circumstances be in a position to participate in the adjudication process. The functions of prosecutor and adjudicator cannot be exercised together in this manner.

. . . .

[para60] ... The fact that the Régie, as an institution, participates in the process of investigation, summoning and adjudication is not in itself problematic. However, the possibility that a particular director could, following the investigation, decide to hold a hearing and could then participate in the decision-making process would cause an informed person to have a reasonable apprehension of bias in a substantial number of cases. It seems to me that, as with the Régie's jurists, a form of separation among the directors involved in the various stages of the process is necessary to counter that apprehension of bias.

. . . .

[para61] The independence of administrative tribunals, which s. 23 of the *Charter* protects in addition to impartiality, is based, inter alia, on the relations the decision makers maintain with others and the objective circumstances surrounding those relations. In *Beauregard* v. *Canada*, [1986] 2 S.C.R. 56, at p. 69, Dickson C.J. defined independence as follows:

> Historically, the generally accepted core of the principle of judicial independence has been the complete liberty of individual judges to hear and decide the cases that come before them: no outsider — be it government, pressure group, individual or even another judge — should interfere

in fact, or attempt to interfere, with the way in which a judge conducts his or her case and makes his or her decision.

The three main components of judicial independence, namely security of tenure, financial security and institutional independence, were identified in *Valente, supra*. The purpose of these objective elements is to ensure that the judge can reasonably be perceived as independent and that any apprehension of bias will thus be eliminated. Independence is in short a guarantee of impartiality.

. . . .

[para65] The respondent relied primarily on the term of office of the directors and the method of dismissal. They are appointed by the government for a term of not more than five years (s. 4). Supplementary directors may also be appointed for as long as the government determines. The orders of appointment adduced in evidence refer to terms of two, three and five years....

. . . .

[para68] In the case at bar, the orders of appointment provide expressly that the directors can be dismissed only for certain specific reasons. In addition, it is possible for the directors to apply to the ordinary courts to contest an unlawful dismissal. In these circumstances, I am of the view that the directors have sufficient security of tenure within the meaning of *Valente*, since sanctions are available for any arbitrary interference by the executive during a director's term of office.

. . . .

[para69] It was suggested that the large number of points of contact between the Régie and the Minister of Public Security was problematic. The Minister is responsible for the application of the Act (s. 175). The Régie is required to submit a report to the Minister each year (s. 21) and the Minister may require information from the chairman on the agency's activities (s. 22). In addition, the Minister of Public Security must approve any rules the Régie might adopt in plenary session for its internal management (s. 24), and the Government must approve the various regulations made by the Régie (s. 116). Each year, the Minister also conducts the evaluation of the chairman of the Régie. Furthermore, the Minister is responsible for the various police forces that may, at the Régie's request, conduct investigations. Finally, the Minister may initiate the permit cancella-

tion process by submitting an application to the Régie under s. 85.

[para70] In light of the evidence as a whole, I do not consider these various factors sufficient to raise a reasonable apprehension with respect to the institutional independence of the Régie. It is not unusual for an administrative agency to be subject to the general supervision of a member of the executive with respect to its management. As Le Dain J. stated in *Valente*, at p. 712, the essential elements of institutional independence may be summed up as judicial control over the administrative decisions that bear directly and immediately on the exercise of the judicial function. It has not been shown how the Minister might influence the decision-making process. The chairman is responsible for monitoring the Régie's day-to-day activities and its various employees, and for preparing the rolls. The fact that the Minister of Public Security is ultimately responsible for both the Régie and the various police forces conducting investigations would not in my view cause an informed person to have a reasonable apprehension with respect to the independence of the directors. The directors swear an oath requiring them to perform the duties of their office honestly and fairly. The Minister's links with the various parties involved are accordingly not sufficient to raise concerns.

. . . .

[para71] The structure of the Régie does not meet the requirements of s. 23 of the *Charter*. However, the various shortcomings I have identified are not imposed by the constituent legislation or regulations made thereunder. Thus, I do not consider it necessary to declare specific provisions of the Act to be inconsistent with the *Charter*. It is sufficient to grant the respondent's motion in evocation and accordingly quash the Régie's decision.

[para72] The respondent is also seeking costs calculated on the basis of expenses actually incurred. Although I am proposing to allow the appeal, I would award costs to the respondent in light in particular of the fact that the issue is one of general interest and the success of the respondent's arguments in this Court. My award is limited to the usual tariff, however.

V — Conclusion

[para73] For these reasons, I would allow the appeal, set aside the judgments of the Court of Appeal and the Superior Court, grant the motion in evocation

and quash the Régie's decision of February 17, 1993 cancelling the respondent's liquor permits, the whole with costs to the respondent.

. . . .

[L'Heureux-Dubé J. delivered separate reasons.]

(g)   Institutional Decisions: *Consolidated-Bathurst*[†]

NOTE

A three-member panel of the Ontario Labour Relations Board decided tentatively that Consolidated-Bathurst had failed to bargain in good faith by not disclosing a planned plant closing during negotiations for a collective agreement. Because the issue involved general policy issues, a meeting of the full Board was held to discuss the panel's draft decision.

At the full Board meeting, the members of the original panel were apparently present. Traditional Board practice required that at such a meeting discussion was to be limited to the policy implications of the draft decision, the facts stated in it were not to be contested, no vote or consensus was to be taken, no minutes were to be kept, and no attendance was to be recorded. Apparently, all aspects of this traditional practice were followed. The panel then wrote their decision, which was against Consolidated-Bathurst.

Consolidated-Bathurst argued that this procedure violated the rules of natural justice, not only by depriving them of an opportunity to know the case against them, but by depriving them of a hearing before an unbiased adjudicator and of the right to the requirement that those who decide must also hear.

EXTRACTS

[The judgment of WILSON, La FOREST, L'HEUREUX-DUBÉ, GONTHIER and McLACHLIN JJ. was delivered by GONTHIER J.:]

I have had the opportunity to read the reasons of my colleague, Sopinka J., and I must respectfully disagree with his conclusions in this case. While I do not generally disagree with the summary of the facts,

decisions and issues, I consider it useful to refer to them in somewhat more detail.

The appeal is from a decision of the Court of Appeal of Ontario dismissing an application for judicial review of two decisions of the Ontario Labour Relations Board ("Board"). In the first decision, a tripartite panel composed of G.W. Adams, Q.C., Chairman of the Board, W.H. Wightman and B. F. Lee representing the management and labour sides respectively, decided, Mr. Wightman dissenting, that the appellant had failed to bargain in good faith with the respondent union because it did not disclose during the negotiations its impending decision to close the plant covered by the collective agreement. Counsel for the appellant then learned that a full board meeting had been called to discuss the policy implications of its decision when it was still in the draft stage. The parties were neither notified of nor invited to participate in this meeting. The appellant applied for a reconsideration of this decision under s. 106 of the *Labour Relations Act*, R.S.O. c. 228, on the ground that the full-board meeting had vitiated the Board's decision and on the ground that the evidence adduced at the first hearing had been improperly considered. The same panel rejected both these arguments in the second decision (the "reconsideration decision").

The Board's decisions were challenged in the Divisional Court on the basis: (1) that the original decision was manifestly unreasonable in fact and in law, and (2) that the full board meeting called by the Board prior to the panel's decision constituted a violation of the rules of natural justice. The Divisional Court rejected the first ground and the appellant did not raise this argument in the Court of Appeal nor in this Court. Thus, the only issue before this Court is whether the impugned meeting vitiated the first decision rendered by the Board on the ground that the case was there discussed with panel

---

[†]   Excerpts from *I.W.A. v. Consolidated-Bathurst Packaging Ltd.*, [1990] 1 S.C.R. 282 (S.C.C.) (15 March 1990) at pp. 308–9, 331–41. (Present: Lamer, Wilson, La Forest, L'Heureux-Dubé, Sopinka, Gonthier and McLachlin JJ.)

members by persons who did not hear the evidence nor the arguments.

In order to determine whether the principles of natural justice have been breached in this case, it is necessary to examine in some detail the facts which led to the initial complaint made by the respondent union. It will also be necessary to examine the evidence as to the purpose and the context of the full board meeting so as to understand the policy matters in issue at that meeting.

.   .   .   .

I am unable to agree with the proposition that any discussion with a person who has not heard the evidence necessarily vitiates the resulting decision because this discussion might "influence" the decision maker. In this respect, I adopt Meredith C.J.C.P.'s words in *Re Toronto and Hamilton Highway Commission and Crabb* (1916), 37 O.L.R. 656 (C.A.), at p. 659:

> The Board is composed of persons occupying positions analogous to those of judges rather than of arbitrators merely; and it is not suggested that they heard any evidence behind the back of either party; the most that can be said is that they — that is, those members of the Board who heard the evidence and made the award — allowed another member of the Board, who had not heard the evidence, or taken part in the inquiry before, to read the evidence and to express some of his views regarding the case to them.... [B]ut it is only fair to add that if every Judge's judgment were vitiated because he discussed the case with some other Judge a good many judgments existing as valid and unimpeachable ought to fall; and that if such discussions were prohibited many more judgments might fall in an appellate Court because of a defect which must have been detected if the subject had been so discussed. [Emphasis added.]

The appellant's main argument against the practice of holding full board meetings is that these meetings can be used to fetter the independence of the panel members. Judicial independence is a long standing principle of our constitutional law which is also part of the rules of natural justice even in the absence of constitutional protection. It is useful to define this concept before discussing the effect of full board meetings on panel members. In *Beauregard* v. *Canada*, [1986] 2 S.C.R. 56, Dickson C.J. described the "accepted core of the principle of judicial independence" as a complete liberty to decide a given case in accordance with one's conscience and opinions without interference from other persons, including judges, at p. 69:

> Historically, the generally accepted core of the principle of judicial independence has been the complete liberty of individual judges to hear and decide the cases that come before them: no outsider — be it government, pressure group, individual or even another judge — should interfere in fact, or attempt to interfere, with the way in which a judge conducts his or her case and makes his or her decision. This core continues to be central to the principle of judicial independence. See also *Valente* v. *The Queen*, [1985] 2 S.C.R. 673, at pp. 686–87, and Benyekhlef, *Les garanties constitutionnelles relatives à l'indépendance du pouvoir judiciaire au Canada*, at p. 48.

It is obvious that no outside interference may be used to compel or pressure a decision maker to participate in discussions on policy issues raised by a case on which he must render a decision. It also goes without saying that a formalized consultation process could not be used to force or induce decision makers to adopt positions with which they do not agree. Nevertheless, discussions with colleagues do not constitute, in and of themselves, infringements on the panel members' capacity to decide the issues at stake independently. A discussion does not prevent a decision maker from adjudicating in accordance with his own conscience and opinions nor does it constitute an obstacle to this freedom. Whatever discussion may take place, the ultimate decision will be that of the decision maker for which he assumes full responsibility.

The essential difference between full board meetings and informal discussions with colleagues is the possibility that moral suasion may be felt by the members of the panel if their opinions are not shared by other Board members, the chairman or vice-chairmen. However, decision makers are entitled to change their minds whether this change of mind is the result of discussions with colleagues or the result of their own reflection on the matter. A decision maker may also be swayed by the opinion of the majority of his colleagues in the interest of adjudicative coherence since this is a relevant criterion to be taken into consideration even when the decision maker is not bound by any *stare decisis* rule.

It follows that the relevant issue in this case is not whether the practice of holding full board meetings can cause panel members to change their minds but whether this practice impinges on the ability of panel members to decide according to their opinions. There is nothing in the *Labour Relations Act* which gives either the chairman, the vice-chairmen or other

Board members the power to impose his opinion on any other Board member. However, this de jure situation must not be thwarted by procedures which may effectively compel or induce panel members to decide against their own conscience and opinions.

It is pointed out that "justice should not only be done, but should manifestly and undoubtedly be seen to be done": *Rex* v. *Sussex Justices*, [1924] 1 K.B. 256, at p. 259. This maxim applies whenever the circumstances create the danger of an injustice, for example when there is a reasonable apprehension of bias, even if the decision maker has completely disregarded these circumstances. However, in my opinion and for the reasons which follow, the danger that full board meetings may fetter the judicial independence of panel members is not sufficiently present to give rise to a reasonable apprehension of bias or lack of independence within the meaning of the test stated by this Court in *Committee for Justice and Liberty* v. *National Energy Board*, [1978] 1. S.C.R. 369, at p. 394, reaffirmed and applied as the criteria for judicial independence in *Valente* v. *The Queen*, supra, at p. 684 (see also p. 689):

> ... the apprehension of bias must be a reasonable one, held by reasonable and right minded persons, applying themselves to the question and obtaining thereon the required information. In the words of the Court of Appeal, that test is "what would an informed person, viewing the matter realistically and practically — and having thought the matter through — [have] concluded...."

A full board meeting set up in accordance with the procedure described by Chairman Adams is not imposed: it is called at the request of the hearing panel or any of its members. It is carefully designed to foster discussion without trying to verify whether a consensus has been reached: no minutes are kept, no votes are taken, attendance is voluntary and presence at the full Board meeting is not recorded. The decision is left entirely to the hearing panel. It cannot be said that this practice is meant to convey to panel members the message that the opinion of the majority of the Board members present has to be followed. On the other hand, it is true that a consensus can be measured without a vote and that this institutionalization of the consultation process carries with it a potential for greater influence on the panel members. However, the criteria for independence is not absence of influence but rather the freedom to decide according to one's own conscience and opinions. In fact, the record shows that each panel member held to his own opinion since Mr. Wightman dissented and Mr. Lee only concurred in part with

Chairman Adams. It is my opinion, in agreement with the Court of Appeal, that the full board meeting was an important element of a legitimate consultation process and not a participation in the decision of persons who had not heard the parties. The Board's practice of holding full board meetings or the full board meeting held on September 23, 1983 would not be perceived by an informed person viewing the matter realistically and practically — and having thought the matter through — as having breached his right to a decision reached by an independent tribunal thereby infringing this principle of natural justice.

(d) Full Board Meetings and the Audi Alteram Partem Rule

Full board meetings held on an *ex parte* basis do entail some disadvantages from the point of view of the *audi alteram partem* rule because the parties are not aware of what is said at those meetings and do not have an opportunity to reply to new arguments made by persons present at the meeting. In addition, there is always the danger that the persons present at the meeting may discuss the evidence.

For the purpose of the application of the *audi alteram partem* rule, a distinction must be drawn between discussions on factual matters and discussions on legal or policy issues. In every decision, panel members must determine what the facts are, what legal standards apply to those facts and, finally, they must assess the evidence in accordance with these legal standards. In this case, for example, the Board had to determine which events led to the decision to close the Hamilton plant and, in turn, decide whether the appellant had failed to bargain in good faith by not informing of an impending plant closing either on the basis that a *"de facto* decision" had been taken or on some other basis. The determination and assessment of facts are delicate tasks which turn on the credibility of the witnesses and an overall evaluation of the relevancy of all the information presented as evidence. As a general rule, these tasks cannot be properly performed by persons who have not heard all the evidence and the rules of natural justice do not allow such persons to vote on the result. Their participation in discussions dealing with such factual issues is less problematic when there is no participation in the final decision. However, I am of the view that generally such discussions constitute a breach of the rules of natural justice because they allow persons other than the parties to make representations on factual issues when they have not heard the evidence.

It is already recognized that no new evidence may be presented to panel members in the absence of the parties: Kane v. *Board of Governors of the University of British Columbia*, supra, at pp. 1113–14. The appellant does not claim that new evidence was adduced at the meeting and the record does not disclose any such breach of the *audi alteram partem* rule. The defined practice of the Board at full board meetings is to discuss policy issues on the basis of the facts as they were determined by the panel. The benefits to be derived from the proper use of this consultation process must not be denied because of the mere concern that this established practice might be disregarded, in the absence of any evidence that this has occurred. In this case, the record contains no evidence that factual issues were discussed by the Board at the September 23, 1983 meeting.

In his reasons for judgment, Rosenberg J. has raised the issue of whether discussions on policy issues can be completely divorced from the factual findings, at p. 492:

> In this case there was a minority report. Although the chairman states that the facts in the draft decision were taken as given there is no evidence before us to indicate whether the facts referred to those in the majority report or the minority report or both. Also without in any way doubting the sincerity and integrity of the chairman in making such a statement, it is not practical to have all of the facts decided except against a background of determination of the principles of law involved. For example, a finding that Consolidated-Bathurst was seriously considering closing the Hamilton plant is of no significance if the requirement is that the failure to bargain in good faith must be a *de facto* decision to close. Accordingly, until the board decides what the test is the findings of fact cannot be finalized.

With respect, I must disagree with Rosenberg J. if he suggests that it is not practical to discuss policy issues against the factual background provided by the panel.

It is true that the evidence cannot always be assessed in a final manner until the appropriate legal test has been chosen by the panel and until all the members of the panel have evaluated the credibility of each witness. However, it is possible to discuss the policy issues arising from the body of evidence filed before the panel even though this evidence may give rise to a wide variety of factual conclusions. In this case, Mr. Wightman seemed to disagree with Chairman Adams with respect to the credibility of the testimonies of some of the appellant's witnesses.

While this might be relevant to Mr. Wightman's conclusions, it was nevertheless possible to outline the policy issues at stake in this case from the summary of the facts prepared by Chairman Adams. In turn, it was possible to outline the various tests which could be adopted by the panel and to discuss their appropriateness from a policy point of view. These discussions can be segregated from the factual decisions which will determine the outcome of the case once a test is adopted by the panel. The purpose of the policy discussions is not to determine which of the parties will eventually win the case but rather to outline the various legal standards which may be adopted by the Board and discuss their relative value.

Policy issues must be approached in a different manner because they have, by definition, an impact which goes beyond the resolution of the dispute between the parties. While they are adopted in a factual context, they are an expression of principle or standards akin to law. Since these issues involve the consideration of statutes, past decisions and perceived social needs, the impact of a policy decision by the Board is, to a certain extent, independent from the immediate interests of the parties even though it has an effect on the outcome of the complaint.

I have already outlined the reasons which justify discussions between panel members and other members of the Board. It is now necessary to consider the conditions under which full board meetings must be held in order to abide by the *audi alteram partem* rule. In this respect, the only possible breach of this rule arises where a new policy or a new argument is proposed at a full board meeting and a decision is rendered on the basis of this policy or argument without giving the parties an opportunity to respond.

I agree with Cory J.A. (as he then was) that the parties must be informed of any new ground on which they have not made any representations. In such a case, the parties must be given a reasonable opportunity to respond and the calling of a supplementary hearing may be appropriate. The decision to call such a hearing is left to the Board as master of its own procedure: s. 102(13) of the *Labour Relations Act*. However, this is not a case where a new policy undisclosed or unknown to the parties was introduced or applied. The extent of the obligation of an employer engaged in collective bargaining to disclose information regarding the possibility of a plant closing was at the very heart of the debate from the outset and had been the subject of a policy decision previously in the *Westinghouse* case. The parties had every opportunity to deal with the matter at the hearing and indeed presented diverging proposals for modifying the policy. There is no evidence that any new grounds were put forward at the meeting and each of the reasons rendered by Chairman Adams and Messrs. Wightman and Lee simply adopts one of the arguments presented by the parties and summarized at pp. 1427–30 of Chairman Adams' decision. Though the reasons are expressed in great detail, the appellant does not identify any of them as being new nor does it contend that it did not have an opportunity to be heard or to deal with them.

Since its earliest development, the essence of the *audi alteram partem* rule has been to give the parties a "fair opportunity of answering the case against [them]": Evans, de Smith's Judicial Review of Administrative Action (4th ed. 1980), at p. 158. It is true that on factual matters the parties must be given a "fair opportunity ... for correcting or contradicting any relevant statement prejudicial to their view": *Board of Education* v. *Rice*, [1911] A.C. 179, at p. 182; see also *Local Government Board* v. *Arlidge*, [1915] A.C. 120, at pp. 133 and 141, and *Kane* v. *Board of Governors of the University of British Columbia*, supra, at pl. 1113. However, the rule with respect to legal or policy arguments not raising issues of fact is somewhat more lenient because the parties only have the right to state their case adequately and to answer contrary arguments. This right does not encompass the right to repeat arguments every time the panel convenes to discuss the case. For obvious practical reasons, superior courts, in particular courts of appeal, do not have to call back the parties every time an argument is discredited by a member of the panel and it would be anomalous to require more of administrative tribunals through the rules of natural justice. Indeed, a reason for their very existence is the specialized knowledge and expertise which they are expected to apply.

I therefore conclude that the consultation process described by Chairman Adams in his reconsideration decision does not violate the *audi alteram partem* rule provided that factual issues are not discussed at a full board meeting and that the parties are given a reasonable opportunity to respond to any new ground arising from such a meeting. In this case, an important policy issue, namely the validity of the test adopted in the *Westinghouse* case, was at stake and the Board was entitled to call a full board meeting to discuss it. There is no evidence that any other issues were discussed or indeed that any other arguments were raised at that meeting and it follows that the appellant has failed to prove that it has been the victim of any violation of the *audi alteram partem* rule. Indeed, the decision itself indicates that it rests on considerations known to the parties upon which they had full opportunity to be heard.

IV — Conclusion

The institutionalization of the consultation process adopted by the Board provides a framework within which the experience of the chairman, vice-chairmen and members of the Board can be shared to improve the overall quality of its decisions. Although respect for the judicial independence of Board members will impede total coherence in decision making, the Board through this consultation process seeks to avoid inadvertent contradictory results and to achieve the highest degree of coherence possible under these circumstances. An institutionalized consultation process will not necessarily lead Board members to reach a consensus but it provides a forum where such a consensus can be reached freely as a result of thoughtful discussion on the issues at hand.

The advantages of an institutionalized consultation process are obvious and I cannot agree with the proposition that this practice necessarily conflicts with the rules of natural justice. The rules of natural justice must have the flexibility required to take into account the institutional pressures faced by modern administrative tribunals as well as the risks inherent in such a practice. In this respect, I adopt the words of Professors Blache and Comtois in "*La décision institutionnelle*", op. cit., at p. 708:

> [TRANSLATION] The institutionalizing of decisions exists in our law and appears to be here to stay. The problem is thus not whether institutional decisions should be sanctioned, but to organize the process in such a way as to limit its dangers. There is nothing revolutionary in this approach: it falls naturally into the tradition of English and Canadian jurisprudence that the rules of natural justice should be flexibly interpreted.

The consultation process adopted by the Board formally recognizes the disadvantages inherent in full board meetings, namely that the judicial independence of the panel members may be fettered by such a practice and that the parties do not have the opportunity to respond to all the arguments raised at the meeting. The safeguards attached to this consultation process are, in my opinion, sufficient to allay any fear of violations of the rules of natural justice provided as well that the parties be advised of any new evidence or grounds and given an opportunity to respond. The balance so achieved between the rights of the parties and the institutional pressures the Board faces are consistent with the nature and purpose of the rules of natural justice.

For these reasons, I would dismiss the appeal with costs.

[The dissenting judgment of LAMER JJ. and SOPINKA J. was delivered by SOPINKA J. (dissenting):]

. . . .

The full Board hearing in this case is said to violate the principles of natural justice in two respects: first, that members of the board who did not preside at the hearing participated in the decision; and second, that the case is decided at least in part on the basis of materials which were not disclosed at the hearing and in respect of which there was no opportunity to make submissions.

Although these are distinct principles of natural justice, they have evolved out of the same concern: a party to an administrative proceeding entitled to a hearing is entitled to a meaningful hearing in the sense that the party must be given an opportunity to deal with the material that will influence the tribunal in coming to its decision, and deal with it in the presence of those who make the decision. As stated by Crane in his comment on the *Consolidated-Bathurst* decision (1988), 1 C.J.A.L.P. 215, at p. 217: "The two rules have the same purpose: to preserve the integrity and fairness of the process." In the first case the party has had no opportunity to persuade some of the members at all, while in the second the party has not been afforded an opportunity to persuade the tribunal as to the impact of material obtained outside the hearing.

. . . .

Notwithstanding that the ultimate decision is made by those who were present at the hearing, where a division of the Board considers that a matter should be discussed before the full Board or a larger division, the parties should be notified and given an opportunity to be heard.

Although I am satisfied that, at least formally, the decision here was made by the three-member panel, that does not determine the matter. The question, rather, is whether the introduction of policy considerations in the decision-making process by members of the Board who were not present at the hearing and their application by members who were present but who heard no submissions from the parties in respect thereto, violates the rationale underlying the above principles.

In answering this question, it is necessary to consider the role of policy in the decision-making processes of administrative tribunals. There is no question that the Labour Board is entitled to consider policy in arriving at its decisions....

. . . .

The Board, then, is obliged by statute to hold a hearing and to give the parties a full opportunity to present evidence and submissions. It is also entitled to apply policy....

. . . .

... The content of [the rules of natural justice] is no longer dictated by classification as judicial, *quasi*-judicial or executive, but by reference to the circumstances of the case, the governing statutory provisions and the nature of the matters to be determined....

. . . .

If a party has the right to attack policy in the same fashion as fact, it follows that to deprive the party of that right is a denial of a full opportunity to present evidence and is unfair. Policy in this respect is not like the law which cannot be the subject of evidence or cross-examination. Policy often has a factual component which the law does not.

Furthermore, under our system of justice it is crucial that the law be correctly applied. The court or tribunal is not bound to rely solely on the law as presented by the parties. Accordingly, a tribunal can rely on its own research and if that differs from what has been presented at the hearing, it is bound to apply the law as found. Ordinarily there is not obligation to disclose to the parties the fruits of the tribunal's research as to the law, although it is a salutary practice to obtain their views in respect of an authority which has come to the tribunal's attention and which may have an important influence on the case....

. . . .

In my opinion, therefore, the full Board hearing deprived the appellant of a full opportunity to present evidence and submissions and constituted a denial of natural justice. While it cannot be determined with certainty from the record that a policy developed at the full Board hearing and not disclosed to the parties was a factor in the decision, it is fatal to the decision of the Board that this is what might very well have happened.

While achieving uniformity in the decisions of individual boards is a laudable purpose, it cannot be done at the expense of the rules of natural justice. If it is the desire of the legislature that this purpose be pursued it is free to authorize the full Board procedure. It is worthy of note that Parliament has given first reading to Bill C-40, a revised *Broadcasting Act* which authorizes individual panels to consult with the Commission and officers of the Commission in order to achieve uniformity in the application of policy (s. 19(4)) [now s. 20(40)]. Provision is made, however, for the timely issue of guidelines and statements with respect to matters within the jurisdiction of the Commission.

POSTSCRIPT

See also the more recent decisions in *Tremblay v. Quebec (Commission des affairs sociales)*, [1992] 1 S.C.R. 259 (S.C.C.) and *Matsqui Indian Band et al. v. Canadian Pacific Limited et al.*, [1995] 1 S.C.R. 3 (S.C.C.).

(h) More Institutional Decisions: *Ellis-Don*†

NOTE

Consolidated-Bathurst said that agencies could consult internally and confidentially on matters of law or policy, as long as the consultations did not focus on disputed issues of fact. But how can a party prove that facts have been discussed if the proceedings are confidential? That was one of the central issues in *Ellis-Don*.

A three-member panel of the Board made an internal draft decision that rejected a union grievance about subcontracting contrary to a collective agreement. The panel held that the union had failed to include Ellis-Don on a list of employers subject to accreditation proceedings. As a result, the union had "abandoned" its bargaining rights with Ellis-Don. After an internal meeting with the full Board, however, the panel issued a final decision, with one member dissenting, that supported the union grievance.

The union learned informally of the nature of the draft decision, and of the internal consultation, and sought a re-hearing. When this was refused, the union claimed that the Board had breached the rules of natural justice. It argued that the differences between the panel's draft and final decision were sufficient evidence that the internal consultation addressed subject matter of a factual nature, contrary to the requirements in the *Consolidated-Bathurst* decision.

Which judgment do you prefer, that of the majority, or that of Binnie J? Why? How clear is the distinction between facts on one hand, and law and policy on the other?

EXTRACTS

[Le BEL J. for himself, McLACHLIN C.J., L'HEUREUX-DUBÉ, GONTHIER, IACOBUCCI, BASTARACHE, and ARBOUR JJ.:]

[para29] In *Consolidated-Bathurst, supra*, Gonthier J. examined whether the existence of this kind of institutional consultation procedure in itself created an apprehension of bias or lack of independence as Sopinka J. feared in his dissent. According to Gonthier J., such a procedure would not of itself raise such an apprehension, provided it was designed to safeguard the ability of the decision-maker to decide independently both on facts and law in the matter. Gonthier J. laid down a set of basic principles to ensure compliance with the rules of natural justice. First, the consultation proceeding could not be imposed by a superior level of authority within the administrative hierarchy, but could be requested only by the adjudicators themselves. Second, the consultation had to be limited to questions of policy and law. The members of the organization who had not heard the evidence could not be allowed to re-assess it. The consultation had to proceed on the basis of

---

† *Ellis-Don Ltd. v. Ontario (Labour Relations Board)*, [2001] 1 S.C.R. 221, aff'g. (1998), 38 O.R. (3d) 737 (O.C.A.), aff'g. (1995), 89 O.A.C. 45, [1995] O.J. No. 3924 (QL) (Div. Ct.), which dismissed the appellant's application for judicial review. Major and Binnie JJ. dissented.

the facts as stated by the members who had actually heard the evidence. Finally, even on questions of law and policy, the decision-makers had to remain free to take whatever decision they deemed right in their conscience and understanding of the facts and the law, and not be compelled to adopt the views expressed by other members of the administrative tribunal. Provided these rules were respected, institutional consultation would not create a reasonable apprehension of bias or lack of independence.

[para30] It is noteworthy that also at issue in the *Consolidated-Bathurst* case were the consultation proceedings followed within the OLRB. The majority decided that such procedures did not create a reasonable apprehension of bias or lack of independence.

[para31] The principles developed in *Consolidated-Bathurst* were also applied in the later case of *Tremblay, supra*. In the *Tremblay* case, the Supreme Court of Canada considered that the consultation procedures were imposed from above on the decision-makers and that they were so formalized that they became binding on the triers of facts, therefore compromising their independence.

2. *Audi Alteram Partem*

[para32] The other issue in *Consolidated-Bathurst* concerned the impact of the consultation proceeding on the application of the *audi alteram partem* rule. The reasons of Gonthier J. conceded that there existed risks in that regard, but held that they could be addressed by ensuring that the parties be notified of any new issue raised during the discussion and allowed an opportunity to respond in an effective manner. The mere fact that issues already litigated between the parties were to be discussed again by the full Board would not amount to a breach of the *audi alteram partem* rule.

[para33] Provided these rules were complied with, the adjudicators retained the right to change their minds and to modify a first draft of a decision. Such changes would not create a presumption that something improper had occurred during the consultation process. In the absence of other evidence to the contrary, the presumption of regularity of administrative procedures would apply.

. . . .

[para34] These principles, as set out in *Consolidated-Bathurst, supra*, and applied in *Tremblay, supra*, gov-

ern the present case. As the appellant bears the burden of establishing that the rules of natural justice have been breached, so it must demonstrate that there was inappropriate tampering with the assessment of evidence.

1. Evidentiary Problems

[para35] The appellant faced difficult evidentiary problems when it launched its application for judicial review. The only facts it knew were that a draft decision dismissing the grievance had been circulated, that a full meeting of the OLRB had been called at the request of Vice-Chair Susan Tacon, that such a meeting had indeed been held and that the final arbitration award upheld the grievance.

[para36] The final decision was silent as to what had happened during the full Board meeting. As stated above, there has been no request for reconsideration, and thus, perhaps, an opportunity was lost to obtain information on the consultation process within the OLRB. From these facts, there is no direct evidence of improper tampering with the decision of the panel. Ellis-Don sought to strengthen its case by obtaining evidence of what had happened during the consultation process. The appellant tried to get this evidence through an interlocutory motion to examine certain members and officers of the OLRB. After the dismissal of its motion by the Divisional Court, Ellis-Don found itself in an impasse, as it could not obtain evidence of the process followed in the particular case from the OLRB through the interrogation of its members or officers.

[para37] The appellant then tried a new tack during the hearing of its application for judicial review. The purpose of its argument remained the same: to establish an improper interference by the full Board in the decision of the panel. Thus, it sought to convince the courts that the change in the decision was of a factual nature and that it could properly be implied that a discussion of the facts had occurred at the full Board meeting. It also suggested that the threshold for judicial review in such a case was an apprehension of breach of natural justice and that there was no need to establish an actual breach of the *audi alteram partem* rule. It argued that such an apprehended breach of natural justice had been established through a displacement of the presumption of regularity of the administrative proceedings of the Board. According to the appellant, it fell to the respondents to establish that the proceedings had not been tainted by any breach of natural justice. Absent evidence to this effect, the Court should find

that there was a breach of natural justice, that the Board had been biased and that the *audi alteram partem* rule had been violated. This unrebutted presumption would justify granting the application for judicial review and quashing the decision of the Board.

. . . .

[para41] In the case at hand, it appears the change in the decision of the panel concerned a matter of law and policy. The general question in issue was the problem of abandonment of bargaining rights. The factual situation as such was well established. It was not disputed that when requested to list the employers for whose employees it held bargaining rights, the IBEW, Local 353 omitted the name of Ellis-Don. It was also conceded that the Union had not offered any evidence at the hearing before the panel as to the reasons for this failure.

. . . .

[para49] In the case of an alleged violation of the *audi alteram partem* rule, even if it can be difficult to obtain evidence to that effect in certain cases, the applicant for judicial review must establish an actual breach. There is no authority for the proposition put forward by the appellant that an "apprehended" breach is sufficient to trigger judicial review. In *Consolidated-Bathurst*, *supra*, the reasons of Gonthier J. clearly distinguished the two problems: bias and *audi alteram partem*. On the one hand, Gonthier J. examined whether the process of institutional consultation created an apprehension of bias. While reviewing the application of the *audi alteram partem* rule, he never indicated that an apprehension of breach was sufficient to justify intervention. Indeed, he found that the record before the Court revealed no evidence that any other issues or arguments had been discussed at the full Board meeting. Therefore, he held that the appellant had failed to prove a breach of the *audi alteram partem* rule: see *Consolidated-Bathurst*, at pp. 339–40. Thus, one has to look at the nature of the natural justice problem involved to determine the threshold for judicial review. *Consolidated-Bathurst* does not stand as authority for the assertion that the threshold for judicial review in every case of alleged breach of natural justice is merely an apprehended breach of natural justice.

. . . .

[para52] The case reveals a tension between the fairness of the process and the principle of deliberative secrecy. The existence of this tension was conceded by Gonthier J. in *Tremblay*, *supra*, at pp. 965–66. Undoubtedly, the principle of deliberative secrecy creates serious difficulties for parties who fear that they may have been the victims of inappropriate tampering with the decision of the adjudicators who actually heard them. Even if this Court has refused to grant the same level of protection to the deliberations of administrative tribunals as to those of the civil and criminal courts, and would allow interrogation and discovery as to the process followed, Gonthier J. recognized that this principle of deliberative secrecy played an important role in safeguarding the independence of administrative adjudicators.

[para53] Deliberative secrecy also favours administrative consistency by granting protection to a consultative process that involves interaction between the adjudicators who have heard the case and the members who have not, within the rules set down in *Consolidated-Bathurst*, *supra*. Without such protection, there could be a chilling effect on institutional consultations, thereby depriving administrative tribunals of a critically important means of achieving consistency.

[para54] Satisfying those requirements of consistency and independence comes undoubtedly at a price, this price being that the process becomes less open and that litigants face tough hurdles when attempting to build the evidentiary foundation for a successful challenge based on alleged breaches of natural justice (see, e.g., H. N. Janisch, "Consistency, Rulemaking and *Consolidated-Bathurst*" (1991), 16 Queen's L.J. 95; D. Lemieux, "L'Équilibre nécessaire entre la cohérence institutionnelle et l'indépendance des membres d'un tribunal administratif: *Tremblay c. Québec (Commission des affaires sociales)*" (1992), 71 Can. Bar Rev. 734). The present case provides an excellent example of those difficulties.

[para55] After the dismissal of its interlocutory motion, the appellant could not examine the officers of the Board on the process that had been followed. In the absence of any further evidence, this Court cannot reverse the presumption of regularity of the administrative process simply because of a change in the reasons for the decision, especially when the change is limited on its face to questions of law and policy, as discussed above. A contrary approach to the presumption would deprive administrative tribunals of the independence that the principle of deliberative secrecy assures them in their decision-making process. It could also jeopardize institutionalized consultation proceedings that have become more necessary than ever to ensure the consistency

and predictability of the decisions of administrative tribunals.

4. Conclusion on the Grounds for Judicial Review

[para56] The record shows no indication of a change on the facts, of impropriety or of a violation of the principles governing institutional consultation. Any intervention would have to be based on mere speculation about what might have happened during the consultation with the full Board. The judicial review of a decision of an administrative body may not rest on speculative grounds. Thus, the Divisional Court and the Court of Appeal of Ontario correctly applied the rules governing judicial review when they dismissed the appellant's application.

. . . .

[BINNIE J. for himself and MAJOR, dissenting:]

[para59] It is occasionally observed that the most important person in the hearing room is the party that has just lost a case. Whatever may be the loser's bitterness or incredulity at the outcome, the overriding imperative is that the outcome was — and was seen to be — reached impartially under a fair procedure. That is the overriding issue in this appeal.

. . . .

[para67] It appears more probable than not that at the full Board meeting in this case there was a discussion about factual matters which likely included "statement[s] prejudicial to [the appellant's] view" because the panel subsequently reversed itself on the appropriateness of an adverse inference against the union for its failure to lead relevant evidence, reversed itself on the issue of abandonment, and thus reversed itself on the outcome of the hearing.

. . . .

[para77] For reasons which are not explained, the Vice-Chair requested a full Board meeting to discuss the panel's initial decision. The Vice-Chair did not formulate a policy issue or notify colleagues that there would be a general review of the policy implications of abandonment. The Vice-Chair just referenced this particular pending decision as the topic for full Board discussion.

[para78] *Consolidated-Bathurst* holds that convening a full board meeting while a particular case is pending is permissible so long as (i) the question for discus-

sion is one of policy rather than fact, (ii) that in the end the panel is free to make its own decision, and (iii) that if the discussion at the full board raises matters not addressed by the parties, that the parties be put on notice and permitted to make representations before a decision is made.

[para79] In my view, the procedure adopted in the present case violates only the first of these limitations. There is no evidence that the second limitation was not observed, and as to the third limitation, the appellant had the opportunity to address the panel on every aspect of the abandonment issue. Its proper complaint is that the initial decision ought not to have been referred to the full Board meeting at all.

Fact versus Policy

[para80] I agree with my colleague LeBel J. that one of the conditions precedent to the validity of a full board meeting is that "the consultation had to be limited to questions of policy and law. The members of the organization who had not heard the evidence could not be allowed to re-assess it. The consultation had to proceed on the basis of the facts as stated by the members who had actually heard the evidence" (para. 29). This limitation is based on what was said by Gonthier J. for the majority in *Consolidated-Bathurst, supra*, at pp. 335–36. In that case, the issue was the scope of the employer's duty to bargain in good faith imposed by what is now s. 17 of the *Ontario Labour Relations Act*. More specifically, the question was whether the duty to bargain in good faith included a duty of candour to disclose without being asked future plans of the employer that would have a significant impact on the economic lives of bargaining unit employees (*Consolidated-Bathurst, supra*, at p. 311). A discussion about the relationship between the obligation to bargain in good faith and a duty of candour raised an abstract policy issue that could be segregated from the facts of that case. Here, the Board's policy had been authoritatively established, i.e., the "active promotion" test. It was for the panel to determine in the factual context of this particular case whether or not this standard was met.

. . . .

[para100] The appellant does not need to establish "external pressure" in this case. It merely has to establish a basis for a reasonable inference that factual matters were referred for discussion at the full Board meeting that ought to have been left to the undisturbed deliberations of the panel.

. . . .

[para105] In my view, the Board cannot have it both ways. It cannot, with the assistance of the legislature [s. 111 of the *Labour Relations Act*, R.S.O. 1990, c. L.2 (now s. 117) granted testimonial immunity to Board members in civil proceedings in regard to information relating to their work], deny a person in the position of the appellant all legitimate access to relevant information, then rely on the absence of this same information as a conclusive answer to the appellant's complaint. We are not in the business of playing Catch 22. The record discloses a change of position by the panel on an issue of fact. This runs counter to *Consolidated-Bathurst* and has to be dealt with properly if confidence in the integrity of the Board's decision making is to be maintained....

. . . .

[para106] In *Tremblay*, of course, the Court was not confronted with a testimonial immunity provision comparable to s. 111 of the *Ontario Labour Relations Act*. Nevertheless, it could not have been intended by the Court to make a distinction between fact and policy, only to have its enforcement rendered impracticable. Where such difficulties of proof are presented, as here, they will have to be factored into the evidentiary burden of proof placed on the appellant.

. . . .

[para112] In my view, subject to the privative clause issue [Binnie J. found the privative clause to be ineffective here], the appellant is entitled to a new hearing before a different panel of the Board. This is not an easy order to make given the fact that this case has been before the Board and the courts for many years. However, the courts in Ontario refused to stay the Board's original order upholding the respondent union's bargaining rights, and the union and its members have not on that account been prejudiced by the delay.

(i)   Bias and Conflict of Interest: *Community Before Cars*[†]

NOTE

In a series of decisions, the federal National Capital Commission decided to widen the Champlain bridge connecting Ottawa to Hull and Aylmer, Québec, from two to three lanes. A community group sought judicial review of the decision, arguing that the fact that the chairperson of the Commission owned properties in Hull and Aylmer very near the bridge gave rise to a reasonable apprehension of bias.

Conflict of interest, and the appearance of conflict of interest is an ever-present problem in government. Where it is not addressed by conflict guidelines — or where there is disagreement about the guidelines — it may have to be resolved in court. Here, as in most cases in which bias is an issue, a key question is the degree of proximity between the decision-maker and the factor allegedly causing the bias.

EXTRACTS

[MULDOON J.:]

[para51] ... The applicant's first bias allegation is that the NCC chairman, Mr. Beaudry, was in a conflict of interest and that his conflict biased the NCC's decisions even though he did not participate in them. That is to say, Mr. Beaudry withdrew from the decision-making process allegedly too late in the day; he tainted the process. This arises out of his interest (latterly, since 1993, held through his wife) in about 1,000 acres of land approximately 3+ kilometres from the north end of the bridge ... and the

---

[†] *Community Before Cars Coalition v. National Capital Commission*, [1997] F.C.J. No. 1060 (F.C.T.D.), online: Q.L. (FCJ); (1997) 135 F.T.R. 1.

fact that after his withdrawal he continued in his capacity as chief executive officer of the NCC. The NCC chairperson, it must be remembered, has two roles under the National Capital Act: chairman of the NCC board of commissioners and the chief executive officer of the NCC. Mr. Beaudry was sworn in as NCC chairman on September 2, 1992.

[para52] The first question to be determined is what the test for bias is in this case. Normally, evidence of a pecuniary interest results in the immediate disqualification of the decision maker because of an appearance of bias.... As Mr. Justice Marceau wrote in *Energy Probe* v. *Canada (Atomic Energy Control Board)*, [1985] 1 F.C. 563 at p. 579–580:

> It was soon "discovered", — it is taught in all the textbooks — that the common law, like the Roman law and the Canon law long before it, did not permit a judge to determine a matter in which he had a pecuniary or proprietary interest (see de Smith's Judicial Review of Administrative Action, (4th Ed. 1980) p. 248).

This, in fact, is the very root of the different types of bias now recognized by Canadian law. Marceau J. went on to describe the evolution of the law of bias at p. 580:

> From that early moment on, the law in that respect has evolved, as I understand it, on the strength of two ideas. One is that there are many interests other than pecuniary which may affect the impartiality of a decision-maker, emotional type interests one might say (see: Pépin and Ouellette, *Principes de contentieux administratifs* (2nd Ed.) p. 253), such as kinship, friendship, partisanship, particular professional or business relationship with one of the parties, animosity towards someone interested, predetermined mind as to the issue involved, etc. The other, which has since become a sort of legal axiom, is that it "is of fundamental importance that justice should not only be done but should manifestly and undoubtedly be seen to be done". The result of the evolution of the law on the basis of these two ideas is that a distinction is today well recognized and acknowledged between situations where the decision-maker has a pecuniary interest in the outcome of the decision, and situations where his interest is of another type. In the first case, since the maxim *nemo judex in causa sua* is readily applicable, the decision-maker is peremptorily disqualified from adjudicating regardless of the importance of the interest, provided however that it is an interest linked and tied to the decision itself and not too remote or too contingent to be devoid of any possible influence. In the second case, the decision-maker is disqualified from adjudicating if the interest is such that it would leave, in the mind of a reasonable man apprised of the facts, a reasonable apprehension of bias.

[para53] The Supreme Court of Canada, in *Newfoundland Telephone* v. *Newfoundland (Public Utilities Board)*, [1992] 1 S.C.R. 623 and *Old St. Boniface Residents Assn.* v. *Winnipeg (City)*, [1990] 3 S.C.R. 1170, has set out guidelines for formulating and applying the test for bias. In *Newfoundland Telephone*, Mr. Justice Cory affirmed that the duty of fairness, which includes impartiality, applies to all administrative bodies, but that "the extent of that duty will depend upon the nature and the function of the particular tribunal" (p. 636). Cory J., after approving the Court's decision written by Mr. Justice Sopinka in the *Old St. Boniface* case, then went on to describe how the application of the bias test should be applied at pp. 638–39:

> It can be seen that there is a great diversity of administrative boards. Those that are primarily adjudicative in their functions will be expected to comply with the standard applicable to courts. That is to say that the conduct of the members of the Board should be such that there could be no reasonable apprehension of bias with regard to their decision. At the other end of the scale are boards with popularly elected members such as those dealing with planning and development whose members are municipal councillors. With those boards, the standard will be much more lenient. In order to disqualify the members a challenging party must establish that there has been a pre-judgment of the matter to such an extent that any representations to the contrary would be futile. Administrative boards that deal with matters of policy will be closely comparable to the boards composed of municipal councillors. For those boards, a strict application of a reasonable apprehension of bias as a test might undermine the very role which has been entrusted to them by the legislature.
>
> ...
>
> Further, a member of a Board which performs a policy formation function should not be susceptible to a charge of bias simply because of the expression of strong opinions prior to the hearing. This does not of course mean that there are no limits to the conduct of board members. It is simply a confirmation of the principle that the courts must take a flexible approach to the problem so that the standard which is applied varies with the role and function of the Board which is being considered. In the end, however, commissioners must base their decision on the evidence which is before them. Although they may draw upon their relevant expertise and their

background of knowledge and understanding, this must be applied to the evidence which has been adduced before the Board.

In sum, the test moves along a sliding scale, from the legislative (which attracts the most lenient application) to the adjudicative end (inevitably the most stringent). So the first step which the Court must take is to determine where the decision-making body falls on the scale.

[para54] Once the administrative body is positioned on the scale, the Court must apply the appropriate test. Where the decision maker is acting in an adjudicative function, such as a human rights tribunal, the standard is whether there is a reasonable apprehension of bias (*Newfoundland Telephone*, p. 638). In the legislative context, such as municipal planning conducted by popularly elected officials — or, as Cory J. wrote in the text excerpted above, administrative boards which deal with policy matters — the test to be applied is the one formulated by Sopinka J. at p. 1197 of the *Old St. Boniface* case:

> The party alleging disqualifying bias must establish that there is a prejudgment of the matter, in fact, to the extent that any representations at variance with the view, which has been adopted, would be futile. Statements by individual members of Council while they may very well give rise to an appearance of bias will not satisfy the test unless the court concludes that they are the expression of a final opinion on the matter, which cannot be dislodged.

That is to say, the decision maker has a closed mind.

[para55] Who determines whether a decision-maker has a so-called closed mind? Mr. Justice Sopinka put it this way: "the reasonably well-informed person" (*Old St. Boniface*, p. 1196 and 1198; from *Committee for Justice* v. *National Energy Board*, [1978] 1 S.C.R. 369).

[para56] What, then, is the test for this case? The NCC falls on the policy-making end of the scale. Although its commissioners are appointed and not elected, the role of the NCC is very similar to that of municipal councils. This is not a startling revelation; the *Munro* case recognized it. Simply stated, the NCC develops policy, decides what course of action to take in terms of administering the national capital region, and then implements the decision. This is analogous to a municipal council.... This is exactly the sort of body contemplated by Justice Cory's words in the above cited passage in *Newfoundland Telephone*: "Administrative boards that

deal with matters of policy will be closely comparable to the boards composed of municipal councillors. For those boards, a strict application of a reasonable apprehension of bias as a test might undermine the very role which has been entrusted to them by the legislature."

[para57] Before applying the tests, it is helpful to recall to whom they are directed. The impugned decisions were made by the NCC board of commissioners and the evidence is clear that Mr. Beaudry, acting on advice from Mr. Wilson, the Ethics Commissioner, withdrew from deliberations and decisions regarding the Champlain bridge. It must be recalled that the applicant's allegations are primarily levied against Mr. Beaudry, and only peripherally at the commissioners. At first blush, one might be tempted to reject the bias argument altogether because Mr. Beaudry was not a decision-maker. Such a solution would not be satisfactory in the face of the applicant's allegations because (1) when Mr. Beaudry was appointed on September 2, 1992, it was relatively early on in the process for making the reconstruction/ rehabilitation decision, (2) after Mr. Beaudry withdrew he remained as head of the NCC staff, which recommended a three lane bridge, (3) it is uncontested that Mr. Beaudry supports a third lane, and (4) his withdrawal occurred almost four years after his appointment. Continuing the inquiry accords with the underlying principle that it is the integrity of the decision-making process which must be examined.

[para58] This complicates the analysis somewhat because the Court must first examine Mr. Beaudry's actions using a different test from that which will be used for the NCC commissioners because partiality by reason of pre-judgment is treated differently from partiality by reason of personal interest. In the *Old St. Boniface* case, Mr. Justice Sopinka made this distinction at p. 1196:

> I would distinguish between a case of partiality by reason of pre-judgment on the one hand and by reason of personal interest on the other. It is apparent from the facts of this case, for example, that some degree of pre-judgment is inherent in the role of a councillor. That is not the case in respect of interest. There is nothing inherent in the hybrid functions, political, legislative or otherwise, of municipal councillors that would make it mandatory or desirable to excuse them from the requirement that they refrain from dealing with matters in respect of which they have a personal or other interest....

[para59] There is no evidence on the record which shows that Mr. Beaudry directly influenced the com-

missioners when each decision was made. In fact, the evidence shows the very opposite. In his affidavit, which was subject to cross-examination, Mr. Beaudry deposed thus:

> I have not at any time either before or after withdrawing from participation in the Commission's decision-making process with respect to the Proposal contacted any members of the Commission to lobby them to favour a three-lane option or otherwise attempted through indirect means to influence the outcome of the process (RR, vol. IV-B, tab 2: p. 2279).

Nor has the applicant pointed to sufficient evidence which would allow the Court to infer that Mr. Beaudry's presence as the NCC chairman for the previous four years had any impact on the commissioners when they made the two decisions. To find bias on the part of the commissioners, the Court must find that any conflict of interest related to Mr. Beaudry's property interests threaded its way to the commissioners' decisions through his influence on the NCC staff. With this in mind, that redoubtable reasonably informed person begins the task at hand.

[para60] The main thrust of the applicant's submissions accords with Justice Sopinka's distinction between pre-judgment and personal interests. That is to say the applicant vigorously attacked Mr. Beaudry's property interests. The applicant's position is that Mr. Beaudry is in a classic conflict of interest. To this Court, the respondent's characterization of this submission is correct: "The real thrust of the allegation seems to be that the Chairman is biased in favour of a three-lane bridge by reason of personal interest and that, through his involvement in certain administrative aspects of the Bridge reconstruction project, his bias tainted the process that led to the decisions under review and therefore tainted the decisions themselves".... If [borne] out by the facts, there is merit to this argument. Compliance with the conflict of interest guidelines only prevents any taint of the commissioners' decisions by reason of Mr. Beaudry's alleged direct influence on the commissioners. It cannot be curative of any influence which he may have already had on the staff unless there is some remedial effect in putting everybody on notice that the chairman had proprietary interest in some land. (It may be recalled that it was found above that there is no evidence of any influence on the commissioners.)

[para61] Sopinka J. suggested that the test (or, when observed as part of the whole bias argument, the sub-test) for determining whether there was a conflict of interest for a municipal counsellor, is to look at whether there was a personal interest under both statute and at common law. If there is, the effect will usually be that the individual is disqualified from participating in any decisions related to the interest. For all intents and purposes this is the applicable test for Mr. Beaudry. Just as the NCC is akin to a municipal council, the position of a commissioner — or, in Mr. Beaudry's case, the Chief commissioner, is similar to a municipal reeve or commissioner. The Court recognizes that, unlike most municipal councillors, NCC commissioners do not run on a platform, so there is no inherent element of prejudgment in their policy postures. When it comes to conflict of interest, however, Sopinka J. has eliminated the "inherent prejudgment" element because it is not an inherent aspect of municipal office to have a personal interest in an issue.

[para62] It is worth emphasizing that Mr. Beaudry withdrew from the decisions. Obviously the Court cannot vitiate the decisions or remove his vote because the normal remedy, disqualification, has been pre-empted. If there be a conflict, however, it would be a significant factor to consider when the reasonable apprehension of bias test is applied to the board of commissioners.

[para63] As with all federally appointed public officials, Mr. Beaudry had to comply with the *Conflict of Interest and Post-Employment Code for Public Office Holders*. According to his sworn affidavit, Mr. Beaudry has done so since his appointment (RR, vol. IV-A, tab 2: p. 2275). His property interests were transferred to his wife in December, 1993.... This, however, does not blow anyone away. This action did, however, conform with the *Code*. Further, Mr. Beaudry's compliance with the *Code* makes it very clear that the chairman had these interests. There was no attempt to conceal them. At no point was any outcry made about this. More importantly, because of the highly charged public debate surrounding the bridge proposals as the time for making the decisions was rapidly approaching, Mr. Beaudry took the extra step of consulting Mr. Howard Wilson, the Ethics Counsellor in June, 1996, and proposed that he withdraw from any discussion or decision regarding the bridge. Mr. Wilson replied that there was no real conflict, but to avoid any appearance of bias, advised the Mr. Beaudry to withdraw....

Based on these facts, the Court finds that Mr. Beaudry committed no wrong. What more could Mr. Beaudry have done, aside from resigning? The applicant suggests that a blind trust would have been appropriate. As the respondent submitted, this would not make any difference. Mr. Beaudry would still know he had an interest in the land. This is very different from a blind trust used for holding publicly traded securities, because the identity of land is very specific; shares much less so.

[para64] To summarize briefly, Mr. Beaudry disclosed all interests in accordance with the *Code*. This is sufficient to fulfil the first part of the conflict of interest test, i.e. compliance with statute. In this case, the *Code* is not even a statutory requirement. On the advice of the Ethics Counsellor, he withdrew from all deliberations and decisions concerning the bridge. The Ethics Counsellor found that Mr. Beaudry was not in a conflict of interest and that withdrawal was recommended to avoid any chance of an appearance of conflict.

[para65] The opinion of the Ethics Counsellor should not, of course, be rubber-stamped by this Court. The opinion is, however, helpful. This goes to the second element of conflict of interest: does a conflict exist at common law? The Federal Court of Appeal articulated the test for public office holders in *Threader* v. *Canada (Treasury Board)*, [1987] 1 F.C. 41 at p. 56

> Whether an appearance of conflict of interest exists must be determined on an objective, rational and informed basis. While the Guidelines contained no definition of the term "appearance of conflict of interest", reference could be made to the concept of apprehension of judicial bias, where mere perception entails legal consequences, in determining the appropriate test. The question to be asked should be phrased as follows:
>
> > Would an informed person, viewing the matter realistically and practically and having thought the matter through, think it more likely than not that the public servant, whether consciously or unconsciously, will be influenced in the performance of his official duties by considerations having to do with his private interests?

... For this case, the test is this: would a reasonable, informed person think that Mr. Beaudry's property interest (now owned by his wife) consciously or unconsciously influenced his performance in his official duties?

[para66] The first point the reasonable person must consider is whether the NCC chairman had anything to gain from a three-lane bridge. The applicant asks the Court to find that as a fact, presumably by drawing an inference from allegedly increased easier access, that Mr. Beaudry's land value will increase.

No evidence in support of this allegation was offered by the applicant. The uncontroverted evidence is that Mr. Beaudry believed that the land value would not increase as a result of the widening of the Champlain bridge....

While instinct may dictate that enhanced, increased access will result in higher land values, this Court cannot take judicial notice of this, especially in face of unchallenged evidence of two things. The first is Mr. Beaudry's evidence that the value would not increase. The second is that the most direct route at this time from the land in question to Ottawa is not by way of the Champlain bridge, but via the MacDonald-Cartier bridge.... The inference which the applicant wishes the Court to draw is fatally weakened by these unchallenged facts. The only fact which the informed reasonable person is left with is that Mr. Beaudry had nothing to gain from a widening of the bridge. On the other hand, Mr. Beaudry himself thought that he ought to consult the Ethics Commissioner and that he ought to divest himself of apparent ownership by transferring the land to his wife, a person not thought to be at "arms length".

[para67] The second point which the reasonable person must consider is whether Mr. Beaudry "engineered" a reversal of NCC opinion, i.e. the applicant alleges that the staff previously favoured a two-lane option. After all, it is admitted that "it is no secret that the Chairman favours a three-lane bridge".... One may speculate that the staff could have asked themselves: "what does the Chairman want?" As noted above, the record shows as an unrefuted fact however that Mr. Beaudry did not believe that any increase in his property interests would result from the widening of the bridge. This is something which the reasonable person cannot ignore, because the applicant adduced no expert or any evidence (speculative as it would have been) that Madame Beaudry's property values would rise as a result of easier river crossing on a three-lane bridge.

[para68] Leaving aside his alleged pecuniary interest altogether, there is no evidence whatsoever from which the Court can infer that Mr. Beaudry influenced the staff in such manner which resulted in a three-lane bridge being portrayed as far and away the preferable option. The issue is solely an evidentiary one....

. . . .

[para70] ... [T]here is no evidence that Mr. Beaudry had any influence one way or another on the NCC

staff with respect to choosing and recommending bridge options.

[para71] For completeness, it may be added that the applicant's assertion, that the NCC staff was in favour of two-lane reconstruction prior to Mr. Beaudry's arrival, is not [borne] out by the evidence either. The hard facts are these: (1) the NCC had considered a three-lane Champlain bridge as early as 1968 (RR, vol. IV-B, tab 2: p. 22672), (2) the December 1992 Fenco Maclaren report which was commissioned in 1990 considered three and four lanes (RR, vol. IV-A, tab 2: p. 2270–71), and (3) the 1989 results of the first phase of the JACPAT, of which the NCC was a participant, found that the Champlain bridge should be widened or twinned if a new bridge were not built at another location (RR, vol. I-A, tab 1: p. 9).

. . . .

[para73] After considering the above, that reasonable person would conclude that there is no evidence which shows that Mr. Beaudry's property interest in certain land in Alymer (now nominally owned by his wife) consciously or unconsciously influenced his performance in his official duties.

[para74] What does all of this mean? In the end, as Mr. Beaudry was not in a conflict of interest, there is no "malignant bias" which can be traced from his involvement as head of the NCC staff through to the NCC commissioners' non-unanimous decisions which would contribute to a reasonable apprehension of bias on the part of the commissioners. When the appropriate test for bias is applied, the reasonably well informed person would find that there is no reasonable apprehension that the NCC commissioners had preconceived that a three-lane bridge was the best option, to the extent that any representations which conflict with this view, which has been adopted, would be futile. There is no evidence to show that the NCC commissioners had their collective mind so fixed. Mr. Beaudry was not in a conflict of interest and had no influence on the consultant's and staff's recommendations. The commissioners had three reconstruction options before them, two two-lane and one three-lane. They knew that the consultant recommended a two-lane bridge and that the NCC staff recommended a three-lane bridge for reasons not considered by the consultant. On September 3, 1996, the commissioners voted seven to five in favour of a three-lane bridge. On October 15, 1996, the margin was nine to four. These numbers by themselves may very well be sufficient to prove no bias according to the test set out by the Supreme Court of Canada. Even so, the foregoing examination exonerates Mr. Beaudry and rejects the notion that any bias emanated from him. Mr. Beaudry did the best he could, short of resigning, in an unfortunate situation.

(j)   Bias and Stereotyping: *Baker*[†]

NOTE

The facts in *Baker* were described in Chapter 4 above. The following extract contains some of the main majority's discussion of bias.

EXTRACT

[L'HEUREUX-DUBÉ   for   herself,   GONTHIER, McLACHLIN, BASTARACHE and BINNIE JJ.]

[para45] Procedural fairness also requires that decisions be made free from a reasonable apprehension of bias, by an impartial decision-maker. The respondent argues that Simpson J. was correct to find that the notes of Officer Lorenz cannot be considered to give rise to a reasonable apprehension of bias because it was Officer Caden who was the actual decision-maker, who was simply reviewing the recommendation prepared by his subordinate. In my opinion, the duty to act fairly and therefore in a manner

---

[†]   *Baker v. Canada (Minister of Citizenship and Immigration)*, [1999] 2 S.C.R. 817, rev'g, [1997] 2 F.C. 127 (F.C.A.), answering a question certified by Simpson J. in [1995] F.C.J. No. 1441 (F.C.T.D.).

that does not give rise to a reasonable apprehension of bias applies to all immigration officers who play a significant role in the making of decisions, whether they are subordinate reviewing officers, or those who make the final decision....

[para48] In my opinion, the well-informed member of the community would perceive bias when reading Officer Lorenz's comments. His notes, and the manner in which they are written, do not disclose the existence of an open mind or a weighing of the particular circumstances of the case free from stereotypes. Most unfortunate is the fact that they seem to make a link between Ms. Baker's mental illness, her training as a domestic worker, the fact that she has several children, and the conclusion that she would therefore be a strain on our social welfare system for the rest of her life. In addition, the conclusion drawn was contrary to the psychiatrist's letter, which stated that, with treatment, Ms. Baker could remain well and return to being a productive member of society. Whether they were intended in this manner or not, these statements give the impression that Officer Lorenz may have been drawing conclusions based not on the evidence before him, but on the fact

that Ms. Baker was a single mother with several children, and had been diagnosed with a psychiatric illness. His use of capitals to highlight the number of Ms. Baker's children may also suggest to a reader that this was a reason to deny her status. Reading his comments, I do not believe that a reasonable and well-informed member of the community would conclude that he had approached this case with the impartiality appropriate to a decision made by an immigration officer. It would appear to a reasonable observer that his own frustration with the "system" interfered with his duty to consider impartially whether the appellant's admission should be facilitated owing to humanitarian or compassionate considerations. I conclude that the notes of Officer Lorenz demonstrate a reasonable apprehension of bias.

.   .   .   .

[para77] ... I would allow the appeal, and set aside the decision of Officer Caden of April 18, 1994, with party-and-party costs throughout. The matter will be returned to the Minister for redetermination by a different immigration officer.

8   Controlling Discretion and Providing Access to Information

(a)   Discretion

Earlier we said that the characteristic functions of the executive include initiating and administering policy and laws. The executive's role in initiating policy which becomes a statute is confined primarily to the political head of the executive, the first minister and Cabinet, and to the senior executive officials who assist them. What of the other functions of the executive and the other members of the administrative process? Are they limited to mechanically applying the letter of a statute to the situation before them? Arguably, they would be limited to this if statutes were all-encompassing and unambiguous.

In fact, no law is all-encompassing, and many policies are far from clear. Consequently, administrators must exercise some choice as to how each should be applied. As the demands on government mounted, legislatures felt it necessary to resort increasingly to large positive grants of statutory discretion. More and more has been left to the judgment of the administrator.

Accordingly, in the well-known case of *Roncarelli v. Duplessis*,[1] the *Alcoholic Liquor Act* provided that the Alcoholic Liquor Commission "may cancel any permit at its discretion";[2] the *Broadcasting Act* states that the Governor in Council "may" by order issue certain kinds of directions from time to time to the Canadian Radio-television and Telecommunications Commission;[3] the *Canada Labour Code* authorizes the Canada Industrial Relations Board to make an interim decision "if it is satisfied" that it can do so without prejudice to the rights of the parties;[4] and in Ontario the *Education Act* says the Minister of Education "may establish such eligibility criteria for appointment to the [Ontario Parent] Council as the Minister considers advisable."[5]

Positive grants of discretion are a common and useful tool, but their application raises important administrative law questions. Where, for example, are grants of this kind necessary? How broadly should they be framed? When should they prevail over the need for concrete, objective standards? Should they preclude the formulation of such standards by the administrator itself? What are their implications for control by the courts and other bodies?

As the American writer K.C. Davis pointed out, not all administrative discretion is the result of a deliberate grant from the legislature.[6] The result is the existence of a large world of "informal" administrative discretion. Informal discretion plays a necessary role in filling in gaps and ambiguities in formal legislation, but provides its own peculiar problems and challenges.

For example, where an administrative scheme imposes obligations on regulated individuals or groups, but provides for enforcement by *ex post facto* penalties, administrators may feel tempted to secure compliance by less drastic (but technically unauthorized) techniques such as informal persuasion and negotiation.[7] These informal techniques may be useful in softening the effect of the formal rules and in promoting an atmosphere that maximizes voluntary cooperation and compliance on the part of those regulated.

On the other hand, where there is a significant gap between the informal discretionary process and the formal rules, what has been authorized is not being done, and the control of the legislature over the executive is weakened proportionately. Moreover, informal discretionary practices of this kind are more vulnerable to abuse than those that are formally authorized. How, for example, can third parties such as consumers or competitors protect themselves against an informal "arrangement" negotiated solely between an administrator and a regulated party?[8] How readily can an administrator or a regulated party secure redress if one or the other fails to honour an informal commitment made outside the statutory framework?

In *Discretionary Justice*, Davis suggested that discretion should be (i) confined by eliminating it where it is unnecessary and formulating rules or policy statements instead; (ii) structured by rules, policy statements, reasons, and openness; and (iii) checked by supervision by others.[9] Are there any other possible alternatives? What do you think of the notion that regulatory discretion should be structured by *ad hoc* arrangements negotiated by the regulator and the regulated party?[10]

Discretion raises special challenges for judicial review. Since judicial review is based on explicit or presumed limitations on statutory power, the broader the discretion, the less the chances of review. Where courts do review discretion, they tend to adopt one of two possible approaches. First, if there is no privative clause purporting to limit judicial review, or other negative signals, they may set aside a decision for fraud, malice, improper purpose, irrelevant considerations, and fettering of discretion. In the presence of a privative clause or its equivalent indication, review of discretion will only occur if the decision was patently unreasonable.

Notes

1. [1959] S.C.R. 121 (S.C.R.).
2. *Ibid.*
3. R.S.C. 1991. c. B-9.01, s. 7(1).
4. *Canada Labour Code*, R.S.C. 1985, c. L-2, s. 20(1).
5. *Educational Act*, R.S.O. 1990, c. E.2, s. 17.1(3)..
6. K.C. Davis, *Discretionary Justice: A Preliminary Inquiry*, 1969 at 2.
7. See, for example, Law Reform Commission of Canada, *Policy Implementation, Compliance and Administrative Law* (Working Paper 51) (Ottawa: Law Reform Commission of Canada, 1986) at 24–26.
8. *Ibid.* at 25 and 73.
9. Davis, *supra* note 6 at 215–17 (## 1–5: statement of problem and confining); 219–20 (## 8–10 and 12: administrative rule-making for confining and structuring); 225–28 (## 15–17: other confining and structuring); and 228–32 (## 18–22: checking, and controlling leniency and privilege).
10. *Supra* note 5.

(b) Discretion and Fettering: *Capital Cities*[†]

NOTE

Section 15 of the *Broadcasting Act* gave the CRTC a mandate to "regulate and supervise all aspects of the Canadian Broadcasting System with a view to implementing the broadcasting policy enunciated in s. 3 of this Act." Purporting to act under this mandate, the CRTC issued a policy statement that encouraged the replacement of commercials from non-Canadian television signals with CRTC-authorized material from Canadian stations. It then amended a cablevision company's licence to permit this kind of replacement. Capital Cities, an American television operator, challenged this decision unsuccessfully before the Federal Court of Appeal. On appeal to the Supreme Court of Canada, they argued, *inter alia*, that the CRTC had fettered its statutory discretion by formulating the policy statement and making the amendment pursuant to it. Laskin C.J.C. gave the reasons for the six-judge majority. Three judges dissented on grounds unrelated to the fettering issue.

Before *Capital Cities*, Canadian courts had tended to stress that a discretion must be enunciated freely and without any fetters. With this decision, the highest court signalled a more lenient approach to the making of policy guidelines and other administrative constraints on discretion.

EXTRACTS

[The judgment of LASKIN C.J.C., MARTLAND, JUDSON, RITCHIE, SPENCE and DICKSON JJ. was delivered by LASKIN C.J.C. Laskin C.J.C. outlined the issues in dispute, addressed the questions of the status of the applicants and of constitutionality (described as "Question 2"), and then continued:]

[†] *Capital Cities Communications Inc. v. Canadian Radio-Television Commission* (1978), 81 D.L.R. (3d) 609 (S.C.C.).

Question 1, Jurisdiction of the *Commission*

This question relates to the scope of the *Broadcasting Act* and to whether it delegates authority to the Canadian Radio-Television Commission to regulate cable distribution systems. The challenge to the authority of the Commission was rejected by the Federal Court of Appeal and, in my opinion, rightly so.

The contentions of the appellants on this issue are based, in the main, on the definition of "broadcasting" in s. 2 of the *Act*, a definition which embraces the definition of "radiocommunication" in the same section and which, in the result, according to the appellants, amounts to a limitation of meaning, as follows: transmission of signals by Hertzian waves intended for direct reception by the general public. Emphasis is placed on the concluding words of the definition of radiocommunication, namely, the words "without artificial guide". What emerges from the submissions of the appellants is a contention of severance of cable distribution systems as receiving systems from broadcasting transmitting stations, a contention not unlike that advanced in respect of the constitutional question.

The [definitions] of "broadcasting" and of "radiocommunication" are as follows:

"broadcasting" means any radiocommunication in which the transmissions are intended for direct reception by the general public;

...

"radiocommunication" means any transmission, emission or reception of signs, signals, writing, images, sounds or intelligence of any nature by means of electromagnetic waves of frequencies lower than 3,000 Gigacycles per second propagated in space without artificial guide;

It may be noted that radiocommunication embraces reception of signals by Hertzian waves as well as transmission of such signals.

What is relevant on the question at hand are the provisions of the Act assigning powers to the Commission. The powers are related to the realization of the objects of the Act set out in s. 3. So far as relevant here (and in relation to Q.3 dealt with below) the objects are as follows:

3. It is hereby declared that
(a) broadcasting undertakings in Canada make use of radio frequencies that are public property and such undertakings constitute a single system, herein referred to as the Canadian broadcasting system, comprising public and private elements:

(b) the Canadian broadcasting system should be effectively owned and controlled by Canadians so as to safeguard, enrich and strengthen the cultural, political, social and economic fabric of Canada;
(c) all persons licensed to carry on broadcasting undertakings have a responsibility for programs they broadcast but the right to freedom to expression and the right of persons to receive programs, subject only to generally applicable statutes and regulations, is unquestioned;
(d) the programming provided by the Canadian broadcasting system should be varied and comprehensive and should provide reasonable, balanced opportunity for the expression of differing views on matters of public concern, and the programming provided by each broadcaster should be of high standard, using predominantly Canadian creative and other resources;

Sections 15, 16 and 17 of the Act define the powers, respectively, of the Commission and of its Executive Committee. They are in the following terms:

15. Subject to this Act and the *Radio Act* and any directions to the Commission issued from time to time by the Governor in Council under the authority of this Act, the commission shall regulate and supervise all aspects of the Canadian broadcasting system with a view to implementing the broadcasting policy enunciated in section 3 of this Act.

16.(1) In furtherance of its objects, the Commission, on the recommendation of the Executive Committee, may
(a) prescribe classes of broadcasting licences;
...

17.(1) In furtherance of the objects of the Commission, the Executive Committee, after consultation with the part-time members in attendance at a meeting of the Commission, may
(a) issue broadcasting licences for such terms not exceeding five years and subject to such conditions related to the circumstances of the licensee
(i) as the Executive Committee deems appropriate for the implementation of the broadcasting policy enunciated in section 3, and
(ii) in the case of broadcasting licences issued to the Corporation, as the Executive Committee deems consistent with the provision, through the Corporation, of the national broadcasting service contemplated by section 3;
(b) upon application by a licensee, amend any conditions of a broadcasting licence issued to him;

(c) issue renewals of broadcasting licences for such terms not exceeding five years as the Executive Committee considers reasonable and subject to the conditions to which the renewed licences were previously subject or to such other conditions as comply with paragraph (a):

Germane to the foregoing provisions are the definitions of "broadcasting licence" and "broadcasting undertaking", found in s. 2 of the Act. They read as follows:

"broadcasting licence" or, in Parts II and III, "licence" means a licence to carry on a broadcasting undertaking issued under this Act;

"broadcasting undertaking" includes a broadcasting transmitting undertaking, a broadcasting receiving undertaking and a network operation, located in whole or in part within Canada or on a ship or aircraft registered in Canada;

It is patent to me that a cable distribution system, at least one which receives signals from a broadcaster and sends them through the system, is a broadcasting receiving undertaking and is in that respect at least within the regulatory and licensing authority of the Commission. This view is reinforced by s. 29(3) of the Act which is as follows:

26.(3) Every person who carries on broadcasting undertaking without a valid and subsisting broadcasting licence therefor, or who being the holder of a broadcasting licence, operates a broadcasting undertaking as part of a network other than in accordance with the condition of such licence, is guilty of an offence and is liable on summary conviction to a fine not exceeding one thousand dollars for each day that the offence continues.

The present case, I should emphasize, is not concerned with closed circuit systems independent of broadcasting as defined in the Act.

There is an element of incongruity in the present case in that the Rogers companies, which operate cable distribution systems and are licensed under the Act, do not [owe] their liability to the authority of the Commission and it is the appellants, although not licensed by the Commission, which object to the licensing control exercised by the Commission over the licensees.

More than general regulatory authority is, however, challenged in the present case under the term of the Act. It is argued that the powers of the Commission do not encompass the regulation of the content of television programmes and, in any event, do not extend to interference with any such programmes once the signals have been received at the antennae

of cable distribution systems. Attention is directed to s. 3(c) of the Act and to s. 17(1)(b), and I set them out again for convenient reference:

(c) all persons licensed to carry on broadcasting undertakings have a responsibility for programs they broadcast but the right to freedom of expression and the right of persons to receive programs, subject only to generally applicable statutes and regulations, is unquestioned;

17.(1) In furtherance of the objects of the Commission, the Executive Committee, after consultation with the part-time members in attendance at a meeting of the Commission, may

(b) upon application by a licensee, amend any condition of a broadcasting licence issued to him;

I find no merit in the submission, made under s. 3(c), that cable distribution systems are protected thereunder against any Commission authority to permit deletion of commercial messages received by them. I can agree that the licensees mentioned in s. 3(c) are broadcasting transmitting stations, but it does not follow that cable distribution systems are covered by the words "the right of persons to receive programs ... is unquestioned". (It was conceded that there are no "generally applicable statutes and regulations" other than the *Broadcasting Act* and any Regulations thereunder.) The words more aptly apply to ultimate receivers of programmes but, whether they do or not, I would not read s. 3(c), a general object clause, as prevailing over the specific licensing authority of the Commission, an authority which is under a generally applicable statute. Mr. Robinette submitted, on behalf of the Commission, that having regard to s. 16(1)(b) (iii) and (iv) of the Act and to s. 28(2) (which refer to "programs, advertisements or announcements"), the word "program" in s. 3(c) should be read as excluding commercial messages or advertising. I do not need to rely on this submission in the present case.

A second contention urged against what the Commission did in this case turns on the scope of s. 17(1)(b) of the Act, empowering the Executive Committee "upon application by a licensee, [to] amend any conditions of a broadcasting licence issued to him". It is alleged that the licences held by the Rogers companies did not contain any conditions which could be said to be amended by what was done here in authorizing deletion of commercial messages and substitution of public service announcements. This seems to me to fly in the face of the provisions of the licences held by the Rogers companies who were authorized thereunder to receive and distribute the signals of the very stations operated by the appellants.

The appellants would give a strictly technical meaning to the word "conditions" and a limited meaning to the word "amend" in s. 17(l)(b). In my opinion, The Act, read as a whole, and s. 17(l) read in its context, make it abundantly clear to me that s. 17(l)(b) refers simply to any change in the terms governing any licence issued by the Executive Committee. The words in s. 17(l) are not to be construed as if they were part of a common law conveyance.

Question 3, Alleged Excess of Jurisdiction

On the assumption of jurisdiction in the sense canvassed in the answer to Q. 1, two further issues are raised touching the exercise of authority by the Commission in the present case. Paragraph (b) of Q. 3 refers to that portion of the Commission's decision in which it made its consent a prerequisite to any settlement by the respondents of litigation initiated against them by the appellants in the Federal Court. I can find no basis in the Act for this requirement. The concern of the Commission that any settlement should not prejudice the ability of the respondents to carry out their obligations under the *Broadcasting Act* is understandable, but the Commission has licensing control which it can exercise to secure such conformity. There may be issues in a settlement which could not be of any concern to the Commission in respect of its authority, and it is an overreaching for it to include a requirement in its decision of its consent to the settlement of private litigation.

This part of the decision is clearly severable; indeed, it was not argued by the appellants that the whole decision must fall if this part was beyond the Commission's authority.

Paragraph (a) of Q. 3 alleges an excess of jurisdiction because the Commission's decision was based on a policy statement and not on law or regulation. Two points are made in respect of this submission: first, s. 3(c) is again invoked to support the assertion that there can be no regulation of programme content unless there are applicable regulations (and none were shown to exist); and s. 16(1) is referred to which authorizes regulations, applicable to all persons holding broadcast licences, with respect to such matters as standards of programmes, the character of advertising and the proportion of time that can be devoted to programmes, advertising or announcements. There are requirements that must be met both under s. 16(2) and under the Statutory Instru-

ments Act, 1970-71-72 (Can.), c. 38, before any regulation becomes effective and it was asserted, without contradiction, that there were as yet no regulations respecting cable distribution systems.

The issue that arises therefore is whether the Commission or its Executive Committee acting under its licensing authority, is entitled to exercise that authority by reference to policy statements or whether it is limited in the way it deals with licence applications or with applications to amend licences to conformity with regulations. I have no doubt that if regulations are in force which relate to the licensing function they would have to be followed even if there were policy statements that were at odds with the regulations. The regulations would prevail against any policy statements. However, absent any regulation, is the Commission obliged to act only ad hoc in respect of any application for a licence or an amendment thereto, and is it precluded from announcing policies upon which it may act when considering any such applications?

Apart from the argument that the Commission's powers do not extend to cable distribution systems, an argument which I have rejected, it is not contended by the appellants that the policy statement, to which reference was made in the decision in this case, deals with matters going beyond the Commission's authority. Reference is, however, made to ss. 16 and 17 of the Act, dealing respectively with power to make regulations and power to issue and amend licences, both of which are qualified by the opening words "in furtherance of its objects". The appellants seemed to regard these provisions as requiring an input of the policy considerations in s. 3 only as regulations are promulgated or on an individual basis when applications are under consideration.

The respondent's position on the foregoing contentions was that since the Commission held a hearing on the application of the Rogers companies, a hearing at which the appellants were heard as to the policy of the Commission and as to the merits of the application, the power of the commission would not be challenged as having been exercised improperly. Reliance was also placed on what was said by Bankes, L.J., in *The King* v. *Port of London Authority, Ex p. Kynoch, Ltd.*, [1919] 1 K.B. 176 at p. 184, and by the House of Lords in *British Oxygen Co. Ltd.* v. *Board of Trade*, [1971] A.C. 610 at p. 624.

In my opinion, having regard to the embracive objects committed to the Commission under s. 15 of the Act, objects which extend to the supervision of "all aspects of the Canadian Broadcasting system with a view to implementing the broadcasting policy enunciated in section 3 of the Act", it was eminently proper that it lay down guidelines from time to time as it did in respect of cable television. The guidelines on this matter were arrived at after extensive hearings at which interested parties were present and made submissions. An overall policy is demanded in the interests of prospective licensees and of the public under such a regulatory regime as is set up by the *Broadcasting Act*. Although one could mature as a result of a succession of applications, there is merit in having it known in advance.

The objection taken under para. (a) of Q. 3 must, accordingly, be dismissed.

. . . .

In the result, I would dismiss the appeal with costs in this Court....

[PIGEON J. dissented, with BEETZ and de GRANDPRE JJ. concurring.]

(c)   Discretion and the *Charter*: *Ontario Film*†

NOTE

Purporting to act under a discretionary power in s. 3(2)(a) of the *Theatres Act* and under their own informal guidelines, the Ontario Board of Censors refused to allow a film society to show a film in public. The film society challenged the constitutionality of the section. They argued that it violated the *Charter* guarantee of freedom of expression and was not saved by s. 1 of the *Charter* because neither the discretionary power nor the guidelines constituted a "limit" within the meaning of s. 1. The Ontario Court of Appeal's decision in this case contrasted with the more expansive approach to discretion and policy guidelines in the *Capital Cities* case.

EXTRACTS

[MacKINNON A.C.J.O.:]

The Divisional Court thoroughly and carefully canvassed the issues that were raised on this appeal and cross-appeal. As we are in substantial agreement with their analysis of these issues and their reasoned conclusions, it would serve no useful purpose to repeat at any length the facts and the issues.

It is argued before us on behalf of the appellant that s. 3(2)(a) of the *Theatres Act*, R.S.O. 1980, c. 498, in view of its lengthy history and the manner in which it is interpreted and applied by the Ontario Board of Censors, is, in some fashion, a recognized restraint on the freedom of expression which falls

outside s. 2(b) of the *Canadian Charter of Rights and Freedoms*. In other words, it is a pre-Charter recognized restraint on the freedom of expression, and there is no need to go to s. 1 of the Charter to salvage it.

Section 3(2)(a) reads:

3(2) The Board has power,
(a) to censor any film and, when authorized by the person who submits film to the Board for approval, remove by cutting or otherwise from the film any portion thereof that it does not approve of for exhibition in Ontario;

We cannot accept that argument. We agree with the conclusion of the Divisional Court that s. 3(2)(a) clearly imposes a limitation on freedom of expression as guaranteed by s. 2(b) of the Charter. We also agree that ss. 35 and 38 of the *Theatres Act* are capable of being interpreted and applied as part of that limitation. The Divisional Court concluded on this point [41 O.R. (2d) 583 at p. 593, 147 D.L.R. (3d) 58 at p. 68]:

These sections, in so far as they purport to prohibit or to allow the censorship of films, may be said to be "of no force or effect"....

We would go further than the Divisional Court on this issue. In our view, s. 3(2)(a), rather than being of "no force or effect", is *ultra vires* as it stands. The subsection allows for the complete denial or prohibition of the freedom of expression in this particular area and sets no limits on the Ontario

---

† *Re Ontario Film & Video Appreciation Society and Ontario Board of Censors* (1984), 45 O.R. (2d) 80 (O.C.A.).

Board of Censors. It clearly sets no limit, reasonable or otherwise, on which an argument can be mounted that it falls within the saving words of s. 1 of the Charter: "subject only to such reasonable limits prescribed by law". Further, like the Divisional Court, we conclude that s. 3(2)(*b*) and ss. 35 and 38 cannot be interpreted and applied in their present form to support the censorship of film although they have a valid role to play otherwise. As pointed out by the Divisional Court, there is no challenge in these proceedings to the system of film classification, nor to the general regulation of theatres and projectionists and other matters dealt with in the statute and regulations.

The Divisional Court stated that they were expressing no view whether the standards issued by the Ontario Board of Censors, if embodied in the legislation, or the regulations properly authorized by the statute, would be considered "reasonable limits" within the meaning of those words found in s. 1 of the Charter. This question is not before us and we express no opinion on whether there can be legislated guide-lines for the Ontario Board of Censors so as to be reasonable limits prescribed by law on the freedom of expression, demonstrably justified in a free and democratic society. In dealing with this point, the Divisional Court stated [at p. 591 O.R., p. 68 D.L.R.]: "One thing is sure, however, our courts will exercise considerable restraint in declaring legislative enactments, whether they be statutory or regulatory, to be unreasonable." We do not think, if they were purporting to enunciate a principle, that there is any such principle to be applied in the determination of what is "reasonable" under s. 1 of the Charter. In approaching the question, there is no presumption for or against the legislation but there are many factors to be considered, in light of the legislation itself and its background, which have been recited in a number of authorities: *Re Federal Republic of Germany and Rauca* (1983), 41 O.R. (2d) 225 at p. 244, 145 D.L.R. (3d) 638 at p. 658, 4 C.C.C. (3d) 385; *Re Southam Inc. and The Queen (No. 1)* (1983), 41 O.R. (2d) 113 at pp. 129–30, 146 D.L.R. (3d) 408 at pp. 424–5, 3 C.C.C. (3d) 515.

The appeal by the Ontario Board of Censors is dismissed.

On the cross-appeal by the respondents, we did not feel it necessary to call on the cross-respondents to respond to the argument. We are in agreement with the Divisional Court in their disposition of the issues in the cross-appeal and it is not necessary to add anything further. The cross-appeal is dismissed.

As success was divided there will be no order as to costs.

J. Polika, Q.C., for appellant.
L. King and C.M. Campbell, for respondent.
K.P. Swan and E.J. Abner, for intervenor, Canadian Civil Liberties Association.

(d) Discretion and Factor-Weighing: *Baker*[†]

NOTE

The facts in *Baker* were described in Chapter 4 above. The following extract contains some of the main majority's discussion of discretion.

EXTRACTS

[L'HEUREUX-DUBÉ for herself, GONTHIER, McLACHLIN, BASTARACHE and BINNIE JJ.]

[para50] ... [Mrs. Baker also submits] that the decision should be held to a standard of review of correctness, that principles of administrative law require this discretion to be exercised in accordance with the *Convention*, and that the Minister should apply the best interests of the child as a primary consideration in H & C decisions....

[para51] As stated earlier, the legislation and regulations delegate considerable discretion to the Minister in deciding whether an exemption should be granted

---

[†] *Baker v. Canada (Minister of Citizenship and Immigration)*, [1999] 2 S.C.R. 817, rev'g, [1997] 2 F.C. 127 (F.C.A.), answering a question certified by Simpson J. in [1995] F.C.J. No. 1441 (F.C.T.D.).

based upon humanitarian and compassionate considerations....

. . . .

[para53] Administrative law has traditionally approached the review of decisions classified as discretionary separately from those seen as involving the interpretation of rules of law. The rule has been that decisions classified as discretionary may only be reviewed on limited grounds such as the bad faith of decision-makers, the exercise of discretion for an improper purpose, and the use of irrelevant considerations.... A general doctrine of "unreasonableness" has also sometimes been applied to discretionary decisions: *Associated Provincial Picture Houses, Ltd.* v. *Wednesbury Corporation*, [1948] 1 K.B. 223 (C.A.). In my opinion, these doctrines incorporate two central ideas — that discretionary decisions, like all other administrative decisions, must be made within the bounds of the jurisdiction conferred by the statute, but that considerable deference will be given to decision-makers by courts in reviewing the exercise of that discretion and determining the scope of the decision-maker's jurisdiction. These doctrines recognize that it is the intention of a legislature, when using statutory language that confers broad choices on administrative agencies, that courts should not lightly interfere with such decisions, and should give considerable respect to decision-makers when reviewing the manner in which discretion was exercised. However, discretion must still be exercised in a manner that is within a reasonable interpretation of the margin of manoeuvre contemplated by the legislature, in accordance with the principles of the rule of law (*Roncarelli* v. *Duplessis*, [1959] S.C.R. 121), in line with general principles of administrative law governing the exercise of discretion, and consistent with the *Canadian Charter of Rights and Freedoms* (*Slaight Communications Inc.* v. *Davidson*, [1989] 1 S.C.R. 1038).

[para54] It is, however, inaccurate to speak of a rigid dichotomy of "discretionary" or "non-discretionary" decisions. Most administrative decisions involve the exercise of implicit discretion in relation to many aspects of decision making. To give just one example, decision-makers may have considerable discretion as to the remedies they order. In addition, there is no easy distinction to be made between interpretation and the exercise of discretion; interpreting legal rules involves considerable discretion to clarify, fill in legislative gaps, and make choices among various

options. As stated by Brown and Evans, *supra*, at p. 14-47:

> The degree of discretion in a grant of power can range from one where the decision-maker is constrained only by the purposes and objects of the legislation, to one where it is so specific that there is almost no discretion involved. In between, of course, there may be any number of limitations placed on the decision-maker's freedom of choice, sometimes referred to as "structured" discretion.

[para55] The "pragmatic and functional" approach recognizes that standards of review for errors of law are appropriately seen as a spectrum, with certain decisions being entitled to more deference, and others entitled to less....: *Pezim...*, at pp. 589–90; *Southam...*, at para. 30; *Pushpanathan...*, at para. 27. Three standards of review have been defined: patent unreasonableness, reasonableness simpliciter, and correctness: *Southam*, at paras. 54–56. In my opinion the standard of review of the substantive aspects of discretionary decisions is best approached within this framework, especially given the difficulty in making rigid classifications between discretionary and non-discretionary decisions. The pragmatic and functional approach takes into account considerations such as the expertise of the tribunal, the nature of the decision being made, and the language of the provision and the surrounding legislation. It includes factors such as whether a decision is "polycentric" and the intention revealed by the statutory language. The amount of choice left by Parliament to the administrative decision-maker and the nature of the decision being made are also important considerations in the analysis. The spectrum of standards of review can incorporate the principle that in certain cases, the legislature has demonstrated its intention to leave greater choices to decision-makers than in others, but that a court must intervene where such a decision is outside the scope of the power accorded by Parliament. Finally, I would note that this Court has already applied this framework to statutory provisions that confer significant choices on administrative bodies, for example, in reviewing the exercise of the remedial powers conferred by the statute at issue in *Southam*, *supra*....

[para56] Incorporating judicial review of decisions that involve considerable discretion into the pragmatic and functional analysis for errors of law should not be seen as reducing the level of deference given to decisions of a highly discretionary nature. In fact, deferential standards of review may give substantial leeway to the discretionary decision-maker in deter-

mining the "proper purposes" or "relevant considerations" involved in making a given determination. The pragmatic and functional approach can take into account the fact that the more discretion that is left to a decision-maker, the more reluctant courts should be to interfere with the manner in which decision-makers have made choices among various options....

[para58] The first factor to be examined is the presence or absence of a privative clause, and, in appropriate cases, the wording of that clause....

[para59] The second factor is the expertise of the decision-maker....

[para60] The third factor is the purpose of the provision in particular, and of the Act as a whole....

[para61] The fourth factor outlined in *Pushpanathan* considers the nature of the problem in question, especially whether it relates to determination of law or facts....

[para62] These factors must be balanced to arrive at the appropriate standard of review. I conclude that considerable deference should be accorded to immigration officers exercising the powers conferred by the legislation, given the fact-specific nature of the inquiry, its role within the statutory scheme as an exception, the fact that the decision-maker is the Minister, and the considerable discretion evidenced by the statutory language. Yet the absence of a privative clause, the explicit contemplation of judicial review by the Federal Court — Trial Division and the Federal Court of Appeal in certain circumstances, and the individual rather than polycentric nature of the decision, also suggest that the standard should not be as deferential as "patent unreasonableness". I conclude, weighing all these factors, that the appropriate standard of review is reasonableness simpliciter.

[para63] I will next examine whether the decision in this case, and the immigration officer's interpretation of the scope of the discretion conferred upon him, was unreasonable in the sense contemplated in the judgment of Iacobucci J. in *Southam...*, at para. 56:

> An unreasonable decision is one that, in the main, is not supported by any reasons that can stand up to a somewhat probing examination. Accordingly, a court reviewing a conclusion on the reasonableness standard must look to see whether any reasons support it. The defect, if there is one, could presumably be in the evidentiary foundation itself or in the logical process by

which conclusions are sought to be drawn from it....

. . . .

[para65] In my opinion, the approach taken to the children's interests shows that this decision was unreasonable in the sense contemplated in *Southam....* The officer was completely dismissive of the interests of Ms. Baker's children....

. . . .

[para67] ... In my opinion, a reasonable exercise of the power conferred by the section requires close attention to the interests and needs of children. Children's rights, and attention to their interests, are central humanitarian and compassionate values in Canadian society....

. . . .

[para69] Another indicator of the importance of considering the interests of children when making a compassionate and humanitarian decision is the ratification by Canada of the *Convention* on the Rights of the Child.... I agree with the respondent and the Court of Appeal that the *Convention* has not been implemented by Parliament. Its provisions therefore have no direct application within Canadian law.

[para70] Nevertheless, the values reflected in international human rights law may help inform the contextual approach to statutory interpretation and judicial review....

. . . .

[para72] Third, the guidelines issued by the Minister to immigration officers ... emphasize that the decision-maker should be alert to possible humanitarian grounds, should consider the hardship that a negative decision would impose upon the claimant or close family members, and should consider as an important factor the connections between family members.

[para73] ... I conclude that because the reasons for this decision do not indicate that it was made in a manner which was alive, attentive, or sensitive to the interests of Ms. Baker's children, and did not consider them as an important factor in making the decision, it was an unreasonable exercise of the power conferred by the legislation, and must, therefore, be overturned. In addition, the reasons for decision failed to give sufficient weight or consideration to the hardship that a return to Jamaica might cause Ms. Baker, given the fact that she had been in Canada for 12 years, was ill and might not be able

to obtain treatment in Jamaica, and would necessarily be separated from at least some of her children.

. . . .

[para76] Therefore, both because there was a violation of the principles of procedural fairness owing to a reasonable apprehension of bias, and because the

exercise of the H & C discretion was unreasonable, I would allow this appeal.

[para77] ... I would allow the appeal, and set aside the decision of Officer Caden of April 18, 1994, with party-and-party costs throughout. The matter will be returned to the Minister for redetermination by a different immigration officer.

(e) Access to Information

Why should you and I know about information in the hands of the administrative process? The answer varies with the specific situation. In the context of natural justice and fair procedure, we have seen that it could be important to know about information that may lead to impending administrative action prejudicial to us, so we can try to defend ourselves against it. Even where there is no specific threat, an individual may have a similar concern about even the possibility of adverse government action.

The media or others (such as administrative law students!) may be seeking information in pursuit of a specific research objective. More generally, knowledge of what government and other parts of the administrative process are doing helps us all plan our lives (e.g., by heeding weather forecasts, consumer products news, or warnings about tax deadlines or water quality, or by taking advantage of government benefits such as new libraries, unemployment insurance, or vaccination clinics).

At the most basic level, information about government and the administrative process is necessary to enable citizens to know that the government is accountable to them. Without a clear knowledge of what the administrative process does, we lose control of it, and loss of public control erodes democracy itself.

There are at least nine main avenues of access to information that are available to Canadians. We have already considered some of these in regard to natural justice and fairness, but will review them all briefly before going on to the ninth, formal access to information legislation.

1. Informal Requests

Often government information can be obtained "simply" by asking. The catch is to know what

to ask, whom to ask, and how to phrase one's question. A government telephone directory, patience, and persistence are three key requirements.

2. Openness

The principle of openness can be used sometimes to compel administrators to conduct their hearings openly, rather than *in camera*. Reviewing courts presume that all judicial proceedings and all administrative proceedings resembling those of courts should be conducted openly. Like all presumptions, this can be rebutted by statutory provisions to the contrary. Sometimes an openness requirement is stipulated or implied in a specific statutory provision, such as s. 20 of the *National Energy Board Act*, considered in the *Dow Chemical* case. Alternatively, it may be required in a general code-like statute, such as s. 9 of the Ontario *Statutory Instruments Procedure Act*, considered in Chapter 5.

3. Natural Justice and Fairness

We addressed the principles of natural justice and fairness in Chapters 4 to 7. Here we will only note that they provide for access to information for specific defensive purposes. They enable a party to proceedings before an ordinary court or before an administrator with enough notice and other information to enable that party to have an opportunity to defend himself or herself. Where they are based on common law, these principles do not provide absolute rights, but presumptions, capable of being defeated by express statutory provisions to the contrary or simply by factors militating against disclosure. In special situations, these principles may also be stipulated expressly in statute, or may be enforceable through s. 7 of the *Charter*. Some administrators attempt to reconcile the needs of disclosure and confidentiality in their own procedural rules.

4. Reasons for Decisions and Annual Reports

At common law, there is no general presumption requiring administrators to provide reasons *after* their decisions, and pre-decision reasons are obtainable only in the context of the rules of natural justice and fairness. However, administrators may be required to provide reasons after decisions as a result of requirements in statutes. One such general requirement is s. 17 of the Ontario *Statutory Powers Procedure Act* (see Chapter 5, above). Statutes may also require that administrators provide reports of their decisions and other actions on an annual or other basis. This is a common requirement for independent government agencies and Crown corporations, which are free of direct ministerial controls.

5. Publication and Pre-publication of Subordinate Legislation

We looked at the making and control of subordinate legislation in Chapter 3. Except where a finite number of parties are in an adversarial situation strongly resembling that of litigation before a court (as in the *Wiswell* case, Chapter 5, above), reviewing courts do not apply natural justice presumptions to subordinate legislation.

The main information requirement for subordinate legislation is publication. The federal *Statutory Instruments Act* imposes publication requirements on some kinds of federal subordinate legislation, along with other requirements such as monitoring by the Justice Department, availability for inspection, and referral to a Parliamentary committee. The provincial *Regulations Acts* contain publication requirements for certain provincial subordinate legislation. At both levels, though, many informal government guidelines and circulars escape these requirements.

Section 4 of the American *Administrative Procedure Act* contains a "notice and comment" provision requiring federal administrative agencies to provide notice of proposed rule-making and to offer interested parties the opportunity to comment on them. The Quebec *Regulations Act* requires that proposed regulations be published in the *Gazette officielle du Québec* prior to being made and coming into effect. The federal government has imposed a similar requirement for federal government departments and major regulatory agencies, not by statute, but as a matter of policy. Perhaps the intention is to make the federal requirements more flexible and less susceptible to judicial review.

6. Parliamentary Assent to Bills

In regard to primary legislation, we should remember one of the most traditional and basic access requirements of all: the requirement that all bills be given assent after public deliberation in Parliament or the relevant provincial or territorial legislature. Related to assent are the investigatory powers of Parliamentary committees and individual legislators.

7. The *Charter*

We encountered s. 7 of the *Charter* in the *Singh* case in Chapter 5. Section 7 provides that:

> Everyone has the right to life, liberty and security of the person, and the right not to be deprived thereof except in accordance with the principles of fundamental justice.

Note that this right is limited to deprivations of "life, liberty, and security of the person." In content, this provision occupies at least the procedural ground covered by natural justice, and probably guarantees open hearings as well. (In *Singh*, we also saw a somewhat similar hearing requirement in the *Canadian Bill of Rights*.)

Two other *Charter* sections that can be used to require access are s. 2(b), guaranteeing the right of "freedom of ... expression, including freedom of the press and other media of communication"; and s. 11(d), stating that "[a]ny person charged with an offence has the right ... to be presumed innocent until proven guilty in a fair and public hearing by an independent and impartial tribunal."

Sections 2, 7, and 11 are all subject to the override section of the *Charter*, s. 33, and to the "reasonable justification" qualification in s. 1.

8. Special Investigatory Bodies

In some cases, an individual's quest for information in specific areas may be aided by special investigatory bodies. Auditors general, human rights commissions, ombudsmen, and individual MPs or MLAs may all play this role.

9. Access to Information Legislation

The federal government and all provinces and territories have enacted formal access to information legislation: Canada (1982); Nova Scotia (1977); New Brunswick (1978); Newfoundland (1981); Quebec (1982); Manitoba (1985, proclaimed 1988); Ontario (1988, extended to Ontario municipalities on 1 January 1991); British Columbia (1993, proclaimed for local government, 1994); Yukon (1996); N.W.T. (1994); Nunavut (1999); and Prince Edward Island (2002). In two other provinces (Alberta and Saskatchewan), denials of requests for information can be appealed to the provincial ombudsman.

Like other access mechanisms, freedom of information legislation must balance between competing needs of disclosure and confidentiality. Some topics that are most often subject to confidentiality claims are Cabinet documents; law enforcement, defence, and national security matters; personal information; policy advice; and commercial secrets.

Clearly, the exemption provisions relating to these and other possible topics are critical to the strength of an access statute. So are the provisions that define the general scope of the legislation: does it apply only to the central administrative process, or does it include the outlying and quasi-administrative processes as well? If it is a provincial statute, does it include the structures of municipal government?

How much does access cost? Is there a threshold point below which searches are free? What is this point? What are the fees for search time and photocopying?

Another critical aspect of access legislation is the nature of the appeal process. Some legislation provides for an appeal to a semi-independent access commissioner (who may also administer protection of privacy legislation) and, ultimately, to the courts. In other provinces, the appellate body at first instance is the provincial ombudsman. In Nova Scotia, appeals used to be routed to the relevant Cabinet minister and ultimately to the legislative assembly. (This procedure changed in 1993: there is now a review by a special body appointed by Cabinet, with appeal to the courts, or an appeal directly to the courts.) Appeals rarely succeeded under the old régime in Nova Scotia. This suggests the importance of having independent appeal structures.

(f)   Access to Information Act[†]

SHORT TITLE

Short title

1. This Act may be cited as the *Access to Information Act*.

PURPOSE OF ACT

Purpose

2.(1) The purpose of this Act is to extend the present laws of Canada to provide a right of access to information in records under the control of a government institution in accordance with the principles that government information should be available to the public, that necessary exceptions to the right of access should be limited and specific and that decisions on the disclosure of government information should be reviewed independently of government.

Complementary procedures

(2) This Act is intended to complement and not replace existing procedures for access to government information and is not intended to limit in any way access to the type of government information that is normally available to the general public.

．   ．   ．   ．

[†] R.S.C. 1985, c. A-1.

ACCESS TO GOVERNMENT RECORDS

Right of Access

Right to access to records

4.(1) Subject to this Act, but notwithstanding any other Act of Parliament, every person who is

(a) a Canadian citizen, or

(b) a permanent resident within the meaning of the *Immigration Act*,

has a right to and shall, on request, be given access to any record under the control of a government institution.

Extension of right by order

(2) The Governor in Council may, by order, extend the right to be given access to records under subsection (1) to include persons not referred to in that subsection and may set such conditions as the Governor in Council deems appropriate.

Records produced from machine readable records

(3) For the purposes of this Act, any record requested under this Act that does not exist but can, subject to such limitations as may be prescribed by regulation, be produced from a machine readable record under the control of a government institution using computer hardware and software and technical expertise normally used by the government institution shall be deemed to be a record under the control of the government institution.

Information about Government Institutions

Publication on government institutions

5.(1) The designated Minister shall cause to be published, on a periodic basis not less frequently than once each year, a publication containing

(a) a description of the organization and responsibilities of each government institution, including details on the programs and functions of each division or branch of each government institution;

(b) a description of all classes of records under the control of each government institution in sufficient detail to facilitate the exercise of the right of access under this Act;

(c) a description of all manuals used by employees of each government institution in adminis-

tering or carrying out any of the programs or activities of the government institution; and

(d) the title and address of the appropriate officer for each government institution to whom requests for access to records under this Act should be sent.

.   .   .   .

Requests for Access

Request for access to record

6. A request for access to a record under this Act shall be made in writing to the government institution that has control of the record and shall provide sufficient detail to enable an experienced employee of the institution with a reasonable effort to identify the record.

Notice where access requested

7. Where access to a record is requested under this Act, the head of the government institution to which the request is made shall, subject to sections 8, 9 and 11, within thirty days after the request is received,

(a) give written notice to the person who made the request as to whether or not access to the record or a part thereof will be given; and

(b) if access is to be given, give the person who made the request access to the record or part thereof.

.   .   .   .

Where access is refused

10.(1) Where the head of a government institution refuses to give access to a record requested under this Act or a part thereof, the head of the institution shall state in the notice given under paragraph 7(a)

(a) that the record does not exist, or

(b) the specific provision of this Act on which the refusal was based or, where the head of the institution does not indicate whether a record exists, the provision on which a refusal could reasonably be expected to be based if the record existed,

and shall state in the notice that the person who made the request has a right to make a complaint to the Information Commissioner about the refusal.

.   .   .   .

Fees

11.(1) Subject to this section, a person who makes a request for access to a record under this Act may be required to pay

(a) at the time the request is made, such application fee, not exceeding twenty-five dollars, as may be prescribed by regulation;

(b) before any copies are made, such fee as may be prescribed by regulation reflecting the cost of reproduction calculated in the manner prescribed by regulation; and

. . . .

Additional payment

(2) The head of a government institution to which a request for access to a record is made under this Act may require, in addition to the fee payable under paragraph (1)(a), payment of an amount, calculated in the manner prescribed by regulation, for every hour in excess of five hours that is reasonably required to search for the record or prepare any part of it for disclosure, and may require that the payment be made before access to the record is given.

. . . .

Access

Access to record

12.(1) A person who is given access to a record or a part thereof under this Act shall, subject to the regulations, be given an opportunity to examine the record or part thereof or be given a copy thereof.

. . . .

EXEMPTIONS

Responsibilities of Government

Information obtained in confidence

13.(1) Subject to subsection (2), the head of a government institution shall refuse to disclose any record requested under this Act that contains information that was obtained in confidence from

(a) the government of a foreign state or an institution thereof;

(b) an international organization of states or an institution thereof;

(c) the government of a province or an institution thereof; or

(d) a municipal or regional government established by or pursuant to an Act of the legislature of a province or an institution of such a government.

Where disclosure authorized

(2) The head of a government institution may disclose any record requested under this Act that contains information described in subsection (1) if the government, organization or institution from which the information was obtained

(a) consents to the disclosure; or

(b) makes the information public.

Federal-provincial affairs

14. The head of a government institution may refuse to disclose any record requested under this Act that contains information the disclosure of which could reasonably be expected to be injurious to the conduct by the Government of Canada of federal-provincial affairs, including, without restricting the generality of the foregoing, any such information

(a) on federal-provincial consultations or deliberations; or

(b) on strategy or tactics adopted or to be adopted by the Government of Canada relating to the conduct of federal-provincial affairs.

International affairs and defence

15.(1) The head of a government institution may refuse to disclose any record requested under this Act that contains information the disclosure of which could reasonably be expected to be injurious to the conduct of international affairs, the defence of Canada or any state allied or associated with Canada or the detection, prevention or suppression of subversive or hostile activities....

. . . .

Law enforcement and investigations

16.(1) The head of a government institution may refuse to disclose any record requested under this Act that contains

(a) information obtained or prepared by any government institution, or part of any government institution, that is an investigative body specified in the regulations in the course of lawful investigations pertaining to

(i) the detection, prevention or suppression of crime,

(ii) the enforcement of any law of Canada or a province, or

    (iii) activities suspected of constituting threats to the security of Canada within the meaning of the *Canadian Security Intelligence Service Act*,

if the record came into existence less than twenty years prior to the request;

(b) information relating to investigative techniques or plans for specific lawful investigations;

(c) information the disclosure of which could reasonably be expected to be injurious to the enforcement of any law of Canada or a province or the conduct of lawful investigations....

. . . .

Security

(2) The head of a government institution may refuse to disclose any record requested under this Act that contains information that could reasonably be expected to facilitate the commission of an offence, including, without restricting the generality of the foregoing, any such information

(a) on criminal methods or techniques;

(b) that is technical information relating to weapons or potential weapons; or

(c) on the vulnerability of particular buildings or other structures or systems, including computer or communication systems, or methods employed to protect such buildings or other structures or systems.

Policing services for provinces or municipalities

(3) The head of a government institution shall refuse to disclose any record requested under this Act that contains information that was obtained or prepared by the Royal Canadian Mounted Police while performing policing services for a province or municipality pursuant to an arrangement made under section 20 of the *Royal Canadian Mounted Police Act*, where the Government of Canada has, on the request of the province or municipality agreed not to disclose such information.

. . . .

Safety of individuals

17. The head of a government institution may refuse to disclose any record requested under this Act that contains information the disclosure of which could reasonably be expected to threaten the safety of individuals.

Economic interests of Canada

18. The head of a government institution may refuse to disclose any record requested under this Act that contains

(a) trade secrets or financial, commercial, scientific or technical information that belongs to the Government of Canada or a government institution and has substantial value or is reasonably likely to have substantial value;

(b) information the disclosure of which could reasonably be expected to prejudice the competitive position of a government institution;

(c) scientific or technical information obtained through research by an officer or employee of a government institution, the disclosure of which could reasonably be expected to deprive the officer or employee of priority of publication; or

(d) information the disclosure of which could reasonably be expected to be materially injurious to the financial interests of the Government of Canada or the ability of the Government of Canada to manage the economy of Canada or could reasonably be expected to result in an undue benefit to any person....

. . . .

Personal Information

Personal information

19.(1) Subject to subsection (2), the head of a government institution shall refuse to disclose any record requested under this Act that contains personal information as defined in section 3 of the *Privacy Act*.

Where disclosure authorized

(2) The head of a government institution may disclose any record requested under this Act that contains personal information if

(a) the individual to whom it relates consents to the disclosure;

(b) the information is publicly available; or

(c) the disclosure is in accordance with section 8 of the *Privacy Act*.

Third Party Information

Third party information

20.(1) Subject to this section, the head of a government institution shall refuse to disclose any record requested under this Act that contains

(a) trade secrets of a third party;

(b) financial, commercial, scientific or technical information that is confidential information supplied to a government institution by a third party and is treated consistently in a confidential manner by the third party;

(c) information the disclosure of which could reasonably be expected to result in material financial loss or gain to, or could reasonably be expected to prejudice the competitive position of, a third party; or

(d) information the disclosure of which could reasonably be expected to interfere with contractual or other negotiations of a third party.

.   .   .   .

Operations of Government

Advice, etc.

21.(1) The head of a government institution may refuse to disclose any record requested under this Act that contains

(a) advice or recommendations developed by or for a government institution or a minister of the Crown,

(b) an account of consultations or deliberations involving officers or employees of a government institution, a minister of the Crown or the staff of a minister of the Crown,

(c) positions or plans developed for the purpose of negotiations carried on or to be carried on by or on behalf of the Government of Canada and considerations relating thereto, or

(d) plans relating to the management of personnel or the administration of a government institution that have not yet been put into operation,

if the record came into existence less than twenty years prior to the request.

Exercise of a discretionary power or an adjudicative function

(2) Subsection (1) does not apply in respect of a record that contains

(a) an account of, or a statement of reasons for, a decision that is made in the exercise of a discretionary power or an adjudicative function and that affects the rights of a person; or

(b) a report prepared by a consultant or an adviser who was not, at the time the report was prepared, an officer or employee of a government institution or a member of the staff of a minister of the Crown.

Testing procedures, tests and audits

22. The head of a government institution may refuse to disclose any record requested under this Act that contains information relating to testing or auditing procedures or techniques or details of specific tests to be given or audits to be conducted if the disclosure would prejudice the use or results of particular tests or audits.

Solicitor-client privilege

23. The head of a government institution may refuse to disclose any record requested under this Act that contains information that is subject to solicitor-client privilege.

Statutory Prohibitions

Statutory prohibitions against disclosure

24.(1) The head of a government institution shall refuse to disclose any record requested under this Act that contains information the disclosure of which is restricted by or pursuant to any provision set out in Schedule II.

.   .   .   .

Refusal of Access

Refusal of access where information to be published

26. The head of a government institution may refuse to disclose any record requested under this Act or any part thereof if the head of the institution believes on reasonable grounds that the material in the record or part thereof will be published by a government institution, agent of the Government of Canada or minister of the Crown within ninety days after the request is made or within such further period of time as may be necessary for printing or translating the material for the purpose of printing it.

THIRD PARTY INTERVENTION

Notice to third parties

27.(1) Where the head of a government institution intends to disclose any record requested under this Act, or any part thereof, that contains or that the head of the institution has reason to believe might contain

(a) trade secrets of a third party,

(b) information described in paragraph 20(1)(b) that was supplied by a third party, or

(c) information the disclosure of which the head of the institution could reasonably foresee might effect a result described in paragraph 20(1)(c) or (d) in respect of a third party,

the head of the institution shall, subject to subsection (2), if the third party can reasonably be located, within thirty days after the request is received, give written notice to the third party of the request and of the fact that the head of the institution intends to disclose the record or part thereof.

. . . .

COMPLAINTS

Receipt and investigation of complaints

30.(1) Subject to this Act, the Information Commissioner shall receive and investigate complaints

   (a) from persons who have been refused access to a record requested under this Act or a part thereof;

   (b) from persons who have been required to pay an amount under section 11 that they consider unreasonable;

   (c) from persons who have requested access to records in respect of which time limits have been extended pursuant to section 9 where they consider the extension unreasonable;

   (d) from persons who have not been given access to a record or a part thereof in the official language requested by the person under subsection 12(2), or have not been given access in that language within a period of time that they consider appropriate;

. . . .

   (e) in respect of any publication or bulletin referred to in section 5; or

   (f) in respect of any other matter relating to requesting or obtaining access to records under this Act.

. . . .

Information Commissioner may initiate complaint

(3) Where the Information Commissioner is satisfied that there are reasonable grounds to investigate a matter relating to requesting or obtaining access to records under this Act, the Commissioner may initiate a complaint in respect thereof.

Written complaint

31. A complaint under this Act shall be made to the Information Commissioner in writing unless the Commissioner authorizes otherwise and shall, where the complaint relates to a request for access to a record, be made within one year from the time when the request for the record in respect of which the complaint is made was received.

INVESTIGATIONS

Notice of intention to investigate

32. Before commencing an investigation of a complaint under this Act, the Information Commissioner shall notify the head of the government institution concerned of the intention to carry out the investigation and shall inform the head of the institution of the substance of the complaint.

Notice to third parties

33. Where the head of a government institution refuses to disclose a record requested under this Act or a part thereof and receives a notice under section 32 of a complaint in respect of the refusal, the head of the institution shall forthwith advise the Information Commissioner of any third party that the head of the institution has notified under subsection 27(1) in respect of the request or would have notified under that subsection if the head of the institution had intended to disclose the record or part thereof.

. . . .

Investigations in private

35.(1) Every investigation of a complaint under this Act by the Information Commissioner shall be conducted in private.

Right to make representations

(2) In the course of an investigation of a complaint under this Act by the Information Commissioner, a reasonable opportunity to make representations shall be given to

   (a) the person who made the complaint,

   (b) the head of the government institution concerned, and

   (c) where the Information Commissioner intends to recommend under subsection 37(1) that a record or a part thereof be disclosed that contains or that the Information Commissioner has reason to believe might contain

     (i) trade secrets of a third party,

(ii) information described in paragraph 20(1)(b) that was supplied by a third party, or

(iii) information the disclosure of which the Information Commissioner could reasonably foresee might effect a result described in paragraph 20(1)(c) or (d) in respect of a third party,

the third party, if the third party can reasonably be located,

but no one is entitled as of right to be present during, to have access to or to comment on representations made to the Commissioner by any other person.

. . . .

Findings and recommendations of Information Commissioner

37.(1) If, on investigating a complaint in respect of a record under this Act, the Information Commissioner finds that the complaint is well-founded, the Commissioner shall provide the head of the government institution that has control of the record with a report containing

(a) the findings of the investigation and any recommendations that the Commissioner considers appropriate; and

(b) where appropriate, a request that, within a time specified in the report, notice be given to the Commissioner of any action taken or proposed to be taken to implement the recommendations contained in the report or reasons why no such action has been or is proposed to be taken.

Report to complainant and third parties

(2) The Information Commissioner shall, after investigating a complaint under this Act, report to the complainant and any third party that was entitled under subsection 35(2) to make and that made representations to the Commissioner in respect of the complaint the results of the investigation, but where a notice has been requested under paragraph (1)(b) no report shall be made under this subsection until the expiration of the time within which the notice is to be given to the Commissioner.

. . . .

Right of review

(5) Where, following the investigation of a complaint relating to a refusal to give access to a record requested under this Act or a part thereof, the head

of a government institution does not give notice to the Information Commissioner that access to the record will be given, the Information Commissioner shall inform the complainant that the complainant has the right to apply to the Court for a review of the matter investigated.

REPORTS TO PARLIAMENT

Annual report

38. The Information Commissioner shall, within three months after the termination of each financial year, submit an annual report to Parliament on the activities of the office during that financial year.

Special reports

39.(1) The Information Commissioner may, at any time, make a special report to Parliament referring to and commenting on any matter within the scope of the powers, duties and functions of the Commissioner where, in the opinion of the Commissioner, the matter is of such urgency or importance that a report thereon should not be deferred until the time provided for transmission of the next annual report of the Commissioner under section 38.

. . . .

REVIEW BY THE FEDERAL COURT

Review by Federal Court

41. Any person who has been refused access to a record requested under this Act or a part thereof may, if a complaint has been made to the Information Commissioner in respect of the refusal, apply to the Court for a review of the matter within forty-five days after the time the results of an investigation of the complaint by the Information Commissioner are reported to the complainant under subsection 37(2) or within such further time as the Court may, either before or after the expiration of those forty-five days, fix or allow.

. . . .

Order of Court where no authorization to refuse disclosure found

49. Where the head of a government institution refuses to disclose a record requested under this Act or a part thereof on the basis of a provision of this Act not referred to in section 50, the Court shall, if it determines that the head of the institution is not authorized to refuse to disclose the record or part thereof, order the head of the institution to disclose the record or part thereof, subject to such conditions as the Court deems appropriate, to the person who requested access to the record, or shall make such other order as the Court deems appropriate.

Order of Court where reasonable grounds of injury not found

50. Where the head of a government institution refuses to disclose a record requested under this Act or a part thereof on the basis of section 14 or 15 or paragraph 16(1)(c) or (d) or 18(d), the Court shall, if it determines that the head of the institution did not have reasonable grounds on which to refuse to disclose the record or part thereof, order the head of the institution to disclose the record or part thereof, subject to such conditions as the Court deems appropriate, to the person who requested access to the record, or shall make such other order as the Court deems appropriate.

Order of Court not to disclose record

51. Where the Court determines, after considering an application under section 44, that the head of a government institution is required to refuse to disclose a record or part of a record, the Court shall order the head of the institution not to disclose the

record or part thereof or shall make such other order as the Court deems appropriate.

. . . .

OFFICE OF THE INFORMATION COMMISSIONER

Information Commissioner

Information Commissioner

54.(1) The Governor in Council shall, by commission under the Great Seal, appoint an Information Commissioner after approval of the appointment by resolution of the Senate and House of Commons.

Tenure of office and removal

(2) Subject to this section, the Information Commissioner holds office during good behaviour for a term of seven years, but may be removed by the Governor in Council at any time on address of the Senate and House of Commons.

Further terms

(3) The Information Commissioner, on the expiration of a first or any subsequent term of office, is eligible to be re-appointed for a further term not exceeding seven years.

(g)   Access, Privacy, and Discretion: *Bland*†

NOTE

Ms. Bland, a researcher for a newspaper columnist, was looking for information relating to rumours of improper deals involving NCC rental properties. She filed an access to information request asking the NCC for "a current list of all rental properties owned and administered by the [NCC] (excluding garden plots) ... also ... the names and rental charges of the tenants of all NCC properties." When the request was refused on the ground that the information was exempt from disclosure because it was personal, Ms. Bland sought judicial

review. Both the Information Commissioner and the Privacy Commissioner intervened in the case.

EXTRACTS

[MULDOON J. (Reasons for Order):]

It was bound to happen that the two interveners (hereinafter the Privacy Comm'r and the Info. Comm'r respectively) would clash, since there is an inherent conflict between their respective roles and duties. Here is an example of those two high State officials locked in litigation as opponents.

† *Bland v. Canada (National Capital Commission)*, [1991] 3 F.C. 325; 41 F.T.R. 202; 36 C.P.R. (3d) 289; [1991] F.C.J. No. 435 (F.C.T.D.). Copyrighted by the Office of the Commissioner for Federal Judicial Affairs.

[Muldoon J. related the facts.]

. . . .

Despite the great weight of paper filed in this case, counsel aver that there are few litigious issues. Counsel for the applicant enumerates as follows: (1) What is "personal information" defined in section 3 of the *Privacy Act*, S.C. 1980-81-82-83, Chap. 111, ... (2) Are the tenants' names and rental charged for their premises personal information? (3) If the previous question be answered against the applicant's contentions, then is there that degree of public interest in such disclosures which would clearly outweigh any resulting invasion of privacy? The respondent's counsel agrees, in effect, saying that the legal issue is the meaning of "personal information" and what is involved in it. There is yet another issue such that, if it be established that the rent payable to the NCC by the residential tenants is less than fair market rent, does that reduction constitute "information relating to any discretionary benefit of a financial nature ... conferred on an individual, including the name of the individual and the exact nature of the benefit"? If so, the identity and the exact nature of the benefit are excepted from "personal information" "for the purposes of sections 7, 9 and 26 [*of the Privacy Act*] and section 19 of the *Access to Information Act*", as provided in paragraph 3(l) of the *Privacy Act*.

The matter arose because of rumours of "sweetheart deals" and reduced rentals accorded to partisan "hacks" of the political party whose adherents enjoyed majority status in Parliament prior to 1984. Now, usually, rumours are like inconsequential ripples against the hull of the ship of State. One pays scant attention to them unless the source provides hard facts, in which case the allegations are lifted out of the trough of mere rumours, to a higher plane of serious consideration. Again, one pays scant attention to rumours unless the source be, himself or herself, an ordinarily reliable source, or a person of such station and credibility as demand serious attention.

There is a supreme irony in this matter, in that one of the primary and most insistent sources of those rumours conveyed directly to the author of The Bureaucrats, someone pressing for verification and public disclosure in the newspaper was none other than Jean E. Pigott, now chairman of the NCC, now resisting the very disclosure which she once sought. It is regrettable to have such evidence before the Court, a regret glumly shared by counsel for the NCC, as recorded at pp. 435 and 436 of the transcript. But there is no gainsaying the fact, recorded in The Bureaucrats columns of October 3, 1987 ... and of "12.1.88" and "4/l/89...."

[Counsel for the NCC argued that the rumours that some people were paying lower than market value price for their leases were unfounded, even though one of the people who had made the allegations was now the chairperson of the NCC.]

. . . .

Counsel for the NCC did not go further and assert that the chairman, in her earlier career, and without the responsibilities of chairman of the NCC, was simply wrong in herself spreading those rumours of serious wrongdoing before she herself took command of the NCC's helm. That does appear to be the inescapable implication of counsel's argument.

All this silliness certainly could, and did, have an effect upon the public interest. In Canada it is not permitted to any appointed, or even elected, officials to assume aristocratic airs in the management of public money or property by telling the citizen-taxpayers that the officials' stewardship is just none of the citizens' business There is a well known compulsiveness on the part of government officials to keep secret matters which are of interest to the public in regard to the management of the taxpayers' money and property. Is that a gratuitous assumption? It is an inference from the fact that despite the powers and activities of the Auditor-General of Canada and of the committees of Parliament, and of the responsibility of the government-of-the-day to possess the confidence of the House of Commons, Parliament still thought fit to enact, and to promote its stated purpose in promulgating the *Access to Information Act*:

> 8.(2) The purpose of this Act is to extend the present laws of Canada to provide a right of access to information in records under the control of a government institution in accordance with the principles that government information should be available to the public, that necessary exceptions to the right of access should be limited and specific and that decisions on the disclosure of government information should be reviewed independently of government.

That definite purpose is expressed no less resolutely in the other official language of this statute. Both versions are equally definite and assertive.

The NCC is a "government institution" as defined in section 3 of the Act and designated in Schedule I thereto. The independent review of the decision to refuse access to the information sought by the applicant is provided in section 41, and exemplified in these very proceedings.

Now this matter of the rumours is emplaced in this litigation because of their alleged impact on the public interest, their potential for diluting public confidence in the administration of the government in general, and of the NCC in particular. The destruction of public confidence never leaves a vacuum in its place.

History, as the Court is entitled to note, notoriously demonstrates that destroyed public confidence is soon replaced by that most accursed, corrosive, dangerous and pernicious of all public attitudes, cynicism. So, what in this situation is in the public interest? That is abundantly clear. It is that, whatever and whenever rumours fly, the conduct of the NCC should be an open book, with all the explanations it cares or needs to make about rental levels, the process of establishing them, or whatever.

It is always in the public interest to dispel rumours of corruption or just plain mismanagement of the taxpayers' money and property. Naturally, if there has been negligence, somnolence or wrongdoing in the conduct of a government institution's operations it is, by virtual definition, in the public interest to disclose it, and not to cover it up in wraps of secrecy. In that case government officials arrogate to themselves, by their refusal to give requested information, the role of judges in their own cause. In this free and democratic society nothing, apart from a direction from the responsible Minister, prevents the government institution from giving whatever explanations it judges appropriate, along with the requested information lawfully disclosed. The Court is not here adjudicating on the validity of the NCC's explanations about its rental levels. The true explanations themselves might in many situations amply dispel the rumours, as it appears from the confidential record placed before this Court.

The Court, in any event, does not relish, but can hardly ignore, the NCC chairman's personal involvement in the generation of this litigation. The interpretation of those paired statutes in *pari niateria*, the *Access to Information Act* and the *Privacy Act* deserves a better, less personal basis of elaboration by the Court. So, while the Court is forced not to disregard that personal element, it will attempt to proceed as far as possible along regular, basic lines, just as if the chairman had evinced no personal connection with the rumours alleged to bear on the determination of the public interest versus any alleged invasion of privacy which results from disclosure of the information.

Is the Court empowered by law to prefer the Court's view of the public interest over that of the NCC? The statutory provision under consideration here is emplaced in the *Privacy Act*, thus:

> 8.(2) Subject to any other Act of Parliament, personal information under the control of a government institution may be disclosed.
>
> ...
>
> (m) for any purpose where, in the opinion of the head of the institution,
>
> (i) the public interest in disclosure clearly outweighs any invasion of privacy that could result from the disclosure, or
>
> ...

(emphasis not in original text)

What outweighs something else is clearly a matter of opinion — and oftentimes a very subtle adjustment of opinion — which, in the statute, resides primarily at least in the head (or chairman) of the government institution (here, the NCC). In the *Access to Information Act* and in the *Privacy Act* the respective sections numbered 41 both begin with the headline, "Review by the Federal Court," and they both provide, in the same words, for a "person" or an "individual" to "apply to the Court for a review of the matter...". This, then, is the review of the matter which subsection 2(l) of the information legislation exacts "be reviewed independently of government (... recours indépendants du pouvoir exécutif.)".

The meaning of this latter provision for the matter to be reviewed independently of government in the total context of the legislation — that is, independently of the decision made or discretion exercised by the head of the government institution, was conveyed forcefully and lucidly by Mr. Justice Heald, for the unanimous Appeal Division of this Court in *Ken Rubin* v. *President of Canada Mortgage and Housing Corporation*, [[1989] 1 F.C. 265], (1988) 86 N.R. 186, (hereinafter cited to F.C.).

. . . .

The passage beginning on page 276 of the Rubin case is of great import here. It runs:

. . . .

[The passage stressed that the government's discretion must be exercised in the context of the general purpose of the *Act*, and continued]:

> In my view Parliament enacted section 46 [of the *Act*] so that the Court would have the informa-

tion and material necessary to the fulfilment of its mandate to ensure that the discretion given to the administrative head has been exercised within proper limits and on proper principles. Judicial deference to the exercise of discretion by an administrative tribunal must, necessarily, be confined to the proper limits of the tribunal's power of decision. The determination of those proper limits is a task for the Court.

What then did the NCC, by its chairman, consider when it concluded that the invasion of its tenants' privacy clearly outweighed the public interest in disclosure of the rental charge exacted for each tenant's right to peaceful exclusive possession of his or her rented premises during the term of the lease? Was the decision to bar disclosure in regard to invasion of privacy versus public interest taken "within proper limits and on proper principles" in deference to the "general intent and purpose of the *Act*, as expressed in section 2 supra"?

. . . .

The NCC, speaking and acting by and through its chairman, evinces no weighing of the factor of invasion of privacy against that of the public interest in disclosure, which weighing exercise is mandated by subparagraph 8(2)(m)(i) of the *Privacy Act*. The "public interest in disclosure" is a statutory Polaris, and it is not to be cursorily denigrated by the simple assertions that it is "less than apparent in this situation" and that "there would be no general benefit for or advantage to the public to be provided with that information". Such assertions do not constitute any weighing of one statutory factor against the other. In any event, under section 2 of the information legislation, "the public interest in disclosure" exists as a paramount value which is to be suppressed only when and if it clearly does not outweigh any invasion of privacy. That requires that "any invasion of privacy" must be a weighty matter, indeed, for if not, it will inevitably be clearly outweighed by "the public interest in disclosure".

. . . .

... The mere assertion of the result falls far short of justification by appropriate reasons....

. . . .

[Muldoon J. went on to find that the chair of the NCC gave hardly any weight to the countervailing public interest.]

... [T]he disclosure of how much residential rent a person pays to a government institution pales into comparative insignificance when one thinks of a really serious invasion of privacy such as disclosure of a criminal record, or of marital infidelity or medical condition for examples of matters which, along with income tax returns, most folks would not wish to disclose, or to have disclosed about themselves.

. . . .

[Muldoon J. went on to find that the tenants' names, addresses and rental payments did not constitute "personal information" protected from disclosure under subsection 19(1) of the *Act* and that in any event the tenants received a "discretionary benefit of a financial nature" excluded by paragraph 3(1) of the *Privacy Act*, which referred to any "personal information" under subsection 19(1),]

Thus, the Court finds that because of their contractual relationships with the NCC, its residential tenants have had conferred upon them, each individually, a "discretionary benefit of a financial nature". The sought-after information, "including the name of the individual and the exact nature of the benefit" in these circumstances is not personal information, and it is not justifiable to refuse to disclose it.

The intent of the *Access to Information Act* is, after all, to establish and enforce the principles that government information, not defined as personal information, should be available to the public. If it be personal information then, when the public right to disclosure clearly outweighs any invasion of privacy which could result from disclosure, it should also be available to the public. The Court finds herein that the public right to disclosure clearly outweighs the noted invasion of privacy. Section 49 of that *Act* commands the Court when it determines, as here, that the refusal to disclose the requested information is not authorized, to order the head of the government institution to disclose the record of that information. So, the Court will order that the NCC do disclose to the applicant, Mary Bland, the NCC's record of the names and residential addresses of all of its residential tenants, together with the exact amount of the annual rent charged to each in regard to NCC residential lands and premises as of May 10, 1984.

. . . .

This has been a long, perhaps quite unnecessarily long, proceeding. Without exaggeration it can be estimated that a goodly portion of a forest was sacrificed just to generate the paper involved in this litigation. In truth, there never was any good reason for the unfortunately not-unusual conditional reflex on the part of the NCC, with or without the advice of its legal counsel, to refuse to disclose its records of the information sought by the applicant. The head of the NCC really ought to have disclosed the requested information with alacrity.

(h) Access, Privacy, and Discretion: *Dagg*†

NOTE

Mr. Dagg filed an access to information request for records of employees entering and leaving Department of Finance premises on weekends. Dagg was a professional access consultant who thought the records might show that the employees were working without compensation, and hoped that they might persuade the employees' union to hire him. Although the Minister provided the records, he deleted from them the employees' names, identification numbers, and signatures. He claimed that this was personal information that was exempted from disclosure by s. 19(1) of the *Access to Information Act*. After a review of his decision as requested by Dagg, the Minister confirmed his original decision and the Information Commissioner refused to intervene on Dagg's behalf. Dagg then sought judicial review of the Minister's decision pursuant to 41. Although the case hinged ultimately on a technical question of statutory interpretation, it required the courts to weigh the openness principle behind the *Access to Information Act* against the opposing values protected by the *Privacy Act*, R.S.C., 1985, c. P-21. [Note that Section 3 of the *Privacy Act* says "that personal information means information about any identifiable individual...."]

EXTRACTS

[CORY J. for himself, LAMER C.J., SOPINKA, McLACHLIN and IACOBUCCI JJ.:]

[para1] I have read the careful and extensive reasons of Justice La Forest. I agree with his approach to the interpretation of the *Access to Information Act* and the *Privacy Act*, particularly that they must be interpreted and read together. I also agree that the names on the sign-in logs are "personal information" for the purposes of s. 3 of the *Privacy Act*. However, I arrive at a different conclusion with respect to the application of s. 3 "personal information" (j) (hereinafter s. 3(j)) of that Act.

[para2] Subsection 3(j) of the *Privacy Act* provides that:

> ... for the purposes of sections 7, 8 and 26 and section 19 of the *Access to Information Act*, ['personal information'] does not include
> (j) information about an individual who is or was an officer or employee of a government institution that relates to the position or functions of the individual including,
>
> ...
>
> (iii) the classification, salary range and responsibilities of the position held by the individual,
> (iv) the name of the individual on a document prepared by the individual in the course of employment.

. . . .

[para3] I agree with La Forest J. that the names on the sign-in logs do not fall under s. 3(j)(iv) of the *Privacy Act*. It would be difficult to conclude that the sign-in logs were "prepared by" the employees, as that expression is commonly understood.

[para4] However, I am of the view that both the opening words of s. 3(j) and the specific provisions of s. 3(j)(iii) of the *Privacy Act* are sufficiently broad to encompass the information sought by the appellant.

[para5] La Forest J. holds that the purpose of s. 3(j) and s. 3(j)(iii) of the *Privacy Act* is:

---

† *Dagg v. Canada (Minister of Finance)*, [1997] S.C.R. 2 S.C.R. 403 (June 26, 1997); rev'g. [1995] 3 F.C. 199, 124 D.L.R. (4th) 553, 181 N.R. 139 (F.C.A.); rev'g. (1993), 70 F.T.R. 54, 22 Admin. L.R. (2d) 171 (F.C.T.D.).

... to exempt only information attaching to posi-tions and not that which relates to specific indi-viduals. Information relating to the position is thus not "personal information", even though it may incidentally reveal something about named persons. Conversely, information relating primar-ily to individuals themselves or to the manner in which they choose to perform the tasks assigned to them is "personal information". [Emphasis in original.]

[para6] I agree. Moreover, I agree with La Forest J. that "generally speaking, information relating to the position will consist of the kind of information dis-closed in a job description"....

.   .   .   .

[para7] However, in applying these considerations to the facts, La Forest J. concludes that the information requested by the appellant is not information about the nature of a particular position. It is on this point that I must differ.

.   .   .   .

[Cory J. said that ordinarily employees come to the workplace only because their work requires it. He distinguished *Canada (Information Commis-sioner) v. Canada (Solicitor General)*, [1988] 3 F.C. 551 (F.C.T.D.) on the ground that the informa-tion there involved qualitative evaluations of an employee's performance. He distinguished *Rubin v. Clerk of Privy Council (Can.)* (1993), 62 F.T.R. 287 (F.C.T.D.) on the ground that the salary infor-mation there related to the individual rather than the position.]

.   .   .   .

[para14] My conclusion that the names on the sign-in logs fall within the opening words of s. 3(j) of the *Privacy Act* and, alternatively, within s. 3(j)(iii) of the Act, is sufficient to dispose of this appeal. It follows that the information must be disclosed.

[para16] ... [I]n light of the conclusion that the infor-mation must be disclosed, it is not necessary for me to consider whether the Minister erred in his exer-cise of the discretion conferred upon him pursuant to s. 19(2) of the *Access to Information Act* and s. 8 of the *Privacy Act*. In general, I agree with La Forest J.'s conclusion that a Minister's discretionary decision under s. 8(2)(m)(i) is not to be reviewed on a *de novo* standard of review. Perhaps it will suffice to

observe that the Minister is not obliged to consider whether it is in the public interest to disclose per-sonal information. However in the face of a demand for disclosure, he is required to exercise that discre-tion by at least considering the matter. If he refuses or neglects to do so, the Minister is declining juris-diction which is granted to him alone.

[para17] Furthermore, it could be determined that the Minister committed an error in principle result-ing in a loss of jurisdiction when he stated:

I do not believe that *you have demonstrated* that if there were any public interest that it clearly overrides the individual's right to privacy. [Emphasis added.]

[para18] From this, it appears that the Minister of Finance placed upon the appellant the burden of demonstrating that the public interest in disclosure clearly outweighed any privacy interest. Yet, s. 8 of the *Privacy Act* does not mention any burden of proof....

[para19] In the result, I would allow the appeal, with costs.

[LA FOREST J., dissenting, for himself, L'HEUREUX-DUBÉ, GONTHIER and MAJOR JJ.:]

.   .   .   .

[para46] The appellant contends that the personal information exemption in the *Access to Information Act* should be construed narrowly so as to favour full disclosure. The Act, he points out, provides that members of the public have a "right of access" to government information (ss. 2, 4) and that exceptions to this right should be "limited and specific" (s. 2). He argues, in effect, that where there is any ambigu-ity as to whether a record constitutes personal infor-mation, the right to disclosure should prevail over the right of privacy.

.   .   .   .

[La Forest J. said the relevant legislative history and statutory wording suggest that the *Access to Information Act* was not intended to prevail over the *Privacy Act*.]

[para47] ... [T]he *Access to Information Act* and the *Privacy Act* are parallel statutes, designed to work in concert to restrict the federal government's control over certain kinds of information. The *Access to Information Act* gives individuals a right of access to

government information. The *Privacy Act* permits them to gain access to information about themselves held in government data banks, and limits the government's ability to collect, use and disclose personal information.

. . . .

[para51] It is clear, therefore, that Parliament did not intend access to be given preeminence over privacy. The appellant correctly points out that under the *Access to Information Act*, access is the general rule. It is also true that exceptions to that rule must be confined to those specifically set out in the statute and that the government has the burden of showing that information falls into one of these exceptions. It does not follow, however, that the "personal information" exemption should receive a cramped interpretation. To do so would effectively read the *Privacy Act* as subordinate to the *Access to Information Act....*

. . . .

[para58] Before attempting to determine whether the sign-in logs requested by the appellant in this case constitute "personal information" within the meaning of s. 3 of the *Privacy Act*, it will be helpful to consider the purposes of the Acts in somewhat greater detail.

[para59] As earlier set out, s. 2(1) of the *Access to Information Act* describes its purpose, *inter alia*, as providing "a right of access to information in records under the control of a government institution in accordance with the principles that government information should be available to the public". The idea that members of the public should have an enforceable right to gain access to government-held information, however, is relatively novel. The practice of government secrecy has deep historical roots in the British parliamentary tradition; see Patrick Birkinshaw, *Freedom of Information: The Law, the Practice and the Ideal* (1988), at pp. 61–84.

[para60] As society has become more complex, governments have developed increasingly elaborate bureaucratic structures to deal with social problems. The more governmental power becomes diffused through administrative agencies, however, the less traditional forms of political accountability, such as elections and the principle of ministerial responsibility, are able to ensure that citizens retain effective control over those that govern them; see David J. Mullan, "Access to Information and Rule-Making",

in John D. McCamus, ed., *Freedom of Information: Canadian Perspectives* (1981), at p. 54.

[para61] The overarching purpose of access to information legislation, then, is to facilitate democracy. It does so in two related ways. It helps to ensure first, that citizens have the information required to participate meaningfully in the democratic process, and secondly, that politicians and bureaucrats remain accountable to the citizenry. As Professor Donald C. Rowat explains in his classic article, "How Much Administrative Secrecy?" (1965), 31 Canadian Journal of Economics and Political Science 479, at p. 480:

> Parliament and the public cannot hope to call the government to account without an adequate knowledge of what is going on; nor can they hope to participate in the decision-making process and contribute their talents to the formation of policy and legislation if that process is hidden from view.

See also: Canadian Bar Association, *Freedom of Information in Canada: A Model Bill* (1979), at p. 6.

[para62] Access laws operate on the premise that politically relevant information should be distributed as widely as reasonably possible.

[La Forest J. referred to comments by political philosopher John Plamenatz in *Democracy and Illusion* (1973), at pp. 178–79.]

[para63] Rights to state-held information are designed to improve the workings of government; to make it more effective, responsive and accountable. Consequently, while the *Access to Information Act* recognizes a broad right of access to "any record under the control of a government institution" (s. 4(1)(b)), it is important to have regard to the overarching purposes of the Act in determining whether an exemption to that general right should be granted.

[para64] The purpose of the *Privacy Act*, as set out in s. 2 of the Act, is twofold. First, it is to "protect the privacy of individuals with respect to personal information about themselves held by a government institution"; and second, to "provide individuals with a right of access to that information". This appeal is, of course, concerned with the first of these purposes.

[para65] The protection of privacy is a fundamental value in modern, democratic states; see Alan F. Westin, *Privacy and Freedom* (1970), at pp. 349–50. An expression of an individual's unique personal-

ity or personhood, privacy is grounded on physical and moral autonomy — the freedom to engage in one's own thoughts, actions and decisions; see *R. v. Dyment*, [1988] 2 S.C.R. 417, at p. 427, per La Forest J.; see also Joel Feinberg, "Autonomy, Sovereignty, and Privacy: Moral Ideas in the Constitution?" (1983), 58 Notre Dame L. Rev. 445.

[para66] Privacy is also recognized in Canada as worthy of constitutional protection, at least in so far as it is encompassed by the right to be free from unreasonable searches and seizures under s. 8 of the *Canadian Charter of Rights and Freedoms*; see *Hunter v. Southam Inc.*, [1984] 2 S.C.R. 145. Certain privacy interests may also inhere in the s. 7 right to life, liberty and security of the person; see *R. v. Hebert*, [1990] 2 S.C.R. 151, and *R. v. Broyles*, [1991] 3 S.C.R. 595.

[para67] Privacy is a broad and somewhat evanescent concept, however. It is thus necessary to describe the particular privacy interests protected by the *Privacy Act* with greater precision....

. . . .

[para76] In the present case, the information on the sign-in logs was collected in order to determine who was in the building in the case of a fire or other emergency. Although the logs were occasionally used for other purposes, there is no evidence that they were ever used to verify overtime claims. More important, it is clear that the persons signing the logs would not have expected that they might be released to the general public....

. . . .

[para96] In any event, even if the logs can be said to record accurately an employee's overtime hours, I am of the view that information concerning when an individual works overtime is "personal information". Whether a person works overtime, and for how long, relates to how he or she performs his or her duties and not to the responsibilities and functions inherent in the position itself....

. . . .

[para113] There is no evidence, as was the case in *Rubin*, supra, that the Minister failed to examine the evidence properly. It is apparent that he considered the appellant's request for a public interest waiver in the light of the objects of the legislation and came to a determination that the public interest did not "clearly outweigh" the violation of privacy that could result from disclosure. This was a conclusion that he was entitled to make....

[para114] In essence, the appellant's objection to the Minister's decision is that he did not give sufficient reasons for it. Generally speaking, however, in the absence of a specific statutory requirement, administrative decision makers have no duty to give reasons for their decisions; see *Supermarchés Jean Labrecque Inc. v. Flamand*, [1987] 2 S.C.R. 219, at p. 233; *Canadian Arsenals Ltd. v. Canadian Labour Relations Board*, [1979] 2 F.C. 393 (C.A.); *Macdonald v. The Queen*, [1977] 2 S.C.R. 665; *Northwestern Utilities Ltd. v. City of Edmonton*, [1979] 1 S.C.R. 684. While it has been suggested that the failure to give reasons, even when there is no statutory requirement to do so, may amount to a breach of the duty to be fair in certain circumstances (David Jones and Anne de Villars, *Principles of Administrative Law* (2nd ed. 1994), at p. 299), the Minister's failure to give extensive, detailed reasons for his decision did not work any unfairness upon the appellant.

[para115] [It was asserted that the Minister incorrectly reversed the onus set out in s. 48 of the *Access to Information Act*.] ... As I have discussed in relation to s. 49 of that Act, the Minister satisfied this burden when he showed that the information in the sign-in logs constituted "personal information". Once that fact is established, the Minister's decision to refuse to disclose pursuant to s. 8(2)(m)(i) of the *Privacy Act* may only be reviewed on the basis that it constituted an abuse of discretion. The Minister did not have a "burden" to show that his decision was correct because that decision is not reviewable by a court on the correctness standard. Reading his statement in context, it is clear that the Minister weighed the conflicting interests at stake. The fact that he stated that the appellant failed to demonstrate that the public interest should override the privacy rights of the employees named in the sign-in logs is therefore irrelevant.

Disposition

[para116] From the foregoing, I have concluded that the appeal should be dismissed....

[para117] ... I would dismiss the appeal, but would award the appellant's costs from the respondent.

9 | National Energy Board

(a) Some General Questions about Public Authorities

A. FRAMEWORK, FUNCTIONS, AND STRUCTURE

1. What part of the administrative process is the public authority?
2. What is the governing legislation of the public authority?
3. What are the public authority's main functions?
4. What is the size and shape of the public authority?
5. What "internal" controls affect decisions of the public authority?

B. INDEPENDENCE

1. How independent is the public authority of the central administrative process? To what governmental controls is it subject? (finality of decisions: role in regulation-making and rule-making; appeal, review procedures; other aspects of independence or subordination)
2. How independent is the public authority from those it is supposed to regulate?

C. JUDICIALIZATION AND JUDICIAL CONTROL

1. How court-like is the public authority?
2. What are the main stages of a typical hearing before the public authority?
3. What rule-making or policy-making functions has the public authority?

D. SOME POTENTIAL ISSUES AND CHALLENGES

1. Constitutional issues (division of powers, *Charter*)
2. Balancing control by central administrative process with independence and impartiality
3. Need to balance expertise and responsiveness to those regulated vs. need to consider third-party and public interests (e.g., membership, accessibility to third parties, costs, etc.)
4. Responding to generally worded mandates (discretion, rules)
5. Balancing fairness and judicial procedure with efficiency
   (a) avoiding undue delay;
   (b) disclosure vs. confidentiality
      (i) re evidence submitted by parties,
      (ii) re staff studies, and
      (iii) re information from other sources;
   (c) subject matter complexity vs. need for simplicity and uniformity;
   (d) role of board counsel, staff, and staff studies;
   (e) general policy guidelines or rules vs. case-by-case adjudication;
   (f) negotiated settlements between parties;
   (g) pre-hearing procedures; etc.
6. Compliance (how to secure mechanisms)

(b) National Energy Board Act†

SHORT TITLE

Short title

1. This Act may be cited as the *National Energy Board Act*, R.S., c. N-6, s. 1.

. . . .

PART I
NATIONAL ENERGY BOARD

Establishment of the Board

Board established

3.(1) There is hereby established a Board, to be called the National Energy Board, consisting of not more than nine members to be appointed by the Governor in Council.

Tenure of members

(2) Subject to subsection (3), each member of the Board shall be appointed to hold office during good behaviour for a period of seven years, but may be removed at any time by the Governor in Council on address of the Senate and House of Commons.

Re-appointment and retirement

(3) A member appointed pursuant to subsection (2) is eligible to be re-appointed to hold office during good behaviour for any term of seven years or less and every member ceases to hold office on attaining the age of seventy years.

Eligibility

(4) A person is not eligible to be appointed or to continue as a member of the Board if that person is not a Canadian citizen or permanent resident within the meaning of the *Immigration Act* or is, as owner, shareholder, director, officer, partner or otherwise, engaged in the business of producing, selling, buying, transmitting, exporting, importing or otherwise dealing in hydrocarbons or electricity or holds any bond, debenture or other security of a corporation engaged in any such business.

Temporary members

4.(1) In addition to the number of members that may be appointed under subsection 3(l), the Governor in Council may, notwithstanding subsection 3(2), appoint temporary members of the Board on such terms and conditions as the Governor in Council may prescribe and any temporary member so appointed shall carry out such duties as may be assigned to that member by the Chairman of the Board.

Maximum number

(2) Not more than six temporary members of the Board shall hold office at any one time.

Temporary members, other employment

(3) A member appointed under subsection (1) shall not, during his term of office, accept or hold any office or employment inconsistent with the member's duties under this Act.

Remuneration

5.(1) Each member, other than a member appointed under subsection 4(l), shall be paid such remuneration for the services of that member as the Governor in Council may from time to time determine.

Idem

(2) Each member appointed under subsection 4(l) shall be paid such remuneration for the services of that member as the Governor in Council may from time to time determine.

. . . .

Executive Officers

Chairman and Vice-Chairman

6.(1) The Governor in Council shall designate one of the members to be Chairman of the Board and another of the members to be Vice-Chairman of the Board.

---

† R.S.C. 1985, c. N-7.

Duties of Chairman

(2) The Chairman is the chief executive officer of the Board, and has supervision over and direction of the work and staff of the Board.

Duties of Vice-Chairman

(3) If the Chairman is absent or unable to act or if the office is vacant, the Vice-Chairman has all the powers and functions of the Chairman.

Acting Chairman

(4) The Board may authorize one or more of its members to act as Chairman for the time being in the event that the Chairman and Vice-Chairman are absent or unable to act or if the offices are vacant.

Head Office and Meetings

Head office

7.(1) The head office of the Board shall be at Calgary, Alberta.

Quorum

(2) Three members constitute a quorum of the Board.

Vacancy

(3) A vacancy in the membership of the Board does not impair the right of the remaining members to act.

Time and place of sittings

(4) The Board may sit at such times and places as it considers necessary or desirable for the proper conduct of its business.

Rules

Rules

8. The Board may make rules respecting
  (a) the sittings of the Board;
  (b) the procedure for making applications, representations and complaints to the Board and the conduct of hearings before the Board, and generally the manner of conducting any business before the Board;
  (c) the apportionment of the work of the Board among its members, and the assignment of members to sit at hearings and to preside threat; and

  (d) generally, the carrying on of the work of the Board, the management of its internal affairs and the duties of its officers and employees.

Staff

Secretary and other officers and employees

9.(1) The Secretary and the other officers and employees necessary for the proper conduct of the business of the Board shall be appointed in the manner authorized by law.

. . . .

Powers of the Board

Board a court

11.(1) The Board is a court of record.

Official Seal

(2) The Board shall have an official seal, which shall be judicially noticed.

Powers with respect to witnesses, etc.

(3) The Board has, with respect to the attendance, swearing and examination of witnesses, the production and inspection of documents, the enforcement of its orders, the entry on and inspection of property and other matters necessary or proper for the due exercise of its jurisdiction, all such powers, rights and privileges as are vested in a superior court of record.

Jurisdiction

12.(1) The Board has full and exclusive jurisdiction to inquire into, hear and determine any matter
  (a) where it appears to the Board that any person has failed to do any act, matter or thing required to be done by this Act or by any regulation, certificate, licence or permit, or any order or direction made by the Board, or that any person has done or is doing any act, matter or thing contrary to or in contravention of this Act, or any such regulation, certificate, licence, permit, order or direction; or
  (b) where it appears to the Board that the circumstances may require the Board, in the public interest, to make any order or give any direction, leave, sanction or approval that by law it is authorized to make or give, or with respect to any matter, act or thing that by this

Act or any such regulation, certificate, licence, permit, order or direction is prohibited, sanctioned or required to be done.

Idem

(1.1) The Board may inquire into any accident involving a pipeline or international power line or other facility the construction or operation of which is regulated by the Board and may, at the conclusion of the inquiry, make

(a) findings as to the cause of the accident or factors contributing to it;

(b) recommendations relating to the prevention of future similar accidents; or

(c) any decision or order that the Board can make.

Matters of law and fact

(2) For the purposes of this Act, the Board has full jurisdiction to hear and determine all matters, whether of law or of fact.

Mandatory orders

13. The Board may

(a) order and require any person to do, forthwith, or within or at any specified time and in any manner prescribed by the Board, any act, matter or thing that such person is or may be required to do under this Act, or any regulation, certificate, licence or permit, or any order or direction made or given under this Act; and

(b) forbid the doing or continuing of any act, matter or thing that is contrary to this Act or any such regulation, certificate, licence, permit, order or direction.

Delegation

14. The Board may delegate to one or more of its members, either jointly or severally, all or any of its powers, duties and functions under this Act, except those under subsection 45(3), section 46, 47, 48, 52, 54, 56, 58, 58.11, 58.14, 58.16, 58.32, 58.35, 58.37 or 129 or under Part IV, VI or VII.

Powers of member authorized to report

15.(1) The Board or the Chairman may authorize one or more of its members to report to the Board on any question or matter arising in connection with the business of or any application or proceeding before the Board, and the member so authorized has all the powers of the Board for the purpose of tak-

ing evidence or acquiring the necessary information for the purpose of making the report and the recommendations contained in it as to the decision or order of the Board to be made on the question or matter.

Not a quorum

(1.1) Notwithstanding subsection 7(2) of this Act and paragraph 22(2)(a) of the *Interpretation Act*, three or more members authorized to report to the Board pursuant to subsection (1) do not constitute a quorum of the Board.

Board to deal with report

(2) When a report is made to the Board under subsection (1), it may be adopted as the decision or order of the Board or otherwise dealt with as the Board considers advisable.

Board may act on own motion

(3) The Board may of its own motion inquire into, hear and determine any matter or thing that under this Act it may inquire into, hear and determine.

. . . .

Orders and Decisions

Enforcement of Board orders

17.(1) Any decision or order made by the Board may, for the purpose of enforcement thereof, be made a rule, order or decree of the Federal Court or of a superior court of a province and shall be enforced in like manner as a rule, order or decree of that court.

Procedure for enforcement

(2) To make a decision or order of the Board a rule, order or decree of the Federal Court or a superior court, the usual practice and procedure of the court in such matters may be followed, or in lieu thereof the Secretary may produce to the court a certified copy of the decision or order under the seal of the Board and thereupon the decision or order becomes a rule, order or decree of the court.

General or particular orders

18. Where under this Act the Board may make or issue any order or direction or prescribe any terms or conditions or do any other thing in relation to any person, the Board may do so, either generally or in any particular case or class of cases.

Conditional orders, etc.

19.(1) Without limiting the generality of any provision of this Act that authorizes the Board to impose terms and conditions in respect of a certificate, licence or order issued by the Board, the Board may direct in any certificate, licence or order that it or any portion or provision thereof shall come into force at a future time or on the happening of any contingency, event or condition specified in the certificate, licence or order or on the performance to the satisfaction of the Board of any conditions that the Board may impose in the certificate, licence or order, and the Board may direct that the whole or any portion of the certificate, licence or order shall have force for a limited time or until the happening of a specified event.

Interim orders

(2) The Board may, instead of making an order final in the first instance, make an interim order, and may reserve its decision pending further proceedings in connection with any matter.

Granting of relief may be partial

20. On any application made to the Board, the Board may make a decision or order granting the whole or part only of the application, or may grant such further or other related relief, in addition to or in lieu of that applied for, as to the Board may seem just and proper, to the same extent as if the application had been for such partial or related relief.

Review, etc., of decisions and orders

21.(1) Subject to subsection (2), the Board may review, vary or rescind any decision or order made by it or rehear any application before deciding it.

Variation of certificates, licences and permits

(2) The Board may vary a certificate, licence or permit but the variation of a certificate or licence is not effective until approved by the Governor in Council.

. . . .

Appeal to Federal Court of Appeal

22.(1) An appeal lies from a decision or order of the Board to the Federal Court of Appeal on a question of law or of jurisdiction, after leave to appeal is obtained from that Court.

Application for leave to appeal

(1.1) An application for leave to appeal must be made within thirty days after the release of the decision or order sought to be appealed from or within such further time as a judge of that Court under special circumstances allows.

Entry of appeal

(2) No appeal lies after leave has been obtained under subsection (1) unless it is entered in the Federal Court of Appeal within sixty days from the making of the order granting leave to appeal.

Board may be heard

(3) The Board is entitled to be heard by counsel or otherwise on the argument of an appeal.

Decisions final

23.(1) Except as provided in this Act, every decision or order of the Board is final and conclusive.

. . . .

Public hearings

24.(1) Subject to subsection (2), hearings before the Board with respect to the issuance, revocation or suspension of certificates or of licences for the exportation of gas or electricity or the importation of gas or for leave to abandon the operation of a pipeline shall be public.

Exception

(2) A public hearing need not be held where the Board, on the application or with the consent of the holder, revokes or suspends
  (a) a licence;
  (b) a certificate issued in respect of an international or interprovincial power line, regardless of whether the power line has been brought into commercial operation under that certificate; or
  (c) a certificate issued in respect of a pipeline, if the pipeline has not been brought into commercial operation under that certificate.

Other matters

(3) The Board may hold a public hearing in respect of any other matter if it considers it advisable to do so.

Fees, Levies and Charges

Regulations imposing fees, etc.

24.1(1) Subject to the approval of the Treasury Board, the National Energy Board may, for the purposes of recovering all or a portion of such costs as the National Energy Board determines to be attributable to its responsibilities under this or any other Act of Parliament, make regulations

   (a) imposing fees, levies or charges on any person or company authorized under this Act to

      (i) construct or operate a pipeline or an international or interprovincial power line,

      (ii) charge tolls,

      (iii) export or import oil or gas, or

      (iv) export electricity; and

   (b) providing for the manner of calculating the fees, levies and charges in respect of the person or company and their payment to the National Energy Board.

. . . .

PART II
ADVISORY FUNCTIONS

Board to make continuing studies and reports

26.(1) The Board shall study and keep under review matters over which Parliament has jurisdiction relating to the exploration for, production, recovery, manufacture, processing, transmission, transportation, distribution, sale, purchase, exchange and disposal of energy and sources of energy in and outside Canada, shall report thereon from time to time to the Minister and shall recommend to the Minister such measures within the jurisdiction of Parliament as it considers necessary or advisable in the public interest for the control, supervision, conservation, use, marketing and development of energy and sources of energy.

Request of Minister

   (2) The Board shall, with respect to energy matters and sources of energy,

   (a) provide the Minister with such advice as the Minister may request, including advice relating to the export pricing of oil and gas;

   (b) prepare such studies and reports as the Minister may request; and

   (c) recommend to the Minister the making of such arrangements as it considers desirable for cooperation with governmental or other agencies in or outside Canada.

. . . .

PART III
CONSTRUCTION AND OPERATION OF PIPELINES

General

Companies only

29.(1) No person, other than a company, shall construct or operate a pipeline.

. . . .

Operation of pipeline

30.(1) No company shall operate a pipeline unless

   (a) there is a certificate in force with respect to that pipeline; and

   (b) leave has been given under this Part to the company to open the pipeline.

Compliance with conditions

   (2) No company shall operate a pipeline otherwise than in accordance with the terms and conditions of the certificate issued with respect thereto.

. . . .

Determination of Detailed Route and Approval

Notice to owners

34.(1) Where a company has prepared and submitted to the Board a plan, profile and book of reference pursuant to subsection 33(1), the company shall, in a manner and in a form to be determined by the Board,

   (a) serve a notice on all owners of lands proposed to be acquired, in so far as they can be ascertained; and

   (b) publish a notice in at least one issue of a publication, if any, in general circulation within the area in which the lands are situated.

Contents of notices

   (2) The notices mentioned in subsection (1) shall describe the proposed detailed route of the pipeline, the location of the offices of the Board and the right of the owner and of persons referred to in subsection (4) to make, within the time referred to in subsection (3) or (4), as the case may be, repre-

sentations to the Board respecting the detailed route of the pipeline.

Written statement of interest and grounds for opposition

(3) Where an owner of lands who has been served with a notice pursuant to subsection (1) wishes to oppose the proposed detailed route of a pipeline, the owner may, within thirty days of being served, file with the Board a written statement setting out the nature of the owner's interest in the proposed detailed route and the grounds for his opposition to that route.

Opposition by persons adversely affected

(4) A person who anticipates that his lands may be adversely affected by the proposed detailed route of a pipeline, other than an owner of lands referred to in subsection (3), may oppose the proposed detailed route by filing with the Board within thirty days following the last publication of the notice referred to in subsection (1) a written statement setting out the nature of that person's interest in those lands and the grounds for the opposition to the proposed detailed route of the pipeline.

Public hearing

35.(1) Where a written statement is filed with the Board pursuant to subsection 34(3) or (4) within the time limited for doing so under that subsection, the Board shall forthwith order that a public hearing be conducted within the area in which the lands to which the statement relates are situated with respect to any grounds of opposition set out in any such statement.

Notice of public hearing

(2) The Board shall fix a suitable time and place for the public hearing referred to in subsection (1) and cause notice of the time and place so fixed to be given by publishing it in at least one issue of a publication, if any, in general circulation within the area in which the lands proposed to be acquired are situated and by sending it to each person who filed a written statement with the Board pursuant to subsection 34(3) or (4).

Opportunity to be heard

(3) At the time and place fixed for the public hearing pursuant to subsection (2), the Board shall hold a public hearing and shall permit each person who filed a written statement with the Board pursuant to subsection 34(3) or (4) to make representa-

tions and may allow any other interested person to make such representations before it as the Board deems proper.

Inspection of lands

(4) The Board or a person authorized by the Board may make such inspection of lands proposed to be acquired for or affected by the pipeline construction as the Board deems necessary.

. . . .

Certificates

Issuance

52. The Board may, subject to the approval of the Governor in Council, issue a certificate in respect of a pipeline if the Board is satisfied that the pipeline is and will be required by the present and future public convenience and necessity and, in considering an application for a certificate, the Board shall have regard to all considerations that appear to it to be relevant, and may have regard to the following:

(a) the availability of oil or gas to the pipeline;
(b) the existence of markets, actual or potential;
(c) the economic feasibility of the pipeline;
(d) the financial responsibility and financial structure of the applicant, the methods of financing the pipeline and the extent to which Canadians will have an opportunity of participating in the financing, engineering and construction of the pipeline; and
(e) any public interest that in the Board's opinion may be affected by the granting or the refusing of the application.

. . . .

Revocation and Suspension

Revocation or suspension of certificate

56.(1) Subject to subsection (2), the Board may, by order, with the approval of the Governor in Council, revoke or suspend a certificate if any term or condition thereof has not been complied with or has been contravened.

Notice and hearing

(2) No order shall be made under subsection (1) unless notice of the alleged non-compliance or contravention has been given to the holder of the certificate and the Board has afforded the holder an opportunity of being heard.

Revocation or suspension on application, etc., of holder

(3) Notwithstanding subsections (1) and (2), the Board may, by order, revoke or suspend a certificate on the application or with the consent of the holder thereof.

Conditions to Certificate

Compliance

57. Every certificate is subject to the condition that the provisions of this Act and the regulations in force at the date of issue of the certificate and as subsequently enacted, made or amended, as well as every order made under the authority of this Act, will be complied with.

· · · ·

Permits

Issuance

58.11(1) Except in the case of an international power line designated by order of the Governor in Council under section 58.15 or in respect of which an election is made under section 58.23, the Board shall, on application to it and without holding a public hearing, issue a permit authorizing the construction and operation of an international power line.

Information

(2) The application must be accompanied by the information that under the regulations is to be furnished in connection with the application.

Publication

58.12 The applicant shall publish a notice of the application in the Canada Gazette and such other publications as the Board considers appropriate.

Further information

58.13 The Board may, within a reasonable time after the publication of the notice, require the applicant to furnish such information, in addition to that required to accompany the application, as the Board considers necessary to determine whether to make a recommendation pursuant to section 58.14.

Delay of issuance

58.14(1) The Board may make a recommendation to the Minister, which it shall make public, that an international power line be designated by order of the Governor in Council under section 58.15, and may delay issuing a permit during such period as is necessary for the purpose of making such an order.

· · · ·

Certificates

Where certificate required

58.15(1) The Governor in Council may make orders
  (a) designating an international power line as an international power line that is to be constructed and operated under and in accordance with a certificate issued under section 58.16; and
  (b) revoking any permit issued in respect of the line.

Exception

(2) No order may be made under subsection (1) in respect of a line more than forty-five days after the issuance of a permit in respect of the line.

Effect of order

(3) Where an order is made under subsection (1),
  (a) no permit shall be issued in respect of the line; and
  (b) any application in respect of the line shall be dealt with as an application for a certificate.

Issuance

58.16(1) The Board may, subject to section 24 and to the approval of the Governor in Council, issue a certificate in respect of
  (a) an international power line in relation to which an order made under section 58.15 is in force,
  (b) an international power line in relation to which an election is filed under section 58.23, or
  (c) an interprovincial power line in relation to which an order made under section 58.4 is in force,
if the Board is satisfied that the line is and will be required by the present and future public convenience and necessity.

Criteria

(2) In deciding whether to issue a certificate, the Board shall have regard to all considerations that appear to it to be relevant.

Revocation of permit

(3) Any permit issued in respect of an international power line in relation to which an order made under section 58.15 is in force and that is not revoked by the order is revoked on the Board's deciding not to issue a certificate in respect of the line.

Location and Construction under Provincial Law

Provincial regulatory agency

58.17 The lieutenant governor in council of a province may designate as the provincial regulatory agency the lieutenant governor in council of the province, a provincial minister of the Crown or any other person or a board, commission or other tribunal.

. . . .

Incorporation of provincial functions

58.21 A provincial regulatory agency designated under section 58.17 has, in respect of those portions of international power lines that are within that province, the powers and duties that it has under the laws of the province in respect of lines for the transmission of electricity from a place in the province to another place in that province, including a power or duty to refuse to approve any matter or thing for which the approval of the agency is required, even though the result of the refusal is that the line cannot be constructed or operated.

. . . .

PART IV
TRAFFIC, TOLLS AND TARIFFS

. . . .

Powers of Board

Regulation of traffic, etc.

59. The Board may make orders with respect to all matters relating to traffic, tolls or tariffs.

Filing of Tariff

Tolls to be filed

60.(1) A company shall not charge any tolls except tolls that are

(a) specified in a tariff that has been filed with the Board and is in effect; or

(b) approved by an order of the Board.

. . . .

Just and Reasonable Tolls

Tolls to be just and reasonable

62. All tolls shall be just and reasonable, and shall always, under substantially similar circumstances and conditions with respect to all traffic of the same description carried over the same route, be charged equally to all persons at the same rate.

Board determinations

63. The Board may determine, as questions of fact, whether or not traffic is or has been carried under substantially similar circumstances and conditions referred to in section 62, whether in any case a company has or has not complied with the provisions of that section, and whether there has, in any case, been unjust discrimination within the meaning of section 67.

Interim tolls

64. Where the Board has made an interim order authorizing a company to charge tolls until a specified time or the happening of a specified event, the Board may, in any subsequent order, direct the company

(a) to refund, in a manner satisfactory to the Board, such part of the tolls charged by the company under the interim order as is in excess of the tolls determined by the Board to be just and reasonable, together with interest on the amount so refunded; or

(b) to recover in its tolls, in a manner satisfactory to the Board, the amount by which the tolls determined by the Board to be just and reasonable exceed the tolls charged by the company under the interim order, together with interest on the amount so recovered.

Disallowance of Tariff

Disallowance of tariff

65. The Board may disallow any tariff or any portion thereof that it considers to be contrary to any of the provisions of this Act or to any order of the Board, and may require a company, within a prescribed time, to substitute a tariff satisfactory to the Board in lieu thereof, or may prescribe other tariffs in lieu of the tariff or portion thereof so disallowed.

Suspension of tariff

66. The Board may suspend any tariff or any portion thereof before or after the tariff goes into effect.

Discrimination

No unjust discrimination

67. A company shall not make any unjust discrimination in tolls, service or facilities against any person or locality.

. . . .

PART VI
EXPORTS AND IMPORTS

Division I
Oil and Gas

Prohibition

Prohibition

116. Except as otherwise authorized by or under the regulations, no person shall export or import any oil or gas except under and in accordance with a licence issued under this Part.

Issuance of Licences

Issuance of licences

117.(1) Subject to the regulations, the Board may, on such terms and conditions as it may impose, issue licences for the exportation or importation of oil or gas.

Compliance

(2) Every licence is subject to the condition that the provisions of this Act and the regulations in force at the date of issue of the licence and as subsequently enacted, made or amended, as well as every order made under the authority of this Act, will be complied with.

Criteria

118. On an application for a licence, the Board shall have regard to all considerations that appear to it to be relevant and shall
  (a) satisfy itself that the quantity of oil or gas to be exported does not exceed the surplus remaining after due allowance has been made

for the reasonably foreseeable requirements for use in Canada having regard to the trends in the discovery of oil or gas in Canada; and
  (b) [Repealed, 1990, c. 7, s. 32]
  (c) where oil or gas is to be exported and subsequently imported or where oil or gas is to be imported, have regard to the equitable distribution of oil or gas, as the case may be, in Canada.

Revocation and Suspension

Revocation and suspension of licences

119.(1) Subject to subsection (2) and the regulations, the Board may, by order, with the approval of the Governor in Council, revoke or suspend a licence if
  (a) any term or condition of the licence has not been complied with or has been contravened; or
  (b) the Board is of the opinion that the public convenience and necessity so require.

. . . .

Regulations

Regulations

119.01(1) The Governor in Council may make regulations for carrying into effect the purposes and provisions of this Division, including regulations respecting
  (a) the information to be furnished by applicants for licences and the procedure to be followed in applying for licences and in issuing licences;
  (b) the duration of licences, not exceeding twenty-five years, from a date to be fixed in the licence, the approval required in respect of the issue of licences, the quantities that may be exported or imported under licences and any other terms and conditions to which licences may be subject.

. . . .

Division II
Electricity

Prohibition

Prohibition

119.02 No person shall export any electricity except under and in accordance with a permit issued under section 119.03 or a licence issued under section 119.08.

. . . .

Regulations

Regulations

127. The Governor in Council may make regulations for carrying into effect the purposes and provisions of this Part, including regulations respecting

(a) the information to be furnished by applicants for licences and the procedure to be followed in applying for licences and in issuing licences;

(b) the duration of licences from a date to be fixed in the licence, the approval required in respect of the issue of licences, the quantities that may be moved out of the designated province or area under the authority of a licence, and any other terms or conditions to which licences may be subject;

(c) units of measurement and measuring instruments or devices to be used in connection with the movement of designated oil or gas out of the designated province or area; and

(d) the inspection of any instruments, devices, plant, equipment, books, records or accounts or any other thing used for or in connection with the movement of designated oil or gas out of the designated province or area.

Offences, Punishment and Enforcement

Offence and punishment

128.(1) Every person who contravenes any of the provisions of this Part or the regulations made under this Part is guilty of an offence and liable

(a) on summary conviction, to a fine not exceeding one hundred thousand dollars or to imprisonment for a term not exceeding one year or to both; or

(b) on conviction on indictment, to a fine not exceeding one million dollars or to imprisonment for a term not exceeding five years or to both.

. . . .

PART VIII
GENERAL

Regulations

Regulations respecting accounts, etc.

129.(1) The Board may, with the approval of the Governor in Council, make regulations

(a) respecting the manner in which the accounts of a company shall be kept;

(b) respecting the classes of property for which depreciation charges may properly be included under operating expenses in the accounts and the accounting method or methods that may be used in computing and charging depreciation in respect of each of the classes of property;

(c) respecting a uniform system of accounts applicable to any class of company; and

(d) requiring

(i) companies that have been authorized under Part III to construct or operate a pipeline,

(ii) persons exporting oil, gas or electricity or importing oil or gas, and

(iii) persons holding a licence under Part VI or VII,

to keep and make available to the Board for inspection by the Board or a person authorized by the Board at a place of business in Canada such records, books of account and other documents in such form as may be prescribed by the regulations and submit to the Board, at such times and in such form as may be so prescribed, returns and information respecting capital, traffic, revenues, expenses and other matters so prescribed and deemed by the Board to be matters that should be considered by it in carrying out its powers and duties under this Act in relation to those companies and persons.

Exemptions

(1.1) The Board may, by order made on such terms and conditions as it considers appropriate, exempt a company or person from the application of a regulation made under subsection (1).

Contravention and punishment

(2) Every person who contravenes a regulation made under this section is guilty of an offence punishable on summary conviction.

General regulations

130.(1) The Governor in Council may make regulations for carrying the purposes and provisions of this Act into effect and may, by those regulations, designate as an oil product or as a gas product any substance resulting from the processing or refining of hydrocarbons or coal if that substance

(a) is asphalt or a lubricant; or

(b) is a suitable source of energy by itself or when it is combined or used in association with something else,

Exemptions

(2) The Governor in Council may by regulation exempt any oil or gas or any kind, quality or class thereof or any area or transaction from the operation of all or any of the provisions of this Act.

. . . .

Report to Parliament

Report to Parliament

133. The Board shall within three months after December 31 in each year submit to the Minister a report on the activities of the Board under this Act for that year, and the Minister shall cause the report to be laid before Parliament within fifteen days after the receipt thereof or, if Parliament is not then sitting, on any of the first fifteen days next thereafter that either House of Parliament is sitting.

(c)   Note on National Energy Board[†]

The National Energy Board (NEB) is part of the outlying administrative process. It is a regulatory body, although it has less to regulate since the deregulation changes in 1985. Its main governing statutes include the *National Energy Board Act*[1], the *Energy Administration Act*[2], and the *Northern Pipeline Act*[3]. Its main regulatory functions are licensing pipeline and powerline proposals (Part III: ss. 52[4] and 58.16); licensing the import and export of oil, gas, and power (Part VI: s. 117); and approving utility rates (Part IV: s. 62). The NEB also has an advisory function (Part II: ss. 26–8), although it is less important than it was in the 1970s.

The NEB has a staff of under 300 [1998], down from pre-deregulation days when it numbered over 460. It has up to nine full-time members, each appointed for up to seven years and with tenure during good behaviour, and up to six part-time members. It operates with a quorum of three members. When a quorum of three makes a decision, it informs the full Board but does not consult with it. There is no formal review committee, and there are no set rules as to where review should be carried out by differently constituted panels.

How independent is the NEB? Cabinet approval is required for NEB decisions

(a)   granting pipeline and some powerline certificates (ss. 52 and 58.15), and
(b)   licensing the import or export of gas or the export of oil (in all cases for longer-term contracts duration), or power (for longer-term contracts: s. 119.08).

Denials of applications do not require Cabinet approval. As a result of the recent deregulation changes, Cabinet approval is not required for orders authorizing the import or export of oil or gas (for under two years), or power (for under three years). Similarly, it has never been required for rate (toll and tariff) decisions (s. 62). Thus far, there has been no case in which Cabinet has denied approval to a Board decision.[5]

Cabinet makes most of the substantive regulations governing the NEB's operations (e.g., s. 119.01 re imports and exports, and s. 119.094 general). The NEB can make regulations regarding the accounts of regulated companies, but these regulations are subject to Cabinet approval: s. 129. The NEB is permitted to make its own procedural rules (s. 8).[6]

There are no appeal, petition, or other review channels from the NEB to the Cabinet or Ministers.

Many members have industry experience (e.g., *Crowe* case). The regulated parties are typically large companies, many of whom have a much more direct interest (backed by more information resources and money) in the subject matter of decisions than consumer and public interest groups.

Although subject to potentially close Cabinet control, the NEB is very court-like. It is the only one of the four authorities we look at that is a court of record (s. 11). Hearings are required to be public, and are very formal. They may be either oral or written. Although the Board does not require that parties in oral or written hearings be represented by legal counsel, they almost always

---

[†]   For the most current situation and further background material, see <http://www.neb-one.gc.ca/index_e.htm>.

are.[7] The average length of oral hearings is about eight days,[8] and important hearings can last considerably longer. In its 1992 *Annual Report*, after noting that it had conducted an usually large number of oral public hearings (15) during the year the Board's chairman made the following comment:

> The Board recognizes that oral hearings can be costly for itself and for the public taking part. It therefore seeks to keep the use of this process to a reasonable minimum by, for example, conducting written hearings where this is appropriate. And when oral hearings are held, the Board tries to reduce their length by encouraging parties to reach prior settlements on issues, by extensive use of written information requests and then by conducting the most efficient and expeditious oral process. In this connection, an innovation introduced in 1992 requires parties to notify applicants which issues they intend to examine. This eliminates the need for the appearance of witnesses whose evidence is not going to be challenged. However, the Board also recognizes that oral hearings are often the best way of examining facts and of hearing an argument in cases which involve opposing interests.

The NEB participates in appeals from its own decisions, subject to the usual bar on participating in purely procedural issues.

The NEB is subject to appeals on law or jurisdiction to the Federal Court of Appeal (s. 22). It used to be subject to review in the Trial Division or the Federal Court of Appeal pursuant to ss. 18 and 28 of the old *Federal Court Act*. In the amended *Act*, it is one of 14 tribunals reviewable only by the Federal Court of Appeal. Many judicial appeals have involved distinguishing between interprovincial and (provincially controlled) intraprovincial pipelines. From 1981 to 1992, there were about nine reported appeals including Board decisions on oil and gas issues and in six of these cases Board decisions were upheld.[9]

Hearing Stages

The main stages of a typical oral hearing before the NEB are as follows:

(a) pre-application consultation;
(b) application;
(c) deficiency letters (sent by NEB if additional material is needed);
(d) NEB decision as to whether oral or other hearing is required;
(e) issue of hearing order (notice of hearing);

(f) receipt of interventions;
(g) pre-hearing conference (optional);
(h) hearing: examination-in-chief of applicant's witnesses, cross-examination by intervenors, cross-examination by board counsel; re-examination of applicant's witnesses by applicant; similar procedure for intervenors' evidence; applicant's rebuttal evidence; concluding arguments by applicants and intervenors; replies by intervenors;
(i) post-hearing meeting, preparation of report; and
(j) reasons (if not approved) or submission for Cabinet approval if received for approval.

Possible Issues

1. **Constitutional issues:** (division of powers: many challenges: e.g., Where does an interprovincial pipeline start and stop? *Charter*: not as many issues here yet?)

2. **Balancing Cabinet control with independence and impartiality:** The NEB takes note of official government policy statements by placing them on the record. Cabinet approval appears not to be a serious problem for the NEB: so far, it has always been given. Is this because the NEB is always well aware of government policy? Is it because the NEB almost never makes mistakes? Since Cabinet approval is not normally preceded by a formal communication to the Board, this is difficult to tell. On another matter, is there any risk that the NEB's advisory function could prejudice its impartiality?

3. **Accessibility to third-party and public interests:** The NEB has an official open-door policy but its formality may still deter participants. Parties are almost always represented by counsel. Does the NEB have any general power to award costs? Some claim that its "court of record" provision implies this, but nobody knows exactly what a "court of record" really is.

4. **Vaguely worded statutory mandate:** see, for example, the requirement in s. 62 of the *National Energy Board Act* that all tolls shall be "just and reasonable."

5. **Balancing fairness and judicial procedure with efficiency:**
   (a) avoiding undue delay; where to hold hearings:

(i) Regulations now dispense with need for a hearing re import/export applications for less than two (heavy crude oil, gas) or three (power) years and with the need to approve price (it is now determined by the parties);

(ii) The Board's recent "low intensity" approach to regulating tolls of smaller pipeline companies on a complaint-only basis also reduces the number of hearings likely to be required; and

(iii) The NEB attempts to use written rather than oral hearings where possible, or to conduct all but a portion of a hearing in writing (see extracts from 1992 *Annual Report*, above). On the other hand, attempts to limit hearings carry an element of risk, and must be done even-handedly (see *Dow Chemical*).

(b) disclosure vs. confidentiality:

(i) Re evidence submitted by parties: "If you file it, it will be on the public record," appears to be the general NEB approach, and

(ii) staff studies: does the NEB release any of these?

(c) subject matter complexity vs. the need for simplicity and uniformity: Much of the subject matter before the Board is extremely technical and complex: what are the implications for accessibility and cost?

(d) **general policy guidelines vs. case-by-case adjudication:** Which is the best way to formulate policy?

(e) **delay:** Is this a problem? Should the National Energy Board Act impose time limits on decisions? How would this be reconciled with hearing requirements?

(f) **compliance:** The NEB has less to regulate, and has taken a more complaint-oriented, hands-off approach to regulation, rather similar to that of the NTA. What specific enforcement mechanisms does it have? Which of these does it use?

Law Reform Commission

In a 216-page study for the Law Reform Commission of Canada, published in 1977,[10] Alastair Lucas and Trevor Bell praised the NEB for using rule-making hearings for formulating policy, but expressed a number of concerns. They criticised the NEB for not releasing staff studies; said the complexity of the subject matter increased dependence on experts and discouraged public participation; argued that the NEB's dual advisory/decision-making role left it open to possible conflicts of interest; and criticised the vagueness of the NEB's statutory mandate. Which of these concerns, if any, is still valid today? Why, or why not?

Notes

1. R.S.C. 1985, c. N-7.
2. R.S.C. 1985, c. E-6.
3. R.S.C. 1985, c. N-26.
4. Unless otherwise indicated, all section references are to provisions in the *National Energy Board Act*.
5. Source: *National Energy Board*.
6. See *National Energy Board Rules of Practice and Procedure*, 1986, as am. Revised NEB Rules of Practice and Procedure were made on 22 January 1993 but are subject to review by the Privy Council Office and Department of Justice and to Cabinet approval.
7. *ibid.*
8. *ibid.*
9. *ibid.*
10. Law Reform Commission of Canada, *The National Energy Board: Policy, Procedure and Practice* by A.R. Lucas & T. Bell (Ottawa: Law Reform Commission of Canada, 1977).

(d) *Dow Chemical*[†]

NOTE

The *Dow Chemical* case was a classic confrontation between the needs of administrative efficiency and those of procedural fairness. When a large petro-chemical company applied to the National Energy Board for a licence to export ethylene, evidence had already been heard on other aspects of the pro-

---

[†] *Re Attorney-General of Manitoba et al. and National Energy Board et al.* (1975), 48 D.L.R. (3d) 73 (F.C.T.D.).

posed project, and time was at a premium. The Board permitted only the applicant to give oral evidence, limiting its opponents to written submissions. Only the counsel for the Board was allowed to cross-examine the applicant. The opponent challenged the Board's decision to proceed in this manner. What was the basis of the court's decision? The common law rules of natural justice? The wording of the relevant statute? Both? Do you agree with the result?

EXTRACTS

[CATTANACH, J.:]

This matter was begun by a notice of motion filed by the Attorney-General of Manitoba as applicant naming the National Energy Board (hereinafter for convenience referred to as the Board) as respondent.

Subsequently the six additional parties named in the above style of cause moved to be joined with the Attorney-General of Manitoba as applicants to which I assented and similarly the three additional parties named in the style of cause as respondents sought to be so added to which requests I also assented.

. . . .

... [O]n motion by the applicants I permitted para. (a) to be amended by its deletion and the substitution of the following:

  (a) an order of Certiorari to quash the following decisions of the National Energy Board namely:
   (i) the decision given on or about June 11, 1974 to hold an ex parte hearing to deal with the application of Dow Chemical of Canada Limited for licences to export some 10 billion pounds of ethylene during a 10 year period commencing on or about July, 1977;
   (ii) the decision pronounced and delivered on the 26th day of June, 1974, whereby the Board decided not to alter its decision to hold an ex parte hearing to deal with the application of Dow Chemical of Canada Limited for licences to export some 10 billion pounds of ethylene during a 10 year period commencing on or about July, 1977;

To fully appreciate the issue and the question which evolve for determination it is expedient to review the background.

Basically, the National Energy Board was created by the *National Energy Board Act*, 1959 (Can.),

c. 46, as amended [now R.S.C. 1970, c. N-6], to exercise a regulatory licensing and advisory supervision on matters relating to the manufacturing, processing, transmission, transportation, distribution, sale, purchase, exchange and disposal of energy and sources of energy within and outside Canada over which the Parliament of Canada has jurisdiction. The paramount consideration of the Board in exercising its jurisdiction is the public interest particularly that the export of energy or its sources will not deplete the supply before the requirements for domestic consumption [are] guaranteed and that the price to be charged therefor is just and reasonable: see s. 83 of the *National Energy Board Act*.

In 1971 Dome Petroleum Limited (hereinafter referred to as "Dome") entered into a contract with a company in Ohio, U.S.A., for the sale of ethane, propane and condensates which Dome considered would make the supplying of ethane originating in Alberta by pipeline an economically feasible project. Accordingly, Dome applied to the Board for amendment to existing licences to increase the volume it might export over a 10-year term and Cochin Pipe Lines Limited (hereinafter referred to as "Cochin") concurrently applied for a certificate of public convenience and necessity for the construction of a pipeline. The Board, due to the rapidly changing energy situation in Canada in 1971 and 1972, limited its decision to propane. This matter was heard in January, 1972.

By its decision given in May, 1973, consequent upon the hearing in January, 1972, the Board allowed the export of an additional volume of propane but restricted the term to five years rather than the requested term of 10 years.

At that time, *i.e.*, May, 1973, the Board directed that Dome and other parties who had taken part in the hearing in January, 1972, should file additional and more current evidence. This further hearing took place in July, August and September, 1973.

From the additional evidence it was readily apparent to the Board that the nature of the over-all project had changed.

Dow Chemical of Canada, Limited (hereinafter referred to as "Dow") had undertaken and committed itself to the construction of a large ethylene manufacturing plant at Fort Saskatchewan, Alberta. It had become the co-shareholder with Dome in equal proportions in Cochin.

Cochin now sought authorization from the board to construct twin pipelines, one as originally contemplated to carry light hydrocarbons to Sarnia, Ontario, and the other to carry ethylene.

The Board issued its decision in January, 1974. It approved the export of ethane as requested but restricted the term of the licence to six years to coincide with the amendments to Dome's licences to export propane and the Board approved the construction of the twin pipeline system.

At the time of the hearings in July, August and September, 1973, the question arose and was argued before the Board whether ethylene fell under the jurisdiction of the Board as being gas or oil within the meaning of Part VI of the *National Energy Board Act.*

However, the evidence before the board established that ethylene would not be transported by the pipeline system until 1977 and accordingly the Board found it unnecessary to decide that issue at that time.

While the Board made no express finding on this issue it was aware of the importance of the issue. This is demonstrated in its report of January, 1974, in which it took into account the amount of ethane which would be required to produce ethylene in determining if there would be a surplus of natural gas and ethylene to the domestic needs.

In April, 1974, the Board concluded that it had jurisdiction over the export of ethylene under Part VI of the Act and its conclusion in this respect was made known to the interested parties.

Dow thereupon made application to the Board for a licence to export ten billion pounds of ethylene over a 10-year period beginning on or about July, 1977; that is one billion pounds annually.

The parties before me appear to accept the Board's conclusion that it has jurisdiction under Part VI of the Act to entertain an application for the export of ethylene. In any event it was not an issue before me that the Board had found facts contrary to the reality thereof thereby conferring jurisdiction upon itself and I am not obliged, therefore, to express any opinion on this particular matter.

From the Board's decision given in January, 1974, on the matters of Dome's application to export propane and Cochin's application to construct twin pipelines, one for light hydrocarbons and the other for ethylene, which pursuant to the direction of the Board when it issued its decision in May, 1973, on the application of Dome to export propane should be heard on additional information on all aspects of the over-all project which was done in July, August and September, 1973, it is apparent that the Board was particularly conscious of the public interest as is its duty to be.

.   .   .   .   .

... [T]he Board considered the two separate applications as part of a single overall project. It is logical to conclude that the Board considered the whole project to consist of three stages:

(1) Dome's application to export propane in January, 1972, the decision on which was given by the Board in May, 1973,

(2) the concurrent and respective applications of Dome and Cochin to export ethane and to construct twin pipelines, one to carry light hydrocarbons and the other to carry ethylene, the decision on which was given in January, 1974, and

(3) the present Dow application to export ethylene. It would be naive to think that the Board was not aware that the ultimate application by Dow to export ethylene was part and parcel of the project in its entirety.

There was ample evidence before the board to this effect. An agreement between Dow and Cochin respecting ethylene was an exhibit before the Board in its 1973 hearings. Officers of Dow testified at length on all aspects of the Dow ethylene project and were cross-examined by counsel for each of the intervenants who chose to do so. The evidence was clear that the ethylene pipeline and the Dow ethylene project were interdependent and that one was essential to the other and that if both ethane and ethylene pipe lines were not authorized the one pipeline would not be built. It was a case of all or nothing.

This being so I have no doubt that the Board regarded each individual and separate application as an integral part of a whole mammoth project:

(1) the manufacture of ethylene by Dow in Alberta,

(2) providing for its transportation to supply the needs of the Canadian market, and

(3) the export of surplus ethylene and other hydrocarbons.

The Board deferred its consideration of the export of ethylene

(1) until it concluded that it had jurisdiction to do so and

(2) because it was not necessary to do so since ethylene would not be exported until 1977.

As was argued, I think that the manner in which the Board considered the three applications piecemeal, that is by first restricting Dome's application to export ethane, propane and condensates to the export of propane, then approving Dome's application to export ethane and approving Cochin's application to construct twin pipelines and finally considering Dow's application to export ethylene, is susceptible of the interpretation that there was but one continuing application before the Board which was considered in three stages.

In my view this interpretation was adopted by the Board and was the underlying factor which prompted the Board to proceed as it did but in so saying I do not overlook the fact that the Board held three distinct and separate hearings.

In April, 1974, as indicated above, the Board concluded that it had jurisdiction over the export of ethylene and made its conclusion known.

Dow then made application for a licence to export ethylene.

The secretary of the Board thereupon dispatched a telex message dated June 11, 1974, to the parties indicated in the body of the message which reads:

> As a party of record at the National Energy Board hearings of the applications of Dome Petroleum Limited, Cochin Pipe Lines Limited, et al., in 1972 and 1973, please be advised as follows:
>
> On Tuesday, the 25th day of June, 1974 at 2:00 p.m., the Board will hear publicly the application of Dow Chemical of Canada, Limited, ex parte, for licences to
>
> 1. Export from Elmore, Saskatchewan, 15 billion pounds of ethylene during a 10-year term commencing upon startup of the plant at Fort Saskatchewan or the 1st day of July, 1977, whichever is the earlier:
> 2. Import at Windsor, Ontario, the said 15 billion pounds of ethylene during the said 10-year term:
> 3. Export from Sarnia, Ontario, 10 billion pounds of ethylene during the said 10-year term, and
> 4. Drop off a portion of the ethylene at Joliet, Illinois, as an alternate point of delivery to Marysville, Michigan.
>
> And take notice that prior to its decision upon the said application, the Board will consider only written representations in respect of the said application subject to the following conditions:
>
> (i) That the representations shall contain sufficient facts to establish that the representor is directly interested in or affected by the said application:
> (ii) That the said representations shall be served on the applicant and be received by the Board on or before the 21st day of June, 1974.

> And further take notice that copies of the said application and written representations may be examined at the office of the Secretary of the Board at:
>
> National Energy Board,
> Trebla Building,
> 473 Albert Street,
> Ottawa, Ontario.
>
> or at the office of the applicant at:
>
> Dow Chemical of Canada Limited,
> Modeland Road,
> Sarnia, Ontario.

The significant content of that message was that the Board would hear "publicly" the Dow application *ex parte* and that the Board would "consider only written representations" subject to the conditions that the representations established that the [representor] was "directly interested in" or "affected by" the application and should be served on the applicant and received by the Board on or before June 21, 1974.

It was moved before the Board, when it convened on June 25, 1974, that the board should alter its decision "to hold an *ex parte* public hearing" in the format set out in the telex notice and instead to hold a public hearing by which was meant that all interested parties should be afforded the opportunity of cross-examining the witnesses called by the applicant in support of its application and to introduce oral evidence in contradiction thereof at the conclusion of which the applicant would be permitted to make oral argument as would counsel for the interested parties who opposed the application.

The Board had announced that it would hear oral evidence on behalf of the applicant and that the applicant might make an oral submission in support of the application but that the parties opposing the application would be restricted to written submission and would not be permitted to cross-examine witnesses called by the applicant.

After having heard argument on the request to so vary the format of the hearing of the application, the Board announced its decision, on June 26, 1974, not to vary its prior decision to hold an "*ex parte* public hearing".

In short, the Board denied the motion made before it on the grounds that "the procedure it has selected in disposing of the Dow application is consistent with the requirements of the *National Energy Board Act* and with the requirements of the rules of natural justice".

However, in view of the expressed concern of a number of the interested parties with respect to the time allowed to make written representations, the

Board announced that it would afford the persons involved in the hearing the opportunity to make further representations with a comparable opportunity to the applicant to make a written reply thereto.

The Board also announced that it would review the application on "an *ex parte* basis" within the framework of the surplus calculations contained in the Board's decision of January, 1974, relating to the Cochin and Dome applications, that the Board's natural gas surplus calculations made provision for a 1.2 billion-pound ethylene plant of Dow using ethane as a feedstock and that the Board's report recognized that Dow's intent to expand the plant using propane and butane as a feed-stock which latter two hydrocarbons do not have to meet the Board's surplus test for natural gas.

The Board still further announced that quantities of ethylene in excess of the quantities determined earlier by the Board would not be dealt with until what was termed "full public hearings" on inquiry into the demand, supply, deliverability and surplus of natural gas with respect to which notices had been sent to all interested parties inviting submissions by September 3, 1974, with the opportunity to those parties to be heard and take an active part in the hearing which I believe is to take place in September, 1974.

What has happened in fact with respect to the Dow application, when the hearing began, was that Dow called three witnesses each of whom had been called and had given evidence at the Dome and Cochin applications. Each witness was shown a transcript of the testimony given by him in the earlier proceedings, which was an exhibit in the current proceedings, with which each acknowledged his familiarity. Each of the three witnesses was asked if he adopted the evidence given by him at the prior proceedings and in response each stated that he did. The oral examination-in-chief consisted of two questions to each of the three witnesses and was no more than the adoption by each witness of the evidence that had been given earlier. It was an incorporation in the Dow proceeding of evidence given in the Dome and Cochin applications by reference thereto.

Counsel for the Board and the members of the Board questioned the witnesses on significant matters raised in the written representations made by Alberta Gas Trunk Line, Dupont of Canada, Esso Chemical of Canada, the Province of Ontario and Polymar and did so generally for the purpose of testing the evidence and putting to the witnesses issues raised by the interveners.

In argument before me, it was pointed out as being significant that counsel for the applicants on the present motion who had been present at the hearing before the Board did not indicate that they wished to cross-examine the witnesses, that they suggested to counsel for the Board or members of the Board any questions which they thought should be put in cross-examination of these witnesses, that they might call witnesses in contradiction, that their positions were not fully understood and that they had not objected to the reception of written argument rather than oral representations.

Generally speaking, when the question of fairness is involved, if the procedure adopted is acquiesced in by a party with that party's full knowledge, then that party is in a disadvantageous position to complain of the procedure so adopted.

The simple answer in the present matter is that the parties in opposition to the application did complain of the procedure at the very outset of the hearing and moved to vary that procedure. The Board denied that request. In view of the Board's ruling that only the applicant may present oral evidence and make an oral argument (which was later changed to written argument and that was done), that the opponents were to be limited to written representations and would not be afforded the right to cross-examine, counsel would be entitled to assume that, if they had made the suggestions or requests [that it] had been suggested that they ought to have made, the suggestions or requests would not be entertained by the Board and that it would have been abortive to make them.

The frequent and repeated use of the words *ex parte* in conjunction with the word "publicly" and sometimes "in public" was a most unfortunate choice. The Latin words *ex parte*, translated literally mean from one side or party only and in a legal sense mean a proceeding that is taken or granted at the instance of and for the benefit of one party only without notice to or contestation by any person adversely interested.

What the Board did was nothing of the sort. It gave notice to interested persons and invited written representations from these persons. The application was not intended to be, nor was it heard *ex parte*. The use of those words in the context was a contradiction and therefore meaningless.

Immediately following the Board's conclusion in April, 1974, that ethylene was gas within the meaning of Part VI of the *National Energy Board Act*, Dow made application for a licence to export ethylene.

On June 20, 1974, the Governor in Council approved an amendment [P.C. 1974-1457, SOR/74-

391, s. 1] of the *National Energy Board Part VI Regulations*, P.C. 1959-1411, SOR/59-435, by adding thereto, immediately after s. 16 thereof, the following heading and section:

Ethylene

16.1(1) Notwithstanding anything in these Regulations, any person may import ethylene without a licence.

(2) The Board may, by order, authorize any person, upon such terms and conditions as the Board may prescribe, to export ethylene.

(3) Every person who exports or imports ethylene shall, when requested by the Board, furnish the Board with such information as the Board may require respecting the exportation or importation.

(4) When a person named in an order made under subsection (2) exports ethylene, he shall do so in accordance with the terms and conditions prescribed by the Board in the order.

2. Subsection 24(2) of the said Regulations is amended by striking out the word "and" at the end of paragraph (g) thereof, by adding the word "and" at the end of paragraph (h) thereof and by adding thereto the following paragraph:

"(i) ethylene."

This amendment became effective on June 24, 1974. The canon of interpretation is that when the effect of an enactment (which canon is applicable to a Regulation authorized under a statute) is to take away a right, *prima facie* it does not apply to existing rights, but when it deals with procedure only, *prima facie* it applies to all matters pending, as well as future.

Assuming the enactment is procedural only, as it appears to be, but which question it is not incumbent upon me to decide for reasons I shall outline, then the Board could by order authorize an applicant to export ethylene and it is clear from the language of the amendment, that the Board can make that order *ex parte* within the correct meaning of those words.

At the outset of the hearing, counsel for Dow moved to the Board that the application for the issue of a licence for the exportation of ethylene should be considered by the Board as an application for an order to authorize Dow to export ethylene pursuant to the amendment to the Part VI Regulations.

This the Board did not decide. In my opinion it was obligatory upon the Board to decide the fundamental character of the application before embarking upon the hearing. The application had to be one thing or the other and not a hybrid of both because different procedures and consequences would follow depending upon which of the two categories into which the application fell.

Because the Board did not decide or make its decision publicly known, I am of the opinion that I am left with no alternative other than to deal with the motion before me on the basis that the application stands as it was originally made to the Board, that is an application by Dow for the issue of a licence for the exportation of ethylene.

Counsel for the Board sought to introduce before me a press release issued by the Board prior to the hearing of the Dow application, and certified copies of the decision and reasons therefor given by the Board on the prior applications of Dome and Cochin. Counsel for the applicants objected to the admission of the material on the ground that the present motion was limited to the Dow application and the material had no relevance thereto. I admitted the material subject to reserve of the objection for the reason that the prior decisions would have a bearing on the question whether the procedure adopted by the Board accorded a fair hearing which I might be well called upon to decide and because there had been no prior motion for direction as to what would constitute the record on *certiorari*. Having so admitted that material, counsel for the applicants requested that the transcript of the evidence at these prior hearings should also be produced. I acceded to that request on the same basis.

Upon more mature reflection, I am satisfied that all material above is properly admitted to ensure that the matter in dispute may be effectually determined and adjudicated upon.

In the *National Energy Board Act*, there are procedural provisions and, pursuant to the authority in s. 7 thereof, rules relating to practice and procedure in proceedings before the Board were made.

If the Board complies with the express procedural provisions, it is the master of its own procedure, but, where there is a complaint, as is here the case, then the Court must decide whether there has been a failure to observe the principles of natural justice by being unjust or unfair in some material way to the persons who complain.

Thus the question to be first determined is whether the Board had authority to proceed in the way it did.

If that question is determined in the negative that, in my opinion, concludes the matter and the applicants are entitled to relief.

On the contrary, if the question is answered in the affirmative, then a second question arises for determination and that is whether the procedure that was adopted by the Board was just and fair to the applicants.

I have been referred to a multitude of cases by counsel. A review of those cases would seem to establish that there is almost no rule with reference to a particular problem that is universally applicable to every type of case in all circumstances. In each of the decisions what was decided was that what was done in that case was, or was not, a compliance with the requirements of natural justice in the circumstances of the case and not that some particular thing must be done, or not done, in all circumstances.

Regardless of how the board may be characterized, that is as exercising administrative or executive functions as opposed to judicial or *quasi*-judicial functions, Parliament did impose procedural duties on the Board.

Section 20 [rep. & sub. R.S.C. 1970, c. 27 (1st Supp.), s.8], of the *National Energy Board Act* provides:

> 20(1) Subject to subsection (2), hearings before the Board with regard to the issue, revocation or suspension of certificates or licences for the exportation of gas or power or the importation of gas, or for leave to abandon the operation of a pipeline or international power line, shall be public.
>
> (2) Where the Board revokes or suspends a certificate or licence upon the application or with the consent of the holder thereof, a public hearing need not be held if the pipeline or international power line to which the certificate or licence relates had not been brought into commercial operation under that certificate or licence.
>
> (3) The Board may hold a public hearing in respect of any other matter if it considers it advisable to do so.

In s-s. (3) the expression used is "public hearing". The exception is s-s. (1) to s-s. (2) is not applicable in the present circumstances. However, the expression "public hearing" is used in s-s. (2). Subsection (1) provides that "hearings" before the Board with regard to the issue of a licence for the exportation of gas (which for the reasons expressed above I have concluded the Dow application to be) shall be "public". The marginal note to s. 20 is "Public hearings". The marginal note does not form part of the statute but is merely *temporanea expositio*. While the marginal note ought not to be relied on in interpreting the statute, it is helpful. Despite the fact that the words "hearings" and "public" are not in juxtaposition in s-s. (1), nevertheless the language of s-s. (1),

when the section as a whole is considered, must be construed as synonymous to "public hearings".

It was contended that the word "public" as an adjective modifying the word "hearing" means that the proceedings of the Board shall be conducted "in public" as contrasted with the proceedings being held *in camera*.

I do not agree with that contention. The word "public" in the context, in my opinion, means that every member of the public, subject to the qualification that such person has a demonstrable interest in the subject-matter before the Board over and above the public generally, shall have the right to participate in the hearing.

I find support for this conclusion in the language of Lord Moulton in *Local Government Board* v. *Arlidge*, [1915] A.C. 120. Lord Moulton considered the meaning of the word "public" in the term "public local inquiry". He said at pp. 147–8:

> The effect of the insertion of the word "public" appears to me to be that every member of the public would have a *locus standi* to bring before the inquiry any matters relevant thereto so as to ensure that everything bearing on the rights of the owner or occupier of the house affected, or the interests of the public in general, or of the public living in the neighborhood in particular, would be brought to the knowledge of the Local Government Board for the purpose of enabling it to discharge its duties in connection with the appeal.

Section 7 of the *National Energy Board Act* provides:

> 7. The Board may make rules respecting
>   (a) the sittings of the Board;
>   (b) the procedure for making applications, representations and complaints to the Board and the conduct of hearings before the Board, and generally the manner of conducting any business before the Board;

(I have omitted paras. (c) and (d) as they have no bearing on the matter in issue.)

Pursuant to that authority, the Board has made Rules relating to practice and procedure before the Board.

Section 6 of those Rules provides:

> 6(1) Except where the Board directs that an application may be heard and determined *ex parte* or makes an expedited proceedings order, the Board shall, as soon as possible after the filing of an application, set the application down for hearing.
>
> (2) Where an application has been set down for hearing, the Secretary shall forthwith notify

the applicant of the time and place fixed for the hearing thereof and shall, by such notification, indicate

(a) the persons to whom and the time within which notice of the application shall be given by the applicant,

(b) the manner, whether by public advertisement, personal service or otherwise, in which notice of the application shall be given by the applicant, and

(c) the form and contents of the notice to be given by the applicant and the information to be included therein, including the time and place fixed for the hearing of the application and the time within which any reply or submission shall be filed with the Secretary.

(3) Upon receipt of the notification referred to in subsection (2) the applicant shall give notice of the application in accordance with such notification.

Section 7 provides for reply or submission by an intervener who intends to oppose or intervene in any application and the content thereof.

Provisions respecting hearings are contained in ss. 15 to 19, which are reproduced:

.   .   .   .

17(1) The witnesses at the hearing of any application shall be examined *viva voce*, but the Board may at any time order that any particular facts may be proved by affidavit or that the affidavit of any witness may be read at the hearing on such terms and conditions as the Board considers reasonable, or that a witness whose attendance ought for good and sufficient cause to be dispensed with be examined before a commissioner or other person authorized to administer oaths, before whom the parties or their solicitors shall attend.

.   .   .   .

Section 3 of the Rules provides:

3(1) Subject to the Act and the regulations and except as otherwise provided in these Rules, these Rules apply to every proceeding before the Board upon an application.

(2) The Board may, in any proceeding before the Board upon an application, direct either orally or in writing that the provisions of these Rules or any of them shall not apply, or shall apply in part only, and without restricting the generality of the foregoing the Board may, for the purpose of ensuring the expeditious conduct of the business of the Board and the hearing and determination of any such proceeding,

(a) extend or abridge the time fixed by these Rules for the doing of any act or thing,

(b) dispense with compliance with any provision of these Rules requiring the doing of any act or thing, or

(c) substitute other rules for the provisions of these Rules or any of them.

(3) In any case not expressly provided for by the Act, the regulations or these Rules, the general rules of practice in the Exchequer Court of Canada may, in the discretion of the Board, be adopted and made applicable to any proceeding before the Board upon an application.

There was no material before me that any application was made to the Board to depart from the Rules nor was my attention directed to any material that the Board so directed either orally or in writing.

While the Board no doubt felt that consideration by it of the Dow application was urgent, the Board did not expressly so state as a condition for the Board initiating on its own motion a substitution of other Rules for those existing for the purpose of the expeditious conduct of the hearing of the Dow application.

Possibly, the telex message of June 11, 1974, might be so construed but, in my opinion, that message should have been predicated upon an express statement that a degree of emergency prevailed which would justify the Board in departing from the Rules ordinarily applicable to a hearing in the absence of which the recipients of the message were entitled to assume that the usual Rules are applicable. This, I think, is inherent in s. 3(1).

Further, s. 3 is "subject to the Act". The crucial question, therefore, is whether the meaning to be ascribed to the word "hearing" as used in s. 20 of the Act is that of a normal "oral hearing" by which I mean a hearing at which the Board would be prepared to hear both sides, to make available to and allow both sides to comment upon or contradict any information that the Board has obtained, to permit the parties to adduce oral evidence, to be represented by counsel, to permit cross-examination of witnesses adverse to their position and for the Board to act only on information of probative value.

I fully appreciate that in many instances a hearing need not be an oral one but may be on written representations. If a tribunal is left by the legislation creating it with unfettered discretion as to how to proceed, then the tribunal can work out an acceptable procedure that does not include an oral hearing, but even then there may be cases where fairness may dictate an oral hearing. That is why I consider that what is contemplated by the use of the word "hearing" in s. 20 of the *National Energy Board Act* is of such crucial importance.

The word "hearing" is defined in the Shorter Oxford English Dictionary as "3. The listening to evidence and pleadings in court of law; the trial of a cause; *spec.* a trial before a judge without a jury 1576." However, the etymological meaning of a word is not necessarily the meaning which the context requires and dictionaries are only to be resorted to for the purpose of ascertaining the use of word in popular language.

I take it as a cardinal rule that the meaning of a word in a statute is to read not according to the mere ordinary general meaning of the word but according to the meaning of the word as applied to the subject-matter unless in the context that word is used in common parlance.

I think the word "hearing" in the context of s. 20 of the *National Energy Board Act* is used in a technical sense.

In endeavouring to discover the meaning of the word "hearing" I must first look to s. 20 itself and I may also look to other sections in the Act and the Act as a whole, as well as Regulations thereunder.

When the word "hearing" is used in legislation, it almost always denotes a hearing at which oral evidence and argument is made but while that is generally so, there may be exceptions when written representations may suffice.

Section 10 of the *National Energy Board Act* reads:

10(1) The Board is a court of record.

(2) The Board shall have an official seal, which shall be judicially noticed.

(3) The Board has, as regards the attendance, swearing and examination of witnesses, the production and inspection of documents, the enforcement of its orders, the entry upon and inspection of property and other matters necessary or proper for the due exercise of its jurisdiction, all such powers, rights and privileges as are vested in a superior court of record.

Section 15 of the Act provides:

15(1) Any decision or order made by the Board may, for the purpose of enforcement thereof, be made a rule, order or decree of the Exchequer Court or of any superior court of any province of Canada and shall be enforced in like manner as any rule, order or decree of such court.

(2) To make a decision or order of the Board a rule, order or decree of the Exchequer Court of Canada or a superior court, the usual practice and procedure of the court in such matters may be followed, or in lieu thereof the Secretary may file with the Registrar of the court a

certified copy of the decision or order under the seal of the Board and thereupon the decision or order becomes a rule, order or decree of the court.

Section 17(l) of the Rules of Practice and Procedure, which has been quoted above, contemplates generally that witnesses shall be called at a "hearing" of any application and shall be examined "*viva voce*" and it seems to me that the words "shall be examined" *viva voce* of necessity includes *viva voce* cross-examination by opponents to the application or their counsel and is not restricted to examination and cross-examination by members of the Board and counsel to the Board. The converse is also the right of the applicant or its counsel with respect to witnesses called by the opponents.

Under s. 10 of the *National Energy Board Act* the Board is constituted as "a court of record".

In *Wharton's Law Lexicon*, 14th ed., at p. 846, "courts of record" are defined as

... those whose judicial acts and proceedings are enrolled on parchment, for a perpetual memorial and testimony, which rolls are called the Records of the Court, and are of such high and supereminent authority that their truth is not to be called in question.

The fact that the statute designates the Board "a court of record" does not constitute the Board a Court of law or justice in the legal sense of that term.

The authorities are clear to show that there are tribunals with many of the trappings of a Court which, nevertheless, are not Courts in the strict sense.

Under s. 10 of the Act, the Board is vested with the powers of a superior Court of record, that is a Court strictly so-called. Under its rules of practice and procedure, it sits and holds hearings. It has all the power to summon and compel the attendance of witnesses, to administer an oath to witnesses, to compel the production and inspection of documents, to enter upon and inspect property, to enforce its decisions and orders, to conduct the examination of witnesses and all the rights and privileges that are vested in a superior Court.

In many instances, its decisions are final and conclusive subject only to review under s. 20 of the *Federal Court Act*, R.S.C. 1970, C. 10 (2nd Supp.), and to the extraordinary remedies under s. 18 of that Act.

In other instances its decisions are not effective until approved by the Governor in Council.

In view of the express statutory provisions in the *National Energy Board Act*, I do not think it is necessary, at this point, to embark upon a discussion of the principles to determine if the function of the Board is purely administrative or executive.

The Board is called upon to decide questions of great public interest. The protection of that interest is the paramount duty of the Board in deciding whether an application for a licence to export natural gas should be granted. In doing so, however, it is confronted with a contest between the applicant for the licence on the one hand and those interested persons who oppose that application on the other.

While there may not be a *lis inter partes* in the true sense of that term, because there is a third party not present, which is the public interest, nevertheless there is a contest between the applicant and the objectors. In some cases the objector may be said to represent the public interests and in others the objector may be a competitor of the applicant.

In the present matter, there was a combination of both.

Such situation has been described and established by authority as a *quasi-lis* between *quasi*-parties.

Because the *National Energy Board Act* has bestowed upon the Board the attributes of a Court and because the statute and the Regulations contemplate the panoply of a full adversary hearing it follows that the word "hearing" in s. 20 of the Act must have attributed to it the same meaning as it has in a Court of law.

In that sense, a "hearing" before the Board is analogous to and imports a "trial" before a court of law.

That being so the applicant for a licence and the opponents thereto must be treated on an equal footing with no discriminatory advantage being bestowed on one side or the other.

Accordingly, if one side is permitted to give oral evidence that same facility must be afforded to the opponents with the right by both sides to cross-examine the witnesses giving the oral testimony adverse to their respective positions. That is what is done in a Court of law, and because I have concluded for the reasons given above that the word "hearing" in s. 20 of the *National Energy Board Act* is to be construed as analogous to and importing a "trial" before a Court of law, it follows that the Board must do the same thing in such a hearing.

This the Board failed to do. If afforded Dow, the applicant, the right to adduce oral evidence and make oral argument while it restricted the interveners to making written representations, which I assume to mean evidence and argument in writing.

No doubt there were cogent reasons present to the Board which influenced it to proceed as it did but this does not detract from the fact that the applicant and the interveners were treated differently.

At the hearing before the Board, Dow did present oral testimony. In other respects the proceedings were changed. Dow did not make oral argument. The interveners were given the opportunity to make further written representations in addition to those originally made, by a specified date, July 8, 1974. Two did and others did not. Dow made written reply to these further representations but the interveners were not permitted to adduce oral evidence nor did they cross-examine the witnesses called by Dow even though the members of the Board and counsel to the Board questioned these witnesses at length.

The oral testimony of the witnesses on behalf of Dow was minimal. It consisted merely of them affirming and adopting for the purpose of this hearing their testimony given at a previous hearing.

If that was the sole purpose in permitting Dow to lead oral testimony I fail to see how this purpose could not have been accomplished simply by receiving that evidence in the current hearing in accordance with s. 18 of the Board's Rules of Practice and Procedure. However, that could not have been the sole purpose because the Board and its counsel subjected these witnesses to lengthy questioning. No doubt the purpose of that questioning was to test and satisfy the Board as to the adequacy of that prior testimony. This is understandable and proper. No doubt a second purpose was to obtain the views of these witnesses in respect of the matters raised in the written representations by the interveners. This too is understandable and proper but it does amount to usurping the privilege and function of the opponents to the application and their counsel if that similar right is not afforded to them.

For the reasons expressed above I have concluded that the manner of conducting this particular hearing before the Board does not conform to the hearing contemplated in s. 20 of the *National Energy Board Act*.

Therefore it is not necessary to consider whether the hearing so conducted was fair and just within the principles of natural justice.

It follows that the applicants herein are entitled to relief.

The relief sought is by way of the prerogative writs of *certiorari*, prohibition and *mandamus*.

These writs are extraordinary remedies and at common law there is a discretion to grant or refuse them which discretion is to be exercised on well-defined principles established at common law.

The appropriate remedy, in my opinion, is by way of an order for prohibition such as is sought in para. (b) of the amended notice of motion but not in the express terms of para. (b).

Accordingly, there shall be an order prohibiting the Board from rendering any decision on the application by Dow Chemical of Canada Limited, dated May 30, 1974, for licences to export ethylene from Canada, to import ethylene into Canada and to re-export ethylene from Canada consequent upon the hearing of that application held in Ottawa, Ontario, on June 25, 26 and 27, 1974.

I deliberately refrain from granting an order in the nature of *certiorari* as sought in para. (a) of the amended notice of motion because the relief granted is more appropriate and adequate.

I also refrain from granting an order for prohibition in the express terms sought in para. (b) of the amended notice of motion and the order for *mandamus* sought in para. (c) thereof.

I do so because the hearing referred to in para. (b) having been concluded, a prohibition to that effect would be abortive and because the hearing was not conducted *ex parte*. I consider the hearing as separate and distinct from rendering a decision consequent thereupon.

I decline to grant an order for *mandamus* directing the Board to hold a full public hearing as sought in para. (c) of the amended notice of motion and from including in the order of prohibition any direction or reference to a full public hearing and the incidences thereof and prohibiting the Board from making an order.

This I decline to do because of the amendment to the *National Energy Board Part VI Regulations* by Order in Council P.C. 19741457, SOR/74-391, dated June 20 1974, by virtue of which any person may import ethylene without a licence and the Board may, by order, authorize any person to export ethylene subject to terms and conditions as are prescribed by the Board.

As indicated above and for the reasons also indicated above, I have considered this motion exclusively on the basis that the application by Dow was for a licence to import and export ethylene and not a request to the Board for an order to export ethylene.

The validity of the Order in Council and the authority of the Board, pursuant thereto, to authorize the export of ethylene by order, without a public hearing, was not in issue before me and accordingly was not fully and completely argued and adjudicated upon.

There shall be no order as to the costs.

Order accordingly

(e)   *CNG*†

NOTE

CNG and a partner were competing with TransCanada Pipeline and partners for permission to transport gas to New York State. The NEB heard an application by TransCanada to transport the gas, but denied it. Subsequently, representatives connected with the TransCanada project met with the Chairman and Vice Chairman of the NEB and noted that the American portion of their project had just been approved by the American regulatory authority. It was agreed that TransCanada would apply to the NEB to conduct an expedited internal review of its decision in the light of this new development. When the NEB agreed to go ahead with the review, CNG objected, and sought an opportunity to show why there should be no review. CNG was denied permission to do this. They then challenged the NEB's decision to proceed with the review, arguing that the earlier meeting between the TransCanada project representatives and the NEB executives gave rise to a reasonable apprehension of bias.

---

† *CNG Transmission Corp v. National Energy Board*, [1992] 1. F.C. 346; 48 F.T.R. 201; [1991] F.C.J. No. 1028 (F.C.T.D.). Copyrighted by the Office of the Commissioner for Federal Judicial Affairs.

EXTRACTS

[CULLEN J.:]

. . . .

On July 29, 1991, Mr. Edge [a consultant associated with the TransCanada project] and [other representatives of this group] met with Chairman Priddle, Vice Chairman Fredette and a member of the NEB's legal staff. The pipeline representatives expressed negative views and reactions to the NEB's decision; they made representations on aspects of the case and expressed the view that the FERC decision [approving the American portion of the TransCanada project] was a changed circumstance ... and therefore a review of the decision [of the NEB to deny the TransCanada application] was warranted. Mr. Edge proposed that the NEB initiate a review on its own volition. The Chairman and Vice Chairman indicated that they did not think it likely that the NEB would initiate such a review. It was then agreed that those corporations represented at the meeting could submit a section 21 review application in which they could request that the review process be expedited by the NEB. This expeditious review would be achieved by dispensing with the two-step review process and proceeding directly with a review on the merits with a short but fair comment period. At the outset of the meeting Mr. Priddle agreed to report back to the members of the NEB on the results of the meeting. A few days later, the 11 members named in this motion received a summary of the meeting.

. . . .

[TransCanada's request for an expedited internal review was granted, and CNG's request for an opportunity to argue against the need for such a review was dismissed.]

. . . .

The NEB derives its powers from the *National Energy Board Act*, R.S.C. 1985, c. N-7, as amended. Section 11 stipulates that the NEB is a "court of record". It is given a broad mandate to discharge various functions under the Act, including the granting of authorizations to construct pipelines and related facilities.... The Chairman is designated by the Governor in Council under section 6 of the Act as the chief executive officer of the NEB to have supervision over and direction of the work and staff of the NEB.

Section 21 of the Act empowers the NEB to review, vary or rescind any order or decision made by it or to rehear any application before deciding it.

Pursuant to section 8 of the Act, the NEB may make rules respecting, *inter alia*, the procedure for making applications, representations and complaints to the Board, the conduct of hearing and generally the manner of conducting any business before the Board (Subsection 8(2)). The NEB's Draft Rules Part V provide that applications for review are required to be filed with the Secretary of the NEB and must be served on every person who was a party to the original proceeding. The party served then has 20 days in which to submit a written statement, file it and serve it. The applicant then has 10 days in which to submit a reply (Rules 41, 42 and 43). It is an established practice of the NEB, as prescribed by Rule 45 (Determination), to deal with applications for review in a two-step process. First, the NEB determines whether a decision should be reviewed once it hears from interested parties, i.e., public comment on the question of whether the decision should be reviewed. Second, if it decides to review, the NEB then disposes of the application or determines the appropriate procedures to govern the conduct of that review. However, under Rule 5 of the Draft Rules, the NEB has the power to dispense with, vary or supplement any provisions of these Rules and under Rule 7 the NEB has the power to abridge the time prescribed in the Rules for the review.

Comments

I agree with the respondent's view that the decision of August 9th to abridge the two-step review process in respect of the GH-1-91 decision is not *quasi*-judicial in nature but is a procedural decision. Therefore the question that I have to deal with is whether the NEB is obliged to comply with the principles of fairness and if so, to what extent does the fairness go?

I disagree with TransCanada's argument that procedural fairness does not apply in the circumstances as the NEB's decision is a preliminary decision. I think the proper approach to resolving the question of whether procedural fairness applies is the approach noted by Sopinka J. in *Old St. Boniface Residents Association Inc.* v. *Winnipeg (City) et al.* (1990), 116 N.R. 46 at p. 57:

> The content of the rules of natural justice and procedural fairness were formerly determined according to the classification of the functions of the tribunal or other public body or official. This

is no longer the case and the content of these rules is based on a number of factors including the terms of the statute pursuant to which the body operates, the nature of the particular function of which it is seized and the type of decision it is called upon to make....

. . . .

It has been argued that the principles of fairness normally applied in respect of NEB hearings into the merits of a case should not be applied with the same rigour to the process by which the NEB determines to rehear. I agree that the degree of procedural fairness to be applied in this case should be lower, but fairness should still apply. In the circumstances it can be argued that the applicant CNG has been prejudiced by the NEB decision in that the respondents ANR, St. Clair and RG & E have been effectively given two opportunities to make out their case, one of which took place privately and in the absence of any of the parties opposed in interest. Further, CNG has been denied the opportunity to address the issue of whether review should take place.

The jurisprudence is clear on the fact that the rules of fairness cover the *audi alteram partem* rule and the *nemo judex* rule....

. . . .

With respect to the question of reasonable apprehension of bias, there is no dispute that the issue is not whether the members named are actually biased (and counsel for the applicant made it quite clear they were not making such an allegation) but whether the circumstances could properly cause a reasonably well informed person to have a reasonable apprehension of a biased appraisal or judgment by the member, however unconscious or unintentional it might be.

The major problem with the NEB's decision is that the source of the idea to abridge the review procedure came from a group representing the losing pipeline interests during a private meeting with certain members of the NEB, notably the Chairman and the Vice Chairman. Had the decision come from the NEB itself without any input from outside sources it could not be subject to attack as the Act does allow for procedural changes.

. . . .

... The Board's policy/rules require that all contacts with the Board be made through the Secretary. This policy is outlined in a NEB letter, dated April

23..., addressed to all companies under the NEB's jurisdiction....

. . . .

Mr. Edge would have been aware of that and also aware of the fact that he was in clear violation of them when he contacted the Chairman directly....

. . . .

In my view it was wrong to have such a meeting unless Mr. Priddle was convinced that it was to discuss procedure only. The NEB has a powerful mandate and with it goes a heavy responsibility to be fair, not to favour one side to the detriment of the other, or not to seem to do so.... [Here] matters of substance were discussed and the introduction of any one of them should have been stopped or the meeting should have been cancelled....

. . . .

... I was somewhat taken aback to hear that the respondents made, and the Chairman and Vice-Chairman heard, negative comments on the reasons for the decision.... I think one is entitled to assume that this should hardly be an item on the agenda dealing with procedure....

. . . .

It is also clear that a decision was taken by the Board, namely, that they would not be initiating a review on their own volition and then went on to suggest or recommend or point out the most expeditious way of getting the respondents' point of view across.

. . . .

In light of the circumstances noted above, including the fact that the NEB had been on notice that TransCanada was likely to file a review application, I agree with the applicant that a reasonably informed person could envisage that the NEB was going to be asked at some point to make some decision and that there was some risk that the information discussed at the meeting could possibly find its way into such a decision.

After reviewing the arguments, I agree with the respondents that NEB members should not be precluded from meeting with members of the "industry" and that a reasonable apprehension of bias is not automatically triggered as a result of preliminary discussions or meetings. Clearly a situation where a party whose application for pipeline construction has been granted meets with NEB members to discuss when pipeline construction can commence, would not warrant and should not warrant judicial interference. However, in the case before me we have a number of extraordinary circumstances which have raised a number of concerns and which I feel warrant intervention. As such, a determining factor in my coming to this decision, was the context of and the overall substance of what transpired, bearing in mind the NEB's mandate as well as its policies and procedures. This was not merely a situation where an NEB member participated in a preliminary meeting of a procedural or investigative nature. Instead, we have a situation where the NEB is on notice that the "losing party" would be filing an application for a review; the Chairman and Vice-Chairman meet with certain pipeline representatives who make up the "losing parties"; this meeting is arranged through direct contact by the former Chairman, who is now acting on behalf of one of the pipeline companies, with the Chairman, which is contrary to the rules and policy of the NEB; significant and substantive issues are discussed; arguments are advanced in support of representatives' [positions] and ideas are advanced as to how the NEB should proceed, i.e. that the NEB should initiate a review on its own volition. A few days later an application for review is filed and shortly after that the NEB decides to conduct a review and states that it has acceded to the applicants' (in the section 21 application) arguments.

.   .   .   .

Clearly the July 29th meeting and how it was conducted was unfair to the applicant and others

involved in the original proceeding. Further, in the circumstances I do not think that the applicant and other interested parties can be said to have had a reasonable or fair opportunity to address the issue of whether the review should even take place.

I am also of the view that Messrs Priddle and Fredette's participation in the July 29th meeting, given what was discussed at this meeting and their participation in the August 9th decision to proceed with a review of the GH-1-91 decision, gives rise to a reasonable apprehension of bias which a reasonably well informed person could properly have, of a biased appraisal and judgment of the issue.

Therefore, for the reasons noted above, the application for *certiorari* will be granted quashing the decision of the NEB, dated August 9, 1991, to proceed with an internal review of the NEB decision dated July 4, 1991 in respect of Hearing Order GH-1-91.

With respect to the application for prohibition, on the basis of the evidence I cannot find that the named members of the NEB, other than Messrs Priddle and Fredette, should be prohibited from participating in any review or rehearing of the July 4, 1991 decision. I agree with the respondents' position that the issuance of a writ of prohibition against the other NEB members would not be appropriate in the circumstances. Therefore, prohibition will be granted prohibiting Messrs Priddle and Fredette from participating in any review or rehearing of the July 4, 1991 decision in respect of Hearing Order GH-1-91.

The applicant is entitled to its costs.

(f)   *Hydro-Québec*†

NOTE

After long public hearings, the National Energy Board granted Hydro-Québec's applications for licences to export electrical power to New York and Vermont. At the hearings, the Board did not require Hydro-Québec to disclose in full the assumptions and methodologies on which its cost-benefit review was based.

Representatives of the Cree people of Quebec opposed the licence application. They argued, *inter alia*, that the Board's failure to require full disclo-

---

† *Quebec (Attorney General) v. Canada (National Energy Board)*, [1994] 1 S.C.R. 159; rev'g. [1991] 3 F.C. 443, 83 D.L.R. (4th) 146, 7 C.E.L.R. (N.S.) 315, 132 N.R. 214; which severed conditions from licences granted by the National Energy Board, [1991] 2 C.N.L.R. 70, but upheld the licences as modified.

sure of the information from Hydro-Québec breached the requirements of procedural fairness by depriving them of the opportunity to participate fully in the review process. The Cree also contended that the Board owed them a higher duty of disclosure as a result of the Crown's special fiduciary (trust-like) obligations to aboriginal peoples.

EXTRACTS

[IACOBUCCI J. for the Court:]

. . . .

[para29] In general, included in the requirements of procedural fairness is the right to disclosure by the administrative decision-maker of sufficient information to permit meaningful participation in the hearing process: *In re Canadian Radio-Television Commission and in re London Cable TV Ltd.*, [1976] 2 F.C. 621 (C.A.), at pp. 624–25. The extent of the disclosure required to meet the dictates of natural justice will vary with the facts of the case, and in particular with the type of decision to be made, and the nature of the hearing to which the affected parties are entitled.

[para30] The issue in this case, then, is not the sufficiency of the disclosure made by Hydro-Québec. That relates to the question, discussed above, of whether there was evidence before the decision-maker on which it could reasonably have reached the decision which it did: *Parke, Davis & Co.* v. *Fine Chemicals of Canada Ltd.*, [1959] S.C.R. 219, at p. 223, per Rand J. Rather, the issue is whether the Board provided to the appellants disclosure sufficient for their meaningful participation in the hearing, such that they were treated fairly in all the circumstances: *Martineau* v. *Matsqui Institution Disciplinary Board*, [1980] 1 S.C.R. 602, at pp. 630–31; *Cardinal* v. *Director of Kent Institution*, [1985] 2 S.C.R. 643, at p. 654; *Lakeside Colony of Hutterian Brethren* v. *Hofer*, [1992] 3 S.C.R. 165, at p. 226, per McLachlin J. (dissenting on another ground).

[para31] In carrying out its decision-making function, the Board has the discretion to determine what evidence is relevant to its decision. It has not been shown that, in this case, the discretion was improperly exercised so as to result in inadequate disclosure to the appellants. As noted above, the Board had sufficient evidence before it to make a valid finding that all costs would be recovered. The appellants were given access to all the material that was

before the Board. The Board specifically found that the appellants themselves presented no evidence of added social costs, and did not call into question the veracity of Hydro-Québec's report. Therefore, it cannot be said that, on this basis, the Board erred in its decision to grant the licences.

C. Fiduciary Duty

[para32] The appellants claim that, by virtue of their status as aboriginal peoples, the Board owes them a fiduciary duty extending to the decision-making process used in considering applications for export licences. The appellants' argument is that the fiduciary duty owed to aboriginal peoples by the Crown, as recognized by this Court in *R.* v. *Sparrow, supra*, extends to the Board, as an agent of government and creation of Parliament, in the exercise of its delegated powers. The duty applies whenever the decision made pursuant to a federal regulatory process is likely to affect aboriginal rights.

[para33] The appellants characterize the scope of this duty as twofold. They argue that it includes the duty to ensure the full and fair participation of the appellants in the hearing process, as well as the duty to take into account their best interests when making decisions. The appellants argue that such an obligation imports with it rights that go beyond those created by the dictates of natural justice, and that in this case, at a minimum, the Board should have required disclosure to the appellants of all information necessary to the making of their case against the applications. The respondents to this appeal, on the other hand, dispute both the existence of a duty, and, if it does exist, that the Board failed to meet it.

[para34] It is now well settled that there is a fiduciary relationship between the federal Crown and the aboriginal peoples of Canada: *Guerin* v. *The Queen*, [1984] 2 S.C.R. 335. Nonetheless, it must be remembered that not every aspect of the relationship between fiduciary and beneficiary takes the form of a fiduciary obligation: *Lac Minerals Ltd.* v. *International Corona Resources Ltd.*, [1989] 2 S.C.R. 574. The nature of the relationship between the parties defines the scope, and the limits, of the duties that will be imposed. The courts must be careful not to compromise the independence of quasi-judicial tribunals and decision-making agencies by imposing upon them fiduciary obligations which require that their decisions be made in accordance with a fiduciary duty.

[para35] Counsel for the appellants conceded in oral argument that it could not be said that such a duty should apply to the courts, as a creation of government, in the exercise of their judicial function. In my view, the considerations which apply in evaluating whether such an obligation is impressed on the process by which the Board decides whether to grant a licence for export differ little from those applying to the courts. The function of the Board in this regard is quasi-judicial: *Committee for Justice and Liberty* v. *National Energy Board*, [1978] 1 S.C.R. 369, at p. 385. While this characterization may not carry with it all the procedural and other requirements identical to those applicable to a court, it is inherently inconsistent with the imposition of a relationship of utmost good faith between the Board and a party appearing before it.

. . . .

[para37] ... I conclude that the fiduciary relationship between the Crown and the appellants does not impose a duty on the Board to make its decisions in the best interests of the appellants, or to change its hearing process so as to impose superadded requirements of disclosure. When the duty is defined in this manner, such tribunals no more owe this sort of fiduciary duty than do the courts. Consequently, no such duty existed in relation to the decision-making function of the Board.

[para38] Moreover, even if this Court were to assume that the Board, in conducting its review, should have taken into account the existence of the fiduciary relationship between the Crown and the appellants, I am satisfied that, for the reasons set out above relating to the procedure followed by the Board, its actions in this case would have met the requirements of such a duty. There is no indication that the appellants were given anything less than the fullest opportunity to be heard. They had access to all the evidence that was before the Board, were able to make submissions and argument in reply, and were entitled to cross-examine the witnesses called by the respondent Hydro-Québec. This argument must therefore fail for the same reasons as the arguments relating to the nature of the review conducted by the Board.

. . . .

[After addressing several other issues, Iacobucci J. concluded as follows:]

[para76] At issue in this appeal are jurisdictional facts. While it is the proper function of this Court to determine whether the Board erred in the exercise of its jurisdiction, this Court will not interfere with the factual findings of the Board on which it bases that exercise, where there is some evidence to support its findings. I conclude that the appellants were given a full and fair opportunity to be heard before the Board, and that the Board had sufficient evidence to reach the conclusions which it did. In particular, I find that the order as set out by the Board neither exceeded nor avoided the scope of the Board's review in the area of the environmental impact of the proposed exports.

10 Canadian Radio-television and Telecommunications Commission

(a) Broadcasting Act[†]

PART I
GENERAL

Interpretation

Definitions

2.(1) In this Act,

"broadcasting"

> "broadcasting" means any transmission of programs, whether or not encrypted, by radio waves or other means of telecommunication for reception by the public by means of broadcasting receiving apparatus, but does not include any such transmission of programs that is made solely for performance or display in a public place;

"broadcasting receiving apparatus"

> "broadcasting receiving apparatus" means a device, or combination of devices, intended for or capable of being used for the reception of broadcasting;

"broadcasting undertaking"

> "broadcasting undertaking" includes a distribution undertaking, a programming undertaking and a network;

"Commission"

> "Commission" means the Canadian Radio-television and Telecommunications Commission established by the *Canadian Radio-television and Telecommunications Commission Act*;

"Corporation"

> "Corporation" means the Canadian Broadcasting Corporation....

. . .

Broadcasting Policy for Canada

Declaration

3.(1) It is hereby declared as the broadcasting policy for Canada that

(a) the Canadian broadcasting system shall be effectively owned and controlled by Canadians;

(b) the Canadian broadcasting system, operating primarily in the English and French languages and comprising public, private and community elements, makes use of radio frequencies that are public property and provides, through its programming, a public service essential to the maintenance and enhancement of national identity and cultural sovereignty;

(c) English and French language broadcasting, while sharing common aspects, operate under different conditions and may have different requirements;

(d) the Canadian broadcasting system should

(i) serve to safeguard, enrich and strengthen the cultural, political, social and economic fabric of Canada,

(ii) encourage the development of Canadian expression by providing a wide range of programming that reflects Canadian attitudes, opinions, ideas, values and artistic creativity, by displaying Canadian talent in entertainment programming and by offering information and analysis concerning Canada and other countries from a Canadian point of view,

---

[†] S.C. 1991, c. 11 (assented to 1 February 1991).

(iii) through its programming and the employment opportunities arising out of its operations, serve the needs and interests, and reflect the circumstances and aspirations, of Canadian men, women and children, including equal rights, the linguistic duality and multicultural and multiracial nature of Canadian society and the special place of aboriginal peoples within that society, and

(iv) be readily adaptable to scientific and technological change;

[The section lists 16 further objectives].

. . . .

PART II
OBJECTS AND POWERS OF THE COMMISSION IN RELATION TO BROADCASTING

Objects

Objects

5.(1) Subject to this Act and the *Radiocommunication Act* and to any directions to the Commission issued by the Governor in Council under this Act, the Commission shall regulate and supervise all aspects of the Canadian broadcasting system with a view to implementing the broadcasting policy set out in subsection 3(1) and, in so doing, shall have regard to the regulatory policy set out in subsection (2).

Regulatory policy

(2) The Canadian broadcasting system should be regulated and supervised in a flexible manner that

(a) is readily adaptable to the different characteristics of English and French language broadcasting and to the different conditions under which broadcasting undertakings that provide English or French language programming operate;

(b) takes into account regional needs and concerns;

(c) is readily adaptable to scientific and technological change;

(d) facilitates the provision of broadcasting to Canadians;

(e) facilitates the provision of Canadian programs to Canadians;

(f) does not inhibit the development of information technologies and their application or the delivery of resultant services to Canadians; and

(g) is sensitive to the administrative burden that, as a consequence of such regulation and supervision, may be imposed on persons carrying on broadcasting undertakings.

Conflict

(3) The Commission shall give primary consideration to the objectives of the broadcasting policy set out in subsection 3(1) if, in any particular matter before the Commission, a conflict arises between those objectives and the objectives of the regulatory policy set out in subsection (2).

. . . .

Policy guidelines and statements

6. The Commission may from time to time issue guidelines and statements with respect to any matter within its jurisdiction under this Act, but no such guidelines or statements issued by the Commission are binding on the Commission.

Policy directions

7.(1) Subject to subsection (2) and section 8, the Governor in Council may, by order, issue to the Commission directions of general application on broad policy matters with respect to

(a) any of the objectives of the broadcasting policy set out in subsection 3(1); or

(b) any of the objectives of the regulatory policy set out in subsection 5(2).

Exception

(2) No order may be made under subsection (1) in respect of the issuance of a licence to a particular person or in respect of the amendment, renewal, suspension or revocation of a particular licence.

Directions binding

(3) An order made under subsection (1) is binding on the Commission beginning on the day on which the order comes into force and, subject to subsection (4), shall, if it so provides, apply with respect to any matter pending before the Commission on that day.

Exception

(4) No order made under subsection (1) may apply with respect to a licensing matter pending before the Commission where the period for the fil-

ing of interventions in the matter has expired unless that period expired more than one year before the coming into force of the order.

Publication and tabling

(5) A copy of each order made under subsection (1) shall be laid before each House of Parliament on any of the first fifteen days on which that House is sitting after the making of the order.

Consultation

(6) The Minister shall consult with the Commission before the Governor in Council makes an order under subsection (1).

Procedure for issuance of policy directions

8.(1) Where the Governor in Council proposes to make an order under section 7, the Minister shall cause the proposed order to be
  (a) published by notice in the Canada Gazette, which notice shall invite interested persons to make representations to the Minister with respect to the proposed order; and
  (b) laid before each House of Parliament.

Referral to committee

(2) Where a proposed order is laid before a House of Parliament pursuant to subsection (1), it shall stand referred to such committee thereof as the House considers appropriate to deal with the subject-matter of the order.

Implementation of proposal

(3) The Governor in Council may, after the expiration of forty sitting days of Parliament after a proposed order is laid before both Houses of Parliament in accordance with subsection (1), implement the proposal by making an order under section 7, either in the form proposed or revised in such manner as the Governor in Council deems advisable.

Consultation

(4) The Minister shall consult with the Commission before a proposed order is published or is laid before a House of Parliament under subsection (1).

Definition of "sitting day of Parliament"

(5) In this section, "sitting day of Parliament" means a day on which either House of Parliament sits.

General Powers

Licences, etc.

9.(1) Subject to this Part, the Commission may, in furtherance of its objects,
  (a) establish classes of licences;
  (b) issue licences for such terms not exceeding seven years and subject to such conditions related to the circumstances of the licensee
     (i) as the Commission deems appropriate for the implementation of the broadcasting policy set out in subsection 3(1), and
     (ii) in the case of licences issued to the Corporation, as the Commission deems consistent with the provision, through the Corporation, of the programming contemplated by paragraphs 3(1)(l) and (m);
  (c) amend any condition of a licence on application of the licensee or, where five years have expired since the issuance or renewal of the licence, on the Commission's own motion;
  (d) issue renewals of licences for such terms not exceeding seven years and subject to such conditions as comply with paragraph (b);
  (e) suspend or revoke any licence;
  (f) require any licensee to obtain the approval of the Commission before entering into any contract with a telecommunications common carrier for the distribution of programming directly to the public using the facilities of that common carrier;
  (g) require any licensee who is authorized to carry on a distribution undertaking to give priority to the carriage of broadcasting; and
  (h) require any licensee who is authorized to carry on a distribution undertaking to carry, on such terms and conditions as the Commission deems appropriate, programming services specified by the Commission.

. . . .

Regulations generally

10.(1) The Commission may, in furtherance of its objects, make regulations
  (a) respecting the proportion of time that shall be devoted to the broadcasting of Canadian programs;
  (b) prescribing what constitutes a Canadian program for the purposes of this Act;
  (c) respecting standards of programs and the allocation of broadcasting time for the purpose of giving effect to the broadcasting policy set out in subsection 3(1);

214

(d) respecting the character of advertising and the amount of broadcasting time that may be devoted to advertising;

(e) respecting the proportion of time that may be devoted to the broadcasting of programs, including advertisements or announcements, of a partisan political character and the assignment of that time on an equitable basis to political parties and candidates;

(f) prescribing the conditions for the operation of programming undertakings as part of a network and for the broadcasting of network programs, and respecting the broadcasting times to be reserved for network programs by any such undertakings;

(g) respecting the carriage of any foreign or other programming services by distribution undertakings;

(h) for resolving, by way of mediation or otherwise, any disputes arising between programming undertakings and distribution undertakings concerning the carriage of programming originated by the programming undertakings;

(i) requiring licensees to submit to the Commission such information regarding their programs and financial affairs or otherwise relating to the conduct and management of their affairs as the regulations may specify;

(j) respecting the audit or examination of the records and books of account of licensees by the Commission or persons acting on behalf of the Commission; and

(k) respecting such other matters as it deems necessary for the furtherance of its objects.

Application

(2) A regulation made under this section may be made applicable to all persons holding licences or to all persons holding licences of one or more classes.

Publication of proposed regulation

(3) A copy of each regulation that the Commission proposes to make under this section shall be published in the Canada Gazette and a reasonable opportunity shall be given to licensees and other interested persons to make representations to the Commission with respect thereto.

Regulations respecting licence fees

11.(1) The Commission may make regulations

(a) with the approval of the Treasury Board, establishing schedules of fees to be paid by licensees of any class;

(b) providing for the establishment of classes of licensees for the purposes of paragraph (a);

(c) providing for the payment of any fees payable by a licensee, including the time and manner of payment;

(d) respecting the interest payable by a licensee in respect of any overdue fee; and

(e) respecting such other matters as it deems necessary for the purposes of this section.

. . . .

Inquiries

12.(1) Where it appears to the Commission that

(a) any person has failed to do any act or thing that the person is required to do pursuant to this Part or to any regulation, licence, decision or order made or issued by the Commission under this Part, or has done or is doing any act or thing in contravention of this Part or of any such regulation, licence, decision or order, or

(b) the circumstances may require the Commission to make any decision or order or to give any approval that it is authorized to make or give under this Part or under any regulation or order made under this Part, the Commission may inquire into, hear and determine the matter.

Mandatory orders

(2) The Commission may, by order, require any person to do, forthwith or within or at any time and in any manner specified by the Commission, any act or thing that the person is or may be required to do pursuant to this Part or to any regulation, licence, decision or order made or issued by the Commission under this Part and may, by order, forbid the doing or continuing of any act or thing that is contrary to this Part or to any such regulation, licence, decision or order.

Referral to Commission

(3) Where an inquiry under subsection (1) is heard by a panel established under subsection 20(1) and the panel issues an order pursuant to subsection (2) of this section, any person who is affected by the order may, within thirty days after the making thereof, apply to the Commission to reconsider any decision or finding made by the panel, and the Com-

mission may rescind or vary any order or decision made by the panel or may rehear any matter before deciding it.

Enforcement of mandatory orders

13.(1) Any order made under subsection 12(2) may be made an order of the Federal Court or of any superior court of a province and is enforceable in the same manner as an order of the court.

Procedure

(2) To make an order under subsection 12(2) an order of a court, the usual practice and procedure of the court in such matters may be followed or, in lieu thereof, the Commission may file with the registrar of the court a certified copy of the order, and thereupon the order becomes an order of the court.

Effect of variation or rescission

(3) Where an order that has been made an order of a court is rescinded or varied by a subsequent order of the Commission, the order of the court shall be deemed to have been cancelled and the subsequent order may, in the same manner, be made an order of the court.

Research

14.(1) The Commission may undertake, sponsor, promote or assist in research relating to any matter within its jurisdiction under this Act and in so doing it shall, wherever appropriate, utilize technical, economic and statistical information and advice from the Corporation or departments or agencies of the Government of Canada.

Review of technical matters

(2) The Commission shall review and consider any technical matter relating to broadcasting referred to the Commission by the Minister and shall make recommendations to the Minister with respect thereto.

Hearings and reports

15.(1) The Commission shall, on request of the Governor in Council, hold hearings or make reports on any matter within the jurisdiction of the Commission under this Act.

Consultation

(2) The Minister shall consult with the Commission with regard to any request proposed to be made by the Governor in Council under subsection (1).

Powers respecting hearings

16. The Commission has, in respect of any hearing under this Part, with regard to the attendance, swearing and examination of witnesses at the hearing, the production and inspection of documents, the enforcement of its orders, the entry and inspection of property and other matters necessary or proper in relation to the hearing, all such powers, rights and privileges as are vested in a superior court of record.

Authority re questions of fact or law

17. The Commission has authority to determine questions of fact or law in relation to any matter within its jurisdiction under this Act.

Hearings and Procedure

Where public hearing required

18.(1) Except where otherwise provided, the Commission shall hold a public hearing in connection with

   (a) the issue of a licence, other than a licence to carry on a temporary network operation;

   (b) the suspension or revocation of a licence;

   (c) the establishing of any performance objectives for the purposes of paragraph 11(2)(b); and

   (d) the making of an order under subsection 12(2).

Idem

(2) The Commission shall hold a public hearing in connection with the amendment or renewal of a licence unless it is satisfied that such a hearing is not required in the public interest.

Where public hearing in Commission's discretion

(3) The Commission may hold a public hearing, make a report, issue any decision and give any approval in connection with any complaint or representation made to the Commission or in connection with any other matter within its jurisdiction under this Act if it is satisfied that it would be in the public interest to do so.

Place of hearing

(4) A public hearing under this section may be held at such place in Canada as the Chairman of the Commission may designate.

Notice of hearing

19. The Commission shall cause notice of

(a) any application received by it for the issue, amendment or renewal of a licence, other than a licence to carry on a temporary network operation,

(b) any decision made by it to issue, amend or renew a licence, and

(c) any public hearing to be held by it under section 18 to be published in the *Canada Gazette* and in one or more newspapers of general circulation within any area affected or likely to be affected by the application, decision or matter to which the public hearing relates.

Panels of Commission

20.(1) The Chairman of the Commission may establish panels, each consisting of not fewer than three members of the Commission, at least two of whom shall be full-time members, to deal with, hear and determine any matter on behalf of the Commission.

Powers

(2) A panel that is established under subsection (1) has and may exercise all the powers and may perform all the duties and functions of the Commission in relation to any matter before the panel.

Decision

(3) A decision of a majority of the members of a panel established under subsection (1) is a decision of the panel.

Consultation

(4) The members of a panel established under subsection (1) shall consult with the Commission, and may consult with any officer of the Commission, for the purpose of ensuring a consistency of interpretation of the broadcasting policy set out in subsection 3(1), the regulatory policy set out in subsection 5(2) and the regulations made by the Commission under sections 10 and 11.

Rules

21. The Commission may make rules

(a) respecting the procedure for making applications for licences, or for the amendment, renewal, suspension or revocation thereof, and for making representations and complaints to the Commission; and

(b) respecting the conduct of hearings and generally respecting the conduct of the business of the Commission in relation to those hearings.

Licences

Conditions governing issue, amendment and renewal

22.(1) No licence shall be issued, amended or renewed under this Part

(a) if the issue, amendment or renewal of the licence is in contravention of a direction to the Commission issued by the Governor in Council under subsection 26(1); and

(b) subject to subsection (2), unless the Minister certifies to the Commission that the applicant for the issue, amendment or renewal of the licence
(i) has satisfied the requirements of the *Radiocommunication Act* and the regulations made under that Act, and
(ii) has been or will be issued a broadcasting certificate with respect to the radio apparatus that the applicant would be entitled to operate under the licence.

Exception

(2) The requirement set out in paragraph (1)(b) does not apply in respect of radio apparatus, or any class thereof, prescribed under paragraph 6(1)(m) of the *Radiocommunication Act*.

Suspension or revocation of broadcasting certificate

(3) No licence is of any force or effect during any period when the broadcasting certificate issued under the *Radiocommunication Act* with respect to the radio apparatus that the holder of the licence is entitled to operate under that Act is suspended or revoked.

Issue, etc., contravening this section

(4) Any licence issued, amended or renewed in contravention of this section is of no force or effect.

Consultation between Commission and Corporation

23.(1) The Commission shall, at the request of the Corporation, consult with the Corporation with regard to any conditions that the Commission proposes to attach to any licence issued or to be issued to the Corporation.

Reference to Minister

(2) If, notwithstanding the consultation provided for in subsection (1), the Commission attaches any condition to a licence referred to in subsection (1)

that the Corporation is satisfied would unreasonably impede the Corporation in providing the programming contemplated by paragraphs 3(1)(l) and (m), the Corporation may, within thirty days after the decision of the Commission, refer the condition to the Minister for consideration.

Ministerial directive

(3) Subject to subsection (4), the Minister may, within ninety days after a condition is referred to the Minister under subsection (2), issue to the Commission a written directive with respect to the condition and the Commission shall comply with any such directive issued by the Minister.

Consultation

(4) The Minister shall consult with the Commission and with the Corporation before issuing a directive under subsection (3).

Publication and tabling of directive

(5) A directive issued by the Minister under subsection (3) shall be published forthwith in the *Canada Gazette* and shall be laid before each House of Parliament on any of the first fifteen days on which that House is sitting after the directive is issued.

Conditions governing suspension and revocation

24.(1) No licence shall be suspended or revoked under this Part unless the licensee applies for or consents to the suspension or revocation or, in any other case, unless, after a public hearing in accordance with section 18, the Commission is satisfied that

(a) the licensee has contravened or failed to comply with any condition of the licence or with any order made under subsection 12(2) or any regulation made under this Part; or

(b) the licence was, at any time within the two years immediately preceding the date of publication in the *Canada Gazette* of the notice of the public hearing, held by a person to whom the licence could not have been issued at that time by virtue of a direction to the Commission issued by the Governor in Council under this Act.

Licences of Corporation

(2) No licence issued to the Corporation that is referred to in the schedule may be suspended or revoked under this Part except on application of or with the consent of the Corporation.

Publication of decision

(3) A copy of a decision of the Commission relating to the suspension or revocation of a licence, together with written reasons for the decision, shall, forthwith after the making of the decision, be forwarded by prepaid registered mail to all persons who were heard at or made any oral representations in connection with the hearing held under subsection (1), and a summary of the decision and of the reasons for the decision shall, at the same time, be published in the *Canada Gazette* and in one or more newspapers of general circulation within any area affected or likely to be affected by the decision.

Report of alleged contravention or non-compliance by Corporation

25.(1) Where the Commission is satisfied, after a public hearing on the matter, that the Corporation has contravened or failed to comply with any condition of a licence referred to in the schedule, any order made under subsection 12(2) or any regulation made under this Part, the Commission shall forward to the Minister a report setting out the circumstances of the alleged contravention or failure, the findings of the Commission and any observations or recommendations of the Commission in connection therewith.

Report to be tabled

(2) The Minister shall cause a copy of the report referred to in subsection (1) to be laid before each House of Parliament on any of the first fifteen days on which that House is sitting after the report is received by the Minister.

General Powers of the Governor in Council

Directions

26.(1) The Governor in Council may, by order, issue directions to the Commission

(a) respecting the maximum number of channels or frequencies for the use of which licences may be issued within a geographical area designated in the order;

(b) respecting the reservation of channels or frequencies for the use of the Corporation or for any special purpose designated in the order;

(c) respecting the classes of applicants to whom licences may not be issued or to whom amendments or renewals thereof may not be granted; and

(d) prescribing the circumstances in which the Commission may issue licences to applicants that are agents of a province and are otherwise ineligible to hold a licence, and the conditions on which those licences may be issued.

Idem

(2) Where the Governor in Council deems the broadcast of any program to be of urgent importance to Canadians generally or to persons resident in any area of Canada, the Governor in Council may, by order, direct the Commission to issue a notice to licensees throughout Canada or throughout any area of Canada, of any class specified in the order, requiring the licensees to broadcast the program in accordance with the order, and licensees to whom any such notice is addressed shall comply with the notice.

Publication and tabling

(3) An order made under subsection (1) or (2) shall be published forthwith in the Canada Gazette and a copy thereof shall be laid before each House of Parliament on any of the first fifteen days on which that House is sitting after the making of the order.

Consultation

(4) The Minister shall consult with the Commission with regard to any order proposed to be made by the Governor in Council under subsection (1).

Directions re Free Trade Agreement

27.(1) The Governor in Council may, either on the recommendation of the Minister made at the request of the Commission or on the Governor in Council's own motion, issue directions of general application respecting the manner in which the Commission shall apply or interpret paragraph 3 of Article 2006 of the Agreement.

Effect of directions

(2) A direction issued under subsection (1) is binding on the Commission from the time it comes into force and, unless otherwise provided therein, applies in respect of matters pending before the Commission at that time.

Request of Commission

(3) The Commission may, in order to request the issuance of a direction under subsection (1), suspend the determination of any matter of which it is seised.

Definition of "Agreement"

(4) In this section, "Agreement" has the same meaning as in the *Canada-United States Free Trade Agreement Implementation Act*.

Setting aside or referring decisions back to Commission

28.(1) Where the Commission makes a decision to issue, amend or renew a licence, the Governor in Council may, within ninety days after the date of the decision, on petition in writing of any person received within forty-five days after that date or on the Governor in Council's own motion, by order, set aside the decision or refer the decision back to the Commission for reconsideration and hearing of the matter by the Commission, if the Governor in Council is satisfied that the decision derogates from the attainment of the objectives of the broadcasting policy set out in subsection 3(1).

Order on reference back

(2) An order made under subsection (1) that refers a decision back to the Commission for reconsideration and hearing shall set out the details of any matter that, in the opinion of the Governor in Council, may be material to the reconsideration and hearing.

Powers on reference back

(3) Where a decision is referred back to the Commission under this section, the Commission shall reconsider the matter and, after a hearing as provided for by subsection (1), may

(a) rescind the decision or the issue, amendment or renewal of the licence;

(b) rescind the issue of the licence and issue a licence on the same or different conditions to another person; or

(c) confirm, either with or without change, variation or alteration, the decision or the issue, amendment or renewal of the licence.

Setting aside after confirmation

(4) Where, pursuant to paragraph (3)(c), the Commission confirms a decision or the issue, amendment or renewal of a licence, the Governor in Council may, within sixty days after the confirmation, on

petition in writing of any person received within thirty days after that date or on the Governor in Council's own motion, by order, set aside the decision or the issue, amendment or renewal, if the Governor in Council is satisfied as to any of the matters referred to in subsection (1).

Reasons

(5) An order made under subsection (4) to set aside a decision or the issue, amendment or renewal of a licence shall set out the reasons of the Governor in Council therefor.

Filing of petitions

29.(1) Every person who petitions the Governor in Council under subsection 28(1) or (4) shall at the same time send a copy of the petition to the Commission.

Notice

(2) On receipt of a petition under subsection (1), the Commission shall forward a copy of the petition by prepaid registered mail to all persons who were heard at or made any oral representation in connection with the hearing held in the matter to which the petition relates.

Register

(3) The Commission shall establish and maintain a public register in which shall be kept a copy of each petition received by the Commission under subsection 28(1) or (4).

Amendment of schedule

30. The Governor in Council may, on the recommendation of the Minister made on the request of the Commission and with the consent of the Corporation, amend the schedule.

Decisions and Orders

Decisions and orders final

31.(1) Except as provided in this Part, every decision and order of the Commission is final and conclusive.

Appeal to Federal Court of Appeal

(2) An appeal lies from a decision or order of the Commission to the Federal Court of Appeal on a question of law or a question of jurisdiction if leave therefor is obtained from that Court on application made within one month after the making of the decision or order sought to be appealed from or within such further time as that Court under special circumstances allows.

Entry of appeal

(3) No appeal lies after leave therefor has been obtained under subsection (2) unless it is entered in the Federal Court of Appeal within sixty days after the making of the order granting leave to appeal.

Document deemed decision or order

(4) Any document issued by the Commission in the form of a decision or order shall, if it relates to the issue, amendment, renewal, revocation or suspension of a licence, be deemed for the purposes of this section to be a decision or order of the Commission.

Offences

Broadcasting without or contrary to licence

32.(1) Every person who, not being exempt from the requirement to hold a licence, carries on a broadcasting undertaking without a licence therefor is guilty of an offence punishable on summary conviction and is liable

(a) in the case of an individual, to a fine not exceeding twenty thousand dollars for each day that the offence continues; or

(b) in the case of a corporation, to a fine not exceeding two hundred thousand dollars for each day that the offence continues.

Contravention of regulation or order

(2) Every person who contravenes or fails to comply with any regulation or order made under this Part is guilty of an offence punishable on summary conviction and is liable

(a) in the case of an individual, to a fine not exceeding twenty-five thousand dollars for a first offence and not exceeding fifty thousand dollars for each subsequent offence; or

(b) in the case of a corporation, to a fine not exceeding two hundred and fifty thousand dollars for a first offence and not exceeding five hundred thousand dollars for each subsequent offence.

Contravention of conditions of licence

33. Every person who contravenes or fails to comply with any condition of a licence issued to the person is guilty of an offence punishable on summary conviction.

(b) Canadian Radio-television and Telecommunications Act†

SHORT TITLE

1. This Act may be cited as the *Canadian Radio-television and Telecommunications Commission Act*.

INTERPRETATION

Definitions

2. In this Act,

"broadcasting"

> "broadcasting" has the same meaning as in the Broadcasting Act;

"Chairman"

> "Chairman" means the Chairman of the Commission designated by the Governor in Council pursuant to subsection 6(1);

"Commission"

> "Commission" means the Canadian Radio-television and Telecommunications Commission;

"Executive Committee"

> [Repealed, 1991, c. 11, s. 75]

"member"

> "member" means a member of the Commission and includes a full-time member and a part-time member;

"Minister"

> "Minister" means the Minister of Communications;

. . . .

"telecommunications undertaking"

> "telecommunications undertaking" means an undertaking in the field of telecommunication that is carried on in whole or in part within Canada or on a ship or aircraft registered in Canada;

"Vice-Chairman"

> "Vice-Chairman" means any Vice-Chairman of the Commission designated by the Governor in Council pursuant to subsection 6(1).

ESTABLISHMENT AND CONSTITUTION OF COMMISSION

Commission established

3.(1) There is hereby established a commission, to be known as the Canadian Radio-television and Telecommunications Commission, consisting of not more than thirteen full-time members and not more than six part-time members, to be appointed by the Governor in Council.

Tenure

(2) A member shall be appointed to hold office during good behaviour for a term not exceeding five years but may be removed at any time by the Governor in Council for cause.

Re-appointment

(3) Subject to section 5, a member is eligible for reappointment.

Duties of full-time members

4. A full-time member shall devote the whole of his time to the performance of his duties under this Act.

Disqualifications

5.(1) A person is not eligible to be appointed or to continue as a member of the Commission if the person is not a Canadian citizen ordinarily resident in Canada or if, directly or indirectly, as owner, shareholder, director, officer, partner or otherwise, the person

> (a) is engaged in a telecommunications undertaking; or
>
> (b) has any pecuniary or proprietary interest in
>
>> (i) a telecommunications undertaking, or
>>
>> (ii) the manufacture or distribution of telecommunication apparatus, except where the distribution is incidental to the general merchandising of goods by wholesale or retail.

Disposal of interest

(2) A member in whom any interest prohibited by subsection (1) vests by will or succession for the

---

† *Canadian Radio-television and Telecommunications Commission Act*, R.S.C. 1985, c. C-22.

member's own benefit shall, within three months thereafter, absolutely dispose of that interest.

CHAIRMAN AND VICE-CHAIRMEN

Chairman and Vice-Chairmen

6.(1) The Governor in Council shall designate one of the full-time members to be Chairman of the Commission and two of the full-time members to be Vice-Chairmen of the Commission.

Chairman chief executive officer

(2) The Chairman is the chief executive officer of the Commission, has supervision over and direction of the work and staff of the Commission and shall preside at meetings of the Commission.

Chairman's absence, incapacity or office vacant

(3) In the event of the absence or incapacity of the Chairman or if the office of Chairman is vacant, the Commission may authorize one of the Vice-Chairmen to exercise the powers and to perform the duties and functions of the Chairman.

Acting Chairman

(4) The Commission may authorize one or more of its full-time members to act as Chairman for the time being if the Chairman and both Vice-Chairmen are absent or unable to act or if the office of Chairman and each office of Vice-Chairman are vacant.

REMUNERATION

Salaries and fees

7.(1) Each full-time member shall be paid a salary to be fixed by the Governor in Council and each part-time member shall be paid such fees for attendances at meetings of the Commission or any committee thereof or at any public hearing before the Commission that the part-time member is requested by the Chairman to attend as are fixed by by-law of the Commission.

Expenses

(2) Each member is entitled to be paid such travel and living expenses incurred in the performance of his duties as are fixed by by-law of the Commission.

STAFF

Appointment

8. The officers and employees necessary for the proper conduct of the Commission's business shall be appointed in accordance with the *Public Service Employment Act.*

SUPERANNUATION

Full-time members' superannuation

9.(1) The full-time members of the Commission shall be deemed to be persons employed in the Public Service for the purposes of the *Public Service Superannuation Act.*

Compensation

(2) For the purposes of any regulations made pursuant to section 9 of the *Aeronautics Act*, the full-time members of the Commission shall be deemed to be persons employed in the public service of Canada.

OFFICES, MEETINGS AND RESIDENCE

Head office

10.(1) The head office of the Commission shall be in the National Capital Region described in the schedule to the *National Capital Act* or at such other place within Canada as may be designated by the Governor in Council.

Regional offices

(1.1) The Governor in Council may direct the Commission to establish an office of the Commission in any region of Canada and the Commission shall comply with any such direction.

Meetings

(2) The Commission shall meet at least six times in each year.

Quorum

(3) A majority of the full-time members from time to time in office and a majority of the part-time members from time to time in office constitute a quorum of the Commission.

Telephone conferences

(4) A member may, subject to the by-laws of the Commission, participate in a meeting of the Commission or a committee of the Commission by means of such telephone or other communication facilities as permit all persons participating in the meeting to hear each other, and a member who participates in such a meeting by those means is deemed for the purposes of this Act to be present at the meeting.

Residence of members

10.1(1) Subject to subsection (2), the full-time members of the Commission shall reside in the National Capital Region as described in the schedule to the *National Capital Act* or within such distance thereof as may be determined by the Governor in Council.

Idem

(2) Where a regional office of the Commission is established under subsection 10(1.1), a full-time member of the Commission who is designated for the purposes of this section by the Governor in Council shall reside in the region and within such distance of the regional office as may be determined by the Governor in Council.

BY-LAWS

By-laws of Commission

11.(1) The Commission may make by-laws
  (a) respecting the calling of meetings of the Commission;
  (b) respecting the conduct of business at meetings of the Commission, the establishment of special and standing committees of the Commission, the delegation of duties to those committees and the fixing of quorums for meetings thereof; and
  (c) fixing
    (i) the fees to be paid to part-time members for attendances at meetings of the Commission or any committee thereof or at public hearings before the Commission that they are requested by the Chairman to attend, and
    (ii) the travel and living expenses to be paid to members.

By-law subject to Minister's approval

(2) No by-law made under paragraph (1)(c) has any effect unless it has been approved by the Minister.

OBJECTS, POWERS, DUTIES AND FUNCTIONS

In relation to broadcasting

12.(1) The objects and powers of the Commission in relation to broadcasting are as set out in the Broadcasting Act.

Telecommunications

(2) The full-time members of the Commission and the Chairman shall exercise the powers and perform the duties vested in the Commission and the Chairman, respectively, by the *Telecommunications Act* or by any special Act within the meaning of that Act.

By-laws

(3) The full-time members of the Commission may
  (a) make by-laws respecting the establishment of special and standing committees of the full-time members, the delegation of the powers, duties and functions of the full-time members to those committees and the fixing of quorums for meetings thereof; and
  (b) by any such by-law, provide that any act or thing done by any such committee in the exercise of the powers or the performance of the duties and functions so delegated to it shall be deemed to be an act or thing done by the full-time members.

Annual report

13. The Commission shall, within three months after the end of each fiscal year, submit to the Minister a report, in such form as the Minister may direct, on the activities of the Commission for that fiscal year, and the Minister shall cause a copy of the report to be laid before each House of Parliament on any of the first fifteen days on which that House is sitting after the Minister receives it.

14. [Repealed, 1991, c. 11, s. 80]

(c)   Telecommunications Act†

Her Majesty, by and with the advice and consent of the Senate and House of Commons of Canada, enacts as follows:

SHORT TITLE

Short Title

1. This Act may be cited as the *Telecommunications Act.*

. . . .

Application

Broadcasting excluded

4. This Act does not apply in respect of broadcasting by a broadcasting undertaking.

. . . .

Powers of Governor in Council, Commission and Minister

Directions

8. The Governor in Council may, by order, issue to the Commission directions of general application on broad policy matters with respect to the Canadian telecommunications policy objectives.

. . . .

Publication of proposed order

10.(1) The Minister shall have an order proposed to be made under Section 8 published in the *Canada Gazette* and laid before each House of Parliament and a reasonable opportunity shall be given to interested persons to make representations to the Minister with respect to the proposed order.

Consultation

(2) The Minister shall consult the Commission with respect to an order proposed to be made under section 8 before it is published or laid under this section and shall consult the Commission again with respect to the order in its definitive form before it is made.

Transmittal and tabling of exemption orders

(3) The Commission shall send to the Minister an order proposed to be made under section 9 and the Minister shall have the order laid before each House of Parliament

Reference to committees

(4) A proposed order laid before a House of Parliament stands referred to such committee as is designated by order of that House to receive such orders.

Modification publication after

(5) A proposed order that is modified after publication need not be published again under section (1).

Making of order

(6) After the fortieth sitting day of Parliament following the first day on which a proposed order has been laid before both Houses, the Governor in Council or the Commission, as the case may be, may make the order either as proposed or with any modifications the Governor in Council or the Commission considers advisable.

Tabling of orders

(7) After an order is made under section 8, the Minister shall have it laid before each House of Parliament on any of the first fifteen days on which that House is sitting after the order is made.

Transmittal and tabling of orders exemption

(8) After an order is made under section 9, the Commission shall immediately send it to the Minister who shall have it laid before each House of Parliament on any of the first fifteen days on which that House is sitting after the order is sent.

---

† S.C. 1993, c. 38 (assented to 23 June 1993).

Meaning of "sitting day"

(9) For the purposes of this section, a "sitting day" is a day on which either House of Parliament is sitting.

Effect of order

11.(1) An order made under section 8 is binding on the Commission beginning on the day on which the order comes into force.

.   .   .   .

Variation, rescission or referral

12.(1) Within one year after a decision by the Commission, the Governor in Council may, on petition in writing presented to the Governor in Council within ninety days after the decision, or on the Governor in Council's own motion, by order, vary or rescind the decision or refer it back to the Commission for reconsideration of all or a portion of it.

Copy of petition to Commission

(2) A person who presents a petition to the Governor in Council shall, at the same time, send a copy of the petition to the Commission.

Copies to other parties

(3) On receipt of a petition, the Commission shall send a copy of it to each person who made any oral representation to the Commission in relation to the decision that is the subject of the petition.

Notice of petition

(4) On receipt of a petition, the Minister shall publish in the *Canada Gazette* a notice of its receipt indicating where the petition and any petition or submission made in response to it may be inspected and copies of them obtained.

Order for reference back

(5) An order made under subsection (1) that refers a decision back to the Commission for reconsideration and hearing

(a) shall set out the details of any matter that the Governor in Council considers to be material to the reconsideration; and

(b) may specify a date before which the Commission shall complete its reconsideration.

Reconsideration

(6) The Commission shall, before any date specified under paragraph (5)(b), reconsider a decision

referred back to it under subsection (1) and may confirm, vary or rescind the decision.

Variation or rescission by Governor in Council

(7) Where the Commission confirms or varies a decision under subsection (6) or does not complete its reconsideration of the decision before any date specified under paragraph (5)(b), the Governor in Council may, by order, vary or rescind the decision within ninety days after the confirmation or variation of the decision or the specified date, as the case may be.

Reasons

(8) In an order made under subsection (1) or (7), the Governor in Council shall set out the reasons for making the order.

Provincial consultation

13. The Minister, before making a recommendation to the Governor in Council for the purposes of any order under section 8 or 12, or before making any order under section 8 or 12, or before making any order under section 15, shall notify a minister designated by the government of each province of the Minister's intention to make the recommendation or the order and shall provide an opportunity for each of them to consult with the Minister.

Report

14. The Governor in Council may require the Commission to make a report on any matter within the Commission's jurisdiction under this Act or any special Act.

.   .   .   .

Just and reasonable rates

27.(1) Every rate charged by a Canadian carrier for a telecommunications service shall be just and reasonable.

Unjust discrimination

(2) No Canadian carrier shall, in relation to the provision of a telecommunications service or the charging of a rate for it, unjustly discriminate or give an undue or unreasonable preference toward any person, including itself, or subject any person to an undue or unreasonable disadvantage.

.   .   .   .

PART IV
ADMINISTRATION

Exercise of Powers

Commission subject to orders and standards

47. The Commission shall exercise its powers and perform its duties under this Act and any special Act
  (a) with a view to implementing the Canadian telecommunications policy objectives and ensuring that Canadian carriers provide telecommunications and services and charge rates in accordance with section 27; and
  (b) in accordance with any orders made by the Governor in Council under section 8 or any standards prescribed by the Minister under section 15.

Inquiries and determinations

48.(1) The Commission may, on application by any interested person or on its own motion, inquire into and make a determination in respect of anything prohibited, required or permitted to be done under Part II, except in relation to international submarine cables, Part III or this Part or under any special Act, and the Commission shall inquire into any matter on which it is required to report or take action under section 14.

Interested persons

(2) The decision of the Commission that a person is or is not an interested person is binding and conclusive.

Quorum

49. For the purposes of this Act, a quorum of the Commission consists of two members, but in uncontested matters a quorum consists of one member.

Extension of time

50. The Commission may extend the period, whether fixed by regulation or otherwise, for doing anything required to be done in proceedings before it or under any of its decisions.

Mandatory and restraining orders

51. The Commission may order a person, at or within any time and subject to any conditions that it determines, to do anything the person is required to do under this Act or any special Act, and may for-bid a person to do anything that the person is prohibited from doing under this Act or any special Act.

Questions of law and fact

52.(1) The Commission may, in exercising its powers and performing its duties under this Act or any Act, determine any question of law or of fact, and its determination on a question of fact is binding and conclusive.

Factual findings of court

(2) In determining a question of fact, the Commission is not bound by the finding or judgment of any court, but the finding or judgment of a court is admissible in proceedings of the Commission.

Pending proceedings

(3) The power of the Commission to hear and determine a question of fact is not affected by proceedings pending before any court in which the question is in issue.

Counsel assigned by Minister of Justice

53. Where an issue of particular importance affecting the public interest arises, or may arise, in the course of proceedings before the Commission, the Minister of Justice may, at the request of the Commission or of the Minister's own motion, instruct counsel to intervene in the proceedings with respect to the issue.

In camera *hearings*

54. A hearing or a portion of a hearing before the Commission may, on the request of any party to the hearing, or on the Commission's own motion, be held *in camera* if that party establishes to the satisfaction of the Commission, or the Commission determines, that the circumstances of the case so require.

Judicial powers

55. The Commission has the powers of a superior court with respect to
  (a) the attendance and examination of witnesses;
  (b) the production and examination of any document, information or thing;
  (c) the enforcement of its decisions;
  (d) the entry on and inspection of property; and
  (e) the doing of anything else necessary for the exercise of its powers and the performance of its duties.

Award of costs

56.(1) The Commission may award interim or final costs of and incidental to proceedings before it and may fix the amount of the costs or direct that the amount be taxed.

Payment of costs

(2) The Commission may order by whom and to whom any costs are to be paid and by whom they are to be taxed and may establish a scale for the taxation of costs.

Rules, orders and regulations

57. The Commission may make rules, orders and regulations respecting any matter or thing within the jurisdiction of the Commission under this Act or any special Act.

Guidelines and Advice

Guidelines

58. The Commission may from time to time issue guidelines and statements with respect to any matter within its jurisdiction under this Act or any special Act, but the guidelines and statements are not binding on the Commission.

. . . .

Review of decisions

62. The Commission may, on application or on its won motion, review and rescind or vary any decision made by it or re-hear a matter before rendering a decision.

Enforcement in Federal Court

63.(1) A decision of the Commission may be made an order of the Federal Court or of a superior court of a province and may be enforced in the same manner as an order of that court as if it had been an order of that court on the date of the decision.

Procedure

(2) A decision of the Commission may be made an order of a court in accordance with the usual practice and procedure of the court in such matters, if any, or by the filing with the registrar of the court of a copy of the decision certified by the secretary to the Commission.

Effect of revocation or amendment

(3) Where a decision of the Commission that has been made an order of a court is rescinded or varied by a subsequent decision of the Commission, the order of the court is vacated and the decision of the Commission as varied may be made an order of the court in accordance with subsection (2).

Saving

(4) The Commission may enforce any of its decisions whether or not the decision has been made an order of a court.

Appeals

Appeal to Federal Court of Appeal

64.(1) An appeal from a decision of the Commission on any question of law or of jurisdiction may be brought in the Federal Court of Appeal with the leave of that Court.

. . . .

Regulations

Regulations

67.(1) The Commission may make regulations
  (a) prescribing standards governing the height of transmission lines of Canadian carriers, not inconsistent with standards prescribed under any other Act of Parliament;
  (b) establishing rules respecting its practice and procedure;

. . . .

  (c) establishing the criteria for the awarding of costs; and
  (d) generally for carrying out the purposes and provisions of this Act or any special Act.

Application

(2) Regulations made by the Commission may be of general application or applicable in respect of a particular case or class of cases.

Incorporation by reference

(3) Regulations made by the Commission incorporating any standard or enactment by reference may incorporate it as amended from time to time.

. . . .

227

Pre-publication of regulations

69.(1) Any regulations proposed to be made under section 67 or 68 shall be published in the *Canada Gazette* at least sixty days before their proposed effective date, and a reasonable opportunity shall be given to interested persons to make representations to the Commission with respect to the proposed regulations.

Idem

(2) Proposed regulations that are modified after publication need not be published again under subsection (1).

PART V
INVESTIGATION AND ENFORCEMENT

Inquiries

Appointment by Commission

70.(1) The Commission may appoint any person to inquire into and report to the Commission on any matter

    (a) pending before the Commission or within the Commission's jurisdiction under this Act or any special Act; or

    (b) on which the Commission is required to report under section 14.

(d) Note on the Canadian Radio-television and Telecommunications Commission†

Two Oppositions

The public authorities we are studying are situated in the middle of two sets of oppositions — at the micro level, the tension between efficiency and fairness that underlies all administrative law; and at the macro level, the tension between independence and accountability that affects all tribunals that purport to act with some degree of freedom from the centre. In the everyday world of public authorities, each of these tensions manifests itself in the form of practical problems and challenges. Some of them can be addressed by the public authority itself; others may require the intervention of statute. Here we are looking at a tribunal that attempts to meet this challenge through two distinct sets of procedures: the Canadian Radio-television and Telecommunications Commission (CRTC).

Two Different Tribunals

Substantively and procedurally, the CRTC is two quite different tribunals under the same roof. Common structural matters are governed by the *Canadian Radio-television and Telecommunications Commission Act.*[1] The *Broadcasting Act* governs the Commission's proceedings in broadcasting matters, where it is concerned mainly with licensing broadcasting operations and regulating their rates. The *Telecommunications Act*[2] is the main statute governing telecommunications proceedings,[3] which relate mainly to regulating telephone and other telecommunications rates. The broadcasting side is concerned with such public interest questions as quality of programming and Canadian culture content, involving dozens of private companies and the CBC. The telecommunications side tends to deal with much more technical issues, such as those that affect giant Bell Telephone, a relatively small number of other fairly large private concerns, and their consumers. The broadcasting side has the more informal procedure; telecommunications, the more formal.

Collegial Decision-Making

Like the other public authorities we are studying, the CRTC is a collegiate body. With a total staff of 420 in 1997, it has a maximum of 13 full-time and six part-time members, each with a tenure for up to five years. Part-time members participate only in broadcasting decisions. A panel of three members constitutes the quorum in broadcasting, at least two of whom must be full-time members. However, this panel must consult with the Commission in regard to policy matters and the making of

---

† For the most current situation and further background material, see <http://www.crtc.gc.ca/eng/welcome.htm>.

regulations. Before 1991, most broadcasting licensing decisions started with a panel having a quorum of at least one full-time member. After hearing the parties, they would make a tentative decision. This decision would then be considered at a meeting of the full Commission (including part-time members), but only a tentative position would be taken there. Finally, after considering this tentative decision, the full-time members would make a final decision. Although the old procedure was intended to combine efficiency needs with consultation, it was cumbersome which meant that the final decision could be made by members who were not present at the hearing (cf. the *Consolidated-Bathurst* decision in Chapter 7). Telecommunications decisions are made by the full-time members, with a quorum of two members in contested cases.

Independence

As with the NEB and the old CTC, there has been controversy as to the best relationship between this public authority and the central executive. The CRTC has more independence than the NEB — Cabinet is not required to approve its decisions or regulations — and less than the CIRB. There is a Cabinet power to issue directions to the CRTC on broadcast licensing and telecommunications matters, review by the Cabinet of broadcasting and telecommunications decisions, and a report to the Minister on disputed CBC licence decisions. In his 1980 study on the CRTC for the Law Reform Commission of Canada, C.C. Johnston suggested that the *ex post facto* Cabinet review power be replaced by a more general Cabinet power to issue broad policy directions, after prior consultation with the CRTC, publication, and opportunity for Parliamentary input.[4] The 1991 amendments to the *Broadcasting Act* implemented most of these recommendations. Note, though, that the old petition to Cabinet is retained in broadcasting (and telecommunications) proceedings.[5] How do the new Cabinet direction powers[6] in broadcasting compare with those in telecommunications and under the *National Transportation Act*? Did the 1991 *Broadcasting Act* changes mean greater accountability and less independence for the CRTC?

Hearings

A problem common to many public authorities is just when to hold a public hearing when the statute doesn't make this clear. Typically, the *Broadcasting Act* confers considerable discretion

here. It says public hearings must be held where the CRTC issues, revokes or suspends a broadcasting licence, or where Cabinet so orders, but everywhere else it gives the CRTC an effective discretion whether to hold a public hearing. What criteria does the CRTC use? In one situation, where there is a licence amendment or renewal, the Act requires the CRTC to consider whether it would be in the public interest *not* to hold a hearing; otherwise the CRTC is directed to consider whether it would be in the public interest to hold a hearing. There is a converse problem where the statute expressly requires a public hearing, but there is no real reason to hold one.[7] Generally speaking, the CRTC tends to convene public hearings for applications for new licences, major policy issues, and amendments to regulations.[8]

Notice

Notice is a key aspect of the rules of natural justice, and is mentioned specifically in the amended *Broadcasting Act*.[9] One interesting aspect of this Act is the statutory requirement of notice before the CRTC makes regulations. This recalls the "notice and comment" requirement of s. 4 of the American *Administrative Procedure Act*, which applies generally to rule-making by federal American administrative agencies. There is no such general statutory requirement in Canada.

Disclosure and Confidentiality

Disclosure and confidentiality are among the most difficult of all procedural problems confronting public authorities. There are two aspects here — a question of balancing the interests of competing parties before the tribunal, and where staff documents are concerned, a question of information-gathering efficiency, on one hand, and court-like fairness on the other.[10] On the first question, the CRTC tackles disclosure and confidentiality with differing degrees of formality depending on whether broadcasting or telecommunications are concerned.[11]

Cross-examination

We noted that on the broadcasting side, procedure is more informal than in telecommunications. In his 1980 Law Reform Commission study, Johnston felt that in areas such as use of cross-examination, broadcasting was too informal, but this informality has generally continued. It is useful to attempt to add up the potential pros and cons of cross-examination — a process very useful for many fact-finding needs, but also very expensive and time-consuming, and thus helpful for those whose main interest is delay.

Guidelines

Johnston complimented the CRTC for its use of policy guidelines, and this practice was given the judicial seal of approval in the *Capital Cities* case. The amended *Broadcasting Act* and *Telecommunications Act* carry this approach even further by formally empowering the CRTC to make non-binding guidelines.

Judicial Control

The CRTC has not been designated as a "court of record" under the old legislation, and neither the amended *Broadcasting Act* nor the *Telecommunications Act* has changed this condition. Under the amended *Federal Court Act*,[12] it is one of the 14 federal tribunals that are reviewable only in the Federal Court of Appeal. There continues to be an appeal on law or jurisdiction from CRTC decisions to the Federal Court of Appeal.

Hearing Procedure

Broadcasting hearings tend to be much less formal than telecommunications hearings. In broadcasting, parties aren't necessarily represented by legal counsel, cross-examination isn't inevitable, and Commission members play a more active role. In telecommunications, legal counsel and cross-examination are a part of almost every oral hearing. Compare the *Broadcasting Act CRTC Rules of Procedure*, C.R.C., c. 375, with the more elaborate *CRTC Telecommunications Rules of Procedure*, SOR/79-554.

Other Possible Issues

1. *Constitutional issues*: Both division of powers and *Charter* issues are important here.
2. *Responding to generally worded mandates*: Has the broadcasting policy so many factors it is little more than an open-ended discretion?
3. *Balancing fairness and judicial procedure with efficiency*:
   (a) avoiding undue delay
   (b) subject matter complexity vs. need for simplicity and uniformity

(c) role of board counsel, staff, and staff studies
(d) general policy guidelines or rules vs. case-by-case adjudication: see *Capital Cities*
(e) pre-hearing procedures, etc.
(f) CRTC participation in judicial control proceedings
4. *Compliance*: How to secure compliance mechanisms

Law Reform Commission Study

In his CRTC study for the Law Reform Commission of Canada,[13] C.C. Johnston was not overly critical of either the broadcasting or the telecommunications side of the CRTC. Nevertheless, he was concerned about matters such as Cabinet review, as mentioned above, and delay, inadequate disclosure, and insufficient reasons for decisions. How, if at all, has the CRTC or Parliament responded to Johnston's concerns in subsequent years? What are the key problems today?

Technological Change and the CRTC

Two important recent CRTC decisions on the future roles of cable and telephone companies were Telecom Decision CRTC 92-12 of 12 June 1992, ending monopolies in long-distance telephone service; and Decision CRTC 94-19 of 16 September 1994, calling for greater competition and lower long-distance rates, as well as allowing telephone company involvement in information services. As well, in the spring of 1995, after written submissions and a 78-party oral public hearing, the CRTC issued a long report on competition and culture on Canada's information highway.

In December 1994, the CRTC allowed ExpressVu Inc. to start operating a direct-to-home satellite service without a licence, provided that it use a Canadian-owned satellite. Its rival, Power DirecTv, had planned to use an American satellite, and complained that the decision would give ExpressVu a virtual monopoly. In April 1995, after intense lobbying and a federal review panel recommendation, the federal government proposed to overrule the CRTC decision. The CRTC chairman said that would interfere with CRTC regulatory responsibilities. There were questions about the legality of the proposed directive because it seemed to go beyond general matters of policy and to affect a specific case. On 7 July 1995, the Cabinet issued a directive permitting ExpressVu to operate without a licence on 1 September 1995 as before, pending the opening of competitive licences on 1 November 1995. The new DTH technology was already generating regulatory turmoil.

Notes

1. R.S.C. 1985, c. C-22.
2. S.C. 1993, c. 38.
3. See also the *Bell Canada Act*, S.C. 1987, c. 19.
4. C.C. Johnston, *The Canadian Radio-television and Telecommunications Commission*, 1980 (144 pp.)
5. In the period from 1984 to 1997, approximately 55 Cabinet petitions were considered. In about 75% of these petitions, Cabinet upheld the CRTC decision. In most of the remaining petitions, Cabinet referred the matter back to the CRTC.
6. These have not been used frequently. For two examples, see SOR/95-319 and SOR/95-320.
7. For example, in a routine situation involving an uncontested application.
8. *CRTC Public Process* <www.crtc.gc.ca/eng/publicpar_1htm#ph>.
9. Section 19. See, however, *Telecommunications Workers' Union v. Canada (Radio-television and Telecommunications Commission)*, [1995] 2 S.C.R. 781 (S.C.C.), below, involving a telecommunications decision.
10. See, generally, *London Cable*.
11. Compare the *Broadcasting Act CRTC Rules of Procedure*, C.R.C., c. 375, s. 20 with the *CRTC Telecommunications Rules of Procedure*, SOR/79-554, s.19.
12. The *Federal Court Act* amendments were proclaimed in force on 1 February 1992.
13. Johnston, *supra* note 4.

(e) *Telecommunications Workers*†

NOTE

The CRTC made a decision determining that Shaw Cable could perform installation work on BC Tel's support structures using Shaw's own contractors. This contradicted the collective agreement between BC Tel and its employees' union, TWU. The agreement required that any work on BC Tel's support structures must be performed exclusively by TWU members. TWU argued that the CRTC decision should be quashed because the CRTC had failed to ensure that TWU had been given notice of the application and proceedings leading to the CRTC decision. TWU had been a party to earlier CRTC proceedings that addressed a similar question.

EXTRACTS

[SOPINKA J., dissenting, for himself, LAMER C.J., and CORY J.:]

. . . .

[para6] In her reasons, my colleague suggests that TWU's interest in the proceedings before the CRTC was merely indirect as Decision 92-4 [awarding the work right to Shaw Cable] was addressing telecommunications policy and not labour relations. With respect, the fact that the CRTC was specifically concerned with telecommunications policy in accordance with its mandate does not detract from the fact that its decision would have a substantial impact on the work jurisdiction of TWU, thereby directly affecting the rights of the union and its members. The very question before the CRTC concerned who had the right to perform the work on the support structures belonging to BC Tel. The CRTC was well aware of the impact that its decision would have on TWU. Although the purpose behind Decision 92-4 may not have been related to the "work jurisdiction" of TWU and the CRTC may have been seeking to avoid entering the realm of labour relations, this is no answer to a violation of natural justice where a decision could potentially override the union's rights.

[para7] The principal, if not the sole, reason for BC Tel's application to the CRTC was to determine who could do the work....

. . . .

[para8] ... Generally, I am in agreement that it would potentially be unduly onerous on regulatory agencies if notice had to be provided to all individuals having contractual relations with a regulated party. As my colleague observes, there are a myriad of decisions of a regulatory agency which could have an indirect impact on individuals simply because they are privy to a contract with the regulated party....

---

† *Telecommunications Workers Union v. Canada (Radio-television and Telecommunications Commission)*, [1995] 2 S.C.R. 781 (S.C.C.: June 22, 1995); aff'g. [1993] F.C.J. No. 444 (F.C.A.), dismissing appellant's the TWU's application for judicial review of a decision of the Canadian Radio-television and Telecommunications Commission.

. . . .

[para9] However, in my view, there are special circumstances which arise in this case such that the *audi alteram partem rule* mandates that formal notice be given to TWU. The central focus of the ruling of the CRTC specifically concerns the very subject matter of the contract between the BC Tel and TWU. Thus, the interest at stake is not simply a contingent one flowing solely from the effect of the decision on BC Tel....

. . . .

[para11] Given the fact that TWU was a party to the [similar] proceedings in 1987, the CRTC would have been aware that the interests of the union were substantially and equally at stake in the application leading to Decision 92-4 since the question to be considered was essentially identical....

. . . .

[para18] ... Procedural fairness is the right of the interested parties and the duty of the administrative tribunal. This does not change where an additional notice obligation [the requirement in section 72 that the employer notify the union of the proceedings] is placed on one of the regulated parties.

. . . .

[para24] As a result, I am of the view that the failure to notify TWU of the proceedings before the CRTC amounted to a denial of natural justice. While notice need not be given to every union which has a collective agreement with a company that is regulated by the CRTC, I believe that the unique circumstances of this case, which I have discussed above, required that notice be furnished to TWU.

. . . .

[L'HEUREUX-DUBÉ J. for herself, La FOREST, GONTHIER, McLACHLIN, IACOBUCCI and MAJOR JJ:]

. . . .

[para29] The *audi alteram partem* rule, which is a component of the principles of natural justice and of procedural fairness, requires that a person who is a party to proceedings before a tribunal be informed of the proceedings and provided with an opportunity to be heard by the tribunal.

. . . .

[para32] ... In my view, the TWU's interest in the proceedings before the CRTC was purely indirect. The CRTC decision concerned questions of telecommunication policy. The CRTC was required to decide on the best way to regulate a monopoly telephone company in order to preserve the public interest. The purpose behind the CRTC decision was totally unrelated to the "work jurisdiction" of the TWU. In fact, such a consideration would have been irrelevant to the CRTC decision. Consequently, the TWU had no relevant interest to represent before the CRTC. While the TWU may have been affected by the CRTC decision, the effect of this decision on the TWU was purely indirect. Accordingly, I conclude that *audi alteram partem* did not require that the TWU be provided with notice of the CRTC hearing. The TWU was not a party nor did it have a direct interest in the proceedings before the tribunal.

[para33] In this respect, it is important to note that a finding in the case at hand that the TWU was entitled to notice would have grave consequences that could paralyse regulatory agencies. Effectively, it would mean that all individuals with contractual relations with a regulatee would have to be given notice of regulatory proceedings concerning that regulatee if such proceedings were likely to affect, even indirectly, the person in question. Given the wide scope of many regulatory agencies, their decisions are likely to have an indirect effect on a large number of individuals in contractual relations with the regulatee. As a result, all such parties would have to be provided with notice of the regulatory proceedings. This is particularly problematic in light of the extreme difficulty of ascertaining exactly who these parties are in advance of the hearing and the possibility that, in the absence of notice, these parties would be able to challenge the legality of the regulatory decision. This could result in an endless series of challenges that would effectively paralyse regulatory agencies. Accordingly, the *audi alteram partem* rule should not be interpreted as requiring that notice be provided to parties indirectly affected by regulatory proceedings.

However, even if I am wrong and the *audi alteram partem* rule would normally have required the CRTC to notify the TWU of the proceedings in question, in my view, s. 72 ... effectively relieves the CRTC of this obligation.

. . . .

[para38] For the reasons outlined above, I would dismiss this appeal with costs throughout.

11   Canadian Transportation Agency

(a) Canada Transportation Act
— *Table of Provisions*†

---

†   S.C. 1996, c. 10 (assented to 29 May 1996), Table of Provisions.

(b)   Canada Transportation Act†

Her Majesty, by and with the advice and consent of the Senate and House of Commons of Canada, enacts as follows:

SHORT TITLE

Short title

1. This Act may be cited as the *Canada Transportation Act*.

HER MAJESTY

Binding on Her Majesty

2. This Act is binding on Her Majesty in right of Canada or a province.

APPLICATION

Application generally

3. This Act applies in respect of transportation matters under the legislative authority of Parliament.

.   .   .   .

NATIONAL TRANSPORTATION POLICY

Declaration

5. It is hereby declared that a safe, economic, efficient and adequate network of viable and effective transportation services accessible to persons with disabilities and that makes the best use of all available

---

† S.C. 1996, c. 10 (assented to 29 May 1996).

modes of transportation at the lowest total cost is essential to serve the transportation needs of shippers and travellers, including persons with disabilities, and to maintain the economic well-being and growth of Canada and its regions and that those objectives are most likely to be achieved when all carriers are able to compete, both within and among the various modes of transportation, under conditions ensuring that, having due regard to national policy, to the advantages of harmonized federal and provincial regulatory approaches and to legal and constitutional requirements,

(a) the national transportation system meets the highest practicable safety standards,

(b) competition and market forces are, whenever possible, the prime agents in providing viable and effective transportation services,

(c) economic regulation of carriers and modes of transportation occurs only in respect of those services and regions where regulation is necessary to serve the transportation needs of shippers and travellers and that such regulation will not unfairly limit the ability of any carrier or mode of transportation to compete freely with any other carrier or mode of transportation,

(d) transportation is recognized as a key to regional economic development and that commercial viability of transportation links is balanced with regional economic development objectives so that the potential economic strengths of each region may be realized,

(e) each carrier or mode of transportation, as far as is practicable, bears a fair proportion of the real costs of the resources, facilities and services provided to that carrier or mode of transportation at public expense,

(f) each carrier or mode of transportation, as far as is practicable, receives fair and reasonable compensation for the resources, facilities and services that it is required to provide as an imposed public duty,

(g) each carrier or mode of transportation, as far as is practicable, carries traffic to or from any point in Canada under fares, rates and conditions that do not constitute

(i) an unfair disadvantage in respect of any such traffic beyond the disadvantage inherent in the location or volume of the traffic, the scale of operation connected with the traffic or the type of traffic or service involved,

(ii) an undue obstacle to the mobility of persons, including persons with disabilities,

(iii) an undue obstacle to the interchange of commodities between points in Canada, or

(iv) an unreasonable discouragement to the development of primary or secondary industries, to export trade in or from any region of Canada or to the movement of commodities through Canadian ports, and

(h) each mode of transportation is economically viable,

and this Act is enacted in accordance with and for the attainment of those objectives to the extent that they fall within the purview of subject-matters under the legislative authority of Parliament relating to transportation.

. . . .

PART I
ADMINISTRATION

Canadian Transportation Agency

Continuation and Organization

Agency continued

7.(1) The agency known as the National Transportation Agency is continued as the Canadian Transportation Agency.

Composition of Agency

(2) The Agency shall consist of

(a) not more than seven members appointed by the Governor in Council, and

(b) such temporary members as are appointed under subsection 9(1),

each of whom must, on appointment or reappointment and while serving as a member, be a Canadian citizen or permanent resident within the meaning of the Immigration Act.

Chairperson and Vice-Chairperson

(3) The Governor in Council shall designate one of the members appointed under paragraph (2)(a) to be the Chairperson of the Agency and one of the other members appointed under that paragraph to be the Vice-Chairperson of the Agency.

Term of members

8.(1) Each member appointed under paragraph 7(2)(a) shall hold office during good behaviour for a term of not more than five years and may be removed for cause by the Governor in Council.

Reappointment

(2) A member appointed under paragraph 7(2)(a) is eligible to be reappointed on the expiration of a first or subsequent term of office.

. . . .

Temporary members

9.(1) The Minister may appoint temporary members of the Agency from the roster of individuals established by the Governor in Council under subsection (2).

Roster

(2) The Governor in Council may appoint any individual to a roster of candidates for the purpose of subsection (1).

Maximum number

(3) Not more than three temporary members shall hold office at any one time.

Term of temporary members

(4) A temporary member shall hold office during good behaviour for a term of not more than one year and may be removed for cause by the Governor in Council.

. . . .

Remuneration

11.(1) A member shall be paid such remuneration and allowances as may be fixed by the Governor in Council.

. . . .

Chairperson

Duties of Chairperson

13. The Chairperson is the chief executive officer of the Agency and has the supervision over and direction of the work of the members and its staff, including the apportionment of work among the members and the assignment of members to deal with any matter before the Agency.

Absence of Chairperson

14. In the event of the absence or incapacity of the Chairperson or if the office of Chairperson is vacant, the Vice-Chairperson has all the powers and shall perform all the duties and functions of the Chairperson.

Absence of both Chairperson and Vice-Chairperson

15. The Chairperson may authorize one or more of the members to act as Chairperson for the time being if both the Chairperson and Vice-Chairperson are absent or unable to act.

. . . .

Rules

Rules

17. The Agency may make rules respecting
   (a) the sittings of the Agency and the carrying on of its work;
   (b) the manner of and procedures for dealing with matters and business before the agency, including the circumstances in which hearings may be held in private; and
   (c) the number of members that are required to hear any matter or perform any of the functions of the Agency under this Act or any other Act of Parliament.

. . . .

Staff

Secretary, officers and employees

19. The Secretary of the Agency and the other officers and employees that are necessary for the proper conduct of the business of the Agency shall be appointed in accordance with the Public Service Employment Act.

. . . .

Powers of Agency

Policy governs Agency

24. The powers, duties and functions of the Agency respecting any matter that comes within its jurisdiction under an Act of Parliament shall be exercised and performed in conformity with any policy direction issued to the Agency under section 43.

Agency powers in general

25. The Agency has, with respect to all matters necessary or proper for the exercise of its jurisdiction, the attendance and examination of witnesses, the production and inspection of documents, the enforcement of its orders or regulations and the entry on and inspection of property, all the powers, rights and privileges that are vested in a superior court.

Power to award costs

25.1(1) Subject to subsections (2) to (4), the Agency has all the powers that the Federal Court has to award costs in any proceeding before it.

. . . .

Compelling observance of obligations

26. The Agency may require a person to do or refrain from doing any thing that the person is or may be required to do or is prohibited from doing under an Act of Parliament that is administered in whole or in part by the Agency.

Relief

27.(1) On an application made to the Agency, the Agency may grant the whole or part of the application, or may make any order or grant any further or other relief that to the Agency seems just and proper.

. . . .

Time for making decisions

29.(1) The Agency shall make its decision in any proceedings before it as expeditiously as possible, but no later than one hundred and twenty days after the originating documents are received, unless the parties agree to an extension of this Act or a regulation made under subsection (2) provides otherwise.

Period for specified classes

(2) The Governor in Council may, by regulation, prescribe periods of less than one hundred and twenty days within which the Agency shall make its decision in respect of such classes of proceedings as are specified in the regulation.

Pending proceedings

30. The fact that a suit, prosecution or proceeding involving a question of fact is pending in any court does not deprive the Agency of jurisdiction to hear and determine the same question of fact.

Fact finding is conclusive

31. The finding or determination of the Agency on a question of fact within its jurisdiction is binding and conclusive.

Review of decisions and orders

32. The Agency may review, rescind or vary any decision or order made by it or may re-hear any application before deciding it if, in the opinion of the Agency, since the decision or order or the hearing of the application, there has been a change in the facts or circumstances pertaining to the decision, order or hearing.

Enforcement of decision or order

33.(1) A decision or order of the Agency may be made an order of the Federal Court or of any superior court and is enforceable in the same manner as such an order.

Procedure

(2) To make a decision or order an order of a court, either the usual practice and procedure of the court in such matters may be followed or the Secretary of the Agency may file with the registrar of the court a certified copy of the decision or order, signed by the Chairperson and sealed with the Agency's seal, at which time the decision or order becomes an order of the court.

Effect of variation or rescission

(3) Where a decision or order that has been made an order of a court is rescinded or varied by a subsequent decision or order of the Agency, the order of the court is deemed to have been cancelled and the subsequent decision or order may be made an order of the court.

Option to enforce

(4) The Agency may, before or after one of its decisions or orders is made an order of a court, enforce the decision or order by its own action.

. . . .

Approval of regulations required

36.(1) Every regulation made by the Agency under this Act must be made with the approval of the Governor in Council.

Advance notice of regulations

(2) The Agency shall give the Minister notice of every regulation proposed to be made by the Agency under this Act.

Inquiries

Inquiry into complaint

37. The Agency may inquire into, hear and determine a complaint concerning any act, matter or thing prohibited, sanctioned or required to be done under any Act of Parliament that is administered in whole or in part by the Agency.

Appointment of person to conduct inquiry

38.(1) The Agency may appoint a member, or an employee of the Agency, to make any inquiry that the Agency is authorized to conduct and report to the Agency.

Dealing with report

(2) On receipt of the report under subsection (1), the Agency may adopt the report as a decision or order of the Agency or otherwise deal with it as it considers advisable.

Powers on inquiry

39. A person conducting an inquiry may, for the purposes of the inquiry,

  (a) enter and inspect any place, other than a dwelling-house, or any structure, work, rolling stock or ship that is the property or under the control of any person the entry or inspection of which appears to the inquirer to be necessary; and

  (b) exercise the same powers as are vested in a superior court to summon witnesses, enforce their attendance and compel them to give evidence and produce any materials, books, papers, plans, specifications, drawings and other documents that the inquirer thinks necessary.

Review and Appeal

Governor in Council may vary or rescind orders, etc.

40. The Governor in Council may, at any time, in the discretion of the Governor in Council, either on petition of a party or an interested person or of the Governor in Council's own motion, vary or rescind any decision, order, rule or regulation of the Agency, whether the decision or order is made inter partes or otherwise, and whether the rule or regulation is general or limited in its scope and application, and any order that the Governor in Council may make to do so is binding on the Agency and on all parties.

Appeal from Agency

41.(1) An appeal lies from the Agency to the Federal Court of Appeal on a question of law or a question of jurisdiction on leave to appeal being obtained from that Court on application made within one month after the date of the decision, order, rule or regulation being appealed from, or within any further time that a judge of that Court under special circumstances allows, and on notice to the parties and the Agency, and on hearing those of them that appear and desire to be heard.

Time for making appeal

(2) No appeal, after leave to appeal has been obtained under subsection (1), lies unless it is entered in the Federal Court of Appeal within sixty days after the order granting leave to appeal is made.

Powers of Court

(3) An appeal shall be heard as quickly as is practicable and, on the hearing of the appeal, the Court may draw any inferences that are not inconsistent with the facts expressly found by the Agency and that are necessary for determining the question of law or jurisdiction, as the case may be.

Agency may be heard

(4) The Agency is entitled to be heard by counsel or otherwise on the argument of an appeal.

Report of Agency

Report of Agency

42.(1) Each year the Agency shall, before the end of May, make a report on the activities of the Agency for the preceding year and submit it to the Governor in Council through the Minister describing briefly, in respect of that year,

  (a) applications to the Agency and the findings on them; and

  (b) the findings of the Agency in regard to any matter or thing respecting which the Agency has acted on the request of the Minister.

Assessment of Act

(2) The Agency shall include in every report referred to in subsection (1) the Agency's assessment of the operation of this Act and any difficulties observed in the administration of this Act.

Tabling of report

(3) The Minister shall have a copy of each report made under this section laid before each House of Parliament on any of the first thirty days on which that House is sitting after the Minister receives it.

Governor in Council

Directions of Agency

Policy directions

43.(1) The Governor in Council may, at the request of the Agency or of the Governor in Council's own motion, issue policy directions to the Agency concerning any matter that comes within the jurisdiction of the Agency and every such direction shall be carried out by the Agency under the Act of Parliament that establishes the powers, duties and functions of the Agency in relation to the subject-matter of the direction.

Limitation on directions

(2) A direction issued under subsection (1) shall not affect a matter that is before the Agency on the date of the direction and that relates to a particular person.

Delay of binding effect

44. A direction issued under section 43 is not binding on the Agency until the expiration of the thirtieth sitting day of Parliament after the direction has been laid before both Houses of Parliament by or on behalf of the Minister, unless the direction has been previously laid before both Houses of Parliament in proposed form by or on behalf of the Minister and thirty sitting days of Parliament have expired after the proposed direction was laid.

Referral to committee

45. Where a direction referred to in section 43 is issued or a proposed direction referred to in section 44 is laid before a House of Parliament, it shall be referred without delay by that House to the committee of that House that it considers appropriate to deal with the subject-matter of the direction or proposed direction.

Consultation required

46. Before a direction referred to in section 43 is issued or a proposed direction referred to in section 44 is laid before a House of Parliament, the Minister shall consult with the Agency with respect to the nature and subject-matter of the direction or proposed direction.

Extraordinary Disruptions

Governor in Council may prevent disruptions

47.(1) Where the Governor in Council is of the opinion that

   (a) an extraordinary disruption to the effective continued operation of the national transportation system exists or is imminent, other than a labour disruption,

   (b) failure to act under this section would be contrary to the interests of users and operators of the national transportation system, and

   (c) there are no other provisions in this Act or in any other Act of Parliament that are sufficient and appropriate to remedy the situation and counter the actual or anticipated damage caused by the disruption, the Governor in Council may, on the recommendation of the Minister and the minister responsible for the Bureau of Competition Policy, by order, take any steps, or direct the Agency to take any steps, that the Governor in Council considers essential to stabilize the national transportation system, including the imposition of capacity and pricing restraints.

Minister may consult affected persons

(2) Before recommending that an order be made under this section, the Minister may consult with any person who the Minister considers may be affected by the order.

Order is temporary

(3) An order made under this section shall have effect for no more than ninety days after the order is made.

Order to be tabled in Parliament

(4) The Minister shall cause any order made under this section to be laid before both Houses of Parliament within seven sitting days after the order is made.

Reference to Parliamentary Committee

(5) Every order laid before Parliament under subsection (4) shall be referred for review to the Standing committee designated by Parliament for the purpose.

Resolution of Parliament revoking order

(6) Where a resolution directing that an order made under this section be revoked is adopted by both Houses of Parliament before the expiration of thirty sitting days of Parliament after the order is laid before both Houses of Parliament, the order shall cease to have effect on the day that the resolution is adopted or, if the adopted resolution specifies a day on which the order shall cease to have effect, on that specified day.

. . . .

Inquiry

Minister may request inquiry

49. The Minister may direct the Agency to inquire into any matter or thing concerning transportation to which the legislative authority of Parliament extends and report the findings on the inquiry to the Minister as and when the Minister may require.

. . . .

Review of Act

Statutory review

53.(1) The Minister shall, no later than four years after the day this Act comes into force, appoint one or more persons to carry out a comprehensive review of the operation of this Act and any other Act of Parliament for which the Minister is responsible that pertains to the economic regulation of a mode of transportation and transportation activities under the legislative authority of Parliament.

. . . .

PART II
AIR TRANSPORTATION

. . . .

Licence for Domestic Service

Issue of licence

61. On application to the Agency and on payment of the specified fee, the Agency shall issue a licence to operate a domestic service to the applicant if

(a) the applicant establishes in the application to the satisfaction of the Agency that the applicant

  (i) is a Canadian,

  (ii) holds a Canadian aviation document in respect of the service to be provided under the licence,

  (iii) has the prescribed liability insurance coverage in respect of the service to be provided under the licence, and

  (iv) meets prescribed financial requirements; and

(b) the Agency is satisfied that the applicant has not contravened section 59 in respect of a domestic service within the preceding twelve months.

(c) Note on Canadian Transportation Agency[†]

GENERAL

The Canadian Transportation Agency (CTA) is part of the outlying administrative process. It is a regulatory body that came into operation in 1996, when it replaced the National Transport Agency (NTA). The NTA, in turn, was created in 1993 to replace the Canadian Transport Commission that had been in existence since 1967.

Creatures of deregulation, the CTA and NTA have been given progressively smaller regulatory roles than the old Canadian Transport Commission. Air transport statutory requirements, transport merger and acquisition rules, and rail line abandonment processes are all less stringent. Unlike the NTA, but like the CTC, the CTA has jurisdiction in regard to rail safety.

The CTA's main governing statute is the *Canada Transportation Act,*[1] together with other legislation.[2] The *Canada Transportation Act* declares that a "safe, economic, efficient and adequate network of viable and effective transportation services

---

[†] For the most current situation and further background material, see <http://www.cta-otc.gc.ca/index_e.html>.

accessible to persons with disabilities and that makes the best use of all available modes of transportation at the lowest total cost is essential to serve the transportation needs of shippers and travellers...."[3]

The CTA's main regulatory functions include:

(i) issuing air and rail carrier licences;
(ii) setting maximum rates in certain rail contexts;
(iii) responding to complaints, including those in the federal marine sector;
(iv) monitoring railway safety;
(iv) removing undue obstacles to the mobility of disabled persons; and
(vi) inquiring into specific transportation concerns.

The CTC's air licensing responsibilities are less rigorous than those of the NTA and the CTC. The CTC had to consider the "public convenience and necessity," including the effect on existing licences, before it could issue an air licence. The NTA had a similarly demanding set of criteria to consider for northern air routes. For both southern and northern routes, the CTA needs only to determine, in effect, if the applicant is "fit, willing, and able." Before issuing a licence, the CTA requires:

(i) that the applicant has not advertised or sold tickets for an air service;
(ii) compliance with Canadian ownership and minimum insurance regulations;
(iii) minimum financial requirements for the operation of medium or large aircraft; and
(iv) authorization from Transport Canada. The CTA patrols international air tariff agreement conditions on a complaint basis.

The CTA's rate monitoring roles are very specific and limited. The CTC had a general power to review the adequacy of rates and rate floors in the rail sector. The CTA can disallow a proposed rate increase by a domestic rail carrier, but only in response to a complaint. The CTA can also set interswitching and competitive line rates for railways and shippers. For western grain, the CTA sets maximum rates. For general rate disputes in the rail and marine sectors, the agency can refer parties to a final arbitration process.

For shipping, the CTA controls licensing and approval of fares in northern Canada and a variety of other concerns.

The *Canada Transportation Act* requires the CTA to render all its decisions "as expeditiously as possible",[4] and in any event, within 120 days of receipt of an application.[5]

The CTA has a staff of about 260 (including seven legal counsel: 1997), well down from the 700-plus staff of the CTC. It has up to seven full-time members, each appointed for up to five years and with tenure during good behaviour (the CTC had up to 17 members with 10-year tenures),[6] and up to three part-time members who serve during good behaviour for up to two consecutive one-year terms, and can be removed for cause.[7] The CTA has power to review its own decisions. Like the NTA and unlike the CTC, it has no formal review committee.

How independent is the CTA? Unlike those of the CTC (but like those of the NTA), most CTA decisions are subject to Cabinet policy directions. Before a Cabinet direction is binding, the Minister must consult with the CTA, and the direction or proposed direction must be laid before Parliament. Moreover, Cabinet directions must not affect specific cases already before the CTA. So far, though, few directions have been issued. CTA decisions are not subject to Cabinet approval. However, all CTA rules and regulations do require Cabinet approval. There is no right of appeal from the CTA to a Minister (as there was from the CTC), but CTA decisions, like those of the CTC and NTA, are subject to petitions to Cabinet[8] and to unilateral amendment by Cabinet. Although the CTA can conduct inquiries on its own initiative in some areas, and in response to complaints, the Minister has a general power to direct the CTA to hold an inquiry. Note, too, the shorter tenure of CTA members. Most CTA members have industry experience.

Like the NTA and unlike the CTC, the CTA is not a court of record.[9] It is not normally required to hold hearings. As with the NTA, most hearings are not oral, but are written "file" hearings.[10] Parties directly affected tend to be represented by legal counsel; those without legal counsel tend to submit written interventions rather than appear personally.

The CTA is subject to appeals on law or jurisdiction to the Federal Court of Appeal. It is one of about a dozen tribunals that are reviewable only by the Federal Court of Appeal.[11]

Hearing Stages

As indicated, NTA and CTA oral hearings have been rare. Where they are held, the following stages are usually involved:

(a) pre-application consultation
(b) application
(c) notice of application

(d)   reply

(e)   interventions

(f)   decision by Agency whether to convene an oral hearing

(g)   pre-hearing conference

(h)   hearing (with examination, cross-examination, reply, and final argument, for each of the parties)

(i)   decision.

Where there is no oral hearing, stage (h) is omitted. The CTA's procedural rules are based on those of the NTA,[12] which are similar to those of the CTC.[13] Recently, there have been indications that oral hearings may become less formal.

Possible Issues

1.   **Direction procedure:** The relationship between the CTA and Cabinet remains to be worked out.[14]

2.   **Cabinet petition procedure:** The Cabinet has rarely overturned Agency decisions.[15] Is this procedure consistent with decision-making by an independent regulatory body?

3.   **Railway abandonment:** The railway abandonment procedure is now largely self-executing. As federally subsidized rail transport is cut back, is the burden shifted to provincially funded road transport?

4.   **Fewer oral hearings:** As noted, the NTA and the CTA have held proportionately fewer oral hearings than the CTC. Why? Is this a positive or negative development?

5.   **Deregulation:** Has it meant less regulation or a different kind of regulation?

6.   **Confidentiality, notice, and disclosure:** How liberal are the CTA's policies here? Compare CTA disclosure cases with the NTA cases such as *Ogilvie Mills v. Canadian National Railways Co. (CNR)*, [1992] F.C.J. No. III (F.C.A.) and *Manitoba v. Canada (N.T.A.)*, [1994] F.C.J. No. 1719 (F.C.A.).

7.   **Agency policy rules:** Should the CTA have more specific rule-making powers?

8.   **Third-party accessibility:** How readily can intervenors appear? What are the rules re costs?

9.   **Agency participation in judicial control proceedings:** How actively does/should the CTA participate?

Law Reform Commission Study

In 1978, the Law Reform Commission of Canada published a 151-page study about the predecessor of the CTA and NTA, the CTC.[16] The author, H.N. Janisch, was concerned about delays in file hearings, inadequate reasons for decisions, disclosure of staff studies, lack of criteria as to when oral public hearings should be held, and lack of accessibility to public interest groups. Which of these old concerns about the CTC are resolved under the *Canada Transportation Act* and the CTA? Which concerns remain unresolved today? Are other issues more important?

Notes

1.   S.C. 1996, c. 10; R.S.C. 1985, c. N-20.01.

2.   For example, *Pilotage Act*, R.S.C. 1985, c. P-14; *Railway Relocation and Crossing Act*, R.S.C. 1985, c. R-4; *Railway Safety Act*, R.S.C. 1985, c. 32 (4th Supp.); *Shipping Conferences Exemption Act, 1987*, R.S.C. 1985, c. 17 (3rd Supp.); and *St. Lawrence Seaway Authority Act*, R.S.C. 1985, c. S-2.

3.   Section 5.

4.   Section 29.

5.   *Ibid.*

6.   *Ibid.*, ss. 7 and 8.

7.   *Ibid.*, s. 9.

8.   *Ibid.*, s. 40. Between 1992 and 1996 there were 39 petitions to the Governor in Council. Of these, 20 were upheld. Source: CTA.

9.   However, the CTA does have the powers of a superior court for enforcing its decisions and executing other matters within its jurisdiction.

10.   In 1995, the Agency held only three oral public hearings; in 1996, it held only one. The average length of the hearings was two days. Source: CTA.

11.   Between 1988 and 1991, Agency action was upheld in about 90% of judicial review decisions. Source: NTA. Thus far, judicial appeal or review of CTA decisions has been relatively infrequent. More recent figures are comparable. For example, in 1995–96 the Federal Court of Appeal heard six appeals and one application for review in regard to decisions of the NTA: In all seven cases, the NTA's decisions were upheld.

12.   *National Transportation Agency General Rules*, SOR/88-23.

13.   See *Canadian Transport Commission General Rules*. SOR/83-448.

14.   For examples of Cabinet directions to the NTA, see SOR/95-502 and SOR/95-443.

15.   For examples of Cabinet orders varying NTA decisions, see SOR/95-89-488, SOR/88-590, and SOR/94-496. The best known example of an effective Cabinet reversal of an NTA decision occurred in the *Greyhound Air* case. In April 1996, the NTA refused Greyhound Air an air carrier licence on the ground that it failed to meet Canadian ownership requirements. A review decision by the NTA in May 1996 came to the same conclusion. In June 1996, after a corporate restructuring agreement, Cabinet issued an order exempting Greyhound Air from the normal ownership requirements.

16.   Law Reform Commission of Canada, *The Regulatory Process of the Canadian Transport Commission* by H.N. Janisch (Ottawa: Law Reform Commission of Canada, 1977).

(d) *Canadian National Railway*[†]

NOTE

The National Transportation Agency, which is the Canadian Transportation Agency's predecessor, made an interswitching decision that had the effect of switching rail traffic from the lines of the C.N.R. to those of the C.P.R. The C.N.R. appealed the decision to the Federal Court of Appeal. The C.N.R. argued, *inter alia*, that the National Transportation Agency "breached the rules of natural justice by failing to allow [the C.N.R.] the opportunity to address the information it had gathered at a closed-door meeting between its staff and the respondent Domtar." [Domtar was the shipper.]

EXTRACTS

[MacGUIGAN J.A. for the Court:]

. . . .

On the second point, the affidavit of Wayne Douglas Gregory Kay (Appeal Book at 83) makes it clear that Agency staff held separate closed door meetings on April 6, 1988, with officials of both the appellant and the respondent Domtar, followed in both cases the following day by inspection of facilities. Before us, the Agency admitted that the minutes taken at those meetings by Agency staff were considered by the Agency in the process of reaching its decision, even though they were not available to the parties until well after the Agency decision had been rendered.

It is apparent from the minutes that the meeting with the appellant focused on calculations of distances, but that the respondent Domtar in its turn laid before the Agency detailed submissions as to such matters as its competitive disadvantage *vis-à-vis* other pulp-and-paper producers and its losses from shortage of railway equipment as supplied by the appellant.

In these circumstances, where the Agency acted on information that was not put before it in the course of its hearings (which in this case were properly conducted through written submissions rather than orally), and no opportunity was given to the appellant to answer such information, to avoid breach of the fair-hearing rule the respondent would have had to show that the information had no bearing whatsoever on the decision reached. This onus the respondent was unable to meet. Consequently, this case falls under the rule laid down by Le Dain J. for a unanimous Court in *Cardinal v. Director of Kent Institution*, [1985] 2 S.C.R. 643 at 661: "the denial of a right to a fair hearing must always render a decision invalid, whether or not it may appear to a reviewing court that the hearing would likely have resulted in a different conclusion."

The appeal must therefore be allowed, the decision of the Agency set aside, and the matter returned to the Agency for redetermination after all the interested parties have been provided with an opportunity to comment on all the information gathered by and put before the Agency. There should be no order as to costs.

[†] *Canadian National Railway Co. v. Canada (National Transportation Agency)*, [1990] F.C.J. No. 240 (F.C.A.) (12 March 1990).

(a) Canada Labour Code†

DIVISION II
CANADA INDUSTRIAL RELATIONS
BOARD

Establishment and Organization

Establishment of Board

9.(1) A board is established, to be known as the Canada Industrial Relations Board.

Composition of Board

(2) The Board is composed of

(a) a Chairperson, to hold office on a full-time basis;

(b) two or more Vice-Chairpersons, to hold office on a full-time basis, and any other Vice-Chairpersons, to hold office on a part-time basis, that the Governor in Council considers necessary to discharge the responsibilities of the Board;

(c) not more than six other members, of which not more than three represent employees, and of which not more than three represent employers, to hold office on a full-time basis;

(d) any other part-time members, representing, in equal numbers, employees and employers, that the Governor in Council considers necessary to discharge the responsibilities of the Board; and

(e) any other part-time members that the Governor in Council considers necessary to assist the Board in carrying out its functions under Part II.

Appointment of Chairperson and Vice-Chairpersons

10.(1) The Chairperson and Vice-Chairpersons of the Board are to be appointed by the Governor in Council, on the recommendation of the Minister, to hold office during good behaviour for terms not exceeding five years each, subject to removal by the Governor in Council at any time for cause.

Appointment of other members

(2) Subject to subsection (3), the members of the Board other than the Chairperson and the Vice-Chairpersons are to be appointed by the Governor in Council on the recommendation of the Minister after consultation by the Minister with the organizations representative of employees or employers that the Minister considers appropriate, to hold office during good behaviour for terms not exceeding three years each, subject to removal by the Governor in Council at any time for cause.

Exception

(3) The members of the Board appointed pursuant to paragraph 9(2)(e) are to be appointed by the Governor in Council, on the recommendation of the Minister, to hold office during good behaviour for terms not exceeding three years each, subject to removal by the Governor in Council at any time for cause.

·   ·   ·   ·   ·

---

† R.S.C. c. L-1, ss. 111, 116; S.C. 1972, c. 18, s. 1; S.C. 1977–78, c. 27, ss. 37, 38; S.C. 1984, c. 39, s. 23; S.C. 1998, c. 26, s. 2.

Chairperson and Vice-Chairpersons

(5) The Chairperson and Vice-Chairpersons must have experience and expertise in industrial relations.

. . . .

Reappointment

12.(1) A member of the Board is eligible for reappointment on the expiration of any term of office in the same or another capacity.

. . . .

Chief executive officer

12.01(1) The Chairperson is the chief executive officer of the Board and has supervision over and direction of the work of the Board, including

(a) the assignment and reassignment of matters that the Board is seized of to panels;

(b) the composition of panels and the assignment of Vice-Chairpersons to preside over panels;

(c) the determination of the date, time and place of hearings;

(d) the conduct of the work of the Board;

(e) the management of the Board's internal affairs; and

(f) the duties of the staff of the Board.

. . . .

Quorum

(2) For the purposes of subsection (1), five persons, namely, the Chairperson, two Vice-Chairpersons and two other members representing, respectively, employees and employers, constitute a quorum.

Equal representation

(3) At a meeting referred to in subsection (1) at which there is an unequal number of members representing employers and employees, the Chairperson shall designate an equal number of members who are authorized to vote on any matter and who represent employers and employees respectively.

. . . .

Staff

13.1 The employees who are necessary for the proper conduct of the work of the Board are to be appointed in accordance with the *Public Service Employment Act*.

Panels

14.(1) Subject to subsection (3), a panel of not less than three members, at least one of whom is the Chairperson or a Vice-Chairperson, may determine any matter that comes before the Board under this Part.

Equal representation

(2) Where a panel formed under subsection (1) is composed of one or more members representing employees, an equal number of members representing employers must also form part of the panel and *vice versa*.

Exception — single member

(3) The Chairperson or a Vice-Chairperson may alone determine a matter that comes before the Board under this Part with respect to [matters such as uncontested applications and preliminary proceedings, and measures to avoid undue delay].

. . . .

Powers, rights and privileges

(5) A panel has all the powers, rights and privileges that are conferred on the Board by this Part with respect to any matter assigned to the panel under this Part.

. . . .

Decision of panel

14.2(1) A decision made by a majority of the members of a panel or, where there is no majority, by the chairperson of the panel is a decision of the Board.

Time limit

(2) The panel must render its decision and give notice of it to the parties no later than ninety days after the day on which it reserved its decision or within any further period that may be determined by the Chairperson.

Powers and Duties

Regulations

15. The Board may make regulations of general application respecting

(a) the establishment of rules of procedure for its pre-hearing proceedings and hearings;

(a.1) the use of means of telecommunication that permit the parties and the Board or its members to communicate simultaneously for pre-hearing conferences, hearings and Board meetings;

(b) the determination of units appropriate for collective bargaining;

(c) the certification of trade unions as bargaining agents for bargaining units;

(d) the conduct of representation votes;

(e) the specification of the period of time after which the Board may receive an application from a trade union for certification as the bargaining agent for a unit where the Board has refused an application from the trade union for certification in respect of the same or substantially the same unit;

(f) the specification of the period of time after which the Board may receive an application from an employee for revocation of a trade union's certification as the bargaining agent for a unit where the Board has refused an application for revocation in respect of the same unit;

(g) the hearing or determination of any application, complaint, question, dispute or difference that may be made or referred to the Board;

(g.1) an expeditious procedure and matters that may be determined under that procedure;

(h) the forms to be used in respect of any proceeding that may come before the Board;

(i) the time within which and the circumstances under which the Board may exercise its powers under section 18;

(j) any inquiry that the Board may make under subsection 34(2);

(k) the form in which and the period during which evidence and information may be presented to the Board in connection with any proceeding that may come before it;

(l) the specification of the time within which and the parties or persons to whom notices and other documents shall be sent and the circumstances in which such notices or other documents shall be deemed to have been given or received by the Board or any party or person;

(m) the determination of the form in which and the period during which evidence as to

   (i) the membership of any employees in a trade union,

   (ii) any objection by employees to the certification of a trade union, or

   (iii) any signification by employees that they no longer wish to be represented by a trade union

shall be presented to the Board on an application made to it pursuant to this Part;

(n) the criteria for determining whether an employee is a member of a trade union;

(o) the circumstances in which evidence referred to in paragraph (m) may be received by the Board as evidence that any employees wish or do not wish to have a particular trade union represent them as their bargaining agent, including the circumstances in which the evidence so received by the Board may not be made public by the Board;

(o.1) the conditions for valid strike or lockout votes;

(p) the authority of any person to act on behalf of the Board and the matters and things to be done and the action to be taken by that person, including the authority of an employee of the Board to make decisions on uncontested applications or questions; and

(q) such other matters and things as may be incidental or conducive to the proper performance of the duties of the Board under this Part.

General power to assist parties

15.1(1) The Board, or any member or employee of the Board designated by the Board, may, if the parties agree, assist the parties in resolving any issues in dispute at any stage of a proceeding and by any means that the Board considers appropriate, without prejudice to the Board's power to determine issues that have not been settled.

Declaratory Opinions

(2) The Board, on application by an employer or a trade union, may give declaratory opinions.

16. The Board has, in relation to any proceeding before it, power

(a) to summon and enforce the attendance of witnesses and compel them to give oral or written evidence on oath and to produce such documents and things as the Board deems requisite to the full investigation and consideration of any matter within its jurisdiction that is before the Board in the proceeding;

(a.1) to order pre-hearing procedures, including pre-hearing conferences that are held in private, and direct the times, dates and places of the hearings for those procedures;

(a.2) to order that a hearing or a pre-hearing conference be conducted using a means of telecommunication that permits the parties and the Board to communicate with each other simultaneously;

(b) to administer oaths and solemn affirmations;

(c) to receive and accept such evidence and information on oath, affidavit or otherwise as the Board in its discretion sees fit, whether admissible in a court of law or not;

(d) to examine, in accordance with any regulations of the Board, such evidence as is submitted to it respecting the membership of any employees in a trade union seeking certification;

(e) to examine documents forming or relating to the constitution or articles of association of
   (i) a trade union or council of trade unions that is seeking certification, or
   (ii) any trade union forming part of a council of trade unions that is seeking certification;

(f) to make such examination of records and such inquiries as it deems necessary;

(f.1) to compel, at any stage of a proceeding, any person to provide information or produce the documents and things that may be relevant to a matter before it, after providing the parties the opportunity to make representations;

(g) to require an employer to post and keep posted in appropriate places, or to transmit by any electronic means that the Board deems appropriate, any notice that it considers necessary to bring to the attention of any employees any matter relating to the proceeding;

(h) subject to such limitations as the Governor in Council may, in the interests of defence or security, prescribe by regulation, to enter any premises of an employer where work is being or has been done by employees and to inspect and view any work, material, machinery, appliances or articles therein and interrogate any person respecting any matter that is before the Board in the proceeding;

(i) to order, at any time before the proceeding has been finally disposed of by the Board, that
   (i) a representation vote or an additional representation vote be taken among employees affected by the proceeding in any case where the Board considers that the taking of such a vote would assist the Board to decide any question that has arisen or is likely to arise in the proceeding, whether or not such a representation vote is provided for elsewhere in this Part, and
   (ii) the ballots cast in any representation vote ordered by the Board pursuant to subparagraph (i) or any other provision of this Part be sealed in ballot boxes and not counted except as directed by the Board;

(j) to enter on the premises of an employer for the purpose of conducting representation votes during working hours;

(k) to authorize any person to do anything that the Board may do under paragraphs (a) to (h), (j), or (m) and to report to the Board thereon;

(l) to adjourn or postpone the proceeding from time to time;

(l.1) to defer deciding any matter, where the Board considers that the matter could be resolved by arbitration or an alternate method of resolution;

(m) to abridge or extend the time for doing any act, filing any document or presenting any evidence in connection with a proceeding;

(m.1) to extend the time limits set out in this Part for instituting a proceeding;

(n) to amend or permit the amendment of any document filed in connection with the proceeding;

(o) to add a party to the proceeding at any stage of the proceeding; and

(o.1) to summarily refuse to hear, or dismiss, a matter for want of jurisdiction or lack of evidence;

(p) to decide for all purposes of this Part any question that may arise in the proceeding, including, without restricting the generality of the foregoing, any question as to whether
   (i) a person is an employer or an employee,
   (ii) a person performs management functions or is employed in a confidential capacity in matters relating to industrial relations,
   (iii) a person is a member of a trade union,
   (iv) an organization or association is an employers' organization, a trade union or a council of trade unions,
   (v) a group of employees is a unit appropriate for collective bargaining,
   (vi) a collective agreement has been entered into,
   (vii) any person or organization is a party to or bound by a collective agreement, and
   (viii) a collective agreement is in operation.

Determination without oral hearing

16.1 The Board may decide any matter before it without holding an oral hearing.

Determination of the wishes of the majority of the employees

17. Where the Board is required, in connection with any application made under this Part, to determine the wishes of the majority of the employees in a unit, it shall determine those wishes as of the date of the filing of the application or as of such other date as the Board considers appropriate.

Review or amendment of orders

18. The Board may review, rescind, amend, alter or vary any order or decision made by it, and may rehear any application before making an order in respect of the application.

Review of structure of bargaining units

18.1(1) On application by the employer or a bargaining agent, the Board may review the structure of the bargaining units if it is satisfied that the bargaining units are no longer appropriate for collective bargaining.

Agreement of parties

(2) If the Board reviews, pursuant to subsection (1) or section 35 or 45, the structure of the bargaining units, the Board

  (a) must allow the parties to come to an agreement, within a period that the Board considers reasonable, with respect to the determination of bargaining units and any questions arising from the review; and

  (b) may make any orders it considers appropriate to implement any agreement.

Orders

(3) If the Board is of the opinion that the agreement reached by the parties would not lead to the creation of units appropriate for collective bargaining or if the parties do not agree on certain issues within the period that the Board considers reasonable, the Board determines any question that arises and makes any orders it considers appropriate in the circumstances.

Content of orders

(4) For the purposes of subsection (3), the Board may

  (a) determine which trade union shall be the bargaining agent for the employees in each bargaining unit that results from the review;

  (b) amend any certification order or description of a bargaining unit contained in any collective agreement;

  (c) if more than one collective agreement applies to employees in a bargaining unit, decide which collective agreement is in force;

  (d) amend, to the extent that the Board considers necessary, the provisions of collective agreements respecting expiry dates or seniority rights, or amend other such provisions;

  (e) if the conditions of paragraphs 89(1)(a) to (d) have been met with respect to some of the employees in a bargaining unit, decide which terms and conditions of employment apply to those employees until the time that a collective agreement becomes applicable to the unit or the conditions of those paragraphs are met with respect to the unit; and

  (f) authorize a party to a collective agreement to give notice to bargain collectively.

Application of orders

19. Where, under this Part, the Board may make or issue any order or decision, prescribe any term or condition or do any other thing in relation to any person or organization, the Board may do so, either generally or in any particular case or class of cases.

Interim orders

19.1 The Board may, on application by a trade union, an employer or an affected employee, make any interim order that the Board considers appropriate for the purpose of ensuring the fulfilment of the objectives of this Part.

Interim decision

20.(1) Where, in order to dispose finally of an application or complaint, it is necessary for the Board to determine two or more issues arising therefrom, the Board may, if it is satisfied that it can do so without prejudice to the rights of any party to the proceeding, issue a decision resolving only one or some of those issues and reserve its jurisdiction to dispose of the remaining issues.

Decision final

(2) A decision referred to in subsection (1) is, except as stipulated by the Board, final.

Definition of "decision"

(3) In this section, "decision" includes an order, a determination and a declaration.

251

Exercise of powers and duties

21. The Board shall exercise such powers and perform such duties as are conferred or imposed on it by this Part, or as may be incidental to the attainment of the objects of this Part, including, without restricting the generality of the foregoing, the making of orders requiring compliance with the provisions of this Part, with any regulation made under this Part or with any decision made in respect of a matter before the Board.

Review and Enforcement of Orders

Orders not to be reviewed by court

22.(1) Subject to this Part, every order or decision of the Board is final and shall not be questioned or reviewed in any court, except in accordance with the *Federal Court Act* on the grounds referred to in paragraph 18.1(4)(a), (b) or (e) of that Act.

Standing of Board

(1.1) The Board has standing to appear in proceedings referred to in subsection (1) for the purpose of making submissions regarding the standard of review to be used with respect to decisions of the Board and the Board's jurisdiction, policies and procedures.

No review by certiorari, etc.

(2) Except as permitted by subsection (1), no order, decision or proceeding of the Board made or carried on under or purporting to be made or carried on under this Part shall
  (a) be questioned, reviewed, prohibited or restrained, or
  (b) be made the subject of any proceedings in or any process of any court, whether by way of injunction, *certiorari*, prohibition, *quo warranto* or otherwise,

on any ground, including the ground that the order, decision or proceeding is beyond the jurisdiction of the Board to make or carry on or that, in the course of any proceeding, the Board for any reason exceeded or lost its jurisdiction.

Filing of Board's orders in Federal Court

23.(1) The Board shall, on the request in writing of any person or organization affected by any order or decision of the Board, file a copy of the order or decision, exclusive of the reasons therefor, in the Federal Court, unless, in the opinion of the Board,
  (a) there is no indication of failure or likelihood of failure to comply with the order or decision; or
  (b) there is other good reason why the filing of the order or decision in the Federal Court would serve no useful purpose.

· · · ·

Effect of registration of order or decision

(3) When a copy of any order or decision of the Board is registered pursuant to subsection (2), the order or decision has the same force and effect as a judgment obtained in the Federal Court and, subject to this section and the *Federal Court Act*, all proceedings may be taken thereon by any person or organization affected thereby as if the order or decision were a judgment of that Court.

Filing of orders in provincial superior court

23.1 The Board may, on application by a person or organization affected by an order or decision of the Board, file a copy of the order or decision, exclusive of the reasons for it, in the superior court of a province. Section 23 applies, with the modifications that the circumstances require, to an order or decision filed in such a superior court.

(b) Note on Canada Industrial Relations Board†

GENERAL

The Canada Industrial Relations Board (CIRB) is part of the outlying administrative process.[1] It is a regulatory body governed by the *Canada Labour Code*.[2] The CIRB was established on 1 January 1999,[3] in response to the recommendations of the *Sims* task force on the *Code*.[4] On that date, the

---

† For the most current situation and further background material, see <http://www.cirb-ccri.gc.ca/index_e.asp>. See also Selected Readings, Chapter 14, below.

CIRB replaced the Canada Labour Relations Board, which was created in 1948.[5]

The CIRB's main functions are licensing, resolving disputes, and imposing sanctions in regard to federally regulated private undertakings and to some independent government bodies under federal jurisdiction. These functions include:

(a) granting or revoking certification (and determining successor rights, etc.);
(b) resolving complaints of unfair labour practices;
(c) resolving illegal strikes or lockouts; and
(d) hearing referrals from safety officers under Part III of the *Code*.

Unlike the former Canada Labour Relations Board (but like labour relations boards in most of the provinces), the CIRB is a "representational" board. Apart from the Chairperson and two or more Vice-Chairpersons, members are appointed to represent the interests of employees and employers, respectively. There can be up to six full-time representative members, allocated equally to employees and employers. An indefinite number of part-time representative members can be appointed, but the principle of equality of representation must be maintained.

The Chairperson and Vice-Chairpersons are appointed by the Governor in Council, on the recommendation of the Minister. They have tenure during "good behaviour" for up to five years. The full-time representative members are appointed in a similar way (but after the Minister has consulted with the organizations' representative of employees or employers), with the same tenure, but for three-year terms.

The total size of the Board, including both members and staff, is about 70 persons.[6]

The CIRB is very independent of the central administrative process. Its decisions are not subject to Cabinet or Ministerial approval, and it makes its own rules and regulations,[7] free of Cabinet or Ministerial approval requirements. There is no appeal from its decisions to Cabinet or a Minister. The rationale for this extreme independence is the delicate nature of the Board's work.

Unlike its predecessor, the Canada Labour Relations Board, but similar to the Canadian Transportation Agency, the CIRB is required by statute to make its decisions within a stipulated time period. For the CIRB, the deadline for deciding is 90 days.[8]

Like its predecessor, the CIRB has a discretion to make a decision without holding a hearing. The Canada Labour Relations Board tended to consider the following factors in deciding whether to hold an oral hearing:

(i) the importance of the case;
(ii) whether or not there is an unfair labour practice case.

The CIRB tends to limit oral hearings to cases where oral evidence is necessary to help clarify conflicting evidence or to establish credibility.

Under the CLRB, fewer than 20% of cases decided involved hearings. The CLRB developed numerous devices to shorten or reduce hearings: e.g., use of labour relations officers to help resolve differences first; holding partial hearings; and not recording hearings. Where CLRB hearings were held, they took about 1.1 day, on average, per case,[9] but the time varied greatly with the nature of the case and other issues, such as the location and availability of the parties, Board members, and counsel, etc.

In light of the its general 90-day deadline for decision-making, it seems likely that the CIRB will be even more anxious than its predecessor to avoid lengthy oral hearings. As well, the new Board has an express power to defer a decision where it feels an issue could be settled by arbitration or some alternate form of resolution.[10]

Although the CIRB has no separate statutory review committee, the *Code* allows for internal review of its own decisions.[11] Under the CLRB, internal review was regarded as exceptional, and was limited to claims of errors of law, inconsistency of Board policy in interpreting Part I of the *Code*, or new information or evidence that could alter the original decision.[12] Review requests were considered by a special "reconsideration panel," and could be referred to the original panel or to a full Board, depending on the allegation.

The CIRB's decisions cannot be appealed but are subject to limited review by the Federal Court of Appeal.[13] A small proportion of the CLRB's decisions were subject to judicial review, and a smaller proportion of these resulted in a Board decision being overturned.[14]

CLRB participation in Federal Court judicial review proceedings depended on prior authorization from the Court.[15] Accordingly, the CLRB tended to limit requests to participate to cases where it considered it necessary to explain its practice, policy, or jurisprudence.[16] The CIRB has express statutory standing in regard to "the standard of review to be used with respect to decisions of the Board and the Board's jurisdiction, policies and *certiorari*, etc."[17]

253

HEARING STAGES

A full certification hearing before the CLRB generally included the following steps:

1. application for certification (and notice given to interested persons, reply by employer, interventions, etc.);
2. assignment of labour relations officer to assist parties and/or identify scope of bargaining unit;
3. report by labour relations officer: public part sums up records on employment classifications and union membership, and confidential part addresses individual employees' support or lack of support for union;
4. decision by Board on whether to convene a hearing, and refuse certification, either with or without hearing; and
5. (if the decision is yes), informal pre-hearing meeting (to narrow issues and discuss proposed procedure);
6. hearing (a simplified representation: procedure does not necessarily follow this sequence and parties may or may not be represented by legal counsel):
   (a) applicant union gives evidence-in-chief supporting application
   (b) cross-examination of union by employer and intervenors, if any
   (c) clarification (by way of re-examination, if legal counsel present) by union
   (d) similar procedure for evidence from employer
   (e) replies and concluding arguments by union and employer
   (f) questions by board counsel and board members throughout.

Where it does decide to convene a hearing, the new Board has been following the general approach set by its predecessor, at least until its new procedural rules are completed. Certainly labour relations officers are being employed as extensively under the CIRB as under the CLRB.

POSSIBLE ISSUES

(a starting point only: for further important issues, see the Law Reform Commission study and Sims Report sections below)

1. **Constitutional issues:** Generally, as a result of judicial interpretation, the provinces have jurisdiction over labour relations. For federal labour relations jurisdiction, it must be established that the work in question is an integral part of a federal undertaking (see *Canada Labour Relations Board v. Yellowknife*, [1977] 2 S.C.R. 729, 736).

   Beyond this, the CIRB's powers are further limited by federal legislation that limits the Board to the federally regulated private sector. As a result, about 700,000 employees and their employers, including activities in the northern territories, aboriginal institutions on *Indian Act* reserves, and some Crown agencies, are subject to regulation by the Board. How should the Board address this large and complex mandate, and how should it deal with the evolving new constraints under the *Charter*?

2. **Balancing control by central administrative process with independence and impartiality:** Why are there few central controls? Does this minimise political interference or political responsibility?

3. **Need to balance expertise and responsiveness to those regulated vs. need to consider third-party and public interests:** Do the advantages of the move to a representational structure outweigh the disadvantages? What has been gained? Lost? How are more general community concerns accommodated? Is there sufficient accessibility for third parties? Is there adequate publication of important reports?

4. **Response to generally worded mandates:** Has the Board enough discretion to grapple with sensitive and fast-changing situations? On the other hand, what are the safeguards against arbitrary or inconsistent use of discretion?

5. **Balancing fairness and judicial procedure with efficiency:** How did the CLRB approach the following challenges?
   (a) avoiding undue delay;
   (b) disclosure vs. confidentiality re:
      (i) evidence submitted by parties
      (ii) use of staff studies, such as reports of labour relations officers; and
      (iii) information from other sources
   (c) subject matter complexity vs. need for simplicity and uniformity;
   (d) role of board counsel, staff, and use of staff studies and members' personal notes;
   (e) general policy guidelines or rules vs. case by case adjudication;

(f) negotiated settlements between parties: should there be a presumption in favour of agreements reached by the parties?

(g) pre-hearing procedures; etc.

What changes are likely under the CIRB?

6. **Working within judicial framework:** How did decisions of the Federal Court and the Supreme Court of Canada influence the answers to these and other administrative law challenges confronting the CLRB? What is the experience so far under the CIRB?

7. **Compliance: How to secure mechanisms**
   (i) cease and desist orders
   (ii) declaration re illegal strike, lockout, etc.
   (iii) consent to criminal prosecution
   (iv) filing of order with Federal Court (has same effect as if order of the court)
   (v) informal compliance techniques

1980 LAW REFORM COMMISSION STUDY

In 1980, the Law Reform Commission of Canada published a 106-page study paper on the CLRB, written by Stephen Kelleher.[18] Some but not all of the study paper's recommendations were subsequently implemented. They include those on delay, disclosure, frequency of hearings, recording of hearings, restriction of review, representation of Board in review proceedings, Board formulation of policy, and non-representational structure.

1996 SIMS REPORT

In June 1995, the federal minister of labour appointed a task force chaired by Andrew Sims to review Part I of the *Canada Labour Code* and its administration. Sims was the former chair of the Alberta Labour Relations Board and also of the Alberta Public Service Employees Relations Board. In February, 1966, the task force released a report called *Seeking a Balance: Review of Part I of the Canada Labour Code*. The report's 70 recommendations called for wide-ranging changes to federal labour law, including a major re-design of the Canada Labour Relations Board. Among other things, the report recommended:

(a) the establishment of a labour relations board with a representational composition (a neutral chair, and equal numbers of other members representing labour and management);

(b) participation by labour, management, and the chair of the board in the appointment of board members;

(c) a shorter (three- to five-year) term for board members;

(d) special board powers in regard to pre-hearing conferences, production of documents, and other procedural matters;

(e) a variety of procedural recommendations to reduce delay in decision-making and processing of cases; and

(f) legislative confirmation of the board's right to appear as a party in judicial review proceedings.

More general recommendations included:

(a) a streamlining of the collective bargaining process; and

(b) a clarification of the rights and obligations of parties during work stoppages, and a requirement that public health and safety services be maintained during such stoppages.

On 4 November 1996, the Minister of Labour introduced Bill C-66 to make extensive changes to Part I of the *Canada Labour Code*. The Bill would have implemented almost all of the key Sims recommendations. The Bill died on the Order Paper just before third reading in the Senate Paper in April 1997, but was reintroduced on 6 November 1997, as Bill C-19, and enacted as S.C. 1998, c. 26, s. 2.

Compare the Sims recommendations with the concerns of Kelleher. Are there some common concerns? To what extent does the re-structured Canada Industrial Relations Board meet them?

Notes

1. Defined in Chapter 1 as "the part of the executive branch of government that is outside the direct control of a Cabinet minister."
2. *Canada Labour Code*, R.S.C. 1985, c. L-1, ss. 111, 116; S.C. 1972, c. 18, s. 1; S.C. 1977–78, c. 27, ss. 37, 38; S.C. 1984, c. 39, s. 23; S.C. 1998, c. 26, s. 2. as am.
3. Pursuant to amendments to Part I (Industrial Relations) of the *Canada Labour Code*. The amendments were introduced as Bill C-19 on 6 November 1997, received Royal Assent on 17 June 1998, and came into force on 1 January 1999.
4. A. Sims, Chair, *Seeking a Balance: Review of the Canada Labour Code* (Hull, Québec: Public Works and Government Services Canada, 1985).
5. The predecessor of the Canada Labour Relations Board was the Wartime Labour Relations Board, created in 1944 by Order in Council P.C. 1003, 17 February 1944.
6. As of summer, 1999.

7. *Canada Labour Relations Board Regulations*, 1992, SOR/ 91-622.
8. *Code*, s. 14.2(2). A longer deadline can be set by the Chairperson.
9. Source: informal estimate derived after communication with Board officer, summer 1997.
10. *Code*, s. 16(l.1).
11. *Code*, s. 18.
12. CLRB internal review policy was addressed in *Telecommunications Workers Union v. British Columbia Telephone Company* (1979), 38 di. 124; [1980] 1 Can. L.R.B.R. 340 and 80 C.L.L.C. 16008 (CLRB no. 220); and *CanWest Pacific Television Inc. (CKCU) et al. v. NABET* (1981), 84 di 19; and CLRB, *Applications for review*, Information Circular No. 3-92. Source: CLRB.
13. *Code*, s. 22 (1), and *Federal Court Act*, R.S.C. 1985, c. F-7, s. 28(1)(h).

14. As well, the courts were prepared to defer to the Board on matters considered to fall within its area of specialized expertise: *Canadian Broadcasting Corporation v. Canada (Labour Relations Board)*, [1995] 1 S.C.R. 157 (S.C.C.). See, however, the narrow interpretation given to the Board's remedial and procedural powers, respectively, in *Syndical des employés de production du Québec et de l'Acadie v. Canada (Labour Relations Board)*, [1984] 2 S.C.R. 142 (S.C.C.) and *Canadian Pacific Air Lines v. Canadian Air Line Pilots Assn.*, [1993] 3 S.C.R. 724 (S.C.C.).
15. Federal Court Rule 1611.
16. Source: CLRB.
17. *Code*, s. 22(1.1).
18. Stephen Kelleher for Law Reform Commission of Canada, *Canada Labour Relations Board*, 1980.

(c)   Shortening the Hearing: *Eastern Provincial*†

NOTE

Labour relations administrators tend to regard flexibility, informality, and speed as essential for effective regulation of labour disputes. These same goals tend to clash with the higher-level procedural safeguards possible under the rules of natural justice. One of the strongest of these safeguards, the oral hearing, can be lengthy, expensive, and — as the Canada Labour Relations Board discovered in this case — difficult to control.

During a bitter labour dispute between an airline and a pilots' union, the Board conducted a hearing into complaints of unfair labour practices made by both parties. The hearing began in March and then lasted another four days in April. Cross-examination of one witness alone took over nine hours. Finally, the Board attempted to expedite the hearing by closing off further presentation of oral evidence. When the Board later issued its decision favouring the union, the airline sought judicial review. It argued that by closing off further evidence, the Board had deprived the airline of the right to be fully heard on its own behalf, and had breached the rules of natural justice. Compare the majority and dissenting responses to this argument. Which is more persuasive?

EXTRACTS

Canada Labour Code, R.S.C. 1970, c. L-1, ss. 119, 122, 148(*a*), 184, 186, 1878, 188, 189 (all re-enacted 1972, c. 18, s. 1; am. 1977–78, c. 27).

Canadian Charter of Rights and Freedoms, s.1

Federal Court Act, R.S.C. 1970, c. 10 (2nd Supp.), s.28.

APPLICATION for judicial review of a decision of the Canada Labour Relations Board.

.   .   .   .

Roy L. Heenan and *Peter M. Blaikie*, for applicant.

Ian G. Scott, Q.C., for respondent, Canada Labour Relations Board.

John T. Keenan, Lila Stermer and *Luc Marineau*, for respondent, Canadian Air Line Pilots Association.

Eric Durnford, for "New Pilots".

[THURLOW C.J.:]

I have had an opportunity to read and consider the reasons for judgment prepared by Mr. Justice Mahoney. I share his opinion that the evidence establishes that the Canada Labour Relations Board

---

† *Re Eastern Provincial Airways Ltd. and Canada Labour Relations Board et al.* (1984), 2 D.L.R. (4th) 597 (F.C.A.).

failed to observe a principle of natural justice by denying the applicant a fair opportunity to present its case and in particular in reaching conclusions on evidence which the applicant, though ready with witnesses, was not afforded an opportunity to refute. Nor am I persuaded that in the circumstances any inference should be drawn that the applicant's right to call witnesses to refute such evidence was waived.

Moreover, the board's order having been made and having become effective immediately on May 27, 1983, the manoeuvre initiated on July 27, 1983, by the board itself, without the concurrence and over the objections of the applicant, to exercise power under s. 119[1] of the *Canada Labour Code*, R.S.C. 1970, c. L-1, after the applicant had applied to this court for review of the board's order and after the court had given special directions for expediting the proceedings, should I think be viewed as evidence of the board's failure to afford the applicant the opportunity to which it was entitled to present its evidence and as an attempt by the board to alter the situation and forestall the review of its order by the court. Under para. 188(1)(*b*) of the Code, at the stage which the proceedings had reached in the latter part of April, it was the duty of the board "to hear and determine" the complaints before it. The applicant was entitled to a fair hearing of its case on the complaints before the matter was decided. It was no substitute to offer the applicant afterwards an opportunity to dispel, if it could, conclusions already reached and cogently expressed by the board.

. . . .

I would dispose of the matter as proposed by Mr. Justice Mahoney.

[MAHONEY J.:]

In the course of a legal strike against the applicant, Eastern Provincial Airways Limited, hereafter "EPA", by its pilots, their certified bargaining agent, the respondent, the Canadian Air Line Pilots Association, hereafter "CALPA", made three complaints of unfair labour practices against EPA and EPA countered with two complaints against CALPA. CALPA's complaints alleged EPA's failure to bargain in good faith contrary to s. 148(*a*) of the *Canada Labour Code*, R.S.C. 1970, c. L-1 (as amended by 1972, c. 18 and 1977–78, c. 27); interference in the administration of a trade union contrary to s. 184(1)(*a*) and discriminating against, intimidating and threatening striking employees contrary to s. 184(3)(*a*)(v). EPA's complaints alleged CALPA's failure to bargain in

good faith contrary to s. 148(*a*) and intimidation and coercion to compel persons to join and quit the union contrary to s. 186. The conduct of the hearing on those complaints by the respondent, Canada Labour Relations Board, hereafter "the Board", and the orders ensuing upon the hearing are subject of this s. 28 application. EPA alleges that it was denied natural justice in the course of the proceeding and that the Board was without jurisdiction to make the orders it did.

The Board sat on March 28 and 29, 1983. It adjourned at the request of the parties. The hearing was resumed at the request of CALPA. It continued on April 18th, 19th, 20th and 21st. No verbatim transcript of the proceeding was kept. We have the documentary evidence received by the Board but, as to what transpired at the hearings, we have only the affidavit evidence submitted by EPA and CALPA. The undated and unverified "public hearing reports" (Case, pp. 602 and 609 ff.), prepared in circumstances unknown to the court, are of no evidentiary value. CALPA tendered the affidavit of Ronald Young. He was cross-examined on it. EPA tendered the affidavits of Ralph D. Farley (Case, pp. 710–7), Danny J. Kaufer (pp. 718–20), Genevieve Payne (pp. 721–2), William J. Verrier (pp. 723–7), Chester Walker (pp. 728–33), Eero O. Lahtinen (pp. 734–7), Kevin C. Howlett (pp. 738–40) and Peter D. Chalmers (pp. 741–2). Farley and Kaufer were cross-examined. The Board's decision was rendered and order made May 27th (pp. 615–707). It dismissed EPA's complaints and upheld CALPA's. This s. 28 application was filed June 1st. On June 29th, the court made an order of directions scheduling proceedings with a view to hearing this application as soon as possible after August 15th. On July 26th, after affidavits as to what had occurred at its hearings had been filed in this court and their deponents cross-examined thereon, the Board called the parties to a rehearing of the complaints pursuant to s. 119 of the Code. EPA attended but declined to participate in the rehearing. CALPA filed, *inter alia*, a copy of the case prepared for this application including EPA's affidavits. The proceeding, which resulted in no change to the order, was held August 2nd and 3rd. It was transcribed verbatim by the Board. On application by the Board, the record of the proceeding was added to the case at the hearing of this application.

The violations of the principles of natural justice alleged by EPA are, briefly, as follows:

1. The Board heard EPA argue only an inscription in law in respect of the CALPA com-

plaints yet it decided, on their merits, all five complaints.

2. The Board did not permit EPA to complete its evidence on CALPA's complaint under s. 184(1)(*a*) and, except to the extent that the evidence as to that complaint pertained to them, had no evidence at all as to the other four.

. . . .

As to the April sittings, Kaufer, one of EPA's counsel, deposes, with respect to Louis Vachon, a secretary employed by EPA, that the chairman "informed the parties that any notes taken by Vachon could not ever be used in any court" and, after noticing that Vachon was using a tape recorder to assist her, the Chairman called counsel to the bench and stated:

> ... that he had ruled in St. John's that no stenography or recording of the hearing would be allowed, and that he was directing the parties to stop any recording of the proceedings.

That all transpired during the first hour of the sitting of April 18. I am satisfied that the Board prevented EPA from making a verbatim record of the proceedings by any practical means whatsoever.

The Board's policy *vis à vis* the recording of its proceedings was explained at length in *Canadian Merchant Service Guild and Canadian Pacific Ltd.*, [1980] 3 Can. L.R.B.R. 87 at p. 91ff. The reason for the policy change appears to have been twofold. A verbatim record was, in its view, unnecessary once its decisions were no longer subject to judicial review on the grounds of error in law or perverse error in finding facts. For numerous reasons, verbatim transcription was seen as inhibiting the Board in its fulfilment of its mission as "a forum for labour relations principals — employees, employers and unions — not a court or forum for lawyers". It is to be remarked that the Board conducts many sorts of hearings, not just the sort in issue here. The rationale of the policy may be more plausible when applied to some sorts than to others.

It is a fair conclusion to be drawn from its reasons that the Board had determined that it could do its job better if those before it were discouraged from recourse to the court. Parliament had already agreed. It had limited the grounds of judicial review to denial of natural justice and issues of jurisdiction. The Board, at p. 148 of the report, continued:

> For the same reasons we have decided not to allow one party to have recording facilities at a

hearing. To do so will reintroduce, on a selected basis, that atmosphere we seek to eliminate by discontinuing recording and act contrary to the purposes we seek to achieve. Although we see and our experience has shown us little advantage during the conduct of the hearing a recording may be of some advantage afterward. Otherwise why would a party want it? That advantage could be in written propaganda surrounding a dispute, or to play edited versions of the proceedings on radio or television, or to prepare future witnesses where there has been an exclusion of witnesses or adjournment, or for other reasons within the imagination of parties. The Board will not allow its proceedings and mediative efforts to be open to this potential for compromise.

An obvious reason a party might want a record, not mentioned, is to facilitate pursuit of its remaining right to judicial review.

A verbatim record would unquestionably have made easier the fulfilment by this court of its duty. However, the refusal to permit EPA to make a verbatim record was not, *per se*, a denial of natural justice even though intended, *inter alia*, to make more difficult the pursuit of its remedy in this court. Applicable as it was to both parties in this dispute, indeed to all parties in all disputes generally, implementation of the policy cannot be found to have been procedurally unfair to EPA. The refusal does, however, expose the Board to having issues of natural justice determined on evidence as to what happened led by the parties, while it cannot, itself, be heard on the subject unless it elects to file affidavits and offer their deponents for cross-examination.

I turn now to the alleged denials of natural justice numbered 1 and 2. There are undisputed facts as to the conduct of the resumed hearing April 18th to 21st.

a. At its outset, April 18th, EPA raised an inscription in law and CALPA asked to have the evidence apply, as relevant to all five complaints.

b. Rulings on both evidence and argument on the inscription were deferred and the Board proceeded to receive evidence on the CALPA complaint under s. 184(1)(*a*).

c. CALPA completed its evidence on that complaint late in the afternoon of April 19th.

d. The evidence of one EPA witness was completed April 20th. The second EPA witness, CALPA's president who had been called by *subpoena duces tecum*, was unable to identify certain documents and his testimony was suspended. A third EPA witness had been testifying about 20 minutes when the hearing adjourned for the day.

e. When the hearing reconvened at 9:00 a.m., April 21st, the third EPA witness resumed the stand but had not begun to testify when the public hearing was suspended and the Board called counsel to an *in camera* meeting.

f. When the public hearing resumed, after 11:00 a.m.,

    i. the parties submitted and the Board received, or made provision to submit and receive, all the remaining documentary evidence by agreement;

    ii. the Board ruled that it would accept the evidence theretofore received in respect of the one complaint as evidence in the other four;

    iii. the Board announced that it would hear argument after the lunch recess and then recessed for lunch. Argument on inscription in law was specifically mentioned by the Chairman, who explained the concept.

g. There were, at the recess, EPA witnesses, including the witness in the box, present and available to testify. (It appears that the need to resume examination of CALPA's president had been obviated by the agreement on documentary evidence.)

h. After lunch, EPA's counsel argued first.

i. After hearing argument in the afternoon, the Board recessed.

j. Following the recess, April 21st, the Board did not resume the public hearings nor receive further evidence from the parties, except the documents as had been agreed, nor receive further argument prior to rendering its decision on the merits of all five complaints.

What is disputed is whether EPA was denied opportunities (1) to complete its evidence on CALPA's s. 184(1)(*a*) complaint; (2) to present evidence at all, beyond the common evidence, on the remaining complaints, including its own, and (3) to argue anything but the inscription in law.

. . . .

Farley's affidavit and the cross-examination thereon is the only evidence as to the *in camera* meeting. The cross-examination (pp. 8, 10 to 9, 6) and re-examination ([pp.] 20, 3 to 22, 23) do not modify the evidence of his affidavit (Case, p. 713 ff., paras. 16 to 36). After dealing with the documents and the application of the evidence received to all complaints, the affidavit continues:

22. That Mr. Lapointe then declared that the Board had the power to decide when they had heard enough proof to order the parties to argue;

23. That Mr. Heenan of Counsel of Applicant, indicated his disagreement with the declaration that the Board had the power to order argument at any time;

24. That Mr. Marc Lapointe stated that the Board intended to finish all five complaints by that evening;

25. That Mr. Heenan of Counsel of Applicant stated that that would be impossible;

Then, after describing the exchange between Heenan and the chairman, the affidavit concluded, as to the meeting, with:

35. That immediately following this statement by Mr. Heenan, Mr. Lapointe stated that the Board was directing the parties to produce what documents they could by consent, and that he was directing them to argue immediately after lunch;

36. That at no time during this meeting did the Board ask Counsel for Applicant to declare their client's defense closed or to waive their client's defense or even to seek instructions from their client to close or waive its defense, nor did counsel do so;

EPA ought to have been in no doubt after the *in camera* meeting that it was expected to argue the merits, not just the inscription in law. The absence from Farley's affidavit of an explicit statement that EPA argued only the inscription and not the merits, a distinction he would clearly have appreciated, is conspicuous, and the inference to be drawn obvious. Considering also Young's detailed list of the subjects covered by EPA in argument, I am entirely satisfied that EPA did argue the merits and that there is no basis in fact for the allegation of denial of natural justice, No. 1.

It is also clear that the Board, at the *in camera* meeting, indicated in no uncertain terms its intention to receive no further evidence than the documents. Accordingly, no inference is to be drawn from the failure of EPA to express its objection when the public hearing resumed. The objection had been emphatically, if unsuccessfully, taken while the Board sat *in camera*. Farley's affidavit, para. 10, also establishes that the Board did disallow questions, while receiving *viva voce* evidence on the complaint under s. 184(1)(*a*), on the grounds that they were not relevant to that complaint.

. . . .

Steele [Mr. Harry Steele, the president of E.P.A., whose comments were found by the Board to be an unfair labour practice] was present April 21st and EPA intended to call him (Case, p. 735). While the Board's decision is not subject to review on the basis of its findings of fact, those findings are to be considered in the context of whether EPA was denied natural justice by being denied a fair opportunity to make out its own case and to answer CALPA's.

The nature of the arrangement made by EPA with the replacement pilots was a central issue before the Board. It is the uncontroverted evidence of Kevin C. Howlett, EPA's director of employee relations, that the Board's findings of fact on that issue are dead wrong and that he was present and was intended to testify. Similarly, the provision of the back-to-work agreement proposed by EPA, identified by the Board as an unfair labour practice, was to have been addressed by Captain Walker. He was the witness in the box when the Board decided it had heard enough. Whether its decision would have been different had it heard the evidence referred to in, for example, para. 23 of his affidavit (Case, p. 731) is not our concern. That it hear it is. The paragraph states:

> 23. That at the time of the decision of the Board, none of the pilots still on strike were qualified to fly, all of whom have to be requalified after ground school, simulator training, aircraft training and flying under supervision, some of this being conducted under Ministry of Transport supervision, and taking about a week.

Nothing in the case leads me to suspect that the proposed evidence of either Howlett or Walker was repetitious or otherwise abusive of the Board's process.

The instances recited are examples. There are others to be found.

I conclude that the alleged denial of natural justice, No. 2, is well founded. It is evident from the Board's own decision that, on points it considered significant, EPA was denied a fair opportunity to make out its own case and to answer CALPA's case by the refusal of the Board to receive evidence. It is also evident that EPA was, by the same refusal, denied the opportunity to lead evidence on subjects which the Board specifically found to have been unfair labour practices.

CALPA argues that, even if a denial of natural justice is found, the action taken by the Board to review the decision under s. 119 either cured the defect or estopped EPA from complaining of it or both. The section provides:

> 119. The Board may review, rescind, amend, alter or vary any order or decision made by it, and may rehear any application before making an order in respect of the application.

That provision was considered by this Court in an unreported decision (*St. Lawrence Seaway Authority et al.* v. *Canada Labour Relations Board et al.*, File A-102-79, decision rendered November 5, 1979 [now reported 31 N.R. 196]) where it was said [at pp. 201–1], by way of *obiter dicta*, that (translation):

> It is quite true that this provision confers on the Board the extraordinary power of reviewing its own decision. In exercising this power, the Board may correct its decisions, especially those which it may have made in disregard of the rules of natural justice; but the mere existence of this power does not have the effect of validating these decisions and of placing them beyond the power of review of the court under s. 28(1)(*a*) of the *Federal Court Act*.

Here, the Board did not correct its decision; it offered to review it and gave the parties the opportunity to make representations and call evidence to that end. That offer, at the stage of the proceedings in this s. 28 application it was made, did not have the effect of validating the decision nor estopping EPA from pursuing its right to its judicial review any more than did the mere existence of the Board's power to review. The correction of a decision with a view to obviating a denial of natural justice may prove difficult in practice once the Board has communicated it. A s. 28 application must, by s. 28(2), have been filed within 10 days of the Board's first communication of its decision to the aggrieved party and the court is, by s. 20(5), required to dispose of it expeditiously. While the Board's [rescission] of a decision might render a s. 28 application moot, an offer to review the decision does not.

I see no alternative but to quash the decision entirely notwithstanding the considerable investment of the Board and parties in the proceedings.

The decision runs to just over 94 typed foolscap pages. It is eloquent and, in places, impassioned. In view of the vehemence with which the decision has been expressed, it would be most unwise for the same members of the Board to undertake any rehearing of the complaints and I would direct that the panel rehearing them not include any of those members.

[COWAN D.J. (dissenting):]

I have read the reasons for judgment of Mahoney J., and agree with his reasoning on the points raised on behalf of the applicant, EPA, with the exception of those relating to the alleged action in excess of jurisdiction on the part of the Board and to the alleged failure of the Board to observe a principle of natural justice.

. . . .

With regard to the allegation that the Board failed to observe a principle of natural justice it is submitted that EPA was denied the opportunity to complete its evidence on the CALPA complaint under s. 184(1)(*a*) and to present any evidence at all, beyond the common evidence, on the remaining complaints, including its own.

The hearing before the Board began on the morning of April 18, 1983, and three days had been scheduled for completion of the hearing of evidence and the argument on behalf of the parties, CALPA and EPA. On April 19th and 20th the hearing continued until late in the evening and, on the evening of April 20th, the chairman of the Board stated that the Board would finish the hearing by the end of the day on April 21st, an additional fourth day having been scheduled. All CALPA's witnesses had been heard with respect to the first complaint of CALPA and three witnesses had been called on behalf of EPA, the last of whom had been giving evidence for approximately twenty minutes when the hearing adjourned at 10:40 p.m. on April 20th.

Captain Lacey, one of the CALPA witnesses, had been cross-examined by EPA counsel for nine hours. On at least one occasion the chairman reminded EPA counsel that some of the questions were repetitious and on a number of occasions he mentioned the limitations of time set by the Board. When the hearing reconvened on April 21st at 9 a.m., there was a discussion about exhibits and the Board held an *in camera* meeting with counsel. The proceedings at that meeting are described in the affidavit of Farley and in his cross-examination on that affidavit. There is no other record of what happened at that meeting and it must be accepted that the chairman stated that the Board had the power to decide when it had heard enough proof to order the parties to argue; that the Board intended to finish

all five complaints by that evening; that EPA counsel stated that this would be impossible; that the chairman stated that the Board was directing the parties to produce what documents they could by consent and that he was directing them to argue immediately after lunch, and that at no time during that meeting, or during the public hearing, did the Board ask EPA counsel to declare his client's case closed.

The parties then met and agreed to the admission in evidence as exhibits of a considerable number of documents. The Board reconvened the public hearing after 11 a.m. and it is clear that all available documentary evidence with respect to all complaints was then placed before the Board by the parties. The Board stated that it would accept the evidence already given in respect of the first CALPA complaint as evidence in the other four complaints and that it would hear argument after the lunch recess which then took place.

. . . .

It is to be noted that EPA did not, at the resumption of the public hearing, object to the action of the Board in closing off the taking of further oral evidence. Counsel for EPA had objected at the *in camera* meeting and stated that he had further witnesses to be called, but he did not repeat that objection at the public hearing. I would have expected him to object and ask that his objection be noted by the Board for the record if he did not, in fact, agree that all necessary evidence, documentary and oral, was before the Board with respect to all the complaints after the parties had produced the additional exhibits following the morning recess. The person who prepared the hearing report ... was, apparently, careful to note a number of objections made from time to time by counsel.

There is no affidavit from Mr. Harry Steele, president of EPA, setting out in detail the kind of evidence he would have given if called to give evidence or denying the making of statements attributed to him in the documents produced and in the oral evidence given before the Board.

. . . .

Having regard to the whole of the evidence I am not convinced that EPA was not given a fair hearing and an adequate opportunity to present its case before the Board, or that the Board failed to observe a principle of natural justice.

After the filing of the s. 28 application the Board invited the parties to appear before the Board and take part in a review by the Board of its May 27, 1983 decision and order including the submission of any relevant additional evidence or argument. CALPA appeared and offered no additional pertinent evidence and EPA appeared as a matter of courtesy to the Board but declined to adduce any additional evidence or argument on the ground that since judicial review proceedings had been taken by it EPA objected to a reopening of the hearing.

It seems clear that the existence of the power in the Board under s. 119 of the code to review its own decision does not have the effect of validating that decision or of placing that decision beyond the power of review of the court under s. 28(1)(*a*) of the *Federal Court Act*, R.S.C. 1970, c. 10 (2nd Supp.). In my view, however, the fact that the applicant, EPA, is complaining that the Board did not, in April, 1983, afford it the opportunity of presenting all the evidence it had available to it, that the Board offered a

rehearing on August 2 and 3, 1983, in order that any relevant additional evidence might be adduced by the parties, and that EPA refused to participate in that rehearing and to adduce additional evidence, lends support to the conclusion that on April 21, 1983 it really did not have any relevant additional evidence to adduce before the Board and was content to rely upon what it thought was the weakness in law of CALPA's case and the absence of power in the Board to grant the kind of relief sought by CALPA, whatever the state of the evidence might be.

For the foregoing reasons I would dismiss the s. 28(1)(*a*) application of EPA.

Application granted.

Note

1. The Board may review, rescind, amend, alter or vary any order or decision made by it, and may rehear any application before making an order in respect of the application.

(d) *Canadian Pacific*†

NOTE

A pilots' union asked the Canadian Labour Relations Board to declare that there had been a change in Canadian Pacific's status as an employer or its business. In a pre-hearing investigation, the Board asked Canadian Pacific informally to produce certain documents and information. Canadian Pacific refused. Relying on its general powers under s. 118(a) 121 of the *Canada Labour Code*, R.S.C. 1970, c. L-1, the Board ordered the production of the material requested. Canadian Pacific challenged the order, claiming that the Board's disclosure powers were limited to oral hearings, where parties could object effectively to the disclosure requested.

Although the case focused on the construction of specific legislative provisions, the majority decision suggested a general reluctance to construe broadly a tribunal's powers to compel disclosure, and a preference for the protections afforded in oral hearings. What do you think of this approach? Should a tribunal's disclosure powers vary accord-

ing to whether it seeks business or personal information? What is the likely effect of this decision on the formality of tribunal proceedings? Compare the majority approach and the dissenting reasons of L'Heureux-Dubé J.

Section 16(f.1) of the amended *Canada Labour Code* gives the Canada Labour Relations Board's successor, the Canada Industrial Relations Board, explicit power "to compel, at any stage of a proceeding, any person to provide information or produce the documents and things that may be relevant to a matter before it, after providing the parties the opportunity to make representations."

EXTRACTS

[GONTHIER J. for himself, LAMER C.J., and La FOREST and IACOBUCCI JJ.:]

[para1] This case raises the issue of whether the appellant, the Canada Labour Relations Board (the "Board"), may act to compel parties, interveners or

---

† *Canadian Pacific Air Lines Ltd. v. Canadian Air Line Pilots Assn.*, [1993] 3 S.C.R. 724 (21 October 1993), aff'g. (1989), 95 N.R. 255, 59 D.L.R. (4th) 384 (F.C.A.), setting aside a decision of the Canada Labour Relations Board.

interested persons to produce documents prior to and outside of the context of a formal hearing held by the Board.

. . . .

[para5] The following two questions are now before this Court:

1. May the Board, for the purposes of its inquiry into the matters raised by the Association, act pursuant to s. 118(a) of the *Code* to require the production of documents and written testimony other than in a hearing *viva voce*?
2. Alternatively, did the Board act outside its jurisdiction when it founded its order on s. 121 of the *Code*?

IV — Relevant Legislative Provisions

[para6] The *Canada Labour Code* provides as follows:

118. The Board has, in relation to any proceeding before it, power
(a) to summon and enforce the attendance of witnesses and compel them to give oral or written evidence on oath and to produce such documents and things as the Board deems requisite to the full investigation and consideration of any matter within its jurisdiction that is before the Board in the proceeding;

. . . .

(f) to make such examination of records and such inquiries as it deems necessary;

. . . .

121. The Board shall exercise such powers and perform such duties as are conferred or imposed upon it by, or as may be incidental to the attainment of the objects of this Part including, without restricting the generality of the foregoing, the making of orders requiring compliance with the provisions of this Part, with any regulation made under this Part or with any decision made in respect of a matter before the Board.

. . . .

VI — Conclusions

[para29] The extent of the power granted by s. 118(a) of the *Code* appears from the plain mean-

ing of the words of the provision. The Board may exercise its power to compel the production of documents only in the context of a formal hearing. This conclusion is supported also by the fact that the nature of the power is coercive, and that the limits on its exercise must be respected. The fact that the power is also judicial in character makes extension of its application to an administrative context, one which would require clear words to that effect. The structure of the provision makes the power to compel the production of documents a part of a complete process which is limited to a formal hearing to which witnesses may be summoned and where they may give evidence on oath. The scope of s. 118(a) cannot be enlarged by means of reference to s. 118(f), which is permissive in nature. Similarly, the presence of broader provisions cannot here operate to allow the special limits imposed on powers such as this to be disregarded. As there is no basis for the conclusion that such a confinement of the power would be inconsistent with the purposes of the Board, when its administrative and judicial functions are considered, the power which is conferred on the Board by s. 118(a) is a power to require witnesses to attend a proceeding before the Board and there to give oral or written testimony and produce documents deemed requisite. In these circumstances, the powers conferred on the Board by ss. 118(a) and 121 do not include a power to compel the production of documents outside the context of a formal hearing.

. . . .

[para30] As the respondents declined taking any part in this appeal, whereupon an *amicus curiae* was appointed by the Court and costs have not been requested, no order for costs will be made.

VII — Disposition

[para31] The appeal is, therefore, dismissed.

[L'HEUREUX-DUBÉ J., dissenting:]

. . . .

[para32] I have had the advantage of reading my colleague Gonthier J.'s reasons and, with all due respect, I do not share his views. For reasons which follow, I consider that, when the Canada Labour Relations Board directs that written testimony and documents be filed pursuant to s. 118(a) of the *Canada Labour Code*, R.S.C. 1970, c. L-1 (now s. 16 of

R.S.C., 1985, c. L-2), the exercise of that power is not subject to any duty to hold a *viva voce* hearing.

. . . .

[para59] First, there is no question in my mind that the intent of Parliament was to give the Board complete control over its own procedure. Accordingly, it is not contested that neither the *Code* nor the Regulations adopted thereunder impose on the Board any duty to hold a *viva voce* hearing....

. . . .

[para61] Finally, the principle that the Board has complete control over its own procedure is especially important in connection with the inquiries which its function mandates it to conduct. In matters concerning the acquisition and protection of bargaining rights, the Board's function enables it to intervene in ways which, in view of the complex nature of labour relations and industrial relations, must be both flexible and effective....

. . . .

[para62] In my view, unduly emphasizing the classification, judicial or quasi-judicial, of the power conferred by s. 118(a), as both the Court of Appeal and my colleague have, runs the risk of masking this special dimension of the Board's function and, in so doing, of bypassing the particular nature of its role....

. . . .

[para70] Moreover, so far as I know, of all the enabling legislation for bodies performing administrative and quasi-judicial functions, only the *Canadian Human Rights Act*, R.S.C., 1985, c. H-6, confers a power to compel the appearance of witnesses and filing of documents in language similar to s. 118(a) of the *Code*. Section 50(2) of that Act provides, however, that this power is conferred on the tribunal in relation to a hearing....

. . . .

[para76] ... [T]he mere fact of requiring written testimony and the filing of documents does not imply that a party is *ipso facto* deprived of its right to, for example, submit its objections as to the admissibility and relevance of the testimony and documents. In the case of privileged documents, there is nothing to

prevent the person required to produce them from asserting his or her rights and asking the Board to make a decision thereon, expressly identifying the documents affected and the rights relied on before forwarding them to the Board.

[para77] Second, a person affected by an order to file documents and written testimony is not without means of indicating his or her reluctance to comply. To provide protection for the rights of parties concerned in a proceeding before the Board, there is an internal procedure (the Board's power to review, rescind, amend, alter or vary its own decisions, mentioned in s. 119) and an external procedure (the Federal Court of Appeal's power of judicial review, mentioned in s. 122) to review decisions and orders of the Board.... In these circumstances, I cannot see how the procedural guarantees of the parties affected are compromised by the absence of a *viva voce* hearing as such.

[para78] Finally, it would seem illogical for Parliament, on the one hand, to intend that the Board should have complete control of its procedure, and, on the other, to impose upon it a duty to hold a *viva voce* hearing, solely in order to obtain relevant information or documents that a party refuses to provide voluntarily. This would appear to be especially illogical as the Board has the right to render its decisions on the merits without any formal hearing. Such an interpretation would establish an absolute right to a *viva voce* hearing. Rather than simply a parenthesis in the procedure of inquiry and decision, this result would deprive the Board of complete control of its procedure and place it at the mercy of the parties, who would then have an ideal means of delaying or indeed paralysing the entire decision-making process....

. . . .

IV — Conclusion

[para85] For all these reasons, I conclude that the Board did not err in interpreting s. 118(a) of the *Code*.... Since, in my view, the exercise of the power to order the filing of written testimony and documents is not subject to any duty to hold a *viva voce* hearing, I would allow the appeal, set aside the judgment of the Federal Court of Appeal and dismiss the applications for judicial review filed pursuant to s. 28(1)(a) of the Federal Court Act, the whole with costs in all courts.

13   Research and Study

(a)   Thirteen Suggestions for Preparing a Good Research Paper in Law

1. **Start early**
   A good research paper won't materialize overnight.

2. **Focus on a specific legal problem or on a set of legal problems**

3. **Use primary as well as secondary sources**
   Secondary sources are most useful at the beginning and end of research — at the beginning to help point to general problem areas, and at the end to provide comparisons with your own analysis of the primary sources.

4. **Ensure that you have the most current statements of the law that exist**
   Has that important decision been reversed on appeal or distinguished in a more recent case? Has the troublesome statutory provision been amended in the past year or two?

5. **Be thorough**
   Investigate all sources, issues, and arguments that might possibly be relevant.

6. **Develop a logical structure**
   One structural outline that is often workable is as follows:
   (a) statement of problem (or posing of question);
   (b) statement of law;
   (c) assessment of problem (or question), including reference to policy and other non-legal considerations; and
   (d) statement of conclusions (including, where appropriate, general implications and suggested reforms).
   The law stated, the assessment made, and the conclusions reached must all be clearly and directly related to the particular problem stated or question posed. In terms of scope, a logical — although not essential — progression for a research paper is from the general to the particular, and then back to the general in the conclusions and implications.

7. **Be analytical**
   Do more than describe. Compare and contrast; assess; weigh pros and cons; argue points; use concrete examples; consider practical implications; draw conclusions; and where possible, prescribe possible reforms.

8. **Be original**
   Evaluate sources and draw conclusions independently; when you agree or disagree with other writers, show why; when referring to ideas or arguments of other writers, always err on the generous side in giving full credit for the authorship of the material referred to; instead of just assembling the thoughts of other writers, try to add something new to academic knowledge and understanding of the topic.

9. **Be accurate**
   Legal writing is an exact art, no matter how complex or uncertain its subject matter; ensure that the law is stated correctly — and grammatically.

10. **Use correct legal form**
    Case and statute references, citations, footnotes, and bibliography must be accurate and in proper legal form.

11. **Get the maximum benefit from drafts**
    Make drafts of the proposed outline of the paper, especially in the early stages of work; don't write and re-write the entire text four

times if what is really needed is drafting and re-drafting one or two specific sections; everything in the final draft, though, should have been written at least once before.

12. **Be concise**

   A good research paper has something in common with an iceberg: the visible (written) part is compact in comparison with the invisible (investigation and organization) part that lies beneath the surface.

13. **Be clear**

   Ensure that your ideas are clear, and then do them full justice in a style that is smooth, concise, and direct.

(b)   Note on Legal Citations

The standard guide to Canadian Legal Citation is the McGill Law Journal's *Canadian Guide to Uniform Legal Citation*, 5th ed. (Scarborough: Carswell, 2002). Chapter 7 of the Guide contains a new section on citing electronic media. The *Guide* should be consulted at all times; the note below is just an introduction.

For law reports, a typical legal citation consists of a title that is underlined or in italics, followed by the date, followed by the volume number (if any), and the abbreviation and the initial page number of the report referred to. When pinpointing a particular paragraph (preferably, if paragraph numbers are available) or page, use ", at 334" or ", at para. 44" after the initial page reference. Reporters that are organized according to year of publication generally use brackets around the year, preceded by a comma. The abbreviation of the jurisdiction and court normally comes at the end of the citation. Reporters that are organized according to volume number generally use parentheses around the year, followed by a comma. Two examples are as follows:

   Smith v. Jones, [1984] 1 S.C.R. 346.

   Smith v. Jones (1984), 1 D.L.R. (4th) 346 (S.C.C.).

(Where the jurisdiction and court are not apparent from the report, this should be indicated in parentheses at the end of the citation. Hence the "(S.C.C.)" in the second example above.)

Law reporters may be either official, semi-official, or unofficial; either multi-jurisdictional or uni-jurisdictional; and either general or topical. Some of the main Canadian reporters are the *Supreme Court Reports* ("S.C.R.": official), *Federal Court Reports* ("F.C.R.": official), *Ontario Reports* ("O.R.": semi-official), *Western Weekly Reports* ("W.W.R.": unofficial, multi-jurisdictional); *Receuils de jurispru-*

dence du Québec ("R.J.Q.": semi-official); *Dominion Law Reports* ("D.L.R.": unofficial, multi-jurisdictional); *Canadian Criminal Cases* ("C.C.C.": unofficial, multi-jurisdictional, topical); *Administrative Law Reports* ("Admin. L.R.": unofficial, multi-jurisdictional, topical). Where possible, more official reporters should be used in preference to those that are less official, and where more than one is cited, the more official reporters should be cited first. Cases (and other legal sources) may also be reported in electronic data base services, such as QUICKLAW, LEXIS-NEXUS WESTLAW (U.S. and some Canadian materials), and eCARSWELL, or on the Internet. If a case citation is available on paper, the electronic data base citation (in abbreviated form) and the Internet URL address can follow it. If a case citation is unavailable on paper, the electronic data base citation (in full form) and/or the Internet URL address should be provided.

   If available in paper:

   Smith v. Jones, [1984] 1 S.C.R. 346, online: QL (SCJ) <http://taxnet.carswell.com>.

   If unavailable in paper:

   Smith v. Jones, [1984] 1 SCJ No. 22, online: QL (SCJ) <http://taxnet.carswell.com>.

(Note that the Internet World Wide Web address is indicated inside angled brackets.)

For legislation, a typical legal citation consists of a short title that is underlined or in italics, followed by a comma, then the abbreviation of the revised statutes (if available) or statute volume, and, lastly, by the chapter number and section or section abbreviation. An example:

   Access to Information Act, R.S.C. 1985, c. A-1, s. 22.

Some special constitutional legislation:

Constitution Act, 1867 (U.K.), 30 & 31 Vict., c. 3, reprinted in R.S.C. 1985, App. II, No. 5.

Canada Act 1982 (U.K.), 1982, c. 11.

Constitution Act, 1867 (U.K.), being Schedule B to the *Canada Act 1982* (U.K.), 1982, c. 11.

Canadian Charter of Rights and Freedoms, Part 1 of the *Constitution Act, 1867* (U.K.), being Schedule B to the *Canada Act 1982* (U.K.), 1982, c. II

As with case reports, online and Internet citations follow paper citations.

(c) Recommendations on Agencies[†]

Law Reform Commission of Canada

Independent administrative agencies will continue to exist and to be selected from time to time as a model for particular administrative purposes. We view it as our role, then, to recommend guidelines that will serve to assist Parliament and Government to choose an appropriate framework for conferring statutory decision-making authority upon these agencies. Accordingly, we recommend that:

1. The accountability that agencies owe to Parliament should, in the normal course, be rendered directly to Parliament through its committee structure, not through the executive.

2. The constituent and enabling Acts relating to an independent administrative agency should define its broad objectives as clearly and in as plain and as unambiguous language as possible. However, they should not normally attempt to spell out the detailed policies required to implement these objectives. The dynamic nature of administration frequently requires that policy making be further structured within a subordinate legislative process as well as with the agency's own rule-making and decision-making processes.

3. Parliamentary assent is essential where the goal is not merely to clarify how the agency pursues legislative objectives, but to redefine its role and duties. Consequently, parliamentary approval should be required through an affirmative resolution procedure whenever the authority provided for by the *Public Service Rearrangement and Transfer of Duties Act* is used.

4. Because of the relationship between statutory decision making and the development of policy that informs administrative decisions, and because of the importance of broad participation in the setting of the policies that guide administrative decision making, independent administrative agencies should play a dominant role in whatever subordinate legislative process is provided for by statute.

5. It is frequently desirable that regulation-making authority be given formally to an agency. Where the mandate of an agency necessarily involves it in matters of policy, it should, in principle, be authorized to develop policy in the form of regulations. These regulations should not normally be subject to executive approval.

6. A pilot project should be undertaken exempting agency regulations that are submitted to a public notice and comment procedure from those requirements of the *Statutory Instruments Act* that precede registration and publication.

7. Authority to issue policy directions to independent administrative agencies should only exist where the agency has a broad mandate to develop and apply policies in areas of activity that Parliament determines, on a statute-by-statute basis, to be suitable for executive guidance. It should not be possible to issue directions to agencies that perform solely adjudicative or courtlike functions. Where authorized to be issued, directions should be issued

---

[†] Excerpts from Law Reform Commission of Canada, *Independent Administrative Agencies* (Report 26) (Ottawa: Law Reform Commission of Canada, 1985) at 44–46, 70–72. Source of Information: Justice Canada. Reproduced with the permission of the Minister of Public Works and Government Services Canada, 2002.

by Cabinet, not by an individual minister, and should take the form of regulations. Thus, they should be legislative, not decisional in nature and effect, addressing general policy issues in advance of specific cases.

8. Agencies should be given the statutory authority to formulate non-binding policy statements about how they will exercise their discretion or interpret their legislation. In turn, authority should be given to permit non-binding policy statements to crystallize into binding ones whenever the agency develops a firm view of the policy that ought to condition its exercise of discretion in individual cases.

9. All subordinate legislation prescribing policy for statutory decision making by independent administrative agencies, and all binding policy statements adopted by an agency, should fall within the purview of the Standing Joint Committee on Regulations and Other Statutory Instruments.

10. The *Statutory Instruments Act* should be amended to allow for a general procedure by which Parliament could disallow regulations or policy statements adopted by the executive or an agency.

11. Parliament should take steps to ensure that administrative policy evolves in an orderly and open fashion. In order to help achieve this objective, Parliament and parliamentary committees should be more active in monitoring and reviewing the exercise of subordinate legislative authority relating to agency activities. Committees should have a clear mandate to scrutinize the activities of particular agencies, and should exert influence over the shape and content of agency reports.

12. Although a strengthened committee system would make the use of new techniques of agency accountability such as "sunset" provisions more feasible than they are at present, Parliament should use more efficiently the existing mechanisms of parliamentary democracy to hold agencies accountable.

13. Decisions by independent administrative agencies should not be open to executive appeal or review at the instance of an interested party. Appeal or review should be to other agencies or to courts, not to political authorities.

14. Intrusive executive authority affecting administrative decision making should be both visible and politically accountable. If a political check on an agency's decisions is imposed by statute, the Cabinet, but not a minister, should be authorized to act on its own initiative to vary or rescind the decision or to remove the power of decision from the agency. The availability and exercise of this power should be exceptional, but where authorized it should be clear that the issue is taken away from the agency and brought within the political arena. Interested persons should, nevertheless, on the political level, be given an opportunity to make representations before the decision is made.

15. Where a high incidence of political control is contemplated, it may be preferable to subject agency decisions to routine executive approval. In these cases Cabinet should be required to refer a matter back to the agency before refusing approval because of a concern not addressed before the agency; communicate to the agency an explanation of its refusal to approve any decision; and give policy directions to the agency from time to time to assist it in making its decisions. Even when an agency's decisions are subject to systematic approval, there remains an element of independence that should be respected if the integrity of the agency process is to be maintained.

16. Privative clauses, as they are presently composed, should be abolished. If a special provision is felt necessary to insulate agency decisions from judicial review, it should be expressed in plain language. It should direct courts to show deference to agency expertise and, therefore, not to exercise their discretion to intervene unless the interpretation placed by an agency on a legislative provision it is required by law to administer is patently unreasonable.

17. Agencies should be encouraged to intervene to support their jurisdiction when it is challenged in judicial review proceedings.

18. Parliament should enact legislation setting out process standards that would serve as guidelines for rules of procedure to be adopted by independent administrative agencies. These standards should be developed along the following lines:

    (a) An agency should ensure that interested persons (that is, those whose interests may be affected or who are in a position to contribute) are given reasonable and adequate notice of its proceedings.

(b) An agency should accord those who are sufficiently interested to be entitled to receive notice of a proceeding[,] the right to participate by providing them with a reasonable opportunity to have their information and views made known to the agency, including their views on the submissions of other participants.

(c) An agency should provide interested persons with reasonable access to information about agency procedures and with reasonable assistance in complying with them, for example in the completion of forms.

(d) An agency should allow a participant to employ a representative whose specialized services can reasonably assist him to participate in an agency proceeding.

(e) An agency should ensure the disclosure to participants of all information that is relevant to the decision the agency will make, subject to reasonable accommodation for confidentiality.

(f) An agency should be impartial in carrying out its duties as a statutory decision maker. Members should be required, while holding office, to divest their conflicting financial interests, to disclose those of their spouses and close relatives, and to withdraw from individual proceedings whenever, for any reason, there is a reasonable apprehension of bias.

(g) An agency should give reasons for a decision whenever the decision amounts to a total or partial denial of a requested action, or is otherwise adverse to the interests of a participant.

(h) An agency should provide for the reconsideration or review of its decisions.

19. Parliament should empower agencies to give full effect to the legislated standards. This should include:

(a) The power to secure information that is relevant to the matter in question, including the power to summon witnesses and documents during any proceeding at which a decision must be made.

(b) The power to maintain control over its proceedings and to remove disruptive persons.

(c) The power to initiate contempt proceedings in the Federal Court of Canada.

(d) The power to compel preliminary sessions.

(e) The power to adjourn proceedings.

(f) The power to make interim orders and to provide interim relief.

(g) The power to adjust from an adjudicative to a rule-making format.

(h) The power to add participants.

(i) The power to consolidate proceedings.

20. Except where otherwise specifically prescribed by statute, an agency should not be obliged to follow the rules of evidence that apply in courts of law, other than the rules of evidentiary privilege. Rules of evidence should be developed by agencies as incidents of administrative procedure.

21. Agencies should be encouraged to make and review periodically rules of procedure, using the legislated standards as guidelines. By the same account, Parliament should refrain, wherever possible, from inserting detailed procedural requirements in agency legislation.

22. The rules of procedure an agency adopts should be subject to scrutiny by a parliamentary committee, and to disallowance in Parliament, but not to judicial review on grounds of nonconformity with the standards.

23. An advisory body comprising representatives of public and private sector institutions having an interest in the federal administrative process should be required to file with the parliamentary committee that considers a set of agency rules of procedure[,] a report of its assessment of the appropriateness of these rules. This report should be filed through a politically responsible official such as the Attorney General.

24. Work should be undertaken to develop a series of model rules of procedure that would accommodate different decision-making styles and activities. These models should serve as the starting-point for the development of rules of procedure by any newly created agency, and for periodic review by an existing one.

25. To help eliminate unnecessary diversity in federal administrative procedure, agencies should have the political onus, when adopting rules of procedure, to justify deviations from the model rules.

26. Further work should be undertaken towards improving the information sharing, education, consultation, screening and co-ordination that are required for an integrated procedural framework for agency decision making at the federal level. In this respect, further consideration should be given to the creation of a permanent administrative council.

(d) Federal Administrative Hearings Act

In April 1995, the federal government proposed a new *Federal Administrative Hearings Powers and Procedures Act*.[1] The Act was to be a general procedural code for oral hearings and aspects of written proceedings of federal administrative agencies. It would:

> ... give agencies powers (or clarify existing powers) to effectively conduct hearings; set out the rights of participants and the public; make it easier for non-legally trained individuals to be appointed to agencies and appear before agencies; and cut delays in start-up time of administrative agencies. Agencies would be given the authority to use alternative dispute resolution processes; order pre-hearing disclosure; control the presentation of cases; reconsider their decisions; dismiss applications for abuse of process, lack of evidence or jurisdiction; creatively enforce their decisions; and issue directions as to the service of documents and other procedural matters.[2]

After consultations, the Act was re-named the *Federal Administrative Hearings Act* and was considerably shortened. However, it would still be extensive, addressing over 70 topics and over 300 subtopics, and affecting over 60 federal agencies. Even in its revised version, the Act would be more detailed than Ontario's *Statutory Powers Procedure Act*, and would address additional matters, such as alternative dispute resolution. The proposed Act would be accompanied by a non-binding guide on intent and implementation. If enacted, it would have a significant effect on federal administrative law.

Notes

1. Canada, Department of Justice, *Proposal for a Federal Administrative Hearings Powers and Procedures Act* (18 April 1995), online: QL (LNPR). The original text was dated 21 December 1995.
2. *Ibid.* at i.

(e) A Case Study on Procedural Problem

The Canadian Food Commission has been given the following jurisdiction under the federal *Good Food Act*, R.S.C. 1970, c. FO-33 (s. 5):

> The Commission shall have exclusive jurisdiction and absolute discretion to grant or refuse food distribution franchises.

Pungent Products Ltd. applied to the Canadian Food Commission for a food distribution franchise that would confer on them the exclusive rights to distribute a new variety of odourless onions across the country. A clerk at the Commission telephoned Pungent Products' main competitor in the food distribution business, Rancid Relays Ltd., and advised Rancid Relays that they might wish to attend "a hearing involving Pungent Products Ltd." at the Commission's national hearing office in Carp, Ontario. Thinking his competitor company was in some kind of difficulty and envisioning an entertaining afternoon, the President of Rancid Relays travelled out to Carp to attend the hearing. When he discovered that the subject matter involved an application to distribute the very food his own company was hoping to apply to distribute — odourless onions — the President of Rancid Relays asked the Commission to adjourn the hearing in time for his company to prepare a case. The Commission agreed to adjourn for several hours, during which time the President of Rancid Relays glanced over Pungent Products' application and prepared his own counter-comment. When the hearing re-convened, the Chairman of the Commission disagreed with several points raised by the President of Rancid Relays, saying that these had already been discounted in a staff study prepared by an officer of the Commission. When the President of Rancid Relays asked to see this staff study, the Chairman refused, indicating that the study contained confidential material relating to a new container transport process being developed by Pungent Products. After the hearing, the Chairman left for supper at a Carp restaurant with his elderly aunt (who was a shareholder in Pungent Products Ltd.). Two days after the hearing, the President of Rancid Relays received the following letter from the Canadian Food Commission:

> This is to advise you that pursuant to section 5 of the *Good Food Act*, R.S.C. 1970, c. FO-33, we have granted Pungent Products Ltd. a franchise to serve as sole distributor of Acme Odourless Onions in Canada. We wish to further advise you that in deciding to grant this franchise, we placed no reliance on the "staff study" referred to at the hearing. (On subsequent examination, it proved not to be a genuine staff study at all, but rather a prank on the part of our former janitor.) Instead, we based our decision on the Commission's long-standing policy of encouraging distribution franchises by companies with nationwide distribution facilities, and those of Pungent Products currently service every province and territory.
>
> We hope you enjoyed your trip to our new national headquarters in Carp, and are enclosing some promotional material by the Carp Tourist Board, which we ask you to distribute to members of your company.

The President of Rancid Relays has sought your advice as to whether the decision of the Canadian Food Commission can be successfully challenged in court on procedural grounds. Advise him. (Assume that the Commission has constitutional authority to deal with matters of this kind. If you have to make any other assumptions as a necessary part of your answer, state clearly what they are.)

14   Selected Readings

1. Introduction: General Works

Anisman, P., & R.F. Reid, *Administrative Law: Issues and Practice* (Toronto: Carswell, 1995).

Baum, D.J., *Cases and Materials on Administrative Law* (Toronto: Butterworths, 1987).

Blake, S., *Administrative Law in Canada*, 2d ed. (Markham, Ont.: Butterworths, 1997).

Braverman, L., *Administrative Tribunals: A Legal Handbook* (Aurora, Ont.: Canada Law Book, 2001).

Brown, D.J.M., & J.M. Evans, *Judicial Review of Administrative Action in Canada*, looseleaf (Toronto: Canvasback Publishing, 1998).

Canada, *Guide to Federal Programs and Services*, 10th ed. (Ottawa: Supply and Services Canada, 1990).

Canadian Bar Association, *Current and Emerging Issues: Administrative and Constitutional Law* (Ottawa: Canadian Bar Association, 1993).

Craig, P.P., *Administrative Law*, 4th ed. (London, U.K.: Sweet & Maxwell, 1999).

Delisle, D., *Droit public et administratif* (Cowansville, Qc.: Yvon Blais, 1995).

Dussault, R., & L. Borgeat, *Administrative Law: A Treatise*, 2d ed., trans. M. Rankin (Toronto: Carswell, 1985) (5 vols.).

Evans, J.M., et al., *Administrative Law: Cases, Text, and Materials*, 5th ed. (Toronto: Emond Montgomery, 2002) [hereinafter *Administrative Law*].

Federal Guidebook (Perth, Ont.: J.K. Carruthers, 1996–) (Annual).

Garant, P., *Droit administratif*, 4th ed. (Cowansville, Qc.: Yvon Blais, 1996) (2 vols.).

——, *Précis de droit des administrations publiques*, 3d ed. (Cowansville, Qc.: Yvon Blais, 1995).

Hoffman, R., et al., *Public Administration, Canadian Materials* (Concord, Ont.: Captus Press, 1993).

Janisch, H., "What is Administrative Law?" (1995) 1 Adm. Agen. 3

Jones, D.P., & A.S. de Villars, *Principles of Administrative Law*, 3d ed. (Toronto: Carswell, 1999).

Kernaghan, K., & D. Siegel, 4th ed. *Public Administration in Canada* (Scarborough, Ont.: Nelson Canada, 1999).

Lordon, P., *Crown Law* (Toronto: Butterworths, 1991).

Macaulay, R.W., *Practice and Procedure Before Administrative Tribunals* (Toronto: Carswell, 1988–) (3 vols.).

MacKinnon, D., *A Compendium of the Northern Regulatory Regime* (Don Mills, Ont.: CCH Canadian, 1986).

Mac Neil, M., et al., *Law, Regulation, and Governance* (Don Mills, Ont.: Oxford University Press, 2002).

Mullan, D.J., *Administrative Law* (Toronto: Irwin Law, 2001).

Stein, J., *The Cult of Efficiency* (Toronto: Anansi, 2001).

Tardi, G., *The Legal Framework of Government: A Canadian Guide* (Aurora, Ont.: Canada Law Book, 1992).

Tindal, C.R., & S.N. Tindal, *Local Government in Canada*, 4th ed. (Toronto: McGraw-Hill Ryerson, 1995).

Van Loon, R.J., & M.S. Whittington, *The Canadian Political System: Environment, Structure, and Process*, 4th ed. (Toronto: McGraw-Hill Ryerson, 1987).

2. Scope and History of Administrative Process

Abel, A., "The Dramatis Personae of Administrative Law" (1972) 10 Osgoode Hall L.J. 61

Arthurs, H.W. " 'Mechanical Arts and Merchandise': Canadian Public Administration in the New Economy" (1997) 42 McGill L.J. 29.

Arthurs, H.W., *'Without the Law': Administrative Justice and Legal Pluralism in Nineteenth-Century England* (Toronto: University of Toronto Press, 1985) (esp. c. 4).

Bourinot, J.G., *Local Government in Canada: An Historical Study* (Montreal: Dawson Brothers, 1886).

Cairns, A.C., "The Past and Future of the Canadian Administrative State" (1990) 40 U.T.L.J. 319.

Canada, Library of Parliament Research Branch, *Central Agencies: Their Role* by L. Fortin (Ottawa: Library of Parliament, 1989).

Canada, Privy Council Office, *Decision-Making Processes and Central Agencies in Canada: Federal, Provincial, and Territorial Practices* (Ottawa: Privy Council Office, 1998).

Cheffins, R.I., & R.N. Tucker, *The Constitutional Process in Canada*, 2d ed. (Toronto: McGraw-Hill Ryerson, 1976) at 51–57.

De Smith, S.A., Lord Woolf & J. Jowell, *Judicial Review of Administrative Action*, 5th ed. (London, U.K.: Stevens, 1995) Appendix 1.

Dussault, R., & L. Borgeat, *Administrative Law: A Treatise*, 2d ed., trans. M. Rankin (Toronto: Carswell, 1985) vol. 1.

Economic Council of Canada, *The Emergence of the Regulatory State in Canada: 1867–1939* (Technical Report No. 15) by C.D. Baggaley (Ottawa: Economic Council of Canada, 1981).

Feltham, I.R., ed., *International Trade Dispute Settlement: Implications for Canadian Administrative Law* (Ottawa: Centre for Trade Policy and Law, 1996).

Henderson, E.D., *Foundations of Administrative Law: Certiorari and Mandamus in the Seventeenth Century* (Cambridge, Mass.: Harvard University Press, 1963).

Hodgetts, J.E., *Pioneer Public Service: An Administrative History of the United Canadas, 1841–1867* (Toronto: University of Toronto Press, 1955).

Hoehn, F., *Municipalities and Canadian Law: Defining the Authority of Local Governments* (Saskatoon, Sask.: Purich Publishing, 1996).

Howard, L., & W.T. Stanbury, "Measuring Leviathan: the Size, Scope and Growth of Governments in Canada" in G. Lermer, ed., *Probing Leviathan* (Vancouver: Fraser Institute, 1982) c. 4.

Howse, R., et al., "Smaller or Smarter Government?" (1990) 40 U.T.L.J. 498.

Hutchinson, A.C., "Mice Under a Chair: Democracy, Courts, and the Administrative State" (1990) 40 U.T.L.J. 374.

Kernaghan K., & D. Siegel, *Public Administration in Canada*, 4th ed. (Scarborough, Ont.: ITP Nelson, 1999), Part III.

Law Reform Commission of Canada, *Independent Administrative Agencies* (Working Paper 25) (Ottawa: Law Reform Commission of Canada, 1980).

———, *The Legal Status of the Federal Administration* (Working Paper 40) (Ottawa: Law Reform Commission of Canada, 1985).

Powrie, T.L., "The Growth of Government," in T.C. Pocklington, ed., *Liberal Democracy in Canada and the United States* (Toronto: Holt, Rinehart and Winston, 1985) c. 2.

Priest, M., & Aron Wohl, "The Growth of Federal and Provincial Regulation of Economic Activity," in W.T. Stanbury, ed., *Government Regulation: Scope, Growth, Process* (Montreal: Institute for Research on Public Policy, 1980).

Rubinstein, A., *Jurisdiction and Illegality* (Oxford: Clarendon Press, 1965).

Stanbury, W.T., "Direct Regulation and its Reform: A Canadian Perspective" [1989] Brigham Young University Law Review 467.

Strick, J.C., *The Public Sector in Canada: Programs, Finance and Policy* (Toronto: Thompson Educational Publishing, 1999).

Taggart, M., ed., *The Province of Administrative Law* (Oxford: Hart Publishing, 1997).

3. Policy Options, Statutes, and Statutory Interpretation

(a) Policy Options

Cotterrell, R., *The Sociology of Law: An Introduction*, 2d ed. (London, U.K.: Butterworths, 1992).

Economic Council of Canada, *The Choice of Governing Instrument* by M. Trebilcock et al. (Ottawa: Supply and Services Canada, 1982).

Hart, H., Jr., & A. Sacks, *The Legal Process, Basic Problems in the Making and Application of Law* (Westbury, N.Y.: Liberty Foundation Press, 1984, based on unpub. ed., 1958).

Janisch, H., "The Choice of Decisionmaking Method: Adjudication, Policies and Rulemaking" in Spec. Lect. L.S.U.C. *Administrative Law: Principles, Practice, and Pluralism* (Scarborough, Ont.: Carswell, 1993) 259.

———, "Further developments with respect to Rulemaking by Administrative Agencies" (1995) 9 C.J.A.L.P. 1.

Laskin, J., "Enforcement Powers of Administrative Agencies" in Spec. Lect. L.S.U.C. *Administra-*

tive Law: Principles, Practice, and Pluralism (Scarborough, Ont.: Carswell, 1993) 226.

Law Reform Commission of Canada, *Policy Implementation, Compliance and Administrative Law* (Working Paper 51) (Ottawa: Law Reform Commission of Canada, 1986) esp. 87–102.

————, *Inspection: A Case Study and Selected References; A Study Paper* (Study Paper) by J.C. Clifford (Ottawa: Law Reform Commission of Canada, 1988).

————, *Pollution Control in Canada: The Regulatory Approach in the 1980s* (Ottawa: Law Reform Commission of Canada, 1988).

————, *Administrative Policing: Some Federal Inspectorates* by J.C. Clifford (Ottawa: Law Reform Commission of Canada, 1990).

Ross, A.L., "The Canadian Environmental Assessment Act: An Analysis of Legislative Goals and Administrative Law in Conflict" (1994) 8 C.J.A.L.P. 21.

Stanbury, W.T., "Direct Regulation and its Reform: A Canadian Perspective" [1989] Brigham Young U. Law Rev. 467.

Summers, R.S., *Law: Its Nature, Functions and Limits*, 3d ed. (Englewood Cliffs, N.J.: Prentice-Hall, 1986).

————, "The Technique Element in Law" (1971) 59 California Law Review 733.

Webb, K., "Thumbs, Fingers, and Pushing on String: Legal Accountability in the Use of Federal Financial Incentives" (1993) 31 Alta. L. Rev. (No. 3) 501.

(b) The Making and Control of Legislation

Bernier, I., *Regulations, Crown Corporations, and Tribunals* (Ottawa: Supply and Services Canada, 1985).

Canada, Department of Justice, *The Federal Legislative Process in Canada* (Ottawa: Supply and Services Canada, 1987).

————, Department of Justice, Administrative Law Section, *Designing Regulatory Laws that Work: a Manual of Precedents for Regulatory Reform*, looseleaf (Ottawa: Department of Justice, 1994).

Canada, Office of Privatization and Regulatory Affairs, *Federal Regulatory Plan, 1997* (Ottawa: Office of Privatization and Regulatory Affairs, 1996).

Evans, *Administrative Law*, c. 4

Ganz, G., *Quasi-Legislation: Recent Developments in Secondary Legislation*, 2d ed. (London, U.K.: Sweet & Maxwell, 1987).

Holland, D.C., & J.P. McGowan, *Delegated Legislation in Canada* (Scarborough, Ont.: Carswell, 1989).

Keyes, J.M., *Delegated Law Making by the Executive Branch* (Toronto: Butterworths, 1992).

Saskatchewan, *Regulatory Code of Conduct* (Regina, Sask.: Government of Saskatchewan, 1993).

Treasury Board of Canada, *Managing Regulation in Canada: Regulatory Reform and Regulatory Processes* (Ottawa: Supply and Services Canada, 1996).

(c) Statutory Interpretation

Gall, G., *The Canadian Legal System*, 4th ed. (Scarborough, Ont.: Carswell, 1995).

Macdonald, R.A., "Understanding Regulation by Regulations" in I. Bernier & A. Lajoie, eds., *Regulations, Crown Corporations and Administrative Tribunals* (Toronto: University of Toronto Press, 1985).

MacLauchlan, H.W., "Judicial Review of administrative interpretation of Law: How Much Formalism Can We Reasonably Bear?" (1986) 36 U.T.L.J. 343

Molot, H.L., "The *Carltona* Doctrine and the Recent Amendments to the Interpretation Act" (1994) 26 Ottawa L. Rev. 257.

Yalden, R., "Deference and Coherence in Administrative Law: Rethinking Statutory Interpretation" (1988) 46 U.T. Fac. L. Rev. 136.

4. Administrative Procedure; Procedural Fairness

Anisman, P. "Jurisdiction of Administrative Tribunals to Apply the *Canadian Charter of Rights and Freedoms*" in Spec. Lect. L.S.U.C. *Administrative Law: Principles, Practice, and Pluralism* (Scarborough, Ont.: Carswell, 1993) at 99–130.

Baum, D.J., *Cases and Materials on Administrative Law* (Toronto: Butterworths, 1987) c. 3–8.

Blake, *supra* c. 3.2.

Blue, I.A., "Administrative Law Hearings: a Comparison of U.S. and Canadian Practices" (1990) 6 Admin. L.J. 5.

Brown & Evans, *supra* c. 4–12.

Cowan, J.G., & T.D. Hancock, "Administrative Remedies: Tribunal Creativity and Judicial

Control" in Spec. Lect. L.S.U.C. *Law of Remedies: Principles and Proofs* (Scarborough, Ont.: Carswell, 1995) 341.

Crane, B.A., "Identifying the Forms of Bias" (1996) 1 Admin. Agen. P. 139.

———, "Comment on Consolidated-Bathurst Packaging case" (1988) 1 C.J.A.L.P. 207.

Evans, J.M., "Administrative Tribunals and Charter Challenges" (1988) 2 C.J.A.L.P. 13.

———, "The Principles of Fundamental Justice: The Constitution and the Common Law" (1991) 29 Osgoode Hall L.J. 51 at 51–92.

———, *Administrative Law* c. 2 ("Fairness: The Threshold"), c. 3 ("The Choice of Procedures"), c. 4 ("Rulemaking"), c. 5 ("Bias and Lack of Independence"), c. 6 ("The Duty To Give Reasons"), c. 7 ("Institutional Decisions").

Galligan, D.J., *Due Process and Fair Procedure: A Study of Administrative Procedures* (New York: Oxford University Press, 1996).

Gauk, C., "The Annotated Alberta Administrative Procedures Act" (1996) 2 Admin. Agen. P. 60.

Janisch, H.N., "Consistency, Rulemaking and Consolidated-Bathurst" (1991) 16 Queen's L.J. 95.

Jones & de Villars, *supra* c. 8.

Kuttner, T.S., "Bias and the Arbitral Forum" (1991) 1 Lab. Arb. Y.B. 23.

Lordon, J.P., "The Independence of Administrative Tribunals: Checking Out the Elephant" (1996) 45 U.N.B.L.J. 123.

Macaulay, R.M., ed., *Practice and Procedure Before Administrative Tribunals*, looseleaf (Scarborough, Ont.: Carswell, 1988–) (3 vols.).

———, *Hearings Before Administrative Tribunals* (Scarborough, Ont.: Carswell, 1995).

MacKay, A.W., "Fairness After the Charter: A Rose By Any Other Name?" (1985) 10 Queen's L.J. 263.

Mashaw, J.L., *Due Process and the Administrative State* (New Haven, Conn.: Yale University Press, 1985).

Mullan, D., "Natural Justice: The Challenges of Nicholson, Deference Theory and the Charter" in N.R. Finkelstein & B.M. Rogers, *Recent Developments in Administrative Law* (Toronto: Carswell, 1987) 1.

———, "The Procedural Obligations of Tribunals and Agencies that do not hold Hearings" (1991) 47 Admin. L.R. 130.

Mullan D.J., & D. Harrington, "The Charter and Administrative Decision-Making: The Dampening Effects of Blencoe" (2002) 27 Queen's L.J. 879.

Ontario, Department of Justice and Attorney General, *Manual of Practice on Administrative Law and Procedure in Ontario under the Statutory Powers Procedure Act, 1971; the Public Inquiries Act, 1971; the Judicial Review Procedure Act, 1971 and related Statutes* (Toronto: Department of Justice and Attorney General, 1972).

Pue, W.W., *Natural Justice in Canada* (Vancouver: Butterworths, 1981).

Ratushny, E., "Rules of Evidence and Procedural Problems Before Administrative Tribunals" (1989) 2 C.J.A.L.P. 157.

Roman, A., *Effective Advocacy Before Tribunals* (Scarborough, Ont.: Carswell, 1989).

Snider, J.A., & C.K. Yates, "Alternative Dispute Resolution: Use and Abuse of Information and Specialized Knowledge" (1995) 33 Alta. L. Rev. 301.

Sopinka, J., "The Role of the Commission Counsel" (1990) 12 Dalhousie L.J. 75.

Sossin, L., "An Intimate Approach to Fairness, Impartiality and Reasonableness in Administrative Law" (2002) 27 Queen's L.J. 809.

Sprague, J.L.H., "Evidence Before Administrative Agencies: Let's All Forget the 'Rules' and Just Concentrate on What We're Doing" (1995) 8 C.J.A.L.P. 263.

Tucker, E., "The Political Economy of Administrative Fairness" (1987) 25 Osgoode Hall L.J. 355.

5. Discretion and Access to Information

(a) Discretion

Blake, *supra* c. 3.1.

Bryner, G.C., *Bureaucratic Discretion: Law and Policy in Federal Regulatory Agencies* (New York: Pergamon, 1987).

Davis, K.C., *Discretionary Justice: A Preliminary Inquiry* (Baton Rouge: Louisiana State University, 1969).

———, *Discretionary Justice in Europe and America* (Urbana: University of Illinois Press, 1976).

Evans, *Administrative Law*, c. 8, ("Findings of Fact and Questions of Law"), c. 10 ("Questions of Law: Standards of Review"), c. 13 ("The Misuse of Discretion"), c. 14 ("Discretion, Rules, and Policy").

Finkle, P., & D. Cameron, "Equal Protection in Enforcement: Towards More Structured Discretion" (1989) 12 Dalhousie L.J. 34.

Gillespie, C.J., "Enforceable Rights from Administrative Guidelines?" (1990) 3 C.J.A.L.P. 204.

Glasbeek, H., & E. Tucker, *Death by Consensus: The Westray Story* (North York, Ont.: Centre for Research on Work and Society, 1992).

Handler, J.F., *The Conditions of Discretion: Autonomy, Community, Bureaucracy* (New York: Sage, 1986).

Harlow, C., *Law and Administration* (London, U.K.: Weidenfeld & Nicolson, 1984).

Jones & de Villars, *supra* c. 7.

Jowell, J., "The Legal Control of Administrative Discretion" (1973) Public Law 178.

Lordon, P., *Crown Law* (Toronto: Thompson Educational, 1994).

McLachlin, Hon. Justice Beverly, "Rules and Discretion in the Governance of Canada" (1992), 56 Sask. L. Rev. 167.

Shumavon, D.H., & H.K. Hibbeln, eds., *Administrative Discretion and Public Policy Implementation* (New York: Praeger, 1986).

(b) Access to Information

Canada, Standing Committee on Justice and Solicitor General, House of Commons, *Open and Shut: Enhancing the Right to Know and the Right to Privacy* (Ottawa: Supply and Services Canada, 1987).

Holland, D.C., & J.P. McGowan, *Delegated Legislation in Canada* (Scarborough, Ont.: Carswell, 1989).

Huscroft, G.A., "The Freedom of Information and Protection of Privacy Act: A Roadmap for Requesters" (1990) 11 Advocates' Q. 436.

Iacono, P.M., "Sunshine on the Insurance Industry: The Ontario Freedom of Information Act" (1989) 1 Can Ins. L. Rev. 195.

Information Commissioner of Canada, *Annual Reports* (Ottawa: Minister of Public Works and Government Services Canada, ongoing).

———, *Access to Information Act: A Critical Review* (Ottawa: Supply and Services Canada, 1994).

———, *Access to Information Act: 10 Years On* (Ottawa: Supply and Services Canada, 1994).

———, *Information Technology and Open Government* (Ottawa: Supply and Services Canada, 1994).

Kalson, M.S., & M. Pelletier, "Access to Information and the Parliamentary Context" (1989) 5 Admin. L.J. 84.

Law Reform Commission of Canada, *Unemployment Insurance Benefits: A Study of Administrative Procedure in the Unemployment Insurance Commission* by P. Issalys & G.

Watkins (Ottawa: Supply and Services Canada, 1977).

———, *Access to information: Independent Administrative Agencies* (Study Paper) by R.T. Franson (Ottawa: Law Reform Commission of Canada, 1979).

McNairn, C.H.H., & C.D. Woodbury, *Government Information: Access and Privacy*, looseleaf (Don Mills, Ont.: De Boo, 1989).

Onyshko, T., "Access to Personal Information: British and Canadian Legislative Approaches" (1989) 18 Man. J.L. 213.

Roberts, A., "New Strategies for Enforcement of the Access to Information Act" (2002) 27 Queen's L.J. 647.

———, "Structural Pluralism and the Right to Information" (2001) 51 U.T.L.J. 243.

Treasury Board of Canada, *Information and Administrative Management: Access to Information* (Ottawa: Supply and Services Canada, 1993).

———, *Info Source: Sources of Federal Government Information*, looseleaf (Ottawa: Supply and Services Canada, 1990–).

6. Administrative Agencies

(a) General

Anthony, R.J., *A Handbook on the Conduct of Public Inquiries in Canada* (Toronto: Butterworths, 1985).

Alberta Law Reform Institute, *Public Inquiries* (Issues Paper 3) (Edmonton, Alta.: Alberta Law Reform Institute, 1991).

Berzins, C., "Policy Development by Labour Relations Boards in Canada: Is There A Case for Rulemaking?" (2000) 25 Queen's L.J. 479.

Blake, *supra* c. 2.3.

Cameron, S., "So Long, and Thank You Very Much" (appointments process and patronage), *The [Toronto] Globe and Mail* (5 June 1993) D1 and D3.

Canadian Bar Association, *Report of the Canadian Bar Association Task Force on the Independence of Federal Administrative Tribunals and Agencies in Canada* ("Ratushny Report") (Ottawa: Canadian Bar Association, 1990).

Canada, Department of Justice, *Revised Proposal for a Federal Administrative Hearings Powers and Procedures Act* (21 December 1987), online: QL (LNPR).

Canada, Library of Parliament, Information and Reference Branch, *Commissions of Inquiry under the Inquiries Act, Part I: 1967 to Date* (Ottawa: Library of Parliament, 1986).

Ellis, S.R., "Administrative Tribunal Design" (1987) 1 C.J.A.L.P. 134.

Feltham, I.R., ed., *International Trade Dispute Settlement: Implications for Canadian Administrative Law* (Ottawa: Centre for Trade Policy and Law, 1996).

Janisch, R.N., "Administrative Tribunals and the Law" (1988) 2 C.J.A.L.P. 263.

Law Reform Commission of Canada, *Administrative Law: Commissions of Inquiry* (Working Paper 17) (Ottawa: Supply and Services Canada, 1977).

————, *Pension Appeals Board: A Study of Administrative Procedure in Social Security Matters* by P. Issalys (Ottawa: Law Reform Commission of Canada, 1979).

————, *Political Control of Independent Administrative Agencies* by L. Vandervort (Ottawa: Law Reform Commission of Canada, 1979)

————, *Public Participation in the Administrative Process* (Study Paper) by D. Fox (Ottawa: Law Reform Commission of Canada, 1979).

————, *Independent Administrative Agencies* (Working Paper 25) (Ottawa: Law Reform Commission of Canada, 1980).

————, *Independent Administrative Agencies* (Report 26) (Ottawa: Law Reform Commission of Canada, 1985).

Law Reform Commission of Nova Scotia, *Agencies, Boards and Commissions: The Administrative Justice System in Nova Scotia* (Halifax: Law Reform Commission of Nova Scotia, 1996).

————, *Reform of the Administrative Justice System in Nova Scotia: Final Report* (Halifax: Law Reform Commission of Nova Scotia, 1997).

MacDonald, R.A., "Reflections on the Report of the Quebec Working Group on Administrative Tribunals (Ouellette Commission Report)" (1987–88) 1 C.A.L.P. 337.

McCormack, J., "Nimble Justice: Revitalizing Administrative Tribunals in a Climate of Rapid Change" (1995) 59 Sask. L. Rev. 385.

Ministère de la justice du Québec, News Release, "Orientations de la réforme de la justice administrative" (20 February 1992).

Mullan, D., "Common and Divergent Elements of Practice of the Various Tribunals: An Overview of Present and Possible Future Developments" in Spec. Lect. L.S.U.C. *Administrative Law: Principles, Practice, and Pluralism* (Scarborough, Ont.: Carswell, 1993) 461.

————, "Reform of Judicial Review of Administrative Action — the Ontario Way" (1974) 12 Osgoode Hall L.J. 125.

Murphy, P.T., *An Inventory of Canadian Provincial Administrative Boards and Other Entities* (Ottawa: Canadian Legal Information Centre, 1990) (2 vols.).

Ontario, Department of Justice & Attorney-General, *Manual of Practice on Administrative Law in Ontario* (Toronto: Queen's Park, 1972).

————, Legislative Research Service, *Agencies, Boards and Commissions in Ontario: Accountability and Control* (Current Issue Paper No. 24) by J. Eichmanis (Toronto: Legislative Library, Legislative Research Service, 1984).

————, Management Board of Cabinet, *Directions: Review of Ontario's Agencies: Report* ("Macaulay Report") by R.W. Macaulay (Toronto: Queen's Printer for Ontario, 1989).

Ontario Law Reform Commission, *Report on Public Inquiries* (Toronto: Ontario Law Reform Commission, 1991).

Priest, M., "The Privatization of Regulation: Five Models of Self-Regulation" (1997–1998) 29 Ottawa L. Rev. 233.

Priest, M.D., "Structure and Accountability of Administrative Agencies" in Spec. Lect. L.S.U.C. *Administrative Law: Principles, Practice, and Pluralism* (Scarborough, Ont.: Carswell, 1993) 63.

Québec, Groupe de travail sur les tribunaux administratifs, *Les Tribunaux administratifs: l'heure est aux décisions: rapport* (Québec, Québec: Groupe de travail sur les tribunaux administratifs, 1987).

Ratushny, E., "What are Administrative Tribunals? The Pursuit of Uniformity in Diversity" (1987) 30 Can. Pub. Admin. 1.

McRuer, Hon. J.C., Chair, *Royal Commission Inquiry into Civil Rights* ("McRuer Commission") (Toronto: Queen's Printer for Ontario, 1969–71) (3 reports, comprising five vols.).

Science Council of Canada, *Public Inquiries in Canada* by L. Salter et al. (Ottawa: Supply and Services Canada, 1981).

Scott, S., "The Continuing Debate over the Independence of Regulatory Tribunals" in Spec. Lect. L.S.U.C. *Administrative Law: Principles, Practice, and Pluralism* (Scarborough, Ont.: Carswell, 1993) 79.

Siegel, D., & K.A. Graham, *Agencies, Boards, and Commissions in Canadian Local Government* (Toronto: Institute of Public Administration of Canada, 1994).

Winberg, J.D., "The Judicial Review Procedure Act and the Divisional Court" in J. Cowan, ed. for Law Society of Upper Canada, *Public Law, 1988–1989* (Toronto: Carswell, 1988) at. 69.

Wyman, K.M., "Appointments to Adjudicative Tribunals: Politics and the Courts" (1999) 57(2) U.T. Fac. L. Rev 101.

(b) National Energy Board

Canada, National Energy Board, *Improving the Regulatory Process* (Ottawa: National Energy Board, 1988).

———, *Annual Reports*; *Regulatory Agenda*; and *Rules of Practice and Procedure* [National Energy Board Internet address: http://www.neb.gc.ca/index.htm].

Gray, E., *Forty Years in the Public Interest: A History of the National Energy Board* (Vancouver: Douglas & McIntyre, 2000).

Law Reform Commission of Canada, *The National Energy Board: Policy, Procedure, and Practice* (Study Paper) by A.R. Lucas & T.R. Bell (Ottawa: Law Reform Commission of Canada, 1977).

Priddle, R., "Reflections on National Energy Board Regulation 1959–98: From Persuasion to Prescription and on to Partnership" (1999) 37 Alta. L. Rev. (No. 2) 524.

(c) Canadian Radio-television and Telecommunication Commission

CRTC, *Annual Reports; Policy Statements; Broadcasting and Telecommunications Rules of Procedure* [CRTC Internet address: http://www.crtc.gc.ca/toc.htm].

Intven, H., "New Developments in Communications Law" in N.R. Finkelstein & B.M. Rogers, eds., *Recent Developments in Administrative Law* (Toronto: Carswell, 1987) 285.

Kaufman, D.S., *Broadcasting Law in Canada: Fairness in the Administrative Process* (Toronto: Carswell, 1987).

Law Reform Commission of Canada, *The Canadian Radio-television and Telecommunication Commission* (Study Paper) by C.C. Johnston (Ottawa: Law Reform Commission of Canada, 1980).

Scott, S., "The New Broadcasting Act: An Analysis" (1990) 1 Media and Communications Law Rev. 24.

(d) Canadian Transportation Agency

Canadian Transportation Agency, *Rules of procedure* [Canadian Transportation Agency Internet address: http://www.cta-otc.gc.ca/eng/toc.htm].

Law Reform Commission of Canada, *The Regulatory Process of the Canadian Transport Commission* (Study Paper) by H. Janisch (Ottawa: Law Reform Commission of Canada, 1977).

Wetson, H.W., "Transportation Reform and the Proposed National Transportation Agency" in N.R. Finkelstein & B.M. Rogers, eds., *Recent Developments in Administrative Law* (Toronto: Carswell, 1987) 321.

(e) Canada Industrial Relations Board

Canada Labour Relations Board, *Annual Reports: Case Summaries and Information Circulars*; *Procedural Rules*; *Estimates* [Canada Industrial Relations Board Internet address: http://home.istar.ca/~clrbccrt].

Clarke, G.J., *Clarke's Canada Industrial Relations Board: An Annotated Guide*, looseleaf (Aurora, Ont.: Canada Law Book, 1999–).

Dorsey, J.E., *Canada Labour Relations Board: Law and Practice* (Toronto: Carswell, 1983).

Foisey, C.H., et al., *Canada Labour Relations Board: Policies and Procedures* (Toronto: Butterworths, 1986).

Law Reform Commission of Canada, *Canada Labour Relations Board* (Study Paper) by S. Kelleher (Ottawa: Law Reform Commission of Canada, 1980).

Sims, A., Chair, *Seeking a Balance: Review of Part I of the Canada Labour Code* (Report of the Task Force to Review Part I of the Canada Labour Code) (Ottawa: Minister of Public Worker and Government Services Canada, 1996).